The Higley
Lesson Commentary

International Uniform
Sunday School Series

EDITOR
  Wesley C. Reagan

CONTRIBUTING WRITERS
  Ron Durham, Ph.D.
  Doug deGraffenried
  Phil Woodland, D.D.
  John Wright

ILLUSTRATOR
  David Chrane (cover)

> **The Higley Lesson Commentary**, in this 70th year of its life, renews its commitment to careful and reverent scholarship, clear and understandable language, practical and insightful application, and interesting and readable writing. We send it to you with a prayer that it will be a powerful resource to you.

Higley Publishing Corporation
P. O. Box 5398
Jacksonville, FL 32247-5398
Tel. (904) 396-1918

i

FOREWORD

In periods of health and prosperity there may be an illusion that one has no urgent need of biblical knowledge and a relationship with God. During times of turbulence and anxiety, however, minds turn quickly to these resources that transcend human ingenuity. We want more wisdom than we have within ourselves. We yearn for power when our own abilities seem impotent compared to the size of the problems. We long for peace in a world that is confusing, frustrating, and dangerous. We are desperate for hope that will penetrate the dark clouds that are on our horizon.

During times like these many begin a serious search for God and a highly motivated study of His Word. We believe that *The Higley Commentary* which has been available for 70 years has soared to a new level of relevance in this troubled world. Thousands who have been devoted students of the Word for years have used this resource to deepen their knowledge. Many more who have neglected their study of the Bible will find here an accessible storehouse of information, illustration, and stimulation.

The old expression, "Strike while the iron is hot," has application here. We should teach while there are so many who are eager to learn. Nothing improves the educational process more than an appetite for knowledge. This is an exciting time to be involved in this enterprise of communicating the Word of God. I am thankful to be included. I am sure that you are also.

Wesley C. Reagan, Editor

Copyright © 2002, Higley Publishing Corporation
P. O. Box 5398, Jacksonville FL 32247-5398

Soft Cover ISBN: 1-886763-22-4
Hard Cover ISBN: 1-886763-23-2
Large Print Student Book ISBN: 1-886763-24-0

Lessons and/or readings are based on International Sunday School Lessons. The International Bible Lessons for Christian Training, copyright © 1992 by the Committee on the Uniform Series.

PREFACE

The apostle Paul urged Christians to "be instant"—literally to *stand firm*—on Christian principles "*in season* and *out of season*" (2 Tim. 4:2). Paul was concerned that we learn and follow Christ's teachings whether it is convenient or not, and regardless of changes in the format and context of our drawing from the refreshing wells of Bible teaching.

Late in the last century an exciting new movement called the "Sunday School" came to be "in season" as the way for churches to provide this training and encouragement. In many places this is still the chosen practice, not only for children but for adults. In some churches, the "adult Sunday School class" led by a popular teacher is as large or larger than the worship service.

In more recent times, the small group movement has provided this opportunity. With fewer members than the large Sunday School class, the small group seeks an atmosphere that is more conducive for personal participation. Often the group leader is more a "facilitator" than a teacher, helping group members apply the Bible text to their own experience. Prayer and sharing often become an important part of these meetings.

The Higley Commentary is designed to be useful "in season and out of season"—in the context of the traditional Sunday School classes at church, in the more informal small groups meeting in homes, even at retreats and Bible conferences. Various helps, including questions, make the material easy to present and accessible to all. Understanding and applying God's Word is its unchanging focus, whatever the format that's "in season."

Ron Durham, Contributor

Editor's Note: Ron Durham has for many years written the exposition sections of *The Higley Commentary*. His rich background includes periods as a missionary, minister, teacher, journalist, and author. In addition to his commentary writing, he has two books in print: *Jacob I Loved* and *Happily Ever After (and Other Myths About Divorce)*. He does contract editing and assignment writing for several publishers.

FALL QUARTER
Judgment and Exile
Challenge to Change (Lessons 1–5)
Limited Hope (Lesson 6–9)

WINTER QUARTER
Portraits of Faith (New Testament Personalities)
Personalities Involved in Messiah's Coming (Lessons 1–5)
Personalities in Jesus' Life and Ministry (Lessons 6–9)
Personalities in the Early Church (Lessons 10–13)

SPRING QUARTER
Jesus: God's Power in Action
Jesus' Early Ministry (Lessons 1–5)
Jesus' Crucifixion and Resurrection (Lessons 6–8)
Jesus' Responses to Faith (Lessons 9–13)

SUMMER QUARTER
God Restores a Remnant
Beginning the Return (Lessons 1–5)
The Renewal of the Nation (Lessons 6–9)
The Message of the Prophets (Lessons 10–14)

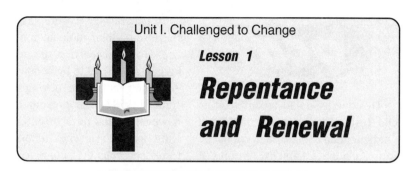

Lesson 1

Repentance and Renewal

2 Chronicles 30:1-6, 8-12

And Hezekiah sent to all Israel and Judah, and wrote letters also to Ephraim and Manasseh, that they should come to the house of the LORD at Jerusalem, to keep the passover unto the LORD God of Israel.

2 For the king had taken counsel, and his princes, and all the congregation in Jerusalem, to keep the passover in the second month.

3 For they could not keep it at that time, because the priests had not sanctified themselves sufficiently, neither had the people gathered themselves together to Jerusalem.

4 And the thing pleased the king and all the congregation.

5 So they established a decree to make proclamation throughout all Israel, from Beer-sheba even to Dan, that they should come to keep the passover unto the LORD God of Israel at Jerusalem: for they had not done it of a long time in such sort as it was written.

6 So the posts went with the letters from the king and his princes throughout all Israel and Judah, and according to the commandment of the king, saying, Ye children of Israel, turn again unto the LORD God of Abraham, Isaac, and Israel, and he will return to the remnant of you, that are escaped out of the hand of the kings of Assyria.

8 Now be ye not stiffnecked, as your fathers were, but yield yourselves unto the LORD, and enter into his sanctuary, which he hath sanctified for ever: and serve the LORD your God, that the fierceness of his wrath may turn away from you.

9 For if ye turn again unto the LORD, your brethren and your children shall find compassion before them that lead them captive, so that they shall come again into this land: for the LORD your God is gracious and merciful, and will not turn away his face from you, if ye return unto him.

10 So the posts passed from city to city through the country of Ephraim and Manasseh even unto Zebulun: but they laughed them to scorn, and mocked them.

11 Nevertheless divers of Asher and Manasseh and of Zebulun humbled themselves, and came to Jerusalem.

12 Also in Judah the hand of God was to give them one heart to do the commandment of the king and of the princes, by the word of the LORD.

Memory Selection
2 Chronicles 30:9

Background Scripture
2 Chron. 29–30; 2 Kings 18–20

Devotional Reading
Psalm 122:1-9

This quarter's study focuses on an Old Testament period we might call "Judgment and Exile." Selections are from 2 Chronicles and the writings of some of the prophets who were active from the reign of Hezekiah, beginning about 726 B.C., to the fall of Jerusalem in 587 B.C.

In general, these were sad times. Because of their idolatry and injustice, God allowed first the northern kingdom of Israel to be conquered in 722, then the southern kingdom of Judah in 587. The present lesson, however, opens on a brighter note. King Hezekiah launches important reforms and calls the people to repentance. The remnant left in the northern kingdom ignores his pleas, but Judah responds more favorably and is given a few more years of freedom.

Make a visual aid by lettering on a large poster board the words REPENT OR PERISH! Parade the sign before the group for a few moments, then ask group members if they have seen modern "prophets" with such signs on street corners. How do they feel when they see such displays?

Responses may include disdain, sympathy, and the feeling that such people are an embarrassment to the faith. Yet when we can get past the embarrassment about the messengers, perhaps we can admit that they have a message for those willing to listen.

The Judean reform king Hezekiah "bears the sign" of repentance in this lesson. Who will mock him? Who will heed?

Teaching Outline	Daily Bible Readings	
	Mon.	Hezekiah Calls for Renewal 2 Chronicles 29:1-11
I. Plans for Renewal—1-5	Tue.	Purify and Consecrate 2 Chronicles 29:15-24
A. Hezekiah's reform, 1-3		
B. Plans for a Passover, 4-5	Wed.	The People Worship 2 Chronicles 29:25-30
II. Passover Proclamation—6, 8-9	Thu.	Sing to the Lord Psalm 149:1-9
A. 'Repent and return!' 6		
B. In hope of leniency, 8-9	Fri.	Thank Offerings Brought 2 Chronicles 29:31-36
III. People's Response—10-12	Sat.	Passover Celebrated 2 Chronicles 30:1-12
A. Mockery in Israel, 10-11		
B. Obedience in Judah, 12	Sun.	God Hears Their Prayers 2 Chronicles 30:21-27

Verse by Verse

I. Plans for Renewal—1-5

A. Hezekiah's reform, 1-3

1 And Hezekiah sent to all Israel and Judah, and wrote letters also to Ephraim and Manasseh, that they should come to the house of the LORD at Jerusalem, to keep the passover unto the LORD God of Israel.

2 For the king had taken counsel, and his princes, and all the congregation in Jerusalem, to keep the passover in the second month.

3 For they could not keep it at that time, because the priests had not sanctified themselves sufficiently, neither had the people gathered themselves together to Jerusalem.

Except for David and Solomon, the books of Chronicles devote more favorable attention to the reform king Hezekiah than to any other king. Although he inherited a weak and depraved realm from his father, King Ahaz, Hezekiah (whose name means "strengthened by Yahweh") was of such strong character that he made sweeping reforms both in governance and religion. As a result, God blessed his rule and enabled his kingdom, Judah, to repel the Assyrians, who conquered the northern tribes of Israel (2 Chron. 32:21-22).

Here, King Hezekiah plans the restoration of the Passover, following a campaign to restore Temple worship and purification sacrifices (chap. 29). This important feast, also called the feast of Unleavened Bread, commemorated the Lord's "passing over" the houses of the Israelites instead of rendering to the Egyptians the horrible punishment of the death of their firstborn child. In calling the people to renewal, Hezekiah is returning to the first mass ritual observance of the Jews' special peoplehood under God.

Although by now God's people had long been divided, this southern king reaches out to all Israel and Judah in his attempts at reform (vs. 1). Ephraim and Manasseh are mentioned specifically because they were the largest of the tribes in the northern kingdom. Aware that his brethren in Israel are under siege by the Assyrians, Hezekiah rightly sees that the best defense for both kingdoms is a return to God, not mere military might. Inviting them to Jerusalem had both political and religious implications, since part of the northern kingdom's apostasy was to set up alternate worship sites (1 Kings 12:26-29). The significance of this departure from God's plan was still important enough by New Testament times that the woman at the well in Samaria asks Jesus about it (John 4:20-22).

Verse 2 shows that Hezekiah wisely consults the people in planning his reforms, resulting in wider involvement than would have been the case had he attempted changes under his edict alone. Originally, the Passover was to be observed in the *first* month of the Jewish new year (Exod. 12:18). Hezekiah's reform, however, had not begun in time for the neglected priesthood to be restored, and the priests sanctified, "at that time" (the first month); so the feast is planned for the second month. Even under the ritual strictness of the Old Law, the God of grace at times allowed the intent of the heart to suffice for ceremonial accuracy—a forecast of Jesus' teaching (see Matt. 23:23).

Another reason for the postponement was that even in Judah the people and the priests alike had carelessly ceased to make the Temple in Jerusalem the center of worship. Temple services had been so neglected that even the doors had to be repaired in order to enter the sacred place (29:3). Inside, "filthiness" (NIV "defilement")—probably referring to idols and various objects used in their worship—had been allowed to accumulate (29:5), thus polluting true worship of the true God. Little wonder that cleanup and other preparations took so long that the Passover had to be postponed.

B. Plans for a Passover, 4-5

4 And the thing pleased the king and all the congregation.

5 So they established a decree to make proclamation throughout all Israel, from Beer-sheba even to Dan, that they should come to keep the passover unto the LORD God of Israel at Jerusalem: for they had not done it of a long time in such sort as it was written.

"From Beer-sheba" in the south . . . "to Dan" in the north was a common way to describe the entire Promised Land. The phrase is another indication of Hezekiah's inclusive vision of reuniting both northern and southern kingdoms in common obedience, symbolized by the restored Passover observance in Jerusalem, rather than in Samaria, to the north.

Why had the feast "not been celebrated in large numbers according to what was written" (vs. 5, NIV)? Because God's people had been preoccupied and distracted with making a living, striking pacts with foreign governments, and a reluctance to worship regularly because they knew their lives were so out of touch with the holiness of God—reasons that are also often painfully present in the case of the neglect of Christian worship today.

II. Passover Proclamation—6, 8-9

A. 'Repent and return!' 6

6 So the posts went with the letters from the king and his princes throughout all Israel and Judah, and according to the commandment of the king, saying, Ye children of Israel, turn again unto the LORD God of Abraham, Isaac, and Israel, and he will return to the remnant of you, that are escaped out of the hand of the kings of Assyria.

The "posts" or "couriers" (NIV) served as the government mail service does today, taking various communiqués and pronouncement from the king's court to the farthest reaches of the realm. This time, the content of their message is not only to come to a Passover of renewal, but is painfully like the message of street-corner preachers today bearing their signs of "Repent or perish!" (see "For a Lively Start"). While the methods employed by such modern "prophets" may be ineffective and even questionable, it is really their message that most people find repulsive. Few of us welcome demands that we repent or "change our minds" and turn from our preoccupation with worldly pursuits to true worship and obedience.

While many Israelites could be expected to ignore and even deride the king's message, those who respond favorably can expect God to "return to the remnant." This is God's way of keeping His covenant made with Abraham that his descendants would be multiplied (as in Gen. 12:1-3). While the willfully disobedient will disqualify themselves to receive the covenant, God will ensure that a remnant will prove Him to be a faithful promise-keeper.

B. In hope of leniency, 8-9

8 Now be ye not stiffnecked, as your fathers were, but yield yourselves unto the LORD, and enter into his sanctuary, which he hath sanctified for ever: and serve the LORD your God, that the fierceness of his wrath may turn away from you.

9 For if ye turn again unto the LORD, your brethren and your children shall find compassion before them that lead them captive, so that they shall come again into this land: for the LORD your God is gracious and merciful, and will not turn away his face from you, if ye return unto him.

Here Hezekiah seems to speak especially to the northern tribes who are in the very process of being conquered by the Assyrians. This tragic event, along with detailed reasons for it, is recorded in 2 Kings 17:6-18. God's patience with injustice and idolatry among His own people had finally been exhausted. Even child sacrifice, borrowed from surrounding pagan worship, had crept into their religious practices (2 Kings 17:17).

In part, their fate was also a direct result of forsaking the sanctuary of the Temple in Jerusalem; so the king promises that if they return to Him their secure haven will be restored. Hezekiah even proceeds to enter briefly into a prophetic ministry, looking ahead to the day when the conquered tribes would model obedience and true worship so faithfully that their captors would allow them to return to the lands God had given to them. Thus their repentance or "turning" would trigger God's responsive "turning" as well, in the form of forgiveness and restoration to the land.

III. People's Response—10-12
A. Mockery in Israel, 10-11

10 So the posts passed from city to city through the country of Ephraim and Manasseh even unto Zebulun: but they laughed them to scorn, and mocked them.

11 Nevertheless divers of Asher and Manasseh and of Zebulun humbled themselves, and came to Jerusalem.

The "remnant" theme is nowhere more evident than in the response of the northern tribes to Hezekiah's invitation to reform, and signify their renewed commitment by coming to a Passover in Jerusalem. Most of "Ephraim and Manasseh," or northern Israel, rejected God's overtures through Hezekiah. The "nevertheless" in verse 11, however, is significant, showing that a minority from among the northern tribes were open to the call to repentance and renewal. Here is a poignant reminder of what the apostle Paul would say some 600 years later: "They are not all Israel, which are of Israel" (Rom. 9:6).

B. Obedience in Judah, 12

12 Also in Judah the hand of God was to give them one heart to do the commandment of the king and of the princes, by the word of the LORD.

Hezekiah's reform movement gained a better hearing in the southern kingdom. God gives mercy to those with open hearts, and in this case He also gives both grace and unity to those who receive the summons to reform, which, as the author pointedly adds, are actually from God.

Evangelistic Emphasis

Bill Adams has been active in personal evangelism at the Eastside Church. His "success record" has come to be regarded with considerable pride among the people at Eastside. Perhaps the most effective part of Bill's evanelistic efforts is his ability to "close the sale." He has cultivated a valuable gift for putting at ease the fears of people that would prevent them from embracing fatih. Bill has learned that much of the time the underlying obstacle to repentance is fear—fear of change.

Although for years Bill Adams has successfully helped people get past their fears of change that prevented their repentance, it never dawned on him that he might need to repent himself. Recently he was challenged by some ideas that shook him to the core. In his attempt to "convert" one of his neighbors, the neighbor proved to be much more knowledgable than Bill expected. Indeed, as Bill became enlightened about some biblical truths he had completely overlooked, he realized that for him to embrace them would truly be . . . frightening.

ℰↃↄℛ

Memory Selection

For if ye turn again unto the LORD, your brethren and your children *shall find* compassion before them that lead them captive, so that they shall come again into this land: for the LORD your God *is* gracious and merciful, and will not turn away his face from you, if ye return unto him.—*2 Chronicles 30:9*

Repentance is an interesting human situation. Rarely will anything surpass it for mending a relationship—any relationship. Yet, for some strange reason, there is within many of us a reluctance to embrace repentance because of our fear of what it will produce.

Perhaps it is something selfish such as our fear of "losing face" or of being placed in a situation of vulnerability. Sometimes our reluctance grows out of our inability to be sure that we will persevere in our attempt to straighten out our life. The fear of failure is the culprit in this situation.

More often than not the fear of repentance that intimidates us is linked with a fear of the wrath or scorn of the one before whom we must repent. In our human arena we've had individuals exploit our contrite spirit to take revenge. These human experiences make us reluctant to repent before God, lest He use the occasion for revenge, too.

Weekday Problems

Faith House of Prayer has a long history of chronic unhappiness. Most of the members have lost count of how many pastors have passed through its revolving doors. Most have stayed only a year or so. The vast majority left unhappily, either due to a forced resignation or due to relentless strife with some of the members that prompted them to decide to seek greener pastures.

Pastor Doug Hines has just finished his first year at Faith House of Prayer. Some of the younger families have begun to gather in whispering clusters, speculating about how much longer he will last. Most of those younger families would like to think that he will stay for a long tenure, yet they are not sure that they ought to set themselves up to be disappointed. Dare they dream that he will be able to bring peace to their home church, even though no previous pastor has been able to do so?

* Is it possible for one pastor to succeed where so many have failed?

* What characteristics might be especially helpful to such a pastor to equip him for a lasting ministry in such a dysfunctional church?

* What can this concerned group of young adults do to contribute to a lasting peace and a long tenure for their pastor?

Nutcracker Sweets

Psychiatrist—Congratulations, Mr. Young. You're finally cured of your delusion. But why are you so sad?
Patient—Wouldn't you be sad if yesterday you were President of the United States, but today you're a nobody?

❖❖❖❖❖

Anyone who sees a psychiatrist should have his head examined.

❖❖❖❖❖

Patient—I'm worried, Doc. I keep thinking I'm a pair of curtains.
Doc—Stop worrying, and pull yourself together.

❖❖❖❖❖

Roger—I used to think I was a beagle, but my psychiatrist cured me.
Dodger—Good! How to do you feel now?
Roger—See for yourself. Just feel my nose.

❖❖❖❖❖

My shrink tells me he's discovered what makes me tick, but he can't explain what makes me chime on the hour.

This Lesson in Your Life

Pete Gomez has been part of Lodge 1845 since he was fresh out of high school. He has earned every decoration possible for excellence and leadership. Through the years, nearly every program or committee has drawn from his time and talent. Pete has long dreamed of the day when his own son would be inducted into the Lodge.

Last month, these long-standing dreams of Pete Gomez were suddenly thrown into doubt. For years, Pete has been painfully aware of declining membership. Many of the surrounding business community have sold out and moved into one of the more affluent suburbs. One by one businesses have closed, leaving a vacant building with windows protected by sheets of plywood. At last month's executive committee meeting, one of the members raised the question whether the lodge should simply close its doors. "Can we really justify our existence any longer? Or, should we do the honorable thing and concede that times have changed and our time is long gone" ? The club's charter prohibits it from simply moving to the suburbs.

For Pete Gomez, the thought of dissolving Lodge 1845 is almost more than he can bear. He has invested far too much of his life there, simply to walk away. Unfortunately, most of the younger members do not understand his intensity of emotion over the matter. They see it simply as a matter of *being pragmatic*. The thought of casting one's membership to the Rotary Club or the Lion's Club even has a certain appeal, due to the strength of membership to be found there. Furthermore, they would rather see Lodge 1845 receive an "honorable burial" than watch it continue to die a slow death of shame.

As Pete stewed about it last evening at dinner, his wife, Gloria, commented that *Pete has become his father.* Somewhat stunned by the remark, he asked what she meant by that. Gloria then reminded Pete how, years ago, when he led the effort to build a new church facility to replace the present, outdated structure, his own father had fought the project adamantly. At the time, Pete failed to understand why anyone would want to hold on to an outdated, sorely limited building that always was in need of more repairs than the church could do. Pete's father, however, had spent much of his life in the old building and had worked tirelessly to keep it presentable.

Though painful, Gloria's observation cast a new light on the situation. For the first time, Pete understands his father's position that had caused such a strain in their relationship, so he can also understant the opinions of his younger lodge companions. Though he still finds the prospect of folding the lodge terribly painful, he is feeling fewer hard feelings toward those who have initiated the discussion.

1. Why was Hezekiah sending out invitations to all Israel, Judah, Ephraim and Manasseh?

He was inviting the people to come to Jerusalem to celebrate the Passover.

2. Why was the Passover being celebrated in the second month instead of the first month, as prescribed in the Law?

There had not been enough priests sanctified to carry out the celebration when the time prescribed date arrived.

3. In Hezekiah's letters, what did he promise to those who would return to the Lord?

He promised that their brothers and children would be shown compassion by their captors.

4. How far did the couriers go who went from town to town in Ephraim and Manasseh?

They went as far as Zebulun.

5. How did the people of Ephraim and Manasseh respond to the invitation of Hezekiah?

The people scorned and ridiculed them.

6. Did all of the people respond negatively?

No. Some men of Asher, Manasseh and Zebulun humbled themselves and went to Jerusalem.

7. What other positive results come from this initiative of King Hezekiah?

In Judah the hand of God was on the people to give them unity of mind to carry out what the king and his officials had ordered, following the word of the Lord.

8. What did the people do with the altars in Jerusalem and the incense altars?

They removed them and threw them into the Kidron Valley.

9. On what day of the second month was the Passover lamb slaughtered?

On the 14th day.

10. Why did the Levites have to kill so many Passover lambs?

The crowd had not consecrated themselves, and so were not ceremonially clean to kill the lambs themselves.

9

I don't really know where the article originated, but it first arrived on my desk about two years ago. At first I laughed out loud, thinking it was a joke. Lately, however, I've wondered whether it is legit. You've probably seen it. It is a brochure promoting "The Lite Church of the Valley" to all those interested. Basically, it reads as follows:

Has the heaviness of your old-fashioned church got you weighted down? Try us! We are the New and Improved Lite Church of the Valley. Studies have shown we have 24 percent fewer commitments than other churches. We guarantee to trim off guilt, because we are Low-Cal . . . low Calvin, that is. We are the home of the 7.5-percent tithe. We promise 35-minute worship services, with seven-minute sermons. Next Sunday's exciting text is the story of "The Feeding of the 500."

We have only six Commandments—your choice!! We use just 3 gospels in our contemporary New Testament, Good Sound Bites for Modern Human Beings. *We take the offering every other week, all major credit cards accepted, of course. We are looking forward with great anticipation to our 800-year Millennium.*

Yes, the New and Improved Lite Church of the Valley could be just what you are looking for. We are everything you want in a church . . . and less!!

The more I thought about this fake(?) brochure, the more it sounded like "Casual Cal," as he calls himself at the new big church across town. Pastor Calvin Weathers at The Big Valley Church has cultivated a image for himself as "the Polo shirt preacher." He not only dresses casually, his preaching style displays the same casual mood. I contacted "Casual Cal" and asked him if that was his brochure, but he denied it. In fact, he quickly laughed off the whole thing as a joke. Apparently, I was not the first to ask.

I don't know what Casual Cal has working for him, but something certainly is attracting the numbers. Big Valley has been growing at record levels. I've lost several families to his band wagon, myself. It hasn't concerned me much, though. So far, every family I've lost has been "dead wood" — people who talked a great piety but out of whom I was able to get very little in the way of commitment. I sincerely hope that he is able to get them seriously involved. If he does, he will be doing more for them than I was ever able to do.

All of this has made me wonder if I should buy some Polo shirts, and maybe a bright red Bible to match. Is black outdated? Somebody will have to help me with all of these new trends. I'm already in 'way over my head!

Lesson 2

God Restores a Sinner

2 Chronicles 33:1-13

Manasseh was twelve years old when he began to reign, and he reigned fifty and five years in Jerusalem:

2 But did that which was evil in the sight of the LORD, like unto the abominations of the heathen, whom the LORD had cast out before the children of Israel.

3 For he built again the high places which Hezekiah his father had broken down, and he reared up altars for Baalim, and made groves, and worshipped all the host of heaven, and served them.

4 Also he built altars in the house of the LORD, whereof the LORD had said, In Jerusalem shall my name be for ever.

5 And he built altars for all the host of heaven in the two courts of the house of the LORD.

6 And he caused his children to pass through the fire in the valley of the son of Hinnom: also he observed times, and used enchantments, and used witchcraft, and dealt with a familiar spirit, and with wizards: he wrought much evil in the sight of the LORD, to provoke him to anger.

7 And he set a carved image, the idol which he had made, in the house of God, of which God had said to David and to Solomon his son, In this house, and in Jerusalem, which I have chosen before all the tribes of Israel, will I put my name for ever:

8 Neither will I any more remove the foot of Israel from out of the land which I have appointed for your fathers; so that they will take heed to do all that I have commanded them, according to the whole law and the statutes and the ordinances by the hand of Moses.

9 So Manasseh made Judah and the inhabitants of Jerusalem to err, and to do worse than the heathen, whom the LORD had destroyed before the children of Israel.

10 And the LORD spake to Manasseh, and to his people: but they would not hearken.

11 Wherefore the LORD brought upon them the captains of the host of the king of Assyria, which took Manasseh among the thorns, and bound him with fetters, and carried him to Babylon.

12 And when he was in affliction, he besought the LORD his God, and humbled himself greatly before the God of his fathers,

13 And prayed unto him: and he was intreated of him, and heard his supplication, and brought him again to Jerusalem into his kingdom. Then Manasseh knew that the LORD he was God.

Memory Selection
2 Chronicles 33:13

Background Scripture
2 Chron. 33:1-20; 2 Kings 21

Devotional Reading
2 Chronicles 6:36-42

11

In dizzying turnabouts, good kings are followed by evil during this period in Israel's history. Wicked King Ahaz had been succeeded by the good king Hezekia. Now Hezekiah has died and the mantle of leadership falls on his son Manasseh, who begins to cancel the reforms his father brought about. Yet this pattern of sin and judgment is shown to be far from inevitable. After being led captive into Babylonia, Manasseh realizes the error of his way, repents, and is restored to his throne.

The lesson shows that Israel's tragic fate was not the fault of God, who waits as a loving Father to forgive and restore. Manasseh and most of the other kings paved their own road to destruction. All this shows God's *foreknowledge* of what would occur, but it does not portray a fatalistic *fore-ordination* that robbed Judah's leaders of free choice that could have resulted in the nation's survival.

೮೦೧೪

Introduce this lesson with illustrations that show both joy for the privilege of "second chances" granted by a gracious God, and the sadness of often having to live with the consequences of sin.

For example, former President Bill Clinton confessed to the nation that he had disgraced his office. While most people are inclined to forgive people who "come clean," what repercussions and consequences lingered after Clinton's confession? A murderer in prison reflects on his actions, and is led to Christ by a prison chaplain. Yet what consequences will he, and his victim's loved ones, have to live with?

Use such illustrations to lead into the lesson of Manasseh's idolatry, followed by his miraculous turnaround.

Teaching Outline	Daily Bible Readings	
I. Manasseh Rules—1-2	Mon.	Manasseh's Evil 2 Chronicles 33:1-6
II. High Places and Altars—3-5 A. Groves to gods, 3 B. Alien altars, 4-5	Tue.	Repentance and Restoration 2 Chronicles 33:7-13
	Wed.	Solomon's Prayer 2 Chronicles 6:36-42
III. Pagan Sacrifices and Idols—6-7 A. Child sacrifice, 6 B. Alien image, 7	Thu.	'If My People Pray' 2 Chronicles 7:11-16
IV. Broken Covenant—8-11 A. Ignoring God, 8-10 B. Reaping results, 11	Fri.	Worship Reform 2 Chronicles 33:14-20
	Sat.	God Hears a Sinner's Prayer Luke 18:9-14
V. Repentance and Restoration— 12-13	Sun.	Repentance to Salvation 2 Corinthians 7:5-13a

Verse by Verse

I. Manasseh Rules—1-2

1 Manasseh was twelve years old when he began to reign, and he reigned fifty and five years in Jerusalem:

2 But did that which was evil in the sight of the LORD, like unto the abominations of the heathen, whom the LORD had cast out before the children of Israel.

Despite Hezeikah's good fatherly influence, his son Manasseh was influenced by the surrounding pagan culture. His rule was "like unto the abominations of the heathen" (NIV "following the detestable practices of the nations")—the very people whose wickedness and idolatry prompted God to empower the Jews to drive them from the Promised Land. Canaanite paganism appealed to the base instincts that motivate those with depraved hearts, and it offered gods that were visible instead of spiritual or abstract.

II. High Places and Altars—3-5
A. Groves to gods, 3

3 For he built again the high places which Hezekiah his father had broken down, and he reared up altars for Baalim, and made groves, and worshipped all the host of heaven, and served them.

Israel had earlier been allowed to build altars of worship to the true God on "high places," sharing the universal primitive perception that worship should be on a spot as elevated as pos-sible since the deity dwells in heaven. Eventually, however, the high places were condemned because God's people began to associate elevated worship sites with the gods of the Canaanites and Assyrians.

The "groves" of the KJV are described by most other translations as "Asherah" (NIV "Asherah poles"), the name of an Assyrian goddess of fertility. Some scholars theorize that pagans chose forested hilltops to worship their gods simply because they were pleasant oases in an otherwise barren landscape, or because they pointed upward to the supposed dwelling place of the gods. When no trees were around, poles would be substituted, planted like trees to point upward to the goddess' dwelling. thus the Assyrian goddess Asherah gave her name to such groves, either natural or man-made. Fertility rites, including ritual sexual relations, added to their eventually being called an "abomination" by the prophets.

B. Alien altars, 4-5

4 Also he built altars in the house of the LORD, whereof the LORD had said, In Jerusalem shall my name be for ever.

5 And he built altars for all the host of heaven in the two courts of the house of the LORD.

Standing alone, verse 4 may be thought to indicate no sin, since God's altar belonged in His house, or the

Temple. Verse 5, however, indicates that the altars Manasseh built were to other gods, and that he was practicing "syncretism," or the blending of false religions with the true.

"The host of heaven" is a reference to the stars and other heavenly bodies often worshipped by pagans. Unlike Manasseh, his son Josiah would be commended for banning worship "to the sun, and to the moon, and to the planets, and to all the host of heaven" (2 Kings 23:5).

III. Pagan Sacrifices and Idols—6-7

A. Child sacrifice, 6

6 And he caused his children to pass through the fire in the valley of the son of Hinnom: also he observed times, and used enchantments, and used witchcraft, and dealt with a familiar spirit, and with wizards: he wrought much evil in the sight of the LORD, to provoke him to anger.

As though worshipping Asherah and the host of heaven were not enough apostasy, Manasseh also took the inconceivable step of aping pagans whose gods demanded child sacrifice. Although the exact nature of the ritual called "passing through the fire" is unknown, it almost certainly refers to child sacrifice similar to that offered to the Ammonite god Molech. Some authorities believe that a hollow idol, with arms outstretched, would be made of bronze or other metal. Fires would be build on the inside of the image, and a child, whose life was demanded as a sign that the worshippers were willing to give their most precious possession to the god, would be placed on the idol's arms and burned

alive. Manasseh's practice of this horrible ritual in the valley of Hinnom just outside Jerusalem branded it as "Gehenna," a place so despicable a place that it became a symbol of the eternal destruction of the wicked (see Matt. 5:22).

The enchantments, witchcraft, familiar spirits, and wizards in verse 6 show that Manasseh dabbled in the occult. Such practices appear to be wrong for at least two reasons. First, the supposed "spirits" contacted in witchcraft too often vie for the true God for worship, making the practice idolatrous. Second, God, with His messengers from heaven, rather than Satan's messengers from hell, are to be our source of revelation about the "other world." Both these practices and child sacrifice are clearly condemned in Deuteronomy 18:10-11.

B. Alien image, 7

7 And he set a carved image, the idol which he had made, in the house of God, of which God had said to David and to Solomon his son, In this house, and in Jerusalem, which I have chosen before all the tribes of Israel, will I put my name for ever:

This incident is a more specific reference to Manasseh's idolatrous tendencies described in verse 5. Adding the term "carved image" is designed to remind us that the true God, being invisible, cannot be reduced to representations in wood or stone. Specifically condemned by the first Commandment, carving a "god" is reduced to exquisite ridicule by the prophet Isaiah, who pokes fun at a person who burns one end of a log to warm him-

14

self and bows down to the other end which he has carved to represent a god! (Isa. 44:13-17). Ever since the Jews' violation of the first Commandment resulted in their captivity, the prohibition against "graven images" has been generally observed so strictly that it has severely restricted religious art among them.

IV. Broken Covenant—8-11

A. Ignoring God, 8-10

8 Neither will I any more remove the foot of Israel from out of the land which I have appointed for your fathers; so that they will take heed to do all that I have commanded them, according to the whole law and the statutes and the ordinances by the hand of Moses.

9 So Manasseh made Judah and the inhabitants of Jerusalem to err, and to do worse than the heathen, whom the LORD had destroyed before the children of Israel.

10 And the LORD spake to Manasseh, and to his people: but they would not hearken.

Verse 8 continues a recitation beginning in verse 7 of God's covenant to keep Israel safe in the Promised Land. This promise was secure until such kings as Manasseh led the people to forsake their part of the covenant by outstripping the Canaanites by engaging in such practices as the idolatry described here. The covenant thus broken, this statement is to warn the people that God is released from His part. The last line is one of the saddest in Scripture: "But they would not hearken."

B. Reaping results, 11

11 Wherefore the LORD brought upon them the captains of the host of the king of Assyria, which took Manasseh among the thorns, and bound him with fetters, and carried him to Babylon.

Now begins the long siege against Judah, which, though finally abandoned by the Assyrians, would be resumed by Babylon, where Manasseh is taken as judgment against his faithlessness. "Among the thorns" probably refers not to the king's having hidden in thorny brush, but to spiked and thorn-like staves and harnesses by which captives were led (cp. the NIV).

V. Repentance and Restoration—12-13

12 And when he was in affliction, he besought the LORD his God, and humbled himself greatly before the God of his fathers,

13 And prayed unto him: and he was intreated of him, and heard his supplication, and brought him again to Jerusalem into his kingdom. Then Manasseh knew that the LORD he was God.

As tragic as Manasseh's story is, it also reveals the "God of second chances." Retaining some kernel of sensitivity to God, the king finally sees that his plight is the result of disobedience, and his repentance and prayer restores the covenant. Although this dramatic reversal in his fortune was cause for personal rejoicing, we can only speculate about how his previous evil practices led thousands of his people into spiritual and physical death. Many Christians have also experienced the good news/bad news situation of having been forgiven of personal sin, but having to live with its consequences.

Evangelistic Emphasis

At age 40, Sam Tishon had spent most of his adult life in prison, mostly for drug-related offences. Amazingly, his wife Margaret did not divorce him. Of course, each time Sam was released he promised Margaret *again* that he was going to straighten up this time. Yet, before his lips were dry from his promise, he was involved in something else that would end up putting him away again.

Sam had again been released when I met him. During his last stay behind bars, he decided that *if* he was going to have a chance at staying clean, he was going to have to "get God back in his life." As a young boy he had been taken to church by his mother. By the time he was 12, however, he was steeped in rebellion, and refused to go. Now he had the initiative to "look up" the church. Much to his encouragement, he found the people there receptive without being judgmental of his squandered life.

It has now been seven years that Sam has remained "clean." His wife testifies that their marriage is better than she ever dreamed it could be. His new career is helping others to go straight like he has done.

ℰᗞᑫᔕ

Memory Selection

And prayed unto him: and he was intreated of him, and heard his supplication, and brought him again to Jerusalem into his kingdom. Then Manasseh knew that the LORD he *was* God.
—*2 Chronicles 33:13*

David Grant had been reared in a Christian home. He knew very well the ways of God, for his dad was a preacher. All his growing years he had heard his father proclaiming the virtues of living a life of faith. Like Manasseh, though, he spurned it all, once he reached adulthood and went "his own way." Deaf to the pleas of his parents and his sister, David indulged freely in the pleasures of this world.

Then one fateful afternoon on a ski slope in Colorado, David ran smack-dab into the back-hand of reality. He hit a tree. The carelessness of his life had spilled over into his skiing. Unlike Sonny Bono, David lived. With several bones badly broken, he had a whole lot of time to think about life. That *thinking* gave birth to *thankfulness*. The spirit of thankfulness yielded rebirth to his faith.

Like Manasseh, David proved that just because a boy goes astray does not necessarily mean that all hope for him is gone. Today, David's life is a dynamic testimony of faith.

Weekday Problems

Sandra Bartlet has been a Christian all of her life. She teethed on the third pew on the left side of the sanctuary. Any time one of the leaders has asked her to assume a responsibility, Sandra has responded with immediate compliance. From the leaders' point of view, Sandra is a model Christian.

What the leaders do not know, however, is that Sandra is up-to-her-ears in astrology. It's not merely a idle fascination with her, though it began that way. By now she actually runs her life according to her astrological reading for the day. That is where Sandra finds the courage to move ahead with any initiative. That's where she seeks her security. As a result, Sandra has come to be in bondage to astrology.

* Is there anything *really wrong with* consulting astrology as an idle curiosity or fascination?

* If Sandra were your best friend, how would you deal with your new awareness of Sandra's secret bondage?

* How can Sandra best break her bondage to astrology in her life? What is an alternative way to gain courage and security amid the uncertainties of life?

Reflections on Repentance

Whatever stress some may lay upon it, a death-bed repentance is but a weak and slender plank to trust our all upon.— *Laurence Sterne*

The dream is short, repentance long.—*Friedrich von Schiller*

It is one thing to mourn for sin because it exposes us to hell, and another to mourn for it because it is an infinite evil; one thing to mourn for it because it is injurious to ourselves, and another thing to mourn for it because it is wrong and offensive to God. It is one thing to be terrified; another to be humbled.—*Gardiner Spring*

True repentance requires great tenderness of heart. Living with the consequences of the deeds that called for repentance requires great strength of faith.—*Anonymous*

This Lesson in Your Life

Bill Simpson has been a deacon at Faith Community Fellowship for nearly 10 years. Though he was raised in a mainline denomination, his wife, Jill, introduced him to the idea of "trying" Faith Community due to the multitude of programs available for their three children. Almost immediately, Bill fell in love with the church and became one of its most outspoken advocates, even before they became members there. Bill, Jill and their children have been active members now for more than 12 years.

Last Sunday, however, Pastor Jim said something that really shook Bill to the foundations of his faith. Preaching on the Prodigal Son from Luke 15, the pastor had made the passing comment that, like the prodigal son, all of us at some point in our lives have been sinners in desperate need of God's mercy. He then proceeded to recite a whole list of famous and infamous sinners, suggesting that we all belong among them.

Initially, Bill laughed out loud. He thought Pastor Jim was making a joke. As he continued to listen, though, he realized that the pastor was dead serious. A stunned silence within Bill quickly turned to anger. *"How dare he stand up there and accuse me of guilt equal to that of Cain or Judas or David with Bathsheba! Who does he think he is, anyway?"*

Bill has never thought of himself as a sinner. Oh, he realizes that he is not perfect. He will readily admit that. So, in a technical sense, Bill will agree he is a "sinner"—*sort of.* Yet, he has been in church all of his life. Never was he a "rebellious young kid" while growing into adulthood. Never did he go through a time of "waywardness," sowing his wild oats. Never did he turn his back on God in some kind of defiant mutiny. Consequently, Bill cannot disagree more strongly with the idea that he be grouped with those who are profanely sinful.

Bill has not yet confronted the pastor about the matter, but he certainly plans to do so. Before initiating that discussion, though, Bill wants to make sure that he's done his homework. He wants to be able to walk into the pastor's office with his Bible in hand to defend his honor. He refuses to accept his place along side of Manasseh, who sacrificed his child to a pagan deity on a altar.

Although Jill strongly agrees with the pastor, she has been very cautious with her words this week. She's never seen her husband like this before and doesn't know how best to respond. It is difficult for her to watch her husband of 15 years become so upset over this matter. How can she help him to understand better the pastor's point of view? What Scriptures can she lead him to that will bring understanding to his faith? How can she express her agreement with the pastor without placing herself in path of her husband's unleashed anger?

1. How old was Manasseh when he became king of Judah?

He was 12 years old.

2. How is Manasseh's reign generally characterized?

As evil. The Bible says that he "did that which was evil in the sight of the Lord."

3. What was the nature of the "evil" that Manasseh did?

Essentially, Manasseh's sin was the participation in and encouragement of idolatry in the land. He worshipped Canaanite gods and enticed the nation to do so.

4. What did Manasseh rebuild that his father had torn down?

He rebuilt the "high places" that his father, Hezekiah had aggressively broken down.

5. What does it mean when it says that Manasseh *"worshipped all the host of heaven, and served them?" Was he worshipping the angels*?

The translation is not clear. NIV renders it, "He bowed down to all the starry hosts and worshiped them." If that is correct, it may have involved in the practice of astrology.

6. What did Manasseh place in the Temple that angered the Lord?

An image (idol) he had carved.

7. In what way did Manasseh's sin spread to others?

Since he was king, Manasseh was held responsible for leading Judah as a nation into the sin in which he indulged.

8. How did Manasseh and the people of Judah respond initially to the Lord's warnings?

Initially, both Manasseh and the people refused to hearken to the word of the Lord.

9. What did the King of Assyria do with Manasseh?

The king of Assyria "bound him with fetters, and carried him to Babylon."

10. How old was Manasseh when he died, leaving the throne of Judah to his son?

Manasseh died at age 67.

Are you easily persuaded to courses of action that you would not have taken otherwise, or are you "a hard sale?" Certainly, we don't wish to become sorely obstinate in our interactions with people simply for the sake of proving to be difficult. At the same time, neither do we wish to be "tossed to and fro with every wind" that blows our way.

One way that most of us can measure our pliability is in our level of *sales resistance.* Some people are helplessly "led to the slaughter" by even the novice hacker. The story is told about such an individual who fell into the clutches of an eager sales clerk, who actually broke a sales record during the transaction. "How did you do it?" his boss asked.

"Well," the clerk said, "a customer came in and I sold him some fishhooks. 'You'll need a line for those hooks,' I said to him, and he bought some line. Then I told him, 'You'll want a rod to go with that line.' So he bought the rod. So I said, 'You ought to have a boat so you can use your rod in deep water,' and the guy bought a boat. When I told him that he needed a boat trailer, he said, 'Well, I'll take one of those, too.' Finally, I said, 'How are you going to pull that boat without a car?' and guess what! He bought my car, too!"

The manager said, "But I assigned you to the greeting card department."

The salesman said, "I know that. This guy came in for a get-well card for his girlfriend, who had a broken hip. When I heard that I said to him, 'You haven't got anything to do for six weeks, so you might as well go fishing.'"

How about it? Does that describe you? When you walk though your house, do you find a host of items you really didn't need? Is there an unused exercise machine that promised to do miracles for your health and form, or a computer you haven't turned on since the second week after your purchased it? Is there a boat in your back yard that only gets wet when it rains, and camping gear that's only been out of the box twice?

None of us likes to think of ourselves as "push-overs." Yet, that is precisely what some of us are. In the merchandise realm, that may be relatively harmless, though expensive. In the spiritual realm, however, the cost can go much higher than we even like to consider. Here, it can start our children on a track that we will regret for the rest of our lives. Carelessly buying into any and every idea can cost us fellowship that is precious to us, because of the wedge it drives between Christians and other friends. Ultimately, it can cost us our relationship with God.

Persuasion has a legitimate place in the realm of the gospel. Each of us yielded to persuasion when we said, *Yes* to the gospel's call. Furthermore, as we grow in Christ, we must remain pliable to the call for change and growth and new understandings. Yet, we should use caution when accepting "new ideas." We buy into those ideas with the same careful examination that would prove advisable when our life's savings are at stake. It may not be our life's savings; it may be our soul.

Present and Future

Zephaniah 1:12; 3:1-5, 11-13

A nd it shall come to pass at that time, that I will search Jerusalem with candles, and punish the men that are settled on their lees: that say in their heart, The LORD will not do good, neither will he do evil.

3:1 Woe to her that is filthy and polluted, to the oppressing city!

2 She obeyed not the voice; she received not correction; she trusted not in the LORD; she drew not near to her God.

3 Her princes within her are roaring lions; her judges are evening wolves; they gnaw not the bones till the morrow.

4 Her prophets are light and treacherous persons: her priests have polluted the sanctuary, they have done violence to the law.

5 The just LORD is in the midst thereof; he will not do iniquity: every morning doth he bring his judgment to light, he faileth not; but the unjust knoweth no shame.

11 In that day shalt thou not be ashamed for all thy doings, wherein thou hast transgressed against me: for then I will take away out of the midst of thee them that rejoice in thy pride, and thou shalt no more be haughty because of my holy mountain.

12 I will also leave in the midst of thee an afflicted and poor people, and they shall trust in the name of the LORD.

13 The remnant of Israel shall not do iniquity, nor speak lies; neither shall a deceitful tongue be found in their mouth: for they shall feed and lie down, and none shall make them afraid.

Memory Selection
Zephaniah 3:5

Background Scripture
Zephaniah 1–3

Devotional Reading
Isaiah 55:6-11

The evil reign of King Manasseh of Judah was followed, in the by-now familiar zig-zag pattern, by the rule of the reform king Josiah (see Lesson 4). The present lesson from the book of Zephaniah reveals the opposition Josiah faced. Many priests and princes were too entrenched in profitable injustices to be interested in changing. Zephaniah warned that ignoring God's will and tolerating corruption would bring judgment upon the land.

Many among God's people would no doubt ask how God could forsake His people after making an "everlasting" covenant with them. As in Lesson 1, this question is answered by the assurance that a faithful "remnant" would remain in the land. This theme brightens Zephaniah's otherwise doom-and-gloom pronouncements.

಄ಞ಄

A church, say, in Anytown, U.S.A., is declining both in numbers and enthusiasm, but its leaders are indifferent to this decay. A young schoolteacher moves to town and joins the church. "I know a firebrand of a preacher who could come in and turn this church around!" he says. However, his pleas are met at best with a yawn: "What's wrong with the status quo?"

Will the minority among the church members be so stifled in their desire for revival that they split off and form a new church? Will the complacency of the majority, and of their entrenched leaders, soon result in closing the church's doors for lack of interest?

The prophet Zephaniah faced this kind of scene about 630 B.C. A new king has called for reform, but is opposed in both religious and political circles. How will present attitudes influence future hope?

Teaching Outline	Daily Bible Readings

I. Searching for the Just—1:12
  A. God's quest, 12a
  B. Complacency punished, 12b
II. Woe to the Disobedient!—3:1-5
  A. Corporate deafness, 1-2
  B. Personal corruption, 3-5
III. Promise of a Remnant—11-13
  A. Addition by subtraction, 11
  B. Poor but fulfilled, 12-13
	Mon. Seek the Lord
	      Zephaniah 1:12–2:3
	Tue. Wait for the Lord to Work
	      Zephaniah 3:1-10
	Wed. Refuge for a Remnant
	      Zephaniah 3:11-20
	Thu. Plans for a Future
	      Jeremiah 29:10-14
	Fri. Surely There Is a Future!
	      Proverbs 23:15-23
	Sat. A New Thing
	      Isaiah 43:14-21
	Sun. Hope in the Lord
	      Psalm 130:1-8

Verse by Verse

I. Searching for the Just—1:12
A. God's quest, 12a

12a And it shall come to pass at that time, that I will search Jerusalem with candles,

The prophet Zephaniah portrays God aggressively seeking out those who oppose King Josiah's reform. His quest reveals both the righteous and the unjust. Some 300 years later this imagery will be reflected in the story of the Greek philosopher Diogenes, who became so cynical that he is supposed to have carried about a lantern in broad daylight searching for a single honest person.

"That time" apparently refers to the "day of the Lord" which is said to be "at hand" in verse 7. This is an approaching time of judgment, whether soon, as in the approaching fall of Jerusalem, or afar, as in the end of the world. The desired effect of such prophecy is to call believers to reform immediately: *today* is a day of evaluation, whenever it occurs.

B. Complacency punished, 12b

and punish the men that are settled on their lees: that say in their heart, The LORD will not do good, neither will he do evil.

"Deist" views conceive of God as a distant Being uninterested in our daily choices of good and evil and uninvolved in administering the consequences of such choices. Unlike this notion, Zephaniah shows that God can descend into the midst of our work-

places, courtrooms, homes, and stock markets and will respond in kind to the evil that He finds there. Those who ignore this active role God takes in their everyday activities are so morally sluggish that they are compared to the "lees" or sediment in the winemaking process which settle heavily to the bottom of the vat.

II. Woe to the Disobedient!—3:1-5
A. Corporate contrariness, 1-2

1 Woe to her that is filthy and polluted, to the oppressing city!

2 She obeyed not the voice; she received not correction; she trusted not in the LORD; she drew not near to her God.

Although 1:12 explicitly refers to the city of Jerusalem, there is some question as to what city is referred to here in 3:1. If the immediate context governs our interpretation, the reference is to the city of Nineveh, the capital of the Assyrian invaders (2:13-15). Indeed, Zephaniah's net of prophetic judgments is flung wide enough to include many cities, in Moab and Ammon and elsewhere (2:8). Certainly the Ninevites, in their idolatry, had earned God's judgment.

However, the reference to the "sanctuary" and the "law" in verse 4 may indicate a shift in the prophet's aim, and that here he refers to Jerusalem, the capital of Judah and thus the primary center of the evils protected by the enemies of the reform king Josiah.

23

The filth and pollution here probably stand for idolatry and injustice in the city, not a garbage collection or air-and-water problem. Yet the passage assures us that frustration with not being able to "fight City Hall" is an ancient problem. Injustice can become so imbedded in the workings of government that it becomes *structural* evil. Perhaps the example with the most far-reaching consequences in the 20th century was Hitler's Germany, which perpetrated injustices and crimes with worldwide effects, even though thousands of individual German people opposed his rule. On a smaller scale, structural evil can be seen when it is a constant battle to hold "absentee landlords" responsible for maintaining decaying tenements. Even as this is being written, lawmakers are debating the justice of "racial profiling," and the government's authority to stop and search individual people on a categorical suspicion based merely on the color of their skin.

Recalling that Judah was a "theocracy," its capital was supposed to acknowledge the rule of God, and make civic decisions accordingly. Thus disobedient city officials were not just a civic affront, but sinners.

B. Personal corruption, 3-5

3 Her princes within her are roaring lions; her judges are evening wolves; they gnaw not the bones till the morrow.

4 Her prophets are light and treacherous persons: her priests have polluted the sanctuary, they have done violence to the law.

5 The just LORD is in the midst thereof; he will not do iniquity: every morning doth he bring his judgment to light, he faileth not; but the unjust knoweth no shame.

No corporate or governmental entity becomes corrupt unless its leaders make corrupt decisions. The principle was illustrated several years ago in a history textbook that argued that "nations don't make war, people do." Zephaniah charges that Judah has come under God's judgment as a direct result of unjust princes and judges, prophets and priests. For example, priestly injustice can be traced at least back to the time of Eli, judge over Israel. Instead of settling for their authorized portion of sacrifices brought to Lord, they would take more than their allotment—by force, if necessary (1 Sam. 2:12-17).

Such unscrupulous leaders in both religion and government "gnaw not the bones till the morrow" or, as in the NIV, "leave nothing for the morning." That is, they are so voracious in devouring others and their rights that there is nothing left of them to gnaw on the next day. Unfortunately for such officials, God is in their midst daily, observing their deeds, weighing them against His own nature that ensures us that He will not do iniquity, and recording departures from this standard for judgment.

III. Promise of a Remnant—11-13
A. Addition by subtraction, 11

11 In that day shalt thou not be ashamed for all thy doings, wherein thou hast transgressed against me: for then I will take away out of the midst of thee them that rejoice in thy pride, and thou shalt no more be haughty because of my holy mountain.

Again the difference between "the one and the many," corporate Judah and just individuals, must be noted to understand this verse. Those who shall "*not* be ashamed" on the day of the Lord's judgment are those just and obedient people who *have* in fact been ashamed for all the "doings" of corporate Judah and its priests. This is because the unjust and idolatrous leaders who were said to have no shame, and who here are said to "rejoice in [their] pride," will be removed. Then "thou"—referring to the people of God who have been purged by the removal of the corrupt from among them—will have no haughty pretensions.

The fact of both shame and deliverance on the day of the Lord was often lost in the expectation of the Jews. Some expected that the Day would be a great party, regardless of how they had lived. The prophet Amos tried to correct this by warning, "Woe unto you that desire the day of the LORD! to what end is it for you? the day of the LORD is darkness [for the wicked], and not light" (Amos 5:18).

History would prove the truth of Zephaniah's prophecy that the faithful remnant would no longer be shamed, at least by idolatry. After Jerusalem was destroyed and most of the people were carried away into Babylonian captivity a century and a half later, a remnant was allowed to return and rebuild the city. Their lesson had been learned so well that Jews as a whole have never again had reason for shame because of the practice of idolatry. Also, as noted in the previous lesson, this "remnant theology"

is God's way of proving faithful in His promise to "eternally" bless the faithful—that minority of people who choose to live under His rule.

B. Poor but fulfilled, 12-13

12 I will also leave in the midst of thee an afflicted and poor people, and they shall trust in the name of the LORD.

13 The remnant of Israel shall not do iniquity, nor speak lies; neither shall a deceitful tongue be found in their mouth: for they shall feed and lie down, and none shall make them afraid.

Although the population of both Israel in the north and Judah in the south was decimated by their respective captivities (in 722 and 587 B.C. respectively), remnants of Jews were left in the land. Those who remained in the north failed to resist the inroads of foreign gods, and the land became known for its mixture of Yahweh worship with idolatry (2 Kings 17:24ff.). Those who were left in the south after Babylon conquered Judah were poor, menial laborers (2 Kings 25:12).

Yet these remaining inhabitants had a possession that the wicked lacked. They had integrity, trust, and the peaceful heart that comes from the worship of the true God and from treating others with justice. We know that "Better is the poor that walketh in his integrity, than he that is perverse in his lips, and is a fool" (Prov. 19:1). In a metaphor that compares these people to God's flock, the prophet describes the security that only God's "lambs" enjoy, exceeding any that can be purchased by wealth or achieved by power.

Evangelistic Emphasis

Perhaps the most often echoed question among unbelievers in their rejection of professors of faith is the question, *If there is a God, why doesn't he do somthing?* Perceiving themselves to be "good" and those around them to be corrupt and abusive, they call out for someone more powerful (perhaps God?) who will step in and stop those who abuse and oppress them. When God does not promptly act, they easily dismiss the claim of the religious that God exists.

In much the same way, those who make no attempt to be "good" easily dismiss the thought that "an accounting" will be made of their evil deeds. Ironically, they may even profess a belief in God. Yet, in all of their years, they have never once seen convincing evidence of God punishing the evil (or at least, not the "smart" evil). So, assuming that it's a "dog-eat-dog world," action is taken against the gullible and the weak without fear of the consequences that *might* come on some future "judgment day."

Between these two groups that reject God (either in theory or in practice) are those who want desperately to believe but struggle with the doubts that arise due to God's inaction. This was part of the struggle of the people living in Zephaniah's world. For those people, Zephaniah's oracle was a message of hope.

ॐ◌ॐ

Memory Selection

The just LORD *is* in the midst thereof; he will not do iniquity: every morning doth he bring his judgment to light, he faileth not; but the unjust knoweth no shame. —Zephaniah 3:5

Connie Stanton was a problem employee at Children's Palace daycare. She had been hired without the appropriate background check, because she was a member of Wildwood Bible Church that ran Children's Palace. Initially, Connie appeared to be an excellent worker. She was obviously a very high energy person. Her interaction with the children could not have been better. Connie's fault was that she was a habitual liar. Always, her lies carried an attempt to make herself look heroic, but they did so at the expense of the daycare center and her fellow staff members.

For months, it seemed to Connie and to the rest of the staff that nothing would be done, "because she is a member of Wildwood Bible Church." Each time Connie was caught in a lie, the Director talked to her about it, but no *real* consequences appeared. What neither Connie nor her coworkers realized was that documentation was patiently being gathered. The day of judgment eventually came.

Weekday Problems

Amber Winston has never been a political activist or any other kind of activist, for that matter. In fact, her general impression of such people has not been very favorable. "Troublemakers" is the term she has often assigned to them in her private thoughts. Last week, however, Amber became aware of an injustice in her neighborhood that generated the most intense fury she can ever remember feeling.

Last week Amber became aware that a good friend of hers from her college days was moving from the west coast to her neighborhood. She was thrilled until she learned that the neighborhood association was planning to block the sale of the house that her friend was purchasing. The official reason was based on an obscure technicality. The real reason was because her friend was from Laos. Due to the fact that Laos is currently one of the most oppressive nations in the world regarding freedom of religion, it was decided by those in control that *"We don't need that kind of people here!"*

* How ought Amber address this matter? Should she go to the homeowner association, city hall, her pastor, or her attorney?

* Should she attack the matter with the obvious determination of an Army sergeant or proceed gently as a diplomat?

* How can Amber enlist others of the neighborhood who would be just as outraged as she is about this racial descrimination?

Headache Hassles

Mom: Doctor, Doctor! My little Billy swallowed a dozen aspirin. What should I do?

Doctor: Are you sure it was a dozen?

Mom: Absolutely. I'm scared to death!

Doctor: Is he sleeping, is his color bad, or did he throw up?

Mom: No, nothing like that. But all that aspirin. What can I do?

Doctor: Just *see* if you can give him a headache.

❖❖❖❖

Dan: What does your mother do for a headache?

Stan: She sends me outside to play.

❖❖❖❖

Have you heard about the amazing new discovery? It's a pill that's half aspirin and half glue, for people who have splitting headaches.

This Lesson in Your Life

Henrietta White grew up in Yazoo City, Mississippi, and her husband Bill is from Tulsa, Oklahoma. When they were teenagers during the race riots of the 1960s, they overheard their parents discussing their strong views concerning the widespread racial unrest that seemed to being tearing apart the country. Henrietta, who is black, griew up fearing the oppressive power of "the whites." Bill, who is white, feared that "those militant blacks" were determined to ruin the country.

The idea that the day would come when Henrietta and Bill would meet and marry someone of the other race was unthinkable for both of in 1968. Yet, meet they did. The year was 1975, and the place was Minneapolis, where they had both gone for a training seminar being conducted by the firm they worked for in Jackson, Mississippi. The first evening Henrietta and Bill went out together for dinner, they told themselves it was a working session, not a "date." Yet, they enjoyed the evening more than they could remember ever having enjoyed a date. It had hardly ended until they were looking forward to the next.

By the end of the week (and the seminar) Henrietta was struggling sorely with her emotions. Though everything seemed so *right* in Minneapolis, she knew well that it would never be acceptable back in Yazoo City. Bill's mind was wrestling with almost exactly the same issues. They were both relieved and pained when the seminar was over.

Less than a month had passed following the seminar when Bill first called Henrietta's office. He "just happened" to be in town on business and wanted to know if she would let him take her to dinner. Before she could stop herself, Henrietta had accepted. Though Jackson is "the big city" compared to Yazoo City, it is still Mississippi. All through dinner, Henrietta felt as though the eyes of the whole world were staring at them. Still, she was not sorry that she had accepted the dinner invitation.

Less than a year later, Henrietta and Bill announced to their families that they were to be married. The strong disapproval that they expected from their families was, instead, outrage. Virtually disowned by their families, the Whites realized that neither Jackson nor Tulsa would be very accepting of their marriage. Seattle, however, offered them a place where they did not feel "out of place." Fortunately, Seattle has also become a major center for those seeking software careers.

A lot has happened in the past 25 years. Both the Washingtons of Yazoo City and the Whites of Claremore have come to love their grandchildren born to Henrietta and Bill and to accept the marriage that gave them birth. Henrietta and Bill have learned that prejudice is not a one-way street. Both of them are thankful that their children have been blessed to grow up in a world with a little bit less of it.

GETTING THE FACTS STRAIGHT

1. During what time period did Zephaniah prophesy?
Zephaniah prophesied during the reign of Josiah.

2. Who was the primary recipient of this message from the Lord that came through Zephaniah?
The people of Judah.

3. Upon what or whom was the wrath of the Lord to be poured?
The Lord's wrath would come upon man and beast, as well as fish and fowl.

4. What were the primary reasons for the Lord's anger?
The Lord's primary grievance was idolatry of various kinds.

5. In order to communicate the thorough nature of His punishment, how did God say He would search Jerusalem?
He said, "I will search Jerusalem with candles."

6. What was the basic attitude of the people toward the judgment of the Lord?
They were saying in their hearts, "The Lord will not do good, neither will he do evil."

7. Of what two offences were the priests said to be guilty?
They had polluted the sanctuary and had done violence to the law.

8. What image did the oracle coming through Zephaniah use to describe the princes?
The princes were described as "roaring lions."

9. What did the Lord profess He would do every morning?
He said that every morning He would bring His judgment to light.

10. To whom of Judah did the Lord promise mercy?
He promised mercy to a faithful remnant.

Humility is not something that comes to most of us easily. And, even when it does, it is often discovered later that it is only pride-of-another-form. Certainly, a truly humble man is hard to find, yet God delights in such people and shows his joy in the ways that he brings honor to them.

A legend that has followed Booker T. Washington demonstrates this truth quite well. It is said that shortly after he took over the presidency of Tuskegee Institute in Alabama, he was taking a stroll in a nice section of town when he was stopped by a wealthy white woman. Not knowing the famous Mr. Washington by sight, she asked if he would like to earn a few dollars by chopping wood for her. Because he badly needed exercise, and had no pressing business at the moment, the request did not distress him, at all. Instead, Professor Washington smiled, rolled up his sleeves, and proceeded to do the humble chore she had requested. When he was finished, he carried the logs into the house and stacked them by the fireplace, and the lady paid him a small fee for the task.

As Mr. Washington departed the lady's home, a little girl from the neighborhood recognized him. Later that evening she knocked on the door of the woman who had "hired" him, expressing her great delight that the lady had been privileged to have the noted Mr. Washington as a guest. She was full of questions about the occasion of his visit. What had the woman of the house served him? Would he be returning soon?

Very much embarrassed, the woman was able to dodge most of the little girl's questions, and early the next morning she went to see Mr. Washington to apologize. Once in his office at the Institute, with the door closed, the lady proceeded to apologize profusely.

"It's perfectly all right, Madam," he replied. "Occasionally I enjoy a little manual labor. Besides, it's always a delight to do something for a friend." It is said that the woman shook his hand warmly and assured him that his meek and gracious attitude had truly touched her and had taught her a lesson that she would never forget.

As the lady told of her embarrassment to her close friends, the word spread far and wide among the wealthy community. The tale that she told persuaded many of her acquaintances to join her in donating thousands of dollars to the Tuskegee Institute.

It is so easy for us to forget a truth so very important to life's relationships: *Arrogance spawns arrogance; humility returns humility.* When we treat people with actions that display a prideful spirit, we inadvertently set them up to respond most naturally with the same prideful spirit. Indeed, it would be "unnatural" for them to respond any other way. Yet, when we relate to people in a spirit of humility, we make it easy for them to respond to us in a humble and loving way—even if that is not their most natural demeanor.

30

Lesson 4

A New Beginning

2 Chronicles 34:1-3, 21, 29-33

Josiah was eight years old when he began to reign, and he reigned in Jerusalem one and thirty years.

2 And he did that which was right in the sight of the LORD, and walked in the ways of David his father, and declined neither to the right hand, nor to the left.

3 For in the eighth year of his reign, while he was yet young, he began to seek after the God of David his father: and in the twelfth year he began to purge Judah and Jerusalem from the high places, and the groves, and the carved images, and the molten images.

21 Go, inquire of the LORD for me, and for them that are left in Israel and in Judah, concerning the words of the book that is found: for great is the wrath of the LORD that is poured out upon us, because our fathers have not kept the word of the LORD, to do after all that is written in this book.

29 Then the king sent and gathered together all the elders of Judah and Jerusalem.

30 And the king went up into the house of the LORD, and all the men of Judah, and the inhabitants of Jerusalem, and the priests, and the Levites, and all the people, great and small: and he read in their ears all the words of the book of the covenant that was found in the house of the LORD.

31 And the king stood in his place, and made a covenant before the LORD, to walk after the LORD, and to keep his commandments, and his testimonies, and his statutes, with all his heart, and with all his soul, to perform the words of the covenant which are written in this book.

32 And he caused all that were present in Jerusalem and Benjamin to stand to it. And the inhabitants of Jerusalem did according to the covenant of God, the God of their fathers.

33 And Josiah took away all the abominations out of all the countries that pertained to the children of Israel, and made all that were present in Israel to serve, even to serve the LORD their God. And all his days they departed not from following the LORD, the God of their fathers.

Memory Selection
2 Chronicles 34:27

Background Scripture
2 Chron. 34—35 2 Kings 22—23

Devotional Reading
Psalm 119:1-8

31

Israel's downward spiral is halted temporarily in this lesson, which portrays the work of one last reform king, Josiah. Like Hezekiah before him (Lesson 1), Josiah cleanses the land of idolatry, and reintstitutes the Passover.

Another important feature of Josiah's reform is the discovery of a scroll which the text calls "a book of the law of the LORD given by Moses" —perhaps the book of Deuteronomy. The fact that it had been lost in the recesses of the Temple shows the priests' and the people's profound departure from active worship and attention to God's will. Josiah, however, leads the nation in a renewal of respect for the Word, and a revival that results in a postpone of God's judgment.

ഇൟൟ

Ask group members to imagine that they had no Bibles. What might happen to Christian faith and practice without the ability to consult the Scriptures over a period of several years, or generations. Would some believers be able to reconstruct some passages from memory? What would happen to important ordinances such as baptism and the Lord's Supper? How might Christian worship be changed? What specific Bible teachings would your miss most?

This was precisely the situation during the reign of King Josiah of Judah. Jewish faith and practice had been neglected so long that their Scriptures had been lost. Idolatry and pagan practices had swept the land. Imagine also the renewed spiritual strength that the people experienced when this book was discovered and its teaching restored!

Teaching Outline	Daily Bible Readings	

I. Reform Under Josiah—1-3
  A. In the ways of King David, 1-2
  B. Eliminating idolatry, 3
	Mon.	Josiah Doest Right
		2 Chronicles 34:1-7

	Tue.	Hilkiah Finds a Scroll 2 Chronicles 34:8-18

II. Recovery of the Law—21
  A. 'The book that is found,' 21a
  B. Grief at the loss, 21b
	Wed.	The King Is Grieved
		2 Chronicles 34:19-28

	Thu.	Josiah Makes a Covenant 2 Chronicles 34:29-33

III. Renewal of the Covenant—29-33
  A. Reading the Word, 29-30
  B. Renewing the Covenant, 31-32
  C. Josiah's heritage, 33
	Fri.	Josiah Keeps the Passover
		2 Chronicles 35:1-10

	Sat.	No King Like Josiah 2 Kings 23:24-30
	Sun.	Call to Renewal Ephesians 4:17-24

Verse by Verse

I. Reform Under Josiah—1-3

A. In the ways of King David, 1-2

1 Josiah was eight years old when he began to reign, and he reigned in Jerusalem one and thirty years.

2 And he did that which was right in the sight of the LORD, and walked in the ways of David his father, and declined neither to the right hand, nor to the left.

At least until Israel was captured by Assyria, when a king died his eldest son inherited the throne regardless of his age or qualifications. The roots of this practice, which still continues in some monarchies, are to be found in God's promise to David that "thine house and thy kingdom shall be established for ever before thee: thy throne shall be established for ever" (2 Sam. 7:16). After that, regardless of the king's name, he was said to occupy "the throne of David" (e.g., Jer. 17:25).

For many kings, this blood-kinship was their only connection with David; but young Josiah took his heritage more seriously. King David had been called "a man after God's own heart." Under his rule, Israel had expanded its territory, riches, and influence; and his success was attributed to God's blessings for having kept Israel true to the worship of Yahweh and free from the influence of pagan religions. Unlike most other kings in the years

of both Judah and Israel, Josiah had the spiritual maturity and wisdom to model his rule after the positive aspects of his forefather David.

B. Eliminating idolatry, 3

3 For in the eighth year of his reign, while he was yet young, he began to seek after the God of David his father: and in the twelfth year he began to purge Judah and Jerusalem from the high places, and the groves, and the carved images, and the molten images.

Josiah's concentrated efforts to use David as his "mentor" began when he was age 16, eight years after ascending the throne at age 8 (vs. 1). Perhaps this focus on David, whose heart was inclined toward the true God instead of to pagan idols, led to Josiah's opposition to idolatry. It was only after another four years that he began a systematic effort to stamp out the pagan worship that had become a continual obsession with the nation.

As noted in Lesson 2, altars on "high places" and worship in "groves" (sometimes only represented by erecting poles) characterized the practice of Assyrian and Canaanite idolatry. Here Josiah begins both to eliminate these worship centers and the images of wood, metal, stone, or even geometrical designs associated with various pagan cults. Whatever the carvings, they were in violation of the first and second commandments (see Exod. 20:3-4).

II. Recovery of the Law—21

A. 'The book that is found,' 21a

21a Go, inquire of the LORD for me, and for them that are left in Israel and in Judah, concerning the words of the book that is found:

Temple worship had been so neglected, in favor of idolatrous worship under groves and on high places, that Josiah's reformers even discovered a considerable sum of money that had been dedicated to the Temple's upkeep, then lost (vs. 17). Along with the money, Hilkiah the priest had also found "a book of the law of the LORD given by Moses" (vs. 14). Hilkiah gave this "book," which was actually a scroll, to Shaphan the scribe, who had direct access to King Josiah.

This document was perhaps the book of Deuteronomy, since that book contains a restatement of the Ten Commandments and the rest of the Law of Moses on which Josiah would base his reform. Deuteronomy is also probably the source of the "curses" which Huldah the prophetess (34:22ff.) later said would be visited upon Judah for having neglected that Law (see Deut. 27:15-26). As important as the discovery of this document was, Josiah is also to be commended for having already made great strides in his campaign for reform, even without the guidance of Scripture. Here is evidence of the power of "oral tradition" and godly customs which had already guided the king to follow in the footsteps of his ancestor David.

B. Grief at the loss, 21b

21b for great is the wrath of the LORD that is poured out upon us, because our fathers have not kept the word of the LORD, to do after all that is written in this book.

Reading the powerful words of God through Moses condemning idolatry and other ungodly practices, Josiah grieves because of the gap between those words and the lives of people, princes, and priests. God had been careful to warn that disobeying Him would bring punishment not only on those who defied His rule, but on their descendants. Especially pointed was the law that idolatry would trigger the wrath of "a jealous God, visiting the iniquity of the fathers upon the children unto the third and fourth generation of them that hate me" (Exod. 20:5). Josiah had good reason to grieve, although the people also had good reason to rejoice that they finally had a king who was sensitive enough to be hurt when God's law was ignored.

III. Renewal of the Covenant—29-33

A. Reading the Word, 29-30

29 Then the king sent and gathered together all the elders of Judah and Jerusalem.

30 And the king went up into the house of the LORD, and all the men of Judah, and the inhabitants of Jerusalem, and the priests, and the Levites, and all the people, great and small: and he read in their ears all the words of the book of the covenant that was found in the house of the LORD.

We can imagine the drama of this important gathering of the leaders of Judah, assembling for the express purpose of hearing again the precious words of the Law that had been discovered. Calling the scroll "the book of the covenant" might lead us to think that Hilkiah the priest had found the entire Pentateuch, or first five books of the Bible. It was that collection that was widely known as the "Torah" (meaning law, teaching, or instruction). However, since the reading of the book was apparently in one sitting, it is more likely that the discovery was only a the part of the Law called Deuteronomy.

Note again the central role played by Jerusalem and its leaders. This reminds us that the books of Chronicles (which were originally a single book) were written in part as a witness to, and rebuke of, the northern tribes of Israel. These rebels had largely forsaken Jerusalem for Samaria, and the ceremony is described partly to remind them that Jerusalem was the center God had chosen to be the center of worship under His covenant with David (see 1 Kings 12:27).

B. Renewing the Covenant, 31-32

31 And the king stood in his place, and made a covenant before the LORD, to walk after the LORD, and to keep his commandments, and his testimonies, and his statutes, with all his heart, and with all his soul, to perform the words of the covenant which are written in this book.

32 And he caused all that were present in Jerusalem and Benjamin to stand to it. And the inhabitants of Jerusalem did according to the covenant of God, the God of their fathers.

Standing in "his place," probably in a throne room, Josiah shows that he understands that the scroll that had been discovered was not merely *law,* but *covenant.* That is, it included God's promise to be with and to bless His people, as well as to curse them if they forsook Him. It was the commitment with Israel that the God of grace would love and protect them, not just a threat from a God of judgment. In verse 32, "stand to it" does not refer to the posture of the people, standing as the law was read, but "standing *for*" the covenant, or pledging themselves to keep it (as in the NIV).

C. Josiah's heritage, 33

33 And Josiah took away all the abominations out of all the countries that pertained to the children of Israel, and made all that were present in Israel to serve, even to serve the LORD their God. And all his days they departed not from following the LORD, the God of their fathers.

The "abominations" Josiah removed are more specifically referred to in the NIV as "detestable idols," repeating the king's purge of idolatry referred to in verse 3. The people's response was supportive enough that they participated in the restoration of the Passover feast, described in 35:18 as unlike any other.

Yet, as heartening as Josiah's reform was, there is also a note of sadness in saying that the people supported his renewal of the covenant with the true God only "all his days." Important though a leader's personal commitment is as a "role model" fc the people, loyalty to eternal prir ciples must arise out of the hearts the people themselves if a nation is remain on the true path.

Evangelistic Emphasis

Throughout the month of June, Pastor Thompson addressed the need for the people of God to be thoroughly penitent, willing to confess openly their sins. He emphasized strongly the need for confession to be specific, not simply in general terms.

He cannot remember a time when people took his words more seriously. Since the last of June, every Sunday morning assembly has caused the sanctuary to seem like a great "confession booth." The only thing missing is the classic prelude, "Forgive me father for I have sinned."

Initially, the pastor thought that it would simply last a Sunday or two and then fade gradually, as most such responses do. Instead, the depth and seriousness of the people's confessions grew stronger each week. It's almost as though the more people hear others confessing, the more courage they have for their own confessions.

It would seem that such a strong response to his sermons would please Pastor Thompson. Instead, he finds himself severely stressed over the matter. He worries how all of this is affecting the visitors. Surely, they will leave thinking this is the worst group of people on the face of the earth.

How can he let strangers know that these really are good people and this really is a great church, when the people, themselves, are standing in the assembly confessing horrible sins?

℘℘℘

Memory Selection

Because thine heart was tender, and thou didst humble thyself before God, when thou heardest his words against this place, and against the inhabitants thereof, and humbledst thyself before me, and didst rend thy clothes, and weep before me; I have even heard thee also, saith the LORD.—*2 Chronicles 34:27*

Tearing one's clothes no longer communicates distress and sorrow, but we certainly do weep before God when our heart breaks because of our guilt. Often, it is when we are suddenly made aware of the cost of our sin that we weep the most. A child dies in an automobile accident, and the policeman ands you the ticket marked DWI. Yes, you've known for years that you needed change your behavior. But suddenly the sorrow you feel because of your vior is more than you can bear. So you take it to God.

you lose your job because of a random drug test at work. You lose your hen she learns of your cheating ways. You lose your business when nbling debts catches up with you. You lose your self-respect when et sin" breaks into your public life. Whatever the price we pay, it is consequence of our sin that finally makes us sorrowful. Yet in the may be the very thing that saves our soul.

Weekday Problems

When Pastor Willams reads the biblical account of Josiah's reform, there arises within him a deep longing to be able to move forward with such candor. Thirty years of ministry has taught him, however, that pastors do not have the freedom to "be up-front" about their short-comings. Too many of his colleagues have lost their career because of such idealism. One friend, struggling with lust, sought the prayers of his board to assist him with the battle. After his confession to them, he was out of a job and was forced to find another vocation.

Pastor Willams is not haunted by any closet skeletons like that. His longing is for confessing his sins and the sins of his church in regard to some treasured "doctrinal possitions" that he has become convinced grossly misrepresent the biblical text. He would love to lead his church into God's richer truths, but he knows that it would cost him both his job and his career.

* Does Pastor Williams have a legitimate fear, or is he merely overly timid?

* If he decides to press ahead with his prophet-like challenge to his church's "errors," how can he do so in a way that minimizes losses?

* Should he press ahead, trusting in the goodness of his people, or should he expect the worst and prepare in advance for his financial survival?

Roots of Reform

He who reforms himself has done much toward reforming others; and one reason why the world is not reformed is because each would have others make a beginning, and never thinks of himself doing it.—*Thomas Adams*

Reform should be more than a test of our beliefs . . . but rather a re-examination of them to determine whether we are following the dead letter or the living spirit which they embody.—*Anne Morrow Lindbergh*

The true reformer is the seminal reformer, not the radical. And this is the way the Sower, who went forth to sow his seed, did really reform the world.—*Anonymous*

The great fundamental principle of the Reformation was the individual responsibility of the human soul to its Maker and Judge.—*T. W. Chambers*

This Lesson in Your Life

Bill Wilson, Pastor of Franklin Street Church, was deep in preparation of his Sunday morning sermon when his secretary interrupted him to tell him that an angry woman wished to speak to him. What timing! Nevertheless, he accepted the call and attempted to listen sympathetically.

The woman on the phone was the parent of one of the children enrolled in the church's daycare program. Her complaint was about the driving and language of some of the high school students who parked their cars in the church parking lot, across from their high school. Bill told her that he would call the high school office to report the problem. They would probably send a patrolman over to monitor the kids' driving, he said.

"I can't believe you're not going to do any more than that!" the woman responded. Bill was amazed, because he thought his response was quite generous. Before the conversation ended, however, Bill learned the caller wanted him to say, "Ok. We'll stop the high school students from parking in our parking lot." Nothing less than that was going to satisfy her.

Though Bill Wilson was never sure that he ever communicated successfully with the lady, he tried to tell her that the church was not primarily a daycare center. "This is a church." he told her. "We attempt to minister in a variety of ways to our community. Our daycare center is only one of many ministries. We also feed the hungry, clothe the needy, counsel with the hurting, reach out to the lost, house community service groups, and provide a safe place for high school students to park their cars."

At one point, the woman made the statement, "Well, it seems to me that you ought to be more concerned with keeping your paying customers happy than with where those hoodlums are going to park."

Although Bill knew by then that the woman would not be satisfied, he stuck by his guns. Daycare was not his primary focus. Neither was food and clothing distribution, community service, counseling, or any of those other ministries. He was pastor of a church. That was central. All of those other things were merely outgrowths of and expressions of the church's primary function as a church. If either Bill or his church were to lose sight of that fact, the church would lose its primary identity.

In much the same way, the Temple in King Josiah's day was the House of God. As the place ordained for the worship of God, worship wasn't a sideline. It was there that sacrifices were made to God's glory. There also the Law was stored, read, hallowed, and enforced.

Unfortunately, as the Temple grew old these functions declined in significance. The problem was reflected vividly in the fact that, over the years, the Law fell into such disregard that it was actually lost. For the Temple to lose its Law was for the Temple to lose its identity.

STRAIGHT

1. How old was Josiah when he began to seek God's will for his life?
He was 15or 16 (he became king at eight years old and he began seeking God in the eighth year of his reign).

2. In what year of his reign did Josiah begin purging Judah of the "high places" and their images?
He began the purge in the 12th year of his reign.

3. What did Josiah have done with the bones of the priests of idolatry?
He had their bones burned on their own altars.

4. In the 18th year of his reign, whom did Josiah send to repair the house of God?
He sent Shaphan the son of Azaliah, and Maaseiah the governor of the city, and Joah the son of Joahaz the recorder.

5. Who is described with the words, "did their work faithfully"?
The craftsmen who did the repairs on the Temple.

6. Who found the book of the Law in the Temple?
Hilkiah the priest.

7. Who took the book of the Law that Hilkiah had found to the king to inform him?
Shaphan the scribe took the book to the king.

8. To whom did the delegation from King Josiah go to inquire of the Lord about their findings?
They went to Huldah the prophetess.

9. What word from the Lord did Huldah have for the king's delegation?
Because of Judah's idolatry, she would be severely punished. Because of Josiah's humbled heart, he would be spared.

10. What action did King Josiah then take in regard to the people?
The king gathered all the people together and read to them the words written in the Law that had been found.

Have you ever indulged in fantasies of being in a position of great power? Perhaps your dream had you in the position of CEO of the company for which you work. Or, maybe you imagined yourself as a court judge, or mayor of the city. If you are truly reckless in your fantasy life, you might even have played with the idea of serving as President of the United States.

In all likelihood, one element of such a fantasy had to do with forcing others to do what you wanted them to do. The power of command or force often dominates what we think of when we consider "leadership" or "authority." In reality, true leadership or authority is more complex than that.

For instance, William Oncken, Jr., in a 1970 *Colorado Institute of Technology Journal*, gave an analysis of authority that suggests it is comprised of four elements:

1. *The Authority of Competence.* The more competent the other fellow knows you are, the more confident he will be that you know what you are talking about and the more likely he will be to follow your orders, requests, or suggestions. He will think of you as an authority in the matter under consideration and will feel it risky to ignore your wishes.

2. *The Authority of Position.* This component gives you the right to tell someone, "Do it or else." It has teeth. "The boss wants it" is a bugle call that can snap many an office or shop into action.

3. *The Authority of Personality.* The easier it is for the other fellow to talk to you, to listen to you, or to work with you, the easier he will find it to respond to your wishes.

4. *The Authority of Character.* This component is your "credit rating" with other people as to your integrity, reliability, honesty, loyalty, sincerity, personal morals, and ethics. Obviously you will get more and better from a person who has respect for your character than from one who doesn't.

As one reads the story of Josiah's leadership of Judah, it is vividly clear that his leadership was not in name only. His effectiveness was found in the multi-dimensional nature of his position with the people. The fact that he sat on the throne was no doubt one source of his influence. Yet, his power of character obviously was the element that allowed him not only to call for reform, but to have the people widely embrace that reform.

Today's leaders in the church would be wise to examine the character of Josiah. If today's leaders are to take the people with them to the "higher ground of the Kingdom," they must move beyond orders and mandates to prayerfulness in behalf of the people they attempt to lead, and the humility that gives them authenticity for service.

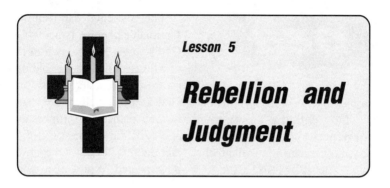

Lesson 5

Rebellion and Judgment

Jeremiah 6:16-21, 26-28

Thus saith the LORD, Stand ye in the ways, and see, and ask for the old paths, where is the good way, and walk therein, and ye shall find rest for your souls. But they said, We will not walk therein.

17 Also I set watchmen over you, saying, Hearken to the sound of the trumpet. But they said, We will not hearken.

18 Therefore hear, ye nations, and know, O congregation, what is among them.

19 Hear, O earth: behold, I will bring evil upon this people, even the fruit of their thoughts, because they have not hearkened unto my words, nor to my law, but rejected it.

20 To what purpose cometh there to me incense from Sheba, and the sweet cane from a far country? your burnt offerings are not acceptable, nor your sacrifices sweet unto me.

21 Therefore thus saith the LORD, Behold, I will lay stumblingblocks before this people, and the fathers and the sons together shall fall upon them; the neighbour and his friend shall perish.

26 O daughter of my people, gird thee with sackcloth, and wallow thyself in ashes: make thee mourning, as for an only son, most bitter lamentation: for the spoiler shall suddenly come upon us.

27 I have set thee for a tower and a fortress among my people, that thou mayest know and try their way.

28 They are all grievous revolters, walking with slanders: they are brass and iron; they are all corrupters.

Memory Selection
Jeremiah 6:16

Background Scripture
Jeremiah 6

Devotional Reading
Psalm 16:5-11

41

During the reign of the reform king Josiah, God called a young man named Jeremiah to enter the prophetic ministry. Sometimes he is called "the "weeping prophet" because of the profound sorrow he expressed at Judah's apostasy and the resulting judgment of God.

The present lesson emphasizes Jeremiah's plea for Israel to return to God's ways, as set down in the Law of Moses. Since the people defiantly refuse to listen, Jeremiah warns that God would actually place roadblocks in their path. The prophet does not apologize for his message of "gloom and doom." No other response could be expected from a man who loved his people, who was charged to call them back to God, but was unable to see the fruits of his labor.

Ask members of your group to share any travel "adventures" they may have had when they got lost. You may even want to exploit the "guy thing" of not wanting to stop and ask directions, or the charge some men make that women simply can't read a map—all in good fun, of course.

Ask whether anyone in the group gets impatient at having to follow a map. Point out that while some adventurous types think it's more fun just to strike out in the general direction of where the think their destination is, once we get hopelessly lost, the common sense thing to do is to go to the map and to submit to its guidance.

In this lesson, the prophet Jeremiah calls the people back to the "map of life"—the Law that God gave them at Sinai. However, they found his message dull and regressive. What they failed to realize is that a map functions not as a dead relic from the past, but a living guide into the future.

Teaching Outline	Daily Bible Readings

I. Rejected Call—6:16-17
 	
II. Reply from God—18-21
  A. The cost of rejection, 18-19
  B. Sacrifices become pitfalls, 20-21
 	
III. Response of Grief—26-28
  A. Jeremiah's lament, 26
  B. A failed test, 27-28
	Mon. Look for the Good Way
	      Jeremiah 6:16-21
	Tue. Tried as Silver
	      Jeremiah 6:22-30
	Wed. Amend Your Ways
	      Jeremiah 7:1-7
	Thu. The People Do Not Listen
	      Jeremiah 7:16-28
	Fri. Return and Rest
	      Isaiah 30:15-19
	Sat. Those Who Enter God's Rest
	      Hebrews 4:1-11
	Sun. Invitation to Christ's Rest
	      Matthew 11:25-30

Verse by Verse

I. Rejected Call—6:16-17

16 Thus saith the LORD, Stand ye in the ways, and see, and ask for the old paths, where is the good way, and walk therein, and ye shall find rest for your souls. But they said, We will not walk therein.

17 Also I set watchmen over you, saying, Hearken to the sound of the trumpet. But they said, We will not hearken.

God's people are standing at a junction of several roads, and Jeremiah urges them to choose the path that will keep them walking in the light of God's Law. Far from a mere return to the past, the Law is the gateway into a faithful future. It is "the good way," leading toward rest for their souls. In short, God is calling them to what people the world over have longed for—peace and tranquillity, deliverance from the multitude of false paths that keep their lives so stressful and uncertain.

The people, however, want to be free from the restraint of the old paths. They want to experiment with forbidden pleasures, such as those offered in the immoral worship of pagan gods. They want to make alliances with nations instead of depending on a God they cannot see. So they bluntly reject God's, and Jeremiah's, plea.

In verse 17 the imagery turns from a shepherd to a watchman on the city wall. The prophets had been appointed to "sound the trumpet" as a warning that the enemy of disobedience is ready to storm the walls. A watchman's trumpet call hopefully rang out in time for the people to arm themselves for battle, and was often their salvation. One would think that anyone would be grateful for such a warning; but in this case the people ignore the danger, and decline to take defensive measures. "We will not listen to such alarmist propaganda," they say.

No wonder Jeremiah is called "the weeping prophet." He is in the same situation Jesus was when he lamented that He had cried out again and again to the people of Jerusalem, representing all Jewry, hoping to save them from ruin. "Repent and turn," He called. Then, rejected by His own people, He added one of the most forlorn lines of Scripture: "but ye would not" (Matt. 23:37). Although, like Samuel before him, Jeremiah no doubt knew at one level that the people were rejecting God, not His prophet, the bond between prophet and people was too strong and complex to separate the call from the person issuing the call. Even today every "reform-minded" pastor whose appeals are rejected may experience anguish like that of Jeremiah.

II. Reply from God—18-21

A. The cost of rejection, 18-19

18 Therefore hear, ye nations, and know, O congregation, what is

among them.

19 Hear, O earth: behold, I will bring evil upon this people, even the fruit of their thoughts, because they have not hearkened unto my words, nor to my law, but rejected it.

Now, as a watchman scorned, God turns to "the nations" round about Judah, as a "congregation" who can bear witnesses to the justice of the judgment He will rain down upon His own people. These pagan nations have been enticing Israel to idolatry, so they know very well that forbidden worship is among God's people, and can serve as a "jury" returning a verdict of "guilty as charged."

Verse 19 broadens the scope of the witnesses God summons to include the entire earth. All this is important, lest Gentile nations accuse the God of the Jews of being disloyal to the Covenant they know He made with the Chosen Race. God invites them to be more discerning than His own people, and to exonerate Him from the charge that the people do not deserve the judgment He will bring upon them. It is not a case of divine disloyalty; the people are reaping the "fruit of their [disloyal] thoughts."

A brief glance at the historical background of the judgment predicted here, along with a map of the period (8th to 6th century B.C.) may be helpful. Although it is the Babylonians, to the east of the Promised Land, who will conquer Judah, verse 22 predicts that Judah's punishment will descend "from the *north*." This may raise a question, since at the time Jeremiah wrote, the *Assyrians* were threatening Judah from the north. What occurred

is that the late Assyrian kings, after Sennacherib, were increasingly threatened themselves by the Babylonians, from the south. Eventually, under King Nebuchadnezzar, the Babylonians swept from their native land of Chaldea northward and conquered Assyria. It would have been impossible for them to go eastward, across the great Arabian desert, to attack Judah, so they launched their invasion from the former Assyrian strongholds to the north of Judah. After laying siege to Judah for many months, Babylonian troops conquered the land in 587 B.C.).

B. Sacrifices become pitfalls, 20-21

20 To what purpose cometh there to me incense from Sheba, and the sweet cane from a far country? your burnt offerings are not acceptable, nor your sacrifices sweet unto me.

21 Therefore thus saith the LORD, Behold, I will lay stumblingblocks before this people, and the fathers and the sons together shall fall upon them; the neighbour and his friend shall perish.

This passage provides an interesting side note describing something of the international trade and commerce developed by Judah. For use in their worship, the country imported incense from Sheba, in southwestern Arabia (generally the area that is modern Yemen). "Sweet cane" or "calamus," probably from India, was made into the precious oil of anointing (see Exod. 30:23ff).

Whatever the commercial value and supposed spiritual benefit of such valuable commodities, the sacrifices in which they were used were worse than useless because the people also worshiped foreign gods at alien altars. Jeremiah therefore echoes similar judgments from other prophets who thundered that God rejects sacrifices that are not from pure hearts and obedient people (see Micah 6:6-8; Amos 5:21-24).

Why would God actually take the initiative and "lay stumbling blocks" before His own people? It was because they had deliberately chosen to worship falsely and to disobey God. Although this is in one sense *self*-destructive ("the fruit of their thoughts," vs. 19), the self-imposed sentence carries with it the awful consequence that God actually enables the willfully disobedient to dig their grave deeper. As Paul would later write, God will send to those who deliberately reject Him "strong delusion, that they should believe a lie" (2 Thess. 2:11). This principle of divine help in disbelief underscores the importance of maintaining a heart that actively desires to know and obey God.

III. Response of Grief—26-28
A. Jeremiah's lament, 26

26 O daughter of my people, gird thee with sackcloth, and wallow thyself in ashes: make thee mourning, as for an only son, most bitter lamentation: for the spoiler shall suddenly come upon us.

In verse 24, the "voice" of the text switches from God to Jeremiah. It is as though God's terrible judgments have so moved the prophet that he cries out to his people himself. They have been so hard-hearted that it is too late to repent. Instead they should go into mourning, adorning themselves in sackcloth and ashes as at the funeral for an only child. After all, God had chosen no other nation to be His "son," or chosen people. The ancient custom was to hire mourners to send up a wail from the funeral procession. Jeremiah urges the people to take up this lament because "the spoiler"—the Babylonian army—is at the gates.

B. A failed test, 27-28

27 I have set thee for a tower and a fortress among my people, that thou mayest know and try their way.

28 They are all grievous revolters, walking with slanders: they are brass and iron; they are all corrupters.

Returning to God himself as the speaker, the text shows that God had appointed Jeremiah to serve in the role of the watchman in the watch-tower on the walls of an ancient fortified city. His task is to "try" or test the people, measuring the quality of their commitment to the true God. As verse 28 shows, we are to think here not of a written or oral test, but a testing of ore by an assayer of precious metals for its anticipated silver content.

Unfortunately, Judah fails the test miserably, as indicated in the divine Assayer's report. Instead of yielding silver, the test shows that the people are like throwaway residue of brass and iron. Reading ahead to verse 29 reminds us that at times lead was added to the ore being tested, in hope that its weight would assist the silver in separating from the ore. Even that technique is wasted on these people, however, for they turn out to be only "reprobate" or rejected (NIV) silver, fit only to be discarded by the Lord.

Evangelistic Emphasis

Bill and Ted are both age 22. They've been best friends as long as either of them can remember, living across the street from each other during all of their childhood. Four months ago, they graduated from Princeton together. Bill received his degree in Engineering. Ted was granted a Bachelor's Degree in Psychology. Neither of them see much future in their chosen fields without graduate school, but they suspect their graduate pursuits will take them different directions geographically. For the past four years they've been roommates.

Bill is concerned for Ted, because Ted is not a Christian. In spite of all their years of friendship and all the times Ted has gone with him to church, Ted remains solidly outside Christ. He perceives himself to be "a pretty good guy," without any need to "be saved." Bill, however, knows well the direction of Ted's choices, and he strongly fears that, without his companionship, Ted's walk will be in the direction of increasingly empty secularism.

Yes. Ted is "a pretty good guy," but his choices are not those that build life for eternity. It saddens Bill to know that, one of these days, Ted will find himself empty and lost and horribly lonely. One more course in Psychology will not fix what is wrong. At the same time, Bill is aware that, until that time comes, Ted is unlikely to understand really his need for a Savior.

ଯ୦ରଛ

Memory Selection

Thus saith the Lord, Stand ye in the ways, and see, and ask for the old paths, where is the good way, and walk therein, and ye shall find rest for your souls. But they said, We will not walk therein.—*Jeremiah 6:16*

Throughout the mid to late 1980s, quite a few banks in Texas "went under" due to the large number of loans and investments related to the oil industry. The '80s were not good years for the oil industry. Consequently, they were not good years for Texas banks.

As soon as a bank defaulted so as to be placed under the supervision of the Federal Deposit Insurance Corporation (FDIC), that federal agency reorganized the structure of the defunct bank. The reorganization was not for the purpose of trying some new banking scheme that was touted as highly profitable. Rather, the FDIC brought the banking procedures back to "square one" —the fundamentals.

Such was the call of God to the people of Judah through Jeremiah. The prophet was not calling the people back to traditionalism. Rather, his message was a call to the fundamentals of faithfulness.

Weekday Problems

Jim and Helen have a 10-year-old son. Mark is "an only child," due to some medical complications during his birth that have prevented Helen from being able to have more children. Mark is very much "the pride of their life." Though they try desperately not to spoil him, they realize that they may at times be guilty.

Last week during her morning devotional, Jim became aware of Jeremiah 6:15 and it's rebuke of Judah's inability to feel a sense of shame. Reading those words heightened his concern for the behavior of their son. For at least five years, Jim and Helen have been trying to teach Mark a sense of modesty about his nakedness. So far, their efforts seem fruitless. He will do just fine for a while, then out of the blue he will dart from the bathroom to his room "as naked as a jaybird." Mark seems to have no sense of shame.

* Is the fact that Mark seems to lack any sense of modesty a matter of serious concern, or should his parents just relax and ignore the issue?

* If Mark were your child, would you be concerned enough to take action? If so, what action? If not, at what age would you become concerned?

* Would your concern be different if the child were a daughter? Why or why not?

Out of the Mouths of Babes (and Lawyers)

Children have been heard to quote the Lord's Prayer like this:

Our Father, who are in heaven, hello, what be thy name?
Our Father, who are in heaven. Hollywood be thy name.
Our Father, who art in heaven, Harold be thy name.
Give us this day our jelly bread.
Give us this day our daily breath.
Lead us not into creation.
Deliver us from weevils.
Deliver us from eagles.
Deliver us from e-mail.
And forgive us our debts as we forgive those who are
dead set against us.

First lawyer: I'll bet you don't even know the Lord's Prayer.
Second lawyer: Do to. "Now I lay me down to sleep. . . ."
First lawyer: OK, you win! I didn't know you knew the Bible that well.

47

This Lesson in Your Life

Henry and Velma West have heard many times the analogy of "the frog in the water." Each time they listened to the preacher describe how the frog will leap immediately from the pot if placed into very hot water. Yet, *if the water is warmed slowly,* that same frog will peacefully and obliviously remain in the water until it is completely cooked

Though they nodded approvingly each time the pastor used that illustration, neither Henry nor Velma really saw much relevance to it. They considered themselves very much "on guard" against any invasion of evil into their lives. They found themselves unable to imagine how they would ever blindly accept any such invasion, however slowly it attempted to enter. More than once, they have spoken out firmly when the youth minister attempted to bring some new fad into the worship assembly that was simply not acceptable. Each time, even though the innovation was very subtle, the Wests stepped forward and put a stop to it.

Last year, however, after a lifetime of living in Winchester, Virginia, Henry's company transferred him to Napa, California. Culturally, it has been a major shock to their senses. Henry and Velma expected it to be a more secular community. They were not prepared, though, for how different they would find the church. What happens during the worship hour is not particularly different. What has challenged Velma and Henry the most are the attitudes of Christians toward certain behaviors that they have always considered absolutely unacceptable. By far, the most significant of these is the matter of "social drinking."

For the first time, Henry and Velma are beginning to understand "the frog analogy." Napa is wine country. All the people in Napa Valley, including church members, drink wine with their dinner. At their home church in Winchester, that would be cause for immediate censure. Furthermore, in Napa quite a number of the people at church work in the wine industry. It is obvious to Velma and Henry that at some point Napa culture slowly infiltrated the church until it finally assumed complete control. They see so clearly how it was just like "the frog in the water."

The real irony for the Wests, however, is that they are the ones who are regarded as "morally suspect," because they smoke! In spite of their attempt not to make too much of the "social drinking" issue, it is clear that some of the families at church avoid them because they both smoke. They don't want Henry and Velma to be a negative influence on their children.

Velma is baffled. She grew up on a tobacco plantation. Never has she thought of tobacco as a "moral" issue. She knows that some regard it as a health concern, but never has anyone ever suggested her smoking was a sin. How should she and Henry deal with this clash of cultures?

STRAIGHT

1. **To what had the Lord compared the daughter of Zion?**
   He compared the daughter of Zion to a comely and delicate woman.

2. **For what purpose were the trees to be cut?**
   For "mounts" or siege ramps to be raised against Jerusalem.

3. **What image did Jeremiah use to describe the outpouring of wickedness from Jerusalem?**
   He said the wickedness was like a spewing fountain.

4. **How did the Lord describe the "ear" of the people of Jerusalem? What did he mean by that?**
   He said their ears were uncircumcised. They were incapable of listening.

5. **Why did Jeremiah say that the word of the Lord had become "a reproach" to the people of Judah?**
   The people of Judah no longer delighted in the word of the Lord.

6. **Whom did the Lord say was covetous?**
   He said that *"from the least of them even unto the greatest of them every one"* is given to covetousness.

7. **Whom did the Lord accuse of being dishonest?**
   The prophets and the priests were accused of dealing falsely.

8. **How were the prophets ans priests treating this illness in the land?**
   They were treating it as a surface wound.

9. **Were they ashamed of the wickedness in the land?**
   No. They had lost all sense of shame.

10. **Where did the Lord tell the people they would find rest for their souls?**
    Walking in "the old paths."

Under the headline, "Sing a New Song," a newspaper story told of a Los Angeles church replacing hymns with Broadway hits. Rather than "Amazing Grace," worshipers sang "Let Me Call You Sweetheart." Instead of the traditional sermon, the pastor simply asked provocative one-sentence questions between the sing-along numbers. These changes were simply Rev. John Griffin's attempt to "make worship meaningful," he claimed.

In his book, *Watching the World Go By*, W. E. Thorn told of a man who was celebrating his 100th birthday being approached by a news reporter who remarked, "I suppose you've seen a lot of changes in your day."

"Yes," said the centenarian, "and I've been against every one of them." Obviously, that centenarian was not a member of that Los Angeles church.

Howard Hendricks suggests that people basically have five attitudes toward change. (1) Early Innovators (2.6 percent), run with new ideas. (2) Early Adaptors (13.4 percent), are influenced by early innovators but not initiators. (3) The Slow Majority (34 percent), are "herd-followers." (4) The Reluctant Majority totals 34 percent. (5) The Antagonistic (16 percent), say they will never change. Hendricks goes on to suggest that the majority of ministers are being nibbled at by the last group. They focus on the minority opinion.

In all fairness, however, it is precisely the fear of radical departure from what one holds as high and holy that prompts such strong resistance to even the smallest and most productive change.

Unfortunately, our fear-based obstinance can carry far-reaching consequences. Leith Anderson, in his book, *Dying for Change,* reminds us that Charles Spurgeon became the pastor of the New Park Street Baptist Chapel in London when he was only 19 years old. The building boasted a seating capacity of 1,500, but the attendance was less than 200. Nine years later they built the Metropolitan Tabernacle to accommodate the large crowds. They established a school to train pastors and began a book distribution business. Metropolitan became one of the most famous and significant religious institutions in 19th-century England, attracting people from every walk of life. During his 38 years as pastor, he built up the congregation to 6,000 members.

When Anderson attended the Metropolitan Tabernacle in 1972, however, they had but 87 worshipers present on that particular Sunday. The speaker lamented over the difficulty in reaching the people in the immediate community of the church.

Much had changed in 75 years. London had changed, the neighborhood had changed, society had changed, all the world had changed. But the church had failed to keep up with the changes. Consequently, the church lost the battle of change.

Lesson 6

Another Strong Warning

Jeremiah 25:1-7; 26:12-13

The word that came to Jeremiah concerning all the people of Judah in the fourth year of Jehoiakim the son of Josiah king of Judah, that was the first year of Nebuchadrezzar king of Babylon;

2 The which Jeremiah the prophet spake unto all the people of Judah, and to all the inhabitants of Jerusalem, saying,

3 From the thirteenth year of Josiah the son of Amon king of Judah, even unto this day, that is the three and twentieth year, the word of the LORD hath come unto me, and I have spoken unto you, rising early and speaking; but ye have not hearkened.

4 And the LORD hath sent unto you all his servants the prophets, rising early and sending them; but ye have not hearkened, nor inclined your ear to hear.

5 They said, Turn ye again now every one from his evil way, and from the evil of your doings, and dwell in the land that the LORD hath given unto you and to your fathers for ever and ever:

6 And go not after other gods to serve them, and to worship them, and provoke me not to anger with the works of your hands; and I will do you no hurt.

7 Yet ye have not hearkened unto me, saith the LORD; that ye might provoke me to anger with the works of your hands to your own hurt.

26:12 Then spake Jeremiah unto all the princes and to all the people, saying, The LORD sent me to prophesy against this house and against this city all the words that ye have heard.

13 Therefore now amend your ways and your doings, and obey the voice of the LORD your God; and the LORD will repent him of the evil that he hath pronounced against you.

Oct. 6

Memory Selection
Jeremiach 26:13

Background Scripture
Jeremiah 25–26

Devotional Reading
Proverbs 4:20-27

51

This lesson summarizes God's case against Judah for its apostasy from the true God. This necessarily involves a repetition of much of what Jeremiah has already said. The events and sayings in his book are not arranged in chronological order. Thus the lesson warns about the evil that will befall the nation if its people do not repent, even though Nebuchadnezzar, king of Babylon, had already conquered Judah (see 24:1).

Jeremiah faithfully warned the people, unlike the false prophets who were at work at the same time. They preached only what the king and the people wanted to hear. Viewing these events from the vantage point of historical hindsight, we learn how valuable even unpopular messages can be.

How long would God withhold His promised judgment on Israel for worshiping idols and dealing unjustly with the needy?

&)CR

FOR A LIVELY START...

Since the relationship between God and Judah is similar to that between a parent and a wayward child, you might begin this session by asking such questions as the following.

Do good parents give their children second chances, or administer punishment at the first instance of disobedi-ence? What do you think about the warning from experts not to use threats? Does it work for parents who promise dire punishment for disobedience to fail to follow through? Where do the biblical principles of law and grace come to play in parenting?

Whatever the responses, this lesson reveals a God who is running out of patience. He has blessed His people, but they have responded with unfaithfulness. Judgment is coming.

Teaching Outline	Daily Bible Readings

I. Scene and Setting—25:1-2
  A. Rulers involved, 1
  B. Jeremiah's audience, 2
II. Seers' Warning—3-6
  A. Persistent preaching, 3-4
  B. Clear message, 5-6
III. Sad Response—7
IV. Salvation Available—26:12-13
  A. Jeremiah's defense, 12
  B. 'The Lord will 'repent,' 13
	Mon. The Persistent Lord
	     Jeremiah 25:1-7
	Tue. Jeremiah's Warning
	     Jeremiah 26:1-6
	Wed. 'The Lord Sent Me to You'
	     Jeremiah 26:7-13
	Thu. Officials Believe
	     Jeremiah 26:14-19
	Fri. 'Turn from Evil!'
	     Proverbs 4:20-27
	Sat. 'Listen, Stubborn of Heart'
	     Isaiah 46:8-13
	Sun. Hearing vs. Understanding
	     Matthew 13:10-16

Verse by Verse

I. Scene and Setting—25:1-2

A. Rulers involved, 1

1 The word that came to Jeremiah concerning all the people of Judah in the fourth year of Jehoiakim the son of Josiah king of Judah, that was the first year of Nebuchadrezzar king of Babylon;

After the reform king Josiah's death, the people had crowned a younger son, Jehoahaz, as his successor (2 Chron. 36:1). However, in these turbulent times, the greater powers of Egypt and Babylon were at war with each other and the tiny nation of Judah became something of a political football between them. Thus, after ruling only three months, Jehoahaz was deposed by Egyptian invaders and carted off to Egypt. His brother Eliakim was reduced to a vassal king over Judah, with his named changed to Jehoiakim (36:2-4).

Babylon's star was rising, however, and its king, Nebuchadnezzar, ("Nebuchadrezzar" is an alternate spelling) defeated the Egyptians. In the process, he took control of their holdings, which included Judah. Thus the present passage includes the king of Babylon's name and the year of his reign along with Jehoiakim's; for from now on, Judah is doomed to be a captured, vassal state, marching inexorably to oblivion.

King Jehoiakim failed to follow in his father's footsteps in reforming worship and re-establishing justice in the land. Jeremiah has already given his sad judgment on Jehoiakim and his reign, saying that instead of being lamented in death, his body would be cast outside Jerusalem in disgrace (Jer 22:18-19). The Chronicler added his own judgment, by now familiar: "He did that which was evil in the sight of the LORD his God" (2 Chron. 36:5).

B. Jeremiah's audience, 2

2 The which Jeremiah the prophet spake unto all the people of Judah, and to all the inhabitants of Jerusalem, saying,

"The which" refers to the years just mentioned, the fourth year of Jehoiakim's reign and the first year of Nebuchadnezzar's. The language here seems purposefully designed to show that Jeremiah was not just a "court preacher." So all will know of God's complaint, the prophet aims his message both at the entire capital city, then the surrounding countryside. The sins of idolatry, immorality, and injustice were endemic to the whole land, and no one, from beggar to king, will be able to say they were not warned of the coming judgment earned by forsaking God.

II. Seers' Warning—3-6

A. Persistent preaching, 3-4

3 From the thirteenth year of Josiah the son of Amon king of Judah, even unto this day, that is the

three and twentieth year, the word of the LORD hath come unto me, and I have spoken unto you, rising early and speaking; but ye have not hearkened.

4 And the LORD hath sent unto you all his servants the prophets, rising early and sending them; but ye have not hearkened, nor inclined your ear to hear.

Jeremiah is careful to show that he and other prophets do not have the blood of the doomed nation on their hands. They have faithfully preached God's words of warning. Jeremiah himself has been at this task for 23 years (he is now in the middle of his long ministry). Figuratively, both God and His faithful prophets have been "rising early" to issue warnings that continued disobedience would bring destruction. In addition to Jeremiah, these prophets included Micah, Obadiah, Nahum, Habakkuk, and Zephaniah—prophets whose writings have been preserved and who had preached since the southern kingdom began its decline under King Ahaz.

B. Clear message, 5-6

5 They said, Turn ye again now every one from his evil way, and from the evil of your doings, and dwell in the land that the LORD hath given unto you and to your fathers for ever and ever:

6 And go not after other gods to serve them, and to worship them, and provoke me not to anger with the works of your hands; and I will do you no hurt.

Despite the "gloom and doom" content of the prophets' message, it had a positive rather than negative

purpose. If the people would turn from evil, God would ensure that they continue to enjoy the fruits of the Promised Land, the land of the Covenant. If they would forsake the worship of idols, God would not harm them.

Note again, as in a previous lesson, the specific injunction against making idols, "the works of your hands"—a clear violation of the first and second Commandments. Even from a human standpoint, worshiping what a mere human craftsman had created was foolish. The prophet Isaiah is credited with the finest bit of satire, hilarious if it were not so serious, on this odd practice. A woodcarver takes great pains to carve a stick into the shape of an idol, then bows down before one end of the stick and worships what he just fashioned, while sticking the other end in the fire and warming himself by it! (See Isa. 44:13-17.)

III. Sad Response—7

7 Yet ye have not hearkened unto me, saith the LORD; that ye might provoke me to anger with the works of your hands to your own hurt.

A deep-seated spiritual sickness is hinted at here. The people have been quite deliberate in their idol worship, knowing in the core of their being that it angered God and was self-destructive. It is one thing for pagans to worship idols in ignorance, and another for God's own people, who have enjoyed health, wealth, and blessings from Him, to continue in habits to their own hurt.

This is essentially a description of *addictive* behavior—continuing to participate in habits known to harm oneself. Idolatry is not only an affront to God. With moral standards no higher than humans can devise (just as they craft the object of worship), idolatry sends a people into a downward moral spiral. Judah, and Israel before it, had a corporate addiction to this self-destructive behavior. Here God labels it for what it is, exonerating himself from any charges that He is unjust for punishing them. They have punished themselves.

IV. Salvation Available—26:12-13

A. Jeremiah's defense, 12

12 Then spake Jeremiah unto all the princes and to all the people, saying, The LORD sent me to prophesy against this house and against this city all the words that ye have heard.

The lesson now moves forward to a passage that finds Jeremiah defending his ministry of warning. This scene is the result of the prophet's having stood in the Temple and predicting that if the people did not turn from their evil ways, God's house would become "like Shiloh" (26:6). It was at Shiloh that the Israelites had experienced a defeat at the hands of their enemies (1 Sam. 4:10).

Few religious people welcome such warnings and threats, and Jeremiah's hearers in effect "stone the messenger" instead of heeding his message. Led by false prophets and priests, the people assemble in a mock court and sentence Jeremiah to death (26:7-11). It is important to note that Jeremiah is now considered to be guilty of treason, not just preaching doom and gloom. This charge was substantiated, in the people's minds, when Jeremiah counseled them to submit to the invading Babylonians, knowing that their fate would be easier than if they fought to the death in a resistance movement that even God opposed (see 27:8).

Despite the threat of death in verse 12, cooler heads prevail and Jeremiah's life is spared (26:24).

B. 'The Lord will repent,' 13

13 Therefore now amend your ways and your doings, and obey the voice of the LORD your God; and the LORD will repent him of the evil that he hath pronounced against you.

Remarkably, there is still time for God to "repent"—not in the sense of showing regret for sin, but literally to "change His mind" about His intent to allow Nebuchadnezzar, king of Babylon, to defeat Judah. This is not the only time Scripture speaks of God as "repenting" in this sense. As early as Genesis 6:6 the Bible says that "it repented the LORD that he had made man," because the human race had become so wicked. In that case, the flood resulted, with Noah and his family singled out for salvation. The pattern will be repeated in Israel's history. God "repents" of His promise to Abraham and his descendants and allows general destruction to descend on them, but again preserves a remnant to remind us that in some way His covenant will be kept.

In one sense this divine change of heart could be brought about with amazing ease—merely by returning to God. In another sense, however, given the stubbornness of the people and the by-now ingrained habit of idolatry, their own minds would prove more unchanging than the mind of God.

Evangelistic Emphasis

When God sent Jonah to Ninevah with a message of doom, it was not a message that was absolute. Though not specifically stated, Jonah knew his God well enough to know that, should the people repent, He would have compassion upon them and spare them.

When Virginia heard the preacher's strong words of rebuke for many of the sins in her life, she did not know the story of Jonah and Ninevah. All she heard were the minister's strong words of condemnation. His tone was one of heated anger. The look on his face was equally severe, and his words spoke threats of eternal punishment.

Virginia had gone to church as a guest of her friend, Jill. Not coming from a church-going family, she didn't really know what to expect. She certainly hadn't expected this, though.

As Virginia left the sanctuary that morning, she left with a sense of horror in her heart. Though the preacher greeted her at the exit and smiled warmly at her, she was not able to smile back. All she could remember was the angry treats of his fearsome God. That night, all she could think of as she tried to go to sleep was standing before the judgment seat of that fearsome God and hearing Him pronounce her sentence to eternal damnation.

Fortunately, during the years since that initial visit to church, Virginia has learned about God's mercy as well as His wrath. In the end, it wasn't God's wrath that touched her heart and changed her, but His love.

ಬಿಂಧ

Memory Selection

Therefore now amend your ways and your doings, and obey the voice of the Lord your God; and the Lord will repent him of the evil that he hath pronounced against you.—*Jeremiah 26:13*

For the novice or the uninitiated, the wording of the King James Version can be very disconcerting. It is difficult to imagine the Lord needing to "repent" from the "evil" He had pronounced. It was for that reason that Jill Adams read and reread Jeremiah 26:13 more than 10 times. As a new Christian, she simply did not understand how God could speak "evil" under any circumstances. Though she had been warned that the prophets could be challenging reading, she had not expected this!

Fortunately, Jill felt close enough to those of her "home group" from church to raise the question in one of their studies. They responded to her question with both clarity and kindness, not making her feel stupid for asking such a question. Gently, they showed her that it was the "punishment" or "disaster" that the Lord would graciously withdraw should the people repent.

Weekday Problems

Ray Rayburn has been a pastor for more than 35 years. During all that time, he has had only a few serious confrontations with the congregation he was serving. Never has it been a pleasant experience. Each time, Ray has determined that he was not going to go through anything like that again.

Unfortunately, Ray sees strong evidence that another such confrontation is on the horizon. In his sermons recently, Ray has been emphasizing strongly the destructive nature of racism. His remarks have been strong, because Ray perceives racism to be a growing problem among many of the people of his church. Though, Ray is trying desperately to speak in love, he can tell that some of the people hear his words as personal attacks against them. Since Ray is relatively new at this church, some perceive him to be an "outsider" who has come in to "ruin their church."

* If some perceive Ray to be an "outsider," what are some steps that Ray can take to help counter that perception?

* Is there some way Ray can address the evils of racism without a *confrontational* outcome? Explain.

* Is it possible that Ray could be overreacting? How can he be sure that he is being "prophetic" in his zeal, not simply neurotically "self-destructive"?

Banter Headlines

Newspaper headlines gleaned from the nation's presses:

March Planned For Next August
Blind Bishop Appointed To See
Lingerie Shipment Hijacked—Thief Gives Police The Slip
L.A. Voters Approve Urban Renewal By Landslide
Patient At Death's Door—Doctors Pull Him Through
Latin Course To Be Canceled—No Interest Among Students, Et Al.
Diaper Market Bottoms Out
Stadium Air Conditioning Fails—Fans Protest
Queen Mary Having Bottom Scraped
Man Found Dead in Cemetery
Father of Ten Shot—Mistaken for Rabbit
Dead Policeman on Force for 17 Years

This Lesson in Your Life

Les Hagen was once a rising star in his denomination. Having been careful to excel beyond the minimum requirements for pastoring a church, he proceeded to polish his gifts. Very early in his ministry, Les began to be noticed as "something special." His polish shone more brightly than any other rising star in his immediate surroundings.

As the years passed, it became apparent that Les was not just glitter and polish. He not only spoke with excellence, his insight unlocked windows toward the future that had been boarded up for years. Horizons that appeared dark and dim suddenly glowed with promise and vision.

It was a time of great change in the country. Many of the youth of the nation were remaining unreached by organized religion. The prized traditions of Hagan's denomination did not bend very easily to address the needs of the unchurched. Les, however, quite effectively bridged the gulf that was keeping them on the outside. He used illustrations that connected with their culture. He addressed questions that their peers were asking. He painted a horizon that cultivated understanding among the young and instilled within them visions that welcomed faith.

Unfortunately, Hagen's messages of insight were not favorably received by everybody. Some were made uneasy by his visions for the future. Others were offended by his disregard for the past. In the passing of time, what was once praise and acclaim turned into suspicion and disapproval. Those who were critical of Les accused him of being "out to destroy the church." Even though Les testified strongly that he loved the church and that his only quarrel with his denomination was a lover's quarrel, his words were not heard. Gradually, his critics convinced the people in the pew that he was an "enemy of" the body of Christ, because "he speaks against it."

No, Les did not have a group to rise up intending to kill him, as happened with Jeremiah. Nor was he placed into a well. Yet, the end result was perhaps no less tragic. Shut up inside a cage of ecclesiastical isolation, Les eventually had to decide whether or not he would allow his spirit to die there.

Unwilling to allow that to happen, Les left the denomination of his tradition and ventured into other territories. There his gifts and insights have been valued, instead of feared. There his pastorate has been a blessing to many.

Unfortunately, the history of the Church is filled with Les Hagans. It doesn't matter which denomination or tradition one studies, their prophetic words are nearly always regarded as threatening and adversarial in nature—even when they are spoken in love.

1. How long had Jeremiah been preaching to the people of Judah, while they continued to ignore his sermons?
   For 23 years.

2. What endearing term did the Lord use in reference to King Nebuchadnezzar?
   "My servant Nebuchadnezzar."

3. What kinds of sounds did the Lord say that he would banish from the nation?
   The sounds of joy and gladness.

4. For how long were these sounds to be banished from Jerusalem and Judah?
   For 70 years.

5. The Lord said that his cup will be filled with something. With what would it be filled?
   The wine of His wrath.

6. Where did the Lord tell Jeremiah to stand to preach to the people?
   He told Jeremiah to stand in the courtyard of the Lord's house.

7. Once Jeremiah had finished his sermon, what was the response of the people?
   The priests, the prophets and all the people seized him and said that he must die.

8. Why were the people angry with Jeremiah?
   Because he had prophesied against their city.

9. What other prophet of the Lord had they killed? Who was the King who had him killed?
   King Jehoiakim had the prophet Uriah killed after hearing his message from the Lord.

10. Who is credited with having helped keep Jeremiah alive?
    Ahikam, son of Shaphan supported Jeremiah and prevented the people from putting him to death.

Are you a good listener? Do you wish you were, but know that you fall woefully short in that realm? Be comforted by the fact that you are not alone in that deficiency. Many of us reflect a lack of cultivation of that skill.

Before refrigerators were invented, icehouses were used to preserve foods. These icehouses had thick walls, no windows, and a tightly-fitted door. Large blocks of ice were obtained during the winter and covered with sawdust to prevent melting. This would allow the ice to last well into summer. One day a man lost his valuable watch while working in the icehouse. He and his fellow workers diligently searched for the valued timepiece without success. A small boy heard of the problem and slipped into the icehouse. He soon emerged from the cold with the man's watch. The men were amazed and asked the boy how he found it. He said, "I closed the door, lay down in the sawdust, and kept very still. Soon I heard the watch ticking."

One of the reasons that most of us are not good listeners is that we haven't learned to be still long enough to hear. We're too busy talking and doing and going and running. Rather than thoughts and ideas, we hear only "sound bytes" that fail to establish themselves in our thought processes. I'm reminded of a little ditty that says:

A wise old owl lived in an oak;
The more he saw, the less he spoke;
The less he spoke, the more he heard;
Why can't we all be like that bird?

Or, it may be that we simply are exposed to so much chatter from a variety of sources that our brain suffers from "noise fatigue" and shuts down, blocking out what we really need to hear. Selective listening is generally thought of with negative connotations. Marilyn vos Savant, however, is listed in *The Guinness Book of World Records Hall of Fame* for "Highest IQ." And, in a 1995 article from her weekly column, she said, "Most of the stuff we hear is just audible junk mail." What Ms. Savant was saying is that if we're really smart, we **will** listen selectively.

An old Italian proverb says, *"From listening comes wisdom, and from speaking, repentance."* That is true in our relationships with people. One of the primary reasons that our relationships struggle is our lack of development of that skill. Yet, even more important is our need to learn to listen to God. In the words of the Lord given through Psalmist, *"Be still and know that I am God."* That is something that we need very much to learn.

God Demands a Just Society

Jeremiah 22:13-23

Woe unto him that buildeth his house by unrighteousness, and his chambers by wrong; that useth his neighbour's service without wages, and giveth him not for his work;

14 That saith, I will build me a wide house and large chambers, and cutteth him out windows; and it is cieled with cedar, and painted with vermilion.

15 Shalt thou reign, because thou closest thyself in cedar? did not thy father eat and drink, and do judgment and justice, and then it was well with him?

16 He judged the cause of the poor and needy; then it was well with him: was not this to know me? saith the LORD.

17 But thine eyes and thine heart are not but for thy covetousness, and for to shed innocent blood, and for oppression, and for violence, to do it.

18 Therefore thus saith the LORD concerning Jehoiakim the son of Josiah king of Judah; They shall not lament for him, saying, Ah my brother! or, Ah sister! they shall not lament for him, saying, Ah lord! or, Ah his glory!

19 He shall be buried with the burial of an ass, drawn and cast forth beyond the gates of Jerusalem.

20 Go up to Lebanon, and cry; and lift up thy voice in Bashan, and cry from the passages: for all thy lovers are destroyed.

21 I spake unto thee in thy prosperity; but thou saidst, I will not hear. This hath been thy manner from thy youth, that thou obeyedst not my voice.

22 The wind shall eat up all thy pastors, and thy lovers shall go into captivity: surely then shalt thou be ashamed and confounded for all thy wickedness.

23 O inhabitant of Lebanon, that makest thy nest in the cedars, how gracious shalt thou be when pangs come upon thee, the pain as of a woman in travail!

Oct. 13

Memory Selection
Jeremiah 22:21

Background Scripture
Jeremiah 22

Devotional Reading
Ephesians 5:8-17

So far, this survey has emphasized the prophet Jeremiah's condemnation of idolatry among the kings and the people of the southern kingdom of Judah. In this lesson the focus shifts to a more "earthly" problem—dealing unjustly with *people*—which as a matter of fact often stems from idolatry.

The previous emphasis deals with the doctrine of one God—monotheism. The present emphasis stems from what is often called "*ethical* monotheism"—how faith in one God results in one Source of morality and justice.

Jeremiah's message here is that God's people should apply the will of the one good and just God to society. The lesson shows that worshiping only the true God is not just an abstract, theological issue. It has concrete, human dimensions as well.

80Q8

Introduce this lesson with a brief discussion of the Parable of the Good Samaritan. Summarize the story (from Luke 10:30-37), emphasizing the three main figures who encountered the wounded man along the road.

Ask which God was worshiped by the priest and Levite, who ignored the plight of the man who had been attacked. Of course they worshiped the one true God, the God of their ancestors Abraham, Isaac, and Jacob. In other words, their theology of God was apparently orthodox.

Then note that the first two men who hurried by the wounded man would have considered the third traveler, the Samaritan, to have been "off" on his theology. Why, then, is he the hero of the story? *Because he applied the goodness of the one God to real life, allowing it to lead him to do good to a person.*

Likewise, the emphasis in this lesson is on "the Samaritan factor": *how we treat others is a reflection of what we believe about God.*

Teaching Outline	Daily Bible Readings	
I. Jehoiakim's Folly—13-15a	Mon.	Act Justly Jeremiah 22:1-9
A. Unjust hiring practices, 13	Tue.	House Built by Injustice
B. Self-centered luxury, 14-15a		Jeremiah 22:13-23
II. Josiah's Wisdom—15b-16	Wed.	Shepherds Scatter the Sheep
A. Blessed in his justice, 15b-16a		Jeremiah 23:1-6
B. Evidence of orthodoxy, 16b	Thu.	Do Justice Micah 6:3-8
III. Jehovah's Judgment—17-23	Fri.	The Faithful Disappear
A. Rich king, forgotten tomb, 17-19		Micah 7:1-7
B. Closed ears, 20-21	Sat.	Judge Righteously
C. Ultimate shame, 21-23		Psalm 7:1-11
	Sun.	Righteousness in Christ 1 John 2:28—3:7

Verse by Verse

I. Jehoiakim's Folly—13-15a
A. Unjust hiring practices, 13

13 Woe unto him that buildeth his house by unrighteousness, and his chambers by wrong; that useth his neighbour's service without wages, and giveth him not for his work;

As noted in the "Focus" section, God's case against Judah now moves from theology to ethics, from the sin of not worshiping the one true God to the arena in which that problem is reflected in how believers treat others. At first this problem is stated as a general denouncement of trying to get something for nothing—specifically, conniving to have one's house built without paying the builders. To get even more specific we must jump ahead to verse 18, where God's "attorney," the prophet Jeremiah, identifies King Jehoiachim as the homeowner charged with what amounted to slavelabor.

Although slavery sometimes seems to be taken for granted as a part of Old Testament culture, God issued commands designed to control it—controls that eventually would abolish the practice in nations most influenced by the Judeo-Christian tradition. Egypt of course receives the most obvious indictment because it enslaved God's own people. Prophets such as Amos railed against those who habitually made a practice of forced labor (see Amos 1:6-9). Most carefully controlled was the occasional practice of Hebrews making slaves of other Hebrews. At times, Scripture seems to forbid the practice, and even when it did occur the indentured were to be released every seventh year (Exod. 21:2-4).

The historical record of Jehoiakim's rule in Kings and Chronicles does not mention his enslaving the people. It does, however, note that the king imposed taxes on them to pay the tribute required by the conquering king Pharaoh Necho (see 2 Kings 23:35). It was but a short step to forcing his subjects to build his palace without pay. Building himself an elaborate palace while the nation was threatened both by Egypt and Babylon was an unwise move in the first place. As we have seen, however, Jehoiakim was not a wise king. He is dismissed in a single, by-now tired phrase as yet another king who "did that which was evil in the sight of the LORD" (2 Kings. 23:37), and was generally one of the reasons God allowed first Egypt, then Babylon, to conquer Judah.

B. Self-centered luxury, 14-15a

14 That saith, I will build me a wide house and large chambers, and cutteth him out windows; and it is cieled with cedar, and painted with vermilion.

15a Shalt thou reign, because thou closest thyself in cedar?

Continuing the reason for pronouncing "Woe" on Jehoiakim, he is quoted here as indulging his covetousness for luxury in building his palace. We can easily imagine that part of his motivation was to show Pharaoh by his opulent lifestyle that he was a grand king in his own right. So he proceeds to panel the palace's ceilings with cedar, probably importing them from the famous cedar forests of Lebanon, then painting them a royal red. Through Jeremiah, God reduces to folly this attention to externals while neglecting "the weightier matters" such as justice: "Does it make you a king to have more and more cedar?" (NIV).

II. Josiah's Wisdom—15b-16
A. Blessed in his justice, 15b-16a

15b did not thy father eat and drink, and do judgment and justice, and then it was well with him?

16a He judged the cause of the poor and needy;

King Jehoichim did not have to look far to find a better example of what really made a king in God's eyes. God challenges him to remember how his own father, Josiah, was amply blessed—not because he built himself a luxurious palace but because he exercised just judgment in ruling the people, particularly seeing to it that the poor and needy received justice— that the cause of the powerless who were most easily taken advantage of was not ignored. Also, unlike Jehoiakim, Josiah had first been more concerned about the state of a neglected Temple than he was about his own palace, and second he had been willing to pay for whatever building projects he undertook (see 2 Chron. 34:9-11).

B. Evidence of orthodoxy, 16b

16a then it was well with him: was not this to know me? saith the LORD.

How are we to tell whether we truly "know" God, or are only going through the motions of worshiping Him? Here God says it is by a special kind of "orthodoxy" often overlooked by those whose only measuring stick is right doctrine. We know that "It was well" with King Josiah, and that he actually knew God, not merely because his theology led him to cleanse the land of idolatry. Rather, he exercised the "orthodoxy" of tending to the poor, paying his bills, and ruling with justice.

This very practical point of view is especially apparent in the Old Testament. It is one reason that Judaism in later years did not produce as many "pure theologians" as did Protestant "orthodoxy." The prophets were assuredly concerned about worshiping the true God, but from that point they were more interested in personal and social justice than in theories about the nature of that God. The emphasis is continued by Jesus, who taught that "Not every one that saith unto me, Lord, Lord, shall enter into the kingdom of heaven; but he that doeth the will of my Father which is in heaven" (Matt. 7:21).

III. Jehovah's Judgment—17-23
A. Rich king, forgotten tomb, 17-19

17 But thine eyes and thine heart are not but for thy covetousness, and for to shed innocent blood, and for oppression, and for violence, to do it.

18 Therefore thus saith the LORD concerning Jehoiakim the son of Josiah king of Judah; They shall not lament for him, saying, Ah my

brother! or, Ah sister! they shall not lament for him, saying, Ah lord! or, Ah his glory!

19 He shall be buried with the burial of an ass, drawn and cast forth beyond the gates of Jerusalem.

The sad outcome of Jehoiakim's attention to self-aggrandizement over justice is indicated by the fact that he had no funeral! "Ah my brother (or sister)" was probably a standard phrase for the ritual of mourning. When a man of God died in 1 Kings 13, mourners cried, "Alas, my brother!" (1 Kings 13:30). Imagine, therefore, the disgrace of a wealthy king's burial not being accompanied by mourning and ritual and testimonials to his greatness. Jehoiakim's unjust rule ended with abasement, his body dragged outside the city gates by a donkey and buried without ceremony.

B. Closed ears, 20-21

20 Go up to Lebanon, and cry; and lift up thy voice in Bashan, and cry from the passages: for all thy lovers are destroyed.

21 I spake unto thee in thy prosperity; but thou saidst, I will not hear. This hath been thy manner from thy youth, that thou obeyedst not my voice.

Although King Jehoiakim will die without lament, God raises a lament at the approaching "death" or conquest of Judah. "Mourners" at this funeral include Lebanon and Bashan, lands that had at times been at least conquered by Israel and are therefore presented here as Judah's "lovers"— a figure of speech perhaps derived from treaties. Now it is these lands who cry "Ah, brother!" They bear witness to the way the God of the Jews had blessed His people with prosperity, only to have them, from the "youth" of their existence as a nation until their soon-approaching death, disregard His leadership and turned to idols and injustice instead.

C. Ultimate shame, 21-23

22 The wind shall eat up all thy pastors, and thy lovers shall go into captivity: surely then shalt thou be ashamed and confounded for all thy wickedness.

23 O inhabitant of Lebanon, that makest thy nest in the cedars, how gracious shalt thou be when pangs come upon thee, the pain as of a woman in travail!

"The wind" (Heb. *ruach*) probably stands here for God's Spirit, which is often described as the "breath" of His mouth. Here this "breath" is as hot as a blast from a smelting furnace, destroying all within its path. Specifically, the "pastors" or shepherds of the people who pretended to be their "lovers" are indicted for not being more faithful leaders. They and the people who followed them will be shamed as other nations watch their consignment to captivity in Babylon.

The NIV offers a clearer translation of verse 23, with the help of a footnote. It considers the phrase "inhabitant of Lebanon" to refer to Jehoiakim's living in a house paneled with cedar from Lebanon, thus figuratively nesting in the cedars. In contrast to such luxury, the approaching Babylonian invaders will soon have both the land and the king writhing as a woman in birth pangs.

Evangelistic Emphasis

Timmy Franklin was once the gleam in his father's eye. He and Timmy's mother had waited so long for a child, having been told by a variety of specialists that their dreams for a child were hopeless. Just two days before his dad turned 45, however, Timmy was born. What a thrill his birth was to his excited parents! But, that was 37 years ago. Last week, they learned that Timmy was gone.

Actually, Timmy had been "gone" a long time. At the age of 12, he began making unwise choices in regard to friends. By the time he was 15, he had a rap sheet that was unbelievably long. After that, it was in and out of prison continually. Timmy's life was one of drugs and alcohol and thievery and violence. Somewhere along the way, Timmy decided that "everybody" had it better than he had it. Driven by this illusion, he was eaten up with resentment, envy, and bitterness. He would take whatever he wanted by whatever means was necessary.

Timmy's parents had not heard from him in nearly 20 years. Last week, they learned that he had been killed and left in a remote Arizona desert about two years earlier. Only recently had his skeleton been found and identified. Though Timmy's parents grieve his death, they recognize that long ago, by his violent life, Timmy chose his violent end.

ഇൻ

I spake unto thee in thy prosperity; but thou saidst, I will not hear. This hath been thy manner from thy youth, that thou obeyedst not my voice.—*Jeremiah 22:21*

Mike Thompson was flying high on the "dot.com" craze just two years ago. His company, *Card Search,* started as a hobby in his bedroom. Basically, it was a internet search engine that allowed card collectors to find prized cards on the World Wide Web. Revenues were generated by advertisers who placed banners and links on his web site and from serious collectors who subscribed to the premium search tools available. What began as a hobby, however, quickly became a fortune.

While riding the wave of fast money, Mike's wife could not interest him in anything spiritual. He was always too busy to spend Sunday morning in worship with her. Even their private devotional time, that once was a treasured part of their day, got lost in the press of activity.

Even more quickly than the wave of prosperity came, however, it disappeared. Boom became bust overnight. Suddenly, there was time again—time for anything. There was time even for God.

WEEKDAY PROBLEMS   Fall Quarter, Lesson 07

Weekday Problems

Alfred Johnson has won bonuses five years in a row at Albany's Coats & Clark factory for outstanding production and profits. In addition to the generous financial bonuses, he's been granted several luxury trips and is being groomed for a corporate management position. Alfred and his wife, Thelma, have taken great pride in his achievement.

Never before last Sunday morning had Alfred ever considered that there might be a negative side to his prosperity. In class, though, a question was raised by Helen Franklin, asking if company managers in today's world wield some of the same power once attributed to kings. Helen is a line worker at Coats & Clark. The heart of Helen's question seemed to address the matter of companies, supervisors, and managers growing wealthy at the expense of overworked and underpaid laborers.

*Is there any legitimacy to this line of inquiry, or is Mr. Johnson just suffering under the weight of a guilty conscience from his new prosperity?

* Is it possible for companies and their managers to make windfall profits without mistreating their employees? How?

* What can Alfred Johnson do to make sure that he is not being guilty of getting rich unjustly?

Traffic Tickles

An elderly gent was crossing the street at a busy corner when a large St. Bernard without a leash came bounding around the corner and knocked him down. An instant later, a little foreign sports car skidded around the same corner and inflicted more damage.

"Did that dog do much harm?" asked a bystander, helping him up.

"Well, no, he didn't hurt me so much, but that tin can tied to his tail nearly killed me."

❖❖❖❖

Joe: I know of a man who was going 80 and tried to beat a train to a railroad crossing.

Flo: Did he get across?

Joe: Oh yes—a nice, marble cross.

❖❖❖❖

Slim: According to this report, in this country a man gets hit by a car about every 20 minutes.

Jim: What a glutton for punishment. He should just stay home.

This Lesson in Your Life

Nearly everyone—even some criminals—claims to want justice. Yet, I wonder how often our definition of justice is biased by how personally injustice touches us.

July 13 of last year, Andrew Burnett of San Jose, California, was sentenced to the maximum three years behind bars for killing a dog. After a minor traffic accident involving the dog's owner, Sara McBurnett, Burnett yelled at her, reached through her open car window, grabbed her fluffy white dog and hurled it to its death into oncoming traffic.

According to the Associated Press release, "The courtroom erupted in applause when Judge Kevin J. Murphy, who said Burnett's release would pose a danger to the community, rejected a recommendation for probation and sentenced Burnett to the maximum possible for felony animal cruelty."

People with very strong feelings on both sides were in the court room. Burnett's mother appealed for leniency, claiming that Burnett is an animal lover. Even before the trial, animal rights advocates began lobbying for much harsher penalties, claiming that three years is not sufficient punishment. Some called for life imprisonment. Then, there were the "bean counters" who calculated that locking up Burnett for that long is going to cost the people of California in excess of $200,000. "Surely," they cried, "there has to be a better way!"

Was justice served in the case? I suspect that question will still be debated years from now. Even then, one will find voices speaking out on all sides of the issue, because rarely is justice quite so cut and dried as we would like it to be. Even though we claim to have the best justice system in the world, it is not perfect. Sometimes the media exerts undue influence. Community bias may place a huge psychological weight on the court system to render a specific verdict. Attitudes of family members of the jury sometimes coach and pressure. One's financial assets or public prominence may buy leniency, or prompt a cry for a more severe penalty. On the other hand, one's inability to hire an attorney may force one to accept the defense of an inept public defender.

While perfect justice may never be achieved, our pursuit of it must never cease. A wise man of ancient Athens was asked when injustice would be abolished. "When those who are not wronged feel as indignant as those who are," he said. Nothing has changed since those days. Injustice will never cease until the wealthy pursue justice with the same zeal as the poor, whites understand its absence as well as people of color, and those blessed by its gavel insist that the same blessing is deserved by everyone.

1. Where did the Lord tell Jeremiah to go to proclaim his warning to the leaders of Judah?

The Lord told him to go to the palace of the king of Judah.

GETTING THE FACTS STRAIGHT

2. What positive message did Jeremiah carry to the king's palace?

The Lord told the king do what is right and just and rescue those who had been wronged.

3. What negative message did Jeremiah carry to the king?

He was told to do no wrong to the alien, the orphan or the widow, and not to shed innocent blood.

4. What conduct brought the promise of kings riding in chariots and on horses?

The kings were to be careful to carry out the commands they were being given.

5. What question would be asked by people from various nations?

They would ask why the Lord had allowed the city to become so desolate.

6. What answer would they be given?

They would be told that God's people had broken covenant with Him and had run after other gods.

7. For whom were the people told not to mourn?

They were told not to weep for the dead king.

8. What kind of burial did the Lord say that Jehoiakim would receive?

He would receive the burial of a donkey—his body would be dragged away and thrown outside the gate.

9. If Jehoiakim were to be the signate ring on the Lord's hand, how did the Lord say He would respond?

Should Jehoiakim be the signate ring on the Lord's finger, He would take him off.

10. Why was Jehoiakim to be regarded as childless?

Because, none of his children would prosper nor sit on his throne.

69

Several years ago, *USA Today* ran a story about John Barrier, who didn't like the way a bank manager, in Spokane, Washington, looked at him because of how he was dressed. John was wearing construction clothes and got a look as if he had crawled out from under a rock.

The problem began when Barrier went to Old National Bank to cash a $100 check. When he tried to get his parking slip validated to save 60 cents, a receptionist refused, saying he hadn't conducted a transaction. "You have to make a deposit," she told him. When he told her that he was a substantial depositor, she looked at him as if "she really believed that—NOT!"

John then asked to see the manager, who also refused to validate the ticket. Barrier then went to the bank headquarters and threatened to withdraw his money unless the manager apologized. No apology came. Consequently, the next day John Barrier returned to the bank and closed his account, withdrawing over $2 million dollars.

I suspect this story could be repeated a thousand times or more, only with other names. Far too often, people are devalued on the basis of their appearances, or on the basis of how much money they have, or at least how much we *perceive* them to have. How Mr. Barrier was treated, however, was wrong, regardless his financial status. It just so happened that the bank felt the consequences of its rudeness because he was a man of money. And, of course, there is something inside us that quickly declares, "It serves them right!"

I wonder, though, how many times I've been guilty of the very same transgression. How many times have I dismissed people because of the way they were dressed or how they smelled? How often have I ignored someone's opinion because I did not recognize him as someone who deserved to have an opinion? How many people have I given "a look" that suggested that they had crawled out from under a rock? Father, forgive me.

Usually when we think of "justice" we think of matters that are governmental or official. Dutifully, we attempt to establish laws that are just, and policies that treat everyone fairly. When we hear that someone was "unjustly accused" or "unjustly tried" in our court system, we eagerly become part of the outcry. Yet, we easily forget that justice is not only a matter of government, courts, and laws. It also pertains to our personal treatment of others.

Does the way we treat others embody justice? Is that true even when we are dealing with people who don't measure up to our standards of income, morals or manners? Do we treat people justly simply because they are made in the image of God, even when they do not measure up to our own sense of worth?

Lesson 8

Hope for the Future

Jeremiah 31:23-34

Thus saith the LORD of hosts, the God of Israel; As yet they shall use this speech in the land of Judah and in the cities thereof, when I shall bring again their captivity; The LORD bless thee, O habitation of justice, and mountain of holiness.

24 And there shall dwell in Judah itself, and in all the cities thereof together, husbandmen, and they that go forth with flocks.

25 For I have satiated the weary soul, and I have replenished every sorrowful soul.

26 Upon this I awaked, and beheld; and my sleep was sweet unto me.

27 Behold, the days come, saith the LORD, that I will sow the house of Israel and the house of Judah with the seed of man, and with the seed of beast.

28 And it shall come to pass, that like as I have watched over them, to pluck up, and to break down, and to throw down, and to destroy, and to afflict; so will I watch over them, to build, and to plant, saith the LORD.

29 In those days they shall say no more, The fathers have eaten a sour grape, and the children's teeth are set on edge.

30 But every one shall die for his own iniquity: every man that eateth the sour grape, his teeth shall be set on edge.

31 Behold, the days come, saith the LORD, that I will make a new covenant with the house of Israel, and with the house of Judah:

32 Not according to the covenant that I made with their fathers in the day that I took them by the hand to bring them out of the land of Egypt; which my covenant they brake, although I was an husband unto them, saith the LORD:

33 But this shall be the covenant that I will make with the house of Israel; After those days, saith the LORD, I will put my law in their inward parts, and write it in their hearts; and will be their God, and they shall be my people.

34 And they shall teach no more every man his neighbour, and every man his brother, saying, Know the LORD: for they shall all know me, from the least of them unto the greatest of them, saith the LORD; for I will forgive their iniquity, and I will remember their sin no more.

Oct. 20

Memory Selection
Jeremiah 31:33

Background Scripture
Jeremiah 30–31

Devotional Reading
Hebrews 10:11-18

71

The common cliché, "All good things come to an end" has its opposite. All *bad* things come to an end also, to those who love God. In this lesson we learn that God's repeated promise that He would punish His people has come full course. The prophet Jeremiah has wept his heart out, and has come to the end of his tears. Despite his many lamentations, Jeremiah's message finally matches his name, which means "Yah (or Jehovah) will rise."

Remarkably, Jeremiah predicts the restoration of the people to the Promised Land some 70 years in the future, seeing the day when the Babylonians will be conquered by the Persians, who will allow the Jews to return. A remnant of God's people will return, and be given both a new start and a New Covenant—a hint of what would be fulfilled when Messiah came.

ഇൗരു

Ask group members to share examples of how we use the word "hope"—*"I hope it doesn't rain tomorrow and spoil the picnic"* ... *"I hope the Falcons (or whoever) win the game"* ... *"I hope to have my house paid off before I retire"* ... *"I hope my children (or grandchildren) turn out OK."*

Some such statements indicate mere wishful thinking. In contrast, biblical hope is tinged with realistic anticipation, because *hope has a history*. It is based on God's acts, such as rescuing His people from Egypt, and delivering them from other enemies (Ps. 23). Hope is dimmed only by disobedience, not the loss of God's love. Hope in this lesson therefore does not just have its head in the clouds but also has its feet on the ground.

Teaching Outline	Daily Bible Readings	
	Mon.	God Will Restore Jacob Jeremiah 30:18-22
I. Deliverance Is Coming—23-26	Tue.	An Everlasting Love Jeremiah 31:1-6
A. With behavioral changes, 23		
B. With renewed life, 24-26	Wed.	God Will Satisfy Jeremiah 31:23-30
II. Days of Restoration—27-28	Thu.	The Coming Covenant Jeremiah 31:31-37
III. New Relationship—29-30		
IV. New Covenant—31-34	Fri.	God Will Bring Healing Jeremiah 33:1-13
A. The need, 31-32	Sat.	'You Have Made Me Hope' Psalm 119:49-56
B. The newness, 33-34	Sun.	Eternal Hope

Verse by Verse

I. Deliverance Is Coming—23-26
A. With behavioral changes, 23

23 Thus saith the LORD of hosts, the God of Israel; As yet they shall use this speech in the land of Judah and in the cities thereof, when I shall bring again their captivity; The LORD bless thee, O habitation of justice, and mountain of holiness.

Jeremiah 30–33 interrupts his prophecies of "doom and gloom" with promises that after a period of captivity God will restore His people to their land. Although glimpses of hope have occasionally shone through the weeping prophet's previous tirades, this section is such a remarkable departure from his usual message that it is often called "The Book of Consolation." When God promises to "bring again" the captivity of His people, He means he will *reverse* it. Note, however, that the language of blessings and good tidings must be accompanied by *justice* and *holiness*, which the people had neglected.

Jeremiah therefore is uniquely stationed on the bridge between doom and rescue, captivity and release, the old and the new. It is his role both to counsel that the Jews surrender to the Babylonians, and that the enemy will not have the last word. In chapter 32, the prophet will be told to act out a vivid "action parable" to illustrate the confident hope that has erupted in his preaching. At the very time the foreign invaders are besieging Judah, God tells Jeremiah to invest in Judean property. It is a bold act, showing that it was wise to invest in the future of God's people despite the coming and temporary downturn in their fortunes.

We do not have to wait for the fulfillment of this prophecy. Within about two generations, Babylon was conquered by the Persians, and the Jews were allowed to return under the Persian king Cyrus (as recorded in the books of Ezra and Nehemiah).

B. With renewed life, 24-26

24 And there shall dwell in Judah itself, and in all the cities thereof together, husbandmen, and they that go forth with flocks.

25 For I have satiated the weary soul, and I have replenished every sorrowful soul.

26 Upon this I awaked, and beheld; and my sleep was sweet unto me.

Recent invasions by the Assyrians, Egyptians, and Babylonians had left Judah in economic and social ruin. It was the custom of invaders in this period to sow farms and pastures with salt to temporarily ruin the soil. However, Jeremiah surprisingly predicts a reversal in agricultural prospects and a return of the "husbandmen" who would tend crops, herds, and flocks.

Verse 25 offers a hint of a recurring theme in the otherwise dismal book of Jeremiah: a "remnant" of the people in Judah have remained faithful to God, deploring the idolatry and injustice of the majority. Soon the weary, sin-satiated souls of these faithful people are to be refreshed. In fact, using the "prophetic perfect" tense, Jeremiah speaks as though this replenishment of spirit has already occurred, even though it will actually happen only after some 70 years in Babylonian captivity. It is the certainty of God's promise that enables the prophet to awaken sweetly refreshed from the sleep during which God has sent this vision of hope.

II. Days of Restoration—27-28

27 Behold, the days come, saith the LORD, that I will sow the house of Israel and the house of Judah with the seed of man, and with the seed of beast.

28 And it shall come to pass, that like as I have watched over them, to pluck up, and to break down, and to throw down, and to destroy, and to afflict; so will I watch over them, to build, and to plant, saith the LORD.

Instead of the Judean hillsides and valleys being sown with salt, the days are coming when they will be resown with people and livestock. Instead of tending to the land's destruction and the people's affliction, God will soon oversee with equal concern the restoration of the people to their land, including the recovery of agricultural and other economic enterprise necessary for the defeated country to recover. The vision brings to mind the days in the waning moments of World War II, when Allied forces, seeing that they were on the brink of victory, began to make plans to help Germany and other European lands to recover even before the armistice was signed.

III. New Relationship—29-30

29 In those days they shall say no more, The fathers have eaten a sour grape, and the children's teeth are set on edge.

30 But every one shall die for his own iniquity: every man that eateth the sour grape, his teeth shall be set on edge.

Judaism, the religion of Abraham, Isaac, and Jacob, was above all characterized by its *corporate* relationship with God. The proverb about the effect a father's eating would have on a son reflects this solidarity. However, the renewal Jeremiah foresees will require a more individual response to God. Being born into the faith and relating to God as a nation had given some the excuse to avoid facing their personal responsibility to Him. Here, nearly 600 years before the coming of the Messiah, the basis is being laid for the inclusion into the people of God *anyone,* Jew or Gentile, who will personally commit themselves to Him.

IV. New Covenant—31-34
A. The need, 31-32

31 Behold, the days come, saith the LORD, that I will make a new covenant with the house of Israel, and with the house of Judah:

32 Not according to the covenant that I made with their fathers in the day that I took them by the hand to bring them out of the land of Egypt; which my covenant they brake, although I was an husband unto them, saith the LORD:

This new basis for relating to God leads to the radical concept of a new covenant—which is needed is, as verse 32b says, because the people had broken the old one. Although God was as a husband to His people, they had "divorced" Him in serving other Gods and ignoring the ethical demands of the Law. Yet because God's love is eternal, He does not absolutely destroy the relationship, but revises it.

This drastic step will be profoundly explored by the apostle Paul and the letter to the Hebrews. Although Hebrews will say that God found "fault" with the Old Covenant (Heb. 8:8), it is clear that the main inadequacy lies within the people who did not, and could not, keep the Law perfectly. Yet God foresaw that this would be the case, since He had planned the Covenant of Grace from the beginning. We may therefore conclude that God instituted the Covenant of Law with "planned obsolescence" in mind.

B. The newness, 33-34

33 But this shall be the covenant that I will make with the house of Israel; After those days, saith the Lord, I will put my law in their inward parts, and write it in their hearts; and will be their God, and they shall be my people.

34 And they shall teach no more every man his neighbour, and every man his brother, saying, Know the Lord: for they shall all know me, from the least of them unto the greatest of them, saith the Lord; for I will forgive their iniquity, and I will remember their sin no more.

The distinction between the Old and the New Covenants is said to be that (a) the New emphasizes the heart more than did the Old; and (b) the contents of the New will be known by each individual member of the Covenant people instead of relying on the community to provide instruction.

Again, these changes were called for more by the inadequacy of the people than by the Old Covenant itself. Moses' Law was to be obeyed from the heart, and the external motions of obedience such as circumcision had never been adequate. Instead, the people were to "circumcise therefore the foreskin of your heart" (Deut. 10:16), and to "love the Lord they God with all thine heart, and with all thy soul, and with all thy might" (Deut. 6:5). What was lacking under the Law was *Jesus*—a Messiah who could keep it perfectly for us, or, in Jesus' own words, "fulfill" it.

Yet it must also be observed that the Old Law also emphasized externals more than the New. It was certain commands of the Law, not the words "We are saved by grace," that were to be tacked to the doorposts of one's house and worn as "frontlets" on the brow.

Furthermore, as indicated in verse 34, under the Old Covenant one did not become a part of the community by coming to know personally the forgiveness of sins by a loving Lord, but simply by being born. Of course this is no injunction against learning all we can about the faith. It only indicates that a person who has been forgiven of his sins is already a member of the Covenant, and needs no official community spokesperson such as a rabbi to tell him how to become one.

Evangelistic Emphasis

Jim and Barbara met during their third year at the University of Texas. After a few months of spending a lot of time together, they began to try to figure out what their future would be. It was at this point that they talked about just "sharing an apartment together." When Barbara told her mother what she and Jim were planning, she told her that their reason for living together was as a temporary trial period to see if they were really "meant for each other."

Being from a Christian home, Barbara didn't expect her mother to be happy about her decision. She did not expect, however, her mother's haunting question, "Can you really engage in 'a temporary trial' of a permanent commitment?" Because of that question and Barbara's anguish to answer it to her own satisfaction, she and Ted decided not to live together before their marriage.

That conversation with her mother rebounded strongly into Barbara's memory last Sunday morning as she listen to the visiting evangelist's closing altar call. His appeal was strong and emotional. The church was preparing to sing "Just As I Am" for the fourth time. No one had yet responded in any public way. It was at this point that the evangelist used these words: "Why don't you just give a commitment to the Lord a try. If you decide later that Christianity is not for you, you can always return to your life as it is now." Barbara wonders if one can honestly engage in 'a temporary trial' of a permanent commitment to the Lord.

෨〇෬

Memory Selection

But this shall be the covenant that I will make with the house of Israel; After those days, saith the Lord, I will put my law in their inward parts, and write it in their hearts; and will be their God, and they shall be my people.—*Jeremiah 31:33*

"There ought to be a law!" How many times have we heard someone say those words? How many times have we ourselves echoed them? They may be heard slightly more often among political conservatives than among Libertarians, but not by much. We all seem to be ready to craft our own set of new laws against some public misconduct or an irritating social practice.

When will we learn that more laws will not necessarily make a more civil society? Already, there are a host of laws on our public books that are beyond any reasonable enforcement. Rather than more laws "on the books," we need the law of righteousness written on our hearts. My *want* to do right will do me far more good than your *demand* that I do right. A time will come, Jeremiah promises, when the motivation to do right will come from within.

Weekday Problems

Often it seems as though it is far more difficult for us to accept forgiveness than it is for God to grant forgiveness. Intellectually, we may know that we are forgiven, yet emotionally we do not feel forgiven. With the lack of a true sense of forgiveness, we miss out on much of the joy that God intends for us to have.

Though it has been nearly 15 years since William was involved in a homosexual relationship, he still carries the shame of his sin. At the time of that involvement, William was a teenager. His activity was both experimental and short-lived. Since that time, William has become a Christian, married and become a father. Still William's sin haunts him. He would love to rejoice in the joy of his salvation, but he does not know that joy.

* Is it possible for William to *be* forgiven if he does not *feel* forgiven? Is it possible for William to be saved if he does not feel saved?

* How can William's wife and Christian friends help him to come to know the joy of forgiveness?

* What might William's pastor do to help him to experience emotionally what he "knows" intellectually?

Talking Back to Texans

A Texas cattleman was showing an Easterner around his ranch on a blistering summery day. Suddenly a strange bird scurried in front of them. "What's that?" the visitor asked.

"That's a bird of paradise," said the rancher.

The stranger rode along in silence for awhile, then said, "Long way from home, isn't it?"

On a visit to tiny Israel, a Texan boasted, "Why, in Texas you can get on a train and ride for days, and still be in Texas."

His Israeli companion nodded sympathetically and murmured, "I know the feeling. We have the same trouble with our trains."

Q: What do you have when you find a pair of boots with a 10-gallon hat on top of them?

A: A Texan with the hot air let out.

This Lesson in Your Life

It's been more than five years since she first called the church office. She gave me only a first name, Antoinette. Her reason for calling was her decision to end her life, and she thought somebody should know. Life, she said, had been terribly cruel to her, and she could stand it no longer. It had just dawned on her that in a few months she would be bankrupt, and she could not bear the thought of being homeless or on welfare. Before the conversation ended, however, the voice on the other end of the line assured me that, though she would definitely end her life, it would not be today. She wanted first to find a home for her nine-year-old dog. She did not want it to be taken to animal control and euthanized.

Antoinette did not end her life that day, or the many days that followed. Though she may one day actually carry out her threat, as of a week ago she was still breathing—but with most breaths, complaining.

To hear her tell it, Antoinette's primary enemy was her mother. Nearly every problem she encounters has roots in a negative relationship with her mother. The fact that she is 63 years old and still hiding behind her less-than-perfect mother does not seem to awaken her to her own horribly warped perception of reality.

Antoinette does seem to be making progress, though. When she first called me, she had never had a job. At 57, she was still living off the pampering indulgence of her parents. She was still single, indulging adolescent fantasies of being swept off her feet by a gallant prince. After her mother's death, she sold the family home for several hundred thousand dollars and lived extravagantly until the money was finally gone. It wasn't until all her credit cards were maxed out that it all began to catch up with her. Finally, she was forced to follow through with her threatened suicide or get a job. She got a job.

In fact, she has had a host of jobs, and has lived at a variety of apartments and boarding houses. Every time she encounters problems with other people, someone else is always to blame.

More than once I've told Antoinette frankly that she is her own worst problem. Although it made her angry at first, she didn't remember it for very long. If she runs out of specific people to blame, she will blame "society" or "bad luck" or even God. It's His fault for allowing her to "have far more problems than any person who has ever lived."

Antoinette is a real person, but in fact I've encountered quite a number of other "Antoninette"—people who cannot accept their own contribution to their woeful plight. They see themselves as a "victim" and nearly everyone else as "the enemy." When that becomes the dominant perception of life, change is nearly impossible.

1. To whom did Jeremiah bring this message from the Lord?

Jeremiah brought the message to Israel and Judah.

2. What exactly was the Lord asking when he said, "Ask ye now, and see whether a man doth travail with child?"

He was asking if it is possible for a man to give birth to a child.

3. Whom did the Lord say He was going to "raise up" for them?

He said that He was going to raise up "David their King" for them.

4. How did the Lord say He would correct Israel and Judah? What does that mean?

He said that he would correct them "in measure." That is, He would not place unrestrained punishment upon them.

5. Whom did the Lord say was prepared to defend the cause of Israel and Judah?

He said that there was none to plead their cause.

6. What did the Lord say that He was going to do for His people's grievous wounds?

He said that He was going to heal them.

7. What did Jeremiah say would go forth from the Lord with fury, and what would it do?

He would send a whirlwind, which would "fall with pain upon the head of the wicked."

8. What kind of love did the Lord say that He has for his people?

He said that He has an "everlasting love."

9. What would be the response of the virgin to the Lord's redemption?

The virgin would rejoice in dance.

10. Where did God say He would one day write His laws?

On the hearts of His people.

Though we've pretty much exhausted our exploration of the dry land on Planet Earth, we still have much to learn about what lies in and around the sea. One fascinating bit of information that has come to light, however, is that of the relationship between the oyster and a tiny red crab.

As the tides roll over and around the oyster, it opens its shell so the cool water can refresh its cramped body and bring the food it needs. For the oyster is a living animal that not only gets hungry but knows when it is time to eat. Unfortunately, when the shell opens, there is great danger for the oyster. The body of the oyster is all jelly. Many of the hungry fish that swarm around it are as fond of oysters as we are. The oyster, however, cannot see, hear, smell, nor taste. It can only feel. Often, therefore, it does not know anything has happened to it until it's too late.

Fortunately, the oyster has a friend to protect it—a tiny, red crab. When the oyster opens its shell, the crab slips in and makes itself at home. Consequently, when a predator fish comes along and threatens the oyster, the tiny crab sees it, and stirs. Feeling the stir of the crab, the shell closes and the oyster is safe.

That tiny red crab works for the oyster very much like the conscience works for the soul. Like the little crab, a well-trained conscience can tell when a person is threatened by the predator called sin. The soul cannot hear, see, or smell sin. What it feels of it is rather sweet—at first. The conscience, however, is that something in the soul that has a tender touch. And many a bitter hour can be avoided by heeding it.

When the prophet of God told of the time to come when God's Law would be written on people's hearts, he surely had something in mind more than the conscience. Yet, our conscience is a very important part of the equation. Whether it is to be regarded as a "good thing" or a "not-so-good thing" may rest on how well it has been trained.

A person's happy conscience is a source of peace not only to himself, but to everyone with whom he comes in contact. At the same time, however, the person who is on bad terms with himself is ready to be on bad terms with everybody. In the words of George Morrison, he is "like those widening ripples on the lake which the stone makes when cast into its stillness." They "are the outward goings of the heart. None is so ready to foment a quarrel as he who has a quarrel with his conscience."

It is selling the conscience short to consider it only from the viewpoint of this little ditty credited to Richard Armour:

The conscience is a built-in feature
That haunts the sinner, helps the preacher.
Some sins it makes us turn and run from,
But most it simply takes the fun from.

80

Habakkuk 3:2-6, 17-19

O LORD, I have heard thy speech, and was afraid: O LORD, revive thy work in the midst of the years, in the midst of the years make known; in wrath remember mercy.

3 God came from Teman, and the Holy One from mount Paran. Selah. His glory covered the heavens, and the earth was full of his praise.

4 And his brightness was as the light; he had horns coming out of his hand: and there was the hiding of his power.

5 Before him went the pestilence, and burning coals went forth at his feet.

6 He stood, and measured the earth: he beheld, and drove asunder the nations; and the everlasting mountains were scattered, the perpetual hills did bow: his ways are everlasting.

17 Although the fig tree shall not blossom, neither shall fruit be in the vines; the labour of the olive shall fail, and the fields shall yield no meat; the flock shall be cut off from the fold, and there shall be no herd in the stalls:

18 Yet I will rejoice in the LORD, I will joy in the God of my salvation.

19 The LORD God is my strength, and he will make my feet like hinds' feet, and he will make me to walk upon mine high places. To the chief singer on my stringed instruments.

Oct. 27

Memory Selection
Habakkuk 3:2

Background Scripture
Habakkuk 1–3

Devotional Reading
Hebrews 11:32–12:2

81

In the sixth century B.C., God's terrible threat to allow foreign nations to conquer His People of the Covenant so profoundly affected the prophets that they could not be content to describe it merely in prose. This lesson focuses on the prophet Habakkuk's agonizing attempt to process God's judgment in the crucible of poetry.

According to a reference in the apocryphal book *Bel and the Dragon,*

Habakkuk was a priest. Judging from the presence of such words as "selah" (3:3), he may have been a singer among the Levites. He may also have been a contemporary of Jeremiah. He knew of Assyria's conquest of the northern tribes of Israel, and now realized, as Jeremiah did, that Babylon would soon wreak similar havoc upon Judah.

Habakkuk gave vent both to passionate questions about God's justice and to hymns of faith. His brief writing shows how faith can exist in the midst of doubt, and praise may alternate with deep complaint.

ℰ⋺ℭ⋺

Ask your group to share briefly experiences that wrung from them opposite emotions. For example, a devastating storm has been known to leave both sorrow at the destruction in its wake, and joy as people come together to help each other as never before. The death of a loved one can

produce both expressions of doubt as we ask *Why, Lord?*, and of faith as we affirming that God will be with us.

True religion has room for the full range of human emotions. The brief prophecy of Habakkuk, as well as the Psalms, show people of faith trusting that God is "big" enough to handle their questions. Although they may not have their questions answered, they know that God is greater than their faltering faith.

Teaching Outline	Daily Bible Readings	
I. Plea for Relief—2	Mon.	I Stand in Awe Habakkuk 3:2-6
II. Praise for God's Glory—3-4 A. Universality, 3 B. Radiance, 4	Tue.	The Lord Is My Strength Habakkuk 3:18-19
	Wed.	My Heart Trusts in God Psalm 28:1-9
III. Power of God's Wrath—5-6 A. Suffering, 5 B. Destruction, 6	Thu.	I Will Trust in God Isaiah 12:1-6
	Fri.	Trust in God Isaiah 26:1-6
IV. Psalm of Faith—17-19 A. Faith amid travail, 17-18 B. Strength amid weakness, 19	Sat.	Acknowledge God's Plan Isaiah 26:7-13
	Sun.	The Fight of Faith 1 Timothy 6:11-16

Verse by Verse

I. Plea for Relief—2

2 O LORD, I have heard thy speech, and was afraid: O LORD, revive thy work in the midst of the years, in the midst of the years make known; in wrath remember mercy.

The "speech" heard by the prophet Habakkuk may refer to contemporary prophecies such as those of Jeremiah predicting the Babylonian conquest, or to the writings of the eighth-century prophets warning of the conquest of the 10 northern tribes. Whatever the source of these divine words, they were full of foreboding to the prophet. Although he may have realized that the wholesale worship of idols and the collapse of justice in the land fully earned God's wrath, it is so fearful to contemplate that he begs for a revival of the works of grace God had displayed in the past, such as leading the people out of Egyptian bondage (see vs. 3, below). He prays that such mighty deeds would overcome the people's unfaithfulness "in the midst of [these very] days" as they had in previous times, that "in wrath" God would also remember mercy.

II. Praise for God's Glory—3-4
A. Universality, 3

3 God came from Teman, and the Holy One from mount Paran. Selah. His glory covered the heavens, and the earth was full of his praise.

The prophet calls up two images of the kind of divine deliverance for which he prayed in verse 2. The first was a demonstration of God's power in destroying the Edomites, enemies of Israel, when divine fire fell on the city of Teman (Amos 1:12). The second was the demonstration of God's leadership near Mount Paran, when the heavens were full of the glory of the pillar of cloud God used to guide the Israelites through the wilderness (Num. 10:12). The fact that these two instances show God using both negative and positive acts to deliver His people is an important part of trust in times of despair.

"Selah," a word of unknown origin, appears most often in the Psalms, which were written to be sung, and is therefore often presumed to be a musical notation lost to modern interpreters. Perhaps it was taken much like modern singers may read Latin or Italian words above a line of music, as when they sing louder at the command *"crescendo."* (See the last part of vs. 19 for a note indicating that this prophecy was to be sung.)

B. Radiance, 4

4 And his brightness was as the light; he had horns coming out of his hand: and there was the hiding of his power.

Continuing to use his "prophetic imagination," Habakkuk envisions

83

God as the embodiment of light, one of Scripture's prevailing descriptions of Him. "God is light," the New Testament will say, in single-syllable simplicity (1 John 1:5). The language here seems to anticipate John's vision of the Son of Man as a Being of brightness with stars in his hand (Rev. 1:16). "Horns" is from the same root word as "rays" (as of light), which is the source of the strange horns coming out of Moses' head in the famous statue by Michelangelo. They would more accurately have been rays of light, as described in Exodus 34:30, 35. Having such rays in His hand implies both that God can unleash bolts of light where He wills, and "hide" or restrain His power. Habakkuk is hoping for a full unleashing of this restraint for the healing of Judah.

III. Power of God's Wrath—5-6
A. Suffering, 5

5 Before him went the pestilence, and burning coals went forth at his feet.

Bright though God's overall personage is, He can also be a God of wrath. In Habakkuk's vision, Judeans are dying from disease (NIV "plague") that God either sends or allows Satan to send in punishment of widespread and stubborn disobedience. The phrase translated "burning coals" may also figuratively refer to a burning fever; hence the NIV's translation, "pestilence." The point is that, in His wrath, "Our God is a consuming fire" (Heb. 12:29). Israel had also felt the sting of this side of the God light. If God is One, then both the good and the evil are under His command (see Isa. 45:7).
B. Destruction, 6

6 He stood, and measured the earth: he beheld, and drove asunder the nations; and the everlasting mountains were scattered, the perpetual hills did bow: his ways are everlasting.

"Measuring" is often used in Scripture in much the same way as when we say that a person "took the measure of his enemy," or defeated him (see 2 Sam. 8:2). Here the prophet is describing God's just wrath in terms so powerful that it "flattens out" mountains and hills, as an atomic bomb levels all before its blast. The past tense is often called "the prophetic past," since Habakkuk's view of the land's approaching conquest is so certain that he can describe it as already having occurred. We may suppose that he is not just giving an objective description of God's power, but wants the disobedient to be moved to reform in view that God has their life or death in His hands.

IV. Psalm of Faith—17-19
A. Faith amid travail, 17-18

17 Although the fig tree shall not blossom, neither shall fruit be in the vines; the labour of the olive shall fail, and the fields shall yield no meat; the flock shall be cut off from the fold, and there shall be no herd in the stalls:

18 Yet I will rejoice in the LORD, I will joy in the God of my salvation.

These verses conclude a colorful, if grim, description of God's awesome power as manifested in His ability to make the mountains "tremble" (vs. 10) and to "thresh" the heathen in His anger (vs. 12). What if the prophet himself is subjected to suffering as a consequence of God's wrath being poured out on the disobedient people around him?

Although he is honest enough to confess that the thought makes his lips quiver and "rottenness" enter his bones (vs. 16), he now comes to a place of peace in the midst of such chaos. Although drought sent from heaven may destroy orchards and crops, fruits and flocks, vineyards and herds, Habakkuk is determined to respond with a word of praise on his lips. This remarkable confession of faith is surely a model for what believers everywhere seek: the ability to remain strong within while storms rage without, to believe in the face of personal misfortune that bring the specter of doubt.

The passage reminds us that it is one thing blithely to say we believe when external events are going our way, when our "stock is up"; but quite another to believe when life goes sour. Like Jeremiah, who bought a field near Jerusalem to express his faith that God would one day restore the people to their land (Jer. 32), Habakkuk is making an investment in faith at a time when "the market is down." This is the essence of saving faith.

B. Strength amid weakness, 19

19 The LORD God is my strength, and he will make my feet like hinds' feet, and he will make me to walk upon mine high places. To the chief singer on my stringed instruments.

If the Babylonian invasion produces so much upheaval that it is hard to keep one's spiritual balance, Habakkuk's source of balance and strength is in God, not the presence or absence of warfare. God's strength will give him the grace and balance of a deer (KJV "hind").

The "high places" here are apparently not those noted in an earlier lesson where pagan worship was conducted, but the "mountain tops" or the high road of faith the prophet is determined to take, come what may. It is there that he will find communion with "the high God" and strength to face the chaos below. While the valleys may yawn menacingly in anticipation of swallowing his body, fallen in warfare, Habakkuk has a high road in his soul that will enable him to brave the battle.

There may also be an element of future hope in this affirmation of faith. As noted in the previous lesson, God promised through Jeremiah to return a remnant to the land, and even to issue a New Covenant since the people had broken the Old (Jer. 31:27-33). Habakkuk was thoroughly steeped in a form of "covenant theology" that made faith's main basis the faithfulness of God, not of the people. Because God had made an "everlasting covenant" with the children of Abraham, Habakkuk could find reassurance that somehow the future would demonstrate this covenant of love even though the present could not offer visible evidence of it.

As noted above, the closing line of Habakkuk's brief prophecy shows its poetic suitability for singing, and closes with the author's instruction to the "choir leader." It is to be sung with "my stringed instruments," apparently indicating that Habakkuk was an instrumentalist as well as a lyricist.

Evangelistic Emphasis

Bill Johnson is not a whole lot different from any of several other people that I know. He's fundamentally "skeptical" by nature. Were it not for his mother's adamant testimony to the contrary, I would be sure that he was born in Missouri, "the show me state." It doesn't matter the subject at hand, Bill is not apt to accept any evidence at face value. He has to examine it carefully for himself.

Bill is no different when it comes to the matter of faith and religion than he is with any other concern. It has to be proven to his satisfaction, before he will "buy" it. Unfortunately, because of his skeptical disposition, most who have tried to approach him with the Gospel message, have gone away convinced that he is hard-hearted and unreachable. In return, due to those would-be teachers' frustrated departures, Bill has been left with the impression that the Gospel cannot stand up under close scrutiny. He finds himself more guarded and skeptical about religion than he was before he ever had exposure to the message, at all.

Perhaps, what Bill Johnson needs most is a teacher who came to Christ with his own apprehensions and so understands the reasons behind the questions that Bill is inclined to ask. Certainly, God has never feared our honest inquiry. The teachers who represent Him must aspire to have the same kind of patience.

ઠ૦ભ

Memory Selection

O LORD, I have heard thy speech, and was afraid: O LORD, revive thy work in the midst of the years, in the midst of the years make known; in wrath remember mercy.—*Habakkuk 3:2*

All of us have heard of the God who worked mighty miracles in the long ago. We've heard about how He enabled Abraham to become a father when he was 100 years old, and how He parted the Red Sea. As children we were taught about the walls of Jerico falling down and about Jesus rising from the dead. It's not as though we don't know about God. Surely, we do.

However, we want to see the mighty handiwork of God today. We like the story of the birth of Isaac in the geriatric ward of the Canaan General Hospital. It would be a whole lot more helpful to our good friends Ben and Barbara if He would do something like that now. They've been trying to have a child for more than 15 years, without success.

And certainly, the story of Sodom's destruction was exciting, but why hasn't God done anything about Osama bin Ladin? We like hearing the stories about when God was active long ago, but where is He today?

Weekday Problems

Audra Jackson has been a Christian all of her life. According to her mother, she was in church the very first Sunday after she was born, and there have been very few times that she has missed since. Had anyone ever told her that she would "lose her faith," Audra would have had an instant rebuttal. But, that was before last summer, when that tornado came through her Oklahoma town and destroyed everything she owned. Her house and barn, her livestock and her car—all of it was blown away. Suddenly, everything she had been working for and scraping to acquire was destroyed.

Audra has not darkened the door of the church since. When Pastor Tucker tried to talk with her about it, all he got was the retort, "The God I've believed in all my life would not allow that to happen!" Though Pastor Tucker is sympathetic with Ms. Jackson, he is at a loss how to help her.

* Is it unreasonable for Audra to expect God to protect her from such catastrophic loss? Why or why not?

* Have you ever experienced a terrible loss compared with that of Audra Jackson? Did it cause you to question your faith?

* What do you think is Audra's primary problem? Anger? Disillusionment? Disbelief? What would you say to try to get through to her?

Infamous Last Words

Epitaphs from various cemeteries:
> Seven wives I've buried, with as many a fervent prayer.
> If we all should meet in heaven, won't there be trouble there?

❖❖❖❖❖

This is too deep for me.

❖❖❖❖❖

Pardon me for not rising.

❖❖❖❖❖

Here lies a lawyer—as usual.

❖❖❖❖❖

There's something here I'd like to get off my chest.

❖❖❖❖❖

And on a dog's grave in a pet cemetery:
> He never met a man he didn't lick.

This Lesson in Your Life

Toni turned 40 just two and a half weeks ago. Now she is burying her husband—her second husband. Her first groom had died less than a year after their marriage. Toni was only 21 at the time. The prospect of being widowed a second time was something she had never had the courage to consider. On this day, though, Toni is not only a widow, she is also the mother of two sons. Her loneliness is almost more than she can bear as she considers the responsibility that confronts her.

Toni had been married to Joe for just over 13 years. Unable to have children of their own, they had adopted two boys. As Toni contemplates rearing them alone, she wonders if she is up to the task. She does have an important resource: her faith. When she became a Christian four years ago, she had no idea how important her faith would become.

Joe had been a good husband; perhaps, too good. For the past 13 years he had protected her from every concern. He had taken care of the farm and managed the finances, making virtually every purchase and paying all the bills. Toni had not worked outside the home, so she has little exposure to the business world.

As the numbness of Joe's death begins to fade, Toni realizes how totally alone she is. As she begins to piece together the various responsibilities she must now assume, panic rises up inside her chest. She does not know how much money they have in the bank—or if they have any! She does not know what bills needed to be paid each month, or where she will get the money to pay them. Perhaps most importantly, Toni does not know how she is going to fill the needs of her sons for a father to mentor them. About all Toni is sure of is that she believes that her God will take care of her needs. Though her faith is only a little over four years old, she is determined not to give in to her fears. She will stand strong and allow her faith to carry her through whatever comes in her way.

Though we don't often notice them or give them accolades, heros of faith like Toni are all about us. They do not stop the mouths of lions like Daniel, or walk on water like Peter. Their faith, nevertheless, is heroic, because it stands tenaciously strong in the face of intimidating obstacles. Much like Habakkuk, even though all the circumstances around them deny the presence and faithfulness of God, they still believe. And because of that belief, they march forward as though God is going to sustain them. Not at all to their surprise, but often to the great surprise of those watching from the sidelines, He does sustain them. Often, He does not give them one bit more than they need. Yet, that which essential to their survival, He supplies.

1. What was the central issue of Habakkuk's initial complaint?

His complaint was that the Lord did not seem to be doing anything about the injustices in the Land.

2. Whom did the Lord declare that he was dispatching to correct the waywardness of Judah?

The Lord said that he was sending the Chaldeans to fix the problem.

3. Why did the Lord choose the Chaldeans to apply his justice to the situation?

The Lord sent the Chaldeans because they could not be stopped by any who tried to resist them.

4. What was the central issue of Habakkuk's second complaint?

He was troubled that God would use such a wicked nation as the Chaldeans to punish the less wicked Judah.

5. Where could Habakkuk be found as he waited for the Lord's answer to his complaint?

Habakkuk climbed up into a tower to await the Lord's answer.

6. What did the Lord tell Habakkuk to do with the answer that he would receive?

The Lord told Habakkuk to write the vision on tables (tablets) legible enough for someone to read it as he saw it while running.

7. By what means did the Lord say the just would live?

The Lord said that the just shall live by his faith.

8. Upon whom did the Lord pronounce a "woe"?

Upon the extortionist, the covetous, the violently criminal, the lewd, and the idolater.

9. Using graphic imagery, what did Habakkuk say that the mountains did when they saw the Lord?

The mountains trembled.

10. Come what may, what did Habakkuk say that his response would be?

He said, "Yet I will rejoice in the Lord, I will joy in the God of my salvation."

The word, "awesome" has come to be used quite loosely in recent years. Typing it into the "Yahoo" search engine yields such results as, "Awesome Sport Bikes," "Awesome Aussies," and "Awesome Waffles." Not one of the 200 pages of listings compared favorably to the image of "awesome" that was instilled within me in Sunday School. Rather, "awesome" is that which is so breathtaking that one is prompted to stare with his mouth agape, unable to speak a word. That is awesome.

"Awesome!" was my initial impression of Niagra Falls. There was no other word for it. And ironically, I had not been all that excited about taking the time to go there. I had seen it on television. "What's the big deal?" was my shrug-off response to my wife's suggestion that it be the focus of our vacation. She would not be discouraged, however. So Niagara Falls was selected as our vactation destination. (It was a "mutual decision," of course.)

Yet, when I stepped out of our car and walked over to the rail fence, overlooking the falls I was speechless, and continued to be so for most of the rest of the day. Seeing it on television in no way prepared me for how magnificent the Falls truly are. Viewing them on television might be comparable to receiving a postcard of a western sunset. There is no way that even the finest postcard can capture the splendor of the western sky. So , it is with Niagra Falls. Even a large screen television can not "take you there." Television is seriously handicapped when it comes to the matter of capturing and communicating that quality we know as "awesome."

It is not only God's creation that is awesome, however. So are His actions in the world. Most of us were left speechless last September 11, 2001, following the attack on the World Trade Center. It was not only the tragedy that left us speechless. Several events of rescue and escape could also only be described as "awesome." One fireman I heard about had been on the 83rd floor of the World Trade Center when it crumbled. He rode it all the way down, surviving with only a few broken bones. He literally walked away from it on his own two feet. Only the most serious skeptics doubted that God had been involved in protecting him in the midst of that crumbling structure. Such miraculous escapes are difficult to explain outside the realm of some kind of extraordinary God-involvement.

Like Habakkuk, Americans will probably continue for quite a long time to ask God for a better understanding of why He allowed more than 6,000 people to die at the World Trade Center. At the same time, however, we need to recognize that somewhere in the vicinity of tw25,000 others escaped the disaster— many in almost unbelievably impossible circumstances. That reality evokes praise precisely because it is awesome.

Lesson 10

The Fall
of Jerusalem

2 Chronicles 36:11-21

Zedekiah was one and twenty years old when he began to reign, and reigned eleven years in Jerusalem.

12 And he did that which was evil in the sight of the LORD his God, and humbled not himself before Jeremiah the prophet speaking from the mouth of the LORD.

13 And he also rebelled against king Nebuchadnezzar, who had made him swear by God: but he stiffened his neck, and hardened his heart from turning unto the LORD God of Israel.

14 Moreover all the chief of the priests, and the people, transgressed very much after all the abominations of the heathen; and polluted the house of the LORD which he had hallowed in Jerusalem.

15 And the LORD God of their fathers sent to them by his messengers, rising up betimes, and sending; because he had compassion on his people, and on his dwelling place:

16 But they mocked the messengers of God, and despised his words, and misused his prophets, until the wrath of the LORD arose against his people, till there was no remedy.

17 Therefore he brought upon them the king of the Chaldees, who slew their young men with the sword in the house of their sanctuary, and had no compassion upon young man or maiden, old man, or him that stooped for age: he gave them all into his hand.

18 And all the vessels of the house of God, great and small, and the treasures of the house of the LORD, and the treasures of the king, and of his princes; all these he brought to Babylon.

19 And they burnt the house of God, and brake down the wall of Jerusalem, and burnt all the palaces thereof with fire, and destroyed all the goodly vessels thereof.

20 And them that had escaped from the sword carried he away to Babylon; where they were servants to him and his sons until the reign of the kingdom of Persia:

21 To fulfil the word of the LORD by the mouth of Jeremiah, until the land had enjoyed her sabbaths: for as long as she lay desolate she kept sabbath, to fulfil threescore and ten years.

Nov. 3

Memory Selection
2 Chronicles 36:15-16

Background Scripture
2 Chronicles 36:9-21

Devotional Reading
Psalm 75

The last chapter of 2 Chronicles describes the end of an era. Having exhausted God's patience by continual disobedience, the people and their leaders now suffer the long-threatened consequence. Nebuchadnezzar, king of Babylon, conquers Judah, carries off many of its survivors to captivity in Babylon, plunders the Temple in Jerusalem, then destroys it by fire.

The siege against Jerusalem had begun years earlier, under King Jehoiakim. Jeremiah and other prophets counseled the successive kings during this period to submit to the inevitable, surrender to Babylon, and get on with the urgent task of reforming their lives. King Zedekiah, Babylon's puppet, ignored this counsel, and earned the infamous distinction of being the last king of Judah. The text closes, however, with a glimmer of hope, forecasting the return of a remnant.

ഇരുന്ന

Recall for your group the doctrine of "manifest destiny" in U.S. history—the assumption that just as God chose Israel, so He chose our country as "a light to the nations." Bible texts originally referring to Israel, such as "Blessed is the nation whose God is the LORD" (Ps. 33:12), are still frequently applyed to the U. S.

Ask group members whether they agree with this comparison. If they do, ask also whether we should also apply God's warnings to His people that they must be faithful. Does sin, personal and national, bring judgment against our land as it did Israel? Whatever answers you receive, note that the lesson describes a grim and certain cause-effect relationship between Israel's disobedience and her fall.

Teaching Outline	Daily Bible Readings	
I. Rebellion under Zedekiah—11-13	Mon.	No Remedy 2 Chronicles 36:9-16
A. Against the prophets, 11-12	Tue.	Jerusalem Falls 2 Chronicles 36:17-21
B. Against the invader, 13	Wed.	Weeping Over Jerusalem Psalm 137:1-6
II. Responsible Parties—14-16		
A. Leaders and people, 14	Thu.	'How Long, O Lord?' Psalm 79:5-13
B. Mocking the prophets, 15-16		
III. Raid by Nebuchadnezzar—17-19	Fri.	Will God Keep Silent? Isaiah 64:6-12
A. Mass killings, 17	Sat.	Daniel's Prayer Daniel 9:1-10
B. Razing the Temple, 18-19		
IV. Ray of Hope—20-21	Sun.	'O Lord, Forgive' Daniel 9:11-19

Verse by Verse

I. Rebellion under Zedekiah—11-13
A. Against the prophets, 11-12

11 Zedekiah was one and twenty years old when he began to reign, and reigned eleven years in Jerusalem.

12 And he did that which was evil in the sight of the LORD his God, and humbled not himself before Jeremiah the prophet speaking from the mouth of the LORD.

To say that Zedekiah "began to reign" in Jerusalem may mislead us to think that Judah is still a sovereign nation unless we notice that he has been placed on the throne merely as a puppet king by Nebuchadnezzar of Babylon (vs. 10). At least his 11-year reign eclipsed in length that of his predecessor, Jehoiakin, who ruled for only three months (vs. 9)! Jehoiakin no doubt proved to be an uncooperative ruler under Nebuchadnezzar, so his brother Zedekiah was selected. Yet he earns the same dreary evaluation as did the other four final kings of Judah: his rule was evil. Specifically, the evil of idolatry may be primarily in mind here, since the king's rebellion is said to be against Jeremiah the prophet. As the verse indicates, this amounts to rebellion against God, since Jeremiah has been faithfully speaking God's Word.

B. Against the invader, 13

13 And he also rebelled against king Nebuchadnezzar, who had made him swear by God: but he stiffened his neck, and hardened his heart from turning unto the LORD God of Israel.

The king of Babylon may have taken advantage of the meaning of Zedekiah's name, "My righteousness is Yah (or Jehovah)," in requiring an oath of allegiance. Nebuchadnezzar's far-flung battlefront, from Assyria to Egypt, meant that he needed to place over small nations in his path deputy-kings who knew his subjects, collected the required tribute to go to Babylon, and quelled any rebellion. Because the Babylonian conquest was God's will, Jeremiah had urged these later kings to submit to Babylonian rule, but Zedekiah "hardened his heart" and refused to obey God in this matter, as in most others.

II. Responsible Parties—14-16
A. Leaders and people, 14

14 Moreover all the chief of the priests, and the people, transgressed very much after all the abominations of the heathen; and polluted the house of the LORD which he had hallowed in Jerusalem.

The Chronicler is careful to spread the blame for Judah's fall on king and priests and people. This was not a case of an overall just society suffering the consequences of having a corrupt king. They had allowed the adage "as the ruler, so the people" to cause them to follow their leaders' idolatrous example. Neither priests nor people were content to worship heathen idols in the "high places" outside Jerusalem. They had actually built pagan altars within the Temple itself, polluting the worship of the true God. Earlier reforms under Hezekiah and Josiah had to begin by cleaning out these abominations (NIV "detestable practices"), as well as debris that had been allowed to accumulate in a Temple that was supposed to be in continuous use in the worship of Yahweh (see 29:15-16; 34:8-11). The practice shows that they had little memory that Yahweh is a jealous God (Exod. 20:5), and little awareness of the fact that the nature of monotheism excludes other gods.

B. Mocking the prophets, 15-16

15 And the LORD God of their fathers sent to them by his messengers, rising up betimes, and sending; because he had compassion on his people, and on his dwelling place:

16 But they mocked the messengers of God, and despised his words, and misused his prophets, until the wrath of the LORD arose against his people, till there was no remedy.

Just as the author showed that both the people and their leaders were at fault in the nation's downfall, he proceeds now to exclude the prophets from blame. Although a few false prophets were exceptions, Jeremiah, Zephaniah, Habakkuk and others had faithfully warned both disobedient kings and priests of God's approaching judgment.

The role of the true prophet in Israel is stated very clearly here. It was one that provided a balance in governmental powers similar to the way the executive, legislative, and judicial branches of our own government were designed to counter-balance each other (with a free press, "the fourth estate," as yet another safeguard). To mock and misuse the prophets, therefore, was a sure way to rob the nation of the privilege of hearing God's Word amid the lesser words of kings and priests.

Previously the prophets' warnings had included the promise that there was still time for repentance and reformation to change God's mind about the coming judgment. Now, however, God has no more patience because the people had not responded. The last four words of verse 16 are like a funeral dirge: *"there was no remedy."*

III. Raid by Nebuchadnezzar—17-19

A. Mass killings, 17

17 Therefore he brought upon them the king of the Chaldees, who slew their young men with the sword in the house of their sanctuary, and had no compassion upon young man or maiden, old man, or him that stooped for age: he gave them all into his hand.

"The king of the Chaldees" refers to Nebuchadnezzar. "Chaldea" was the broader term for Babylonia, the ancient land toward the lower end of the Tigris and Euphrates rivers, often called "the cradle of civilization." A more ancient name for the area was Sumer. Since many of Chaldea's strongest rulers came from one of its chief cities, Babylon, the names Babylonia and Chaldea were often used synonymously. Chaldea included the area on modern maps where the borders of Iraq, Iran, and Kuwait converge near the Persian Gulf. How ironic that a Chaldean, from the land where we first meet Abraham, the father of the Jews, should now threaten Abraham's descendants.

The author notes that King Nebuchadnezzar is allowed to conquer the land because he is a tool in God's hand, not because of his superior righteousness. In fact the Chaldean king will also soon be judged for his arrogance (Jer. 51; Dan. 4:18ff.). Yet the rein God gives to Nebuchadnezzar's is loose enough that he wreaks terrible destruction on the land, which is described in even more detail in Jeremiah 52. Here we learn that Jerusalem resisted the final siege for two years. Finally, with famine prevailing in the city, the troops and the king tried to escape. The Chaldean army, however, pursued and overtook them. Nebuchadnezzar cruelly required King Zedekiah to watch as his own sons and princes were slain; then the king's own eyes were put out and he was led in chains to Babylon where he was kept imprisoned until his death.

B. Razing the Temple, 18-19

18 And all the vessels of the house of God, great and small, and the treasures of the house of the LORD, and the treasures of the king, and of his princes; all these he brought to Babylon.

19 And they burnt the house of God, and brake down the wall of Jerusalem, and burnt all the palaces thereof with fire, and destroyed all the goodly vessels thereof.

Again, Jeremiah 52:17-23 describes the looting of the Temple in Jerusalem in more detail. Although recently neglected, this was the Temple built by Solomon that had once been "the glory of the nations." In plundering its treasures, Nebuchadnezzar is not only lining his own coffers; he is following the common practice of attacking a conquered people's morale and spirit by desecrating their center of worship.

IV. Ray of Hope—20-21

20 And them that had escaped from the sword carried he away to Babylon; where they were servants to him and his sons until the reign of the kingdom of Persia:

21 To fulfil the word of the LORD by the mouth of Jeremiah, until the land had enjoyed her sabbaths: for as long as she lay desolate she kept sabbath, to fulfil threescore and ten years.

Although he slaughtered most of the people of Judah, Nebuchadnezzar left "certain of the poor of the land" to prevent an uprising (Jer. 52:16), and carried a remnant to be his servants back in Babylon. As humiliating as this was (and such an anguished lesson that never again would the Jews be generally guilty of idolatry), the author of Chronicles finds a dimly burning light at the end of the tunnel. He foresees that some of God's people will return to the Promised Land after a "sabbath rest" of 70 years. The land has become so polluted by idols that God decrees a timespan long enough for the idolatrous generation to die off. Only then will He move Cyrus, king of Persia, to allow a remnant of the Jews to return and rebuild their holy city and its Temple (vss. 22-23).

Evangelistic Emphasis

Jerry's and Genny's "little boy" Buck is now 17. According to their agreement with him, he is now on his own as far as decisions are concerned. Each year for the past several years more responsibilities and more freedoms have been released to him. So far, each transition has been made smoothly, to the delight of his parents.

During his last year in high school, Buck will make most of his own decisions. His parents will enforce no curfew, no restrictions and no rules. Though the idea frightens them, they know that in one more year, he will be going off to some university, anyway. Out from under their oversight, he will be free to make his own decisions. They prefer to have the privilege of watching him do that.

Several friends of Jerry and Genny have responded with alarm at their "no rules" relationship with Buck. They claim that it is a policy of "permissiveness" that is doomed to bring grief to their lives. Their friends even accuse them of disregarding the Lord's parenting guidelines and of "flaunting modernistic views." Genny and Jerry are somewhat shocked at their friends' strong criticism. They could not disagree more with their accusations of "permissiveness." As they perceive it, they have been involved all their son's life, attempting to help him to develop controls within himself. It is their conviction that self-control and self-discipline will be present long after their "rod of correction" has been left behind.

80Q8

Memory Selection

And the LORD God of their fathers sent to them by his messengers, rising up betimes, and sending; because he had compassion on his people, and on his dwelling place: But they mocked the messengers of God, and despised his words, and misused his prophets, until the wrath of the LORD arose against his people, till there was no remedy.—*2 Chronicles 36:15-16*

We are not very good about accepting bad news. Given an opportunity, we tend to plug our ears against it, lest it spoil our day. Fearful of the unusual mole on our back, rather than risking the doctor giving us the bad news that it is melanoma, we conveniently "forget" to mention it each time we are at the office for a checkup. Our fantasy seems to be that if we pretend that it is not there, it will disappear. Unfortunately, avoiding such "bad news" can be deadly.

When it comes to spiritual bad news, we do not do much better. It is difficult to allow ourselves to be voluntarily exposed to the "bad news" that we need desperately to repent. That's a message for others but not us. Unfortunately, until we allow ourselves to hear the "bad news" that we need to repent, we prevent ourselves from hearing the "good news" that we are forgiven.

Weekday Problems

Veronica tries hard not to be cynical about politicians, but she often does not succeed. Every time she begins to trust some political leader, another scandal appears in the news. Even though the scandal is about a different politician, the distrust spills over onto the one she had begun to trust. Veronica feels herself cringe and harden inside. She's not sure that she will ever trust a politician fully. "They're all a bunch of crooks and opportunists," a voice echoes inside her head. Outwardly, Veronica nods that it is true.

Veronica's mother is not nearly so untrusting. She grew up during the Roosevelt era, long before the Watergate fiasco. "Yes, there are some 'bad eggs,'" she will admit. "But, there are also some statesmen and stateswomen."

* Can Veronica's mother do anything to help "cure" Veronica to have faith

* What from Scripture can Veronica's mother use to help convince her daughter that, although a person makes a moral mistake, it doesn't mean that he is "rotten to the core," as Veronica is inclined to say?

* How does the apostle Paul's comment about our rulers being God's servants (Romans 13) apply to Veronica's strong apprehensions about them?

Marriage Mania

My wife dresses to kill; and she cooks the same way.—*Henny Youngman*

My wife and I were happy for 20 years. Then we met.—*Rodney Dangerfield*

I was married by a judge. I should have asked for a jury.—*George Burns*

Flo (after a quarrel with her husband Joe): You know, I was a fool when I married you.
Joe: Yes, dear, but I was in love and didn't notice.

I haven't spoken to my wife in 18 months. I don't like to interrupt her.

Why didn't I report it when a thief stole my credit card? Because he was spending a lot less than my wife.

This Lesson in Your Life

The summer 2001 will long be remembered by the residents of California as the summer of "rolling blackouts." Long before the 100-degree plus temperatures settled in, the utility companies warned that they were unable to meet the electricity demands. The symptom that most personally affected the general population was random periods of power outages—which always seemed to come at the most inconvenient times. Computers suddenly went blank, losing a vital document or data base. Traffic lights stopped working at rush-hour. Dishwashers stopped in the middle of a run. Air conditioners stopped working in the heat of the day.

Even greater problems occurred behind the scenes. Utility companies filed bankruptcy. The state legislature was called upon to cough up the money to salvage the situation, to keep the power on. Governor Davis threatened an "executive takeover" of the utility companies, should they not cooperate with the state-driven agenda. Credit ratings of both the utility companies and the state of California fell considerably, driving up both the cost of electricity and the cost of borrowing to meet the demand. California tax-payers were sent the bill for all the state-funded emergency actions. Utility rates were increased by 40 percent immediately, and retroactively to the beginning of the crisis.

Blame was thrown about skillfully. Some blamed the Public Utility Commission, others the utility companies. The Democrats blamed the Republicans, and the Republicans blamed the Democrats. The Governor of California blamed Texas-based power generators, and many of the critics blamed the governor.

More than a year later, the question as to who is responsible for the "rolling blackouts of 2001" is still being debated. It is clear, however, that somebody "messed up" terribly. Somebody ought to have been planning for the growing energy requirements of the swelling California population. Long before the situation was at the point of crisis, somebody should have recognized that it was headed that way. Though the ordinary people of California did nothing wrong, they suffered the brunt of the consequences for the irresponsibility of their leaders.

All this was similar to the situation of the people of Judah. The consequences that fell upon them were much more severe than that of rolling blackouts. As Nebuchadnezzar moved in his troops, many young men died in battle. The people's treasured Temple was first ravaged, then destroyed. The city's walls were demolished, along with all of Jerusalem's primary buildings. Those who survived the sword were carried off to a foreign land to serve a king who worshiped a strange god.

Did God still care about His people? They were aware that they had sinned; but they needed to know whether God still loved them.

1. How long did Jehoahaz reign as king of Judah, and how old was he when he became king?

Jehoahaz reigned for three months as king of Judah. He was 23 when he became king.

2. Who was Eliakim, and how was he related to Jehoiakim?

Eliakim, the name given to Jehoiakim when he became king, was the brother of Jehoahaz, who became King of Judah in his place.

3. Who was credited with overthrowing the kingship of Jehoiakim? What happened to him after his overthrow?

Nebuchadnezzar, king of Babylon, overthrew Jehoiakim. He was carried away to Babylon in fetters.

4. What else did Nebuchadnezzar carry off to Babylon at the time he took Jehoiakim?

Nebuchadnezzar also carried off vessels of the house of the Lord to put in his temple in Babylon.

5. Who was assigned to take the place of Jehoiakim as king of Judah?

Jehoiakin, the son of Jehoiakim, was made king of Judah.

6. After Jehoiakin was called to Babylon, who took his place as king?

Zedekiah, Jehoiakin's uncle and Jehoiakim's brother, served as king.

7. How did the leaders of Jerusalem respond to the message of the Lord that was sent by his prophets?

They mocked the messengers of God, despised His words, and misused his prophets.

8. Why did Nebuchadnezzar overthrow Zedekiah?

Because Zedekiah rebelled against Nebuchadnezzar's rule.

9. When Nebuchadnezzar overthrew Jerusalem, what happened to those who escaped the sword?

They were carried away to Babylon, where they became servants to Nebuchadnezzar and his sons.

10. Who remained in Jerusalem?

Only "the poorest sort of the people of the land."

The story is told of an atheist who was taking a walk through the woods, admiring all that the "accident of evolution" had created. "What majestic trees! What powerful rivers! What beautiful animals!" he said to himself.

As he walked alongside the river, he heard a rustling in the bushes behind him. As he turned to look, he saw a seven-foot grizzly charge toward him. He ran as fast as he could up the path. He looked over his shoulder and saw that the bear was closing in on him. He tried to run even faster, so scared that tears were coming to his eyes. He looked over his shoulder again, and the bear was even closer. His heart was pumping frantically as he tried to run even faster, but he tripped and fell on the ground. He rolled over to pick himself up and saw the bear was right on top of him and raising his paw to kill him.

At that instant, he cried out "Oh my God!"

Just then, time stopped. The bear froze; the forest was silent; the river even stopped moving. A bright light shone upon the man, and a voice came out of the sky saying, "You deny my existence all of these years. You teach others I don't exist. You even credit my creation to a cosmic accident. And now you expect me to help you out of this predicament? Does this mean that I am now to count you as a believer?"

The atheist, ever so proud, looked into the light and said, "It would be rather hypocritical to ask to be a Christian after all these years, but could you make the *bear* a Christian?"

"Very well," said the voice.

Time resumed, the bright light went out, the river ran, and the sounds of the forest continued. The bear put down his paw, then brought both paws together, bowed his head and said, "Lord, I thank you for this food which I am about to receive."

God is mocked in a variety of different ways. When the day is over, though, He always has full possession of His dignity. Through it all, He sees it all. Dr. Robert E. Speer tells the story of an old sculptor who was cutting a figure that was to stand in a niche in the wall so that its back would never be seen, yet he was working with the same painstaking care on the back as on the front. Someone asked, "Why are you working on the back of that figure? No one will see it."

"Ah," replied the sculptor, "God will always be looking upon it."

"I am not sure," continues Dr. Speer, "that it is not on the obscurities of our lives that God looks, far more than on what we regard as our real life, upon which men look. What He looks at, after all, is what is back of the life." That is the heart.

100

Grief and Hope

Lamentations 1:12-16; 3:22-24, 31-33

1:12-16

I s it nothing to you, all ye that pass by? behold, and see if there be any sorrow like unto my sorrow, which the Lord hath afflicted me in the day of his fierce anger.

13 From above hath he sent fire into my bones, and it prevaileth against them: he hath spread a net for my feet, he hath turned me back: he hath made me desolate and faint all the day.

14 The yoke of my transgressions is bound by his hand: they are wreathed, and come up upon my neck: he hath made my strength to fall, the Lord hath delivered me into their hands, from whom I am not able to rise up.

15 The Lord hath trodden under foot all my mighty men in the midst of me: he hath called an assembly against me to crush my young men: the Lord hath trodden the virgin, the daughter of Judah, as in a winepress.

16 For these things I weep; mine eye, mine eye runneth down with water, because the comforter that should relieve my soul is far from me: my children are desolate, because the enemy prevailed.

3:22-24

22 It is of the LORD's mercies that we are not consumed, because his compassions fail not.

23 They are new every morning: great is thy faithfulness.

24 The LORD is my portion, saith my soul; therefore will I hope in him.

3:31-33

31 For the Lord will not cast off for ever:

32 But though he cause grief, yet will he have compassion according to the multitude of his mercies.

33 For he doth not afflict willingly nor grieve the children of men.

Memory Selection
Lamentations 3:22-23

Background Scripture
Lamentations 1–5

Devotional Reading
Psalm 42:5-11

Nov. 10

101

Jeremiah earned his nickname, "the weeping prophet," by lamenting his people's sinfulness and wailing, "Oh that my head were waters, and mine eyes a fountain of tears" (Jer. 9:1). His cry became the book of Lamentations, on which today's lesson is based. Apparently the prophet wrote it shortly after the Babylonians destroyed the Holy City in 587/586 B.C.

As the book of Job is the Bible's classic quest to understand personal suffering, Lamentations is a quest for answers amid corporate calamity. Unlike Job, however, Jeremiah has a firm answer to the reason for the city's fate: its people refused to repent of having turned away from God to idols, and from just treatment of people made in His image. Finally, however, just as Job ends with God blessing after all, so Lamentations includes Jeremiah's confident expectation that God will not forever forsake His people.

Imagine aloud that you are a citizen of a widely immoral city. You had warned your fellow-citizens that if they did not reform, God would allow a foreign invader to destroy the city. They refused to listen; and now the enemy is razing your city.

The horror of it all makes such an impact on you that you compose a kind

of "funeral dirge" for the city. For ease of memorization, so others can join you in your lament, you cast your poem as an "acrostic"—with the letters of each verse in the alphabet beginning with succeeding letters, A to Z. You identify with your defeated fellow-citizens, but you defend the justice of God. At the end, you share your confidence that the city will be restored.

This was the origin of the "Lamentations" or, as an ancient Hebrew title has it, "Wailings," of Jeremiah.

Teaching Outline	*Daily Bible Readings*

I. God Is Angry—1:12-16
  A. The day of God's anger, 12
  B. Attacked by God, 13
  C. Abandoned to the enemy, 14
  D. Crushed as in a winepress,
    15-16
 	
II. God Is Just—3:22-24
 	
III. God Will Save—31-33
	Mon. Comfort Is Far from Me
	         Lamentations 1:12-16
	Tue. Great Is God's Faithfulness
	         Lamentations 3:19-24
	Wed. God Will Have Compassion
	         Lamentations 3:25-33
	Thu. Lift Hearts to Heaven
	         Lamentations 3:34-41
	Fri. God Heard My Plea
	         Lamentations 3:49-57
	Sat. Restore Us
	         Lamentations 5:15-22
	Sun. Sow in Tears, Reap in Joy
	         Psalm 126:1-6

Verse by Verse

I. God is Angry—1:12-16
A. The day of God's anger, 12

12 Is it nothing to you, all ye that pass by? behold, and see if there be any sorrow like unto my sorrow, which Lord hath afflicted me in the day of his fierce anger.

As noted in "For a Lively Start," the book of Lamentations is carefully constructed as an "acrostic," a poem with verses that begin with the successive letters of the alphabet. For example, if a modern poet had been writing these laments in English, she might have begun 1:1 something like, "**A**mong the nations Israel was great, but . . ."; then proceeded to start 1:2 with a "B" word, as: "**B**ut she turned from God to idols," and so on. This lesson, beginning with the twelfth verse, begins in Hebrew with the twelfth letter, "lamedh," which corresponds to our letter "L." In English we would have arranged to begin the verse with something like "**L**ook, all ye who pass by . . . ." The acrostic use of the Hebrew alphabet of 22 letters accounts for the number of verses in each chapter except chapter 3, which reflects the added discipline of starting each verse in 22 three-stanza verses with the same letter, yielding 66 verses. (See Psalm 119 for an example of another Bible acrostic.)

Although this rather restrictive style was common in its own right as a part of poetic art in the ancient world, Jeremiah may have used it not just for its artistic value but as a memory aid—for the book was included in the "Megilloth" or "Rolls" which were frequently read and/or recited in public services (along with Ecclesiastes, Psalms, Ruth, and Esther). As verse 12 indicates, Lamentations was an eloquent appeal to anyone hearing the service to pause in their normal pursuits and pay attention to the anguish among God's people caused by the destruction of Jerusalem by the Babylonians.

Note that Jeremiah writes in the first person (there is no sorrow "like unto *my* sorrow"), taking on the suffering of the people as his own. In return, he also wishes for the people to share with him his interpretation of what had happened. For example, it is not just Nebuchadnezzar, king of Babylon, who had "afflicted me"; it was *God* who had used Babylon to punish disobedient Israel, just as He had promised. If the people of Judah blamed Nebuchadnezzar instead of attributing their plight to God, they could not repent of their sins and turn to God as He longed for them to do.

B. Attacked by God, 13

13 From above hath he sent fire into my bones, and it prevaileth against them: he hath spread a net for my feet, he hath turned me back:

he hath made me desolate and faint all the day.

We have previously noted that Nebuchadnezzar's armies burned the Temple and the king's quarters, and no doubt much of the city, during his conquest of Jerusalem (2 Chron. 37:19). Because of the people's love for the holy City of David, this also ignited anguish in the depths of their souls. The invaders blocked the city gates to prevent escapes, thus "spreading a net" that entangled people who might otherwise have fled. The occupation of the city was not only physically oppressive, making them faint; it attacked the morale of the people, making them desolate.

C. Abandoned to the enemy, 14

14 The yoke of my transgressions is bound by his hand: they are wreathed, and come up upon my neck: he hath made my strength to fall, the Lord hath delivered me into their hands, from whom I am not able to rise up.

Now the poetic imagery shifts to that of oxen like those commonly used to pull carts. Jeremiah cuts to the quick of the national soul by saying that it is laboring under the ox-yoke of its own transgressions, rather than attributing their servitude directly to the invaders, or to God. The yoke of disobedience has been borne for so long that it could not be easily lifted; it has become a series of entwined yokes that restrict movement instead of helping pull the load. It is so heavy that the people cannot rise under it.

This imagery is already familiar to Jeremiah. At one point in his ministry, God had told him actually to place

an ox-yoke on his own neck to symbolize the servitude they would serve under Nebuchadnezzar, king of Babylon (Jer. 27:2-8). False prophets, courting the approval of King Zedekiah, brazenly challenged Jeremiah's warning. One of them prophesied that the precious vessels Nebuchadnezzar had already begun to take to Babylon would be returned. He went so far as to break the yoke that Jeremiah had placed on his own neck to defy any notion of servitude (28:10-11). Now, watching the fires destroy Jerusalem, it could have been of no comfort to Jeremiah that his own gloomier prophecy had come true.

D. Crushed as in a winepress, 15-16

15 The Lord hath trodden under foot all my mighty men in the midst of me: he hath called an assembly against me to crush my young men: the Lord hath trodden the virgin, the daughter of Judah, as in a winepress.

16 For these things I weep; mine eye, mine eye runneth down with water, because the comforter that should relieve my soul is far from me: my children are desolate, because the enemy prevailed.

Continuing in the voice of Jerusalem and its inhabitants, Jeremiah's dirge speaks of the impotence of the "mighty men" of Jerusalem. This phrase usually refers, in the Old Testament, to crack troops that were the palace guard. These soldiers might have repelled the invaders had not God himself planned for the city's downfall. In the Chronicler's account of the city's fall, he spoke specifically of Nebuchadnezzar's having included the "mighty men of valor" with the princes, craftsmen and others whom Nebuchadnezzar captured and deported to Babylon (2 Kings 24:14).

A vivid image with mixed metaphors is offered in 15b-15. At first Judah is portrayed as a virgin who was expected to keep herself pure for Yahweh, her betrothed; but the virgin is violated as she changes into grapes trodden in a winepress. Finally, the juice that is extracted from the crushed grapes becomes the tears of the prophet and the entire city as they discover that the God who would have formerly come to their rescue has removed Himself from the scene.

II. God Is Just—3:22-24

22 It is of the LORD's mercies that we are not consumed, because his compassions fail not.

23 They are new every morning: great is thy faithfulness.

24 The LORD is my portion, saith my soul; therefore will I hope in him.

Just as in any calamity, many Judeans asked why God would allow such a disaster to come upon them. Jeremiah is ready for such questions. He had reminded them in 1:5 that God had afflicted Judah because of "the multitude of their transgressions," not because He is an unjust or uncaring God. Now the prophet takes the further step of asserting that it was only by God's mercies that their suffering was not even greater. He can even pause in the midst of his "wailings" to insert a brief psalm of praise in verses 23-24 (which has been set to music by modern Christians). This affirmation of faith and hope forms a transition to the next passage, where the mood will change from a funeral dirge to an expression of confidence that the destruction of Jerusalem will not be the last word.

III. God Will Save—3:31-33

31 For the Lord will not cast off for ever:

32 But though he cause grief, yet will he have compassion according to the multitude of his mercies.

33 For he doth not afflict willingly nor grieve the children of men.

Previous lessons have shown that Jeremiah not only predicted the Babylonian captivity but that it would come to an end (as in Jer. 50:17-10). Following God's instructions, the prophet had even invested in Judean real estate, buying a field near Jerusalem during the siege but before the captivity to show the certainty of the people's restoration to the land (32:6-15). The divinely-inspired optimism appears again in poetic form here.

Note that the fact that God will not cast away His people forever does not depend on their reformation, but on the compassionate and forgiving nature of God. He has not "willingly" caused His people's downfall; and after a time of judgment, He will restore a remnant to the land. The people find themselves conquered not because God enjoys afflicting them, but because of their rebellion against Him. Although Jeremiah will call for a return to God (vss. 40-41), He could still have kept them in captivity with all justice. God's mercy, however, leads Him to plan a brighter future—which will be described in the books of Ezra and Nehemiah as the people are allowed to return and rebuild the city.

Evangelistic Emphasis

It is difficult to believe that incredibly difficult hardships sometimes produce faith. Yet, that was the way it happened for Terry and Janet Moore. Neither, having grown up in homes that gave only lip-service to religion, was inclined to give much thought to such things early in their marriage. It wasn't until their two-year-old daughter, Molly, was hit by a car speeding through their neighborhood, that God became more than an exclamation to them. Suddenly, they found themselves terribly angry at God for allowing this to happen to their little girl.

Yet, as Molly lay for days in a coma in Pediatric Intensive Care, Terry and Janet gradually moved from fierce anger directed toward God to that of desperate begging God to spare their little girl. At first, their prayers were little more than cries of agony. After all, they really didn't know how to pray. But after Molly had spent 15 days in a coma, then six weeks in a body cast, Terry and Janet had done more praying than many Christians in a lifetime of saying dinner grace. Gradually, their angry outbursts became anguished petitions, and their petitions then began to grow into hopeful intercessions. whis finally were actually transformed into thankfulness and faith. Today, Janet and Terry make sure that conversation with God is a regular part of their day.

ഈറ

Memory Selection

It is of the Lord's mercies that we are not consumed, because his compassions fail not. They are new every morning: great is thy faithfulness.
—*Lamentations 3:22-23*

Many of us first encountered these verses at a camp devotional or a youth rally. It was the Revised Standard Version that provided the lyrics for what came to be one of my favorite devotional songs:

The steadfast love of the Lord never ceases,
His mercies never come to an end;
They are new every morning;
Great is thy faithfulness.
The Lord is my portion," says my soul,
"Therefore I will hope in him."

Little did most of us know that these words of hope emerged during the destruction of Jerusalem hundreds of years before Christ. Most of our struggles had to do with Mrs. Stern's grueling math exams or the most recent zits that appeared in the most conspicuous places just before the high school dance. Yet, Jeremiah was able to express his hope and faith even as the City of David was being destroyed!

Weekday Problems

Not long ago I served as the guest speaker at Sierra Bible Camp. Youth from the senior boys' cabin and the senior girls' cabin always have a devotional at the lake the last night at camp. The setting is awesome, with starry skies and a crisp chill in the air. A small campfire provides both warmth and a soft glow. Part of the evening's events involves the "giving of a rose" as each camper spontaneously gives an imaginary rose to one of the other campers or staff to express special appreciation. The "roses" are invisible, but very meaningful.

This year, I was particularly impressed with how many of the campers gave a rose to another camper with the phrase such as, "You were really there for me when I needed you." The two thoughts that came most prominently to my mind were: (1) *How could these young kids have so many problems?* and (2) *What these strongly independent kids are actually affirming is "community"!*

* Can you give an example of a time in your life when your problem seemed enormous because you had no one to share it with?

* Are there in most of us both a yearning for independence and a hunger for community? How can the church best address these needs?

Answers You Didn't Want to Hear to Questions You Didn't Ask

Q: What do you call a cannibal who ate his mother's sister?
A: An aunteater, of course.

Q: Who broadcasted from the station with the smallest number of electrical outlets in the world?
A: Paul Revere. His studio had only one plug.

Q: What birds have learned to talk to policemen?
A: Stool pigeons.

Q: What did they call the man who was killed when he fell from the roof while trying to overhear a conversation in the bedroom below?
A: An eavesdropper.

Q: How much money was made by the man who invented the hay-baling machine?
A: I don't know, but he made a bundle.

This Lesson in Your Life

Rarely do we truly understand another's experience exactly. At best, we have only approximate guesses as to how someone really feels during his moment of trial, pain, crisis, or stress. Yes, a woman who has suffered a miscarriage understands better the pain of another woman with the same kind of loss than one who has never had such a loss. And the widower who lost his wife of 50 years better understands better than the young, newly-married minister the grief of his friend who is now facing a similar loss.

Yet, while there is always a gap between our experience and another's, no one's pain is as singularly superior to the pain of all others as it tends to feel. No trial is quite the magnum prototype that we think it is. Each experiences moments of trial, pain, crisis, or stress that are generally common to the human experience. How we deal with, yield to, or overcome those human challenges ultimately helps determine the kind of person that we choose to be.

The suffering that came upon sixth-century B.C. Jerusalem because of the people's sin was unusually harsh; bu it was not *uniquely* harsh. Others, similarly sinful and similarly punished, also suffered harsh consequences. One of the special traits of Jerusalem and the prophet who wrote Lamentations was their ability to come to terms with their sins, confess them, then praise God in spite of the pain of their punishment.

Though there is justifiable lament, there is also praise. Though there is a crying out to God over His stern countenance, there is also praise for His grace. Lamentations brings to its readers the Bible's greatest concentration of sorrow and complaint; but it also provides some of the most beautiful praise.

Do we really "lament" our own moments of trial, pain, crisis, or stress, looking to God to supply our need and our answer? Or is our complaint more of a "murmur," in that we are found to be crying out against God, and hoping to glean some pity and moral support from our friends? Is our grumbling merely filling the air about us with high-decible sound waves, or are we carrying our petitions to the throne room of God?

I'm afraid that much of what I hear coming from my fellow Christians (and perhaps, myself) is little more than self-indulgent self-pity. Rather than laments that glorify God by calling upon Him to act, they tend to be expressions of resentment against Him because he hasn't blessed us nearly as abundantly as we have come to feel is our due. Rather than prompting God's compassion, I strongly suspect that when we *complain* rather than *lament*, we make ourselves irritations to the patience of the Almighty.

1. To what does the writer first compare the city of Jerusalem?

He compares Jerusalem to a widow who has been left alone.

2. Those who pass by Jerusalem do what with their hands and heads, and what do they say?

They *clap their hands* and *wag their heads.* They say, "Is this the city that men call "The perfection of beauty, The joy of the whole earth"?

3. What scoffing remarks were made by Jerusalem's enemies?

Jerusalem's enemies mocked saying, "We have swallowed her up: certainly this is the day that we looked for; we have found, we have seen it."

4. To whom did the author compare "a bear lying in wait?"

He compared the Lord to a bear lying in wait.

5. What did the author say was "new every morning"?

The Lord's compassions or mercies.

6. What are we to lift unto the Lord?

We are to lift our hearts and our hands to the Lord.

7. What does the text say that it is good to wait quietly for?

The salvation of the Lord.

8. What is said to happen to the infant's tongue because of the seige?

The infant's tongue sticks to the roof of its mouth because of thirst.

9. The punishment of the people of Jerusalem is said to be greater than that of whom?

It is said to be greater than the punishment of Sodom.

10. Whose punishment did the people say that they were being called to bear?

They said, "Our fathers sinned and we bear their punishment."

One of the movies that has delighted my family was "Patch Adams." The story behind the movie is about Doctor Adams, or "Patch," as he has come to be affectionately known, a physician who places a great emphasis on laughter as a means of aiding recovery from illness.

It seems that years ago, when Adams was working as a physician in Washington D.C., he was so deadly serious about everything that he once tried to kill himself. Not having been successful, he regained enough sanity to check himself into a mental hospital. While there, he says, "I grew to respect what matters in life: wonder and curiosity and love and faith and family and friends and nature and humor." Once Dr. Adams was released from the hospital, he added a new dimension to his medical practice. He became a clown and humorist.

Today, Dr. Adams is a popular speaker at medical gatherings all across the nation. Even before the movie brought him broad recognition among the general population, he had already come to wear the title, "the clown prince of physicians" among the in-crowd of medicine.

"Fun," testifies Dr. Adams, "has overwhelming medicinal effects on our patients. So many fewer pain medications! I am amazed at how humor has had a beneficial impact on disease, especially chronic disease such as arthritis and mental illness." Years ago, Archbishop Fulton J. Sheen made the comment, "A smile across the aisle of a bus in the morning could save a suicide later in the day."

Considering, these observations about the complexity of our human nature, I can't help but think not only of humor but of *praise* in the life of the believer. Christians who have walked many years hand-in-hand with God will often testify that an hour of "good worship" (uplifting worship) will nurture their well-being better than a whole bottle of pills. Just as we need to laugh to nurture our personhood, so also we need to praise and rejoice. That need is there even during our times of woe—if not *especially* during our times of woe. Perhaps, that's why we are reminded by the apostle Paul to "Rejoice always!" It is not surprising then, when we find a grand passage of praise in the midst of the greatest outpouring of lament and woe found in Scripture. May we take the apostle's advice seriously and nurture our soul with praise. It might also not be a bad idea to take Dr. Adams' advice seriously. A good laugh would do most of us a world of good.

Ezekiel 18:1-4, 20-21, 25-32

The word of the LORD came unto me again, saying,

2 What mean ye, that ye use this proverb concerning the land of Israel, saying, The fathers have eaten sour grapes, and the children's teeth are set on edge?

3 As I live, saith the Lord GOD, ye shall not have occasion any more to use this proverb in Israel.

4 Behold, all souls are mine; as the soul of the father, so also the soul of the son is mine: the soul that sinneth, it shall die.

20 The soul that sinneth, it shall die. The son shall not bear the iniquity of the father, neither shall the father bear the iniquity of the son: the righteousness of the righteous shall be upon him, and the wickedness of the wicked shall be upon him.

21 But if the wicked will turn from all his sins that he hath committed, and keep all my statutes, and do that which is lawful and right, he shall surely live, he shall not die.

25 Yet ye say, The way of the Lord is not equal. Hear now, O house of Israel; Is not my way equal? are not your ways unequal?

26 When a righteous man turneth away from his righteousness, and committeth iniquity, and dieth in them; for his iniquity that he hath done shall he die.

27 Again, when the wicked man turneth away from his wickedness that he hath committed, and doeth that which is lawful and right, he shall save his soul alive.

28 Because he considereth, and turneth away from all his transgressions that he hath committed, he shall surely live, he shall not die.

29 Yet saith the house of Israel, The way of the Lord is not equal. O house of Israel, are not my ways equal? are not your ways unequal?

30 Therefore I will judge you, O house of Israel, every one according to his ways, saith the Lord GOD. Repent, and turn yourselves from all your transgressions; so iniquity shall not be your ruin.

31 Cast away from you all your transgressions, whereby ye have transgressed; and make you a new heart and a new spirit: for why will ye die, O house of Israel?

32 For I have no pleasure in the death of him that dieth, saith the Lord GOD: wherefore turn yourselves, and live ye.

Memory Selection
Ezekiel 18:4

Background Scripture
Ezekiel 18

Devotional Reading
Romans 6:17-23

Nov. 17

111

The most obvious theme of today's text is that God holds every person individually responsible for his or her sins. He does not hold children responsible for the sins of their parents, nor find parents guilty for the sins of their children. Of equal interest, however, is the reason why, at this time in Israel's history, God communicates this truth about personal responsibility.

Ezekiel was a priestly prophet (1:3), a contemporary of Jeremiah, Habakkuk, and Zephaniah. He thus lived through the horror of Judah's last days, including its captivity by the Babylonians (or Chaldeans). He must have heard questions from the few righteous people left in Judah, who understandably asked why they seemed to be punished for the sins of the majority. Whatever happened to God's Covenant to save Israel? Ezekiel's teaching here is designed to deal with such disturbing questions.

♣♣

Today's lesson can be introduced by leading your group in a discussion of why sin seems to be so contagious. Ask such questions as, *How do you feel about the fairness of God when a "crack baby" is born with an inherited addiction? Who is to blame when a child whose father beats his wife grows up, marries, and abuses his own wife?* Or, *Do you think a modern German youth deserves scorn by a person who survived Nazi atrocities during World War II?*

Note that similar questions could be raised by righteous Israelites who were carried into Babylonian captivity for sins that the majority of their brethren and their leaders committed. The priest-prophet Ezekiel deals with such questions of "inherited guilt" in today's text.

Teaching Outline	Daily Bible Readings	

I. Myth About Guilt—1-4
  A. Misleading proverb, 1-3
  B. All are God's, 4
	Mon.	The Righteous Will Live
		Ezekiel 18:1-9

	Tue.	The One Who Sins Will Die Ezekiel 18:19-24

II. Many vs. One—20-21
  A. Radical individualism, 20
  B. Repentance vs. inheritance, 21
	Wed.	Turn and Live
		Ezekiel 18:25-32

III. Management of Guilt—25-28
  A. God on trial, 25
  B. Conditions for forgiveness, 26-28
	Thu.	Why Will Ye Die?
		Ezekiel 33:7-11

	Fri.	Without Excuse Romans 1:16-25

IV. Make God Happy: Repent!–29-32
  A. Principle's summary, 29-30
  B. 'Turn and live!', 31-32
	Sat.	God Will Repay
		Romans 2:1-8

	Sun.	Belief Brings Life John 3:6-21

Verse by Verse

I. Myth About Guilt—1-4
A. Misleading proverb, 1-3

1 The word of the LORD came unto me again, saying,

2 What mean ye, that ye use this proverb concerning the land of Israel, saying, The fathers have eaten sour grapes, and the children's teeth are set on edge?

3 As I live, saith the Lord GOD, ye shall not have occasion any more to use this proverb in Israel.

Since the prophet Jeremiah also knew of this proverbial saying (Jer. 31:29), it was apparently widespread. In fact, the idea that children inherit their parents' sins is common in many societies; and it is easy to see how common experience would give rise to it. As in "For a Lively Start," one of the saddest illustrations of how such a myth might start is the infant who is born with an addiction inherited from its mother. Other illustrations abound: a son inherits a farm with worn-out soil because his father did not practice crop rotation or other good land management practices. A whole nation suffers from the legacy of a corrupt dictator.

Furthermore, some Jews may have thought that God's own Word supported the idea of inherited guilt. Had not God warned, when giving the Ten Commandments, that he is "a jealous God, visiting the iniquity of the fathers upon the children unto the third and fourth generation" (Exod. 20:5).

Regardless of its widespread use and apparent logic, both Jeremiah (31:30) and Ezekiel explode the myth. They do so by distinguishing distinguish between *guilt* and *the consequences* of sin. The minority of faithful Israelites, especially those who were born in Babylonian exile, no doubt felt that being captured by Babylon implicated them in the sins of the majority since they suffered the same punishment. Ezekiel encourages them by saying, "Not so. The fact that the teeth of your idol-worshiping fathers were set on edge by the sour grapes of Babylonian captivity does not mean that you should have the same taste in your own mouth. Don't use that proverb any more!"

B. All are God's, 4

4 Behold, all souls are mine; as the soul of the father, so also the soul of the son is mine: the soul that sinneth, it shall die.

Ezekiel's encouraging word to the faithful children of the Judean captives continues by reminding them that God has not abandoned them just because they are no longer in the land God had promised to their fathers. We can easily understand how faithful worshipers may have felt bereft without the Temple that symbolized their faith. Some were reduced to wailing, "How shall we sing the Lord's song in a strange land?" (Ps. 137:4). Here God reminds them that His presence is not limited to geography. He is just as much the Father of those born in Chaldea as He had been of their disobedient fathers back in Judah.

We are not to think of "souls" as meaning "disembodied spirits," as though God is saying that our spirits are His, but not our bodies. The Hebrew word *nephesh* which is used here for "soul" also means "life." God is saying that whether our parents sinned or not, whether we inherited the consequences of their sin or not, whether we are at home or elsewhere, we are all in His loving hands.

II. Many vs. One—20-21
A. Radical individualism, 20

20 The soul that sinneth, it shall die. The son shall not bear the iniquity of the father, neither shall the father bear the iniquity of the son: the righteousness of the righteous shall be upon him, and the wickedness of the wicked shall be upon him.

This elaboration on the concept that we are *individually* responsible to God was no doubt necessary because many Jews had carried too far the idea of *corporate* responsibility. The Old Covenant is based in part on the fact that God's promise to Abraham was also to his unborn "seed" or descendants (see Gen. 17:1-8). This idea was so strong that Abraham's descendants as a whole could be referred to by the name "Israel," which in fact was the new name given to Abraham's grandson Isaac. Unfortunately, however, some Israelites took such refuge in God's promise to save His people "Israel" that they had neglected *personal*

morality and responsibility. At the other extreme, especially responsible Israelites who had suffered in the Babylonian conquest, now felt guilty because God's judgment upon the whole had affected them personally. God reassures them with this teaching that balances "corporate personality" with the fact that when it comes to assigning blame or guilt, God deals with us individually.

B. Repentance vs. inheritance, 21

21 But if the wicked will turn from all his sins that he hath committed, and keep all my statutes, and do that which is lawful and right, he shall surely live, he shall not die.

How should a Jew in Babylon deal with having suffered either the guilt or the consequence of Israel's sins? By repenting of any individual sins and turning whole-heartedly to the joyous task of keeping God's Law and doing that which is right. (The promise that such a person would "not die" obviously refers to spiritual death, since even the righteous must lay down their body in physical death.)

III. Management of Guilt—25-28
A. God on trial, 25

25 Yet ye say, The way of the Lord is not equal. Hear now, O house of Israel; Is not my way equal? are not your ways unequal?

The dilemma of God's having promised to enter into an "eternal Covenant" with the children of Israel, then allowing them to be conquered, resulted in widespread questioning God's righteousness. More particularly, Ezekiel must deal with individual Jews who questioned whether their guilt justified actually being banished from the Promised Land. Although God does not fully justify His ways here, He has previously made it abundantly clear that it was Israel's overall disobedience, among both common people and their leaders, that resulted in their conquest. At any rate, the best among us are still unrighteous (or "not equal" in our judgments), giving none of us the right to sit in judgment over God's righteousness.

B. Conditions for forgiveness, 26-28

26 When a righteous man turneth away from his righteousness, and committeth iniquity, and dieth in them; for his iniquity that he hath done shall he die.

27 Again, when the wicked man turneth away from his wickedness that he hath committed, and doeth that which is lawful and right, he shall save his soul alive.

28 Because he considereth, and turneth away from all his transgressions that he hath committed, he shall surely live, he shall not die.

To become almost painfully explicit, God in effect tells us to put "blinders" on, considering our own state before Him and ignoring that of others. God will consider the individual's path in rendering judgment, not the way taken by others: the righteous who rebel and die in sin, and the wicked who repent and turn, are weighed in the balances they create for themselves, not some kind of "corporate" scale.

IV. Make God Happy: Repent!–29-32
A. Summary of the principle, 29-30

29 Yet saith the house of Israel, The way of the Lord is not equal.

O house of Israel, are not my ways equal? are not your ways unequal?

30 Therefore I will judge you, O house of Israel, every one according to his ways, saith the Lord GOD. Repent, and turn yourselves from all your transgressions; so iniquity shall not be your ruin.

Again the vision of "hauling God into court" arises. Yet a righteous Israelite in Babylon need not fear that the Supreme Judge is unjust. Each person who repents will be redeemed from the corporate judgment inflicted on the larger whole. The majority's "iniquity" need not be the individual's ruin; and a former idol-worshiper is still free to turn to God.

B. 'Turn and live!', 31-32

31 Cast away from you all your transgressions, whereby ye have transgressed; and make you a new heart and a new spirit: for why will ye die, O house of Israel?

32 For I have no pleasure in the death of him that dieth, saith the Lord GOD: wherefore turn yourselves, and live ye.

We recall that Jeremiah had predicted that God would give His people a new covenant (Jer. 31:31). What is also needed is a new heart, a spirit that longs to submit to God's will. Although God also promises exactly that (Ezek. 11:19), He also calls us to renew our own hearts so we can meet these gifts with willingness and joy. In one last justification of Israel's fate, God affirms His essential nature: He has no joy in seeing the wicked perish in their sins. Instead, angels rejoice when even one sinner repents and turns to God (Luke 15:10).

Evangelistic Emphasis

It Is all too easy for us to blame someone else for our shortcomings. That is true, not only for the 40-year-old neurotic lying on the psychiatrist's couch, blaming her mother for her "total failure" at life. It is true for most of us sinners when we find ourselves caught in the headlights of exposure. Just like Adam before us, we anxiously look about for someone else to blame for our predicament. When the consequences of our bad choices begin to stack heavily against us, we attempt to persuade ourselves that we have been victimized by the bad parenting we received, the meanness of our third-grade teacher, or the so-cial disadvantages of our upbringing.

The temptation to "pass the buck" that seduces us is nothing new. "The fathers have eaten sour grapes, and the children's teeth are set on edge" had become the easy chant of the masses during Ezekiel's day. They had sung the song for so long, they had come to believe that it was true. Yet, it was no less a cop-out then than it is today. The problems of the people of Judah were not caused by the sins of their parents. The problems of the people of Judah were caused by their own sins. They were unfaithful to God. They had forgotten his statutes. They were mistreating their neighbors. They were indulging their greed. They were exploiting the poor. They were dabbling in idolatry. Consequently, if life was ever going to be right for them, it would be necessary for *them* to repent.

** споз**

Memory Selection

Behold, all souls are mine; as the soul of the father, so also the soul of the son is mine: the soul that sinneth, it shall die.—*Ezekiel 18:4*

Gregory White has always considered himself to be "a self-made man." He has always pulled himself up by his own bootstraps. He bought his own car while still in high school, put himself through college, and built his own business from a moon-lighting enterprise into a multi-billion dollar corporation.

Unfortunately, Gregory has also gone through four marriages. Each wife was in the beginning a prized trophy. Each was strikingly attractive. He poudly paraded them before his peers much like he did his corporate acquisitions. Yet, near the end of each marriage, what had been prized came to be detested. Though Gregory perceived each of these women as belonging to him (i.e., his wife), he never quite ever came to see himself as belonging to her (i.e. her husband). Their relationship was never mutual. In much the same way, Gregory religiously embraces Yahweh as his God, but has never thought of himself as God's man.

Weekday Problems

Helen Simpson has not climbed out of bed except for toilet needs for the past four months. Thelma, Helen's sister has looked in on her each day to make sure that she had something to eat, some fresh water beside her bed, and to ease her own mind that Helen was still among the living. Helen's doctor tells Thelma that her problem is depression. Within the past year, she has lost her marriage, her mother to cancer and her best friend from highschool to a random drive-by shooting. Because of these losses, Helen has convinced herself that she is "under a curse." She isn't sure what she has done wrong, but she is quite certain that these losses have come as a punishment for her sins. The prospect that her sins have caused the deaths of her mother and best friend is almost more difficult than she can bear.

* Is there something fundamentally wrong with Helen's thinking that she is "under a curse" or that she is being punished for her sins? Why? Why not?

* What does Ezekiel 18 have to offer to Helen that might change her perception of her situation?

* Have you ever felt that God might be punishing you for your sins through the hardships suffered by those near you?

Hits and Myths

In addition to the Jewish maxim, "The fathers ate sour grapes and the children's teeth are set on edge," we have our own "stock sayings." Are the following adages foolproof, or are they at best half-truths?

Money talks.
Like father, like son.
You can't teach an old dog new tricks.
We can all pull ourselves up by our own boot-straps.
An apple a day keeps the doctor away.
You always reap what you sow.
Pretty is as pretty does.
You can't squeeze blood out of a turnip.
The customer is always right.
A rolling stone gathers no moss.
Where there's smoke there's fire.
A miss is as good as a mile.
God helps those who help themselves.

This Lesson in Your Life

Jack Priest hasn't been inside a church building in more than 20 years. When he left home for college, he resigned also from the family tradition of going to church every time the door was open. During college, felt compelled to go along with his parents when back at home for school breaks, but since then he has arranged d his visits to avoid Sundays. Now, at age 44, Jack finds himself haunted by his faint memories of faith.

There was a time in Jack's life when his church involvement was filled with zeal. Christianity placed before him a challenge that he found to be personally enticing. He cannot remember which sermon planted the seed or which Bible Class lesson shaped the concept. All Jack remembers was the impression that he and God were involved in a spiritual face-off. His goal was to live the perfect life, keeping all the rules. God's goal was to scrutinize closely his every move and catch him in a mistake. If successful at his attempt to live the perfect life, he would be the winner and God would have to let him into the gates of Heaven. If, however, God caught him in a mistake, that would mean that God was the winner, and he would suffer the consequences of the loss.

It was during Jack's 16th year that he realized that he was "whipped." There was no way that he would ever successfully finish the "contest" with God." What made Jack so certain was his new awareness that "thoughts count." He remembers that Sunday morning in the Teen Class when the lesson was from Ezekiel 18. The teacher decided to use that chapter to talk with the kids about their lascivious fantasy lives. He emphasized the daunting words of Ezekiel 18:4, and those of the first half of 1 Corinthians 4:5. Together, they produced a focus that Jack never was able to shake.

Though it has been nearly 30 years, Jack has never gotten past the image of God that took hold of him that Sunday in the Teen Class. It seemed to him as though God had stacked the cards against him. "If I sin, I will 'die,' and since I can't always control my thoughts, I'm toast," he thought. The thought that God would so unfairly judge him was more than his faith could bear.

Unfortunately, Jack has never gone back and read either the real message of Ezekiel 18 or of 1 Corinthians 4:5. In both passage, the message is about God's grace, not His exacting harshness. First, God tells His people that a man will not have to stand in judgment for what someone else has done, even if it happens to be his father (or his son). Second, God will give credit for even the good thoughts we've had, those things we've longed to do for Him, although we've never had opportunity to bring them to completion.

GETTING THE FACTS STRAIGHT

1. What was the proverb that had come to be often recited in Judah?

The fathers have eaten sour grapes, and the children's teeth are set on edge.

2. Basically, what was God's objection to that popular proverb?

He said that the souls of both parents and children belong to him, and it is the soul that sins who will die.

3. What did God say would happen with the man who lived a just life?

He said that the man who lives a just life will live.

4. If a just man has a son who is not just like his father, what will happen to the son? On whose head does his fate lie?

The son who is not just will die. His blood is upon his own head. His father will not bear the burden of his son's sin.

5. What is the result if an unjust father has a son who lives a just life?

The son will live, but his father will not be credited for his son's righteousness. Neither will the son bear the stain of his father's guilt

6. What did the Lord say would become of the wicked man who turns from his wicked ways and lives righteously?

He shall surely live, he shall not die. The transgressions he has committed will not be held against him.

7. What is the implied answer when the Lord asks the question, "Have I any pleasure at all that the wicked should die? "

The expected response seems to be, **"NO."**

8. What did the Lord say would happen to the righteous man who turns from his life of righteousness to do evil?

He will die. The righteousness that he had done shall not be remembered.

9. What would be the basis of judgment that the Lord would bring upon the house of Israel?

He would judge each and every man according to his own deeds.

10. What call did the Lord send out to the people of Judah?

His call was for them to repent, turn from their wicked ways, and live.

The story is told about a little girl who walked into Bible class late one morning. Her hands were dirty, her dress was soiled, and there was a curious dirty ring around her mouth. Her teacher asked her how she had gotten so dirty so early in the morning. She explained that on her way to Bible school, a neighbor boy asked her to blow up his wading pool. She blew and blew until she had enough air to make the rubber wall stand up. Then, the boy picked up the hose and started filling the pool.

As the boy began filling the pool, the little girl invited him to come to Bible school with her. "No, I want to play in my pool," was the boy's immediate reply.

At this point in the reviewing of the events, and with her pretty blue eyes looking straight toward the teacher, the girl said, "I pulled the stopper out of the air hole and let the air out so the pool would go down, because if he didn't come to Bible school with me, I didn't want God to blame me for it!"

Most of us struggle with blame. There resides a fear deep within us of being blamed for that which is not our fault. At the same time, many of us are inclined to attempt to dodge blame when the problem is very much our fault. Certainly, not many of us are inclined to step forward to accept the blame for something caused by another. It's not usually the American way.

On the other hand, Joe Montana, among the best quarterbacks in NFL history, says he owes part of his success to being able to say, "I dropped the ball," even if he didn't. In his 16-year pro career (he retired in '95), Montana was a leader who both accepted the blame and shared the credit. According to an interview with *USA Weekend,* whenever Montana received a bad handoff from the man playing center, he'd return to the sidelines and tell the coach it was his fault, even if it meant getting chewed out.

"When you're a leader," Montana said, "you've got to be willing to take the blame. People appreciate when you're not pointing fingers at them, because that just adds to their pressure. If you get past that, you can talk about fixing what went wrong." This leadership quality in Montana was one of the significant qualities that made him such an effective quarterback. Yet, its significance had nothing to do with how accurately he was able to throw the football.

It is not unusual that the qualities that are most to be credited to our professional success are little related to our educational degrees, technical acumen, or professional finesse. Often the trait that most enriches us has to do, instead, with our character. When we forget that truth, both we and our profession are the losers.

Ezekiel 36:22-32

Therefore say unto the house of Israel, Thus saith the Lord GOD; I do not this for your sakes, O house of Israel, but for mine holy name's sake, which ye have profaned among the heathen, whither ye went.

23 And I will sanctify my great name, which was profaned among the heathen, which ye have profaned in the midst of them; and the heathen shall know that I am the LORD, saith the Lord GOD, when I shall be sanctified in you before their eyes.

24 For I will take you from among the heathen, and gather you out of all countries, and will bring you into your own land.

25 Then will I sprinkle clean water upon you, and ye shall be clean: from all your filthiness, and from all your idols, will I cleanse you.

26 A new heart also will I give you, and a new spirit will I put within you: and I will take away the stony heart out of your flesh, and I will give you an heart of flesh.

27 And I will put my spirit within you, and cause you to walk in my statutes, and ye shall keep my judgments, and do them.

28 And ye shall dwell in the land that I gave to your fathers; and ye shall be my people, and I will be your God.

29 I will also save you from all your uncleannesses: and I will call for the corn, and will increase it, and lay no famine upon you.

30 And I will multiply the fruit of the tree, and the increase of the field, that ye shall receive no more reproach of famine among the heathen.

31 Then shall ye remember your own evil ways, and your doings that were not good, and shall lothe yourselves in your own sight for your iniquities and for your abominations.

32 Not for your sakes do I this, saith the Lord GOD, be it known unto you: be ashamed and confounded for your own ways, O house of Israel.

Memory Selection
Ezekiel 36:26

Background Scripture
Ezekiel 36–37

Devotional Reading
Jeremiah 32:36-41

Nov. 24

We have noticed the shock experienced by God's Chosen People when He allowed them to be conquered by Babylonia). This lesson's focus on the future Restoration of Israel reveals a more positive but no less surprising aspect of the story of salvation.

This shift is seen in the fact that so much of Ezekiel's prophecy of the Return had no *literal* fulfillment. Although God brought them back to the land under Cyrus, king of Persia, nowhere do we read of the land blossoming and the people united under one ruler (as 37:21-22 predicts). Apparently God is so disillusioned with His people that while He will rescue them from captivity, He has resorted to a *new* "Israel" as His Covenant family. Since the Israel of the flesh has failed to bearing the message of the One God to the nations, God predicts an Israel of the Spirit—a forecast of the day when the Messiah would come and a New Covenant inaugurated (see also Jer. 31:31).

Before the class meets, call various members and ask them to bring any photos they may have of themselves as an infant or young child.

At your meeting, distribute the photos and ask members if they can identify the person portrayed in each youthful picture. Enjoy pointing out features such as the fact that "Bill" has about the same amount of hair now as he did as a baby! The main point, however, is that while we can often see the adult in the child, his final image is still forming, and won't be complete until God's future arrives.

In a similar way, Ezekiel's predictions of the glory of Israel's return from captivity are fulfilled in only rudimentary, "youthful" ways. The final shape of God's people remains for the End time.

Teaching Outline	*Daily Bible Readings*	

I. Sanctifying God's Name—22-24
  A. 'For My Sake, not Yours,' 22-23
  B. 'You shall return!' 24
II. Sprinkled with Grace—25-30
  A. Cleansing the altars, 25
  B. A new spirit, 26-27
  C. A vision of renewal, 28-30
III. Shamed to Glory—31-32
	Mon.
	Tue.
	Wed.
	Thu.
	Fri.
	Sat.
	Sun.
		Israel's Homecoming
		Ezekiel 36:8-12
		The Lord's Holiness
		Ezekiel 36:16-23
		A New Heart
		Ezekiel 36:24-28
		Saved from Uncleanness
		Ezekiel 36:29-33
		They Shall Know God
		Ezekiel 36:34-38
		Can Dry Bones Live?
		Ezekiel 37:1-6
		God's Spirit Within
		Ezekiel 37:7-14

Verse by Verse

I. Sanctifying God's Name—22-24
A. 'For My Sake, not Yours,' 22-23

22 Therefore say unto the house of Israel, Thus saith the Lord GOD; I do not this for your sakes, O house of Israel, but for mine holy name's sake, which ye have profaned among the heathen, whither ye went.

23 And I will sanctify my great name, which was profaned among the heathen, which ye have profaned in the midst of them; and the heathen shall know that I am the LORD, saith the Lord GOD, when I shall be sanctified in you before their eyes.

At first glance, this passage may seem to portray God as more interested in glorifying Himself than in rescuing Israel from Babylonian captivity. In a sense, this is precisely the case; but as we shall see it does not mean that God is self-righteous, as it would mean if a mere human made such a statement.

The passage must be understood in the context of God's sweeping plan of salvation for all ages and all people. Although He called Israel to be His chosen people as a preliminary step in the plan, the nation had failed Him miserably. Both people and priest, citizen and king, had sold out to idolatry and immorality, thus profaning God's Name before the nations (vs. 22). The word "profane," which appears three times here, means "be-fore" (and thus outside) the temple." In other words, in forsaking the worship of the true God in His Temple, Israel gave to Gentiles the false testimony that idols outside the Temple were acceptable objects of worship.

To "sanctify" means to "set apart for holy use." God could no longer use Israel as His "light to the nations" because she had refused to be set apart for His holy purpose. Finding the nation with no saving holiness within itself to exhibit to Gentiles, God had to find that holiness within himself. If the name of Yahweh is to be glorified by the Gentiles, God must act out of a loftier reason than Israel's present state of unrighteousness. That loftier reason is to be found only in Himself, in His unmatched grace, loving Israel despite her unloveliness.

B. 'You shall return!' 24

24 For I will take you from among the heathen, and gather you out of all countries, and will bring you into your own land.

This part of Ezekiel's prophecy is fulfilled in full view on the stage of history. As the books of Ezra and Nehemiah show, a remnant of Israel did return "from among the heathen." This was about 538 B.C., some 70 years after the people first began to be carried into captivity (just as Jeremiah had predicted in Jer. 25:11-12). This historic return puts a dent in what has come to be called the

"Diaspora"—the "scattering" of the Jews from Canaan not only in Babylonia but in Egypt, the Middle East, and as far east as India.

Although this prophecy that a remnant of the people would return to the land was partly literal, it also has figurative overtones. In a secondary sense, Israel also "returned" from the Diaspora at the Day of Pentecost in Acts 2, for the outpouring of the Holy Spirit and the inauguration of God's Kingdom under the risen Messiah.

II. Sprinkled with Grace—25-30
A. Cleansing the altars, 25

25 Then will I sprinkle clean water upon you, and ye shall be clean: from all your filthiness, and from all your idols, will I cleanse you.

The practice of sprinkling, both with water and with blood, had long been a symbol of the forgiveness of sins under the Old Covenant. For example, an elaborate sprinkling ritual is prescribed for "separating" (or "sanctifying") people from their uncleanness after they had handled a dead body (Num. 19:16-22). The fact that there was a physical element to the ritual, ridding oneself of disease-bearing germs, provided a vivid picture of the more deadly disease of sin.

Note, however, that here, unlike the ritual as described in Numbers 19, the people do not sprinkle each other but rely on God's own sprinkling. Here again is the picture of Israel's having become so unclean because of idolatry, injustice, and immorality that she has no moral power to cleanse herself. God's act of sanctifying them for His own name's sake, since there was no sanctifying power left in His people,

is seen to be an act of grace, not of self-righteousness.

B. A new spirit, 26-27

26 A new heart also will I give you, and a new spirit will I put within you: and I will take away the stony heart out of your flesh, and I will give you an heart of flesh.

27 And I will put my spirit within you, and cause you to walk in my statutes, and ye shall keep my judgments, and do them.

Now Ezekiel's prophecy begins to be "spiritualized" or made futuristic, with several elements that would be fulfilled only with the coming of the New Covenant, and among all peoples, not just the Jews. As a previous lesson noted, the prophet Jeremiah had also predicted that in the Age to come, God would give His people a new heart for a new Covenant—a heart that was inclined toward sincere obedience and not just ritual correctness (Jer. 31:31-33). In addition to speaking of this new heart, Ezekiel adds a new *spirit*—God's Spirit (resulting in the "s" being capitalized in many versions to indicate that the Holy Spirit is meant).

According to the apostle Peter, in his famous sermon on the Day of Pentecost, the new reign of Jesus was to be an age of the Holy Spirit (Acts 2:14-18). This, too, had been prophesied by various prophets under the Old Covenant (as in Joel 2:28ff.); but it did not occur immediately upon the return of a remnant of the Jews to the Promised Land.

Ezekiel is not so much interested in the sensational "speaking in tongues" that the Spirit prompted in

Acts 2 as he is in the work of the Spirit on the human heart. In their stubborn disobedience, God's people had exhibited a "stony heart"; but in the Age to come, the Spirit would turn the hearts of the Covenant People into yielding "flesh" instead of stone. In Jesus' Parable of the Soils (Lk. 8:4ff.), we learn that we as hearers of the Word must also do our part in providing "soft soil" or a willing heart.

C. A vision of renewal, 28-30

28 And ye shall dwell in the land that I gave to your fathers; and ye shall be my people, and I will be your God.

29 I will also save you from all your uncleannesses: and I will call for the corn, and will increase it, and lay no famine upon you.

30 And I will multiply the fruit of the tree, and the increase of the field, that ye shall receive no more reproach of famine among the heathen.

Ezekiel's vision of renewal is sometimes used to defend the right of modern Israel to occupy its ancient borders in Palestine. It seems awkward, however, to try to apply the geographical aspect of this prophecy without noting its spiritual elements. The Israel spoken of here is one who is willing to be saved from its uncleanness—whereas many Jews in modern Israel have come to question or neglect the faith of their forefathers. The land spoken of here blossoms—whereas much of modern Israel is stony and barren. Such observations raise the possibility that the fulfillment of this prophecy is to be understood in a spiritual rather than literal sense. Perhaps the "land" is a spiritual "place" to be occupied not by a particular race or nation but by all people with faith and commitment to God and His saving power.

III. Shamed to Glory—31-32

31 Then shall ye remember your own evil ways, and your doings that were not good, and shall lothe yourselves in your own sight for your iniquities and for your abominations.

32 Not for your sakes do I this, saith the Lord GOD, be it known unto you: be ashamed and confounded for your own ways, O house of Israel.

These verses may seem at first reading to be unduly harsh to modern ears. Many people today fear shame, and have rightly been warned against its use as a device for manipulating children into good behavior. For God, however, it was essential that Israel face its profound disobedience directly. To have deliberately worshiped an idol—perhaps one that demanded child sacrifice—when God said "Thou shalt not" would make any person of integrity and conscience ashamed.

However, God is not interested in reducing His people to groveling. Their shame has a redemptive purpose. By being stricken to the depths of their being for their willful sin, Israel fulfills a role it had previously had difficulty fulfilling—being a "light for the Gentiles" (Isa. 42:6, NIV). How true to life that Israel's shame—her authentic sorrow for sin and heartfelt turning to the Lord—becomes a more powerful witness than displays of power or sophisticated orations professing faith but not demonstrating its genuineness by obedience.

Evangelistic Emphasis

As David Washington was nearing the end of his interview at Central Community Church, which had called him to the ministry, he felt vaguely uneasy. Although the church board had admitted to him that the church faced many struggles following a church split, Pastor Washington had a nagging suspicion that the weren't telling him everything.

Their pastor five years ago had left with a third of the congregation after an angry and ongoing struggle with the church board. Unfortunately, the church fuss had become "the talk of the town," while the church was left mangled and bleeding. Tragically, the pastor who was called to replace the departing minister then scandalized the church again in a bitter divorce from his wife. With all that information being openly disclosed to David, it is difficult for him to believe that his haunting suspicions have any validity.

At that point, one of the members, a retired police chief, pulled him aside and informs him that, prior to everything he has been told, the church was much in the news due to a pedophile who abused quite a number of the young boys in the church.

As David leaves to give the matter to prayer, he seriously wonders if a church with so much baggage will ever successfully reach the community with the gospel. God's Name has been profaned among the unbelievers because of them.

ಸಾಂದ್ರ

Memory Selection

A new heart also will I give you, and a new spirit will I put within you: and I will take away the stony heart out of your flesh, and I will give you an heart of flesh.—*Ezekiel 36:26*

At the Dawson High School 20-year class reunion, it was Buff Franklin who sent everyone into a state of disbelief. Buff had been the "class bully" all through school. In addition to that, he was the "class misfit," the "class flunky," and a general all-around embarrassment to the rest of the class. Virtually everybody expected him to spend his life in prison. They certainly had never expected Buff to show up at the class reunion. No one on the planning committee would have ever considered inviting him had they known where to find him. Obviously, he had learned of the reunion on his own.

What surprised everyone more than the fact that Buff came, however, was *the Buff who came.* He was not at all as they remembered him. Buff had met and married a Christian woman. He, too, had become a Christian. Together, they seem to have an impressively beautiful Christian family that bears all the marks of love, faith, and godliness that "the Buff they knew" never possessed.

Weekday Problems

When Brenda Jenkins first opened her law office, her friends at Baxter Street Church proudly celebrated with her. Brenda had grown up at Baxter Street. The people there loved her and were very proud of her.

Today, however, the people at Baxter Street Church wince every time someone mentions Brenda's name. Her law firm has come to be known throughout the state as the sleaze law firm of Birmingham. Repeatedly, the news media have had stories that seem to link Brenda with criminal elements. Even though she still has her membership at Baxter Street, she is no longer a source of pride. Primarily, her membership has come to be the source of shame.

* What is the most constructive way for a church to deal with the reality of "shame" within the membership. Give some tangible examples.

* Ought the pastor of Baxter Street Church approach Brenda Jenkins regarding the negative impact that her law practice is having on the membership? Why or why not?

* If Brenda Jenkins concludes that she is not doing anything illegal, unethical, or immoral, what can she do to present a better understanding of her law practice to the people at Baxter Street Church?

From Daffy's Dictionary

Restitution—A home for chronically tired people.
Debate—Dat woim used to catch defish wid.
Restaurant chains—Cook-alikes.
Humorist—A person who originates old jokes.
Membrane—The part of your brain you remember with.
Mental block—A street on which several psychiatrists live.
Minor operation—One that is performed on someone else.
Mischief—The head man's daughter.
Misjudge—An unmarried lady jurist.
Nag—A woman with no horse sense.
Natural selection—When a child takes the largest piece.
Nitrate—Cheapest price for calling long-distance.
Obesity—Surplus gone to waist.
Octopus—A cat with only eight lives left.
Minnehaha—An Indian princess famous for her one-liners.

This Lesson in Your Life

Terry Harper, who is 45, would not describe himself as a particularly religious man, but he believes in God. For the most part, Terry has not had much to do with organized religion of any brand. Basically, he believes in "fate" or "luck" (good and bad). Mostly, his luck has been bad, he would quickly tell you. Though Terry has never figured out why God chose to send him bad luck, his feeling that way hasn't enhanced his disire to worship. Life is a game of dice, he figures. For some reason, he has thrown a lot more "snake eyes" than "sevens."

As luck would have it, Terry never did do very well in school. He always seemed to get the teachers who "had it in for him." Before he had graduated from elementary school, Terry had lost track of how many times he had been sent to the principal's office. Before he got halfway through high school, Terry decided that he was tired of everybody always being on his back, so he dropped out of school. From that point on, life seemed to spiral rapidly downward.

At first, Terry picked up jobs rather easily. Somehow, the advertised pay always sounded like a whole lot more money than it proved to be when it came to paying the bills. Terry grew quickly bored with each job and moved on to another. Rarely did he find the new one to be any more satisfying. Before long, the transition between jobs became noticeably more difficult. The word spread through the business community that he was undependable, disloyal, and irresponsible. It wasn't long before "unemployed" was his normal state and "employed" was the exception.

Attempting to pick up some quick change by moving some rock cocaine for a friend brought Terry Harper's first arrest, but it was not his last. It wasn't long before every officer in town knew his name and face painfully well. Eventually, "jail time" turned into "prison time" as Terry's luck went from bad to worse. At 45, he is serving his fifth stretch in a state facility. This stretch is different, however. This time Terry is being drawn into a circle of friends who have "come to the Lord" in prison. A preacher comes each week to study the Bible with a group of them, and Terry is being dragged along.

Of all the things that Terry has heard in these Bible studies, the one thing that he finds to be both the most difficult to accept and the most intriguing is the concept of "choice." Terry has never before considered that our lives are shaped not by "luck" or "fate" but by our choices. That idea contradicts Terry's whole world view. Though he is not a rocket scientist, Terry is bright enough to recognize that to accept that concept as true is to accept the idea that his messed up life is his fault. It is due to his very messed up choices."

GETTING THE FACTS STRAIGHT

1. **What does the Lord say was the primary reason He would deliver the house of Israel from those who mocked them?**

He said that he did not do it for their sake but for His holy name's sake.

2. **What had the house of Israel caused to happen to the name of the Lord among the nations?**

Israel had caused God's name to be profaned among the nations.

3. **When did the Lord say that the nations would again know that He is the Lord?**

He said that the nations would again know that He is the Lord when He is hallowed in the house of Israel before the nations' eyes.

4. **After the Lord gathered His people from among the nations, what would he then do?**

He said that He would then take them to their own land.

5. **How did the Lord say that He would cleanse them from their filthiness and from their idols?**

He said that he would sprinkle them with clean water.

6. **How did the Lord say that He would change the people's heart?**

He said that He would remove their heart of stone and replace it with a heart of flesh.

7. **In addition to a new heart, what else did the Lord say that He would put in them, and what would result from that?**

He said that He would place His Spirit within them. As a result, they would keep His statutes and judgments and do them.

8. **Where did the Lord say that the people would live?**

He said that they would live in the land that He gave to their forefathers.

9. **What relationship did God say would then exist between God and the house of Israel?**

He would be their God and they would be His people.

10. **How did the Lord say that the people of the house of Israel would respond when they remembered their evil ways and deeds?**

He said that when they remembered, they would loathe themselves.

First impressions are often lasting ones. Indeed, according to the sage wisdom of Connie Brown Glasser and Barbara Steinberg Smalley, if you play your cards right, you can enjoy the benefits of what sociologists call the "halo effect." This means that if you're viewed positively within the critical first four minutes, the person you've met will likely assume everything you do is positive. Four minutes!

Actually, the formation of our "image" *begins* more quickly than that. Within a mere 10 seconds, people we meet will begin to make judgments about our professionalism, social class, morals, and intelligence. People tend to focus on what they see (dress, eye contact, movement), on what they hear (how fast or slowly we talk, our voice tone and volume), and on our actual words.

Now, you may take comfort in such statistics, but they make chills run up and down my spine. Were I the master of first impressions, it would be a good deal. After the initial meeting, I could relax my guard a bit. Instead, just hearing such ideas dredges up horrible memories of "first impressions" that have been long-buried.

There was that time in fourth grade, for example, when during my very first day in a new school, I mindlessly entered the girl's restroom, instead of the boy's. Then there was that first day on a new job in Minnesota about 18 years later, when my wife and I showed up for a "little get-together" of the elders and deacons. What we understood to be "a casual dinner" was arranged so that we could meet and get acquainted with the church leaders. Unfortunately, we showed up in slacks and sweaters (nice but definitely casual), finding all the men in suits and all the women in to-the-floor evening dresses.

These are only two of a host of ghosts that burst forth from my nightmare closet when I think of "first impressions." Hopefully, I've improved over the years, but even now, I know that "first impressions" is not really my area of strength. Consequently, even though I've continued to work on them, I've worked even harder on making good "lasting impressions."

I've learned that often in our urgency to "make a good first impression" we end up giving some people the idea that we're not real. Christians sometimes try so hard to cause people to think well of Christ by the way they live that they leave, instead, the impression of hypocrisy. It is for that reason that Steve Green decided to try a different method. In his book, *Listening Heart,* Green confesses that although he has a passion for holiness, he recognizes within his own life the tendency we all have of occasionally being dishonest spiritually. To remind himself of this tendency, he says, "I am still a recovering hypocrite." Although we quickly become defensive when someone says the Church is full of hypocrites, we would do better to acknowledge that we are all "recovering hypocrites" who could very easily slip back into sin.

This quarter's focus on people who affected the life of Jesus provides a refreshing glimpse of how real people interacted with the Son of God—affecting His own personality and being affected by Him. Unit I begins at the beginning, with a look at some among Jesus' own family who were privileged to be the first people who influenced His earthly life.

In the first lesson, on the parents of John the Baptist, we find God working mightily in the lives of members of the coming Messiah's extended family. Repeating a pattern that began with Sarah, wife of Abraham, God opens the womb of a woman supposedly past child-bearing age—illustrating that the Messianic Age will be one in which God will revitalize and empower His people.

This lesson can be introduced effectively by discussing the impact often made by an unexpected "blessed event"—the awareness that a baby will be born to an older woman, or the arrival of a baby, by birth or adoption, to a previously childless couple.

Members of your own group might share such an experience (either of their own or of someone near to them). What thoughts, negative or positive, go through the mind of a 45-year-old woman who learns she is pregnant? What impact does an unexpected infant, by natural birth or adoption, have on older children in the family? Do people often have special expectations for an unexpected child that might make the child feel special . . . or spoiled? Elizabeth and Zacharias, parents of John the Baptist, must have faced similar issues.

Teaching Outline	Daily Bible Readings
I. Joyful Announcement—1:5-14 　A. Barren couple, 5-7 　B. Angelic appearance, 8-11 　C. Birth predicted, 12-14 II. Jumping for Joy—39-45 　A. Visit from a cousin, 39-40 　B. Pre-birth awareness, 41-45 III. Jubilance at a Birth—57-58	Mon.　An Angel Visits Zacharias 　　　　Luke 1:5-13 Tue.　Questioning the Promise 　　　　Luke 1:14-20 Wed.　Elizabeth Conceives 　　　　Luke 1:21-25 Thu.　'His Name Is John' 　　　　Luke 1:57-66 Fri.　Zacharias Prophesies 　　　　Luke 1:67-75 Sat.　John's Ministry Predicted 　　　　Luke 1:76-80 Sun.　'Prepare the Way of the Lord' 　　　　Isaiah 40:3-11

Verse by Verse

I. Joyful Announcement—1:5-14
A. Barren couple, 5-7

5 There was in the days of Herod, the king of Judaea, a certain priest named Zacharias, of the course of Abia: and his wife was of the daughters of Aaron, and her name was Elisabeth.

6 And they were both righteous before God, walking in all the commandments and ordinances of the Lord blameless.

7 And they had no child, because that Elisabeth was barren, and they both were now well stricken in years.

Of the several Herods mentioned in the New Testament Scriptures, this is Herod the Great, the father of the rest. He was an Idumean, a land whose people had been converted to Judaism at the point of the sword during the Maccabeean wars of 167–37 B.C. In fact, Herod's wife, Miriamne, whom he eventually murdered, was a descendant of the Maccabees, the revolutionary Jewish family that for years held out against Roman rule in Judea. Although a Jew in name, Herod's loyalty lay with Caesar, and he was hated by Jews despite his rebuilding the Temple.

The "course" (NIV "priestly division") of Abia or Abijah" identifies Zacharias as a member of one of the regiments of priests who served in the Temple for particular terms. Although priests were not required to choose a wife from among the priestly tribe of Aaron, Elisabeth's heritage in that tribe would have been considered a choice selection for both the elderly priest and Elisabeth. Their marriage seems to have been marred only by childlessness. The fact that they were "righteous" and "blameless" would have made them and those who knew them wonder why God had not blessed them with a child.

Recalling that the role of the priests was to stand before God and offer sacrifices for the sins of the people, we can see the significance of God's choosing this aging couple to help herald the coming of the Messiah. Their piety, and Zacharias' role in offering sacrifice, are signs that God is using the best examples of the Old Covenant priesthood to help administer the New Covenant, with its new sacrifice, Jesus. Their advanced age is also being used to repeat the pattern that began with Abraham and Sarah, who also had a child of promise when they were supposedly past the child-bearing days. In both cases, as in the instance of Isaac's wife Rebekah, and Samuel's mother Hannah, God is inaugurating a new and fruitful era of the Spirit by showing His power over nature, which had shut the wombs of these women.

133

B. Angelic appearance, 8-11

8 And it came to pass, that while he executed the priest's office before God in the order of his course,

9 According to the custom of the priest's office, his lot was to burn incense when he went into the temple of the Lord.

10 And the whole multitude of the people were praying without at the time of incense.

11 And there appeared unto him an angel of the Lord standing on the right side of the altar of incense.

Because there were many more priests than Temple duties, the task of offering incense was a rare privilege. Assigned by the casting of lots, it was a service that a priest was allowed to perform only once in his lifetime. Thus God chose an especially auspicious day to send His angel to announce the role Zacharias and Elisabeth would perform in helping prepare the people for the coming Messiah. The people would have been standing outside the area of the Temple where the altar of incense was located, so Zacharias was alone when the angel appeared.

C. Birth predicted, 12-14

12 And when Zacharias saw him, he was troubled, and fear fell upon him.

13 But the angel said unto him, Fear not, Zacharias: for thy prayer is heard; and thy wife Elisabeth shall bear thee a son, and thou shalt call his name John.

14 And thou shalt have joy and gladness; and many shall rejoice at his birth.

Fear is certainly an appropriate reaction to standing in the presence of one of God's holy angels (see also Gideon, Judg. 6:22; and the parents of Samson, Judg. 13:21-22). The usual response of the angel, however, is "Fear not"—their rare appearance is not in order to be treated with awe but to get on with the special work of God that is signaled by their visit. The prayer that God has heard must have been the usual prayers in the Temple service for the salvation of Israel rather than a petition for a son, since Zacharias has trouble believing the angel's announcement (vss. 18, 20).

As the Gospel story unfolds we learn that the infant John who is promised to this elderly couple is John the Baptist. No doubt the promised joy that will accompany him will result not only from the elderly couple finally having a child, but from the glad message he will eventually bear, "The Messiah is coming"!

II. Jumping for Joy—39-45
A. Visit from a cousin, 39-40

39 And Mary arose in those days, and went into the hill country with haste, into a city of Juda;

40 And entered into the house of Zacharias, and saluted Elisabeth.

Our story moves from the angel's announcement that Elisabeth will bear John the Baptist on past the even more startling revelation that Mary, a virgin espoused to a man named Joseph, will actually bear Jesus, the Messiah himself (vss. 26-33). (Although Mary also is "troubled," she receives the angel's news without the doubt expressed by Zacharias, saying "Be it unto me according to thy word" [vs. 38].)

The angel has told Mary about God's related plans for Elisabeth, and that Elisabeth is six months into her pregnancy (vss. 26, 36). This is no doubt why Mary hastens to visit Elisabeth. The KJV says Elisabeth is Mary's "cousin" (vs. 36), giving rise to the common assumption that John the Baptist and Jesus were second cousins. However, the word can also simply mean "relative" (as in the NIV) or "kinswoman."

B. Pre-birth awareness, 41-45

41 And it came to pass, that, when Elisabeth heard the salutation of Mary, the babe leaped in her womb; and Elisabeth was filled with the Holy Ghost:

42 And she spake out with a loud voice, and said, Blessed art thou among women, and blessed is the fruit of thy womb.

43 And whence is this to me, that the mother of my Lord should come to me?

44 For, lo, as soon as the voice of thy salutation sounded in mine ears, the babe leaped in my womb for joy.

45 And blessed is she that believed: for there shall be a performance of those things which were told her from the Lord.

Elisabeth's outburst of praise at Mary's presence indicates the profound humility of the older woman in accepting the fact that the one in her womb is only a forerunner of the babe Mary will bear. She praises Mary for having believed the angel's news about her pregnancy even though she did not "know" a man (vs. 34).

The presence and salutation of the mother of the Messiah is so stupendous that Elisabeth is filled with the Holy Spirit and the babe she is bearing leaps for joy. Elisabeth's interpretation of this sharp movement of the fetus is obviously at some visceral level below the level of consciousness, especially in light of the fact that when he is grown John the Baptist has to ask whether Jesus, his kinsman, is really the Messiah (John 1:32-33; Matt. 11:3).

III. Jubilance at a Birth—57-58

57 Now Elisabeth's full time came that she should be delivered; and she brought forth a son.

58 And her neighbours and her cousins heard how the Lord had shewed great mercy upon her; and they rejoiced with her.

Finally, the infant John is born. In the sisterhood of Jewish women a barren woman was sometimes looked down on; but by the same token Elisabeth's "cousins" or kinfolk are jubilant that God has filled her womb and that she has now delivered a child. Already the angel's announcement in verse 14 is being fulfilled, as "many . . . rejoice at his birth."

Ironically, John's adult life does not seem to be as joyful as these scenes that accompany his birth. His mission of being a forerunner required him to preach a stern message of repentance, and he wound up being beheaded for it. His rugged wilderness lifestyle included none of the ease and convenience popularly associated with happy people. Yet the joy associated with his birth, life, and ministry is no less real, for he was faithful to his assigned task of preparing the way of the Lord.

Evangelistic Emphasis

One of the earliest stories of the Bible is of Abraham and Sarah. At a time when that couple should have been more concerned about the issues related to the end of life, God had them involved in "young people's activities." After God set in motion their move from Ur to the borders of the Promised Land, He got nature involved in changing the lives of Abraham and Sarah. When they should have been more concerned about their health in old age, they found that God was making them parents.

The New Testament begins with a similar story. This time the "joys of an autumn parenthood" fall on Zacharius and his wife Elizabeth. We are not told their age, but only that Elizabeth was barren.

This is the arena in which God seems to operate best. When humans declare a situation or a person as "hopeless," God becomes most active. This good news means that no situation is beyond the answer of a prayer. Elizabeth and Zacharius had been praying for God's blessing. God heard their prayers.

This story of old folks as new parents is a story of hope for all of those people for whom a relationship with Jesus is still in the future. Nothing is impossible for God.

৪০৫৪

Memory Selection

But the angel said unto him, Fear not, Zacharias: for thy prayer is heard; and thy wife Elisabeth shall bear thee a son, and thou shalt call his name John.—*Luke 1:13*

Names are important. The gospel of Luke was sent to Theophilus, whose name meant "friend of God." Quickly Luke mentions several important names so the story of Jesus could be put in historical context. Twice the angel of the Lord gives the name of a child to be born. Both John and Jesus are named from "above."

Names carry with them certain expectations. It is a modern difficulty to name a baby. The baby has to be given a name for a birth certificate to be issued. In history, children were often not named until the time of their baptisms, thus giving the parents time to think about a name. Certain parental expectations are placed on children through their names. Ask any of us who were named after our fathers if we didn't have to live up to certain expectations. Parents should try some adult titles in front of their "cute" baby names before giving the child that name. Would you want "President Buffy Sanders" to be in charge of our nuclear weapons?

John's cousin was named Jesus. "Jesus" means "savior." He lived out the expectation placed on Him by God and reflected in His name. Do you live out the expectation that is found in your name?

136

Weekday Problems

Jim and Terri had been married for 11 years, and had yet to have a child. They had done everything the doctors had suggested; but after 11 years of trying, even their doctor was beginning to suggest adoption as their only option.

Jim and Terri were faithful members of First Church. They both sang in the choir. They worked with the youth and taught in the Sunday school. They loved children, and they were faithful in their discipleship and righteous in their living.

Terri's sister, Theresa announced to her Sunday school class on Sunday that she and her husband were expecting their third child. That very morning, the pastor of First Church preached a sermon on the power of prayer to change reality. Terri was the first parishioner in his office after the sermon.

"Preacher," she said, "I have been praying for a child for 11 years now. So far I have had nothing but frustration. I want to know why God is not answering my prayer? I don't think He really hears me. If He does, I don't think He can do anything about our situation."

*How would you answer Terri's complaint? Do you think she might find some comfort in the story of Elizabeth and Zacharius?

*How are patience, waiting and faithfulness connected, in this "weekday problem" and in the story of Elizabeth?

'Welcome the Little Children'

"Children are God's apostles, sent forth day by day to preach of love and hope and peace."—J. R. Lowell

❖❖❖❖❖

"Be ever gentle with the children God has given you. Watch over them constantly; reprove them earnestly, but not in anger."—Elihu Burritt

❖❖❖❖❖

"Many children, many cares; no children, no felicity.—C. N. Bovee

❖❖❖❖❖

"Man, a dunce uncouth, errs in age and youth: babies know the truth."—A. C. Swinburne

❖❖❖❖❖

"God must love all little boys,/They fit into His plan;/They are the only things He'll use/To make into a man."—Roy Z. Kemp

This Lesson in Your Life

In the world of television any dilemma can be solved in 23 minutes. If Wally and the Beaver had a problem, Ward and June could find a solution to that problem in 23 minutes. That is the length of time that a 30-minute sit-com lasts. We like fast solutions to our problems.

The story of Elizabeth and Zacharius causes us to feel uncomfortable. First, these were faithful servants of the Lord. Luke writes of them, "they were both righteous before God, walking in all the commandments and ordinances of the Lord blameless" (Luke 1: 6). The prominent theological assumption in this country is that God blesses those who are faithful; so we wonder why this couple were childless, in a culture that viewed that condition as a curse. Luke also notes that Elizabeth was getting older and the possibility of having a child was decreasing. The language of the King James Version is striking: "They were both were now well stricken in years" (Luke 1:7). The blessings of God on this couple should have come "faster."

When God did promise Zacharius a son, Zacharius didn't believe the good news. He came out of the Temple after Gabriel's visitation, with all kinds of problems. Zacharius was struck dumb, unable to talk because he didn't believe the words of God's angel. When God is going to bless you, it shouldn't lead to any kind of hardship, should it?

We see from this text that God is not influenced by the 23-minute solution. He works according to His time schedule through His unique, loving ways. What happened to Elizabeth and Zacharius happened when it did and in the manner it did to call attention to God's glory. It might not have been as "clean and tidy" as we would want it, but the results were world changing.

This story is about people who trusted God despite what was happening to them. The lesson is about waiting; but waiting is not something that is done well in today. Children graduate from college and think they deserve a salary commensurate with their parents. These same children want all the things of the world, NOW. Everything is boiled down into a fashion that allows us to get "what we want, when we want it." God is becoming popular with a younger generation because they see Him as a way of fulfilling their desires for material benefit.

Elizabeth and Zacharius waited and prayed. They were faithful in their living. When things didn't work out the way they dreamed, they still trusted God. A hard lesson for us to learn is that God will be God, even if that doesn't fit into our expectations.

1. What significant heritage did both Zacharius and Elizabeth share?

They both were from different lines of the Hebrew Priesthood. Elizabeth was descended from Aaron. Zacharius was descended from Abijah.

2. The events depicted in the text took place during the reign of which king?

Herod was king of Judea at the time of these events.

3. How did Luke describe the kind of life that both Elizabeth and Zacharius led?

Luke wrote, "And they were both righteous before God, walking in all the commandments and ordinances of the Lord blameless" (Luke 1:6).

4. What clue was given about the approximate age of this couple?

Luke states, "They both were now well stricken in years" (Luke 1: 7). In other words, they were very old!

5. What was Zacharius doing when the angel of the Lord appeared to him in the temple?

It was his turn, because of his priestly office, to burn incense before the Lord in the Temple.

6. Who appeared to Zacharius as he served the Lord in the Temple?

The angel Gabriel appeared to Zacharius.

7. What promise did the angel make to Zacharius?

Gabriel assured Zacharius that his prayer had been heard, and Elizabeth would bear a son.

8. What was the promise made about this child?

The child would be great in the sight of the Lord. He would not drink wine or strong drink. He would be filled with the Holy Ghost from his mother's womb.

9. The promised child was compared in personality and function of ministry to what previous prophet?

The ministry of John the Baptizer had many parallels to the ministry of Elijah (Luke 1: 17).

10. As a result of his disbelief, what happened to Zacharius?

He was struck dumb. However, at the birth of the child he was able to speak and gave the child the name John.

Waiting has its rewards!

Don't expect that reasoning to work with a child or grandchild as you are being dragged through the toy section of your local Wal-Mart. Tell the child to be patient and wait, that you are certain someone will surely give them that cherished gizmo on Christmas, and the look you get will be indicative of how most honest people feel about waiting. In a world of high tech gadgetry and wizardry we have become spoiled by speed. Most people want everything YESTERDAY. Even in a sacred place such as the kitchen, we have allowed the microwave to become the symbol of our hurried home life. So many children and parents don't eat together, that the mantra of life has become, "Supper is in the refrigerator, pop it in the microwave when you get home." The food that we are "popping" into the microwave came from the grocery store, a place complete with one through 20 item express lanes. I spend more time counting items to see which express lane to be in than I would have spent in the "normal lanes." We want to brag about how quickly we can hurry through the grocery store, so we can hurry home to make a microwave meal for our hurried families. Are you blushing yet?

God never read a book on time management. When you are the Almighty and not bound by time, then a time management book would be a waste of time. The other thing we notice, to our chagrin, is that God never seems to be in a hurry. Waiting seems to be something God likes for us to do.

Listen to His Word: "But they that wait upon the LORD shall renew their strength; they shall mount up with wings as eagles; they shall run, and not be weary; and they shall walk, and not faint" (Isa. 40: 31). "Wait on the LORD: be of good courage, and He shall strengthen thine heart: wait, I say, on the LORD" (Psalms 27: 14). "Wait on the LORD, and keep His way, and He shall exalt thee to inherit the land: when the wicked are cut off, thou shalt see it" (Ps. 37: 34). "Say not thou, I will recompense evil; but wait on the LORD, and He shall save thee" (Prov.20:22).

Nowhere in the Scriptures can a reference be found to God getting in a hurry. Being hurried and harried is a human trait that is often counter-productive. A major element of a righteous life is knowing how to live in God's time. God is not worried about what the clock says; so much as He is concerned about the "seasons of the soul." God has placed a seed in your soul. He comes and checks the progress of that seed. God is concerned about the sowing season and harvest time. The time in the middle is spent nurturing the soil, not the seed.

The next time you are in a hurry, remember God takes His time. The next time you are delayed, remember to use that time connecting with God. I have learned that those moments of "delay" are often gifts sent my way by God. In moments of delay I can move from activity to contemplation. I have even been known to pray while standing in the grocery store line.

Lesson 2

Mary: Chosen for Blessing

Luke 1:26-38, 46-49

And in the sixth month the angel Gabriel was sent from God unto a city of Galilee, named Nazareth,

27 To a virgin espoused to a man whose name was Joseph, of the house of David; and the virgin's name was Mary.

28 And the angel came in unto her, and said, Hail, thou that art highly favoured, the Lord is with thee: blessed art thou among women.

29 And when she saw him, she was troubled at his saying, and cast in her mind what manner of salutation this should be.

30 And the angel said unto her, Fear not, Mary: for thou hast found favour with God.

31 And, behold, thou shalt conceive in thy womb, and bring forth a son, and shalt call his name JESUS.

32 He shall be great, and shall be called the Son of the Highest: and the Lord God shall give unto him the throne of his father David:

33 And he shall reign over the house of Jacob for ever; and of his kingdom there shall be no end.

34 Then said Mary unto the angel, How shall this be, seeing I know not a man?

35 And the angel answered and said unto her, The Holy Ghost shall come upon thee, and the power of the Highest shall overshadow thee: therefore also that holy thing which shall be born of thee shall be called the Son of God.

36 And, behold, thy cousin Elisabeth, she hath also conceived a son in her old age: and this is the sixth month with her, who was called barren.

37 For with God nothing shall be impossible.

38 And Mary said, Behold the handmaid of the Lord; be it unto me according to thy word. And the angel departed from her.

46 And Mary said, My soul doth magnify the Lord,

47 And my spirit hath rejoiced in God my Saviour.

48 For he hath regarded the low estate of his handmaiden: for, behold, from henceforth all generations shall call me blessed.

49 For he that is mighty hath done to me great things; and holy is his name.

Memory Selection
Luke 1:30-31

Background Scripture
Luke 1:26-56

Devotional Reading
Psalm 146

In ancient times, a king would often communicate important events through his herald, who would go throughout the kingdom proclaiming the news. Today's lesson focuses on the most important royal announcement ever made. The herald is the angel Gabriel, and his "kingdom proclamation" is in the first instance to Mary, who is told that she will actually give birth to the Messiah. Luke accords the tidings the space due an announcement that will affect the whole world.

Since this unit deals with the personalities involved in Jesus' coming to earth, the teacher will want to focus especially on how this young Jewish girl received the angel's news —from her initial uncertainty to her outburst of praise at being chosen for this unimaginable role.

The angel Gabriel's announcment that Mary was pregnant has some quite earthly parallels in our times, when unwed motherhood is a daily reality. Challenge group members to identify with Mary by imagining her questions. They may include:

1. How do I deal with "talk"? Although Mary was not promiscuous, she knew that some in the community would wonder about the father. Her first question (1:34) had social as well as personal dimensions.

2. Should I marry the father? In Mary's culture this question had to be answered Yes. She would be expected to marry Joseph, to whom she was engaged. How should unwed mothers-to-be today deal with this issue?

3. How will we support this child? Fortunately, Joseph was a carpenter. What kinds of "safety nets" do modern unwed mothers have? How can we encourage young people to think responsibly about such issues?

Teaching Outline	Daily Bible Readings	
I. Angelic Announcement—26-33 　A. Mary and Joseph, 26-27 　B. The child to come, 28-33 　　1. Favored mother, 28-30 　　2. Future King, 31-33 II. All-Powerful God—34-37 　A. Fundamental question, 34 　B. Miraculous answer, 35 　C. A similar case, 36-37 III. Acceptance with Joy—38, 46-49 　A. 'My soul submits,' 38 　B. 'My spirit rejoices!' 46-49	Mon. Tue. Wed. Thu. Fri. Sat. Sun.	You Have Found Favor Luke 1:26-33 I Am the Lord's Servant Luke 1:34-38 Elizabeth Greets Mary Luke 1:39-45 Mary's Song of Praise Luke 1:46-56 Praise God for His Deeds Psalm 71:15-21 Great Are God's Works Psalm 111:1-6 Magnify God with Me Psalm 34:1-5

Verse by Verse

I. Angelic Announcement—26-33
A. Mary and Joseph, 26-27

26 And in the sixth month the angel Gabriel was sent from God unto a city of Galilee, named Nazareth,

27 To a virgin espoused to a man whose name was Joseph, of the house of David; and the virgin's name was Mary.

The word "angel" in both Hebrew and Greek means "messenger"; and angels are found throughout the Bible bringing important messages from God to man. Yet none of these messages is bathed in such a glorious light as this announcement of Gabriel (one of the few angels, who, along with Michael the archangel [Jude 9], is named in Scripture.) "The sixth month" refers to the sixth month of Elisabeth's pregnancy which has just been recounted.

Although angels are supernatural beings, they were created by God (Ps. 148:2, 5). They apparently have freedom of choice, since some angels are evil servants of Satan (cf. "the devil and his angels," Matt. 25:41).

God's angels seem to have served as go-betweens between sinful man and the holy God. Before Adam and Eve sinned in the Garden, God spoke with them personally. After they sinned and were expelled from Eden, angels (in the form of the mysterious "cherubim") are mentioned for the first time as guarding the Garden's entrance (Gen. 3:24). Note the contrast between that scene and Gabriel's role here. The Child whose birth he announces to Mary will in a sense "re-open" the gates to closer communion with God.

Although we cannot over-emphasize the importance of this scene, it is often allowed to obscure the fact that an angel (probably Gabriel) also would appear to Joseph in similar "Annunciation," to reassure him that he should marry Mary even though she is pregnant (Matt. 1:20). As a descendant of the house of David, Joseph is also an important part of the story of Christ's birth, since Messiah was to be a descendant of David (2 Sam. 7:12-13).

We are told that Mary is a virgin to prepare us for the fact that the Child's true father is God, through the Holy Spirit—as the angel explains both in verse 35 (see below), and to Joseph in Matthew 1:20.

B. The child to come, 28-33
1. Favored mother, 28-30

28 And the angel came in unto her, and said, Hail, thou that art highly favoured, the Lord is with thee: blessed art thou among women.

29 And when she saw him, she was troubled at his saying, and cast in her mind what manner of salutation this should be.

30 And the angel said unto her, Fear not, Mary: for thou hast found favour with God.

We can well imagine this young Jewish girl's being "troubled" and even fearful at the appearance of a divine messenger from God. Furthermore, he "hails" her ("Hail" is "Ave" in Latin, leading to the classic hymn, "Ave, Maria") as blessed among all women. Perhaps, as an unknown girl from a family without wealth or social stature (note her "low estate," vs. 48), this exalted and exalting greeting was as perplexing to Mary as the appearance of an angel.

In later years, especially when standing at the foot of the Cross, Mary will have cause to remember desperately the angel's reassurance that being chosen to be Christ's mother was a sign she is "highly favored."

2. Future King, 31-33

31 And, behold, thou shalt conceive in thy womb, and bring forth a son, and shalt call his name JESUS.

32 He shall be great, and shall be called the Son of the Highest: and the Lord God shall give unto him the throne of his father David:

33 And he shall reign over the house of Jacob for ever; and of his kingdom there shall be no end.

Although the term "Messiah" is not used here, the august terms imply as much. Not only will His name be "Jesus," which means "savior"; as the "son of the Highest" and the ruler on David's throne this Child is obviously destined to be the long-awaited "Coming One" expected by devout Jews. The Kingdom He will establish

will not be limited to geographical areas but will be in people's hearts, and will last eternally.

II. All-Powerful God—34-37
A. Fundamental question, 34

34 Then said Mary unto the angel, How shall this be, seeing I know not a man?

Sometimes modern critics dismiss the virgin birth as a myth, implying that primitive people did not know the facts about human reproduction. Of course Mary asks this question about the promised infant's paternity precisely because she does know "where babies come from," and that she has not "known" a man (a common Bible euphemism for sexual relations). Her question is similar to Sarah's, who asked how she could bear a child in her old age (Gen. 18:10-11). It prepares us to consider anew that God often chooses to do "mighty acts" or go beyond "the natural" to convince us of His reality and His love.

B. Miraculous answer, 35

35 And the angel answered and said unto her, The Holy Ghost shall come upon thee, and the power of the Highest shall overshadow thee: therefore also that holy thing which shall be born of thee shall be called the Son of God.

Mary could not have been prepared for such an answer, for the world's greatest minds have grappled with it without penetrating its mystery. Speculation about "how this could happen" seems futile; like Mary, we are called not to explain the event but to affirm that the child born of Mary is in some special way God's son, not primarily Joseph's. Historically, the doctrine of the virgin birth has been held to be essential to the doctrine of the Incarnation. It is a way of showing that Christ's nature was both divine and human, and that in Him God became flesh in order to identify with, and save, sinful humanity.

C. A similar case, 36-37

36 And, behold, thy cousin Elisabeth, she hath also conceived a son in her old age: and this is the sixth month with her, who was called barren.

37 For with God nothing shall be impossible.

Gabriel meets Mary's wonder about how she, an unmarried girl, might conceive a child by pointing to her kinswoman Elisabeth (vss. 7-14, Lesson 1). Like Sarah, Abraham's wife, Elisabeth had been enabled to have a son in her old age. The fact is that human birth in its "normal" stages has many mysteries, one of them being why some women are barren, like Elisabeth was. Gabriel is saying that the God who can open wombs in the first place can also "overshadow" Mary's own womb through the Spirit.

III. Acceptance with Joy—38, 46-49
A. 'My soul submits,' 38

38 And Mary said, Behold the handmaid of the Lord; be it unto me according to thy word. And the angel departed from her.

Fortunately, Mary does not require as much detail as theologians do about the how and the why of the virgin birth! She seems to melt before the sheer majesty and mystery of Gabriel's pronouncement, simply declaring herself to be a servant of the Lord and giving herself by faith to whatever He has in mind. In doing so, she not only accepts her own destiny as Jesus' mother but models the essential way to come to God under the New Covenant.

B. 'My spirit rejoices!' 46-49

46 And Mary said, My soul doth magnify the Lord,

47 And my spirit hath rejoiced in God my Saviour.

48 For he hath regarded the low estate of his handmaiden: for, behold, from henceforth all generations shall call me blessed.

49 For he that is mighty hath done to me great things; and holy is his name.

These verses begin the famous "Magnificat," Mary's lovely song "magnifying" or praising God for gracing her with the role of bearing His only-begotten Son. (The song continues through verse 55.) It has long been observed that Mary's outburst of praise resembles the song of Hannah after she was blessed with her son Samuel. We may also recall the song of Miriam and Moses praising God for freeing the Jews from Egyptian slavery (Exod. 15). Despite some similarities, these previous songs have a militant note lacking in Mary's song. She does see God's strength and His power over the pseudo-powerful in His having chosen an unknown and "unempowered" Jewish girl through whom to bless the world (vss. 51-52). The emphasis, however, is in praise without the militance: God has done great things.

Evangelistic Emphasis

God is in the unexpected!

Imagine Mary's excitement as she plans for her wedding feast. Watch her as she shows off the band of coins around her forehead signifying her engagement to Joseph. Watch her as she glows when Joseph's name is mentioned. It might have been over 2,000 years ago, but brides are brides! The date for the celebration was getting close. Then God forever altered Mary's life.

God will not fit neatly into a Franklin Planner. He has a way of breaking out of each box into which we place, or try to place Him. God is sovereign, and sovereignty can't be confined.

That is why we need to look for Him in our interruptions and in the unexpected. The good news is that not only is He there. He often is the creator of the unexpected in our lives. He moves in "strange ways" so that we might come to know His love and presence in different ways.

This season, as you fight mall traffic and look for the perfect gifts, remember that God is in the unexpected and unimaginable. The hand of God drastically changed Mary's plans. Those changes brought some hardship, but a greater joy into her life.

We are preparing to celebrate the birth of His biggest, unexpected surprise, Jesus the Christ. The good news is that when you experience the unexpected, or your life gets "upset" it might be God at work!

ುಂ

Memory Selection

And the angel said unto her, Fear not, Mary: for thou hast found favour with God. And, behold, thou shalt conceive in thy womb, and bring forth a son, and shalt call his name JESUS.— *Luke 1:30-31*

Finding favor with God can be dangerous to your reputation. The scandal of the birth of Jesus is lost on this culture. We take an unwed mother in stride and a child with only one parent has become the norm. In that day, an unwed mother was held in great contempt.

Many of God's servants have had their reputation ruined. At the very least, finding favor with God can cause people to laugh at you. Can you imagine what Noah's neighbors thought when he found favor with God and built the first "cruise ship?" How about Abraham trying to explain God's travel plans to his family?

When we find favor with God it means our character is such that we can accomplish what God wills without worrying about the damage doing His will might have on our reputation. When we find favor with God, we need to take a deep breath and lean on Him, because we can be certain that things are going to be different, and in some ways, they might become rough!

Weekday Problems

The christmas season found Melinda with an overloaded schedule. As chairperson of the hospitality committee, she and her committee would do the majority of the preparation for the open-house the pastor was planning. Somehow she found herself involved with other clubs that were having Christmas functions, too. And as church organist, she was practicing hard for the choir's cantata and for the Christmas Eve service.

Her two children, who had two children each, announced that their families would be coming home for Christmas. While she would be saved the chore of packaging and mailing gifts, she would have to cook and plan for 10 people on Christmas day. Then her brother and mother invited themselves over as well.

It all came down on her at the Christmas Eve service when the preacher asked Melinda to share a word of witness about the meaning of a family Christmas. She declined, and felt guilty about it afterwards.

*Have you found yourself too busy to have a meaningful Christmas?

*How can we return to the simplicity of that first Christmas? Or can we?

*How could Mary's reactions throughout Luke's Christmas account, bring comfort and solace to Melinda's hectic life?

Did Joseph and Mary Have a Marriage Like These?

She knows the honeymoon is over when he no longer smiles gently as he scrapes the burnt toast.

A Kansas cyclone had ripped off the roof of the farm-house and set the couple's beds down over in the next county. "Don't cry," said the farmer to his weeping wife. "We're safe."

"I'm not crying because I'm scared, but because I'm so happy," his wife replied. "This is the first time in 14 years we've been out together."

When my wife needs money, she calls me "Handsome." She says "Hand some over."

Despite the statistics, he denies that married men live longer than single men . . . it only seems longer.

147

This Lesson in Your Life

We either trivialize Mary or give her too much credit in the Christmas story. Mary stands out as a strong witness to a woman's unflinching faith in God; but have you noticed that in the Christmas plays, she doesn't get any lines? Joseph gets to lead the donkey and argue with the innkeeper. Mary remains silent throughout most of these reenactments.

We have glossed over all the social stigmas that the birth of Christ placed on Mary. Throughout her life, she probably heard the whispers of the people as they labeled her immoral and her son illegitimate. Perhaps that is why she convinced Jesus that it was important to do something about the couple who had run out of wedding wine (John 2). She lived with the fear that something dreadful would happen to Jesus, and even misunderstood her son's role, along with the rest of the family. Yet, from Gabriel's visitation to Calvary, Mary's faith in God was unwavering.

She probably had a good sense of humor. We overlook that in God's people. We take the Almighty so seriously that we deny Him and us the ability to laugh. I remind you that God created the giraffe and the ostrich. He even put *you* together in a unique way. Mary must have shared God's sense of humor. God had placed her in an indefensible position. Can you hear her having to explain to Joseph her condition? Can you see her explaining to the Son of God where He was born? It was her faith mixed with her humor that sustained her in those dark days, while Joseph was making up his mind about whether to divorce her.

Mary was a visionary. She was given the promise of God, and nothing else. She risked it all, because in that promise, she could see into the future. How could a child born to peasants in a cave in Bethlehem, raised in a carpenter's shop in Nazareth ever amount to anything? His critics would echo those very same questions. Yet, even with her son dying on the cross, Mary could see with God's vision. She knew what had been spoken about this child. She knew that He was God's Messiah. She knew, at least in part, what that would mean for the human race. She was more than willing to do what needed to be done, because she could see into the future what God was going to do.

Can you imagine the hush in heaven as Gabriel talked to Mary? She had found favor with God. She was being invited to participate in this cosmic adventure of the life of Christ. Yet she, along with all other humans, had the right to refuse God's invitation. There was some nervous shuffling and rustling of angel's wings as Gabriel mapped out God's plan. But there is no hesitation on Mary's part.

How would our world be different if we had real people like Mary? Can you image what could be accomplished if in your own church, people could look beyond present reality and see God's possibilities?

GETTING THE FACTS STRAIGHT

1. **The angel Gabriel appeared to Mary in the sixth month. To what does the sixth month refer?**
The reference is to the sixth month after the conception of John the Baptizer.

2. **What do the announcements to both Mary and Elizabeth have in common?**
The birth of both of the children was announced to the mothers by the angel Gabriel.

3. **What was Mary's marital state when the angel Gabriel visited her?**
Mary was a virgin, and engaged to Joseph. They had not consummated the marriage.

4. **What was Mary's reaction to the angel Gabriel's salutation?**
She was perplexed. She pondered in her heart would kind of greeting this might be.

5. **What did the angel Gabriel tell Mary?**
He told her not to be afraid because she had found favor with God. She would conceive and bear a son, whose name would be Jesus.

6. **What did Mary learn about Elizabeth from her visit with Gabriel?**
Mary was told that Elizabeth had conceived a son. Elizabeth was in the sixth month of her pregnancy.

7. **What did Mary do as a result of the message of the angel?**
She went to Elizabeth and Zacharius's home. She did this before any mention is made of her telling Joseph what had happened.

8. **What happened when Mary and Elizabeth saw each other?**
The baby inside of Elizabeth jumped for joy and Elizabeth was filled with the Holy Spirit.

9. **Is there something about Mary and Elizabeth that you find interesting?**
Neither one of the women should be with child. Elizabeth was "too old," and Mary was a virgin.

10. **How were Jesus and John the Baptizer related to one another?**
Since Mary and Elizabeth were relatives, Jesus and John were cousins to each other.

God saved the world in plain sight.

The Christmas season is our celebration that God came to be born as one of us. Jesus Christ was God in the flesh. Beyond all the commercial trappings of Christmas there is this basic message. God did this wonderful thing in plain sight. He did it where not only could humanity reach out and touch His son, humanity could comment on the ministry of His son.

Think about all the things that happen in our world in secret. Why must a School Board have an executive session? Aren't they about providing for a good education for our children? Why should that be a cause for secrecy? Who does our Congress have to keep information from those who elected them? It seems the longer we live in the information age the more we feel the need for secrecy.

The writer of Hebrews says that God had always been speaking to His children. In the last days God spoke in Son-talk (1:1-2). Son-talk is the language of incarnation—God coming to earth in the person of His Son Jesus Christ. Jesus not only talked about love, He modeled love. Not only did He preach about forgiveness, He offered forgiveness to those who sought it. He lived a life centered in God's will as He talked about centering in God's will. His words were spoken, so that anyone willing could listen to the heart of God. His actions were public, so people could see God's love in action. Jesus didn't do things secretly.

Christianity is a faith that is best shared in the open. The Church can never create a "secret conclave" because it would be contrary to the public nature of the faith. We are a see-and-be-seen Church! We are a talking and noise-making community. We should claim the language of Son-talk and be making God-like noises all over our planet—especially at this time of the year.

As we talk about what God has done in our lives, we become effective witnesses. We make Christmas real to the next generation by showing how Jesus has been born in each of us. Still, 2,000 years later, the best way to share God's love is to mimic Jesus. The simple act of inviting a friend to a meal will get his attention. Helping someone decorate a home for Christmas or helping a homebound shop will get his or her attention. These are the noises the church and individual believers need to make.

Such deeds-in-the-open are powerful tools for the Holy Spirit's action in our world. Do you have a story of God's activity in your life? If God has been working in your life, give a great gift for Christmas; share that story with someone who needs a word of grace and life.

A person in the throws of agony or darkness doesn't need a sermon. He needs to look into the eyes and hold the hands of a person who can say, "I was where you are." When you can identify with that pain and have a story of redemption, you will have a captive audience. Christmas is a great time to share your faith.

Lesson 3

Joseph: A Righteous Man

Matthew 1:18-21, 24-25; 2:13-15, 19-23

Now the birth of Jesus Christ was on this wise: When as his mother Mary was espoused to Joseph, before they came together, she was found with child of the Holy Ghost.

19 Then Joseph her husband, being a just man, and not willing to make her a publick example, was minded to put her away privily.

20 But while he thought on these things, behold, the angel of the Lord appeared unto him in a dream, saying, Joseph, thou son of David, fear not to take unto thee Mary thy wife: for that which is conceived in her is of the Holy Ghost.

21 And she shall bring forth a son, and thou shalt call his name JESUS: for he shall save his people from their sins.

24 Then Joseph being raised from sleep did as the angel of the Lord had bidden him, and took unto him his wife:

25 And knew her not till she had brought forth her firstborn son: and he called his name JESUS.

2:13 And when they were departed, behold, the angel of the Lord appeareth to Joseph in a dream, saying, Arise, and take the young child and his mother, and flee into Egypt, and be thou there until I bring thee word: for Herod will seek the young child to destroy him.

14 When he arose, he took the young child and his mother by night, and departed into Egypt:

15 And was there until the death of Herod: that it might be fulfilled which was spoken of the Lord by the prophet, saying, Out of Egypt have I called my son.

19 But when Herod was dead, behold, an angel of the Lord appeareth in a dream to Joseph in Egypt,

20 Saying, Arise, and take the young child and his mother, and go into the land of Israel: for they are dead which sought the young child's life.

21 And he arose, and took the young child and his mother, and came into the land of Israel.

22 But when he heard that Archelaus did reign in Judaea in the room of his father Herod, he was afraid to go thither: notwithstanding, being warned of God in a dream, he turned aside into the parts of Galilee:

23 And he came and dwelt in a city called Nazareth: that it might be fulfilled which was spoken by the prophets, He shall be called a Nazarene.

Memory Selection
Matthew 1:24-25

Background Scripture
Matthew 1:18-25; 2:13-23

Devotional Reading
Isaiah 11:1-5

This lesson takes us from heavenly concepts to earthly realities; from the sublime announcement to Mary that she would bear the Christ-child to the practical issues of how this news would be taken by the man to whom she was betrothed; and from the grand vision of saving believers throughout the world to the immediate task of saving the life of the Babe of Bethlehem from his enemies.

For all these down-to-earth details, God chooses a humble carpenter from the little-known city of Bethlehem for Jesus' "foster father." This lesson focuses on what kind of man Joseph was. We know from Matthew 2:19 that he was "a just man." Challenge your group to find other character traits implied by the unfolding story.

&&CR

Lead into this lesson by discussing the challenge of being a foster parent or a step parent. Perhaps some in your class will have had that experience, either as a parent or a child. Be sensitive to the fact that some who had parents other than their birth parents may have painful memories (just as many people do even if they had "natural" parents). Without exposing such memories (and thus turning the group into a counseling session), you can ask questions that raise challenges faced by foster, step- or adoptive parents.

Ask how Joseph must have felt when he discovered that Mary was going to have a child who would not be "his" by natural procreation. Can we fault him for planning not to marry her, at first? Would he have likely treated Jesus differently from any natural-born children they had later? How can parents in mixed marriages today treat all their children fairly?

Teaching Outline	Daily Bible Readings	
I. Shocking News—1:18-21	Mon.	Joseph Believes God Matthew 1:18-25
A. Surprise announcement, 18-19	Tue.	Visitors from the East Matthew 2:1-12
B. Startling explanation, 20-21	Wed.	Flight to Egypt Matthew 2:13-18
II. Steadfast Response—24-25	Thu.	Return to Galilee Matthew 2:19-23
III. Sudden Opposition—2:13-15	Fri.	The Righteous Please God Proverbs 15:1-9
IV. Searching for a Home—19-23	Sat.	God's Protection Psalm 1:1-6
A. Return from Egypt, 19-20	Sun.	Branch of Righteousness
B. Settling in Nazareth, 21-23		

Verse by Verse

I. Shocking News—1:18-21
A. Surprise announcement, 18-19

18 Now the birth of Jesus Christ was on this wise: When as his mother Mary was espoused to Joseph, before they came together, she was found with child of the Holy Ghost.

19 Then Joseph her husband, being a just man, and not willing to make her a publick example, was minded to put her away privily.

The previous lesson has introduced us to the mystery of the virgin birth of Jesus. Unlike the focus on Mary in Luke's account, however, the profound event is mentioned here as it regards Joseph and his reaction to the fact that Mary, to whom he was "espoused" (Luke 1:27), "was found with child by the Holy Ghost."

This "espousal" was a much firmer arrangement than an "engagement" in our own culture. The period of betrothal usually lasted for a year. Although the couple continued to live apart with their families of origin, and did not have sexual relations during that time, to break the "engagement" required divorce proceedings just as marriages did. Being found pregnant would certainly be included among the reasons for the relatively rare divorces during such betrothals. Joseph could have easily obtained such a divorce, publically declaring three times, "I divorce you, I divorce you, I divorce

you." However, his just character comes through in his reluctance to bring public shame on Mary; thus his plan to obtain a private divorce.

B. Startling explanation, 20-21

20 But while he thought on these things, behold, the angel of the Lord appeared unto him in a dream, saying, Joseph, thou son of David, fear not to take unto thee Mary thy wife: for that which is conceived in her is of the Holy Ghost.

21 And she shall bring forth a son, and thou shalt call his name JESUS: for he shall save his people from their sins.

The angel of the Lord may have been none other than Gabriel, who appeared to Mary (Luke 1:26). His greeting, "Joseph, thou son of David," is faithfully recorded by Matthew to emphasize Joseph's place in the lineage of David the king (which has already been referred to in 1:6). Here is an announcement not just for Joseph but for the ages to come: this Child is of the seed of David and can therefore lay rightful claim to David's throne, as the Messiah (2 Sam. 7:12-13).

Although the angel reassures Joseph that he can proceed with his plans to make Mary his wife, we wonder what this humble Galilean carpenter would have made of the statement that his betrothed was with

153

child "of the Holy Ghost." The root of the word for "conceived" also gives us our term "genesis"; the angel is saying literally that the Child had been "genesised" not by another man but by the Holy Spirit. As verses 22-23 will explain, the angel ties this supernatural event with the prophecy of Isaiah 7:14.

The salvation from sin that the angel says will accompany the long-awaited Messiah was not as prominent in current Jewish expectations as the hope that He would deliver them from the hated Roman oppressors. Still, the Old Testament itself is clear that forgiveness, not just political liberation, would accompany this descendant of David (see esp. Isa. 53:1-10).

II. Steadfast Response—24-25

24 Then Joseph being raised from sleep did as the angel of the Lord had bidden him, and took unto him his wife:

25 And knew her not till she had brought forth her firstborn son: and he called his name JESUS.

Whatever questions Joseph may have had about how Mary had become pregnant, he holds firmly to his vivid dream, and proceeds to obey the angel's directive. Thus the life and ministry of Jesus is now grounded in the simple obedience of both Joseph and Mary, setting an example for all who would follow their Son's Messianic leadership. Although it would have been common for married couples to abstain from sex during the woman's pregnancy, it is mentioned plainly here to forestall later charges that their first child may

have been Joseph's, instead of being born "of the Holy Spirit."

III. Sudden Opposition—2:13-15

13 And when they were departed, behold, the angel of the Lord appeareth to Joseph in a dream, saying, Arise, and take the young child and his mother, and flee into Egypt, and be thou there until I bring thee word: for Herod will seek the young child to destroy him.

14 When he arose, he took the young child and his mother by night, and departed into Egypt:

15 And was there until the death of Herod: that it might be fulfilled which was spoken of the Lord by the prophet, saying, Out of Egypt have I called my son.

Our selected text now moves beyond the story of the birth of Jesus, beyond the visit of the wise men from the east (2:1-12) and their being questioned by King Herod about the precise place in Bethlehem where the "King of the Jews" was born. The story resumes after God had warned these eastern sages not to report to Herod because of his evil intentions (vs. 12). (The traditional number of three wise men is based only on the three gifts they offered in Jesus' honor [vs. 12], rather than any explicit reference in the text.)

Again "the angel of the Lord" proves indispensable in performing his duties as a "messenger," instructing Joseph, ever the protective father, to flee to Egypt for the Christ-child's safety. Egypt is selected as a temporary refuge for two reasons: (1) It was a safe haven not many days to the south of Bethlehem, and (2) God

154

is allowing a significant historical pattern to help us identify Jesus with Israel. Immediately we recall that God's people themselves were called out of Egypt in the exodus, the event that formed them as never before into a nation. The prophecy Matthew finds "fulfilled" is in Numbers 24:8. We would not think of that text referring to this event in the early life of Jesus if it were not for Matthew's selecting it, not so much as "predictive prophecy" but as an illustration that just as God brought His people out of Egypt so He is now, to people of faith, bringing His Messiah out for His own special mission. (Jewish rabbis were already accustomed to identifying Messiah with the nation, and would be quick to see that Matthew's reference is intended to show the authenticity of Jesus as the long-awaited Deliverer.)

IV. Searching for a Home—19-23
A. Return from Egypt, 19-20

19 But when Herod was dead, behold, an angel of the Lord appeareth in a dream to Joseph in Egypt,

20 Saying, Arise, and take the young child and his mother, and go into the land of Israel: for they are dead which sought the young child's life.

From Roman records we know that King Herod died in 4 b.c. (Hence Jesus must have been born about 5 B.C. instead of in the year "0"; the date of His birth was set about four years too late by the sixth-century scholar Dionysius). Herod's cruel reign lasted 34 years, and was marked not only by the "slaughter of the innocents" (vss. 16-18) but by putting

three of his own sons to death. Once more it is an angel who notifies Joseph that it is safe to bring the boy Jesus out of Egypt.

B. Settling in Nazareth, 21-23

21 And he arose, and took the young child and his mother, and came into the land of Israel.

22 But when he heard that Archelaus did reign in Judaea in the room of his father Herod, he was afraid to go thither: notwithstanding, being warned of God in a dream, he turned aside into the parts of Galilee:

23 And he came and dwelt in a city called Nazareth: that it might be fulfilled which was spoken by the prophets, He shall be called a Nazarene.

No doubt guided in part by the Old Testament prophecy in Micah 5:2 that the Messiah would be born in Bethlehem, Joseph heads first toward that town, in Judea. Herod's heir Archelaus, however, was as cruel as his father; so Joseph returns instead to his own hometown of Nazareth, to the north, in "Galilee of the Gentiles" (Luke 1:26; 2:4). Oddly, the Old Testament does not mention Nazareth; but Matthew apparently relates the town's name to the Hebrew word netser, or "branch," and ties it to the Messianic prediction in Isaiah 11:1— "And there shall come forth a rod out of the stem of Jesse, and a Branch shall grow out of his roots." Thus, by this word-play, Jesus appropriately comes to be known as a "Nazarene" both because it was His home town and because He is David's descendant.

Evangelistic Emphasis

"Unlikely" is a good word to describe the people and methods that God chooses to get his work done. "Unlikely" also is a good description for the people that God is still using and seeking. Joseph was an unlikely candidate for one of the lead roles in the first Christmas saga. If God were going to bring His son to earth to be our redeemer, a more likely father figure could have been found. God chose Joseph to be Mary's husband. God chose Joseph to make sure the accommodations at Bethlehem were acquired. God made Joseph responsible for presenting Jesus in the temple as well as protecting his family during the flight into Egypt. A careful reading of the text would reveal that Joseph, while seeming "unlikely" was very well suited to the task to which God called him.

The unlikely have been serving God faithfully from the start. The Good News is that God seems to seek out people who would be described as "unlikely" to do His bidding. He can even take the "unlikely" and bring them into a new relationship with Him. This choosing of the "unlikely" we call grace. When we witness the power of God changing some of these "unlikely" characters into the saints of the church, we call that kind of grace, Amazing!

The story of Joseph brings hope to all of us "unlikely" people that if we will obey the will of God, He will make out of us the "unlikely" saints.

This good news sounds "unlikely" to some, but to us who believe it remains God's amazing grace.

៚෬

Memory Selection

Then Joseph being raised from sleep did as the angel of the Lord had bidden him, and took unto him his wife: And knew her not till she had brought forth her firstborn son: and he called his name JESUS.—*Matthew 1:24-25*

One of the newest inventions of the technology industry is called a Palm Pilot. It is a fancy notebook that helps us keeps track of names, dates, addresses, phone numbers, and other important stuff. It is annoying to have a conversation with a person who owns one of these, because if he would listen rather than work with his new "memory device" he could remember what was being told to them.

God didn't have technology! He had to use *people* to remember what was important. The Lord had to trust His followers' memories with the sacred things He taught them.

I am amused by the naming of Jesus. If you will look back to the last memory selection, you will see that the angels told Mary what to name Jesus. Did the angels do this just in case Joseph forgot?!

Weekday Problems

Jennifer was in church every Sunday, reluctantly. She was the youngest daughter of her widowed mother who was making certain that she "grow up in church." Jennifer led a deceitful life. Most Sundays she had to fight a hangover in order to make it through the services. But she succeeded in fooling everyone in the church.

So everyone was in shock when Jennifer announced that she was expecting a child in five months. As far as anyone knew, she didn't even have a steady boyfriend. True to their Christian faith, church members tried to surround Jennifer with love and compassion. Her pregnancy and delivery were uneventful, but there were complications with the baby. The doctor said that the baby had a heart defect as a result of Jennifer's abuse of cocaine.

Jennifer's mother, who didn't handle the pregnancy well, was not about to take this latest revelation of her daughter's dark activities "in stride." The doctor had to tell both Jennifer and her mother that there was little or no hope for the child's survival. After only a few days of life, Jennifer's baby died.

A month later, Jennifer was again in church. This time not dutifully, but with a big question hanging over her heart. Jennifer was looking for hope and for comfort in her life.

*What are the advantages of living an obedient life of faith?

*How might Jennifer find comfort in the story of Joseph, especially in regard to his obedience and God's blessing?

Sorry You Asked

Q: Why did the fig go out with a prune?
A: Because it couldn't get a date.

❖❖❖❖❖

Q: How do you fix a broken tomato?
A: With tomato paste, of course.

❖❖❖❖❖

Q: What goes "Woof, woof, tock!"
A: A watch dog, I guess.

❖❖❖❖❖

Q: What's the largest thing ever made from grapes?
A: The grape wall of China.

This Lesson in Your Life

Andy Warhol's axiom that "everyone is famous for 15 minutes" seems to be a driving force in our culture. We have created a whole genre of shows in which ordinary people become famous as "survivors." We have turned game shows into some perverse type of verbal combat. We look for celebrities in the strangest places and find them in the most unsavory characters.

Joseph stands in such stark contrast to this crazy world called modern America. If there were a Christmas pageant produced, Joseph would have very few speaking lines. Unlike the tenor at most Operas, while Joseph is a main character in the birth of Jesus, he is not a loud character. Most of his speaking lines are with angels and Mary. He has no great poems like Mary. He has been given no place of importance in this story like the Magi or the shepherds. Joseph is a quiet character of faithfulness in our biblical saga. He is never mentioned after the time Jesus ran off to the Temple when He was 12. As you ponder this lesson, read your Bible and see if you can decide how long Joseph lived. The interesting thing is that Joseph could have been alive throughout the lifetime of Jesus. He could have been in the carpenter shop, earning a living for his family, including his rabbi son Jesus.

Joseph is a vital part of the Christmas story and a vital part of the early life of Jesus. We know that Jesus took up the profession of his father Joseph. We know that Joseph, in as many ways as possible, provided for his family. We know that Joseph was an honorable man, because he was not willing to embarrass Mary when he discovered her pregnancy. We know that he was probably inventive, because he turned the manger into a place where Mary could give birth. Joseph didn't have many lines in the early Christmas story, but he was a major character in God's plan.

Joseph was a quietly faithful follower of the Lord.

Most of the people who work hard in your church never make the headlines of the local paper. The fact that they are busy in the church is one of the factors that might be keeping them from nefarious deeds that would land their name in the news. Quiet faithfulness will not help any of us achieve our "15 minutes of fame." We will find in our faithful obedience to the Lord an eternity of blessings as we enter into heaven and hear Jesus say, "Well done, thy good and faithful servant."

Indeed, the highest compliment that one can pay to a child of God is not to hang the moniker of "famous" on him. The highest word of affirmation for any of us seeking to live for Jesus is for others to say of us "we were faithful."

GETTING THE FACTS
STRAIGHT

1. According to Matthew what was the marital status of Joseph and Mary?

Mary had been engaged to Joseph, but they were not yet living together when Mary was found to be with child.

2. When Joseph found out that Mary was pregnant, what plans did he made regarding her?

Because Joseph was a righteous man, he didn't want to embarrass Mary so he planned to divorce her quietly.

3. As Joseph was making plans to dismiss Mary, what happened that caused him to change his plans.

As Joseph was planning to dismiss Mary, an angel came to Joseph in a dream and told him not to do as he had planned.

4. What were the specific instructions that Joseph received from the angel speaking to him in a dream?

Joseph was told not to be afraid to take Mary as his wife. He was told the child was conceived of the Holy Spirit and should be named Jesus.

5. After Joseph woke from this angelic dream, what were his next actions?

Joseph did as the Lord commanded and took Mary as his wife, but had no marital relations with her until she bore her son.

6. After the birth of Jesus in Bethlehem, what instructions did he receive from God in another dream?

He was told to take his family and to flee from Bethlehem and go to Egypt.

7. What events had made staying in Bethlehem impossible for Joseph, Mary, and Jesus?

King Herod had ordered the slaughter of all male children in his kingdom who were two years of age or younger.

8. When would it be safe for Joseph to return to the region of Galilee?

Joseph would return home only after the news that King Herod had died.

9. How did Joseph know that Herod had died?

Joseph was told of the death of Herod by an angel in a dream. The angel told him it was safe to return.

10. How many dreams did Joseph have involving angels, and what were the instructions of each?

Joseph had three dreams. The first one was to take Mary as his wife, the second was to flee to Egypt, and the third was to return to Israel.

One family tradition during the holiday season is to drive around and look at Christmas lights. I am particularly interested in how the Holy Family is portrayed in various decorations. Several years ago I noticed an interesting nativity scene in New Orleans. The baby Jesus was the focal point of the Nativity. This one had baby Jesus in a barn-like building. He was surrounded by Wise Men, who were elegantly dressed. There were several shepherds along with their sheep. There to one side was the holy family. Mary was standing beside the manger, hands folded in the attitude of prayer and awe. She was dressed in white and looked like every other Mary I have seen. Over one shoulder, angels were peering at the manger scene. Over her other shoulder, dressed in all his finest, was Santa Claus. I stopped the car. I could find no character in this elaborate nativity that looked anything like Joseph. He was left out.

That is the problem too many modern presentations of the Christmas story. Joseph is relegated to a footnote. Since he is not the "real" father of Jesus, we don't let him be a real part of the Christmas story. He fades obediently into the background. In fact, however, Joseph was a man of character and depth. He was a righteous man. With Mary, who found favor with God, they provided a godly home for God's Son.

Joseph was also a dreamer. In Matthew's account, Joseph is told in the first dream not to hestitate to marry Mary, for that which was conceived in her was from the Holy Spirit, and to name the child Jesus. In the second dream, Joseph was told to flee to Egypt, to avoid "the slaughter of the innocents." In a third dream, Joseph was told to return his family to Israel because Herod was dead.

God sometimes speaks to us in and through our dreams, but it takes a special person to hear His voice in those dreams. Joseph had imagination. He had a big enough imagination to believe that God could work His plan through a simple carpenter. He had enough imagination to believe there was a "logical" answer to Mary's pregnancy. He was a big enough dreamer to see that God could send a baby into the world and through that special Child bring about the redemption of humanity. Joseph had a big enough imagination to believe that God could work his plan for humanity through ordinary human beings, such as a simple carpenter.

What about you? Are you a dreamer? Has God placed big dreams for your life, or for your church, in your heart? One of the spiritual traits we often ignore is the ability of some people to have dreams and visions. Joel prophesied that in the last days God's people would have visions and dream dreams. Do you have enough imagination that God could work through your dreams and visions? Has God made you a dreamer?

Go ahead. God makes His dreams for us come true.

Lesson 4

Mary, Mother of the Messiah

Luke 2:1, 4-20

A nd it came to pass in those days, that there went out a decree from Cæsar Augustus, that all the world should be taxed.

4 And Joseph also went up from Galilee, out of the city of Nazareth, into Judaea, unto the city of David, which is called Bethlehem; (because he was of the house and lineage of David:)

5 To be taxed with Mary his espoused wife, being great with child.

6 And so it was, that, while they were there, the days were accomplished that she should be delivered.

7 And she brought forth her firstborn son, and wrapped him in swaddling clothes, and laid him in a manger; because there was no room for them in the inn.

8 And there were in the same country shepherds abiding in the field, keeping watch over their flock by night.

9 And, lo, the angel of the Lord came upon them, and the glory of the Lord shone round about them: and they were sore afraid.

10 And the angel said unto them, Fear not: for, behold, I bring you good tidings of great joy, which shall be to all people.

11 For unto you is born this day in the city of David a Saviour, which is Christ the Lord.

12 And this shall be a sign unto you; Ye shall find the babe wrapped in swaddling clothes, lying in a manger.

13 And suddenly there was with the angel a multitude of the heavenly host praising God, and saying,

14 Glory to God in the highest, and on earth peace, good will toward men.

15 And it came to pass, as the angels were gone away from them into heaven, the shepherds said one to another, Let us now go even unto Bethlehem, and see this thing which is come to pass, which the Lord hath made known unto us.

16 And they came with haste, and found Mary, and Joseph, and the babe lying in a manger.

17 And when they had seen it, they made known abroad the saying which was told them concerning this child.

18 And all they that heard it wondered at those things which were told them by the shepherds.

19 But Mary kept all these things, and pondered them in her heart.

20 And the shepherds returned, glorifying and praising God for all the things that they had heard and seen, as it was told unto them.

Memory Selection
Luke 2:7
Background Scripture
Luke 2:1-20
Devotional Reading
Isaiah 9:1-7

161

Through the ages, many Christians have so spiritualized the birth of Christ that it loses contact with earthly realities. Ancient legends even portrayed the boy Jesus doing magical tricks like breathing life into a mud-pie dove! Although the true story is about an other-worldly God, we must not forget that it is about God's becoming *man*.

Luke's account focuses on such earthly realities as having to pay high taxes . . . the discomfort of a woman in the late stages of pregnancy having to travel . . . using a stable for a birthing room . . . and the first visitors being humble (and no doubt smelly!) sheep-herders fresh from the pasture.

Ironically, it is the earthiness of the story that makes it so remarkable. For it is the story of a glorious and majestic God literally becoming "down to earth."

☙☙

Encourage group members to share stories of unusual circum-stances of "blessed events" in their family. For example, are any moms present who almost didn't make it to the hospital in time? Did any dads in the group get so excited they almost failed to get the suitcase in the car? One husband, whose wife was two weeks late, finally took her for a ride in a jeep over a bumpy, switch-back mountain road, to hurry things along. Another, trying to be of help during the agony of his wife's birth-pangs, passed out and missed the big event.

Point the discussion to the circum-stances of Christ's birth that are just unique enough to make the scene real —the difficult time Mary must have had traveling to Bethlehem, the trouble in finding room at the inn, having to borrow a manger from the animals in a stable. Even if her new-born had not been the Christ-child, Mary would never have forgotten this birth!

Teaching Outline	Daily Bible Readings	
I. Citizens' Census—1, 4-5	Mon.	Jesus Is Born Luke 2:1-7
A. The Roman tax, 1	Tue.	News for Shepherds
B. Fulfilled prophecy, 4-5		Luke 2:8-14
II. Christ in a Manger—6-7	Wed.	Mary's Reflection Luke 2:15-20
III. Chorus of Angels—8-14	Thu.	Sword in the Soul
A. Tidings of joy, 8-12		Luke 2:21-35
B. Song of praise, 13-14	Fri.	Anna Sees and Believes Luke 2:36-40
IV. Considered Responses—15-20	Sat.	Remembering His Mission
A. The shepherds, 15-18, 20		Luke 2:41-51
B. Mary, 19	Sun.	A Child Is Born! Isaiah 9:1-7

Verse by Verse

I. Citizens' Census—1, 4-5
A. The Roman tax, 1

1 And it came to pass in those days, that there went out a decree from Cæsar Augustus, that all the world should be taxed.

"All the world" was a common way to refer to the far-flung Roman Empire. Of course the term was an over-statement, but the fact is that the world of ordinary travel and commerce known to the people in Palestine was indeed ruled by Rome (see the NIV, "the entire Roman world"). Also as in the NIV, the word for "tax" more accurately refers to a census, which would of course become the basis for taxation. Although this particular census is not referred to in Roman history itself, it is on sound historical ground because Judea had only recently been made part of Syria (note vs. 2's reference to its governor, who is referred to by the historian Josephus). The Emperor would want to know how many subjects lived within the new political boundaries.

B. Fulfilled prophecy, 4-5

4 And Joseph also went up from Galilee, out of the city of Nazareth, into Judaea, unto the city of David, which is called Bethlehem; (because he was of the house and lineage of David:)

5 To be taxed with Mary his espoused wife, being great with child.

Lesson 3 noted that being "espoused" in the Jewish culture was an intensified form of engagement which could be broken only by divorce, as though the couple were married; but that an angel has told Joseph not to divorce Mary since she was with child of the Holy Spirit.

Jewish influence on the region's politics, promoted especially by the Sadducees, is reflected in the fact that registration in the tax census was according to tribe. Thus Joseph travels from Nazareth in the north down to Bethlehem of Judea, "the city of David," since he was of the tribe of Judah. Both Matthew's and Luke's genealogies are careful to list David as one of Joseph's ancestors (Matt. 1:6, 16; Luke 3:23, 31).

This detail is important because it was essential to show that the Christ-child fulfilled Old Testament prophecy of a "Davidic Messiah"—that He would be of the "seed" of David, and sit on the throne that God had promised eternally to David (2 Sam. 7:12-13). Note how carefully God is orchestrating this event: although Joseph lives in Nazareth, the census draws him to Bethlehem, the prophesied birthplace of the Messiah (Mic. 5:2). Despite the vaunted power of the Roman Emperor, a greater Ruler is using him to arrange for specific fulfillment of Messianic prophecy.

II. Christ in a Manger—6-7

6 And so it was, that, while they

were there, the days were accomplished that she should be delivered.

7 And she brought forth her firstborn son, and wrapped him in swaddling clothes, and laid him in a manger; because there was no room for them in the inn.

The days that were "accomplished" refer to Mary's nine-month pregnancy. (Rome obviously felt that its census was more important than the timing of Christ's birth!) In one sense it seems a supreme injustice for the King of kings not to be born in a palace nursery, much less a cozy inn, and to settle instead for a rude stable where animals were kept. Yet the picture fits the prophet Isaiah's prediction that Messiah would be "despised," a prophecy that would only be intensified at His death (Isa. 53:3).

In words that understate the stupendous implications of this event, Luke mentions that the child is Mary's "firstborn." The spectacular acclaim will be reserved for the angels in the verses to follow. Although his first garment is not a royal mantle but the clean birth-cloths called "swaddling clothes," this infant is none other than "Immanuel," or "God with us" (Isa. 7:14).

III. Chorus of Angels—8-14
A. Tidings of joy, 8-12

8 And there were in the same country shepherds abiding in the field, keeping watch over their flock by night.

9 And, lo, the angel of the Lord came upon them, and the glory of the Lord shone round about them: and they were sore afraid.

10 And the angel said unto them,

Fear not: for, behold, I bring you good tidings of great joy, which shall be to all people.

11 For unto you is born this day in the city of David a Saviour, which is Christ the Lord.

12 And this shall be a sign unto you; Ye shall find the babe wrapped in swaddling clothes, lying in a manger.

The extraordinary presence of angels that has been a previous feature of the story of God's preparing Joseph and Mary for this event continues, and is expanded to humble shepherds. Selecting people who would have been considered somewhat "lower class" continues the irony of the King of heaven condescending to people of "low estate," as Mary has said (Luke 1:48). The scene also pre-figures the apostle's Paul's statement that "not many wise men after the flesh, not many mighty, not many noble, are called" (1 Cor. 1:26); and the role that Jesus Himself will play as the Good Shepherd.

The contrast between these common men and the event the angels announce to them is heightened by the "glory of the Lord" that apparently lights up the night. This is the "Shekinah" or shining Presence that often marked the presence of the divine among mortals. It was so powerful that it caused people who saw it to throw themselves face-down on the ground; so it is no wonder that the angels have to reassure the shepherds not to be so frightened that they cannot appreciate the glorious message. Once more, the message includes a pointed reference to Bethlehem as the "city of David" to reinforce the Messianic importance of this birth.

B. Song of praise, 13-14

13 And suddenly there was with the angel a multitude of the heavenly host praising God, and saying,

14 Glory to God in the highest, and on earth peace, good will toward men.

The "announcing" angel is joined by a host of other angels—a heavenly chorus that reminds us that events as glorious as this cannot be "processed" merely by calm discussion: they must be sung about! The "heavenly host" may have been composed not only of angels but of the creatures known as cherubim and seraphim, part of the heavenly court that so awed Isaiah when he found himself in God's throne room (Isa. 6:1-3). The scene is among the emotional foundation stones of singing praises in church to this day.

IV. Considered Responses—15-20
A. The shepherds, 15-18, 20

15 And it came to pass, as the angels were gone away from them into heaven, the shepherds said one to another, Let us now go even unto Bethlehem, and see this thing which is come to pass, which the Lord hath made known unto us.

16 And they came with haste, and found Mary, and Joseph, and the babe lying in a manger.

17 And when they had seen it, they made known abroad the saying which was told them concerning this child.

18 And all they that heard it wondered at those things which were told them by the shepherds.

20 And the shepherds returned, glorifying and praising God for all the things that they had heard and seen, as it was told unto them.

Note that in the present outline verse 19 is treated below, in order to connect the response of the shepherds in verses 18 and 20. These simple herdsman make a twofold response to the astounding event that lit up the night skies near Bethlehem. First they hurry to the village to pay homage to the Child about whom the angels sang. Then they broadcast the angelic message to others. Here is another "incarnation" that believers must imitate: the words of heaven are to be enfleshed in human words. Ever since, in the absence of angels whose glory fills the night, those who have already heard the Good News are to take it into all the world.

B. Mary, 19

19 But Mary kept all these things, and pondered them in her heart.

The text pointedly notes that, unlike the outgoing response of the shepherds, Mary takes the birth, and the shepherds' worship of her new baby, into quiet contemplation. She has already had her own outburst of praise, in the song recorded in 1:46-55. A previously unknown, unmarried Jewish girl has given birth to the Son of God. It would all be too much to contain in one heart without pausing to reflect on what it might mean.

Evangelistic Emphasis

The account of the first Christmas is loaded with irony. The news that Mary was having a baby was in some ways not really "*good* news." An Angel had to reassure Joseph. And the census was bad news, since it was to determine taxes, which aren't good news. Since Mary was very pregnant, the trip was bad news; and the hotel in Bethlehem was full. Yet it all worked out the way that God wanted; and what should have been bad news turned out to be good news.

How would you want your Savior born? Would you feel comfortable with a savior who was born in palace and raised to be royalty? What about a Savior who was born among the aristocratic and had all the luxuries of life? Could you approach that kind of Savior with your daily problems? How about a savior who was born, out back in the barn?

I can approach a Savior who had such humble beginnings. I can relate to that kind of Savior. The good news of Jesus Christ is that He came as one of us for us. His life was filled with that kind of irony that surrounds Christmas. He loved sinners and that made religious people hate Him. He never committed a sin, yet died a sinner's death. He never owned a home, yet prepared a home for us in heaven. One whose life began in a cave and ended in a cross is our savior. His life was so full of contradictions and irony that He certainly can understand our confusion and forgive our sin.

80CR

Memory Selection

And she brought forth her firstborn son, and wrapped him in swaddling clothes, and laid him in a manger; because there was no room for them in the inn.—*Luke 2:7*

If we could "whip up" on one of the characters in the Christmas story, the innkeeper would be the first in line for a little abuse. How dare he turn away this woman who was in such a delicate condition? He must have been a cad to have thought only of his profit margin, rather than helping this find young couple find lodging in the strange town of Bethlehem.

Legend has it that the innkeeper was really a selfish oaf. However the Bible says nothing about him. We have developed this whole persona for the innkeeper based on the small phrase in Luke 2: 7. The text reads, "there was no room for them in the inn."

The innkeeper may actually have been a hero, finding Mary and Joseph a quiet place for the birth to take place. Christmas helps us forget our categories of villain and hero, and causes us to look again with wonder at all the people God loves.

Weekday Problems

Sheila was in a state. Something was going on in the office, and she wasn't in on the secret. Telephone calls were being made, and when she would walk in the room the persons on the phone would grow silent. When Sheila inquired about the secrecy, the secretaries simply gave her an incredulous look and went about their business. That was not so far out of the ordinary; Sheila was not the most popular executive in the firm. She was feeling very left out of whatever was happening. She wondered if a Christmas party was being planned without her being on the guest list. She often felt left out, especially at Christmas time. Sheila was one of those persons whose birthday fell a couple of days before Christmas. She never had a party on her birthday, it was always "too close to Christmas." It bothered her that her birthday had never been celebrated. With all the secret office shenanigans, Sheila was certain that her birthday would be forgotten and she would be excluded from any Christmas party now being planned.

On a Saturday night, Sheila and her husband Glenn attended the Christmas play at their daughter's school. On the way home Sheila began reflecting on obvious secrecy at the office. It all made her very angry. Then when she walked in the house that night 30 people yelled, "Happy Birthday!"

*When have you ever felt "left out?"

*Have you included everyone in your Christmas celebration?

Taxing Times

Sunday School teacher: Now who decreed that "all the world should be taxed"?

Pupil: The Democrats.

❖❖❖❖❖

Hope: What's the difference between a tax collector and a taxidermist?

Dope: No difference at all. Both of them skin the victim.

❖❖❖❖❖

Jack: Did you know that some presidents gave their salaries back to the government?

Zack: Yeah, and now they have us all doing it.

❖❖❖❖❖

God couldn't do without the IRS. He loves the poor, and the IRS creates them for Him to love.

167

This Lesson in Your Life

"In those days a decree went out from Caesar Augustus" (Luke 2:1). We have heard the words so often they don't even register with us. Actually, the decree caused utter chaos. Persons had to pack up their homes and move to strange cities. They couldn't make a reservation in the local Holiday Inn, because it didn't exist. These displaced pilgrims were forced to live with relatives. They had to find work in strange job markets. Children had to make adjustments and find new friends.

It was out of this chaos that God brought His Son into the world. Think about your life. Don't you relate to this chaos, this unpredictability of life? Many of your friends won't go into the work-a-day world without a planner. They want to control every moment of life. Ask your friends about how their lives are working out with their planners. They will tell you that the unexpected and unplanned activities change their plans. This happens almost daily.

Yet, it is often in the unexpected that we find God. Elijah didn't find God in all the expected places. He was neither in the wind, the earthquake, nor the fire. God came to Elijah in "a still small voice" (1 Kings 19: 11-13). As a person who plans worship, I can testify that God comes more in the unplanned moments than in those that are carefully worked out. He turned the world upside down for the birth of His Son, who would turn the world upside down. The first lesson in this story is that God is found in the surprises of life, if you are looking for Him. Think about the shepherds watching their flocks. They hadn't planned on an angelic choir singing to them. The message the choir gave was important, "Fear not!" (Luke 2: 10).

The second lesson of this passage is the call to fearless living. The shepherds had much to fear. They had to keep watch over sheep to protect them from thieves and wild animals. But right in the middle of the shepherd's chaos came the message, "Fear not."

Christmas challenges the church to practice fearless living in a frightening world. We can do that only as we are anchored in Jesus Christ. Jesus was born into a world like ours—a world thrown into chaos by the capricious dictates of Rome. People had been displaced. They were afraid. They had the sense of being lost. Have you noticed that it doesn't sound that much different from the world in which we live?

But the good news is that Jesus understands your fear. He came to give you peace in an upside-down world. That blessing can be yours, but at a cost. You have to relinquish your need to have everything work out the way you planned. Not that you should give up planning; just don't resist God when He decides to take over your plans for you.

GETTING THE FACTS STRAIGHT

1. The birth of Jesus Christ happened at a specific time in world history. What world figures did Luke mention?

Caesar Augustus was the emperor of the Roman Empire. Quirinius was the governor of Syria.

2. What decree had just been issued?

The decree was a call for a census of the Roman Empire. Each member of the empire had to register.

3. What was the significance of the trip that Joseph and Mary made from Nazareth to Bethlehem?

Joseph was going to Bethlehem to pay his taxes. Taxes were collected according to tribes or families.

4. What was the importance of Bethlehem?

Bethlehem was the ancestral home of David, and it was prophesied as the birthplace of the Messiah.

5. What differences do you notice between the lineage of Jesus in Matthew 1:1-17 and Luke 3: 23-38?

Matthew traces the genealogy back to Abraham. Luke traces the genealogy back to God.

6. What else is interesting about the two genealogies of Jesus?

Matthew traces the genealogy through Joseph, and Luke through Mary.

7. According to Luke, were Joseph and Mary married when they traveled to Bethlehem?

According to Luke, Mary and Joseph were still engaged when they made the journey to Bethlehem (Luke 2: 5b).

8. What verse mentions the innkeeper, who is prominent in many Christian traditions?

The innkeeper isn't mentioned in any Scripture. This Scrooge-like person is the product of legends, not the Bible.

9. The long-awaited Savior of the Jews had come. To whom was the great event first announced?

The birth announcement was first made to the shepherds who were watching their flocks at night.

10. What was the significance of the announcement of the birth to the shepherds?

Jesus came for all people. No one was to be excluded from His love, not even lowly shepherds.

It's December 22. Do you have all of your Christmas preparations made? Wednesday will be here before you know it. Christmas exectations abound. You might be the one expected to make the dressing. Or you could be the one expected to put all of those Christmas presents together, especially those that say, "some assembly required." Perhaps in your family you will be expected to offer the Table Grace at the big Christmas meal.

We are a bit like the merchants in the town of Bethlehem on that first Christmas. They were so busy with the throngs in town for the census that they didn't even notice the birth that took place in Bethlehem's manger. There was so much rushing around that the noise of a newborn crying was simply another noise to them.

Mary and Joseph were breathing a collective sigh of relief, for it seemed that the hard part of their journey was over. They had survived the gossips in Nazareth speculating on Mary's condition and what Joseph would do about it. They had made the trip from their hometown to this teeming town of Bethlehem. They had survived the birth and the visits from the shepherds. They had found time to reflect on their special Son and the prophecies that would be fulfilled in Him. They had expectations of raising a child and seeing what God would do through Him.

Expectations are a fact of life. We place expectations on others around us. We expect a person standing behind a sign that says "Customer Service" is actually interested in giving service to us, the customer. We expect to be treated with dignity and courtesy when we are in public. Likewise we place expectations on those around us. Children and grandchildren live out certain expectations, both spoken and unspoken. We place expectations on our church and faith community. We have even placed expectations on our Lord.

Expectations sometimes get us into trouble, because not all of our expectations can be met. There are bound to be disappointments in our lives, when we expect others to do things for us. Not all of your expectations are going to be met, not even by the Lord, Himself.

Expectation carries with it the idea of an agenda. When we have expectations we usually have a list of things that need to happen for our expectations to be met. May I suggest another word as we approach this Christmas season? The word is *anticipation*.

The difference between expectation and anticipation is the difference between an agenda and an outlook. Anticipation is the hope that an event may happen. It is the functional difference between looking forward to Christmas because it is a wonderful celebration with family and friends, and facing Christmas because you are the person expected to do everything. It is the difference between seeing Christmas as a holiday complete with all the trimmings, and seeing it as a time to remember the birth of Jesus Christ.

170

Lesson 5

John the Baptist: Messiah's Forerunner

Matthew 3:1-11; 11:7-10

In those days came John the Baptist, preaching in the wilderness of Judaea,

2 And saying, Repent ye: for the kingdom of heaven is at hand.

3 For this is he that was spoken of by the prophet Esaias, saying, The voice of one crying in the wilderness, Prepare ye the way of the Lord, make his paths straight.

4 And the same John had his raiment of camel's hair, and a leathern girdle about his loins; and his meat was locusts and wild honey.

5 Then went out to him Jerusalem, and all Judaea, and all the region round about Jordan,

6 And were baptized of him in Jordan, confessing their sins.

7 But when he saw many of the Pharisees and Sadducees come to his baptism, he said unto them, O generation of vipers, who hath warned you to flee from the wrath to come?

8 Bring forth therefore fruits meet for repentance:

9 And think not to say within yourselves, We have Abraham to our father: for I say unto you, that God is able of these stones to raise up children unto Abraham.

10 And now also the axe is laid unto the root of the trees: therefore every tree which bringeth not forth good fruit is hewn down, and cast into the fire.

11 I indeed baptize you with water unto repentance: but he that cometh after me is mightier than I, whose shoes I am not worthy to bear: he shall baptize you with the Holy Ghost, and with fire:

11:7 And as they departed, Jesus began to say unto the multitudes concerning John, What went ye out into the wilderness to see? A reed shaken with the wind?

8 But what went ye out for to see? A man clothed in soft raiment? behold, they that wear soft clothing are in kings' houses.

9 But what went ye out for to see? A prophet? yea, I say unto you, and more than a prophet.

10 For this is he, of whom it is written, Behold, I send my messenger before thy face, which shall prepare thy way before thee.

Memory Selection
Matthew 11:10

Background Scripture
Matthew 3; 11:2-19; 14:1-12

Devotional Reading
John 1:1-14

171

The heroic ministry of John the Baptist, whose birth was announced even before that of the Messiah's (Lesson 1), is the focus of this lesson. Both a positive and a negative element are emphasized in our text. Positively, John's work was essential in preparing the way for Jesus. Thanks to his preaching, thousands eagerly anticipated the Messiah.

Negatively, John was faced with the challenge of tearing down attitudes that would hinder Jesus' message. His bold claim that "the axe is at the root" was a revolutionary declaration that the ruling forms of legalistic and pretentious forms of worship were about to be toppled. With his rugged lifestyle and appearance and his fiery preaching, John is one of the most colorful New Testament figures and a "road builder" who smoothed the way for Jesus.

୫୦୦ଃ

Although John the Baptist denied being the Messiah, history tells us that after his death some followers made him into a "cult hero." This makes it all the more remarkable that the real John seemed content to "play second fiddle" to Jesus.

Discuss with your group the qualities required for a person to play such a role: to be vice president of the corporation but never the president . . . to race to second place but never win the blue ribbon (and thus to be labeled an "also-ran") . . . to be salutatorian of your class but never valedictorian . . . to be a right-hand man but never *the man*. John the Baptist was a hero in his own role because he saw its contribution to the Messiah's work. While he did not allow his ego to be bruised because he was not the Messiah, it actually required a strong ego to resist attempts to make him someone he was not.

Teaching Outline	Daily Bible Readings

I. John's Ministry—3:1-6
  A. Preparing the Way, 1-3
  B. John the Person—4
  C. John the Baptizer, 5-6
 	
II. John's Reproach—7-11
  A. The axe at the root, 7-10
  B. The greater One to come, 11
 	
III. Jesus' Valuation—11:7-10
  A. False views, 7-9
  B. 'My messenger," 10
	Mon. John Proclaims Repentance
	      Matthew 3:1-10
	Tue. John Baptizes Jesus
	      Matthew 3:11-17
	Wed. John Testifies to the Light
	      John 1:1-15
	Thu. Not the Messiah
	      John 1:19-28
	Fri. None Greater than John
	      Matthew 11:2-15
	Sat. John's Death
	      Matthew 14:1-12
	Sun. 'By what authority?'
	      Matthew 21:23-32

Verse by Verse

I. John's Ministry, 3:1-6
A. Preparing the Way, 1-3

1 In those days came John the Baptist, preaching in the wilderness of Judaea,

2 And saying, Repent ye: for the kingdom of heaven is at hand.

3 For this is he that was spoken of by the prophet Esaias, saying, The voice of one crying in the wilderness, Prepare ye the way of the Lord, make his paths straight.

John the Baptist was so important a link between the Old and the New Covenants that all four Gospels include his ministry as a preamble to the ministry of Jesus Himself. Only when we pay full attention to John's proclamation of God's demand that we live up to His standards of righteousness can we fully appreciate God's grace in giving Christ to be righteousness in us when we inevitably fall short of that goal.

Repentance and the nearness of the Kingdom were the two main points in John's preaching. Some righteous Jews in his audience bemoaned the widespread unrighteousness among the people, and taught that the Kingdom would not come until they reformed. Note, however, that while John calls the people to repentance (a "change of mind" that leads to reform), the Kingdom will come, regardless.

John may have expected this realm

(which Luke usually refers to as "the kingdom of God") to include an earthly throne and the overthrow of the occupying Roman army. For when Jesus fails to set up this political entity and instead establishes the Kingdom in the hearts of his followers, John asks, "Art thou he that should come, or do we look for another?" (Matt. 11:3). Whether John's precise expectations were fulfilled or not, his message of repentance was an essential step in preparing for Jesus' own message.

John's work is also a fulfillment of the prophecy in Malachi 3:1 that God would send His own messenger to prepare the way for Messiah. Making God's paths "straight" reflects the work of ancient "road crews" going before the caravan of a great king, leveling steep places and straightening out bends in the road that would impede his progress.

B. John the Person—4

4 And the same John had his raiment of camel's hair, and a leathern girdle about his loins; and his meat was locusts and wild honey.

John's lifestyle has all the marks of the wilderness figure that he is. He is not merely striking a radical pose for publicity, but fulfilling the prophecy that the prophet Elijah would precede the Messiah (Mal. 4:5); and Elijah was also a rough-hewn wilderness

173

figure (Zech. 13:4; 2 Kings 1:8). Later, Jesus will explicitly say that John the Baptist is the figurative fulfillment of this Elijah prophecy (Matt. 11:13-14).

It was widely believed among the Jews after the time of Malachi that prophecy had ceased in Israel, God having withdrawn this kind of direct communication from His people. Identifying John the Baptist with the heroic prophet Elijah showed that the prophetic link with God had not been broken, but that it had to be received on God's new terms, which included the prophetic ministries of both John and Jesus.

C. John the Baptizer, 5-6

5 Then went out to him Jerusalem, and all Judaea, and all the region round about Jordan,

6 And were baptized of him in Jordan, confessing their sins.

Obviously the time was right for John and his message. Despite its sternness and judgment (see below), the people sense in it the ring of truth and respond to it in droves. Revival is in the land! Although some rituals under the Old Covenant involved "washings," the practice of baptism itself grew up in the period between the Testaments. (The community that produced the Dead Sea Scrolls practiced it.)

Luke adds that John's message included "the baptism of repentance for the remission of sins" (Luke 3:3). However, the washing away of sins symbolized by John's baptism apparently looked forward to, and depended upon, the atoning sacrifice of Christ. Later, disciples of John who

had not known of the Cross, the resurrection, and the indwelling of the Holy Spirit, would be rebaptized in the name of Jesus (Acts 19:1-6).

II. John's Reproach—7-11
A. The axe at the root, 7-10

7 But when he saw many of the Pharisees and Sadducees come to his baptism, he said unto them, O generation of vipers, who hath warned you to flee from the wrath to come?

8 Bring forth therefore fruits meet for repentance:

9 And think not to say within yourselves, We have Abraham to our father: for I say unto you, that God is able of these stones to raise up children unto Abraham.

10 And now also the axe is laid unto the root of the trees: therefore every tree which bringeth not forth good fruit is hewn down, and cast into the fire.

The Pharisees represented the strict law-keepers among the Jews, and despite the hypocrisy of some (Matt. 23), many of them were genuinely pious. The Sadducees, though smaller in number, were the more politically influential. Neither the righteousness of the Pharisees nor the power of the Sadducees exemplified the purity of heart that would make good soil for Jesus' message; so in John's sweeping judgment all are labeled as "snakes"!

When his good standing before God was questioned, the most natural response of a Pharisee or Sadducee was to appeal to his heritage. How could it be doubted that a person who was a child of Abraham was also acceptable as a child of God? John introduces a new note of individualism in answer to this question. God now seeks an expanded family, those who come to Him with the spiritual fruit of humble hearts and obedient spirits. Those who, instead, can boast only of a "birth certificate" traceable to Father Abraham are now an unfruitful tree that will be cut down.

B. The greater One to come, 11

11 I indeed baptize you with water unto repentance: but he that cometh after me is mightier than I, whose shoes I am not worthy to bear: he shall baptize you with the Holy Ghost, and with fire:

The apostle John's account of John the Baptist's ministry shows that some wondered aloud whether the Baptist was the Messiah. John was quick to relieve them of this notion (John 1:19-21). Here he uses two illustrations to emphasize his subordinate role. He is (a) not worthy to be a valet who bears the noble Messiah's sandals; and (b) his baptism is only with water, whereas Jesus' baptism would be with the Spirit (which is widely held to refer to the incident in Acts 2, when the disciples were "immersed" in the outpouring of the Spirit that resulted in their speaking in tongues (see also Acts 1:5). The baptism of fire likely refers to the "immersion" in suffering that Jesus predicted His disciples would undergo (Matt. 20:21-23). The point of John's statement is that he regards the rite of baptism included in his own ministry to be inferior to the work of Jesus.

III. Jesus' Valuation—11:7-10

A. False views, 7-9

7 And as they departed, Jesus began to say unto the multitudes concerning John, What went ye out into the wilderness to see? A reed shaken with the wind?

8 But what went ye out for to see? A man clothed in soft raiment? behold, they that wear soft clothing are in kings' houses.

9 But what went ye out for to see? A prophet? yea, I say unto you, and more than a prophet.

The text now brings us forward to the time when John the Baptist had become such a threat to civil and religious order that he was jailed. Jesus sends messengers to reassure John that his work of preparation has been successful (11:1-6), then turns to the crowds to give this word of praise for the Baptist's heroic ministry. Those who had gone to hear John in the wilderness should not have expected to find a leader in fine robes and living in a palace. Yet merely focusing faithfully on his task of preparing the way for the Christ was more praise-worthy than living as a religious prince.

B. 'My messenger," 10

10 For this is he, of whom it is written, Behold, I send my messenger before thy face, which shall prepare thy way before thee.

Jesus' final benediction on the life and work of John the Baptist draws again from the prophecy in Malachi 3:1. The reference not only plainly identifies John as the fulfillment of this prediction, but Jesus as the Messiah for whom God's messenger, John, prepared the way.

175

Evangelistic Emphasis

Aren't you relieved that God does not judge us on externals? John the Baptizer certainly would not qualify as one of the Lord's "best dressed saints." John wore funny clothing and had a stranger diet. His strength was his relationship with the Lord. His message was one of repentance and preparation. His mission was to point beyond himself to a "mightier one" who was coming.

The only equivalent one might draw would be if a preacher decided to grow long hair, got himself an earring and a couple of tattoos. What if this same preacher announced to the congregation he was on a macrobiotic diet? That would certainly attract attention. If the same preacher was calling the nation to repentance and preparation to meet the Messiah, he might garner headlines. On second thought, we'd dismiss him as a kook. Anyone who dares question the holiness of America can sometimes find themselves on the receiving end of some nasty comments about their patriotism. We have a curious mix of patriotism and religion. To have one is by default to possess the other.

All of Jerusalem was coming to John. He was a fresh voice in a wilderness of religious noise and ritual. His fresh approach to proclaiming God's message was appealing. His new words harkened back to the old days of the prophets.

Yet John's message was not good news. He called persons to repent and to confess their sins to the Father.

The good news happens after we have repented and opened our lives up to the cleansing presence of Jesus Christ.

℘Q

Memory Selection

For this is he, of whom it is written, Behold, I send my messenger before thy face, which shall prepare thy way before thee.—*Matthew 11:10*

Where I grew up, you were either the first one to launch out on a project or a mere follower. You could either lead the exploration party or you could wait and see what happened to others who went ahead of you.

We have those same basic choices in life, and in the Church. Leaders and followers are both essential to the life of faith and the ministry of the Church. You have to be clear in your own mind which you are. Leadership is not a role you can take; leadership is a role which has to be earned.

In the case of John the Baptizer, leadership meant that he made preparations for the one coming after him. He shows that leadership can involve preparing the way for others to lead. It is the nature of the work of faith that we need to prepare for those who will come behind to us to continue in our place. Leading or following, we are making a way for a new generation to serve Jesus Christ.

Weekday Problems

Thomas announced that he was resigning as president of the firm to take a similar job in the Carolinas. He had risen though the ranks and brought the firm along with him. It was now an industry leader. The board of directors endorsed Thomas' hand-picked successor.

Before the moving truck was packed, Thomas felt as though the troubles had begun at the firm. The first day in the office, the new company president made several changes. No one lost a job or lost money, but the changes were noticed. The new president availed himself of the company policy that allowed for the president to choose and purchase his own company vehicle. The new president traded in Thomas' old station wagon for a sleek luxury sedan.

When Thomas's wife Jane came home later that afternoon, her husband was fuming. He told Jane about all the changes that the new president had made at the firm. "Honey," she said, "you have only one problem."

"What's that?" he snarled.

"You don't work there anymore!"

*Describe a time when you found it difficult to "let go" and "move on."

*Is it hard to build something for others and then watch them take their leadership roles and responsibilities?

Points to Ponder

Be fishers of men. You catch 'em, He'll clean 'em.

❖❖❖❖

A family altar can alter a family.

❖❖❖❖

Forbidden fruits create many a jam.

❖❖❖❖

Give God what's right, not what's left.

❖❖❖❖

Give Satan an inch and he'll be a ruler.

❖❖❖❖

God grades on the Cross, not the curve.

❖❖❖❖

God loves everyone, but probably prefers fruits of the Spirit over religious nuts.

❖❖❖❖

If God is just your co-pilot, swap seats!

This Lesson in Your Life

In light of John the Baptizer's mission to prepare the way for Christ, you might discuss in your class what the "ministry of preparation" is about. One way to make this point is to compare the guy who runs the brush-hog with the fellow who builds the house. The house can't be built until the land has been cleared. Yet, some persons might not find clearing that land a "fulfilling task." John the Baptizer was a true servant. He pointed not to himself, but to his Master.

John and Jesus were cousins whose lives and ministries were intertwined and overlapped. At Caeserea Philippi, one of the answers that Jesus heard about Himself was that people were saying He was John the Baptizer. So, people who saw and heard both of these men affirmed their closeness in ministry. Still, given our penchant for admiring heroes, we have a hard time with John's servant position.

Their ministries converged at Jesus' baptism. The obvious question to ask is, "If Jesus was sinless, why did he need John's baptism for the forgiveness of sins?" It really is a loaded question. The answer is easier than one might expect. Jesus was identifying with John's ministry. By submitting to John's baptism, He was showing everyone that John was doing God's work. Jesus was affirming the prophetic role John was playing in the Messianic ministry. Jesus was identifying with the people who were coming to John. He was acting out his love and identification of them.

As a minister, when I am present for a youth function, I am saying that the youth are important to the church. You do the same thing when you go to a Chamber of Commerce banquet or when you attend a political rally. Jesus was letting those people know He valued them.

Jesus was also dedicating himself to His ministry. In a way, this baptism was his ordination too. He was set aside from that moment for what He would be doing for the next three years.

We are all called into the ministry by virtue of our baptism. God has claimed us and sealed us to work for him. It may be a ministry like John's—you might be a "behind the scenes" person who does the things that are not noticed.

In teaching this very class you may be preparing someone to hear the call of God into the ordained ministry. You might be preparing the way for the next Billy Graham. You might not be in the spotlight, but a life might be transformed because of your quiet, faithful, diligent work.

John the Baptizer is remembered for his outlandish garb and his strange diet. He would better be remembered as the one who made way for Him who is "the Way, the Truth and the Life"—Jesus Christ, our Lord.

GETTING THE FACTS STRAIGHT

1. **Where did John first appear "proclaiming a baptism of repentance for the forgiveness of sins?"**

He first appeared in the wilderness. We have no further detail about where this wilderness was.

2. **Who were the people who were coming to hear John and for baptism?**

People came "from the whole Judean countryside and all the people of Jerusalem."

3. **What was different about John's appearance and his diet?**

John wore camel cloth with a leather belt. He ate locusts and wild honey.

4. **What was John's relationship to the coming Messiah?**

John said that he was not worthy to stoop over and untie the thong of Jesus' sandals.

5. **What promise did John make about the coming Messiah?**

While John baptized with water, the coming Messiah would baptize with the Holy Spirit.

6. **What happened at the baptism of Jesus?**

The heavens split apart and the Spirit descended on Jesus like a dove. A voice came from heaven saying, "This is my Son, the Beloved, with whom I am well pleased" (Matt. 3: 17).

7. **When John saw the religious elite, the Pharisees and Sadducees, coming for baptism, what did he say to them?**

John said, "You brood of vipers! Who warned you to flee from the wrath to come?"

8. **What assumption were the religious elite making about their relationship to God, and how did John counter that assumption?**

The Pharisees and the Sadducees thought that being related to Abraham won them credit with God. John said that God could make stones into children of Abraham.

9. **How did Jesus describe the ministry of John the Baptizer?**

Jesus told the crowds that John was a prophet, and that no man born of woman was greater than John.

10. **To what other Old Testament character did Jesus compare John the Baptizer?**

Jesus said that John was in the line of great Old Testament prophets, and the people could say that John was the "Elijah to come."

179

In typical fashion, when George Allen moved to Washington, D.C., as head coach of the Washington Redskins football team, he promised the the moon. He said he would develop the Redskins into a championship football team. He promised them a trip to the Super Bowl by the second season.

The team, that first year, had a brilliant preseason. Then, early in the regular season, they won several amazing victories. Then they began to lose. And lose. And lose. The blame fell, at least in part, on a quarterback named Sonny Jurgenson. Yet he was, in my opinion, one of the greatest ever to play the game. He was great because of a personality that exuded personal security.

One day after another defeat, Jurgenson was getting ready to take a shower and go home. A sportswriter leaned over to him in the locker room and said, "Say, Sonny, be honest now. Don't all these off-the-wall remarks we write and all this public flack disturb you? Doesn't it make you want to quit when people throw things at you from the stands and when you get those hate letters?"

Sonny Jurgenson leaned back, gave a big toothless grin, and sighed, "No, not really. I don't want to quit. I've been in this game long enough to know that every quarterback, every week of the season, spends his time either in the penthouse or the outhouse."

Leaders are open to criticism and second-guessing by those they are attempting to lead. The irony is that the ones making the criticisms have no desire to lead themselves. They can't decide if they want to follow, either. To the critics who stand on the sideline and second-guess the quarterback, without ever being in the game, we say "Lead, follow, or get out of the way."

While we are not supposed to take that attitude in the Church, we all know the havoc that mere critics reap in the life of the Church. These are people whose only talent is to filibuster. If they can talk long enough and critically enough, they can ruin the vision of the people.

John and Jesus were two powerful leaders who understood their roles in history. John knew that he was to prepare the way for Jesus. He knew that the Lord was God. John was not. His whole ministry was pointing the people to One who would come after him, who was greater than he was. Our ministry today is to point another generation to faith in Jesus Christ. Even as they receive the Lord, they also receive the commissioning to be leaders.

Is it time in your faith community to step aside and let another generation lead? Is it time to pray for the younger leaders of the church? Is it time to hear their concerns and try things their way? A younger generation is hungry to hear the gospel, and once heard, to make that message relevant to their generation. There is a new way of "doing church" and these younger people are excited about it. Have you given them a chance to express their enthusiasm?

We can, in these days, lead, follow, or get out of the way!

Lesson 6

The Rich Man's Wrong Priorities

Mark 10:17-27

And when he was gone forth into the way, there came one running, and kneeled to him, and asked him, Good Master, what shall I do that I may inherit eternal life?

18 And Jesus said unto him, Why callest thou me good? there is none good but one, that is, God.

19 Thou knowest the commandments, Do not commit adultery, Do not kill, Do not steal, Do not bear false witness, Defraud not, Honour thy father and mother.

20 And he answered and said unto him, Master, all these have I observed from my youth.

21 Then Jesus beholding him loved him, and said unto him, One thing thou lackest: go thy way, sell whatsoever thou hast, and give to the poor, and thou shalt have treasure in heaven: and come, take up the cross, and follow me.

22 And he was sad at that saying, and went away grieved: for he had great possessions.

23 And Jesus looked round about, and saith unto his disciples, How hardly shall they that have riches enter into the kingdom of God!

24 And the disciples were astonished at his words. But Jesus answereth again, and saith unto them, Children, how hard is it for them that trust in riches to enter into the kingdom of God!

25 It is easier for a camel to go through the eye of a needle, than for a rich man to enter into the kingdom of God.

26 And they were astonished out of measure, saying among themselves, Who then can be saved?

27 And Jesus looking upon them saith, With men it is impossible, but not with God: for with God all things are possible.

Jan. 5

Memory Selection
Mark 10:21

Background Scripture
Mark 10:17-27

Devotional Reading
1 Timothy 6:6-19

In their search for feeling "right with God," some people travel to far-away lands and sit for months in a monastery at the feet of a guru, only to return with the nagging question, *Is that all there is?* Some enter the ministry expecting "holy work" to satisfy their hunger to experience closeness to the Divine, but are disillusioned. A wealthy person may seek peace of mind by contributing large sums of money to a godly cause, yet still feel that she has "not done enough" to win peace with God.

This lesson focuses on Jesus' remarkable ability to look into a person's heart and identify why feeling close to God is so elusive. In this case, the obstacle is material wealth. Yet the story calls each of us to identify in our own hearts any barrier to discovering that Christ Himself is both the center and the goal of faith.

☙◌☙

Boiled down to a single essential, what enables you to feel secure in your faith, or that you are "on target" in your search for God? Responses might include general answers such as *obedience . . .or regular prayer . . . doing good to others . . . practicing the Golden Rule . . . participating in worship.*

In today's lesson, a man asks Jesus a similar question: "What shall I do that I may inherit eternal life?" We might have responded that nothing we can "do" wins salvation, but that "Jesus did it all." However, this man lived under the Law of Moses; and Jesus tells him too "keep the law." Sadly, this answer wasn't enough for the man; and many today who live under grace, not Law, can identify with his feeling that God was still distant. Only by identifying with the man's question can we arrive at a meaningful answer for ourselves.

Teaching Outline	Daily Bible Readings	
I. Crucial Question—17	Mon.	Sorrowful Rich Man Mark 10:17-22

II. Curious Answer—18-19
  A. Who is 'good'?, 18
  B. The Law's core, 19
	Tue.	Difficulty for the Rich
		Mark 10:23-31

	Wed.	Attempt to Buy Power Acts 8:14-24

III. Critical Barrier—20-22
  A. Obedient but empty heart, 20
  B. Full bank account, 21-22
	Thu.	'I'll Follow, but . . . .'
		Luke 9:57-62

	Fri.	'You Are Lukewarm' Revelation 3:14-20

IV. Christ's Summary—23-27
  A. Human impossibility, 23-25
  B. Christ's possibility, 26-27
	Sat.	What Tomorrow Brings
		James 4:13-17

	Sun.	Saving and Losing Life Matthew 16:24-28

Verse by Verse

I. Crucial Question—17

17 And when he was gone forth into the way, there came one run-ning, and kneeled to him, and asked him, Good Master, what shall I do that I may inherit eternal life?

This story of the dissatisfied Jew seeking the key to eternal life is also recounted in Matthew, who adds that he is a young man (19:20), and in Luke, who tells us that he is a ruler (18:18). It is from verse 23, here, that the story has received the common title, "The Rich Young Ruler."

We can also tell that he is an earnest man, since he both runs to and kneels before Jesus. This does not necessarily mean that the man is actually worshiping Jesus, since the word for "kneel" was often used for the kind of bow one would give to a respected teacher. Also, the KJV's "Master" means only "teacher," as in the NIV. The whole scene portrays a man greeting a person he honors as a good man and an authoritative teacher. Perhaps the man had followed Jesus long enough to perceive this much, before approaching Him personally; but his greeting stops short of identifying Jesus as "good" in the sense that God is the epitome of divine goodness.

"Eternal" or "everlasting life" is mentioned in the Old Testament only once (Dan. 12:2). It is therefore likely that the young ruler has heard Jesus speak of it, especially in terms like that in John 3:36, where it is described not just in future terms of "living forever" but of a divine quality of life that believers have in the present. Despite his earnest endeavors to keep the law (see vs. 20), the man has not experienced anything like the divine quality of life of which he had heard Jesus speak.

II. Curious Answer—18-19
A. Who is 'good'?, 18

18 And Jesus said unto him, Why callest thou me good? there is none good but one, that is, God.

Jesus' surprising response may indicate that He perceives that while the seeker accepts that Jesus is a good person, he does not yet identify Him with God, the Ultimate Good. The difference is summed up in Christ's statement, "I and my Father are one" (John 10:30). Thus His answer bluntly confronts the man with the question, "Whom say ye that I am?" (Matt. 16:15). Unless the man is prepared to move from his perception of Jesus as merely a good man to the belief that He is one with God, he will not be able to internalize any answer Jesus might give to his question; for Jesus Himself is the "eternal life" the man claims to seek.

B. The Law's core, 19

19 Thou knowest the command-ments, Do not commit adultery, Do

not kill, Do not steal, Do not bear false witness, Defraud not, Honour thy father and mother.

Curiously, Jesus draws the man's attention to only the part of the Ten Commandments that deal with persons' treatment of each other, rather than to the commands to love God and have "no other gods before me." Perhaps this is because a rich person is in a special position to respond to other people and their needs, and Jesus knows the man has difficulty in this area. (For loving God and neighbor as the core of the Law, see Matt. 7:12; 22:40.)

We are also drawn to the fact that even keeping those parts of the Law that deal with ministering to the needs of others does not in itself "earn" salvation; and this principle of salvation by grace must also be in Jesus' mind. It is as though He says to the young man, "If you have such difficulty loving people, and the part of the Law that calls you to share your wealth, how can you hope to love God and attain 'eternal life' with Him?"

III. Critical Barrier—20-22
A. Obedient but empty heart, 20

20 And he answered and said unto him, Master, all these have I observed from my youth.

One purpose of the Law is to confront us with the impossibility of keeping it perfectly, thus leading us to throw ourselves on the mercy of the Law-giver (see Rom. 5:13; 7:7). Although the young man has been exemplary in keeping the external rules of the Law, he had not gone far enough in his understanding of the Law's purpose to despair at ever

doing enough for others. Failing to understand his need to throw Himself on the mercy of God and experience His grace, it is no wonder he had not found a sense of God's gracious acceptance.

B. Full bank account, 21-22

21 Then Jesus beholding him loved him, and said unto him, One thing thou lackest: go thy way, sell whatsoever thou hast, and give to the poor, and thou shalt have treasure in heaven: and come, take up the cross, and follow me.

22 And he was sad at that saying, and went away grieved: for he had great possessions.

Despite the man's lack of faith in Him as the divine Son of God, Jesus sees in him something sincere and lovable. The very fact that he bothered to keep the Law's decrees from his youth was admirable, and his pursuit of eternal life indicated an earnestness and willingness to go beyond the external demands of the Law. Seeing all this, Jesus takes the time to share with the man what His divine insight has revealed.

On the surface, Jesus' recommendation that the man sell all his goods and give the proceeds to the poor would seem to indicate that his problem is of a financial nature—not too little money but too much. Actually the love of material treasure is only a symptom of the underlying issue: the man had a case of joyless religion because he was allowing something other than God to pretend to be the center of his faith. The fact that he went away grieved indicates that he simply could not see his way clear to accept Jesus' counsel.

IV. Christ's Summary—23-27
A. Human impossibility, 23-25

23 And Jesus looked round about, and saith unto his disciples, How hardly shall they that have riches enter into the kingdom of God!

24 And the disciples were astonished at his words. But Jesus answereth again, and saith unto them, Children, how hard is it for them that trust in riches to enter into the kingdom of God!

25 It is easier for a camel to go through the eye of a needle, than for a rich man to enter into the kingdom of God.

The issue Jesus has just dealt with is so important that he summons His disciples to gather round Him to listen to Him reflect on what had occurred. Why are they shocked at His conclusion that riches make it hard for a person to enter the Kingdom? Because they were victims of "prosperity theology," the view heard even in modern times that God will materially bless anyone as devoted as the rich man seemed to be.

After all, the Covenant God had made with Abraham promised material reward, including heirs, good crops, large flocks and herds, and the land of Canaan. As a general rule, such blessings did follow the God's people, until they forsook the worship of Yahweh and the just treatment of others. Too often, however, they turned this positive promise into an automatic negative, considering riches an inevitable sign that a person was beloved of God, and poverty or sickness or a barren womb as an indication of sin. (Note the question in John 9:2: "Who sinned, this man or his parents, that he was born blind?" [NIV].)

The fact is, Jesus says, riches are not a sign of God's favor, but can make the Kingdom as hard to enter as it would be to drive a camel through the eye of a needle. Jesus puts together the largest animal well-known in Palestine together with the smallest slit for this comparison. (A commentator during the Middle Ages once suggested that the "eye of a needle" was actually the name of a small gate, too low for a camel to enter, in the wall of Jerusalem; but there is no other evidence for this, or for our not taking Jesus' statement literally.)

B. Christ's possibility, 26-27

26 And they were astonished out of measure, saying among themselves, Who then can be saved?

27 And Jesus looking upon them saith, With men it is impossible, but not with God: for with God all things are possible.

The disciples are as puzzled here as they were when Jesus taught that God sends material blessings such as rain on both the just and the unjust (Matt. 5:45) If the wealthy do not deserve such blessings, along with salvation, how can anyone be saved? This is the question to which Jesus has lead the rich young ruler. No one can be saved, rich or poor, apart from God's grace, which is more often bestowed as an inner blessing than as material gain; and no one can be saved who allows wealth or any other concern to have higher priority than loving and obeying God.

Evangelistic Emphasis

Life's ultimate question is found in our lesson for today: "Good Teacher, what must I do to inherit eternal life?" Our culture judges us on what we "do." When you are in a room where introductions are going on, take note. The name of the person will be given, and what they "do" for a living usually gets added. This is Mike Johns. He is an attorney. This is Mary Smith. She is a C.P.A. We even ask our children, as a query of interest, "What are you going to do when you grow up?"

Jesus answered the man first in terms of the right things to do. The right actions were keeping the commandments and obeying the law.

When the rich man told Jesus he had kept the Law, Jesus looked into his heart and told him one more thing to do. Now we get all bent out of shape about selling everything and giving it to the poor. Those words are fodder for debate in any culture; so much so, we never get to what Jesus told the man to do after selling everything.

Ultimately the Good News is that our relationship to God through Christ is not determined on what we "do." Our relationship is just that, a state of being in which we are properly related to the Lord. As a part of that proper relationship to the Lord certain actions are inevitable. We will live a moral life because we are rightly related. We will do justice, love kindness and walk humbly with our God, because He is giving us the power to do those things.

The Good News is that it is being *and* doing that count!

৪ﾂ৫

Memory Selection

Then Jesus beholding him loved him, and said unto him, One thing thou lackest: go thy way, sell whatsoever thou hast, and give to the poor, and thou shalt have treasure in heaven: and come, take up the cross, and follow me.—*Mark 10:21*

As a practical matter, you can't live without your "god." The rich man's god was the economic security his possessions brought. He trusted in his fortune both as a his ultimate protection. He wanted eternal life more as an adjunct to his possessions than a desire of his heart. Although very moral, the man lacked *faith*.

Look deeply into your soul and ask this question: *What are the people and things I can't live without?* When you have answered that question for yourself, then you have discovered your true god. The answers can sometimes be less than comforting, especially when Christians make Jesus third or fourth on their list of things they can't live without.

Jesus looks into our souls each day and confronts us in many ways about making gods with our own hands. What is He calling you to give up in order to follow Him faithfully?

Weekday Problems

Sara Thibodeaux was poor as a church mouse. However, because everyone that Sara knew was poor, poverty didn't bother her. It was just a fact of life for her.

Sara became a dubious celebrity on a January day when she purchased a lottery ticket. Although poor, a lottery ticket was one luxury that she felt she could indulge. She never seemed to miss the dollar each week, and she at least had something to look forward to. On Saturday night, Sara and her family would gather around the small television set and listen as the numbers of the lottery were read out. This Saturday night, Sara looked at the television and her lottery ticket in total disbelief. She had won! She had won more money than she dreamed was possible to have!

Sara's life changed. She bought the things she had missed in life. She bought a big house and a big car. She took a trip, and actually flew to her destination. She suddenly became a famous resident of her small town.

Sara had always been a good person, and attending church was something she customarily did. She didn't go as much as she should have, but she went.

After winning the lottery, Sara was in church for the first time in a long time. The minister preached about "The Rich Young Ruler and Jesus."

Sara was not happy to hear what the minister, and Jesus, said.

*How does our economic status affect how we hear these words of Jesus?

Out of the Mouths of Babes

Excerpts from children's letters to their minister:

I know that God loves everybody, but He never met my sister. Yours sincerely, Arnold. (Age 9, Nashville)

✦✦✦✦

Please say in your sermon that Peter Peterson has been a good boy all week. Sincerely, Peter Peterson. (Age 9, Phoenix)

✦✦✦✦

I would like to go to heaven some day because I know my brother won't be there. Love, Stephen. (Age 8, Chicago)

✦✦✦✦

I think a lot more people would come to your church if you moved it to Disneyland. Loreen. (Age 9, Tacoma)

✦✦✦✦

Please say a prayer for our Little League team. We need God's help or a new pitcher. Thank you, Alexander. (Age 10, Raleigh)

This Lesson in Your Life

Let's talk about your money!

If you think you can teach this lesson without involving money in the conversation, you are sadly mistaken. You might start out the lesson talking about Christmas bills. They should begin rolling in right about this time from last year's Christmas shopping. Isn't it interesting that we celebrate One who was born in a stable with such extravagant gift-giving that we pay for it the rest of the year? Something is amiss in our living. We have missed the point of Christmas, and we will pay for our "mistakes" for many months to come. So a discussion of money and possessions might strike a nerve at this time of the year. Christmas is over, but is it paid for? All those "things" we thought were so important both to give and receive, how do we look at them two weeks later?

Of course we don't like to hear that Jesus talked more about money and possessions than he did prayer or any other subject. There must be some kind of spiritual connection between how we use or abuse money and Jesus Christ. The broad concept is called *stewardship*. Stewardship is how we should look at all of life. Our lives, and the things in our lives, are held in trust. Everything around us belongs to God. He only allows us to use the things of this earth while we are here. How are you caring for the things around you? Are you being a good steward, or is there a problem with thinking that the things God has lent you actually belong to you? Do you practice stewardship over them, or are you enslaved to them?

The "rich young ruler," as he is popularly called, was blinded to his spiritual weaknesses by the security his "things" brought him. He was certain that anything that could happen in life could be faced because he had the financial resources necessary to handle any eventuality. He was trusting in his bank account to get him through tomorrow.

Although a righteous man, he lacked one thing. He lacked a basic trust in God's goodness to take care of him. He would rather trust in his own abilities to overcome any problem. Imagine his shock when Jesus showed him that his spiritual problem was money! It was a double shock because in that day having money and possession were seen as the blessings of God. Perhaps that same kind of thinking has evolved in our church today.

The other thing that involves money and this lesson is a discussion of poverty and wealth. Jesus never condemned wealth. He condemned those persons who were trusting in their wealth, or who used that position to hurt others. Likewise, Jesus never made poverty a role model for His people. The whole discussion of this story is tempered by how we view and use our money. Before leading a class in this discussion the teacher will have to look at his own use of money and things. We have to be very careful to consider this passage in the light of our own our lifestyles.

1. As Mark recorded the story of the Rich Young Ruler, what event occurred immediately preceding this encounter with Jesus?

Jesus blessing the children immediately preceded the story of the Rich Young Ruler.

2. Jesus had begun to move from one place to another. As this happened, a man approached with a question. What was the question?

The man approached Jesus and asked him, "Good Teacher, what must I do to inherit eternal life."

3. What was the first response that Jesus made to this man's request?

Jesus said, "Why do you call me good? No one is good but God alone."

4. Jesus proceeded with a statement of what would be necessary for eternal life. What is important for eternal life?

Jesus said that keeping the commandments were steps in finding eternal life.

5. How did this man respond to Jesus' statement about keeping the commandments, ?

He told the Lord that he had kept all of the commandments since he was a young man.

6. How did Jesus respond to this man's claim that he had kept the commandments since he was a young man?

Jesus did not contradict the man's claim, but looked at him and "loved him."

7. What one thing did Jesus say the man lacked in order to inherit eternal life?

The man was told to go and sell all that he owned and give the money to the poor, and then he would have treasures in heaven.

8. How did the man respond to the directive to "go and sell all you have and give the money to the poor?"

This man went away grieving because he had many possessions.

9. As the crowd watched this encounter, what did Jesus say to them as this rich man walked away?

Jesus told the crowd that it would be very difficult for the rich to enter the kingdom of God.

10. Why do you think the statement that Jesus made concerning wealth and entering the kingdom perplexed the disciples?

Like most contemporaries of Jesus, the disciples saw wealth as a sign that God had blessed the person who was wealthy.

Have you ever heard of the "Utopian Complex"? It's a term used by psychologists and psychiatrists to describe people who go through life looking for the perfect situation, waiting for the perfect moment to do what they ought to do and be what they ought to be. Meanwhile, life passes them by and they end up feeling frustrated and betrayed and empty and miserable.

The syndrome is illustrated by a story of an Indian princess. One morning, in the early days of this country, a Native American princess visited a neighboring tribe which was known far and wise for its magnificent cornfields. She asked if she might select one ear of corn from their fields to take home to provide seed corn for her own tribe's fields next year.

Graciously her request was granted—on one condition. She would have to make her selection as she walked down a row. That is, she could not turn back and pick an ear of corn she had already passed. So, off she went, walking slowly down each row looking for the perfect ear of corn. She walked and looked and studied and pondered; but she could not bring herself to pick an ear or corn for fear that a better one might be just a few more feet down the row.

Suddenly what she had done hit her with a sickening thud: she had blown her opportunity! She had walked down the entire length of each row without picking a single ear. Now there was no turning back. Sadly she walked out of the field empty-handed because she could not bring herself to make a choice.

Similarly, too many of us wait for perfection before we will act. We come to the end of our days and realize too late that there are no perfect situations, no perfect marriages, no perfect people, no perfect churches.

The man who met Jesus was looking for the perfect answer to his question. He was hoping to obtain information that would allow him to add to the things he had, and thus "achieve" eternal life. He had done everything he had ever been told in order to gain "perfection." He hoped that as he became "perfect" he would acquire eternal life—which to him was just a commodity that could be bought, sold, or bargained. When Jesus heard the man's affirmation that he had kept all the commandments, He loved him. This is one of the few times where Jesus did not point out any overt sin in this person's life.

Yet, Jesus indicated to the man that to have the "perfect life" he must give up this quest of having the perfect answers to his questions, as well as giving up all of his possessions. The man went away sorrowful, because he was very wealthy. He was looking for perfection in the things that he could add to his collection of things; but Jesus told him that perfection is not possible in *things*. Eternal life is found only in loving God.

Are you waiting for something to change, or for something to be perfect before you act? How many excuses do you have for not following Jesus?

Today is the perfect time to follow Him.

Lesson 7

Mary and Martha: Friends of Jesus

Luke 10:38-42; John 11:20-27, 30-32

Now it came to pass, as they went, that he entered into a certain village: and a certain woman named Martha received him into her house.

39 And she had a sister called Mary, which also sat at Jesus' feet, and heard his word.

40 But Martha was cumbered about much serving, and came to him, and said, Lord, dost thou not care that my sister hath left me to serve alone? bid her therefore that she help me.

41 And Jesus answered and said unto her, Martha, Martha, thou art careful and troubled about many things:

42 But one thing is needful: and Mary hath chosen that good part, which shall not be taken away from her.

John 11

20 Then Martha, as soon as she heard that Jesus was coming, went and met him: but Mary sat still in the house.

21 Then said Martha unto Jesus, Lord, if thou hadst been here, my brother had not died.

22 But I know, that even now, whatsoever thou wilt ask of God, God will give it thee.

23 Jesus saith unto her, Thy brother shall rise again.

24 Martha saith unto him, I know that he shall rise again in the resurrection at the last day.

25 Jesus said unto her, I am the resurrection, and the life: he that believeth in me, though he were dead, yet shall he live:

26 And whosoever liveth and believeth in me shall never die. Believest thou this?

27 She saith unto him, Yea, Lord: I believe that thou art the Christ, the Son of God, which should come into the world.

30 Now Jesus was not yet come into the town, but was in that place where Martha met him.

31 The Jews then which were with her in the house, and comforted her, when they saw Mary, that she rose up hastily and went out, followed her, saying, She goeth unto the grave to weep there.

32 Then when Mary was come where Jesus was, and saw him, she fell down at his feet, saying unto him, Lord, if thou hadst been here, my brother had not died.

Jan. 12

Memory Selection
Luke 10:41-42

Background Scripture
Luke 10:38-42; John 11:20-32

Devotional Reading
John 15:12-17

This lesson on Jesus' interaction with friends reminds us that the Gospels are not just interested in "doctrine." They also portray Jesus in ordinary life situations, interacting with people as they face everyday events. Here we become better acquainted with the kind of people Jesus chose as friends, and how we can welcome Him as a friend in our own lives.

This very human touch is remarkably characteristic of the Gospel accounts of Jesus' life. They are not just theological treatises but vignettes of births and deaths, weddings and family dinners, selfish quarrels and companionship, faith and doubt, the certainty of God's love, brushes with the law and speculation about the future. Lessons like this make it easy to welcome Jesus into the everyday events of our own lives, too.

ഇറ

How do we sometimes see the Lord as we interact with our own friends? Ask group members how friends have been instrumental in enabling them to better appreciate the fact that Christ is alive and well in the lives of real people.

Have any group members had a friend who stood up for them when others criticized them? Has a friend ever helped them out of a jam? Do they know stories about, or perhaps have they experienced, an incident in which a life was saved by a friend? What is it like to have a friend in whom you can confide, with full confidence that what you have to say won't be repeated? Has anyone had friends so close that he could even confront them with an unpleasant truth they needed to hear? What would it be like to have Jesus as a friend, as Mary, Martha, and Lazarus do in this story?

Teaching Outline	*Daily Bible Readings*
I. Dining with Friends—Luke 10:38-42	Mon. Jesus Visits His Friends Luke 10:38-42
A. Mary at Jesus' Feet, 38-39	Tue. A Message to Jesus John 11:1-6
B. Martha's complaint, 40	
C. Jesus' response, 41-42	Wed. The Death of Lazarus John 11:7-16
II. Death of a Friend—John 11:20-27, 30-32	Thu. 'If You Had Been Here!' John 11:17-27
A. Jesus' living presence, 20-27	Fri. Jesus Weeps John 11:28-37
1. Two responses to death, 20	
2. 'Lord, I Believe,' 21-22	Sat. 'Lazarus, Come Forth!' John 11:38-44
3. 'Help my unbelief,' 23-27	Sun. Mary Anoints Jesus John 12:1-8
B. Abiding faith, 30-32	

Verse by Verse

I. Dining with Friends–Luke 10:38-42

A. Mary at Jesus' Feet, 38-39

38 Now it came to pass, as they went, that he entered into a certain village: and a certain woman named Martha received him into her house.

39 And she had a sister called Mary, which also sat at Jesus' feet, and heard his word.

Jesus has completed His work in Galilee and left His home country for Jerusalem (Luke 9:51). Together with John 11:1, this enables us to identify the village where Mary and Martha lived as Bethany, which was only about two miles from Jerusalem. As an itinerant preacher, Jesus often accepted the hospitality of friends. These particular friends were especially close to Him, as evidenced by the sisters' description of Lazarus as "he whom thou lovest" (John 11:3).

Since it was "her house," Martha assumes responsibility for preparing the meal for their friend. Yet it is generally assumed that the two sisters, who were perhaps widows, and their brother all lived there.

This Mary, we are told explicitly, also in John's Gospel, was the Mary who anointed Jesus' feet with precious oil at a Passover feast not long before His death (John 11:2; 12:3). Since there were several "Marys" connected with

Jesus' ministry (in addition to His mother), John was apparently concerned that this Mary not be confused with the Mary who was "a sinner" and also anointed Jesus, at an earlier meal in the house of Simon the Pharisee (Luke 7:37-38).

Note that Jesus is not a "professional" who performs only at public events; even at the house of His friends, He is willing to share His message. For a woman to sit at the feet of a teacher such as Jesus was a small departure from the Jewish custom of not including women in Scripture studies, although the informality of the home setting would not have made Mary a "radical."

B. Martha's complaint, 40

40 But Martha was cumbered about much serving, and came to him, and said, Lord, dost thou not care that my sister hath left me to serve alone? bid her therefore that she help me.

Tending to meal preparation as a good Jewish homemaker was taught to do, Martha is "distracted" (NIV) from listening to Jesus. The word for "cumbered" (KJV) means literally to be "dragged around." In other words, Martha was allowing the task to "do a job" on her instead of staying on top of the job; so it isn't surprising that she perceives Mary to be "doing

193

nothing." Her request that Jesus tell Mary to help with the meal preparation is a hint that He is more than a friend to them; they also respect His role as an authoritative Teacher.

C. Jesus' response, 41-42

41 And Jesus answered and said unto her, Martha, Martha, thou art careful and troubled about many things:

42 But one thing is needful: and Mary hath chosen that good part, which shall not be taken away from her.

Saying Martha's name twice indicates a degree of tenderness, as though Jesus is somewhat sympathetic toward her plight. After all, she is devoting herself to serving Him and the others. His defense of Mary is not that her choosing to sit at His feet indicates her superior piety, but that amid the many chores that hosts might find to be "encumbered" about, Martha would do well to reexamine her priorities. After all, Jesus could not have stopped by very often; and Mary, defying custom, has been able to put it into proper perspective.

The "one thing" that is essential is that we learn all we can about Jesus. Eating is also important, but Jesus is defending the priority of spiritual food over physical. He taught the same lesson when he seemed to be not very hungry as His disciples urged him to eat, indicating that in ministering the Word He has been dining on spiritual food (John 4:31ff.).

II. Death of a Friend—John 11:20-27, 30-32

A. Jesus' living presence, 20-27

1. Two responses to death, 20

20 Then Martha, as soon as she heard that Jesus was coming, went and met him: but Mary sat still in the house.

The scene shifts now to another more sober event in the life of Jesus' friends, Mary, Martha, and Lazarus. John is the only Gospel writer who records this incident. Preceding verses have told us that Lazarus was sick, and that his sisters sent word to Jesus, perhaps hoping that He would come and heal their brother. Jesus, however, has plans to perform an even greater miracle, or "sign," which is John's favorite word to describe wonders Jesus did that point to the glory that awaits believers at the consummation of the Kingdom.

Verse 20 again finds Martha in an active mode and her sister Mary "sitting." Although the two may have actually had personalities that differed in this way, it would have been common to find any relative sitting and grieving over the death of a family member. We are not told why Martha cannot sit still and wait for Jesus' arrival. Perhaps the sisters simply have different ways of handling grief, as is true to this day. Some people deal with sorrow by staying in motion, while others need to withdraw for a time.

2. 'Lord, I Believe,' 21-22

21 Then said Martha unto Jesus, Lord, if thou hadst been here, my brother had not died.

22 But I know, that even now, whatsoever thou wilt ask of God, God will give it thee.

At first reading, Martha may sound as though she is complaining that

Jesus did not come sooner. However, she seems to express the hope in verse 22 that Jesus might yet perform the miracle he in fact will do. At any rate, it is an expression of faith, leading to the probability that in verse 21 she is only expressing her sorrow, and in another way, her faith that Jesus' presence would have made a difference.

3. 'Help my unbelief,' 23-27

23 Jesus saith unto her, Thy brother shall rise again.

24 Martha saith unto him, I know that he shall rise again in the resurrection at the last day.

25 Jesus said unto her, I am the resurrection, and the life: he that believeth in me, though he were dead, yet shall he live:

26 And whosoever liveth and believeth in me shall never die. Believest thou this?

27 She saith unto him, Yea, Lord: I believe that thou art the Christ, the Son of God, which should come into the world.

Now Jesus seems to be testing the depth of the faith Martha has expressed. In verse 23 He is probably making a double reference to the miracle of raising Lazarus He is about to perform, and to the eventual resurrection of the dead. Martha's response in verse 24 indicates that she understands Jesus to be referring to the latter, which was the teaching of the Old Testament (although the Sadducees denied it [Mark 12:18]).

In verses 25-26, Jesus wants to lead Martha to a deeper level of faith, one that confesses that wherever Jesus is, there also are the full benefits

of the Kingdom He inaugurated, including the resurrection. Confessing that Jesus is the resurrection is what would lead the apostle Peter to write later that Christians who are being persecuted for their faith can, in the midst of suffering, experience the presence of Christ, and thus "resurrection joy," before the Last Days and the actual resurrection (see 1 Pet. 1:6-7). Martha's final outburst seems to have a note of desperation in it, as though she hopes that confessing her faith that Jesus is the Christ (lit. "the Anointed," or the Messiah) will suffice for whatever deeper and only dimly perceived depths of faith to which Jesus is drawing her.

B. Abiding faith, 30-32

30 Now Jesus was not yet come into the town, but was in that place where Martha met him.

31 The Jews then which were with her in the house, and comforted her, when they saw Mary, that she rose up hastily and went out, followed her, saying, She goeth unto the grave to weep there.

32 Then when Mary was come where Jesus was, and saw him, she fell down at his feet, saying unto him, Lord, if thou hadst been here, my brother had not died.

Sympathizing friends had gathered to sit with Lazarus' grieving relatives. The identity of verse 32 with Martha's statement in verse 21 shows how much alike the sisters were, despite their differences. Mary's going to the tomb to weep sets the scene for "the rest of the story," when Jesus triumphantly raises her brother from the dead.

Evangelistic Emphasis

Who is your best friend? Why is that person your best friend? You might want to make a list of best friends.

The definition of a "best friend" is modified throughout life. As children, a best friend is often the child with the neatest toys. Maybe, a best friend is that person who lives next door and is a constant companion. As teenagers, the first best friend tends to be the one who gets his driver's license and has a car. Then a best friend can become a member of the opposite sex.

As adults, our criterion for choosing a best friend is often more childish than when we were children. Our best friend might be that person who can help us climb the corporate or social ladder. A best friend might have a boat or a cabin or a country club membership that we can "use."

Maturing in the faith means we choose best friends who are true soul mates. A best friend listens openly and honestly. They withhold advice or comment until that is sought. They understand our feelings, our phobias, and our failings. A best friend is there to lift us up when we have fallen. He becomes a best friend not because of what he can give to us, but because of what he allows us to give and share with him.

In the text for this lesson, we learn that Jesus was a good friend to Mary, Martha, and Lazarus. That same Friend can become our "best friend" as well.

ഐ)ൽ

Memory Selection

And Jesus answered and said unto her, Martha, Martha, thou art careful and troubled about many things: But one thing is needful: and Mary hath chosen that good part, which shall not be taken away from her.—*Luke 10: 41-42*

You should copy Luke 10: 41-42 and place it in a conspicuous place in your home. These words might help you avoid a costly trip to the doctor, or a premature trip to the funeral home.

Jesus was speaking to a hurried and harried woman, who had "had enough." Mary was sitting at the feet of Jesus listening to His words, while Martha was in the kitchen "working her fingers to the bone." Martha didn't feel that the situation was equitable. She complained to Jesus and He gently rebuked her.

Even in the church we can have our priorities so out of whack that we lose our focus. What is important is "sitting at the feet of Jesus," whether or not the tablecloths are clean and match the silverware for the church supper.

Jesus reminds us, though His words to Martha, to be less worried with hurry and more concerned about matters of the soul. Honor Jesus by erasing some of those "non-vital" meetings from your schedule.

196

Weekday Problems

Tamara usually worked herself into such a stew about church suppers that the church almost stopped having them. The preacher thought they were important to the spiritual well being of the congregation. Tamara only saw trouble.

In March, after the church remodeled the kitchen and fellowship hall, the preacher invited all the town dignitaries to a service of dedication for the remodeled facility. Tamara dutifully agreed to head up preparation for all of the festivities. Although she made it known to everyone who would listen that she was not happy doing all of that "work."

That entire small town turned out for the pot-luck supper. They all bragged on the beauty of the building, the good food and the fine way table settings. Everyone was bragging about everything—everyone except Tamara.

The next morning she came in the preacher's office in tears. She had worked all week making sure that everything was perfect. She rehearsed for the preacher the near tragedy that occurred when someone left the biscuits unattended. She complained about pouring tea, lack of ice, and the storage for the dishes being too high in the new cabinets.

The preacher listened compassionately and said, "Tamara I think you missed the point of all of this."

*In what ways had Tamara missed the point of what happened at the church that night?

Marriage Mayhem

Never go to bed mad. Stay up and fight.—*Phyllis Diller*

I bought my wife a new car. She called and said that there was water in the carburetor. I said, "Where's the car?" and she said, "In the lake."—*Henny Youngman*

❖❖❖❖❖

The secret of a happy marriage remains a secret.—*Henny Youngman*

❖❖❖❖❖

People are always asking couples whose marriages have endured at least a quarter of a century for their secret for success. Actually, it is no secret at all. I am a forgiving woman. Long ago, I forgave my husband for not being Paul Newman.—*Erma Bombeck*

197

This Lesson in Your Life

"Preacher, what is wrong with . . . ?" You can fill that blank with anything you want to and I have heard the question. The question really means, "Preacher, how much like everyone else can I be and still be Christian?" This lesson goes a long way in answering that question.

Jesus' three friends at Bethany represent the basics of what Christians are called to be and to do in service of the Lord. The meal took place in Martha's home, and her sister Mary and brother Lazarus were there.

In John 11 we find that Lazarus was a witness to the power of God in his life. That is our first task—to be witnesses to the power of God in our lives. Too often, persons want to share what they are doing for God or for his church. This kind of witness is calls attention to the person rather than to God. Lazarus did nothing in this story. God did everything.

We learn that "Martha served." The second element of our faith is to work. "Work" is a four-letter word. It is called "work" for a reason. Were you ever promised that work would be fun, or fulfilling? How about work in the church, such as shining brass, dusting pews, mowing grass, changing light bulbs. Those are not fun things, but the work needs to be done. The key to working faithfully is to use the talents you have in the work of the church. It is foolish when the church puts a carpenter on the finance committee or a banker on the maintenance committee. Martha did for the Lord what she did best—cook.

Mary was also in the picture. She worshipped the Lord. The word "worship" comes from an Old English root meaning "worth-ship." In our worship we are showing the church and the world the value we place on God. Mary gave her absolute best. Nothing was reserved or held back for a rainy day. She opened her heart to the Lord and poured out her love and her adoration.

We can understand being a witness for Christ and working for Him, but worship sometimes causes us to stumble. We sit in the sanctuary like spectators at a sporting event. If the choir is not sharp, if the sanctuary is not the right temperature, if the preacher isn't eloquent, we grumble that the worship service didn't seem "right." But worship is not an hour when we watch, it is an hour in which we perform. As you read the story in John, what is Mary doing? She is right in the middle of things, being conspicuous in her actions. It wasn't important to her what anyone was thinking. It didn't matter if they heard her sing. She wasn't concerned about what she was wearing. She didn't care about what Judas thought or said. She had one focus: Jesus Christ. She poured out her heart to Him.

"Preacher, what's wrong with . . .?" I usually answer, "Nothing, as long as it doesn't affect your witness, work, or worship of the Lord."

1. When was Jesus in Bethany? Why was He there?

Jesus was in Bethany six days before the Passover. He came to Bethany to have a meal celebrating the resurrection of Lazarus.

2. Whose home was in Bethany? What is the significance of that person?

Jesus was at the home of Lazarus, whom Jesus raised from the dead.

3. What was the relationship between Mary, Martha and Lazarus?

These three persons were brother and sisters (although Luke's account gives no indication of their relationship).

4. What did Mary do during the meal that was unusual?

Mary took a pound of nard and anointed the feet of Jesus. She then wiped his feet with her hair.

5. What was significant about Mary's use of her hair to wipe the feet of Jesus?

A woman's hair was her most prized possession. As in modern times, women went to great lengths to care for their hair.

6. What was it about Mary's action that offended Judas Iscariot?

The cost of the nard that Mary used to anoint Jesus' feet would have fed the poor for a significant amount of time. Judas was telling her that her actions were a waste of resources.

7. According to the gospel of John, why did Judas make this statement?

Judas was not concerned for the poor. He was the treasurer of the group and was skimming funds from the common purse.

8. What was Jesus' response to Judas' complaint about Mary's actions?

Jesus told Judas that the poor would always be with them. However, Jesus would not always be with them.

9. What do you think the statement of Jesus to Judas meant?

Jesus was clearly predicting His death, which would take place in a few days in Jerusalem.

10. What was different about John's and Luke's account of this story?

The major difference is the conversation that Martha and Jesus had as recorded in Luke. John omits this detail.

In the 1997 fall semester at Duke University, two sophomores taking organic chemistry did pretty well on all of the quizzes, the midterms, and labs. They each had a solid "A," and were so confident going into the finals that the weekend before finals week, even though the chemistry final was on Monday, they decided to go up to the University of Virginia and party with some friends there. So they did this and had a great time. However, they slept all day Sunday and didn't make it back to Duke until early Monday morning.

Rather than take the final then, they found Professor Aldric after the final and explained to him why they missed the test. They told him that they went up to UVA for the weekend and had planned to come back in time to study, but that they had a flat tire on the way back, didn't have a spare, and couldn't get help for a long time and so were late getting back to campus.

Aldric thought this over, then agreed that they could make up the final on the following day. The two guys were elated and relieved. They studied that night and went in to take the exam the next day. Aldric placed them in separate rooms, handed each of them a test booklet, and told them to begin.

They looked at the first problem, which was something simple about free radical formation and was worth five points. "Cool" they thought, "this is going to be easy." They did that problem and then turned the page. They were unprepared, however, for what they saw on the next page.

It said, "(95 points) *Which tire?*"

If we fail to take our Christian virtues with us on Monday we can end up over our heads before we even realize that we've gotten our feet wet. The story about Mary, Martha and Jesus is the story of our Monday manners. Martha is overworked and frustrated. If Mary would have helped Martha, there would have been peace. She was too busy sitting at the feet of Jesus, even though she knew how busy her sister was in the kitchen.

Jesus put Martha in her place. There is no way around it. Jesus told Martha that Mary had chosen the "better part." Mary's worship was more important than Martha's fussing, fuming, and cooking. Stings doesn't it?

Now, we are not told how the story ended. Did Martha join Mary at the feet of Jesus? Or did she stomp back into the kitchen? How you finish the story is a reflection on how you live your life. If you let Martha sit at the feet of Jesus and worship, the story ends one way. She does not worry about the kitchen stuff. Then you may be allowing room in your life to worship Jesus Christ. Martha made Him a priority. However, if you have Martha go back into that kitchen and work, perhaps you really feel that worship is an interruption keeping you from the really important things. Worship takes a backseat to all of those important things that happen Monday through Saturday.

Pilate: Judge on Trial

John 18:31-38; 19:12-16a

Then said Pilate unto them, Take ye him, and judge him accord ing to your law. The Jews therefore said unto him, It is not lawful for us to put any man to death:

32 That the saying of Jesus might be fulfilled, which he spake, signifying what death he should die.

33 Then Pilate entered into the judgment hall again, and called Jesus, and said unto him, Art thou the King of the Jews?

34 Jesus answered him, Sayest thou this thing of thyself, or did others tell it thee of me?

35 Pilate answered, Am I a Jew? Thine own nation and the chief priests have delivered thee unto me: what hast thou done?

36 Jesus answered, My kingdom is not of this world: if my kingdom were of this world, then would my servants fight, that I should not be delivered to the Jews: but now is my kingdom not from hence.

37 Pilate therefore said unto him, Art thou a king then? Jesus answered, Thou sayest that I am a king. To this end was I born, and for this cause came I into the world, that I should bear witness unto the truth. Every one that is of the truth heareth my voice.

38 Pilate saith unto him, What is truth? And when he had said this, he went out again unto the Jews, and saith unto them, I find in him no fault at all.

John 19

12 And from thenceforth Pilate sought to release him: but the Jews cried out, saying, If thou let this man go, thou art not Caesar's friend: whosoever maketh himself a king speaketh against Caesar.

13 When Pilate therefore heard that saying, he brought Jesus forth, and sat down in the judgment seat in a place that is called the Pavement, but in the Hebrew, Gabbatha.

14 And it was the preparation of the passover, and about the sixth hour: and he saith unto the Jews, Behold your King!

15 But they cried out, Away with him, away with him, crucify him. Pilate saith unto them, Shall I crucify your King? The chief priest answered, We have no king but Caesar.

16a Then delivered he him therefore unto them to be crucified.

Jan. 19

Memory Selection
John 18:37-38

Background Scripture
John 18:31-38; 19:12-16a

Devotional Reading
1 Timothy 2:1-6

Integrity is the central issue in this lesson. Two cultures, Roman and Jewish, clash at Jesus' arrest and trial. Integrity, however, transcends cultural bounds. A lack of integrity results in trumped-up charges against Jesus. A failure of integrity caused Pilate to place political favor above setting an innocent man free.

Shining through this subterfuge is the integrity of Jesus. He does not deny that He is King of the Jews, even though they are at that very moment rejecting Him as their Sovereign. Faced with a death sentence, he declines to save His life by denying who He really is. But because He acts with integrity, He turns the tables on His opponents. They, not Him, are called into judgment. The burden of acting with integrity is now on the shoulders of the Jews . . . on the Romans . . . on us.

ഇൻൽ

Lead into this lesson by asking group members to give examples of people who acted with integrity. A boy received too much change at a shop, and returned it . . . a businessman told the truth when a lie may have seemed safer . . . a person stood up for what they believe instead of being intimidated by a crowd . . . a public figure acted out of conviction instead of currying favor with voters.

Then note that according to the dictionary, the word comes from a Latin word that means "entire" or "whole." This word also gives us the term *integer*, for "a whole number." Point out that when we act without integrity we have a "split personality," morally speaking. When Jesus models integrity in this lesson, He is portraying a whole person, being true to who He is.

Teaching Outline	Daily Bible Readings
I. Who Would Judge Jesus?–31-32	Mon. Jesus Brought Before Pilate John 18:28-32
II. Who Is Jesus?—33-37 A. Interview with Jesus, 33-35 B. The King of hearts, 36-37	Tue. Pilate Questions Jesus John 18:33-37
	Wed. Pilate's Wife's Dreams Matthew 27:15-19
III. What Is Truth?—38	Thu. 'Behold the Man!' John 18:38–19:5
IV. Shall I Crucify Your King?— John 19:12-16a A. A political problem, 12 B. Deceitful claim, 13-15 C. Condemned to die, 16a	Fri. 'I Find No Fault in Him' John 19:6-12
	Sat. Pilate Washes His Hands Matthew 27:21-26
	Sun. Condemned to Die John 19:13-22

Verse by Verse

I. Who Would Judge Jesus?—31-32

31 Then said Pilate unto them, Take ye him, and judge him according to your law. The Jews therefore said unto him, It is not lawful for us to put any man to death:

32 That the saying of Jesus might be fulfilled, which he spake, signifying what death he should die.

Pontius Pilate served as "procurator" of Judea under the Roman Emperor Tiberius for 10 years (A.D. 26-36). He appears on the scene in 18:29, apparently coming to Jerusalem for a court session from his palace in Caesarea. Actually, the Jewish leaders had already decided that Jesus should die, lest His followers foment a revolution that would bring the Romans down in force on all the Jews (John 11:47-50). Verse 32 refers to Jesus' prediction in 12:32-33 to being "lifted up" in death, in an obvious reference to His coming crucifixion.

Pilate's reluctance to get involved seems to stem from the fact that he knew little of the case the Jews had against Jesus. It would have been Pilate's task, as procurator, to sit in judgment of Jesus if He had been charged with rebellion against Rome. However, from more detailed information in the other Gospels we learn that the Jewish leaders had difficulty finding people to testify against the

Lord. Finally they were able to find false witnesses who would testify that Jesus was planning to destroy the Temple (Matt. 26:59-61)—a mainly Jewish issue in which Pilate would have been reluctant to get involved even if he had been informed about it.

Rome refused to give the Jews authority to levy the death sentence. Otherwise, its broad policy was to respect the religious customs of the people they ruled and to allow them to determine the penalty for non-capital offenses.

II. Who Is Jesus?—33-37
A. Interview with Jesus, 33-35

33 Then Pilate entered into the judgment hall again, and called Jesus, and said unto him, Art thou the King of the Jews?

34 Jesus answered him, Sayest thou this thing of thyself, or did others tell it thee of me?

35 Pilate answered, Am I a Jew? Thine own nation and the chief priests have delivered thee unto me: what hast thou done?

Jesus had been taken to the Roman "judgment hall" in verse 28. The Jews who had engineered His arrest declined to enter the hall because doing so would render them ceremonially unclean. Thus, Pilate had to leave the hall to consult them about the charges against Jesus—an indication of the remarkable deference the Romans usually paid to Jewish religious scruples. In verse 33 Pilate returns from this consultation to the hall of judgment. The interchange with Jesus here is unique to John's Gospel, and remarkable, since John usually focuses on the guilt of the Jews in the opposition to and condemnation of Jesus. Here he exposes also the way the Roman judicial system was responsible in its own way for Jesus' death.

To Pilate's question, "Art thou the king of the Jews?" Jesus replies with His own question in verse 34. He wants to know whether Pilate as a person is interested in how to understand Jesus' claim to be a Ruler, or whether he is merely parroting the wrong-headed Jewish charges. Even now, the question of whether, and how, Jesus is truly King must be settled by personally confronting the issue, instead of being kept at the level of hearsay.

In verse 35, Pilate avoids dealing with the question of his personal evaluation of Jesus' Kingship by protesting with exasperation that since he is not a Jew he should not have to decide on the matter. Obviously he hopes to limit the issue to an in-house Jewish matter, and to avoid involving the Roman court in a concern that had become such a hot potato. Yet Pilate shows some independence by not relying solely on the charges of the Jews, but asking Jesus to testify in His own behalf. However, the governor apparently ignores his wife's warning not to get involved in sentencing Jesus, after it was revealed to her in a dream that He was innocent (Matt. 27:19).

B. The King of hearts, 36-37

36 Jesus answered, My kingdom is not of this world: if my kingdom were of this world, then would my servants fight, that I should not be delivered to the Jews: but now is my kingdom not from hence.

37 Pilate therefore said unto him, Art thou a king then? Jesus answered, Thou sayest that I am a king. To this end was I born, and for this cause came I into the world, that I should bear witness unto the truth. Every one that is of the truth heareth my voice.

Although some commentators observe that Jesus did not answer Pilate's question about His kingship, His reference in verse 36 to "My kingdom," and His confession that this was the purpose of His birth (vs. 37) clearly indicate that He does admit to be a King . . . of sorts. The indirect nature of Jesus' reply arises from the fact that He knows Pilate will have difficulty accepting the nature of His rule—a reign over people's hearts, not a direct or armed threat to the political power of Rome.

In verse 37b, Jesus evangelistically confronts Pilate with the opportunity to become a believer. Pilate has heard the Jews' charges and Jesus' own testimony. Now Jesus confesses clearly that He was born to be King over people's hearts, and implies that Pilate could actually understand, and submit to, this Kingship if he were truly "of the truth," or sincere.

III. What Is Truth?—38

38 Pilate saith unto him, What is truth? And when he had said this, he went out again unto the Jews, and saith unto them, I find in him no fault at all.

Earlier, Pilate had tried to evade ruling on the charges against Jesus by asking, "Am I a Jew?" Now he tries to duck the issue by asking an abstract, philosophical question about the definition of "truth." Not waiting for an answer is a sure sign that he is not in fact "of the truth." Yet he has the courage to tell the Jews that he finds Jesus innocent. Unfortunately Jesus is not protected by the rule in our own land that holds that persons are innocent until proved guilty; and Pilate's declaration of Jesus' innocence will not save Him from death.

IV. Shall I Crucify Your King?—John 19:12-16a

A. A political problem, 12

12 And from thenceforth Pilate sought to release him: but the Jews cried out, saying, If thou let this man go, thou art not Caesar's friend: whosoever maketh himself a king speaketh against Caesar.

Although Pilate tried to release Jesus and to satisfy the Jews' bloodlust by executing a thief named Barabbas (18:39–19:11), the crowd will have none of it. They charge that if Pilate releases Jesus he will have set free a man who admitted to being a king, and that this would be a direct threat to the rule of Caesar over the Roman Empire. Pilate will prove to lack the character and courage to defy this political ploy.

B. Deceitful claim, 13-15

13 When Pilate therefore heard that saying, he brought Jesus forth, and sat down in the judgment seat in a place that is called the Pavement, but in the Hebrew, Gabbatha.

14 And it was the preparation of the passover, and about the sixth hour: and he saith unto the Jews, Behold your King!

15 But they cried out, Away with him, away with him, crucify him. Pilate saith unto them, Shall I crucify your King? The chief priest answered, We have no king but Caesar.

Now Pilate seats himself dramatically in an elevated, stone-paved place of judgment (which archeologists are believed to have located in the Temple area). In a last feeble effort to set Jesus free, Pilate describes Him as the Jews' own king, and asks incredulously if they want to crucify such a royal Personage. The crowds' answer is again shrewdly political, and dripping with deceit. Although they actually hate Caesar and his oppressive rule over them, they express total loyalty to him here—again positioning Pilate as Caesar's enemy if He allows King Jesus to live.

C. Condemned to die, 16a

16a Then delivered he him therefore unto them to be crucified.

Death by hanging from a stake or cross had been practiced since the days of the Pharaohs (see Gen. 40:19). It was considered especially shameful by the Jews, since God had pronounced a curse on those so executed (Deut. 21:22-23). As dark a day as this is, God's plan will transform it into the day when He who was accursed became the means of salvation (see Gal. 3:13).

Evangelistic Emphasis

We can become inspired when we read the story of the "good guys" of Scripture. Peter falls and then is redeemed by Jesus. Barnabas is an example of encouragement to the early Christian community. Paul and Timothy dedicate themselves to the ministry. Priscilla and Aquila are a pattern for team ministry. The "good guys" will be the subject of subsequent lessons.

Pontius Pilate, however, isn't one of the good guys. He is a tragic figure in the biblical story. Pilate is one of those people who is "too bad to be good and too good to be bad." He stands as a reminder that the Kingdom of God is reserved for those who make a faith commitment to Christ.

Even though he was close to Jesus, involved in the story of the Cross, Pilate's name will not be on the list of "heroes of the faith." The good news may take the form of a warning, as in this lesson. The warning is that we can be close to sacred things and still not be redeemed. While many congregations call the name of Pilate every Sunday in reciting the Apostles' Creed, it is doubtful God will call his name in glory.

Be warned. You can be close to the trappings of religion, but that doesn't save your soul! A faith commitment to Jesus Christ is the only way to have life eternal.

ഏറ

Memory Selection

Every one that is of the truth heareth my voice. Pilate saith unto him, What is truth?— *John 18: 37-38*

The problem with our world is not what we know. The problem is that so much of what we know is not true. Having a knowledge based on something other than truth is the basis of prejudice and superstition.

Jesus said, "I am the way, the truth, and the life." Truth is a rare commodity in our world. Politicians often don't have much of it. Children and adults, when "caught red-handed," don't seem concerned with expressing it. Even science has a problem with what is truth. (What is the "latest" truth on what foods are good for you?)

In Jesus there is a truth that can guide us through the moral morass in which we find ourselves at the beginning of the 21st century. He is a certainty in an uncertain world. He is the only truth you can trust, who will never change His definition of what truth is. Jesus is "the truth, the whole truth and nothing but the truth."

Weekday Problems

Buster Weatherly was thinking that he would have been better suited to be a wrestling referee than the pastor of First Church. Recently it has seemed that Buster has found himself in the middle of all kinds of messy situations. Most of the people coming to him with problems want Buster to choose sides; of course he was to choose *their* side.

The latest upset was over the matter of whether the choir should buy blue robes with white piping or white robes with blue piping. The issue had clearly divided the choir right down the middle and the sopranos were no longer speaking to the tenors. The battle had begun to enter the "regular church members" as both sides tried to rally support for their choir robe position. The choir director was at odds with the organist.

A committee had been formed to try and settle the matter and they had asked the Rev. Weatherly to weigh in on the matter before the choir. Of course, they didn't want pastoral guidance; they wanted Buster to pick a color. When Buster refused to become engaged in their choral color dilemma, many of the choir members were mad! They doubted the "backbone" of their preacher.

*How many "dumb" things have caused problems in your church?

*How many times have you tried to get people to "join your side?"

Insights on Integrity

Undoubtedly, there is little integration or integrity in most men's characters; there is only habit and a plodding limitation in life and mind; and if social pressure were not added to lack of opportunity disorderly lives would be more common than they are.—*George Santayana*

Nothing more completely baffles one who is full of trick and duplicity, than straightforward and simple integrity in another.—*Nathaniel Cotton*

Give us the man of integrity, on whom we know we can thoroughly depend; who will stand firm when others fail . . . such an one is a fragment of the Rock of Ages.—*A. P. Stanley*

To maintain [integrity] in high places costs self-denial.—*C. Simmons*

This Lesson in Your Life

Pilate asked Jesus, "What is truth?" But I want to know, *what is true about Pilate?* Pontius Pilate is one of the villains of the New Testament. On the wall of shame, hanging some place in the bowels of hell are, Judas, Caiaphas, and Pontius Pilate. There is no way that any of these three characters are walking the streets of heaven right now. We know that to be the truth and we know that to be a fact. Don't we?

Many of the people who walked away from Jesus may have had redemptive "second thoughts." Can you imagine Pilate as an older man, reflecting on life, thinking about Jesus? Can you imagine him living on his retirement pension and calling for Paul or Peter to come from their cell and tell him more about Jesus? It's hard to imagine such scenes, isn't it? We want our heroes to be pure and we want our villains to be purely evil. The truth is that all of us are a mixture of the good and the bad. The truth is that we are engaged in an internal struggle, or as Paul wrote, our members are at war with each other.

Pilate was caught between two warring factions. There is almost a sense that Pilate wanted to free Jesus, but had such contempt for the Jews that he played along with their desire to crucify their own "king." When he asked Jesus "What is truth?," I hear him asking with fatigue in his voice. He knows that no matter what he decides about the truth he would make the wrong decision about Jesus. He could not be true to what he wanted to do as a person, because the Roman procurator side of him got in the way. What is true of Pilate is that he was not true to himself. He made a decision about a life, based on political expediency. That tragic mistake is replayed almost daily in our world.

The truth is that when we think about Pilate we have prejudice in our hearts about who he was and what he did. We make him purely evil and see no redeeming qualities in him at all.

Truth is hard to find in a world swimming in information. Each time a study is released, most of us find out that we have been living life wrong, and the things we are doing are contributing to our demise. The truth is that *living* contributes to our demise. We were born to die, so stop fretting about the amount of fiber in your diet.

Like Pilate, we are a mixture of good and bad. When you have opportunities to make choices, allow your good and truthful side to choose. When you are dealing with others and know they are showing their bad side, give them a redemptive break.

Yet it's also the truth that you can't be neutral about Jesus. Pilate tried to straddle that fence and failed. You can't straddle it either. You choose to make Jesus your Savior or you choose to reject Him. The truth is that often the truth hurts.

1. **The Jews seeking the execution of Jesus would not enter the palace of Pilate, why?**

They wanted to eat the Passover and entering Pilate's palace would have made them unclean.

2. **What was the irony that stands out about these Jews trying to remain clean?**

They are refusing to enter the palace of Pilate, yet they are seeking the execution of an innocent man.

3. **Because the Jews would not enter Pilate's palace, how were they able to communicate with him?**

Pilate came outside the palace to hold conversations with them.

4. **What was Pilate's initial response to the crowd who was seeking to punish Jesus?**

Pilate told the crowd to "judge Jesus by your own laws."

5. **Do you know why it was important for the Jewish leaders to involve Pilate in their plot against Jesus?**

The Sanhedrin could find Jesus guilty of violating Jewish law, but this body had no power to execute Him.

6. **The Gospel writer indicated that this whole scenario was to fulfill Scripture. What was the essence of the fulfillment?**

Jesus had died for our sins as Isaiah 53:4-5 predicted. The soldiers cast lots for his clothing as Psalm 22:18 predicted.

7. **From the text, how many interviews did Pilate hold that evening?**

Pilate held three interviews. The initial one was held with the Jews. He held a private one with Jesus. He told the Jews his verdict.

8. **What was the initial verdict that Pilate rendered concerning Jesus?**

Pilate initially told the Jewish leadership that he found no fault with Jesus.

9. **What did Pilate do next?**

He participated in the custom of releasing a prisoner for the Passover.

10. **What choice did the crowd make when Pilate allowed them to pick a prisoner to be released?**

The crowd chose to have Barabbas released to them, and to have Jesus crucified.

A Sunday school teacher was watching her class draw pictures of the Christmas story. There were the usual pictures of stars and shepherds. Mary and Joseph were pictured in various stages of being "stick figures." One little boy had Mary, Joseph, and baby Jesus in an airplane.

"Johnny," said the teacher, "that is a very interesting picture. But tell me—who is in front flying the plane?"

"That is Pontius the pilot," Johnny said,

Well it is the only funny story I know about Pontius Pilate, and honestly it has been rather difficult to do an uplifting message for you, with him as an example.

Roman rulers bracketed the life of Jesus. According to Luke the whole reason Jesus was born in Bethlehem was that the Roman emperor Augustus demanded a tax enrollment. At the end of his life, Jesus again finds Himself dealing with the Romans, this time with Pilate.

The Romans were always behind the scenes. So many of the teachings of Jesus have Romans as the foil. The people Jesus taught were under their rule. Many of the citizens of Palestine looked for a great Messiah who, like David, would drive the enemy out of the land and return rule the Jewish people.

The religious leaders tried to trap Jesus by questioning whether they should pay taxes to the Romans. It seems that the question of paying taxes is always on the minds of God's people. Jesus' response was indicative of how He lived: "Give to Caesar the things that are Caesar's and to God the things that are God's." Jesus used that notion to rebuke the popular idea that He had come to lead a Jewish revolt. His kingdom was not of this earth

Jesus telling His people to "go the extra mile" and "give your coat" are all understood only in the context of people living in a Roman-occupied land.

The point is simple. We also live under a political system, but our faith in Jesus must not depend on that system. It doesn't matter who is in the White House, Congress, the State House, or the Mayor's mansion in terms of our faith in Jesus. A close reading of the Gospels might lead us to believe that Jesus really doesn't care about our political system, because His kingdom is not of this world. Could it be that one of the ploys of the devil to keep us from winning souls is to get us, as the Church, so involved in political issues? We are best tempted where we are most passionate. We see so many political issues in terms of ultimate justice and human rights. Could it be that we are "chasing ghosts" in the name of being politically astute?

While His whole life was bracketed by the Roman Empire, Jesus kept His spiritual focus. We would do well to learn the lesson. Some things have priority over our political system. We are citizens of both an earthly "kingom" and the Kingdom of God. We must not get our allegiances confused.

Peter: Restored Leader

Luke 22:31-34, 54-62; John 21:17

And the Lord said, Simon, Simon, behold, Satan hath desired to have you, that he may sift you as wheat:

32 But I have prayed for thee, that thy faith fail not: and when thou art converted, strengthen thy brethren.

33 And he said unto him, Lord, I am ready to go with thee, both into prison, and to death.

34 And he said, I tell thee, Peter, the cock shall not crow this day, before that thou shalt thrice deny that thou knowest me.

54 Then took they him, and led him, and brought him into the high priest's house. And Peter followed afar off.

55 And when they had kindled a fire in the midst of the hall, and were set down together, Peter sat down among them.

56 But a certain maid beheld him as he sat by the fire, and earnestly looked upon him, and said, This man was also with him.

57 And he denied him, saying, Woman, I know him not.

58 And after a little while another saw him, and said, Thou art also of them. And Peter said, Man, I am not.

59 And about the space of one hour after another confidently affirmed, saying, Of a truth this fellow also was with him: for he is a Galilaean.

60 And Peter said, Man, I know not what thou sayest. And immediately, while he yet spake, the cock crew.

61 And the Lord turned, and looked upon Peter. And Peter remembered the word of the Lord, how he had said unto him, Before the cock crow, thou shalt deny me thrice.

62 And Peter went out, and wept bitterly.

John 21

17 He saith unto him the third time, Simon, son of Jonas, lovest thou me? Peter was grieved because he said unto him the third time, Lovest thou me? And he said unto him, Lord, thou knowest all things; thou knowest that I love thee. Jesus saith unto him, Feed my sheep.

Jan. 26

Memory Selection
John 21:15

Background Scripture
Luke 22:31-34, 54-62; John 21:1-22

Devotional Reading
Acts 4:1-13

211

Of the personalities in Jesus' life and ministry featured in this unit, none is more colorful than the apostle Peter. Considering Peter's stature in the Church after New Testament times, the Gospels' description of him as head-strong, brash, and wavering in faith is remarkably candid.

Ironically, however, the focus of the present lesson is as much on the character of Christ as on Peter's denial of Him. For every ounce of inconstancy in Peter's nature, Christ supplies a pound of rock-like conviction. For every sign of irresponsibility, Jesus signals His confidence that Peter will become responsible. The lesson is therefore about ourselves as well as Peter. Will we allow Christ to transform out liabilities into assets for the sake of the Kingdom?

Challenge your group to imagine how they would feel if they had been among the 12 apostles, walking and talking daily in Jesus' presence. Think about your every inner thought, your motives, your ambitions, your attitudes, all being exposed before this One who can look into the heart.

Call for one-word descriptions of the predominant feeling group members imagine their having. Is it fear, wishing we could hide at least some of our thoughts from the Lord? Or would we feel intimidation, knowing we could never match His standards? Or would we trust Him enough to bask in a feeling of His acceptance? This lesson portrays Peter, with all his hot-headedness and instability, finally hearing Jesus accept him fully, "warts and all," and even commissioned to pastor God's flock!

Teaching Outline	Daily Bible Readings	

I. Rejection Predicted—Luke 22:31-34
  A. Threat from Satan, 31-32
  B. Protest and prophecy, 33-34
	Mon.	'When You Are Converted' Luke 22:24-34

	Tue.	Peter Denies Jesus Luke 22:54-62

II. Roundly Denying Jesus—54-62
  A. First denial, 54-57
  B. Further denials, 58-60
  C. Bitter regret, 61-62
	Wed.	Peter Goes Fishing John 21:1-6

	Thu.	'It Is the Lord!" John 21:7-14
	Fri.	'Do You Love Me?' John 21:15-19
III. Restored to Service—John 21:17	Sat.	'Repent and Be Baptized' Acts 2:37-42
	Sun.	'Walk, in Jesus' Name!' Acts 3:1-7

Verse by Verse

I. Rejection Predicted—Luke 22:31-34

A. Threat from Satan, 31-32

31 And the Lord said, Simon, Simon, behold, Satan hath desired to have you, that he may sift you as wheat:

32 But I have prayed for thee, that thy faith fail not: and when thou art converted, strengthen thy brethren.

"Simon" (the Greek form of Peter's Hebrew name "Simeon") is the rough-hewn Galilean fisherman whom some assumed to be something of an ignorant country bumpkin (Acts 4:13). He could be quick to act on his faith in Jesus, as when he threw himself into the sea to walk on water, but his faith sometimes proved shallow (Matt. 14:28-31). He could also be given to making dogmatic but wrong-headed statements, as when he rebuked Christ for predicting that He would be killed in Jerusalem (16:21-23). He brandished his sword in defense of Jesus (John 18:10-11), then denied Him only hours later. Given "the keys to the kingdom of heaven," and the first apostle to learn of the inclusion of the Gentiles (Acts 10), Peter still had difficulty being true to this revelation, and Paul later rebuked him for racial discrimination (Gal. 2:11-14).

Christ's prayer that Peter would resist this "sifting" of Satan is a metaphor based on winnowing grain to separate the chaff from the kernel.

A glimpse into the mystery of the Triune God is given us as we see the divine Son, to whom many directed their prayers, directing His own prayers to the Father. Note that Jesus is so confident that His prayer would be answered that He does not tell Peter to feed His sheep if but when he is "converted." (The NIV translates the word for "converted as "turned back," since Peter is obviously already converted here. When he denies Jesus he will not need to be "re-saved" but to return to his faith.)

B. Protest and prophecy, 33-34

33 And he said unto him, Lord, I am ready to go with thee, both into prison, and to death.

34 And he said, I tell thee, Peter, the cock shall not crow this day, before that thou shalt thrice deny that thou knowest me.

Peter's firm protest that it is unthinkable that he would fall to Satan's temptation is typical of the man's impetuous personality. We are not to think that he is anything but honest in affirming constancy, but it will become obvious that he does not have a clear perception of his weaknesses. At least his promise to go "to death" with Jesus indicates that he may have matured in his understanding of the Messiah's true role since the time he rebuked Jesus for even mentioning His approaching death.

Given the previous incidents when Peter has indicated that his faith could come and go, we may think that any perceptive person could make a prediction such as Jesus does; but the knowledge that his denials would be three in number, then punctuated by a rooster's crowing, could only come from supernatural insight.

II. Roundly Denying Jesus—54-62
A. First denial, 54-57

54 Then took they him, and led him, and brought him into the high priest's house. And Peter followed afar off.

55 And when they had kindled a fire in the midst of the hall, and were set down together, Peter sat down among them.

56 But a certain maid beheld him as he sat by the fire, and earnestly looked upon him, and said, This man was also with him.

57 And he denied him, saying, Woman, I know him not.

Peter is sometimes singled out for undue blame in this scene. The fact is that all the disciples fled when the authorities arrested Jesus (Matt. 26:56). At least Peter returned to follow at a distance the events as they unfolded, although hoping he would not be identified as a disciple. As it turned out, however, Peter has been too outspoken, too much in a leadership position, to keep from being recognized. When he joins others around a fire—perhaps not only to find warmth but also to listen for bits of information about the results of Jesus' trials—a simple

serving woman recognizes him as being one of Jesus' fellow-travelers.

B. Further denials, 58-60

58 And after a little while another saw him, and said, Thou art also of them. And Peter said, Man, I am not.

59 And about the space of one hour after another confidently affirmed, saying, Of a truth this fellow also was with him: for he is a Galilaean.

60 And Peter said, Man, I know not what thou sayest. And immediately, while he yet spake, the cock crew.

Peter's threefold denial of Jesus is obviously symmetrical with Jesus' threefold question to Peter, after the resurrection: "Lovest thou me?" (John 21:15-17). We can imagine all kinds of emotions welling up in the apostle with increasing pressure as a second and then a third person insists that they recognize him as a disciple. The pressure becomes so great that according to Matthew's account Peter underlines his second and third denials with oaths and curses (Matt. 26:72-74). He does not merely swear that he is telling the truth, but curses, in an effort to indicate how opposite his sentiments are from this "holy one of Israel." The oaths are not fully issued before the rooster crows, precisely as Jesus predicted!

C. Bitter regret, 61-62

61 And the Lord turned, and looked upon Peter. And Peter remembered the word of the Lord, how he had said unto him, Before the cock crow, thou shalt deny me thrice.

62 And Peter went out, and wept

bitterly.

The cock's raucous crowing must have echoed through Peter's soul like a solemn bell announcing his guilt. Then to have his Lord turn His eyes upon him makes it entirely believable that Peter would flee again, this time not so much in fear as in grief and self-condemnation. Christ's look need not have been one of condemnation, but only of sorrow, for it to pierce Peter's heart in this way.

III. Restored to Service—John 21:17

17 He saith unto him the third time, Simon, son of Jonas, lovest thou me? Peter was grieved because he said unto him the third time, Lovest thou me? And he said unto him, Lord, thou knowest all things; thou knowest that I love thee. Jesus saith unto him, Feed my sheep.

This remarkable passage shows the immeasurable grace of God in giving sinners a second chance to be restored to His good favor, and even given a leadership role ("Feed my sheep"). Jesus matches Peter's threefold denial by extending this grace three times.

An interesting but puzzling feature of this conversation is the use of two different Greek word for "love." The first two times Jesus asks Peter if he loves Him, He uses the word *agapeo*, usually defined as the highest, most selfless form of love. Although Peter answers Yes each time, he uses the word *phileo*, usually defined as only "friendship love." Finally, the third time Jesus asks the question, he seems to condescend to Peter's speech by also using the word *phileo* for love. These differences appear in the Phillips translation, implying that in His first two questions Jesus is asking, "Peter, do you have an absolutely selfless and perfect love for me?" However, since it has only been a few days since Peter's shameful denial of the Lord, the apostle is still filled with remorse; so he can only confess a somewhat lower level of love: "Lord, you know that you are my friend." The third time Jesus puts the question to Peter, perhaps he condescends to use the apostle's own way of describing his love to show either that (1) such "friendship" is sufficient, or, (2) to question whether Peter's "friendship" love (*phileo*) is adequate (cp. Phillips, "Are you my friend?"). That is, "If you can only confess your friendship and not selfless commitment, are you really my friend?"

The first interpretation seems preferable in light of Jesus' commission, "Feed my sheep." It seems more likely that Jesus stoops to using Peter's word phileo or "friendship" love in honor of his humility and honesty, and to indicate that He can take whatever level of love Peter will give Him and transform it into usefulness. At any rate, in commanding Peter three times to "feed" (lit. "be a pastor to") God's flock, Jesus is bestowing full forgiveness and restoration to his apostolic ministry.

How affirming this must have been to Peter! As history shows, his dramatic restoration to service in the early Church resulted in a servant-leader who did not linger permanently in despair over his weakness, but accepted Christ's restorative grace in order to minister to His people.

Evangelistic Emphasis

The picture we have of Simon Peter is a caricature. He was so much like "a bull elephant in a china shop" that we don't take him seriously as a person. Simon Peter was as real and as one could be. His mistakes were legendary.

He wanted to walk on water, but got lead feet only a few steps from the boat. He wanted to build a hotel for Moses, Jesus, and Elijah on the Mount of Transfiguration. He tried to correct Jesus' suffering servant theology. He fell asleep while Jesus prayed in Gethsemane. He cut off the ear of the servant of the High Priest. Three times he denied knowing Jesus. He ran away when the shadow of the Cross loomed large over our Lord's last hours. Rather than waiting for instruction from the Lord after the resurrection, Peter said, "I'm going fishing."

Yet, even with this list, Peter was "the rock." He was the one around which the early Church was built. So many of the pebbles put on that foundation since have been like Peter.

For all of his buffoonery, Peter turned out to be a person who was used mightily by the Lord. More like a "bulldog" than a "bull elephant" Peter's faith and witness grew though sheer tenacity. Since Jesus had not quit on him, Peter would not quit on himself.

If Christ has room in His Church for Simon Peter, He certainly has room in His kingdom for you and me.

৪৩৫৩

Memory Selection

So when they had dined, Jesus saith to Simon Peter, Simon, son of Jonas, lovest thou me more than these? He saith unto him, Yea, Lord; thou knowest that I love thee. He saith unto him, Feed my lambs.—*John 21: 15*

Jesus asked the same question of Simon Peter three times. We all know what Peter had in his mind when Jesus asked the question, "Do you love me?" The third time, Peter had to have thought back to the night of the betrayal. Jesus was working on making Simon Peter the rock upon which the church would be built. Becoming a rock is not a pleasant experience. Rocks are created in an atmosphere of heat and pressure. As a result they become hard.

Jesus forgives our sins and our failures. While He does so with grace, He will not simply "let us off the hook." We must deal with our failures in a way that brings growth and strengthens us for the continuing journey.

At what point is God working in your life to make you a rock? He will find that place of greatest weakness and there work on you. The process might get "hot," and there will be some pressure; but you will be a better disciple if you don't give in—or give up.

Weekday Problems

The problem with this lesson is that on a weekday basis we want forgiveness for ourselves, yet we are slow to give a second chance to others. To prove the point, you will need the Sunday morning paper for your Sunday school class. Using the front section of the newspaper look at all the stories about people who have messed up.

The thing about newspapers is that the people who do "good deeds" are hidden on the inside of the paper. I don't know why we have to start our mornings with all the "bad stuff," but it seems to be our habit. Now look at the stories involving people and their hurts. Where do these people need a second chance? How might a second chance change their lives? Would you be willing to offer a second chance to the people included on the front page of your Sunday morning newspaper?

Fortunately, most of our sins don't make it to the front page of the paper. Our failures don't come with photographs published for our family and friends to read. Our failures, in most cases, are known only to a few. In the quietness of our prayer life we can seek forgiveness and ask for a second chance.

But what about people's public failures. Do we forgive them? Are we willing to allow them less than *we* have sought from God? How does your class feel about Simon Peter's private failure and very public repentance?

Daffynitions

Lame duck: A politician whose goose is cooked.

Coach: A person who is always willing to lay down your life for his job.

Virus: A Latin word meaning "Your guess is as good as mine."

Adolescence: The period when young people suddenly feel a great responsibility to answer the phone.

Budget: A systematic method of worrying before you spend, as well as afterward. Also, an attempt to live below your yearnings.

Waiter: A person who thinks that money grows on trays.

Taxpayer: A person who doesn't have to pass a civil service exam to work for the government.

Optimist: A person who goes into a restaurant without a dime and figures on paying for the meal with the pearl he might find in an oyster.

This Lesson in Your Life

Simon Peter is the hero of almost every preacher! Laypersons seem to identify with Peter, too. Peter began his time with Jesus boldly. One day, as Jesus walked by, He called Simon and Andrew from the fishing boats. Jesus asked them to give up their careers and follow Him on the adventure of faith. From Matthew's telling of the story, it appears that Peter went with Jesus without question. His adventurous spirit was partially responsible for his walking on the water. We tend to forget that Peter actually walked on the water for a moment. He was willing to risk his life for Jesus. We see that in his actions in Gethsemane. He was willing to fight, even though Roman guards were all around him.

But if anything shows through Peter's life, it is his inconsistency. One minute he would die for the Lord, the next he was running from a fight. One minute he was walking on the water, the next he was floundering in the pitching seas. Yet he is an example of what God can do with people. Preachers love him because sometimes we are inconsistent. We want to minister to all the sheep, but sometimes we miss one or two. We want to preach great sermons, but sometimes we fail to get the sermon off the launching pad. Laymen are inconsistent. Some will reach great spiritual heights. They will have vision and commitment. Then a couple of years later they have been added to an "inactive roll."

Simon Peter is an example of God's patience with our inconsistency. The Lord demands our total obedience. God wants us to mold ourselves perfectly to His will. He understands that sometimes we fail to do either. We smile at Peter because we know about his mistakes. Our smile is tempered with the knowledge that Jesus did rebuke him for some of his blunders. We also know that Jesus willingly forgave Peter and reissued the divine call on Peter's life.

Peter was human. He was saint and sinner, hero and villain. He could be sleeping at the moment of Transfiguration and running at the moment Jesus was before Pilate and still the Lord loved him.

Jesus' love for Peter should be a comforting thing. It reminds us that Jesus has called us all. There is no "professional clergy" anymore. In the New Testament, you find that all Christians are called to be ministers or "servants." Simon Peter left all that was familiar to follow Jesus.

Like Peter, you too can know God's grace. Peter once told Jesus how forgiving He was. (Peter was willing to forgive seven times seven.) He found out through his mistakes how forgiving God was. Peter even learned something that many of the saints of God never learn. Peter learned how to forgive himself for his failures.

It is no wonder that we all love Simon Peter. He is so much like us.

GETTING THE FACTS
STRAIGHT

1. As the Last Supper was proceeding, what did Jesus tell Simon Peter?
Jesus said He was praying for Peter that Satan not be able to destroy him.

2. What was Simon's response to the knowledge that Jesus was praying for him?
Peter responded that he would follow Jesus to prison and even to death.

3. How did Jesus respond to Peter's brash claim of loyalty to Jesus?
Jesus told Peter that before the cock crowed that morning, Peter would deny Jesus three times.

4. When Jesus was arrested and taken to the house of the High Priest, what was Peter doing?
Peter was following the procession of people leading Jesus to the High Priest's house.

5. Where did Peter follow in the procession to the High Priest's house?
Peter was following this procession at a distance.

6. What happened as Peter sat by the fire in the courtyard?
A servant girl recognized Peter as a follower of Jesus.

7. From the comments of the servant girl, what might be assumed about the people sitting by the fire?
One might assume the people sitting by the fire were those persons who had arrested Jesus.

8. How many other people asked Peter if he were a follower of Jesus?
Two other people asked Peter if he were a follower of Jesus. A total of three people asked him that question.

9. What was Peter's response to the charge that he was a follower of Jesus?
Peter denied knowing Jesus.

10. What happened the third time Peter denied knowing the Lord?
As predicted, the cock crowed and Jesus looked at Simon Peter. Peter ran out of the courtyard weeping bitterly.

When Johnny and Boots were 6 and 7 respectively and growing up in Texas, they played Texas Rangers in the back yard. Johnny's mother, wanting to take advantage of having law enforcement officers on the place, asked them to go to the hen house and round up and rout out the chicken snake that had been making an appearance there.

They boldly went where they had never gone before, only to find themselves, when they stood on tiptoe to look on the top shelf, nose-to-nose with a chicken snake. Both of them screamed and ran so fast that they did considerable damage to themselves and to the hen house.

Johnny's mother, who stood on the porch when the boys came running and screaming to the house, said, "Boys, boys, what is wrong with you? You know perfectly well a chicken snake cannot hurt you." Whereupon Johnny's friend, Boots, replied, "Yes, Ma'am. But there's some things that will scare you so bad, you hurt yourself."

Peter clung to the edge of the fire where he warmed himself in fear—hurting himself more deeply with each of his three denials. Today, we too are getting scared so badly about some things that we are hurting ourselves in our effort to avoid them. Often our actions are a denial of who we are as God's children.

We fear our economic future. So we take short cuts to economic security to insure our future. Some of the short cuts involve keeping the money that we should be giving to God for ourselves. Our justification for this is that God knows we need to money to take care of our family's needs and to make sure they have a future. Have we ever asked ourselves what kind of economic future God has prepared for us?

Too often we're so busy watching out for our own comfort that we cannot imagine taking any sort of personal risk.

Consider the man who went to see the pastor of an inner-city church. Though the pastor was used to the conditions of poverty and want surrounding his parish, he was touched by the story this man told him.

The man described the needs of a poor widow. "She has four hungry children to feed, is confined to her bed with no money for a doctor, and she owes three months rent and is about to be evicted from her apartment." The man then explained that he was trying to help raise the needed rent money, $600. Digging into his own wallet while racking his brains for other solutions, the pastor applauded the man's concern and commitment. "Of course I'll help," he said, "If you can give your time to this cause, so can I. By the way, how do you know this woman?"

"I'm the landlord," the man replied.

We deny Christ in so many ways. By failing to live boldly as Christians we deny the power of Jesus Christ to help us be what He has called us to be.

Unit III. Personalities in the Early Church

Lesson 10

Barnabas: Encourager and Enabler

Acts 4:36-37; 9:26-27; 11:22-26; 15:36-41

And Joses, who by the apostles was surnamed Barnabas, (which is, being interpreted, The son of consolation,) a Levite, and of the country of Cyprus,

37 Having land, sold it, and brought the money, and laid it at the apostles' feet.

Acts 9

26 And when Saul was come to Jerusalem, he assayed to join himself to the disciples: but they were all afraid of him, and believed not that he was a disciple.

27 But Barnabas took him, and brought him to the apostles, and declared unto them how he had seen the Lord in the way, and that he had spoken to him, and how he had preached boldly at Damascus in the name of Jesus.

Acts 11

22 Then tidings of these things came unto the ears of the church which was in Jerusalem: and they sent forth Barnabas, that he should go as far as Antioch.

23 Who, when he came, and had seen the grace of God, was glad, and exhorted them all, that with purpose of heart they would cleave unto the Lord.

24 For he was a good man, and full of the Holy Ghost and of faith: and much people was added unto the Lord.

25 Then departed Barnabas to Tarsus, for to seek Saul:

26 And when he had found him, he brought him unto Antioch. And it came to pass, that a whole year they assembled themselves with the church, and taught much people. And the disciples were called Christians first in Antioch.

Acts 15

36 And some days after Paul said unto Barnabas, Let us go again and visit our brethren in every city where we have preached the word of the Lord, and see how they do.

37 And Barnabas determined to take with them John, whose surname was Mark.

38 But Paul thought not good to take him with them, who departed from them from Pamphylia, and went not with them to the work.

39 And the contention was so sharp between them, that they departed asunder one from the other: and so Barnabas took Mark, and sailed unto Cyprus;

40 And Paul chose Silas, and departed, being recommended by the brethren unto the grace of God.

41 And he went through Syria and Cilicia, confirming the churches.

Feb. 2

Memory Selection
Acts 11:23-24

Background Scripture
Acts 4:32-37; 9:26-27;
11:19-30; 15:36-40

Devotional Reading
Hebrews 10:19-25

221

Sometimes Christianity is presented as a set of doctrines—and indeed the doctrinal aspect of the faith is crucial. This unit, however, shows also the impact that individual people had in the early Church, just as the previous unit focused on the influence of persons during the life and ministry of Jesus. This emphasis on

Christian personalities should not surprise us, since the faith has always been spread by the impact Christ makes on the human heart.

This lesson focuses on the influence of the early Christian leader Barnabas in the life of the apostle Paul. As noted, Bar-nabas means "Son of Encouragement." It was a nickname truly earned by this good man. As his work unfolds, focus also on how we ourselves can be encouragers in the life of others.

The young missionary was on a speaking tour to raise funds. At several engagements, he was accompanied by an elder from his sponsoring congregation. We can imagine how the young man would find the sage advice and fatherly presence of the older man a steadying influence.

Not! The older man's encouragement hardly took the form of wise counsel. Instead, sitting on the front pew just before the young missionary arose to speak, he would grip the young man's knee with a strong hand and whisper, "Go, baby go!"

In this lesson, Barnabas had the same kind of sensitivity as this elder, in perceiving the kind of mentoring and encouragement appropriate for the moment. What similar roles can we play in the Lord's work today?

Teaching Outline	Daily Bible Readings	
I. A Cypriot's Gift—Acts 4:36-37	Mon.	Son of Encouragement Acts 4:32-37
II. Selfless Mediator—9:26-27	Tue.	Speaking Up for Paul Acts 9:23-30
A. Mistrusted convert, 26	Wed.	Exhorting Believers Acts 11:19-24
B. Ministry of mediation, 27		
III. Supportive Encourager—11:22-26	Thu.	Barnabas Fetches Saul Acts 11:25-30
A. The gift of exhortation, 22-24	Fri.	Ordained as Missionaries Acts 13:1-5
C. The gift of teaching, 25-26		
IV. Strong Feelings—15:36-41	Sat.	Relating What God Has Done Acts 14:21-28
A. Plans for a second journey, 36-37	Sun.	Barnabas Chooses Mark Acts 15:36-41
B. Friends disagree, 38-41		

Verse by Verse

I. A Cypriot's Gift—Acts 4:36-37

36 And Joses, who by the apostles was surnamed Barnabas, (which is, being interpreted, The son of consolation,) a Levite, and of the country of Cyprus,

37 Having land, sold it, and brought the money, and laid it at the apostles' feet.

Although the influence of Barnabas, or "Joses," in the early Church can hardly be over-emphasized, he seems to be a humble man who did not seek the spotlight. He is best known for facilitating Paul's ministry—a task hinted at even by his name, *bar-* or "son of" Encouragement (NIV).

Because the city was teeming with visitors for an unusually long period, the crucial need of feeding them arose. These earliest believers in the resurrected Messiah caught His spirit of caring and sharing early on; and those with means enabled the critical needs of the masses to be met (vss. 32-35; see also 7:1-7). We learn here that Barnabas was also generous— selling property and bringing the proceeds to the apostles to help with the task of feeding the multitudes.

II. Selfless Mediator—9:26-27

A. Mistrusted convert, 26

26 And when Saul was come to Jerusalem, he assayed to join himself to the disciples: but they were all afraid of him, and believed not that he was a disciple.

The scene now moves beyond the stoning of Stephen, a mob attack attended and approved of by Saul of Tarsus, who would later become the apostle Paul (Acts 7:60–8:1); and beyond Saul's subsequent conversion (9:1-18). At first, Saul was distrusted by both Jews and Christians. Disillusioned Jews had tried to kill him when he proved to be a turncoat and joined the opposition (vss. 23-25).

B. Ministry of mediation, 27

27 But Barnabas took him, and brought him to the apostles, and declared unto them how he had seen the Lord in the way, and that he had spoken to him, and how he had preached boldly at Damascus in the name of Jesus.

Now Barnabas' gift of encouragement for which he had been nicknamed proves to provide Saul with just the kind of introduction he needs to win the confidence of the Christians he had so recently persecuted. Barnabas wisely takes the new convert to "the top," to the apostles, trusting that their acceptance of Saul would have a "trickle-down" effect on rank-and-file members of the fast-growing body of believers.

"He had spoken to him" refers to the Lord's having spoken to Saul in the Damascus Road experience. Barnabas may have known such details of Saul's conversion from having heard his testimony while preaching to the Jews of Damascus (vs. 22). He may also have served as Saul's mentor, since as a Jewish-Christian himself he would have had a good grasp of how to link the new faith with the old. At any rate, Barnabas' courageous attempt to integrate Saul into the leadership of the early Christian movement apparently proved successful, in light of the responsibility that will later be given to him.

III. Supportive Encourager–11:22-26
A. The gift of exhortation, 22-24

22 Then tidings of these things came unto the ears of the church which was in Jerusalem: and they sent forth Barnabas, that he should go as far as Antioch.

23 Who, when he came, and had seen the grace of God, was glad, and exhorted them all, that with purpose of heart they would cleave unto the Lord.

24 For he was a good man, and full of the Holy Ghost and of faith: and much people was added unto the Lord.

The "tidings" that reached the Jerusalem church consisted of the news that the gospel was being preached abroad by Christians who had fled Jerusalem after Stephen's martyrdom (Acts 8:4-8). Some of these early "lay missionaries" had

preached to Gentiles (11:20), taking seriously their Lord's saying that He had "other sheep" outside the fold of Judaism. Leaders of the Jerusalem church, who had not yet grasped this universal mission, were anxious to know more.

For this fact-finding mission they chose Barnabas, perhaps because, being from Cyprus, he was a part of the Dispersion of Jews to many lands and would be well-acquainted with issues that arose in communities where they lived side-by-side with Gentiles. They send him to Antioch of Syria, 300 miles north of Jerusalem, which was such a thriving city that it was third in importance in the Empire, following Rome and Alexandria.

In keeping with his positive spirit, Barnabas heartily approves of what he finds; and consistent with his gift of encouragement he exhorts these new believers to be steadfast in their new faith. Note that Luke champions Barnabas as both a good and a Spirit-filled man. The early Christians would not have benefited from the work of a person without integrity, or who was not open to the gifts of the Spirit, regardless of how effective a motivator he was.

B. The gift of teaching, 25-26

25 Then departed Barnabas to Tarsus, for to seek Saul:

26 And when he had found him, he brought him unto Antioch. And it came to pass, that a whole year they assembled themselves with the church, and taught much people. And the disciples were called Christians first in Antioch.

Barnabas is both wise and humble enough to recognize that these new Christians need not only a "cheer leader" to encourage them but a teacher to ground them in the faith. What better candidate for this task than Saul, who had the training of a Jewish rabbi but was raised in a Gentile setting? It was during Saul's year at Antioch that the name "Christian" was first applied to the movement previously referred to simply as "the way." Many commentators believe that the name "Christian" was given with some degree of derision, as though opponents were dismissing them as "little Christs"; but as the movement grew the name would be treated with more respect.

IV. Strong Feelings—15:36-41
A. Plans for a second journey, 36-37

36 And some days after Paul said unto Barnabas, Let us go again and visit our brethren in every city where we have preached the word of the Lord, and see how they do.

37 And Barnabas determined to take with them John, whose surname was Mark.

Paul and Barnabas had taken with them young John Mark (probably the Mark who wrote the second Gospel) on their first missionary journey into Asia Minor (Acts 13:5). We know from Colossians 4:10 that Mark was Barnabas' nephew. Both the family connection and the reasons for having selected Mark as part of the mission in the first place prompt Barnabas to assume that the young man will accompany them again.

B. Friends disagree, 38-41

38 But Paul thought not good to take him with them, who departed from them from Pamphylia, and went not with them to the work.

39 And the contention was so sharp between them, that they departed asunder one from the other: and so Barnabas took Mark, and sailed unto Cyprus;

40 And Paul chose Silas, and departed, being recommended by the brethren unto the grace of God.

41 And he went through Syria and Cilicia, confirming the churches.

Although we are not told why, Mark had left Paul and Barnabas at Perga on the first missionary trip (Acts 13:13). Only now do we learn that whatever his reasons for leaving, Paul considered it as a defection "from the work" ahead. Now, therefore, he declines to enlist Mark again. This disagreement is often treated more seriously than the evidence sustains. It actually resulted in doubling the missionary activity at this point, with Paul and Silas taking one course and Barnabas and Mark another. Also, toward the end of his life, Paul shows that in his estimation Mark was entirely rehabilitated, and was "profitable to me for the ministry" (2 Tim. 4:11).

Their disagreement shows that even the closest of Christians can disagree without animosity. We may also speculate that Barnabas, characteristically the "Son of Encouragement," may have had a better spirit about the dispute than the apostle Paul, whose personality was so intense that it would be hard to imagine his earning the name "Son of Encouragement."

Evangelistic Emphasis

Barnabas was to the ministry of Paul what John the Baptizer was to the ministry of Jesus. Without a Barnabas encouraging Saul of Tarsus, there might not have been a Paul, the Apostle. Barnabas' star shines but for a moment in Scripture, but it shines brightly.

The difference we make in life has nothing to do with the number of years we spend on the earth. Brightening a life has everything to do with the intensity of our faith. Barnabas had a faith that wholly trusted God and defied human nature. A "safe faith" that relied on human skill would have rejected a friendship with Saul of Tarsus. By human standards, Saul could not be trusted. Barnabas could be the "son of encouragement" because he saw beyond what was tangible to what was possible in the kingdom of God.

Encouragement is all about seeing the possibilities in a person and being willing to reach out to those possibilities. The "good news" is that Jesus Christ has looked beyond what is in you and me. He sees, from the vantage of eternity, what could be. That is why He encourages us. He wants to help us reach that point of full and faithful discipleship.

Barnabas also had faith in himself. Knowing he was an instrument of God he could confidently reach out to Saul and help begin the ministry of Paul. Do you believe in yourself enough to claim your place in the kingdom of God?

ഇരൂ

When he (Barnabas) came and saw the grace of God, he rejoiced, and he exhorted them all to remain faithful to the Lord with steadfast devotion; for he was a good man, full of the Holy Spirit and of faith.— *Acts 11:23-24*

There is an old story told about a man who was constantly going to the altar of the church. At every revival he would come asking for the "filling of the Spirit." This went on for years. At one revival, near the end of the week, the fellow once again presented himself for prayer for "the filling of the Holy Spirit." The evangelist had the man kneel at the altar and began praying aloud that this "brother be filled with the Holy Spirit."

Suddenly from the back of the church the voice of an elderly saint in the church was heard, praying, "But be careful Lord, he leaks!"

The term "full of the Holy Spirit" is a rarity in Scripture. It is used of those persons who are walking close to the Father. Barnabas was not the only disciple who was "full of the Spirit," Stephen was another disciple who was described as being "full of the Holy Spirit

Are you "filled with the Holy Spirit," or do you leak?

Weekday Problems

Tony was at the end of his rope. His shift had been notified that the plant was "downsizing" and all workers on the third shift would be laid off. He could either wait for an opening on another shift, or accept transfer across the country. Moving was out of the question because Tony was taking care of his mother, who had recently suffered a stroke.

If the job problem wasn't enough, his wife Pam was giving Tony fits at home. She had wanted a baby for years. The time never seemed to be right, and now it seemed as thought time was running out. She and Tony tried and tried, but failed to have children. This depressed Pam and she took her depression and anger out on Tony.

Hal Martin was a life-long friend of Tony's. They played a few holes of golf together once a month. One afternoon Hal just stopped by. He caught Pam and Tony in on of their tiffs. Sensing the anger in the room, Hal invited himself in for a glass of tea. He sat for a moment in silence.

Tony said, "Boy, I'll bet we look silly, don't we?"

Hal continued to sit. As the minutes unfolded into a couple of hours, Hal listened patiently to both Tony and Pam. He offered no advice. He took no sides. Hal made it clear that he heard and understood each one of them.

*How can one offer encouragement without using words?

In the Presence of the Absent-Minded

A man staggered from his train and complained to his wife, "I'm exhausted, riding backward for two hours."

"Why didn't you ask the person sitting opposite if you could trade places?" his wife asked.

"I couldn't," her husband replied. "There was no one sitting there."

"Where's the car?" demanded the professor's wife. "Don't you remember driving it to town?"

"Oh dear me," he replied. "I do remember that after I got out I turned around to thank the driver for the lift, and wondered where he had gone."

Did you hear about the absent-minded professor who . . .

   . . . Returned from lunch, saw the sign on his door, "Back in 30 minutes," and sat down to wait for himself?

   . . . Struck a match to see if he had blown out the candle?

   . . . Left for town, and slammed his wife and kissed the door?

This Lesson in Your Life

I have vivid memories of trying to talk to my dad about playing football. I had average ability. I played quarterback, but managed to stay injured most of my High School playing days. I remember trying to talk to Dad about giving up football. I talked about wanting to do other things and about getting hurt so much. He really wasn't listening, though, and sent me on my way with a piece of advice: "Remember son, the bigger they are the harder they fall." I found out it was true. Big guys were landing on me all the time, and they did fall hard. I suppose Dad was trying to encourage me to continue playing the sport he loved so.

Encouragement is an elusive concept. I have witnessed ministers "encouraging" a congregation: "If you don't pledge the budget, we'll turn out the lights." I have seen people "encouraging" one another to teach Sunday school: "If you don't take the third grade class, I guess we won't have a class this year." I have been shocked at "encouragement" I have heard at funerals: "Don't worry honey, it'll be all right." Encouragement can't be done on a superficial level. We have to be honest about our hopes and fears before we can enter into another person's hopes and fears. My father had a fear that I wasn't going to fulfill his desire that I play football. He couldn't relate to my fear of being hurt while playing, so he could offer no encouragement.

Barnabas takes up very few pages of the New Testament, but he is the role model for people who are called to the ministry of encouragement. Much like John the Baptizer prepared the way for Jesus' ministry, Barnabas prepared the way for the ministry of Paul the Apostle. In the early days of Paul's mission, it was Barnabas who vouched for the new disciple. Many of the leaders suspected that Paul was trying to infiltrate the Christian movement with his sudden conversion. It was Barnabas who testified to the authenticity of Paul's conversion experience. When you consider what Barnabas did, you are struck by the risks that he took.

Encouragement involves letting down your walls in order to enter the life of another. It is not glad-handing people. It is not "patting them on the back." It is not quoting the verse of the day and telling them that God will not give us more than we can handle. It is entering their lives where they are, and staying with them. Barnabas left Paul only after he was certain the Apostle could stand alone.

This would be a good day to take some time and reflect in the class about persons who have encouraged you and your class members in discipleship. Recall persons who have been an encouragement in a dark time in life. If these persons are still around, why not thank them for what they meant to you?

GETTING THE FACTS STRAIGHT

1. Acts 4:32 indicates a unique economic practice of the early Church. What was that practice?

There was no private ownership. The early Christians placed everything in trust to be used in common by the whole group.

2. Why was the first mention of Barnabas associated with this early Christian practice of sharing all things in common?

Barnabas sold some property and gave the proceeds of that sale to the church to be used as was needed.

3. What was Barnabas' given name and what is its significance?

Barnabas' given name was Joseph. He was called "Barnabas" by the disciples. Barnabas means, "Son of encouragement."

4. What official Hebrew cultic office did Barnabas hold?

Barnabas was a Levite. He was a professional in the interpretation of Jewish Law.

5. How would Barnabas' training naturally draw him to Paul?

Barnabas was a Levite, trained in the Law. Saul of Tarsus was a Pharisee, also trained in the Law.

6. What happened when Paul presented himself at Jerusalem to the disciples?

The disciples were afraid of Paul and were hesitant to let him participate in the life of their community.

7. What evidence did Barnabas give the Jerusalem church in defense of Paul?

Barnabas vouched for Paul's Damascus road experience. He also explained that Paul had boldly preached Jesus to all who would listen.

8. As a result of Barnabas' plea, how did the Jerusalem community act toward Paul?

They put him to work. He continued to preach. He offended the Hellenists, who tried to kill him. The church sent him to Tarsus to save his life.

9. How did Barnabas and Paul meet again?

Barnabas had been sent to Antioch. From there he went to Tarsus to get Paul. Together they returned to minister in Antioch.

10. What significant job was given to Paul and Barnabas?

They were in charge of collecting and transporting the famine relief offering for Jerusalem.

Ignace Jan Paderewski, the famous composer-pianist, was scheduled to perform in a concert hall in America. It was an evening to remember—black tuxedos and long evening dresses, a high-society extravaganza. Present in the audience that evening was a mother with her fidgety nine-year old son. Weary of waiting, he squirmed constantly in his seat. His mother had brought him only because she hoped that he would be encouraged to practice the piano if he could hear the immortal Paderewski.

At one point in the program as the mother turned to talk with friends, her son could stay seated no longer. He slipped away from her side, strangely drawn to the ebony concert grand Steinway and its leather-tufted stool on the huge stage flooded with blinding lights. Without much notice from the sophisticated audience, the boy sat down at the stool, staring wide-eyed at the black and white keys. He placed his small, trembling fingers in the right location and began playing "Chopsticks." The roar of the crowd was hushed as hundreds of frowning faces, turned in the boy's direction. Irritated and embarrassed, they began to shout,

"Get that boy away from there!"

"Who'd bring a kid that young in here."

"Where's his mother."

"Somebody stop him."

Backstage, the master overheard the sounds out front and quickly put together in his mind what was happening. Hurriedly, he grabbed his coat and rushed on stage. Without one word of announcement, he stooped over behind the boy, reached around both sides, and began to improvise a countermelody to harmonize with and enhance "Chopsticks." As the two of them played together, Paderewski kept whispering in the boy's ear, "Keep going. Don't quit, son. Keep on playing. Don't stop. Don't quit."

So, I tell you. Keep on going. Don't stop. Don't quit.

I thought you might like that word of encouragement in your work. We need a whole generation of Barnabases in the church. Not people who stand over each other making guilt the prime motivation factor for service—that is not encouragement. We need people who will lift each other up in prayer, who will call out the giftedness in others. We need folks who have vision, and who see how we can be a part of that vision. Our words and deeds of encouragement make the difference between people who settle for "Chopsticks" and those who master *"Concerto in A Minor."* In the Church it can be the difference between being a "pew sitter" and a person who does great things for Christ.

Encouragement is as simple as making a phone call, writing a note, sending a small gift, or simply saying "I'm praying for you." Those things make us all feel important, and that is goal of encouragement.

Paul: Obedient Messenger

Acts 26:12-23, 27-29

Whereupon as I went to Damascus with authority and commission from the chief priests,

13 At midday, O king, I saw in the way a light from heaven, above the brightness of the sun, shining round about me and them which journeyed with me.

14 And when we were all fallen to the earth, I heard a voice speaking unto me, and saying in the Hebrew tongue, Saul, Saul, why persecutest thou me? it is hard for thee to kick against the pricks.

15 And I said, Who art thou, Lord? And he said, I am Jesus whom thou persecutest.

16 But rise, and stand upon thy feet: for I have appeared unto thee for this purpose, to make thee a minister and a witness both of these things which thou hast seen, and of those things in the which I will appear unto thee;

17 Delivering thee from the people, and from the Gentiles, unto whom now I send thee,

18 To open their eyes, and to turn them from darkness to light, and from the power of Satan unto God, that they may receive forgiveness of sins, and inheritance among them which are sanctified by faith that is in me.

19 Whereupon, O king Agrippa, I was not disobedient unto the heavenly vision:

20 But shewed first unto them of Damascus, and at Jerusalem, and throughout all the coasts of Judaea, and then to the Gentiles, that they should repent and turn to God, and do works meet for repentance.

21 For these causes the Jews caught me in the temple, and went about to kill me.

22 Having therefore obtained help of God, I continue unto this day, witnessing both to small and great, saying none other things than those which the prophets and Moses did say should come:

23 That Christ should suffer, and that he should be the first that should rise from the dead, and should shew light unto the people, and to the Gentiles.

27 King Agrippa, believest thou the prophets? I know that thou believest.

28 Then Agrippa said unto Paul, Almost thou persuadest me to be a Christian.

29 And Paul said, I would to God, that not only thou, but also all that hear me this day, were both almost, and altogether such as I am, except these bonds.

Feb. 9

Memory Selection
Acts 26:19

Background Scripture
Acts 25:23–26:32

Devotional Reading
Ephesians 3:1-13

A modern saying has it that "God does not call the qualified; He qualifies the called." No doubt the adage makes a valid point. No limits can be placed on how God can enable anyone to do the task for which He calls them. Yet the saying doesn't seem to describe all "callings." In the case of the apostle Paul, God called a

Ask group members to call out one-sentence descriptions of the first thing that comes to mind when they think about Paul. Responses to anticipate, or to supply, include: He was at first called "Saul" . . . He was a Jew who at first persecuted Christians . . . Later he became the "apostle to the

person who was already admirably qualified for ministry. Trained at the feet of a famous Jewish rabbi, Saul of Tarsus was also a Greek-speaking Jew familiar enough with non-Jewish cultures to be later selected as "the apostle to the Gentiles."

Today's lesson is drawn from only one of the three accounts of Saul's conversion from Judaism (see also Acts 9 and 22). The space the New Testament devotes to this topic indicates the significance of this, the "13th apostle."

Gentiles". . . He was the 13th apostle, . . . He wrote more of the New Testament than any other single author . . . He supported himself as a tent-maker . . . He championed "salvation by grace" over keeping the works of the Law . . . He was from the Gentile city of Tarsus . . . His preaching often got him into trouble and even thrown in jail. No one in this unit on "Personalities in the Early Church" had a greater influence on early Gentile Christianity than the apostle Paul.

Teaching Outline	Daily Bible Readings

I. Interrupted Journey—12-18
  A. Paul's commission, 12
  B. Accosted by Christ, 13-15
  C. A new assignment, 16-18
 	
II. Instant Obedience—19-23
  A. New message, new
    audience, 19-20
  B. Basis of the charge, 21-23
 	
III. Invitation to a King, 27-29
  A. Persuasive intent, 27-28
  B. 'You and all others!,' 29
	Mon. Paul Before Festus
	       Acts 25: 1-12
	Tue. Festus Explains the Case
	       Acts 25:13-22
	Wed. Paul Before Agrippa
	       Acts 25:23-27
	Thu. Paul Begins His Defense
	       Acts 26:1-8
	Fri. About His Conversion
	       Acts 26:9-18
	Sat. Paul's Obedience
	       Acts 26:19-23
	Sun. Appeal to Agrippa
	       Acts 26:24-32

Verse by Verse

I. Interrupted Journey—12-18

A. Paul's commission, 12

12 Whereupon as I went to Damascus with authority and commission from the chief priests,

This is the third time that the story of Paul's conversion from Judaism to Christianity is recorded (see also Acts 9:1-31; 22:1-21). He is now confronting King Herod Agrippa at one of several official hearings convened to consider the charges by Jews who had caused his arrest (22:30ff.). The grandson of Herod the Great, Agrippa had learned to pander to the Jews by persecuting Christians (Acts 12:1-3).

Paul's persecution of Christians (as the rabbinically trained Saul of Tarsus) had begun in Jerusalem. Jewish authorities, acting in accordance with Roman law, had deputized him to capture Christian leaders and returning them to Jerusalem for trial (22:5). Paul begins the story of his conversion at this point because it shows how scrupulous he had been to keep the Law that was so treasured by the very people who are bringing a case against him now.

B. Accosted by Christ, 13-15

13 At midday, O king, I saw in the way a light from heaven, above the brightness of the sun, shining round about me and them which journeyed with me.

14 And when we were all fallen to the earth, I heard a voice speaking unto me, and saying in the Hebrew tongue, Saul, Saul, why persecutest thou me? it is hard for thee to kick against the pricks.

15 And I said, Who art thou, Lord? And he said, I am Jesus whom thou persecutest.

God is so intent on converting this Jewish zealot into an instrument for His own use that He abandons all subtlety in getting Paul's attention. That the light was a supernatural event was testified to by those who accompanied him on his mission. The account in 22:9 indicates as much. (This verse also says that Paul's companions did not hear the voice from heaven, compared with 9:7, which says they did. Possibly they heard a sound *like* a voice, but did not understand the message.)

As other translations show, "pricks" were sharp poles or goads attached to an ox-cart to keep oxen from straying from side to side. The voice from heaven is asking Paul, then known as Saul, whether it is not uncomfortable to be so zealously working against an all-powerful God.

Understandably shocked by being knocked down by a bright light, Paul's first response is to anxiously ask who is behind this strange event (which, according to previous accounts, included being struck temporarily blind). Since "Lord" can simply mean "Sir," or "Master," Paul is not necessarily acknowdging that he is confronting Jesus as Lord. Whatever he understood at first, the event will later be taken to qualify Paul as an apostle by having "seen the Lord" (1 Cor. 9:1; see also Acts 9:27).

Yet the very fact that Paul perceived this to be a supernatural event may also indicated that he realizes that whoever this "Lord" is, he is somehow involved with Yahweh Himself. We can only imagine the shock Paul felt when he realized that he had been so wrong-headed as to miss the fact that the Jesus whose followers he was persecuting is somehow actually identified with the God he thought he was serving!

C. A new assignment, 16-18

16 But rise, and stand upon thy feet: for I have appeared unto thee for this purpose, to make thee a minister and a witness both of these things which thou hast seen, and of those things in the which I will appear unto thee;

17 Delivering thee from the people, and from the Gentiles, unto whom now I send thee,

18 To open their eyes, and to turn them from darkness to light, and from the power of Satan unto God, that they may receive forgiveness of sins, and inheritance among them which are sanctified by faith that is in me.

The Lord wastes no time rebuking Saul for his mistake. Instead, He immediately says that he is being singled out for this conversion experience not just for his own sake, but because God has in mind a larger mission for him. More than once throughout Christian history, the zeal with which a person opposes God is eventually channeled into the more positive purpose of working equally hard in His behalf. Note that verse 16 promises further appearances, presumably to reveal other Christians truths to Paul.

In verses 17-18 we learn that the Lord also promises to deliver Paul from the Jews ("the people") now clamoring for his death, and from Gentiles, whose courts he will be tried in. Obviously this does not mean that Paul's life will be spared forever, but that he will be delivered long enough to fulfill this new mission God has in mind for him. (Later, as other early Christians are persecuted for the faith, "deliverance" will come to mean not being released from death but from the threat of not confessing their faith.)

II. Instant Obedience—19-23

A. New message, new audience, 19-20

19 Whereupon, O king Agrippa, I was not disobedient unto the heavenly vision:

20 But shewed first unto them of Damascus, and at Jerusalem, and throughout all the coasts of Judaea, and then to the Gentiles, that they should repent and turn to God, and do works meet for repentance.

The man who had been on the way to persecute Christians in Damascus went on to preach Christ there! Luke mentioned this in Acts 9:20, adding that Paul's defection from Judaism so angered the Jews that he had to be helped to escape an attempt on his life (9:23-25). As for Paul's work among the Gentiles, he summarizes three missionary tours in the last half of verse 20.

B. Basis of the charge, 21-23

21 For these causes the Jews caught me in the temple, and went about to kill me.

22 Having therefore obtained help of God, I continue unto this day, witnessing both to small and great, saying none other things than those which the prophets and Moses did say should come:

23 That Christ should suffer, and that he should be the first that should rise from the dead, and should shew light unto the people, and to the Gentiles.

Although "these causes" no doubt refer to Paul's work among Gentiles, the actual charge that he took uncircumcised men into the Temple was false (see 21:27-29). Still, his opponents were able to make the charge stick in hearing after hearing all through the rest of the book of Acts, which ends with Paul having appealed to Caesar and taken to Rome, where he was kept under house arrest while awaiting trial.

In verses 22-23 Paul explains that his teaching is consistent with the Jews' own Law. Although the Sadducees among his accusers would have objected to his doctrine of the resurrection, this would have served to show Agrippa that the whole matter was a doctrinal matter between Christians and Jews, and had no place in a Roman court.

III. Invitation to a King, 27-29

A. Persuasive intent, 27-28

27 King Agrippa, believest thou the prophets? I know that thou believest.

28 Then Agrippa said unto Paul, Almost thou persuadest me to be a Christian.

The Herodian family consisted of Idumeans (Edomites), many of whom had been forcibly converted to Judaism during the days of the Maccabeean rebellion against Rome. Paul therefore knew that Agrippa would have been somewhat acquainted with the Old Testament. Ever the evangelist even while under arrest, Paul does not shy away from confronting the king with the opportunity to confess faith in Jesus as the Messiah predicted by the prophets.

The KJV rendering of verse 28 sounds as though the king is on the verge of becoming a Christian; but most scholars now think the difficult phrase should be translated to show that he is actually dismissing Paul's invitation by saying something like the niv's translation: "Do you think that in such a short time you can persuade me to be a Christian?"

B. 'You and all others!,' 29

29 And Paul said, I would to God, that not only thou, but also all that hear me this day, were both almost, and altogether such as I am, except these bonds.

Paul's more serious reply will not let the king get off the hook with such a light-hearted response. He would wish for all, whether with much argument or little, to share the joy he knew as a Christian—minus, of course, the shackles that bound him.

Evangelistic Emphasis

We are a part of the church because people have vision. The Sunday school class you sit in on Sunday is there because someone had vision. Some individual or group of individuals believed that God was calling them to build the space in which your faith community meets.

We are part of the Church, because other people have had vision. We don't think of the apostle Paul as a visionary, but he was. It was his vision of a mission to the Gentiles that brought the message of Jesus Christ to the rest of the world. Without the apostle Paul, the church may have been a part of the Jewish faith community today.

The struggle that Paul faced most in his ministry was a defense of his ministry to the Gentiles. His Jewish brethren thought that he was being disobedient to the will of God. Paul explained to them that God had given him the vision for the ministry to the Gentiles.

God is a visionary. He sees us not as we are, but as we could be with our lives in tune with His will. On Sunday, when you sit in your class remember that you are there because people had vision and followed their belief in a visionary God.

The good news is that when God gives you a vision, He also gives you the power to accomplish the vision he has given you.

ಬಂಡ

After that, King Agrippa, I was not disobedient to the heavenly vision.—*Acts 26: 19*

As a minister, one of my tasks is to perform wedding ceremonies. It is a joy to share with a young couple the love that brings a man and a woman to the point of making their vows public. In the months and weeks prior to the wedding I meet with the couple to help them prepare for the service and for a life together.

One of the questions that some of the brides have been asking recently is, "You are not going to ask me if I have to be obedient to him, are you?" I reassure them that the promise to "obey" has not been in most marriage rituals since the middle 19th century.

Yet I wonder about couples who don't want to deal with the notion of being obedient, at least to each other. In these times, of course, a trip to the mall leaves one wondering whether any longer think that obedience is an important lesson to teach at all.

I'm glad that Paul was obedient to the vision that God gave him. Paul changed the course of church history. Obedience is a concept that is not outdated, but still sorely needed.

Weekday Problems

The reactions from members of the Finance Committee ranged from resignation to outrage. The financial secretary at Big Church had spent an hour going over the ways in which the church was in violation of current tax law. The indiscretions of Big Church ranged from not reporting income for teenagers working in the nursery to "money laundering."

The main problem as Frank Johnson saw it was how the new laws would hurt Mrs. Mary Grace Wallace. Miss Mary Grace, as everyone knew her, was a widowed saint of Big Church. Her husband Harry had been the church organist for as long as anyone could remember. When he died, members of the church felt compelled to supplement Mary Grace's meager pension. They gave donations to the church in Mary Grace's name. The church treasurer wrote a check from these donations to Miss Mary Grace. For years the members had taken a tax deduction on the amount they gave the church for Miss Mary Grace. Miss Mary Grace never felt that she had to claim this gift as income from the church. The financial secretary told the finance committee that this practice was at best not good business, and at worst, illegal.

Other tax-related issues were also expressed. Several committee members asked, "Why do we have to obey the tax laws? We are a church!"

*How do you feel about being obedient, even to laws you don't like?

Goofs and Glitches

The following errors failed to stop the press:
Mr. Carlson won a 10-pound turkey at Saturday's shurkey toot.

❖❖❖❖❖

At the Ladies' Aid Society meeting many interesting articles were raffled off. Every member brought something they no longer needed. Many members brought their husbands.

❖❖❖❖❖

First printing: Mr. Janelli was a defective in the police force.
Second printing: Mr. Janelli was a detective in the police farce.

❖❖❖❖❖

The Wildwife League will meet tonight.

❖❖❖❖❖

Headline: Nine volunteers put in new church furnace.

❖❖❖❖❖

Dr. Jeremiah is the author of a brand-new book that is expected to outsmell the 2 million copies of his first book.

237

This Lesson in Your Life

The apostle Paul was reviewing his call before King Agrippa. A man who had the power to set him free or to condemn him to death was the audience to whom Paul appealed for justice. Paul stood and spoke clearly of his conviction that Jesus had called him specifically to preach the good news to the Gentiles.

Paul was a man of many talents. He was a tent-maker, and not impressed with professional preachers. I wonder what he would have to say today about our super-star traveling preachers? I wonder if this simple tent-maker would have much patience with a preacher who complains about how tough ministry is, flying from place to place in a $35 million Lear jet. Paul went to a city and went to work making tents and paying his own way as he did evangelism in that place.

Paul was a thinker. The logic that he used witnesses to the tough mindedness of this man. He argued with Jews, Gentiles, and pagans alike. His arguments were to convince them not that he was right, but that Jesus was the Messiah. He called people to "repentance," which means to "change one's mind." How much do we talk about the "transformation of the mind?" Do we use well thought out, articulate arguments to convince people to have faith in Jesus Christ?

Paul was a moral conservative. There is much argument about some of the rules he left for the Church. Many think that some of the things Paul told us not to do, are now fine. Their argument is that Paul's teachings were limited to his own cultural setting. Yet we still need the strong word of "right and wrong." We live in a day where many do not respect absolutes. The word that Paul gave the Church would serve us well as we seek to be faithful in a crazy world.

Paul was a poet. He penned some of the most beautiful poetic images. First Corinthians 13 is the epitome of love's description. He wrote hymns and poems, and used his poetic touch to let his readers know how Jesus had put a "song in his heart."

Paul was above all a visionary leader. A bi-vocational preacher, rabbi, poet, missionary, and visionary leader, he serves as an example of leadership at the dawn of the 21st century. Paul was who he was and did what he did because he followed what was in his heart.

God has also placed a vision and a passion in each of our hearts to follow Him. When we follow that passion and vision we will be faithful and others will be touched for Jesus Christ.

Following our ambition and passion for God is called being obedient. Such a simple, almost quaint notion is a powerful key to change lives. Being obedient to God is being a faithful disciple.

GETTING THE FACTS STRAIGHT

1. **What was Saul doing when his conversion experience took place?**
Saul was on his way to Damascus. The High Priests had given him authority and commission to arrest Christians.

2. **At what time of day did Paul's experience with Jesus happen?**
The experience Paul had with Jesus happened at noon.

3. **On the road to Damascus, was Paul traveling alone?**
No, Paul was not alone. He and his companions were affected by the presence of Jesus.

4. **What strange event happened on the road to Damascus?**
Paul saw a light from heaven brighter than the noonday sun and he heard a voice from heaven.

5. **What interesting detail did Paul give about what the voice said to him?**
Paul noted that the voice spoke to him in Aramaic.

6. **What was the initial question that Jesus asked Paul?**
Jesus asked, "Saul, Saul, why are you persecuting me?"

7. **In asking that question, what did Jesus affirm about His relationship to the church?**
Since Saul was on his way to persecute the Church, in asking that question Jesus showed that He and the Church are one.

8. **After Paul heard the voice, what happened next?**
Jesus told Paul to get up and stand on his feet. He then gave him work to do,

9. **What was the first part of the assignment that Jesus gave to Saul?**
Saul was to be a servant and a witness to what the reality of Jesus he had experienced that day.

10. **What was the promise and the calling that Jesus spoke of?**
That Paul would be rescued from the Jews and the Gentiles, so he could minister to them.

"Without a vision the people perish."

What do those very familiar words mean to you as you teach this lesson?

In most homes there is the ubiquitous junk drawer. It is a drawer, usually in the kitchen but sometimes in a desk or a table, where you stash all the stuff you think you will ever need. In the one in my kitchen there is an odd assortment of things: batteries in all sizes, pens and pencils, paper clips and nails, coupons and sales announcements, letters and invitations, matches, and screwdrivers. The junk drawer in our kitchen grows and grows.

I open the drawer and begin throwing things away, but my wife will catch me and make me put the stuff back. She tells me, "You never now when we might need that stuff."

I submit to you that the junk drawer or the dirty closet in your home is indicative of what happens when your vision fades. The things in those junk places are there because you no longer have a vision for how they need to be used. Although they become junk, we keep those things around because we *might* use them sometime in a distant future.

The same dynamic is present as we talk about vision in our faith journey. If we don't have a vision, the things of our faith walk pile up in a closet and are no longer useful to us or to anyone else.

We need to clean out our spiritual closets. This process begins by taking time to dwell on God. Our vision and passion for ministry is inspired by our connection to God. When we sit alone with Him, he can point out all of the junk in our lives and show us how our vision has faded. God can find those things we thought were junk and show us how to use that part of our lives for Him. He can re-ignite the passion in our souls.

Once we know what is valuable and what is junk in our spiritual closets, we can be more faithful in our service to God. Are you carrying notions of how the church should be in ministry, service, and worship that you had 20 years ago, and you have never updated? Well, you need to get those thoughts out of your spiritual closet and re-examine them. Do you wish that things could "go back the way they used to be?" That idea should be thrown out.

How about the way technology is used in the church? Is your idea of modern technology an electric typewriter? If so, then you have some spiritual cleaning you and God need to do. Has your understanding of the Bible not changed since you were a youth in Sunday school? If so, you need to get rid of some of those notions and hear what God's Word says to you *today*.

If we have a vision and a passion for ministry, we will need to do some spring-cleaning in our spiritual closets. Hold on to what we need to serve God, and get rid of the rest.

When you have vision, you tend to travel light.

Timothy: Valued Helper

Acts 16:1-5; Philip. 2:19-24; 1 Tim. 1:1-3; 2 Tim. 1:3-5

Then came he to Derbe and Lystra: and, behold, a certain disciple was there, named Timotheus, the son of a certain woman, which was a Jewess, and believed; but his father was a Greek:

2 Which was well reported of by the brethren that were at Lystra and Iconium.

3 Him would Paul have to go forth with him; and took and circumcised him because of the Jews which were in those quarters: for they knew all that his father was a Greek.

4 And as they went through the cities, they delivered them the decrees for to keep, that were ordained of the apostles and elders which were at Jerusalem.

5 And so were the churches established in the faith, and increased in number daily.

Philippians 2

19 But I trust in the Lord Jesus to send Timotheus shortly unto you, that I also may be of good comfort, when I know your state.

20 For I have no man likeminded, who will naturally care for your state.

21 For all seek their own, not the things which are Jesus Christ's.

22 But ye know the proof of him, that, as a son with the father, he hath served with me in the gospel.

23 Him therefore I hope to send presently, so soon as I shall see how it will go with me.

24 But I trust in the Lord that I also myself shall come shortly.

1 Timothy 1

1 Paul, an apostle of Jesus Christ by the commandment of God our Saviour, and Lord Jesus Christ, which is our hope;

2 Unto Timothy, my own son in the faith: Grace, mercy, and peace, from God our Father and Jesus Christ our Lord.

3 As I besought thee to abide still at Ephesus, when I went into Macedonia, that thou mightest charge some that they teach no other doctrine,

2 Timothy 1

3 I thank God, whom I serve from my forefathers with pure conscience, that without ceasing I have remembrance of thee in my prayers night and day;

4 Greatly desiring to see thee, being mindful of thy tears, that I may be filled with joy;

5 When I call to remembrance the unfeigned faith that is in thee, which dwelt first in thy grandmother Lois, and thy mother Eunice; and I am persuaded that in thee also.

Memory Selection
Philippians 2:22
Background Scripture
Acts 16:1-5; Philippians 2:19-24; 1 Timothy 1:1-3; 2 Timothy 1:15
Devotional Reading
2 Timothy 2:1-7

Feb. 16

It must have meant a great deal to both Paul and Timothy for the great apostle to the Gentiles to refer to the young man Timothy as "my own son in the faith" (1 Tim. 1:2). This lesson focuses on Timothy, selecting various scenes that illustrate his relationship with Paul.

An interesting application emerges

from this account: the opportunity we today have to develop similar "mentor" relationships. Mentoring shows promise in several areas, not the least of which is the lowering of walls in our highly age-segregated society. As helpful as it may be to approach people's needs by age, this lesson can pose a good question: Can some principles in the relationship between Paul and Timothy show us how both older and younger people can also benefit from being together?

ഇൻരു

Tell your group about a 65-year-old woman who was part of a volunteer group who went to an elementary school "across the tracks" every six weeks. The students were of different ages and races. But as they talked about the students' report cards . . . asked them how things were going at home . . . encouraged them to raise a grade C to a B or even an A next report

period. A bridge was being built.

Invite group members to share similar mentoring stories—in school programs, or boys and girls' clubs. Tell of being a parent-mentor, such as letting little Ruby sift the flour and help bake the cake.

Point out that today's lesson is about one of the Bible's most famous mentor relationships—between the apostle Paul and the young minister Timothy, bridging age and cultural differences. What can we today learn from this relationship?

Teaching Outline	Daily Bible Readings
I. Co-workers in the Faith–Acts 16:1-5	**Mon.** Paul Takes Timothy Acts 16:1-5
A. Timothy's background, 1-2	**Tue.** 'No One Like Him' Philippians 2:19-24
B. Gesture to the Jews, 3	**Wed.** Loyal Son in the Faith 1 Timothy 1:1-5
C. Nourishing churches, 4-5	**Thu.** Man of Sincere Faith 2 Timothy 1:1-7
II. Comfort from Timothy–Philip. 2:19-24	**Fri.** Ministering in Berea Acts 17:10-15
A. A like-minded minister, 19-21	**Sat.** A Mission for Timothy 1 Thessalonians 3:1-6
B. Travel plans, 22-24	**Sun.** 'Come to Me Soon' 2 Timothy 4:9-15
III. Charge to a Preacher–1 Tim. 1:1-3	
IV. Companion's Memories–2 Tim. 1:3-5	

Verse by Verse

I. Co-workers in the Faith–Acts 16:1-5
A. Timothy's background, 1-2

1 Then came he to Derbe and Lystra: and, behold, a certain disciple was there, named Timotheus, the son of a certain woman, which was a Jewess, and believed; but his father was a Greek:

2 Which was well reported of by the brethren that were at Lystra and Iconium.

Derbe and Lystra were cities in central Asia Minor (now Turkey) where Paul and Barnabas had preached and established churches on their first missionary tour (Acts 14:6ff.). Many Jews had been settled there during various "dispersions." Paul is on his second missionary tour, accompanied by Silas. He is also reporting the decision made by the apostles in Jerusalem, that Gentiles were not to be required to come to Christ through Moses, circumcision, and the Law (see Acts 15:28-29).

B. Gesture to the Jews, 3

3 Him would Paul have to go forth with him; and took and circumcised him because of the Jews which were in those quarters: for they knew all that his father was a Greek.

The origin of the practice of cutting away the foreskin of males as a religious ritual is unknown. It preceded the dawn of history, and has been practiced by peoples as widely separated as the Egyptians and the Australian aborigines. Although circumcision doubtless had some health benefits, its significance has always been centered on religion and tribalism. God ordained circumcision as a sign of His Covenant with the Jews (Gen. 17:9-14). Thereafter, circumcision was the mark that distinguished Jew from Gentile, who, regardless of ethnic differences, were all known as "the uncircumcised."

The Greek word for circumcision means literally "to cut around"; and part of the significance of the practice was that it carried the idea of cutting away the sins of the flesh. This moral aspect enabled even the Old Testament to speak of "circumcision of the heart" (Deut. 30:6). However, such "spiritualization" was far from enough for "Judaizing teachers." Disagreeing with the decision at the Jerusalem council, they dogged Paul's steps trying to enforce the practice of circumcision on Gentile believers. This was not just out of Jewish pride; many sincere teachers felt that without circumcision Gentiles could not be included in God's Covenant.

Although Paul would later become the great enemy of circumcision, this

243

Jewish allegiance to the practice explains why he had Timothy circumcised. Although the marriage of Timothy's mother to a Gentile was officially prohibited, Paul knew that the younger man would be accepted more readily in predominantly Jewish churches if he received the mark of Judaism.

C. Nourishing churches, 4-5

4 And as they went through the cities, they delivered them the decrees for to keep, that were ordained of the apostles and elders which were at Jerusalem.

5 And so were the churches established in the faith, and increased in number daily.

We can well imagine how adrift these infant churches would have felt without this supportive, strengthening ministry of Paul and Timothy. Most of the early Christians in these areas would have attended synagogue services where they heard the reading of the Law; but questions had been raised about how binding it was. So what principles and teachings were they to follow, in these days when the New Covenant Scriptures were not yet formed? The visits and communications from Paul and Timothy supplied this need.

II. Comfort from Timothy—Philip. 2:19-24

A. A like-minded minister, 19-21

19 But I trust in the Lord Jesus to send Timotheus shortly unto you, that I also may be of good comfort, when I know your state.

20 For I have no man likeminded, who will naturally care for your state.

21 For all seek their own, not the things which are Jesus Christ's.

The scene now moves from Paul's early days as a Christian preacher to later in his long and active ministry. He had made many dear friends in Philippi (Acts 16:12ff.), and now writes to them, probably from prison in Rome, to thank them for remembering him in his need and to urge them to remain joyfully committed to the faith. Yet this seems inadequate; so in the event that he would not be able to visit them again in person he takes the next best step: sending a "like-minded" person.

That person is, again, the young minister Timothy. Apparently he has proved himself as a worthy student for Paul to mentor. He can both report to Paul on the "state" of the Philippians' faithfulness, and, being selfless, devote himself to any needs or lack among them. While it is sad that Paul could find no other brethren who were not centered on their own concerns, what a tribute to Timothy for the apostle to trust him to have the Philippians' needs, not his own, as a priority.

B. Travel plans, 22-24

22 But ye know the proof of him, that, as a son with the father, he hath served with me in the gospel.

23 Him therefore I hope to send presently, so soon as I shall see how it will go with me.

24 But I trust in the Lord that I also myself shall come shortly.

The Philippians already knew Timothy because the younger man had been privileged to be with Paul and others who first took the gospel to that area, Macedonia, in the first recorded proclamation of the good news in Europe (Acts 16:12). Timothy had proved himself among them by working with Paul as a son apprentices himself to his father in a trade—in this case the service of the gospel. Some traditions hold that Paul was released from prison and may have been able to fulfill the expectations he voices in verse 24, but this cannot be certainly known.

III. Charge to a Preacher–1 Tim. 1:1-3

1 Paul, an apostle of Jesus Christ by the commandment of God our Saviour, and Lord Jesus Christ, which is our hope;

2 Unto Timothy, my own son in the faith: Grace, mercy, and peace, from God our Father and Jesus Christ our Lord.

3 As I besought thee to abide still at Ephesus, when I went into Macedonia, that thou mightest charge some that they teach no other doctrine,

Timothy had also been with Paul on his third missionary tour. After Paul's tumultuous experience in the city of Ephesus (Acts 19:1ff.) he left for Macedonia again, leaving Timothy at Ephesus (20:1-4). Now he writes, late in life, to this young man who had proved himself a true "son in the faith."

The "other doctrine" Timothy was charged to confront included "fables and . . . genealogies" (1 Tim. 1:4). At first glance this seems to refer to the zeal of some Jews to connect with their heritage. Many scholars, however, hold that the terms refer to Gentile notions of similar "connec-

tions" between God and man. Whatever heresy is referred to, Paul insists that salvation is to be found in the wisdom of God, not man (Eph. 1:17-23).

IV. Companion's Memories—2 Tim. 1:3-5

3 I thank God, whom I serve from my forefathers with pure conscience, that without ceasing I have remembrance of thee in my prayers night and day;

4 Greatly desiring to see thee, being mindful of thy tears, that I may be filled with joy;

5 When I call to remembrance the unfeigned faith that is in thee, which dwelt first in thy grandmother Lois, and thy mother Eunice; and I am persuaded that in thee also.

Still later, toward the end of Paul's life, the old warrior was comforted by his memories of Timothy and his faithfulness and concern for his "father" in the faith. In these few verses we catch a glimpse of Paul's personal connection not just with Timothy but with his grandmother, who would have been a faithful Jewess; and his mother, who may have been a convert to Christianity. Obviously the apostle appreciates the kind of faith-heritage that had prepared Timothy to come to believe in Jesus as the Messiah.

In about the year 325, the early church historian Eusebius wrote that Timothy became the first bishop of Ephesus. Long after he died, his remains were thought to be buried in the "Church of the Apostles" in the city of Constantinople (modern Istanbul).

Evangelistic Emphasis

Faith in Jesus Christ starts at home! Timothy's faith was a natural result of the home in which he lived. His grandmother passed her faith to his mother, who passed her faith down to Timothy. This young preacher had learned to love and study the Hebrew Scriptures. He then came to know Jesus Christ as his Lord. Timothy was so versed in the faith that Paul met him and then "called" him into the preaching ministry.

The call for the Church, and for each believer, is to begin sharing our faith at home. We have time for all of our business obligations, our social occasions and our ecclesiastical organizations, but we have little time for family devotionals or Bible reading. One of the hallmarks of the Hebrew faith was that it was passed down from generation to generation. Timothy's faith was passed down for three generations. His faith resulted from his family's participation in his faith development.

As we think about the good news that Jesus brought into the world our goal should be sharing that good news with family first. When we build a strong faith base at home, we can begin reaching out to our world.

The good news is that Jesus died for all. Are there members of your family who have not heard the good news of Jesus Christ? If that is the case, start at home sharing that word.

A person in your family, living under your roof, might be the next great religious leader of our nation.

൹൹ൽ

Memory Selection

But ye know the proof of him, that, as a son with the father, he hath served with me in the gospel.— *Philippians 2: 22*

A favorite childhood pastime used to be flying a kite. Children went to great lengths to get the kite airborne and keep it there. There are two absolute necessities for flying a kite. The first thing that must happen is for there to be sufficient wind blowing that day. No matter how aerodynamically correct a kite is, unless the wind is blowing, a kite will never fly.

The second necessity in kite flying might surprise you. For a kite to fly, the string must be strong. Did you ever have the experience of getting a kite airborne and then having the string break? Unlike a helium balloon, a kite will simply fall back to earth. The kite must have *resistance* to fly. The string creates resistance.

In our faith, we must have that string that anchors us to Christ Jesus. In many cases we follow the examples of others who are living victoriously. Timothy became the "string" that anchored the Corinthians' behavior to Christ.

You are an example for other people of the faith.

Weekday Problems

"For the last one hundred years there has been at least one Lewis serving on the Board of Harmony Church." Joe Lewis was livid as he spoke these words to no one in particular. The church newsletter had just arrived and Joe was reading the slate of officers for 2002. There were no members of the Lewis family on the Board. Of course, there were only three members of that family remaining in the church. Joe and Mary Lou were in their 80s, and their nephew Fred, who didn't attend church.

Joe hadn't dealt well with things at Harmony Church for the past few years. He wasn't in favor of the new preacher, who was only 40. When he was able to go to church, young families annoyed him with squalling babies. The that was selected included many "praise songs" he didn't know.

Mary Lou, who had been a saint in Harmony Church for years, simply patted her husband on the hand. "You know Joe," she said lovingly, "Don't you think it's time for a new generation to take over?

That evening Mary Lou read their devotional from 2 Timothy. "Joe," she said, "how do you think Paul felt abot trusting Timothy with his ministry? Timothy was a younger man you know."

*How do you feel about the younger leadership in the church today?

Weightier Matters

Wife: Honey, will you still love me if I put on a few pounds?
Hubby: Yes I do.

❖❖❖❖

Doctors tell us that more than 7 million of us are overweight. Of course that's in round figures.

❖❖❖❖

Did you hear about the new reducing salon on Wall Street? It's for stocky brokers.

❖❖❖❖

Mae: I don't know what to do to look thinner.
Rae: Well I plan to hang around fatter people.

❖❖❖❖

Wife to husband as she measures his waist: Amazing! It can take an oak tree 200 years to attain that girth!

❖❖❖❖

Joe: Guess what! I've lost 10 pounds.
Flo: Turn around. I think I just found them.

This Lesson in Your Life

Have you ever met someone and knew immediately that he was a person of faith? Did you sense something about his demeanor that hinted of his relationship to Christ? Paul might have had a similar experience when he met Timothy. Although we learn that Paul knew the genealogy of Timothy's faith, he was impressed with this young man. From Paul's experience with John Mark, we know that the apostle could be very impatient with people who didn't measure up to his standards (Acts 13:13, 15:36ff) Yet he and Timothy seemed to have "hit if off." The instant rapport apparently continued throughout Paul's life.

Many issues in their relationship could make a helpful Sunday School lesson. Timothy's faith grew out of how he was raised. Whether we like it or not, the saying, "the nut doesn't fall far from the tree" is true when it comes to parents and children. We are products of how we were raised, as our children will be products of how we raise them. Eunice and Lois planted Timothy's faith. Much of a child's decision about Jesus Christ is dependent on what that child has learned about Christ from watching parents model the faith. If we are faithful witness and workers, if our behavior at church and at home is consistent, our children are likely to embrace the faith we share. The converse of this is true also. If we model a negative kind of faith, children will likely develop that kind of faith. What kind of example are you setting for a younger generation?

Secondly, are we allowing a younger generation to take positions of leadership in the church? The truth is that the generation born between 1920 and 1946 is paying the bills in the church. The people with children are struggling to keep roofs over their head. They have some time to help in the church, and are usually quite capable and faithful. What happens is that the bill-paying generation doesn't want to share the authority with a generation that isn't "giving as much as we are."

Paul gave Timothy responsibility and authority. He kept his eye on young Timothy, but he didn't tell him every step to take. Are you ready to share church leadership? If you are one of the "baby boomer" generation, are you ready to take your leadership role? Age-ism is rapidly raising its head as a major political issue both in America at large and in the church. There was much talk in the 1960s about the "generation gap." The truth is that we have only seen the beginnings of a true "generation gap." The gospel of Christ is the only way of bridging this coming social crisis in our churches and in our land. It will take big people on both ends of the age spectrum to deal with some of the coming issues.

1. **Where did Paul meet Timothy?**

Paul was traveling from Syria and Cilicia to Derbe and Lystra. It was in Lystra that he met Timothy.

2. **What does the text say about Timothy's parents?**

Timothy's mother was a Jewess who was professing faith in Jesus. Timothy's father was a Greek. The implication was that his father was not a believer.

3. **Why did Paul have Timothy circumcised before they left on this preaching tour?**

So his uncircumsion would not offend the Jews in the cities to which they traveled. This was not done previously because his father was a Greek.

4. **What was the purpose of the mission upon which Paul and Timothy were working?**

They were sharing the decision that had been reached at the Jerusalem Conference. This conference was described in Acts 15.

5. **What happened as a result of the work that Paul and Timothy were carrying out?**

"The churches were strengthened in the faith and increased in numbers daily."

6. **What was Paul's purpose in sending Timothy to the Corinthians?**

Paul sent Timothy to remind the Corinthians of Paul's "ways in Christ Jesus."

7. **Why was Paul sending Timothy to the church at Philippi?**

Paul, who probably was in prison, wanted news of the Philippian church so that receiving word of their ministry might cheer him.

8. **How does Paul describe his relationship with Timothy?**

In most cases Paul refers to Timothy as a son. He wrote to the Philippians, "how like a son with a father he has served with me."

9. **What was the genealogy of Timothy's faith?**

His faith lived first in his grandmother Lois, and then in his mother, Eunice.

10. **What ecclesiastical relationship did Paul and Timothy share?**

Timothy had been "ordained" by Paul. "For this reason I remind you to rekindle the gift of God that is within you through the laying on of my hands."

How did you learn to ride a bike?

Most of us learned by first watching others ride bicycles, whether older siblings or children in the neighborhood. We had seen other people ride, and became convinced we could do that.

Our first bicycle came with training wheels. Some adult usually was behind us holding us up and even pushing us and we began the process of riding the bicycle. We were on the bike, but another was doing most of the work for us. After sufficient practice with the training wheels, the day arrived when the adult in our life took those wheels off of the bicycle. On this day he was very close behind us ready to grab the bicycle in case we had an accident. On this day we were finally doing most of the work on moving the bike.

Being a Christian and serving in ministry is a similar process. Paul and Timothy illustrate clearly the role of the mentor and the disciple. In many ways, we learn to serve Jesus like we learn to ride a bike.

We learn what it is like to be a Christian by watching others exercising their faith. We watch them in church participating in worship. We are fortunate to watch them in daily life living out their faith. We watch people serve Jesus and learn by watching. Then the day comes when we are invited to participate in the ministry of Christ. Perhaps that is why Jesus sent the disciples out two by two. I wonder if He paired a more experienced disciple with a less experienced one. Our first "adventures in serving Jesus" were usually done in places where people were close by, who could help us in a moment of crisis. After ministry at this level, we are ready to solo.

The people who have mentored us in the faith now watch us express our faith and ministry. They do so from a distance but still are there encouraging us and praying for us.

I can see this pattern of mentor and disciple playing out in the life of Paul and Timothy. I have seen it happen in my own ministry. It is a wonderful way to teach a new generation how to grow in the faith, how to reach out in love and service to our world.

Are you ready to be a mentor in the faith? It is a special position, and brings many rewards and joys. How long has it been since you "took someone under your wing" and showed them how to live for Jesus Christ? What a wonderful way to serve the Lord by raising up a new generation to work in the church. Is there a young person you can invite to lead a part of your Sunday school lesson? Is there a child or a youth whom you might want to invite to help with your missions project? Is God calling you to mentor someone in the faith?

Remember who guided you through this growing process? Remember how close you were to him? Remember the faith and belief he had in you? Share that powerful Christian relationship with someone else.

Priscilla and Aquila: Partners in the Gospel

Acts 18:1-4, 24-26; Romans 16:3-4
1 Corinthians 16:19; 2 Timothy 4:19

After these things Paul departed from Athens, and came to Corinth;

2 And found a certain Jew named Aquila, born in Pontus, lately come from Italy, with his wife Priscilla; (because that Claudius had commanded all Jews to depart from Rome:) and came unto them.

3 And because he was of the same craft, he abode with them, and wrought: for by their occupation they were tentmakers.

4 And he reasoned in the synagogue every sabbath, and persuaded the Jews and the Greeks.

24 And a certain Jew named Apollos, born at Alexandria, an eloquent man, and mighty in the scriptures, came to Ephesus.

25 This man was instructed in the way of the Lord; and being fervent in the spirit, he spake and taught diligently the things of the Lord, knowing only the baptism of John.

26 And he began to speak boldly in the synagogue: whom when Aquila and Priscilla had heard, they took him unto them, and expounded unto him the way of God more perfectly.

Romans 16

3 Greet Priscilla and Aquila my helpers in Christ Jesus:

4 Who have for my life laid down their own necks: unto whom not only I give thanks, but also all the churches of the Gentiles.

1 Corinthians 16

19 The churches of Asia salute you. Aquila and Priscilla salute you much in the Lord, with the church that is in their house.

2 Timothy 4

19 Salute Prisca and Aquila, and the household of Onesiphorus.

Memory Selection
Romans 16:3-4

Background Scripture
Acts 18:1-4, 24-26; Romans 16:3-4
1 Corinthians 16:19; 2 Timothy 4:19

Devotional Reading
Ephesians 4:1-13

Feb. 23

A "vocational missionary" couple, Priscilla and Aquila, are the focus of this lesson in our continued study of people who made a difference in the Church in New Testament times. Their story includes interesting details about this Jewish-Christian couple and their frequent travels in the Mediterranean world, and also about their unique working relationship with the apostle Paul.

As many modern missionaries have discovered, mission teams are often an effective way to evangelize a previously unreached area. Certainly the faith has been spread by stalwart "loners"; and all teams have unique issues of cooperation and unity of mind (recall the disagreement between Paul and Barnabas, in Lesson 10). The focus in this lesson, however, is on the strengths of the team approach; and the perceptive teacher will find ways to show that Paul and this missionary couple respected the differing gifts each brought to the task of sharing the good news.

ಐಂಐ

Discuss the advantages and disadvantages of working or living with a "partner," as in the lesson title. Everyone in your group will have experience with "flying solo" vs. "partnering"—living as a single person vs. being married, running one's own business vs. a partnership or corporation, etc. What issues does having a partner bring to a living or working relationship? How do we weigh the independence and freedom of not having to consult or consider a partner vs. the advantages of having someone else to count on? What attitudes and character traits are necessary for both "going it alone" and partnering with another? Just such issues are at stake in this lesson.

Teaching Outline	*Daily Bible Readings*

I. Partnership Formed—Acts 18:1-4
 A. Jewish connection, 1-2
 B. A common trade, 3
 C. Christian mission, 4
 	
 II. 'Continuing Ed' Project—24-26
 	
 III. Sacrificial Partners—Rom. 16:3-4
 	
 IV. Continuing Ministry—1 Cor.
 16:19; 2 Tim. 4:19
 A. House-church hosts, 1 Cor. 16:19
 B. Relationship sustained, 2 Tim. 4:19
	Mon. Fellow Tentmakers
	        Acts 18:1-10
	 Tue. Continuing Education
	        Acts 18:24-28
	 Wed. Risking Their Necks
	        Romans 16:1-5
	 Thu. Church in a Home
	        1 Corinthians 16:13-24
	 Fri. Greeting Loved Ones
	        2 Timothy 4:16-22
	 Sat. Unity of the Spirit
	        Ephesians 4:1-8
	 Sun. Equipping Gifts
	        Ephesians 4:9-16

Verse by Verse

I. Partnership Formed—Acts 18:1-4
A. Jewish connection, 1-2

1 After these things Paul departed from Athens, and came to Corinth;

2 And found a certain Jew named Aquila, born in Pontus, lately come from Italy, with his wife Priscilla; (because that Claudius had commanded all Jews to depart from Rome:) and came unto them.

"These things" in verse 1 refer to Paul's preaching in Athens, which had not been very productive. We can imagine, therefore, that Paul proceeded to the Greek city of Corinth with less than buoyant spirits.

If Athens was a center of learning and culture, Corinth was a bustling trade center just down the road across a narrow strip of land (see a map). Paul had no doubt found Aquila and Priscilla. by going to the Jewish quarter, where the couple had taken up residence after leaving Italy.

Although it is obvious that Aquila and Priscilla are also Christians, they had been forced to leave Italy in one of the frequent expulsions of Jews, since the earliest Christians were widely believed to be a Jewish sect. Suetonius, an ancient Roman historian, refers to the command of the emperor Claudius referred to here, in these words: "The Jews were in a constant state of tumult at the instigation of one Chrestus" (a frequent Roman spelling of "Christ"). Even before the "tumult" in many Jewish communities over whether Jesus was truly the Messiah, the tension between their religious scruples and the customs in their new homes caused constant civic unrest.

B. A common trade, 3

3 And because he was of the same craft, he abode with them, and wrought: for by their occupation they were tentmakers.

Small "home manufacturing" businesses were the backbone of industry in the ancient world. The apostle Paul may have wanted to focus on his tentmaking trade for a time, while nursing the wounds from his disappointing experience in Athens. It is therefore not surprising, given their common faith and trade, to find this threesome throwing their lot together in living quarters that also served as a small "tent factory." Although the demand for tents was no doubt greater in lands to the east where nomads roamed, the military and the poor in and around Corinth would have created some demand for the trade. Corinth's location near the seaport city of Cenchrea would have also offered exporting opportunities.

The reference to living and working together understates the human relations issues involved. Despite what they had in common, Paul,

Aquila, and Priscilla would have had to exercise the greatest respect for each other to make such an arrangement work.

C. Christian mission, 4

4 And he reasoned in the synagogue every sabbath, and persuaded the Jews and the Greeks.

Soon after moving to Corinth, Paul takes up his customary method of visiting the local synagogue to share his message. Services there were much more informal than the church assemblies in modern American Christianity, and synagogue leaders were usually eager to invite guests such as Paul to speak. Also, going first to the synagogue with his message was of theological importance to Paul. Because the Israelites were God's chosen race, he had been charged to go "to the Jew first," and only then to the Greek (as in Rom. 1:16, etc.). We are probably to assume here that Aquila and Priscilla accompany Paul on these Sabbath-day synagogue visits.

II. 'Continuing Ed' Project—24-26

24 And a certain Jew named Apollos, born at Alexandria, an eloquent man, and mighty in the scriptures, came to Ephesus.

25 This man was instructed in the way of the Lord; and being fervent in the spirit, he spake and taught diligently the things of the Lord, knowing only the baptism of John.

26 And he began to speak boldly in the synagogue: whom when Aquila and Priscilla had heard, they took him unto them, and expounded unto him the way of God more perfectly.

We sometimes assume that primitive means of travel were more confining than they really were in the world of the first century. We have noted that Apollos, who was born in northern Asia Minor, lived in Italy before being expelled and taking up residence in Corinth. In Acts 18:18 we are told that Aquila and Priscilla go to Syria, then to Ephesus; and in later texts for this lesson we learn they are back in Italy (Rome), then Corinth again. Now, in verse 24, we are introduced to another Jewish-Christian, Apollos, who hails from Alexandria, Egypt. Not only has he come to Ephesus, on the western coast of Asia Minor; he will shortly travel to Achaia, and Corinth, himself (18:27; 19:1). The whole picture is one of surprisingly free movement and a more cosmopolitan atmosphere than is often assumed.

Alexandria was the "Athens of Egypt," and offered all the opportunities an Apollos would need to become a man of learning and eloquence. Its library was famous throughout the known world, and it was an important center for Jews of the Dispersion. Apollos was an early product of Jewish-Christianity in Alexandria, a movement whose growing influence will produce famous Christian teachers such as Clement and Origen.

As educated and eloquent as he was, however, Apollos had apparently not heard that the Christ for whom John the Baptist was only a herald had died, rose again, and instituted His own baptism (see Matt. 28:18-20). Although John had baptized with "the baptism of repentance for the remission of sins" (Luke 3:3), it was not accompanied by the gift of the indwelling Holy Spirit (Acts 2:38). Aquila and Priscilla therefore put their teaching skills to good use, no doubt having them sharpened by the time they have spent with Paul. Since we are not told otherwise, and since Christians in Ephesus give Apollos a hearty recommendation when he leaves(vs. 27), we are to assume that Apollos readily accepts their effective instruction.

III. Sacrificial Partners—Rom. 16:3-4

3 Greet Priscilla and Aquila my helpers in Christ Jesus:

4 Who have for my life laid down their own necks: unto whom not only I give thanks, but also all the churches of the Gentiles.

The text now moves us to the last chapter of Paul's great Epistle to the Romans, and to his concluding greetings to people that are especially dear to him. We should not be surprised, by now, to find that Aquila and Priscilla are among the first that he greets. This time we note that their names are reversed. Since the order of names in a list was often important in Greek writings, some have speculated that Priscilla has by now become recognized as the better-known or better-equipped partner. (She is listed first in four of the six references to them in the New Testament.)

Unfortunately we know nothing of the situation in which this dedicated couple would have laid down their lives for Paul. Later, the apostle will refer to having "fought with beasts at Ephesus" (1 Cor 15:32; whether literally or with "beastly" men is unknown). Perhaps Priscilla and Aquila tried to intervene in Paul's behalf when he was persecuted there.

IV. Continuing Ministry—1 Cor. 16:19; 2 Tim. 4:19

A. House-church hosts, 1 Cor. 16:19

19 The churches of Asia salute you. Aquila and Priscilla salute you much in the Lord, with the church that is in their house.

After yet another move, Aquila and Priscilla are found here at the city of Philippi (where Paul perhaps from wrote 1 Corinthians). Here they are hosts of a house-church, the most frequent meeting place in the early days of Christianity. The fact that Paul sends their greeting to the Corinthians shows their continued importance as ministers, both in Philippi and among the brethren in their former city of Corinth.

B. Relationship sustained, 2 Tim. 4:19

19 Salute Prisca and Aquila, and the household of Onesiphorus.

Our final reference to this Jewish-Christian couple is toward the end of Paul's life. ("Prisca" is a shortened form of "Priscilla".) Now, instead of citing their greetings to other Christians, Paul sends his own greetings to his old friends. Yet again, they have changed locations ; for 2 Timothy is generally assumed to have been to sent to Ephesus (see 1 Tim. 1:3).

Onesiphorus was also a world traveler Paul knew well, since he had ministered to the apostle when he was in prison in Rome (2 Tim. 1:16-17). Obviously several personalities in the early church formed a tight-knit team of Christian missionaries.

255

Evangelistic Emphasis

The word "evangelism" strikes terror in the hearts of some Christians. We all have an image conjured up by our past experience with the word and with believers in that word. I learned the "Four Spiritual Laws" and know all the recruitment "tricks." I can answer every objection to accepting Jesus. I have all the pertinent verses highlighted in my "sword." Strange, I never lead a soul to Christ using those "methods."

In the story of Aquila, Priscilla and Paul there are lessons for us to learn about sharing Christ with our world. We learn that both Paul and Aquila were tent makers. Paul went to work with Aquila. Those two men must have had some deep, wonderful conversations about tent making and about the faith.

The good news of Jesus Christ is more effectively shared over a cup of coffee than over an opened religious tract. When we enter into a person's life, we are able to communicate with him as a friend. Our sharing, whether words of encouragement or our faith, then becomes an act of love and compassion rather than one of simply collecting another scalp.

I believe that we can't share the good news of Jesus with a person until we are willing to become a friend to that person. If we don't care enough about a sinner to drink coffee with them, then it is doubtful we care anything about their eternal destiny.

Evangelism involves finding something in common and building a communication bridge from that. In tent-making Paul and Aquila had something in common. They became friends who shared the adventure of faith.

ಬಿೂಂ

Greet Priscilla and Aquila, who work with me in Christ Jesus, and who risked their necks for my life, to whom not only I give thanks, but also all the churches of the Gentiles. —*Romans 16:3-4*

How many thrill seekers do you know? Has anyone in your family jumped out of an airplane? How about friends who ride on roller coasters? Our lives have become so pedestrian that we look for vicarious thrills. We don't want to take any chances, but we enjoy watching those who do.

Have you ever considered your faith an adventure? Paul said that Aquila and Priscilla "risked their necks" for him. We are not sure what all that risk was about. We do know that Aquila and Priscilla seemed to have traveled a great deal. They were almost vagabonds, yet seemed to have been persons of means.

My feeling is that faith in Jesus Christ was a great adventure of Aquila and Priscilla. Following Him was what these two vagabonds of the faith would enjoy. They were willing to take almost any chance for Jesus. Don't you long for a faith that is adventurous and takes huge risks?

Weekday Problems

Some members of First Church's finance committee had thought from the start that it was a mistake to put Dave Reaves on the committee. Dave was a banker, but hardly a typical banker. He rarely wore a suit. He made loans to people whose business proposals had been turned down by other bankers. Dave said he had little respect for "penny pinching paper pushers."

So it was no surprise that with Dave on the finance committee the meetings would be lively. First Church had always struggled with money. They could do anything they wanted to in ministry, but never were able to build up any sizable savings or nest egg. Everything they did was "pay as you go."

When the youth group needed a van, Dave became their mouthpiece. The discussion about the van went along the usual lines of "How much now and how much later?" The "How much?" question was giving way to the "too much" sentiment on the committee.

It was then that Dave "blew a fuse." He told the committee that First Church did not belong to them, but to the Lord. If the Lord wanted the group to have a van, they would have it. He stated that all it took was a "step in faith." When the van proposal was turned down, Dave said, "I'll buy a van and give it to the church"—and then made a motion to adjourn!

*How do you feel about people like Dave who don't seem to have any respect for "common sense?"

Adam and Eve: Questions You Never Knew You Wanted Answered

Q: Who was created first, Adam or Eve?
(Wrong) A: Eve. She was the first maid.

❖❖❖❖❖

Q: Why was Adam's first day the longest?
A: Because it had no Eve.

❖❖❖❖❖

Q: Why was Eve not afraid of getting the measles?
A: Because she'd Adam.

❖❖❖❖❖

Q: At what time of day was Adam created?
A: A little before Eve.

❖❖❖❖❖

Q: What was Adam and Eve's reaction to being cast out of Eden?
A: They raised Cain.

This Lesson in Your Life

The story is old and all too familiar to preachers and church people alike. Mr. and Mrs. Jones will have a crisis in their family and they will want a preacher with them at that moment. It doesn't matter that they haven't darkened the doors of the church for decades. Overlook the fact that the reason for their absence was the preacher's wife didn't fawn over Mrs. Jones' peach cobbler at a pot-luck dinner back in the '50s. Ignore all the visits, time, and effort that were given to wooing the Joneses back to church. They want a preacher to drop everything and make them the center of his life—at least until the crisis has passed and things are "normal" again.

The aggravation for us ministers is that this happens almost every week. The reason we can live with it, and some times through it, is that so many others are faithful to the church. Like Aquila and Priscilla, they would be wonderful additions to any church. These two people were obviously well-traveled. They were well versed in their faith. They were open to the ministry of Paul.

What makes them appealing is their spirit of adventure. The Memory Selection verse caught my attention. They "risked their necks for Paul's life." They welcomed him, first into their home and lives. Paul and Aquila went into business together for awhile. Wouldn't you have like to have been a fly on the tent canvas as those two worked?

Then Aquila and Priscilla traveled with Paul. They "pulled up stakes" and took a trip with this apostle. They had to have known how dangerous it would have been to travel with him. Paul had the acute ability to anger the Jews in any city.

Aquila and Priscilla were right in the middle of the explosive growth of the church. We learn from their encounter with Apollos that they were also involved in sharing the faith. Some adults are willing to be adventurous in the faith, without thinking through their decisions or faith positions. But from their encounter with Apollos, we can assume that Aquila and Priscilla had a faith that was well reasoned and logical.

The story of Aquila and Priscilla makes one wish for a church full of people with such adventurous faith. They wouldn't spend all of their time complaining about the hymns or the flowers in the sanctuary. They wouldn't be interested in the report of the committee on committees. People with adventurous faith have only one thing on their minds. They want to discover God in every moment and at every turn. They are spiritual thrill seekers. Those of us who are weighed down by the cares of this world look askance at them. Unfortunately our "copping out" of the adventure of faith also forfeits the certainty of faith they had.

1. What information does the 18th chapter of Acts give about the travels of Paul?

After preaching in Athens, Paul traveled to Corinth.

2. What does the same chapter of Acts tell about the travels of Aquila?

He was born in Pontus. He then moved to Rome. When Claudius ordered the Jews out of Rome, Aquila traveled to Corinth.

3. What trade did Paul and Aquila have in common?

They were both tent-makers. Since tents in the first century were made of leather, they could also have been tanners. (The word "tent-makers" is vague in Greek.)

4. While Paul was working with Aquila what else was he doing?

Paul was going to the synagogue and arguing with the Jews and the Greeks about Jesus.

5. How long was Paul in Corinth?

Verse 18 states that Paul stayed in Corinth for "a considerable time."

6. Where did Paul travel from Corinth?

Paul went to Syria. Aquila and Priscilla accompanied him on this trip.

7. Putting the information from chapter 18 together, construct the travel itinerary of Aquila and Priscilla.

From Rome they traveled to Corinth. They then left with Paul for Syria. By the end of the chapter they had arrived in Ephesus.

8. What preacher did Aquila and Priscilla encounter in Ephesus?

Apollos was in Ephesus preaching "the way of the Lord."

9. What happened between Apollos and Aquila and Priscilla?

Apollos did not know the difference between baptism into Christ and the baptism of John. Priscilla and Aquila explained this to him "more accurately."

10. What does Paul's greeting in Romans to Aquila and Priscilla seem to indicate?

That Aquila and Priscilla had traveled back to Rome after Claudius' ban was lifted.

Mt. Moriah was a threshing floor, a place where people would come to thresh their grain. Two brothers owned the threshing floor. Tradition held that in exchange for the use of the threshing floor, the brothers got to keep the leftover grain that wasn't swept up and collected in a day. When several people came to thresh grain on a daily basis, there would be an abundant supply left over.

The two brothers were quite different. One brother had a wife and 12 children. He lived in an area on one side of the threshing floor. The other brother had no wife and had no children. He lived on the other side of the threshing floor.

The business the brothers shared thrived so that each of them had a room where their share of the grain could be stored. Each afternoon they would gather the grain into sacks and store it in their respective storage places.

It came to pass that each night, neither one of the brothers would sleep well. One brother would lie on his pallet and think to himself, "It is not right that I have so much grain. I am all alone. I have no wife. I have no children. My brother has all those hungry mouths of feed." So this brother would arise. And hidden by the darkness would take one of his sacks of grain, cross the threshing floor, and place it in his brother's storage room.

Later that night, the other brother would lie awake and think to himself, "It is not right that I have all this grain. My brother is all alone in the world. When I am an old man, I will have 12 sons to take care of me. Who will take care of my brother in his old age? So this brother would arise, take one of *his* sacks of grain and place it in his brother's storage room.

This went on for years. Each night each brother took a sack from his supply and gave it to the other brother. Until one night . . .

For whatever reason, the rabbis never really said, the brothers were awake at the same time. Each was in bed worrying about the other. So they both arose at the same time. They both went to their supply of grain. This night they met in the middle of the threshing floor. When they looked at one another and saw the sacks, they fell together in an embrace.

God looked down from heaven and smiled. Seeing that kind of love, He decided to honor the place and the brothers by having a Temple built on their threshing floor.

It takes that kind of brotherly love to serve Jesus, but more, it takes that kind of brotherly effort to a make a difference in our world. Paul, Priscilla, and Aquila give us an example of what powerful results are realized when we work together for the cause of Jesus Christ.

Join hands with your brothers and sisters in Christ and get to work.

Unit I. Jesus' Early Ministry

Lesson 1

The Beginning of the Gospel

Mark 1:9-26

And it came to pass in those days, that Jesus came from Nazareth of Galilee, and was baptized of John in Jordan.

10 And straightway coming up out of the water, he saw the heavens opened, and the Spirit like a dove descending upon him:

11 And there came a voice from heaven, saying, Thou art my beloved Son, in whom I am well pleased.

12 And immediately the Spirit driveth him into the wilderness.

13 And he was there in the wilderness forty days, tempted of Satan; and was with the wild beasts; and the angels ministered unto him.

14 Now after that John was put in prison, Jesus came into Galilee, preaching the gospel of the kingdom of God,

15 And saying, The time is fulfilled, and the kingdom of God is at hand: repent ye, and believe the gospel.

16 Now as he walked by the sea of Galilee, he saw Simon and Andrew his brother casting a net into the sea: for they were fishers.

17 And Jesus said unto them, Come ye after me, and I will make you to become fishers of men.

18 And straightway they forsook their nets, and followed him.

19 And when he had gone a little further thence, he saw James the son of Zebedee, and John his brother, who also were in the ship mending their nets.

20 And straightway he called them: and they left their father Zebedee in the ship with the hired servants, and went after him.

21 And they went into Capernaum; and straightway on the sabbath day he entered into the synagogue, and taught.

22 And they were astonished at his doctrine: for he taught them as one that had authority, and not as the scribes.

23 And there was in their synagogue a man with an unclean spirit; and he cried out,

24 Saying, Let us alone; what have we to do with thee, thou Jesus of Nazareth? art thou come to destroy us? I know thee who thou art, the Holy One of God.

25 And Jesus rebuked him, saying, Hold thy peace, and come out of him.

26 And when the unclean spirit had torn him, and cried with a loud voice, he came out of him.

Memory Selection
Mark 1:11

Background Scripture
Mark 1:1-45

Devotional Reading
Luke 4:14-21

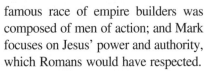

This lesson's focus, "The Beginning of the Gospel," is taken from Mark 1:1. The *way* Mark begins the gospel story is striking. He omits the account of Jesus' birth, and genalogy, and plunges directly and powerfully into His ministry.

This feature points to one of the reasons many scholars believe Mark's Gospel was written for Romans. This famous race of empire builders was composed of men of action; and Mark focuses on Jesus' power and authority, which Romans would have respected.

In swift strokes, Mark first describes Jesus identifying with people in His baptism and temptations; yet He emerges from both as a Victor. Then he proceeds to show His authority in calling the apostles, in teaching, and in casting out a demon. Mark is saying not only to Roman readers but to us today, "Here is God's divine, all-powerful Son! Hear ye him!"

Ask for examples of breath-taking displays of power group members can recall from their own experience or reading. Some may have stood near the edge of an active volcano in Hawaii, or read of the devastation of Mt. St. Helen's in Washington, in 1980. (Check some facts about this disaster in an encyclopedia.) Others may know about the "Big Bang" theory, or the impact of a meteorite, , or the awesome power of an earthquake, flood, or storm.

Point out that many people have a fascination for power in the "natural" world. Mark's Gospel, however, reminds us of the *super*natural display of God's power in Jesus, God's Son. This lesson demonstrates this power in His victory over temptation, and in healing a man who was demon-possessed. Are we as awed by such spiritual power as we are by the forces of "nature"?

Teaching Outline	Daily Bible Readings

I. Baptized by John—9-11
  A. Submission in baptism, 9
  B. Testimony from heaven, 10-11
 	
II. Beset by Satan—12-13
 	
III. Broadcasting the Message—14-15
IV. Calling Four Fishermen—16-20
 	
V. Demonstrating Authority—21-26
  A. Authoritative teaching, 21-22
  B. Casting out a demon, 23-26
	Mon. Baptism and Temptation
	     Mark 1:1-13
	Tue. Calling Four Fishermen
	     Mark 1:14-20
	Wed. 'Follow Me!'
	     John 1:43-51
	Thu. 'You Will Catch People!'
	     Luke 5:1-11
	Fri. Exorcising a Demon
	     Mark 1:21-28
	Sat. Healing the Sick
	     Mark 1:29-38
	Sun. Preaching in Galilee
	     Mark 1:39-45

Verse by Verse

I. Baptized by John—9-11
A. Submission in baptism, 9

9 And it came to pass in those days, that Jesus came from Nazareth of Galilee, and was baptized of John in Jordan.

For background information on baptism, see Lesson 5 of the Second Quarter. As noted there, such outward "washings" had long been associated with being inwardly cleansed of sin. Why, then, was the sinless Son of God baptized? Matthew's Gospel supplies one answer. When John the Baptist himself questioned the need for Jesus to be baptized, He answered, "Suffer it to be so now: for thus it becometh us to fulfil all righteousness" (Matt. 3:15). Probably this means something similar to "fulfilling the Law" (Matt. 5:17). Since baptism was to be a command under the New Covenant, Jesus, as Founder of the New Covenant, wanted to "fill full" any commands He would ask of His followers.

From one standpoint it is an astounding act of humility for God's Son to submit to this ordinance. Yet in another sense it is only an extension of the marvelous act of the Incarnation itself. Having indicated that God is with us by becoming flesh, Jesus now repeats the message by submitting to the same washing to which He will call those who believe in Him.

B. Testimony from heaven, 10-11

10 And straightway coming up out of the water, he saw the heavens opened, and the Spirit like a dove descending upon him:

11 And there came a voice from heaven, saying, Thou art my beloved Son, in whom I am well pleased.

Here is one of the few times that what Christians have come to call the "Trinity" are portrayed in one scene. The Son emerges from the waters of baptism, the Spirit descends in the form of a dove, and the Father speaks the authoritative word of acceptance of Jesus' Sonship.

The dove had been a symbol of reconciliation between God and man for centuries. It appears first in Genesis 8:8-12, when it returns to the ark with a branch showing that the flood had abated. Sacrificial doves were offered in Old Covenant worship. It is in this scene at Jesus' baptism, however, that the tender-natured dove becomes a symbol of the Holy Spirit that endures today.

The voice acknowledging Jesus as God's Son is addressed to Jesus Himself here, whereas in Matthew and Luke it is addressed to John and others at the scene. Some have speculated that Mark's version shows that it was necessary for God to inform Jesus that God was adopting

263

Him at His baptism, and that only then did He become God's Son. Matthew and Luke, they say, revise the statement to oppose this "adoptionist" theory—which, however, contradicts the wider evidence from John 1:1ff. and other passages that speak of Jesus' eternal Sonship with the Father before creation.

II. Beset by Satan—12-13

12 And immediately the Spirit driveth him into the wilderness.

13 And he was there in the wilderness forty days, tempted of Satan; and was with the wild beasts; and the angels ministered unto him.

The Spirit is not just tenderness. Here He is also the instigator of discipline that would try Jesus as by fire and strengthen Him for the trials of His ministry. Typical of his direct brevity, Mark omits the details of the Temptation, and we must rely on the accounts in Matthew 4 and Luke 4 for the account of the three-fold temptations.

In the wilderness, Satan offered Christ demonic powers if He would worship the prince of demons. Jesus resists each temptation by citing Scripture, showing the importance of the Old Testament as an authoritative support in living for God instead of for Satan. "The wilderness" in Scripture is both a haven where believers can shut out the world and hear the voice of God, and a bleak and barren wasteland where bodily needs lower our capacity to resist Satan's overtures. This glimpse into Christ's early experiences reminds us that while we may need to draw away from the crowds temporarily to "re-

hear" God's will, permanently isolating ourselves will likely only serve Satan's purposes, not God's.

III. Broadcasting the Message—14-15

14 Now after that John was put in prison, Jesus came into Galilee, preaching the gospel of the kingdom of God,

15 And saying, The time is fulfilled, and the kingdom of God is at hand: repent ye, and believe the gospel.

John had been imprisoned by King Herod for preaching against the king's adultery (he had taken his brother Phillip's wife (Matt. 14:3-4). It would make sense for Jesus to choose John's arrest as the time to begin His public ministry, since people would be less likely to confuse the two and assume that John was the Messiah (see John 1:19-20). The essence of His message is said to be the nearness of "the kingdom of God." The time predicted by the Messianic prophets had arrived. This "realm" or "rule" has both a present reality and a future aspect. It can be entered immediately by those who "repent" and "believe" (see Col. 1:12-14); and it will be consummated at the Second Coming of Christ.

IV. Calling Four Fishermen—16-20

16 Now as he walked by the sea of Galilee, he saw Simon and Andrew his brother casting a net into the sea: for they were fishers.

17 And Jesus said unto them, Come ye after me, and I will make you to become fishers of men.

18 And straightway they forsook their nets, and followed him.

19 And when he had gone a little

further thence, he saw James the son of Zebedee, and John his brother, who also were in the ship mending their nets.

20 And straightway he called them: and they left their father Zebedee in the ship with the hired servants, and went after him.

As Jesus begins to call the men who will comprise the 12 apostles, He begins with four fishermen. This would have been natural since His ministry was at first centered around the Sea of Galilee, where fishing was an important industry. Further significance is seen in the way verse 17 connects their trade with their future task of seeking disciples instead of fish. This scene no doubt contributed to the emergence of the fish, and the word ICHTHYS (Grk. "fish," the letters also standing for "Jesus Christ, God's Son and Our Savior"), as a symbol of the early followers of Jesus.

V. Demonstrating Authority—21-26
A. Authoritative teaching, 21-22

21 And they went into Capernaum; and straightway on the sabbath day he entered into the synagogue, and taught.

22 And they were astonished at his doctrine: for he taught them as one that had authority, and not as the scribes.

Capernaum, a bustling city on the northwestern shore of Galilee, was Jesus' temporary home (Mark 2:1) and the scene of many of His miracles. As the apostle Paul would do years later, Jesus begins his teaching ministry at a synagogue, since He was sent first to "the lost sheep of the house of Israel."

Unfortunately, the training that enabled Jesus to speak with such authority occurred during the "silent years" of which we know little. Of course in addition to the likely fact that He received schooling that would equip Him to be a rabbi, the special indwelling of the Spirit (vs. 10) and His growing awareness of His own Sonship must have contributed to the power of His presence as He spoke.

B. Casting out a demon, 23-26

23 And there was in their synagogue a man with an unclean spirit; and he cried out,

24 Saying, Let us alone; what have we to do with thee, thou Jesus of Nazareth? art thou come to destroy us? I know thee who thou art, the Holy One of God.

25 And Jesus rebuked him, saying, Hold thy peace, and come out of him.

26 And when the unclean spirit had torn him, and cried with a loud voice, he came out of him.

The second way Jesus demonstrated His power and authority was by exorcising a demon-possessed man. Like the demon named "Legion," this unclean spirit had several voices, each of which begged for Jesus to leave them alone. They know He is God's Messiah because, like Him, they are from the spiritual world (reminding us that not all spirits are "of God"). Jesus ignores their pathetic pleas to be left alone because a human life is at stake, and because He must demonstrate His power over evil in order to be accepted as the victor over the kingdom of evil.

Evangelistic Emphasis

"Are you saved?"

You would never hear that question on the lips of Jesus. Look at His first few encounters with people, as recorded by Mark. He calls His first disciples and He never utters that question to them. He called two sets of brothers, Simon and Andrew, James and John. Not once in the process of inviting these people to come with Him did Jesus ask them, "Are you saved?"

He didn't ask the person in the synagogue if he were saved. Here was an individual who was right in the middle of the congregation, listened to the Word preached at every gathering, may have preached it himself, and he had a demon possessing him. You should smile at this story, because we have all met Christians we thought were possessed. Yet even as Jesus was driving the demon out of the man, He never inquired about the man's salvation.

"Are you saved?"

While well intended, it's a question that makes a relationship with Jesus Christ sound like something that could be had at garage sale prices. It infers that praying the right prayer with the right catch phrases wins a sinner entry into the Kingdom.

The better question, the one the Church should be asking today is, *"Are you following Jesus?"*

Following Jesus involves a life-long process of faith and obedience.

ಶಿಂಡಿ

Memory Selection

And there came a voice from heaven, saying, Thou art my beloved Son, in whom I am well pleased.—*Mark 1:11*

A little validation goes a long way. The words from heaven came early in the ministry of Jesus, and they carried Him all the way through to the next words, which came at the Transfiguration.

We are so afraid of pride in the Church that we have not understood the importance in being "proud" of the accomplishments of those around us. How long has it been since someone said to you, "I'm proud of you"? If you are like most of us, it has been a very long time. If you have heard those words recently, you are in a very select minority.

How long has it been since you expressed pride in the job that another was doing? A simple note expressing your appreciation for another person might encourage him or her to keep going in a positive direction.

The words heard at Jesus' baptism were not for the crowds. They were for Him. To give Him encouragement for the long journey of His ministry is why God spoke.

God is proud of the way you serve Him as well!

Weekday Problems

Jane had been a faithful member of First Church for many years, and had served in every capacity in the church. Deeply devout, she attended weekend retreats, led Bible study groups and even formed a prayer group. She was also careful to notice that she worked more in the church than most of the other members. She talked about serving Jesus with her head tossed back, looking down her nose.

When a new pastor came, he immediately "meddled" in one of Jane's pet areas. She informed him that his position would mean such a drastic change in the way things had always been that she might stop attending that church. The change was desperately needed, and implemented over Jane's loud objections. Jane kept her promise and was notably absent from church.

Two weeks later the pastor went to visit Jane, seeking reconciliation and healing. Jane informed him that she wouldn't be back as long as he was pastor. She said she had prayed about it and felt that God understood her position.

*What is the difference between having pride and being proud?

*Do you think that Jane's position is a result of her pride being hurt?

Jesus Shall Reign Where'er the Sun

Jesus shall reign where'er the sun
Doth his successive journeys run;
His kingdom stretch from shore to shore,
Till moon shall wax and wane no more.
To Him shall endless prayer be made,
And praises throng to crown His head;
His name, like sweet perfume, shall rise
With every morning sacrifice;
People and realms of every tongue
Dwell on His love with sweetest song,
And infant voices shall proclaim
Their early blessings on His name.
. . .
Let every creature rise and bring
Peculiar honors to our King;
Angels descend with songs again,
And earth repeat the loud amen.

—Isaac Watts

This Lesson in Your Life

The thesis sentence for Jesus' ministry is found in part of the reading for this lesson. Jesus' first sermon was this, "The time is fulfilled, the kingdom of God is at hand, repent and believe the gospel." It is nice to know that effective sermons can be short sermons.

"The time is fulfilled." By this Jesus meant that the time to make a decision had arrived for the people living in Palestine. We are faced with making choices each day. Some of our choices are complex, and really don't matter in the "big picture." I can remember returning a cable box because there were too many stations to choose from and yet nothing to watch. The time to make a choice about Jesus had arrived. The time to choose Jesus comes to us each daily. With the important decisions, we choose between being faithful to Jesus and choosing our own path through life.

"The kingdom of God is at hand." Preachers and teachers have written whole libraries of material about the meaning of this phrase. The image gets lost on a people who have never had a king, and don't often think about kingdoms. This statement means that the rule of God has become available to us. We bring the kingdom of God on earth when Jesus rules in our hearts. We bring the kingdom of God when Jesus is the priority by which we make our decisions.

"Repent," Jesus said.

Repentance is another word that has fallen from our Church vocabulary. We know that Jesus said we ought to do it, but we don't require it many times of our own members. Repentance means changing the direction of our lives. We repent when we change our minds about the things we are doing or allowing in our lives. Repentance means walking away from the things that were and walking toward what God wants in our lives. The best illustration of repentance is the story of the Prodigal Son, when we are told, "He came to himself." Once he recognized the untenable situation he was in, he decided to return home.

"Believe in the gospel," Jesus said.

Believing in the gospel is more than mental assent to a bunch of theological ideas. Jesus is not talking about a theological checklist in which we say, "I believe in the virgin birth. I believe in substutionary atonement." Jesus was telling His listeners and us that belief in the gospel will change the way one handles daily activities. A belief in the gospel will cause one to be busy in the work of God. He will be participating in telling people that he knows, "The time is fulfilled, the kingdom of God is at hand, repent, and believe the gospel."

GETTING THE FACTS STRAIGHT

1. Jesus was baptized by John. What were the circumstances surrounding the baptism?

As John was preaching and Jesus was traveling from Nazareth, He was baptized by John in the Jordan.

2. What two things did Jesus see after He was baptized?

Jesus saw the heavens being torn apart (opened) and the Spirit of God descending like a dove.

3. What did Jesus hear after He was baptized?

Jesus heard a voice from heaven saying, "This is my Son, whom I love, with you I am well pleased."

4. After Jesus was baptized by John in the Jordan River, what happened next in His ministry?

The Spirit sent Him into the wilderness to be tempted of the devil for 40 days.

5. What details were given about the temptation of Jesus in the wilderness?

Mark gave none of the specific temptations, but did say that Jesus was with the wild animals and the angels attended Him.

6. According to Mark, when did Jesus begin His public ministry?

The public ministry of Jesus began after John the Baptizer had been put in prison.

7. Who were the first four disciples that Jesus called in His ministry?

Jesus called Simon and his brother Andrew, then he called the brothers James and John.

8. What vocation do Simon, Andrew, James and John appear to have in common?

All four of these disciples of Jesus were fishermen.

9.After Jesus called these four disciples, what happened next in the narrative?

Jesus was in Capernaum and it was the Sabbath. He went into the synagogue and began to teach.

10. In the synagogue in Capernaum, what two things happened?

The people were amazed at the teaching of Jesus, and a demon was driven out of a man who was attending synagogue.

Does God love you? While most preachers proclaim boldly that He does, They somehow usually end up saying that God loves you *more* after you repent of your sins. In order to be obedient to God, you must then be baptized. After you are baptized and join the Church, then God is pleased when you start tithing. After everything you do, a preacher can convince you God wants you to do *more* before He will fully love you. I know that people hear that message even though we don't intend to preach it that way. I have been told, "Preacher I need to start coming to church, but first I've got to get my life straightened out." Or "Preacher I know that God will not hear my prayers because I have not been a very good person." Perhaps right now you are wondering when God is going to let the other shoe drop. When is He going to "get you" for that sin that is hiding in your life? You are wondering if God will withdraw His love and grace from you.

But God loves you unconditionally, just as you are. That is the radical nature of Jesus' love. We come to understand that when we look at the characters that Jesus first called to follow Him. Jesus didn't select His first disciples from a rabbinic school. Jesus found four men who were fishermen and called them to follow Him. He didn't give them any training, or demand that they take some religious vows. He simply said, "Follow me." There is a radical lesson here as the Church deals with people who don't have faith in Jesus.

Jesus didn't tell Peter and Andrew that they had to affirm a prescribed set of religious maxims or clean up their act. He offered them an invitation to follow Him. Some writers maintain that Peter did not have faith in Jesus until after the resurrection. Is it possible that Peter was in the middle of all Jesus' ministry and wasn't completely "redeemed"? It took him the whole ministry of Jesus to "get saved."

The Church is not the place where those who have "arrived" gather. We are the place where those who are on the way are encouraged. When you understand fully the nature of salvation. You must honestly answer. "I was saved, I am being saved and I will be saved." If you are honest, you can't put a definite date or time or place on it. Because salvation is not something you do. It is something God does. God takes His time, often working in ways we don't readily perceive.

Just think of the time and effort it took with Simon Peter, all the setbacks he endured, the guffaws and the false steps that made up his walk with Jesus. However, Jesus in His love would not give up on Peter, Andrew, you, or me. He invited those fishermen and He invites us to take part in this journey of faith. Jesus asks that we "follow Him."

A true salvation experience takes place over a lifetime.

Lesson 2

The Beginning of Conflict

Mark 2:3-17

And they come unto him, bringing one sick of the palsy, which was borne of four.

4 And when they could not come nigh unto him for the press, they uncovered the roof where he was: and when they had broken it up, they let down the bed whcrein the sick of the palsy lay.

5 When Jesus saw their faith, he said unto the sick of the palsy, Son, thy sins be forgiven thee.

6 But there were certain of the scribes sitting there, and reasoning in their hearts,

7 Why doth this man thus speak blasphemies? who can forgive sins but God only?

8 And immediately when Jesus perceived in his spirit that they so reasoned within themselves, he said unto them, Why reason ye these things in your hearts?

9 Whether is it easier to say to the sick of the palsy, Thy sins be forgiven thee; or to say, Arise, and take up thy bed, and walk?

10 But that ye may know that the Son of man hath power on earth to forgive sins, (he saith to the sick of the palsy,)

11 I say unto thee, Arise, and take up thy bed, and go thy way into thine house.

12 And immediately he arose, took up the bed, and went forth before them all; insomuch that they were all amazed, and glorified God, saying, We never saw it on this fashion.

13 And he went forth again by the sea side; and all the multitude resorted unto him, and he taught them.

14 And as he passed by, he saw Levi the son of Alphaeus sitting at the receipt of custom, and said unto him, Follow me. And he arose and followed him.

15 And it came to pass, that, as Jesus sat at meat in his house, many publicans and sinners sat also together with Jesus and his disciples: for there were many, and they followed him.

16 And when the scribes and Pharisees saw him eat with publicans and sinners, they said unto his disciples, How is it that he eateth and drinketh with publicans and sinners?

17 When Jesus heard it, he saith unto them, They that are whole have no need of the physician, but they that are sick: I came not to call the righteous, but sinners to repentance.

Memory Selection
Mark 2:17

Background Scripture
Mark 2:1–3:6

Devotional Reading
Luke 15:1-17

Jesus and His followers were misunderstood from the beginning. Even among those who were expecting the Messiah, some wondered if Jesus was the genuine article, and others misunderstood His plan to die.

This lesson features more hostile objections to Jesus' claims. Was it not blasphemy to claim to forgive sins, as though He were divine? What about His associating with sinners? If He were the Messiah, couldn't He tell good people from bad, and keep a proper distance from those who were not worthy? Jesus showed His awareness of all this when he sent word to John the Baptist in prison and said, "Blessed is anyone who takes no offense at me" (Matt. 11:6, NRSV).

This lesson's focus on those who did take offense also provides a good opportunity to ask ourselves whether we might have been among them.

∞⋘

Ask members of your group if they have ever been involved in a case of "mistaken identity." Has anyone ever called out to someone in a crowd, only to find, when that person turned around, that he didn't know him after all? Have you ever answered the telephone flippantly, thinking it was a friend or family member, then discovered that a stranger was on the line?

Ask what clues we go by to identify a person we think we know. Their height or weight, shape or hair color, the way they walk or talk, or some other mannerism? Then hone in on the fact that we correctly identify another only when our perception matches their reality. In Jesus' case, many rejected Him because He did not fit their preconceptions of what He "should" be. Even today, we must allow Him to define Himself and His own mission, instead of pressing our preconceived ideas about who we wish He was, and what He might do.

Teaching Outline	Daily Bible Readings	

I. Healthy in Spirit—3-5
    A. Zealous friends, 3-4
    B. Body-soul connection, 5
	Mon.	'Your Sins Are Forgiven'
		Mark 2:1-12

II. Whole in Body—6-12
    A. Is this blasphemy?, 6-7
    B. Proof of power, 8-12
	Tue.	Eating with Sinners
		Mark 2:13-17

	Wed.	Joy for One Who Repents Luke 15:1-7
	Thu.	New Wine, Old Wineskins Mark 2:18-22

III. Who Needs Jesus?—13-17
    A. Publican/disciples, 13-15
    B. Answering critics, 16-17
	Fri.	People Come First
		Mark 2:23-28

	Sat.	Healing on the Sabbath Mark 3:1-6
	Sun.	'You are the Son of God!' Mark 3:7-12

Verse by Verse

I. Healthy in Spirit—3-5
A. Zealous friends, 3-4

3 And they come unto him, bringing one sick of the palsy, which was borne of four.

4 And when they could not come nigh unto him for the press, they uncovered the roof where he was: and when they had broken it up, they let down the bed wherein the sick of the palsy lay.

The setting here is in the city of Capernaum (vs. 1), on the northwest shore of the Sea of Galilee, which was Jesus' home base during much of His Galilean ministry. It is a sign of the early attention Jesus drew as a public teacher that crowds pressed around him in numbers that made it impossible for this invalid's friends to get him in touch with this teacher who also had the reputation of being a healer. They knew that these gifts were to be combined in the long-awaited Messiah.

The KJV "palsy" refers to any of several diseases with the symptom of paralysis (see the NIV). Since the man could not walk, and since most houses in the Middle East had stairways to the roof, his friends had no trouble carrying him up. The difficulty was getting him down; but this they accomplished by removing the broad, flat tiles that would have been laid on slats or "stringers" (Luke 5:19). Although Mark describes this as breaking up the roof, the tiles could of course have been replaced without permanent damage. Still, the effort the paralytic's friends went to shows the strength of their friendship as well as their expectations that Jesus could heal him.

B. Body-soul connection, 5

5 When Jesus saw their faith, he said unto the sick of the palsy, Son, thy sins be forgiven thee.

Modern faith healers sometimes say that a person whom they were unable to heal did not have enough faith. In this case, however, we are not told whether the sick man had faith or not; yet Jesus heals him on the basis of the faith of his friends, who had gone to the trouble to get the man to Jesus. Although faith is often an important component of healing, this incident shows that the real power lies in Jesus, not in persons.

Jesus first heals the man's soul, not his body, reminding us that most people in Bible times (Jew and Gentile alike) believed that illness was sent by God (or the gods) as punishment for sin. This is not as "primitive" a view as we might think, since there is often a direct connection between sin and sickness (for example, between habitual drunkenness and liver failure).

273

Jesus, however, taught that this is not an automatic or "supernatural" rule. God, for example, blesses both the just and the unjust with rain (Matt. 5:45). Whether real or imagined, however, the man in this account associated his illness with sin; so Jesus proceeds to tackle the spiritual issue first, and pronounces the man spiritually whole. As verse 10 will show, He could take this supernatural step only if He had divine authority.

II. Whole in Body—6-12
A. Is this blasphemy?, 6-7

6 But there were certain of the scribes sitting there, and reasoning in their hearts,

7 Why doth this man thus speak blasphemies? who can forgive sins but God only?

The scribes, who were something like a combination of lawyers for the Law and religious police, object to Jesus' audacity in pronouncing forgiveness, knowing that this authority belongs only to God. Blasphemy is literally the sin of reviling God, either by speaking evil of Him or intruding as a mere human on His domain, as the scribes suspect Jesus does here. Their question was serious, since blasphemy was punishable by death (Lev. 24:15-16).

No doubt Jesus anticipated their question, and forgave the man's sin not only for the man's own benefit but in order to confront His opponents with the issue of His divinity. Just as in the case of people today, they must now decide whether this healer and teacher is really who He claims to be, or is an impostor.

B. Proof of power, 8-12

8 And immediately when Jesus perceived in his spirit that they so reasoned within themselves, he said unto them, Why reason ye these things in your hearts?

9 Whether is it easier to say to the sick of the palsy, Thy sins be forgiven thee; or to say, Arise, and take up thy bed, and walk?

10 But that ye may know that the Son of man hath power on earth to forgive sins, (he saith to the sick of the palsy,)

11 I say unto thee, Arise, and take up thy bed, and go thy way into thine house.

12 And immediately he arose, took up the bed, and went forth before them all; insomuch that they were all amazed, and glorified God, saying, We never saw it on this fashion.

Although it goes unrecognized, Jesus' very ability to see into the scribes' hearts shows His divinity. Then, true to one of Mark's specific purposes in writing his Gospel, Jesus proves His power in the unseen realm of sin and forgiveness by demonstrating it in the visible realm of sickness and health. "Them all" apparently refers to all but the skeptic scribes, since throughout the Gospels they are portrayed as unconvinced witnesses of such miracles. For those open to faith, however, this story is a reminder that the miracle of forgiveness is as amazing and worthy of praise as are instances of physical healing.

III. Who Needs Jesus?—13-17
A. Publican/disciples, 13-15

13 And he went forth again by the

sea side; and all the multitude resorted unto him, and he taught them.

14 And as he passed by, he saw Levi the son of Alphaeus sitting at the receipt of custom, and said unto him, Follow me. And he arose and followed him.

15 And it came to pass, that, as Jesus sat at meat in his house, many publicans and sinners sat also together with Jesus and his disciples: for there were many, and they followed him.

Moving out of the house and the town to teach on the shores of Galilee, Jesus continues to engage in a style of ministry that will bring criticism from His enemies. This time His offense consists not of claiming divine powers, but acting all too human! In the process of gathering the 12 apostles about Him, he calls a tax collector named Levi to be one of them. According to the parallel account in Matthew 9:9, this "publican" (Luke 5:27) also went by the name "Matthew." Most Jews hated the publicans since they collected taxes for the hated Romans, and were allowed to extort for their own profit far more than was due Rome.

B. Answering critics, 16-17

16 And when the scribes and Pharisees saw him eat with publicans and sinners, they said unto his disciples, How is it that he eateth and drinketh with publicans and sinners?

17 When Jesus heard it, he saith unto them, They that are whole have no need of the physician, but they that are sick: I came not to call the righteous, but sinners to repentance.

By inviting Matthew the publican and others like him to dine with Him, Jesus adds insult to injury. It was bad enough to accept a tax collector as a disciple, but worse to dine with him since that was a sign of friendship, acceptance, and fellowship. In answer to His enemies, Jesus again connects sickness with sin, at least metaphorically, and points out that His actions are exactly consistent with the very reason He came.

This answer is loaded with significance in more ways than one. First, in claiming to have "come" Jesus is identifying Himself as "He who comes," a popular way of describing the Messiah (see Ps. 118:26; Matt. 21:9). He was the Messiah sent from God, not an upstart mortal who emerged a hero from the masses.

Second, Jesus defines His role as Messiah as having to do with loving and saving sinners. This did not at all fit the view of those who expected the Messiah to be such a paragon of righteousness that he would associate only with people "like him." Neither did this "mission to the least, the last, and the lost" fit the expectations of those who thought a "real" Messiah would lead a revolt against their political masters, the Romans. The failure to meet such expectations would cost Jesus His life.

This scene begs to be applied even by the Church in modern times. It is often difficult for Christians to accept the challenge of following in Christ's footsteps to the extent that they associate with society's outcasts in order to take the Great Physician to the spiritually ill.

Evangelistic Emphasis

To what lengths will you go to help another person experience the love of God? For most of us the answer is a simple one. We will pray for a person to experience "saving grace," or perhaps invite a person to join us in church one Sunday. Beyond that, we will basically leave people alone.

The men in this lesson amaze me with their tenacity for getting their friend to Jesus. First these four men had to overcome a transportation problem. Their friend could not walk. They created a way of hauling him to the home where Jesus was preaching.

They could have given up when they saw the great crowd that had gathered outside the door of the home. It was standing room only as the people listened to Jesus teaching.

These four men would not give up. They figured out a way to get on top of the house with their friend on the stretcher and lower him to Jesus. They offended the homeowner by removing a part of their roof. They then found the ropes and made a way to lower this man down to the place where Jesus was. Jesus offered to heal the man partly because He saw the faith of all five of the people involved in the story.

Sometimes we are called to have faith for people around us, to surround them with belief, when their belief is weak.

୫୬ଓଷ

Memory Selection

When Jesus heard it, he saith unto them, They that are whole have no need of the physician, but they that are sick: I came not to call the righteous, but sinners to repentance.—*Mark 2: 17*

Jesus came for people unlike us. He came that those who had no relationship with God, or knowledge of Him, might have both. Jesus spent most of His ministry around people that we try to avoid. He was always the center of attention at dinner parties that were attended by the worst offenders of Jewish law. Tax collectors, prostitutes, and other sinners made up the guest list and according to the Bible, there was enough wine present that his enemies labeled Jesus a drunkard.

The very religious of people had the most unreligious things to say about Jesus Christ. They were the ones that accused Him of being evil because He was always in the company of evil people. The purpose of Jesus was to tell these outcasts of society that God loved them. His ministry was to the very people that the religious leaders had thought God had given up on.

In your area, who are the people who are in most need of a physician? Are these people ones with whom you would share a pew? It is too easy to look down our noses at those God loves. Remember, God loves those people we find most unlovable.

Weekday Problems

Ben Marshall married his high school sweetheart right after graduation from college. He and Cindy have two wonderful children. He has advanced readily through his company's structure, and is now poised for the next step up on the corporate ladder. Along the way, Ben has maintained good family relationships. He also coaches his son's baseball team, is active in the Lion's Club, sings in his church's choir, and substitutes as a high school Sunday school teacher.

The next step up the corporate ladder is to become an Executive Vice President of the firm. His income would be more than he ever imagined. He would have job security and a guaranteed shot at the firm's presidency. In that position, one of his tasks would be to entertain the firm's best clients. These clients like to patronize a club with exotic dancers and expensive liquor. Ben would be expected to entertain these clients in this establishment. He knows that to refuse the next step up the ladder is also to guarantee he will rise no higher in the firm. He tells his wife, who understands about the whole situation. Her response is to stand behind him no matter what choice he makes.

*How do we judge which places are good or bad for Christians to frequent?

*If we judge an establishment to be evil, are we also judging the people who work there? What is our responsibility in sharing the gospel with them?

Quotable Quotes

Many a child who watches television for hours will go down in history . . . not to mention arithmetic, English, and geography.

People seldom think alike except when it comes to buying wedding presents.

A halo has only to fall about 11 inches to become a noose.

A man's horse sense deserts him when he is feeling his oats.

Confucius say: Ostrich who keep head in sand too long during heat of day gets burned in the end.

The worst thing about history repeating itself is that every time it does so, the price goes up.

This Lesson in Your Life

People were listening to every word that came from the lips of Jesus. His teaching with such authority and His ability to work the mighty wonders of God had caused a crowd to gather in that small home in Capernaum. The people were piled in as tightly as they could. The crowd had overflowed outside the doors of the house and the people listened to Jesus with great anticipation of what He would teach them about God.

Suddenly, the roof came off the house, and four men could be seen peeking down from the hole. They had this funny shy but knowing-what-they-were-doing look. After surveying the situation, they took a pallet and rope and lowered a paralyzed man down to where Jesus was. When He saw the faith of all five of the men, He was so impressed that He healed the one who was paralyzed.

Now what He said to this man stirred controversy among those who heard the words. Jesus said, "Son, your sins are forgiven." The religious leaders, who were always hanging around, were aghast at the words that Jesus had spoken. These people didn't have to say the words, Jesus could tell by the look on their face what they were thinking. He responded, "Which is easier to say, be healed or be forgiven?" They tried to engage Him in a religious argument.

Although there is not a clear cause and effect relationship between most illnesses and sin, there is still a lifestyle relationship. There's no mystery when a lifetime of drinking leads to liver problems, or when a lifetime smoker develops lung cancer. It's also true, however, that people can make themselves sick from guilt.

I knew of a man once who had slapped his teenaged son in a fit of justified frustration. Regretting this reaction, he apologized to his son. A couple of weeks later the man developed a very severe cold, which worsened and landed him in the hospital. As the symptoms of the cold vanished, the doctors discovered that the man had lost feeling in his arms, and they were paralyzed. It was assumed that some virus had caused this to happen.

X-rays and tests revealed that the man's nervous system was completely healthy. After eliminating all medical reasons for the paralysis, the hospital chaplain was called in. After talking and praying with the man, the chaplain made a suggestion that the man was punishing himself for the guilt he felt for slapping his son. After several sessions in the hospital, the man slowly regained the use of his hands.

Jesus wants to deal with our real problem, whether physical or spiritual. He knows where we need healing, and we should trust the "Great Physician" to know where to apply the medicine.

GETTING THE FACTS STRAIGHT

1. In what location was Jesus when most of the activity in this text took place?

The opening chapters of Mark's gospel have Jesus in the town of Capernaum.

2. The men carrying the paralyzed man could not get to Jesus. Why?

The crowd that had gathered to hear Jesus teach was so large they were blocking the doorway.

3. When the men saw that they could not get their paralyzed friend to Jesus what did they do?

They climbed on top of the house, made a hole in the roof, and let their friend down through the hole.

4. When Jesus saw their faith, He healed the man. What words did He speak to the man?

Jesus told the man, "Your sins are forgiven."

5. What did the teachers of the Law do in response to Jesus' words to the paralytic man?

They didn't say anything, but were questioning Jesus in their hearts about forgiving the man's sin.

6. What did the religious leaders thinking about Jesus' statement?

They thought that Jesus was guilty of blasphemy, because only God could forgive sins.

7. What did Jesus say to these teachers of the Law?

Jesus asked them, "Which is easier to say, your sins are forgiven or take up your pallet and walk?"

8. After He made His statement to the religious leaders, what did He say to the paralytic man?

He told the man, "I tell you, get up, take up you mat and go home."

9. What happened after Jesus told the man to get up and go home?

The man got up and went out before all of them, and the crowd was amazed at what they had seen.

10. Jesus was once again by the lake, and saw a man. Who was the man and what did Jesus say to him?

The man Jesus met was the tax collector Levi, and Jesus told the man to "follow me."

279

Having a meal is more about social interaction than it is about nutrition. Think about all the meals that stand out in your mind. They were meals around social interactions and celebrations. Thanksgiving and Christmas dinners are two of the times I remember from my childhood. I don't know what kind of food we had but I remember the people sitting around those large family tables. The conversations around those tables mattered more than the food.

When men in our day eat a meal together they are transacting business. When you see two community leaders sitting at a table, they are not sharing soulful thoughts. They are transacting business. That is why the FBI likes to bug restaurants where organized crime figures gather. Those people are not talking about feelings and relationships. They are transacting business.

When Jesus was seen eating with people, it was different than in our culture. When you sat down and ate a meal in that culture you were giving validation to the person with whom you were eating. When Jesus sat down and ate with the sinners, He was by his actions saying, "You people are just fine."

One of the great conflicts about Jesus arose over the fact that He would sit at the table with a group of sinners. The religious leaders would never sit with sinners; they would have no social interactions with these kinds of people. When Jesus sat with them and listened to their life stories, it was the first time these people had experienced that kind of compassion from a religious leader.

Jesus then told a very short parable. "It is not the healthy who need a doctor, but the sick. I have not come to call the righteous but sinners."

The strange paradox is that we are called to live holy lives. In our lifestyle choices we make a witness to the love of God that is in us. At the same time, we are called to bring others to Jesus. One of my favorite questions to ask a church is, "How long has it been since you invited a sinner to dinner?" People look at me funny like they don't know any sinners. I'll bet you have a list of sinners. I know you have put your hands on your hips and said, "I just don't know what this world is coming to" when you have seen some person do something of which you didn't approve? Did you think of inviting that person to dinner?

How many lives might you change by allowing a "sinner" to get to know you and allow you to know them? The gospel of Jesus is not a finger-pointing exercise in conversion. His gospel is gently taking someone by the hand and leading him or her to the Master. We can only do that to the extent that we are willing to take time with people who don't know Jesus. Maybe we all need to join some kind of dinner evangelism club. I think a great compliment as a leader in your church would be for someone to say of you, "I saw him eating with sinners."

Lesson 3

Jesus' Authority

Mark 4:36-41; 5:2-13

And when they had sent away the multitude, they took him even as he was in the ship. And there were also with him other little ships.

37 And there arose a great storm of wind, and the waves beat into the ship, so that it was now full.

38 And he was in the hinder part of the ship, asleep on a pillow: and they awake him, and say unto him, Master, carest thou not that we perish?

39 And he arose, and rebuked the wind, and said unto the sea, Peace, be still. And the wind ceased, and there was a great calm.

40 And he said unto them, Why are ye so fearful? how is it that ye have no faith?

41 And they feared exceedingly, and said one to another, What manner of man is this, that even the wind and the sea obey him?

5:2 And when he was come out of the ship, immediately there met him out of the tombs a man with an unclean spirit,

3 Who had his dwelling among the tombs; and no man could bind him, no, not with chains:

4 Because that he had been often bound with fetters and chains, and the chains had been plucked asunder by him, and the fetters broken in pieces: neither could any man tame him.

5 And always, night and day, he was in the mountains, and in the tombs, crying, and cutting himself with stones.

6 But when he saw Jesus afar off, he ran and worshipped him,

7 And cried with a loud voice, and said, What have I to do with thee, Jesus, thou Son of the most high God? I adjure thee by God, that thou torment me not.

8 For he said unto him, Come out of the man, thou unclean spirit.

9 And he asked him, What is thy name? And he answered, saying, My name is Legion: for we are many.

10 And he besought him much that he would not send them away out of the country.

11 Now there was there nigh unto the mountains a great herd of swine feeding.

12 And all the devils besought him, saying, Send us into the swine, that we may enter into them.

13 And forthwith Jesus gave them leave. And the unclean spirits went out, and entered into the swine: and the herd ran violently down a steep place into the sea, (they were about two thousand;) and were choked in the sea.

Memory Selection
Mark 4:41

Background Scripture
Mark 4:35–5:20

Devotional Reading
John 5:2-17

Like the overall theme of Mark, this lesson portrays Jesus' superhuman power. As noted earlier, Mark may have written especially for Romans, who were impressed with displays of power.

One account in today's text describes Jesus' amazing (a favorite word for Mark) power over the physical world, or nature, as He stills a storm at sea. The other portrays His authority over the spiritual realm, as

he casts out a demon from a crazed sufferer. (Compare Mark's account with those in Matthew 8 and Luke 8.)

Such incidents may at first seem somewhat removed from our experience today, when we have air conditioners and heaters that control the effects of weather, and psychologists who can heal the spirit. Yet we are far from being able to control devastating "natural disasters," and no one is in total control of human nature. We still have occasion to ask in wonder, "What manner of man is this, that even the wind and the sea obey him?"

ഇറ

Ask group members to discuss various ways people learn to restore calm in the outward and inward storms of life. We defend against storms at sea by equipping ships with stabilizers. For earthquake protection we invent better anchoring for buildings, and limit their height. Emergency shelters are prepared for people

who live in flood-prone areas.

For inner calm, we can purchase soothing music and beautiful scenery, or go to the mountains and gaze at majestic peaks. Others go to the beach and allow the sound of the surf to wash peace into their souls. Meditation and prayer bring peace to many.

Today's lesson shows that Jesus is the true Power behind all such secondary measures. The creative Word is behind the power of creation. He knows the need for peace in the soul because He is both God and man.

Teaching Outline	Daily Bible Readings

I. Calming a Storm—4:36-41
  A. Gale on Galilee, 36-37
  B. From sleep to action, 38-39
  C. A matter of faith, 40-41
 	
II. Casting Out a Demon—5:2-13
  A. Demonic power, 2-5
  B. Pleading with Jesus, 6-8
  C. Possessed pigs!, 9-13
	Mon. 'Peace, Be Still!'
	     Mark 4:35-41
	Tue. Walking on Water
	     Mark 6:45-51
	Wed. Confronting a Demon
	     Mark 5:1-10
	Thu. All Are Amazed
	     Mark 5:11-20
	Fri. Turning Water to Wine
	     John 2:1-11
	Sat. The Son Gives Life
	     John 5:19-24
	Sun. Teaching with Authority
	     Matthew 7:24-29

Verse by Verse

I. Calming a Storm—4:36-41

A. Gale on Galilee, 36-37

36 And when they had sent away the multitude, they took him even as he was in the ship. And there were also with him other little ships.

37 And there arose a great storm of wind, and the waves beat into the ship, so that it was now full.

In the midst of His Galilean ministry, Jesus calls for His disciples to take him to "the other side" of the sea (vs. 35), from the northwest shore, where we last left Him, to the eastern side. Those who know the Sea of Galilee report that it is subject to sudden storms, seemingly blowing up out of nowhere. This is partly because of the extremes of altitude in the area, ranging from the lake's surface, which is 700 feet below sea level, to the Golan Heights on the eastern shore, with cliffs that rise to a height of 2,700 feet. Air currents, cooled from these heights and from the mountains to the west, can rush down the slopes and collide turbulently both with each other and with warmer air near the lake's surface. Caught in such a storm, the ship bearing Jesus begins to take on water, and is in danger of sinking.

B. From sleep to action, 38-39

38 And he was in the hinder part of the ship, asleep on a pillow: and they awake him, and say unto him, Master, carest thou not that we perish?

39 And he arose, and rebuked the wind, and said unto the sea, Peace, be still. And the wind ceased, and there was a great calm.

The "hinder part" of the ship (NIV "stern") would have provided a place for Jesus to rest that was less subject than the ship's bow to the normal rise and fall of the waves. No doubt He is exhausted from the intense sessions of teaching and healing recorded in the previous chapters. Nevertheless, the boatmen become impatient as Jesus' nap endures after the dangerous storm strikes. Actually, His trust in His Father's protection is simply weightier than the power of the storm; but the disciples interpret this as indifference.

Despite the disciples' need for more of the kind of faith Jesus had exhibited by continuing to sleep, He arises to calm the wind and the waves with a word of rebuke. It may seem miraculous to us for Jesus to be able to speak to inanimate matter, and for it to respond to His voice. However, this miracle is grounded in the even greater miracle of creation itself, when Jesus as the Word spoke matter into existence in the first place (John 1:1-14). If He could create matter, we should not find it incredible that He could control it.

C. A matter of faith, 40-41

40 And he said unto them, Why

are ye so fearful? how is it that ye have no faith?

41 And they feared exceedingly, and said one to another, What manner of man is this, that even the wind and the sea obey him?

Just as Jesus had rebuked the storm, now He mildly rebukes the disciples for having had greater fear of the storm than respect for His power. Jesus had already demonstrated His power over nature in His healing miracles; so He can rightly ask why they could not carry over the faith that those incidents had created into the situation on the sea.

Their question shows that even Christ's closest disciples did not become "instant believers." Yet their faith, while weak at this point, will grow from mustard-seed size to the mountainous faith it took to take the Good News to all the known world.

II. Casting Out a Demon—5:2-13
A. Demonic power, 2-5

2 And when he was come out of the ship, immediately there met him out of the tombs a man with an unclean spirit,

3 Who had his dwelling among the tombs; and no man could bind him, no, not with chains:

4 Because that he had been often bound with fetters and chains, and the chains had been plucked asunder by him, and the fetters broken in pieces: neither could any man tame him.

5 And always, night and day, he was in the mountains, and in the tombs, crying, and cutting himself with stones.

This event occurs near the town of Gadara (or Gergesenes, Matt. 8:28, from differing manuscripts), on the east side of Galilee (5:1). Although this is one of the Bible's most colorful and striking stories, it is not easy to understand. In the first place, it is not clear how people come under the influence of Satan as described here. (It has rightly been noted that "demon possession" is not a biblical phrase; even those with demons belong not to Satan but to God.)

Some would dismiss these accounts as descriptions of insanity that primitives wrongly attributed to satanic influence. Certainly the insane can have superior strength against restraints, and often are as self-destructive as this man. However, Mark 3:9-10 clearly distinguishes between illness and demonization; and Jesus has previously shown His separate mastery over both maladies.

No doubt the man had been chained to keep him from harming himself as well as others. However, just as God's Spirit had empowered Samson to break the chains that bound him, so Satan had given such strength to this wretch that he broke all restraints. We are not told whether he lived in a cemetery on his own volition, or had been driven there by others for their own protection. Either way, that environment would have made him all the more fearful, since demons are so commonly associated with burial grounds.

B. Pleading with Jesus, 6-8

6 But when he saw Jesus afar off, he ran and worshipped him,

7 And cried with a loud voice, and said, What have I to do with

thee, Jesus, thou Son of the most high God? I adjure thee by God, that thou torment me not.

8 For he said unto him, Come out of the man, thou unclean spirit.

At first it may seem odd that the man both worships Jesus and begs Him to leave him alone. Yet this "split personality" is the essence both of some kinds of mental illness and, apparently, of being demonized. It is merely a demonically enlarged version of the "double mind" many people have when they at one moment want to do right, and at the next to do wrong.

As in earlier cases, the demon(s) recognize Jesus as the Son of God since both He and they are from the spirit-world. Yet this recognition obviously does not translate into a saving knowledge of Christ, reminding us that "the devils also believe, and tremble" (Jas. 2:17).

C. Possessed pigs!, 9-13

9 And he asked him, What is thy name? And he answered, saying, My name is Legion: for we are many.

10 And he besought him much that he would not send them away out of the country.

11 Now there was there nigh unto the mountains a great herd of swine feeding.

12 And all the devils besought him, saying, Send us into the swine, that we may enter into them.

13 And forthwith Jesus gave them leave. And the unclean spirits went out, and entered into the swine: and the herd ran violently down a steep place into the sea, (they were about two thousand;) and were choked in the sea.

In the strangest stroke of all, the finale of this story finds Jesus both accommodating the wishes of the demons, then destroying them in the sea. Jesus may have been asking the man his name both to clarify his sense of who he really was in God's eyes, and to "humanize" him before the onlookers; but it is the demons who answer, and with a name that indicates they are "many." Again, while some compare this with the mental problem called "multiple personalities," the supernatural element of the biblical cases of demonization clearly extends beyond mere mental illness.

Why the demons prefer to be sent into the swine over being banished from the country is another unanswered question. Although Christ seems at first to grant the demons' wish, they send the hogs into such a frenzy that they rush blindly off a cliff overlooking the sea, and are drowned. This development is a kind of mirror-image of an even grander-scaled "trick" Jesus will play on Satan, when He at first allows Himself to be killed on the Cross, then unexpectedly arises from the dead.

In an interesting postscript to this account, verses 14-17 will describe the townspeople's request that Jesus leave the region because of this incident. We are not told whether the swine were kept by Gentiles or by Jews, to whom pork was forbidden. Whoever owned them, the economic loss was apparently of greater importance than the opportunity to witness God at work through Christ in their midst.

Evangelistic Emphasis

The first convert that Jesus and the disciples made would not be a good poster child for mission work. The first convert to the movement lived in a cemetery. He was crazy. He was so crazy that the town members had chained him up in the cemetery in hope that the ghosts and demons of the cemetery could handle him. He was dirty. He was loud. His hair was unkempt. He was a mess. By the time Jesus was finished with him, a whole herd of pigs were dead, but he was a new man.

This story is a comfort to those who wonder if they can ever have a relationship with God. If *this* fellow can be the first convert to the Jesus movement, anyone you can think of would make a possible disciple of Jesus Christ.

Jesus' ministry to the outcasts, rather than coddling the religious elite, is a comforting thought for those who struggle with the notion of a loving God. While God hates sin, he loves the sinner. That is a differentiation that we have yet to master. We lump sinners and their sins together and say, "They ought to clean up their act." Yet we do nothing to encourage them into a renewing relationship with the church or with the Lord.

The next time you are tempted to get down on a member of society and label him hopeless remember this first disciple of the Lord. He was some kind of convert.

ಬಂಡ

Memory Selection

Who then is this, that even the wind and the sea obey him?—*Mark 4: 41*

Peace is not the absence of conflict; it is the ability to be calm in the storm! Watching the disciples facing this storm, one wonders if they felt any peace at all. They were frightened as they faced this tempest on the Sea of Galilee.

The challenge we face is that we not only don't have peace, we get frustrated when we are in the storms of life and water seems to get into our boat. You know, the promise in the pages of Scripture is that no harm will come to Jesus' disciples. He never promised us that we wouldn't get wet!

Too many believe that merely getting wet is a sign that God has abandoned us and that the storms of life will overcome us. Our faith really needs to mature in the face of the rampant "healthy and wealthy" gospel being preached in some corners of the church.

If the storms of life are surrounding you, pray. God will answer. Your feet might get wet, but you will not drown!

Weekday Problems

The new church directories had been held up at the printer's. By the time they arrived in the church office, a year had passed since the photographs had been taken. Dwayne Johnson, who had worked on the directories, was not pleased with the company, nor that so many faces had changed during the year. He told the Pastor that he really didn't want to distribute the directories. He wanted to write the company for a refund and forget the whole project. He was quite adamant and angry.

As the pastor thumbed through his new copy of the directory, he came to the page containing the Johnson family. Dwayne, Katy and their sons Jason and Jonathan were pictured along with their daughter, Jennifer. The pastor remembered the day Jennifer died. She had struggled for two years with leukemia, and lost the battle. The other picture that caught the Pastor's eye was of Dwayne's parents, Helen and Bob. Bob had also died during the last year.

Dwayne Johnson was a faithful member of First Church with a deep abiding faith. Strangely, as the pastor pondered the situation, he realized that Dwayne's attendance and behavior patterns had changed over the last year.

*How have members of your faith community reacted when they have faced the storms of life?

*What can be done with Dwayne to help aid in his struggles with life's pain?

Bringing up Father

Wife: There's an old-clothes man at the door.
Husband: Tell him I have all the old clothes I can use.

First husband: See this rabbit's foot? It saves me lots of money.
Second husband: How's that?
First Husband: I carry it in my change pocket, and every time my wife sticks her hand in there she thinks she has hold of a mouse.

Suzie: My husband embarrasses me so! He has this dreadful habit of holding his little finger out when he holds a cup of tea.
Floozie: Why is that embarrassing? I thought that holding out one's little finger is considered a polite way to hold a teacup.
Suzie: With the tea bag dangling from it?

The Lesson in Your Life

After a day of teaching and ministry, an exhausted Jesus told the disciples to load up the boat and head to the other side of the Sea of Galilee. Making a pillow out of a leather pouch, Jesus fell asleep in the boat. While He slept a gale blew in. It tossed the boat upon the sea. And the disciples did what so many in the church do today. *They panicked!*

Awakening Jesus, they asked if He even cared about them. After rebuking them, He calmed the storm. You have always heard it preached that Jesus calms the storms in your life if you only have faith. So then, why do so many of us panic like the disciples when we are storm-tossed? Let us look at this passage from another angle.

Why did Jesus rebuke those disciples? Why did He call them cowards? What was He really saying? If God incarnate is in a boat with you, do you think that the boat will perish? Do you? Those men had nothing to fear from that storm. God wasn't going to allow His son to succumb to some thunderstorm on a pond in Palestine. I think His rebuke applies more to us if we hear it in terms of adventure. Standing knee-deep in the water, the disciples should have enjoyed the power of nature, and the calmness of having the Son of God in the boat with them.

A storm blew up on the sea. It wasn't the first time. It wasn't the last. It was a fleeting thing. So why didn't those disciples just enjoy the storm?

You see, we think that because we are in that boat with Christ nothing should ever rock that boat. Without spiritualizing the story, boats in the Bible almost always signify salvation. One of the earliest symbols for the Church was a boat. So if Christ is with us in the boat we think that the waters should be a smooth as glass. We think that troubles, upsets, and turmoil shouldn't happen to us as long as we are in the boat. We should be immune, because that's what it means to be a part of the Church.

That's one of our failings. Too many people want the Church to be a quiet, comfortable operation where nobody gets hurt and nobody gets healed. We want to float along on the smooth surface, never rocking the boat, never causing a storm. Until we are willing to "rock the boat" we will never get to the real work of the Church, which is never security but always *salvation*. Because of this line of thinking, we find ourselves in dire conditions. Rather than dealing with all the storms in culture, Church, and personal lives, we have hidden in the harbor. We wait for the right circumstance to come out before trying to be the Church. When we finally are brave enough to come out of the harbor, we won't sail far; and at the first sight of a storm cloud we rush back into safe harbor. We won't even go far enough for Jesus to calm our storms.

GETTING THE FACTS
STRAIGHT

1. **After Jesus had taught all day, He wanted to go across to the other side of the sea of Galilee. How did He travel?**

Jesus left the crowd behind and got into a boat to go over to the other side.

2. **When they were in the boat, going to the other side, what happened?**

A furious storm came up, so violent that the boat was almost swamped.

3. **How did Jesus react to the storm?**

Jesus was in the back of the boat with his head on a cushion, asleep.

4. **What did the disciples do and say?**

The disciples woke Jesus with a very pointed question: "Don't you care that we perish?"

5. **After Jesus was awakened, what did He do with the storm?**

Jesus got up, rebuked the winds, and said to the waves, "Quiet, be still."

6. **After the storm was calmed, Jesus rebuked the disciples. What did He say to them?**

"Why were you so afraid? Do you still have no faith?"

7. **How did the disciples react to the storm and the calming of the storm?**

They were terrified and asked each other, "Who is this that even the wind and the waves obey him?"

8. **After the night on the Sea of Galilee, the boat landed on the other side. Who greeted the disciples and Jesus?**

When Jesus got out of the boat, a man with an evil spirit from the tombs came out to meet Him.

9. **How did Mark describe this man who lived among the tombs?**

As a mad man, who lived in the tombs. People had tried to chain him to control his behavior but he broke the chains.

10. **After the man freed himself from the chains, what kind of behavior did he exhibit?**

The man spent night and day among the tombs crying out and often cutting himself.

I think Jesus rebuked those disciples for their lack of a sense of adventure. Faith is such an adventure. If it isn't, I doubt very much that it is faith. If you are floating on a calm sea, then you are not headed in any definite direction. You are just floating.

The resurrection teaches us we need no longer fear anything. Not even death itself. So what keeps us still spiritually anchored in safe, snug harbors? Are we, perhaps, more afraid of becoming *failures* than of becoming *fatalities?* Are we more afraid of *living* than we are afraid of dying?

That storm didn't blow around the boat just because Jesus was on board. It hit with full force and fury. Nowhere does Jesus promise His followers anything different. A *peaceful* voyage is not the ticket the Church travels on. The ticket guarantees a *peace-filled* journey, with Christ always present. Jesus Christ's promise is not to sail us around every storm, but is to bring us *through* all storms, in one *"peace."*

One more thing I want to say about this story. *I think those who panicked weren't fishermen.* You see, Peter, James and John had fished those waters their whole lives. They were probably standing in the bow of the boat smiling at all the weak-kneed, green-gilled land lovers. It was one of those green-gilled disciples who woke the Lord.

There are always those kinds of people around: telling Noah it will never float, laughing at Abraham as he converted the den into a nursery, telling Moses he was too old to lead, and that the giants were too big in the Promised Land. These same people mocked David as being too young to kill a giant and become king, told Amos and Hosea to preach positive sermons. They even tried to tell Jesus to tone down His rhetoric and try to get along.

Whatever we try to do in the Church, people like that will always be around. People who are always reaching for the life vest, protecting their security in case of a rainy day, living safe lives. They don't like storms. Not even when Jesus himself causes them. They want everything to work out in the end. And they hate unresolved issues.

Well, to those persons I would say, *"I would rather be in a tossing boat with a calm Jesus, than in a calm boat with a shaky captain."* Those who fear the storm, rather than enjoying it, are the ones who may have missed the vital, life-changing experience with Jesus Christ. When Christ is present in your life, and in the Church, there is nothing to fear!

So here we are. I wonder, are we "Standing on the Promises?" Or are we merely sitting on the premises? Are we reaching for that blessed "Higher Ground" that God has promised to us? Or are we satisfied on this plateau?

There are storms ahead. "Things they are a changin'." But just hang on and enjoy the adventure that Christ has set before us. It is called the journey of faith. We don't travel alone. Christ is with us!

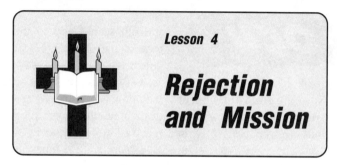

Lesson 4

Rejection and Mission

Mark 6:1-13

A nd he went out from thence, and came into his own country; and his disciples follow him.

2 And when the Sabbath day was come, he began to teach in the synagogue: and many hearing him were astonished, saying, From whence hath this man these things? and what wisdom is this which is given unto him, that even such mighty works are wrought by his hands?

3 Is not this the carpenter, the son of Mary, the brother of James, and Joses, and of Juda, and Simon? and are not his sisters here with us? And they were offended at him.

4 But Jesus said unto them, A prophet is not without honour, but in his own country, and among his own kin, and in his own house.

5 And he could there do no mighty work, save that he laid his hands upon a few sick folk, and healed them.

6 And he marvelled because of their unbelief. And he went round about the villages, teaching.

7 And he called unto him the twelve, and began to send them forth by two and two; and gave them power over unclean spirits;

8 And commanded them that they should take nothing for their journey, save a staff only; no scrip, no bread, no money in their purse:

9 But be shod with sandals; and not put on two coats.

10 And he said unto them, In what place soever ye enter into an house, there abide till ye depart from that place.

11 And whosoever shall not receive you, nor hear you, when ye depart thence, shake off the dust under your feet for a testimony against them. Verily I say unto you, It shall be more tolerable for Sodom and Gomorrha in the day of judgment, than for that city.

12 And they went out, and preached that men should repent.

13 And they cast out many devils, and anointed with oil many that were sick, and healed them.

Memory Selection
Mark 6:4

Background Scripture
Mark 6:1-13

Devotional Reading
John 12:44-50

This lesson has a two-fold emphasis. First we are given a glimpse of how the people at Jesus' "home congregation" viewed him early in his ministry—and what we learn, though understandable, does not flatter them. The second focal-point is what has been called "The Limited Commission," which, in contrast to "The Great Commission," finds Jesus sending the apostles only to Jews.

Both scenes add to the credible tone of the Gospels. Had they been concocted to present a rosy picture of Jesus' success as a preacher, they would not have been so candid in describing the poor reception He received from the local synagogue. Had Mark and the other Gospel writers sought only to paint a "politically correct" picture of a Savior for the whole world (a picture which will emerge later), the limited mission of the 12 would not have been so faithfully described.

∞⧉

A reminder of some of the many everyday "proverbs" that have crept into our language from the Bible can be an inviting way to start this discussion. Ask whether any group members can recall proverbial sayings with biblical origins . . . such as:

"He (or she) is the apple of my eye" (from Prov. 7:2; Lam. 2:18). . . "As you sow, so shall you reap" (Gal. 6:7). . . "Don't hide your light under a bushel" (Matt. 5:15-16). . . "You can't put new wine in old wineskins" (Matt. 9:17). . . "Laughter is medicine for the soul" (Prov. 17:22). . . "Am I my brother's keeper?" (Gen. 4:9).

Finally, note that this lesson will reveal the origin of another well-known proverb: "A prophet is not without honor except in his own country."

Teaching Outline	Daily Bible Readings	
I. Limited Acceptance—1-6	Mon.	Prophet Without Honor Mark 6:1-6
A. Local wonder, 1-3	Tue.	Questions About Messiah John 7:37-44
B. Limited miracles, 4-6	Wed.	Prophet from Galilee? John 7:45-52
II. Limited Commission—7-13	Thu.	The Kingdom Is Near Matthew 10:5-15
A. Limited equipment, 7-9	Fri.	Of Serpents and Doves Matthew 10:16-26
B. Instructions for mission, 10-11	Sat.	Whoever Welcomes You Matthew 10:37-42
C. Obedient ministry, 12-13	Sun.	Sending Out the 12 Mark 6:7-13

Verse by Verse

I. Limited Acceptance—1-6

A. Local wonder, 1-3

1 And he went out from thence, and came into his own country; and his disciples follow him.

2 And when the Sabbath day was come, he began to teach in the synagogue: and many hearing him were astonished, saying, From whence hath this man these things? and what wisdom is this which is given unto him, that even such mighty works are wrought by his hands?

3 Is not this the carpenter, the son of Mary, the brother of James, and Joses, and of Juda, and Simon? and are not his sisters here with us? And they were offended at him.

"Although "his own country" often refers to Jesus' home base of Capernaum, on the northwest shore of Galilee, Luke indicates that the questions raised here about Jesus occurred in Nazareth.

In many ways, the local synagogue attenders in Nazareth saw a different Jesus than the one who left them some weeks earlier. This time He attends the services accompanied by the 12 apostles, which must have caused quite a stir in the small gathering. The young man who had grown up among them and helped in his father's carpentry shop had now become a respected rabbi who attracted disciples.

Furthermore, verse 2 shows that Jesus raised even more eyebrows when he began to teach—for the teaching authority of wisdom begins to pour from his mouth beyond any training they knew about. They had also heard about the miracles or "mighty works" the young carpenter's apprentice had worked elsewhere.

Verse 3, however, shows that while all this produces "astonishment," most of the synagogue members are not impressed enough by the transformation in Jesus to lead them to confess that He is the Christ, the long-awaited Messiah. They know him and his family, as this unique list of his siblings shows; and as the saying goes, familiarity has bred contempt. According to John 7:3-5, even the family members listed here did not believe in Him; and anyone who has known "sibling rivalry" can understand their doubt. Yet the doubters ignore the evidence that Jesus has become a recognized teacher and healer.

Except for Mary and Joseph, the Gospels are almost silent about Jesus' family. However, Protestants often point out that the reference here to four brothers and at least two sisters casts doubt on the Catholic doctrine of the "perpetual virginity" of Mary. The idea that Mary did not have sexual relations with her husband also seems contradictory to her having "known" Joseph (sexually) after the birth of Jesus, as Matthew 1:25 states.

293

B. Limited miracles, 4-6

4 But Jesus said unto them, A prophet is not without honour, but in his own country, and among his own kin, and in his own house.

5 And he could there do no mighty work, save that he laid his hands upon a few sick folk, and healed them.

6 And he marvelled because of their unbelief. And he went round about the villages, teaching.

It is likely that Jesus' statement in response to His rejection in his hometown was already a proverb with which His audience was familiar. Verse 5 indicates the difficulty of accomplishing much remarkable spiritual work in an atmosphere of unbelief, but not the absolute impossibility. He does perform a few healings, as at other times He performs miracles despite the absence of faith. As noted in Lesson 2, He did not ask the man lowered through the roof about his own faith, but nonetheless healed him on the basis of the faith of his friends. Also, Lazarus obviously did not have faith when Jesus raised him from the dead.

Still, the parallel passages in Matthew and Luke show that Jesus held His hometown people guilty for their unbelief. In Luke, Jesus brings up Old Testament instances of God's having selected a single person for special blessing, because of the doubt and disobedience of the majority. This incisive judgment ignited such anger that the people of the synagogue seized Jesus, intending to throw him over a cliff; but somehow He escaped their clutches (Luke 4:24-29).

II. Limited Commission—7-13
A. Limited equipment, 7-9

7 And he called unto him the twelve, and began to send them forth by two and two; and gave them power over unclean spirits;

8 And commanded them that they should take nothing for their journey, save a staff only; no scrip, no bread, no money in their purse:

9 But be shod with sandals; and not put on two coats.

The sending out of the 12 on the "Limited Commission" (in contrast with the "Great Commission" of Matt. 28:18-20) is probably related to the previous account of Jesus' rejection by those in His hometown synagogue. (Compare also the sending of "the 70" in Luke 10:1ff.). Jesus has been rejected in some major cities as he had been in Nazareth, and He has taught and nurtured the 12 in His personal "school." It is time, therefore, to involve them in His mission, and in country areas where the people have not yet heard the message.

Going out "two by two" may be grounded in the Jewish teaching that testimony is to be backed by at least two witnesses. (Deut. 17:6) The disciples are bearing witness that "the kingdom of heaven is at hand" (Matt. 10:7), and that its King, the Messiah, has in fact already come. They are to go without much thought for their personal or financial comfort ("scrip" refers to a bag for carrying personal items, as in the NIV). In other words, the disciples were to live by faith, not by sight—living testimony that the faith to which they will be calling people is actually a livable option.

This strict regimen was not intended to be permanent, as confirmed by the fact that later Jesus will tell them to go equipped with the very articles He forbids them to take here, plus their swords (Luke 22:35-36).

B. Instructions for mission, 10-11

10 And he said unto them, In what place soever ye enter into an house, there abide till ye depart from that place.

11 And whosoever shall not receive you, nor hear you, when ye depart thence, shake off the dust under your feet for a testimony against them. Verily I say unto you, It shall be more tolerable for Sodom and Gomorrha in the day of judgment, than for that city.

Why Jesus tells the apostles not to move about when they find a suitable residence in a village remains a mystery. Perhaps they are not to appear shiftless, unstable, or ungrateful for the hospitality they are offered. Later, the hospitality extended to traveling missionaries had been so abused that the early Christian writing called the *Didache* ("Teaching") warns against hosting them more than two or three nights!

Much clearer is Jesus' stern judgment against people who reject the message of the 12. Strict Jews made it a practice to "shake the dust" off their sandals after traveling in Gentile territory; so the symbolism here is that those who spurn the disciples are to be treated as unfit subjects of the new Israel or "chosen people."

A further restriction is recorded in Matthew's version. There, Jesus tells the 12 not to go into Gentile or Samaritan cities, but to limit their preaching to Jews (Matt. 10:5-6). Not until Acts 10 and the introduction of the Roman soldier Cornelius will the Christian message be endorsed for Gentiles. Jesus goes first to "the lost sheep of the house of Israel" because, as the people chosen to bear the Messiah, they have the right to hear of Him first. Even the apostle Paul, famous as the "apostle to the Gentiles," will preach to "the Jew first," and only then to "the Greek" or Gentile world (Rom. 1:16).

C. Obedient ministry, 12-13

12 And they went out, and preached that men should repent.

13 And they cast out many devils, and anointed with oil many that were sick, and healed them.

Repentance is a fundamental platform of the message that "the kingdom of heaven is at hand." This is simply because all people as unbelievers are serving a "king" other than Jesus—whether it is material gain, Satan himself, or "King Self." To repent is to change our mind about our present course so decisively that we change our course.

The success of the 12 in duplicating the miracles of Jesus, including exorcising demons, grew out of His having equipped them with "power over unclean spirits" (vs. 7). After the commission of the 70, some reported excitedly of their surprising ability to cast out devils. Jesus' reply puts such sensational feats into perspective: "Rejoice not that the spirits are subject unto you; but rather rejoice, because your names are written in heaven" (Luke 10:20).

Evangelistic Emphasis

Are you successful?

Success, American style, is something that is promised to every member of this culture. If one is honest, takes well-thought-out chances, and works hard, success is soon to follow. Success is defined in many ways, but it most often has something to do with money or the things that money provides. It is known as the Horatio Alger myth. It simply does not happen for everyone who keeps his or her nose clean and works hard.

With all the promise of success, we don't talk much about failure. Failure is also an elusive concept. You may be a personal success yet a business failure, and the converse of that is also very true. Most of the really big failures in life end up as some kind of news story.

Did you know that Jesus gives us permission to fail? Not in the moral or ethical sense, but we are given the right to fail in attempting great things for Him. It is more faithful to attempt something great in the name of Jesus and fail than it is to try nothing and constantly succeed at it.

Jesus' ministry in His own hometown was a failure. His inability to minister was not His fault, but resulted from the lack of faith of the people of the village. So many times our ministry failures are not our fault, but a lack of response by those to whom the ministry was directed.

Jesus didn't let this failure stop Him, how about you?

ഇരു

But Jesus said unto them, A prophet is not without honour, but in his own country, and among his own kin, and in his own house.— *Mark 6: 4*

It is tough to do ministry in the place where you grew up. Nothing much has changed since Jesus had the problem in His own hometown.

Most of the problem has to do with those of us who watch people grow up. We can't imagine how God could call that person into ministry. The problem is that we see the foibles and failures of boys and girls as they grow up. We get caught thinking about people as children or youth, when they stand before us as full-grown adults.

For ministers it is equally hard going home. People in your hometown will find out what you are doing and they will say, "I remember when . . . ." Then they always manage to relate some story about when you were younger and much less "minister-like." When I'm in those situations I smile and say, "God isn't finished with me yet."

Be supportive of those in your faith community who are now ministers.

Weekday Problems

It was not the kind of conversation one might expect at a domino tournament. Frank Jackson, Ruddie Cunningham, Ardis Whitman, and John Cole were playing. While harassing each other about their playing, the were actually discussing the person of Jesus Christ, the heart of Christianity. Despite the topic of their talk, none of the men went to church.

Frank claimed that Jesus was a good moral teacher, that if a person lived by the words of the Lord that person should be able to get by and get into heaven. Frank "reckoned about every good person would go to heaven." Ruddie and Ardis were not so sure. They argued that Jesus had lived and died, but all that resurrection stuff was so much "church bunk." They couldn't imagine someone being dead and then suddenly being alive again. They liked how Jesus seemed to have understood the common man—and the idea that He didn't have too high an opinion of the preachers of His day.

John Cole was the lone holdout. Even though he wasn't a church person, he had some valuable insights. "I believe," John said, "that Jesus was who He claimed He was." John went on to affirm that the only reason Christianity has existed for 20 centuries was because Jesus really arose from the dead.

*How did the people of Nazareth view Jesus in His day?

Other Memos from Mission

In the days when some Methodist ministers were "circuit-riding" preachers, a friend asked one minister, "How is it that you're so thin and gaunt while your horse is so fat and sleek."

Replied the preacher, "Because I feed the horse, and the congregations feed me."

The minister habitually told his congregation that if they needed him to visit they should drop a note in the offering plate. One evening after services he discovered a note that read, "I am one of your loneliest members and heaviest contributors. May I have a visit tomorrow evening?" It was signed by his wife.

Remark to the pastor after the morning service: "Every sermon you preach is better than the next one."

Note in the church bulletin: "There will be no healing service tonight due to the illness of our minister."

This Lesson in Your Life

Jesus' commissioning words and directions at the beginning of the disciples' missionary activities reveal that He knew there was a time to get down to work and a time to get out and get on. At the same time, Jesus gave His disciples power to participate in His own authority. Alongside His confident directions to "travel light," Jesus gave His disciples guidance on how to deal with failure.

Following Christ, preaching and teaching and living in the power of his name, *does not mean the life of Christian discipleship is insulated from failure.* In fact, Jesus provided his followers with a "sacrament of failure"—shaking the dust off our feet. Just as there are ways to *live* that teach the world about Christ, there are also ways to *fail* that are uniquely Christian. Failure, or what futurist Don Michael calls "error embracing," is going to be a big part of any Christian ministry.

Understanding how Jesus' own ministry, how His very death on the Cross for our sake and our salvation provided all Christians with a sacrament of failure, can empower all of us with the "nerve of failure" as we witness to the world.

Not all of our relationships are going to work out. Ernest T. Campbell once remarked in a sermon that some relationships which get off on the wrong foot always remain left-footed if not "flat-footed." There comes a time then when we need to shake the dust off our feet, to commend our failed relationships to God and to other Christians, and spend our time building other relationships.

The apostle Paul offered an equally consoling piece of advice to his fellow failure-prone Christians in Rome. *"If it is possible, as far as it depends on you, live peaceably with all."* Paul knew that we will not always succeed in making peace. He knew there would be times when it was impossible, when the clouds of division and rejection would make success beyond our grasp. That is the time when we must "shake the dust off" and move along.

Likewise, not all of the programs we dream up for our success and for the success of others will work out. Have you failed to get your eating under control? Or to get a friend to give up smoking? Maybe it's time for you to shake the dust off that "success program," and commend the problem to other caring Christians and to the Lord.

It's not that we ever give up. By "shaking off the dust" we are making that person, or project, or dream the responsibility of others. We are, by participating in that sacrament of failure, admitting that we have tried and failed!

Do you have enough faith to say that you have failed? Do you have faith to shake the dust off, and give it to the Lord?

1. Where was Jesus immediately before he traveled to His home town?

Jesus was around the Sea of Galilee. He had just raised a child from the dead (Mark 5: 37-43).

2. When Jesus came to His hometown, did He immediately go into the synagogue and teach?

A close reading of the text would indicate that Jesus arrived in his hometown before the Sabbath.

3. What was the reaction to Jesus' teaching in the synagogue?

The people who were in the synagogue and heard Him were amazed.

4. What question did these amazed hearers ask among themselves?

They asked about the source of Jesus' wisdom and teaching, since He was a hometown boy.

5. As they pondered Jesus' teachings and His miracle-working power, what conclusions did they draw about Him?

They said, "Isn't this the carpenter? Isn't this Mary's son?"

6. Who did the people say were siblings of Jesus?

His brothers were James, Joseph, Judas and Simon. His sisters are also mentioned but not named.

7. When Jesus perceived their feelings about Him, what was His response to them?

Jesus said, "Only in his hometown, among His relatives and in His own house is a prophet without honor."

8. As Jesus continued to minister in Nazareth, what were the results of His ministry?

Because of the people's unbelief, He could only lay His hands on a few sick people and heal them.

9. What happened next in Jesus' ministry?

The next event in the ministry of Jesus was sending the disciples out two by two to do ministry.

10. What were the results of the preaching, teaching, and healing ministry of the disciples?

They drove out many demons and anointed many sick people with oil, and healed them.

A man took his first plane ride, reluctantly. He didn't want to go at all, but was finally persuaded to try it. Fearfully, he got on the plane. The pilot took off, circled the field, and returned immediately . . . and safely. Someone asked the "uneasy rider," "Well, now that wasn't so bad, was it? How did you like it?"

The man replied, "I'll tell you this much. I never did put my full weight down in that thing."

Faithfulness means putting our full weight down on God. It means trusting Him when everything we have tried has failed. It means resting in the assurance that He won't ever fail us. With that kind of faith, we can live exciting lives. We can live like that preacher who once prayed, "Lord, we're going to shoot for the stars tonight. But if we come up short, we thank you that we are higher than we have ever been before."

It is a faith that allows us to "shake the dust off" when something doesn't work, and move on to find other fields of ministry and new relationships.

At a girls' softball game a couple of years ago, a mother whispered to her little girl as she came up to bat, "Remember, if you swing at the ball I'll pay you $20. I don't care what happens. Just swing, and the money is yours." I thought that to be a little strange. I was certain that for $20 the child would be flailing away at the ball. But she stood there, bat on her shoulder and never took a swing. The next time she came up, the same thing happened. No matter where or how the pitch was made, the bat never left her shoulder.

We surmised, along with the mother, that she was so afraid of missing the ball that she would rather be called out than taking the chance of swinging and missing. She simply would not swing at the pitch. If that isn't a commentary on the pressures parents place on children, I don't know what is.

I remember being the "commissioner" of our T-Ball league a few years ago. I tried to put in a rule that we wouldn't keep score. I was trying to keep four-year-olds from dealing with winning and losing. Well, you would have had more luck trying to get a pacifist to enlist in the Marines. I don't think the children cared that much, but the parents and the coaches wanted *winners* and *losers!* Watching some of those coaches and parents, it would be more appropriate to say that they only wanted "winners."

We are so much like that little girl at the plate, bat on her shoulders, but afraid to swing at the pitch. So, fearful of failing, we never try. I wonder how many of you ever really tried to live your dream . . . or fulfill your calling . . . or follow your heart . . . because you were afraid of failing. *There are more people afraid of failing than have ever failed.* Fear is keeping us from stepping up to bat in faith.

It seems to me that in giving the disciples permission to shake the dust from their feet Jesus was giving people who *try,* a sacrament—a sacrament of failure. But how sad to fail because we feared even to try.

What Really Defiles

Mark 7:1-15

Then came together unto him the Pharisees, and certain of the scribes, which came from Jerusalem.

2 And when they saw some of his disciples eat bread with defiled, that is to say, with unwashen, hands, they found fault.

3 For the Pharisees, and all the Jews, except they wash their hands oft, eat not, holding the tradition of the elders.

4 And when they come from the market, except they wash, they eat not. And many other things there be, which they have received to hold, as the washing of cups, and pots, brasen vessels, and of tables.

5 Then the Pharisees and scribes asked him, Why walk not thy disciples according to the tradition of the elders, but eat bread with unwashen hands?

6 He answered and said unto them, Well hath Esaias prophesied of you hypocrites, as it is written, This people honoureth me with their lips, but their heart is far from me.

7 Howbeit in vain do they worship me, teaching for doctrines the commandments of men.

8 For laying aside the commandment of God, ye hold the tradition of men, as the washing of pots and cups:

and many other such like things ye do.

9 And he said unto them, Full well ye reject the commandment of God, that ye may keep your own tradition.

10 For Moses said, Honour thy father and thy mother; and, Whoso curseth father or mother, let him die the death:

11 But ye say, If a man shall say to his father or mother, It is Corban, that is to say, a gift, by whatsoever thou mightest be profited by me; he shall be free.

12 And ye suffer him no more to do ought for his father or his mother;

13 Making the word of God of none effect through your tradition, which ye have delivered: and many such like things do ye.

14 And when he had called all the people unto him, he said unto them, Hearken unto me every one of you, and understand:

15 There is nothing from without a man, that entering into him can defile him: but the things which come out of him, those are they that defile the man.

Memory Selection
Mark 7:21

Background Scripture
Mark 7:1-23

Devotional Reading
Psalm 51:10-17

FOCUS

What distinguishes the genuine Christian from one who is Christian in name only? The sad history of divisions within Christendom reveals the weakness of mere human ability to answer this question. Yet we instinctively know that there is a difference; and today's lesson focuses on one answer. True Christians do all they can to serve God from the heart, while "name-only" Christians seek to substitute externals, or human tradition, when they find heart-felt obedience uncomfortable.

Yet only God can look into the heart and determine if obedience is "heart-felt." It therefore becomes the task of each individual Christian to look within, to examine himself for an obedient heart, rather than seeking to label others. In Christianity, the "true-false" test is one we must take ourselves, not assign to others.

ഇറ

FOR A LIVELY START...

Stand before the group and perform a "Christian" act, such as:

1. Lay hands on someone in the group, as though you are healing them.

2. With an offering plate on a table, elaborately go through the process of taking money from your wallet or purse and placing it in the plate.

3. Partake of the bread and wine of communion for all to see, but take the wine first, then the bread.

After your demonstration, ask, "Was what I did just then pleasing in the eyes of God?" Answers may include, "Certainly; you did the right thing," "You did the right thing in the wrong way," and "How can we know? We can't see into your heart."

Note that in today's lesson, Jesus will affirm that the last answer is the correct response.

Teaching Outline	Daily Bible Readings	
I. Emphasizing Tradition—1-5 　A. Finding fault, 1-2 　B. External purity, 3-5 II. Tradition over Obedience—6-13 　A. The trouble with tradition, 6-9 　　1. Externals vs. the heart, 6-7 　　2. Rejecting God's will, 8-9 　B. A specific example, 10-13 III. Evil in the Heart—14-15	Mon.	Holding to Tradition Mark 7:1-8
	Tue.	Defilement from Within Mark 7:9-15
	Wed.	Explaining the Point Mark 7:17-23
	Thu.	God Knows the Heart Luke 16:10-15
	Fri.	Don't Worship Tradition! Col. 2:6-10
	Sat.	'Create in Me a Clean Heart' Psalm 51:10-17
	Sun.	'Take the Log from Your Eye' Luke 6:37-42

Verse by Verse

I. Emphasizing Tradition—1-5

A. Finding fault, 1-2

1 Then came together unto him the Pharisees, and certain of the scribes, which came from Jerusalem.

2 And when they saw some of his disciples eat bread with defiled, that is to say, with unwashen, hands, they found fault.

Even during His Galilean ministry, Jesus was scrutinized and criticized by official Jewry from Jerusalem. Here the complaint of the Pharisees ("the strictest sect" of the Jews, Acts 26:5, NIV) is that Jesus' disciples do not observe their traditional ritual washings before meals.

Although some such washings were commanded in the Law of Moses, the Pharisees' strict observances went far beyond the Law, being based only on oral tradition. Later, they would claim that God also gave Moses this oral tradition, and that it was handed down by the elders (vs. 3) and the prophets. At the time Mark writes, this great body of tradition, consisting of infinite details and arguments about how to apply the written Law, was still taking shape. It was completed in the form of the "Talmud" about A.D. 300. The Pharisees taught that obeying this tradition was important to keep from encroaching on the written Law; thus it became a "hedge about the Law,"

and actually became more important to strict legalists than the Law itself.

B. External purity, 3-5

3 For the Pharisees, and all the Jews, except they wash their hands oft, eat not, holding the tradition of the elders.

4 And when they come from the market, except they wash, they eat not. And many other things there be, which they have received to hold, as the washing of cups, and pots, brasen vessels, and of tables.

5 Then the Pharisees and scribes asked him, Why walk not thy disciples according to the tradition of the elders, but eat bread with unwashen hands?

Since Mark is writing for Gentile readers, he helpfully explains that more was at stake here than washing before meals. The oral tradition further required ritual washings after going to market, since Gentiles and non-kosher items were found there, along with many other cleansing rituals to render various dishes "holy." The real point, of course, is that Jesus and His disciples were not keeping these practices which, although applied externally, were supposed to render the heart "clean" or pure before God. The fact that God had not commanded the rituals, and that performing them seemed no help

303

in making a person more loving or genuinely religious, was no deterrent to these strict traditionalists.

II. Tradition over Obedience—6-13
A. The trouble with tradition, 6-9
1. Externals vs. the heart, 6-7

6 He answered and said unto them, Well hath Esaias prophesied of you hypocrites, as it is written, This people honoureth me with their lips, but their heart is far from me.

7 Howbeit in vain do they worship me, teaching for doctrines the commandments of men.

Jesus wisely answers His critics by quoting the written Law, specifically a prophecy from Isaiah 29:13 ("Esaias" is the Greek form of the prophet's name). Here God, through the great messianic prophet, rebukes Israel for doing precisely what the Pharisees were doing: holding fast to the external form of faith while neglecting the "weightier matters" of the Law: judgment, mercy, and faith (Matt. 23:23).

Here it may be helpful to admit that no religious group has long survived without some customs that support their faith and practice. The existence of church buildings, hymnals, and various worship styles not found in the New Covenant Scriptures are examples. Such practices may rightly be called "tradition," which simply refers to "that which has been handed down." Jesus seems to have little problem with such practices unless they assume the status of "doctrine," or, as will be made clear below, unless they actually cancel the intent of sound doctrine—as indicated in His next counter-charge.

2. Rejecting God's will, 8-9

8 For laying aside the commandment of God, ye hold the tradition of men, as the washing of pots and cups: and many other such like things ye do.

9 And he said unto them, Full well ye reject the commandment of God, that ye may keep your own tradition.

Jesus taught that the essence of "keeping the Law" was to love God and neighbor (Matt. 22:37-38). Instead of being zealous for the Law's essence, however, the Pharisees had become experts in such tiny details as how many pots could be washed before the water was changed. Such details were not harmless additions to the Law; they consumed so much of their efforts that they had lost focus on how to keep the Law itself. Ironically, the "hedge" they had built about the Law to protect it had become a tool for destroying it.

B. A specific example, 10-13

10 For Moses said, Honour thy father and thy mother; and, Whoso curseth father or mother, let him die the death:

11 But ye say, If a man shall say to his father or mother, It is Corban, that is to say, a gift, by whatsoever thou mightest be profited by me; he shall be free.

12 And ye suffer him no more to do ought for his father or his mother;

13 Making the word of God of none effect through your tradition, which ye have delivered: and many such like things do ye.

To show that He is not dealing in

generalities, Jesus now gives a specific example of "straining out a gnat but swallowing a camel" (see Matt. 23:24). The Law included the simple command to honor one's parents. Implied in this command is to see that they are cared for in sickness or old age. As anyone knows who has had infirm elderly relatives, this can be inconvenient.The tradition of the Pharisees made it possible for them to make a contribution to a religious work such as Temple services and be released from the bothersome duty of actually caring for their parents, or seeing that they were cared for. A formal statement had even been developed, in which the person seeking such relief would utter the word "Corban," meaning "It is a gift." What better example of "making the word of God of none effect through your tradition" could be cited?

Implied in this example is Jesus' intent to defend His disciples for not observing ritual hand-washing traditions. It was very possible for a person to so focus on this outward act that gratitude for the food, which is an inner act of the heart and part of the essence of the Law, was also made "of none effect." This intent sets up Jesus' final words in our lesson.

III. Evil in the Heart—14-15

14 And when he had called all the people unto him, he said unto them, Hearken unto me every one of you, and understand:

15 There is nothing from without a man, that entering into him can defile him: but the things which come out of him, those are they that defile the man.

The principle at stake here is so important that Jesus calls together not just the disciples whom the Pharisees had criticized, but all the people around Him. He tells them that the critics had been looking in the wrong place for the source of spiritual defilement. Obviously, cleansing one's hands before eating is helpful from a physical standpoint; but the Pharisees had made it into a method of cleansing the heart, and Jesus denies that mere ritual can do so. Becoming defiled is a matter of a soiled soul, not a dirty body. Being defiled manifests itself in what "comes out" of a person in the form of harsh judgmentalism, evil talk, and evil deeds toward others. It is the product not of something that comes in contact with the skin, but with the heart, and its "thoughts and intents."

A corollary to Jesus' teaching here relates to what to do about defilement. If sin springs from the heart, it is removed not by external ritual but by heartfelt repentance and prayer. When King David became convicted of his sin with Bathsheba, he did not seek a ceremonial washing. Instead, he prayed, "Create in me a clean heart, O God; and renew a right spirit within me" (Ps. 51:10).

According to verses 16-22, the importance of ritual was so engrained even in those who followed Jesus that they sought additional explanation of this teaching. Jesus goes to great detail in showing the difference between external practices, and foods that pass through the body without defiling it, and heart-based evil that in fact pollutes the soul.

305

Evangelistic Emphasis

This lesson causes us to grapple with the concept of good news versus morality. Jesus said, "You shall know the truth and the truth shall set you free." As far as being obedient to the Law, Jesus saw this at two main points. He taught us to love God and love our neighbors as we love our-selves. Beyond those two points of the Law, Jesus didn't give too many details of what it meant to follow Him.

What He left out, the legalists in the Church have run in and filled. It would be interesting in your class to note the number of persons who were once taught, and might still believe, that failing to do the Law's "work" of avoiding card playing, dancing, and attending a movie on Sunday will earn an express ticket to Hell.

While I don't approve of all the changes in society, I'm hesitant to start making lists of new sins. I know some deeply devout Christians who have tattoos and body piercing. They even attend church and sing in the choir.

Jesus made this point with the legalists when He told them that it was those things coming out of a person that defiled them, not those things going into them.

This lesson is good news for those who want Jesus to set them free from the works of the Law. It causes trouble for those of us who would like to point the finger and condemn.

ෆ෦෬

Memory Selection

For from within, out of the heart of men, proceed evil thoughts, adulteries, fornications, murders. —*Mark 7: 21*

One translation takes the list; "evil thoughts, adulteries, fornications, murders" and translates it simply "evil intentions."

The line between heart and hand is a short one. According to Jesus, evil actions arise out of a heart that is evil, or indifferent to the things of God.

The road to hell is paved with good intentions; I wonder what kind of road is paved with evil intentions. Again the truth here is that what is really more important is what is in one's heart. Your lifestyle can be acted out for awhile, but to be a faithful follower of Christ for a lifetime, you need a heart that has been renewed by the grace of God in Jesus Christ.

A renewed heart does not give us a standing excuse to do anything we please, but it does free us from the legal bondage that legalists within the would seek to put on us.

Weekday Problems

Joe was in a quandary. He had a moral problem that would not have bothered anyone but him. He had been a Little League baseball coach for nearly 50 years, working with 10- and 11-year-year-old boys. His standing with them and their parents was one of honor and respect.

Joe was also a leading businessman in the community. His business was known for quality work and ethical business practices. He also held positions on almost every non-profit agency's board, from the Red Cross to the Heart Association.

Joe was a leading member of First Church. None surpassed his knowledge of the Bible and his love for the church. Thus it came as a surprise to the minister when Joe stopped him one Sunday after church and said, "I have a moral problem."

The problem was that Joe was going to receive the "Citizen of the Year" award from the local Chamber of Commerce, and the award banquet was to be held at a local casino. "Kids look up to me," Joe explained, "and I don't want to hurt my reputation. What should I do, preacher? Should I go and receive the reward, or stay home because of the banquet being in a casino?"

*What would be your advice?

Roastings from the Heart

My friend here is full of brother love. He always stops anyone who's beating a donkey.

Was the rock cold when you crawled out this morning?

She has the knack of making strangers immediately.

Whatever is eating him must be suffering from indigestion.

He's a contact man—all con and no tact.

If he had his conscience surgically removed, it would be a minor operation.

She would look nicer if she'd stop applying her makeup with a paint roller.

His breath was so bad that his dentist had to work on his teeth through his ear.

He once directed a movie that was so bad that six states use it in place of capital punishment.

I recommended that he have himself X-rayed to see what other people see in him.

From *The World's Greatest Collection of Clean Jokes*
by Bob Phillips. Used by permission of the author.

307

This Lesson in Your Life

Medical science makes advances daily that help people over come "heart trouble." There are devices that can prolong life until a heart transplant is possible. One device that can shock a heart back into rhythm has been installed in airplanes and hotels, and our church even purchased one recently. So if you have cardiac distress at our church, we can shock you back to life. (I have threatened to use this device on choir members who sleep during my sermon, but have been told that is not politically correct.)

Jesus identified another kind of heart problem that can't be fixed by modern medicine or modern technology. He identified the heart as the center of our will, and thus the locus of our actions. The heart is where a person chooses his or her actions.

The Hebrew Law was set up to protect the body from being rendered "unclean." The Law provided that a Hebrew was not to have contact with a dead body, or a Gentile, or certain foods. But Jesus taught that it is from the *inside* that a person is made unclean.

Religion seeks to keep people from separating from God by keeping their actions consistent. Many groups have rules and regulations for everything from what foods to eat to which kinds of make-up are appropriate. If members can maintain the outward appearance of holiness, everything must be fine with their souls.

Jesus saw humanity in a different light. He knew that people could have the outward form of religion and their hearts be far from God. He knew that it was not what went into a person that made him unclean but rather it was what he did that made him unclean.

The deep truth here is that one can't hide what is in the heart for very long. If a person harbors ill will against another, it won't be long before that ill will takes on a shape and a form. For example, persons who engage in gossip talk about loving their neighbor, then share vicious stories about that same person. They don't do a very good job of masking the hatred that dwells within their hearts. Their words revealed the hypocrisy in their souls.

When I preach to people and am accused of "stepping on their toes," I respond lovingly that when I have one finger pointed at "them" I have three others pointed back at me. The danger of the spiritual elite is that they tend to point out the sins of others while ignoring their own sins.

By telling us that sin comes from the heart, Jesus warns all who would seek to judge only by the exterior activities and actions of others. The key to holy living is a holy heart. If our actions come from a holy heart, we won't have to worry about being defiled.

GETTING THE FACTS STRAIGHT

1. **From Mark 7:1, what group of people are about to give Jesus some trouble?**
   The Pharisees and some of the scribes from Jerusalem.

2. **What criticism did these religious authorities from Jerusalem have against Jesus?**
   They claimed that the disciples were eating with defiled hands, that is, without washing them.

3. **What parenthetical note is given concerning the tradition of the Pharisees and others about washing?**
   The Pharisees and all the Jews don't eat unless they wash their hands.

4. **What other details are given about the Jewish rituals concerning food and eating?**
   They didn't eat anything from the market unless they washed it. They washed their eating utensils.

5. **What was Jesus' first response to those who criticized His disciples for not observing these Jewish cleansing rituals?**
   He called them hypocrites.

6. **What quote from Isaiah did Jesus use to make His point?**
   "This people honors me with their lips but their hearts are far from me" (Isaiah 29:13).

7. **In making a summation about His criticism of the Pharisees and others, what did Jesus say?**
   He said, "You abandon the commandment of God and hold to human tradition."

8. **What commandment did Jesus show that the Pharisees were violating with the rule of "Corban"?**
   They violated the Fifth Commandment, "Honor thy father and mother."

9. **What seemed to be the rule of "Corban"?**
   The rule appeared to be one by which the Jews could avoid supporting their parents by dedicating their money to God.

10. **What did Jesus say about the nature of true defilement?**
    Nothing from outside a person can defile him, but only those things which come from the heart.

You're being watched.

In many cities, that means you'll get a ticket for speeding. Photo radar vans sit beneath freeway. The radar records your speed while the camera focuses on your license plate. The traffic cop doesn't need to be there, and you won't know you're caught until you get the ticket in the mail!

Video cameras are popping up everywhere, like virtual seeing eyes. School districts are installing cameras in school buses to document to unbelieving parents how their children behave. YMCAs have mounted security cameras in weight rooms, mirrored aerobic rooms, gymnasiums, and indoor tennis courts. You can't pause in your workout to blow your nose without being caught at it on camera.

In London, cameras have been posted in some neighborhoods, two or three to a block, putting citizens under constant surveillance. Yet, most people seem to approve. In our own country, day-care dads and minivan moms are getting into the act, using hi-tech tools to monitor their, precocious—or atrocious— children while they are away at work. With Web cams positioned strategically throughout the child-care center, parents can log on to the Internet to see what's happening with their babies.

Parents like this peek-a-boo technology for two reasons: They can be sure their children are safe, and they feel more connected with their kids. Jane logs on about once a day for a few minutes, just long enough to check in on her son Kenny and his 4-year-old brother Andrew. On days when her sons are upset at the time she drops them off, she finds the video images particularly comforting. Web cams placed in strategic locations put people on their best behavior. No matter how they might be feeling at the time, no matter what they might be thinking, their behavior is accessible for public viewing and evaluation.

In other words, we are in an age of "virtual morality." At first, this seems like a sure-fire way to create a well-behaved society. But outward behavior doesn't necessarily reflect inward character. When the cameras aren't rolling, we're more likely to drop the role we've been playing and just "be ourselves."

That's called *character*—who we are when no one is looking.

Jesus says, "Not so fast." Although the Y is watching our workouts, the government filming our behavior on the streets, and parents observing their children at the day-care center, God sees what is in our hearts and minds. God has—God is—the ultimate Web cam, an all-seeing Holy cam, perched inside our souls and pointed in our direction.

Jesus says, "Listen to me, all of you, and understand: There is nothing outside a person that by going in can defile, but the things that come out are what defile" (Mark 7:15).

Maybe we've been playing to the wrong camera.

Lesson 6

Entering Jerusalem and Cleansing the Temple

Mark 11:1-9, 15-18

A nd when they came nigh to Jerusalem, unto Bethphage and Bethany, at the mount of Olives, he sendeth forth two of his disciples,

2 And saith unto them, Go your way into the village over against you: and as soon as ye be entered into it, ye shall find a colt tied, whereon never man sat; loose him, and bring him.

3 And if any man say unto you, Why do ye this? say ye that the Lord hath need of him; and straightway he will send him hither.

4 And they went their way, and found the colt tied by the door without in a place where two ways met; and they loose him.

5 And certain of them that stood there said unto them, What do ye, loosing the colt?

6 And they said unto them even as Jesus had commanded: and they let them go.

7 And they brought the colt to Jesus, and cast their garments on him; and he sat upon him.

8 And many spread their garments in the way: and others cut down branches off the trees, and strawed them in the way.

9 And they that went before, and they that followed, cried, saying, Hosanna; Blessed is he that cometh in the name of the Lord:

15 And they come to Jerusalem: and Jesus went into the temple, and began to cast out them that sold and bought in the temple, and overthrew the tables of the moneychangers, and the seats of them that sold doves;

16 And would not suffer that any man should carry any vessel through the temple.

17 And he taught, saying unto them, Is it not written, My house shall be called of all nations the house of prayer? but ye have made it a den of thieves.

18 And the scribes and chief priests heard it, and sought how they might destroy him: for they feared him, because all the people was astonished at his doctrine.

Memory Selection
Mark 11:15

Background Scripture
Mark 11:1–12:12

Devotional Reading
Luke 19:28-40

311

People reacted in opposite ways to Jesus. At first, "the common people heard Him gladly"; and the "Triumphal Entry," one of the twin focuses of this lesson, is the culmination of the glad reception many gave Him. The second focus in the lesson shows the negative kind of response, this time expressed by the money-changers in the Temple. They were more interested in the "business" of religion than in the Kingdom of God.

The alert teacher will look for examples that show the same extremes of response today to the message of Jesus. Some gather in glad celebrations that honor Him, while others still view Him as a "stumbling-block" to their self-interests. Encourage a climate in your class that lends itself to the psalmist's encouragement: "Enter into his gates with thanksgiving, and into his courts with praise" (Ps. 100:4).

ഇഓ

Remember the former hit tune, "I Love a Parade"? What is there about a parade that excites and attracts us? Why do people often stand for hours along the street, in fair weather or foul, just to watch a parade? Some group members may mention the spirited bands, others the colorful floats, and still others (in some parts of the country) the splendid horses and western regalia of the "Sheriff's Posses" or other riding clubs.

All this can be compared to the spirit of the crowds in Jerusalem for the Passover. Jesus entered the city to the excitement and acclaim of those who had come to believe that He was the Messiah. Of course it is realistic to point out also that the same crowds will flee a few days later when their Messiah is crucified. For now, however, they love the parade!

Teaching Outline	Daily Bible Readings	
I. Clamor of the Crowds—1-9	Mon.	Jesus Enters Jerusalem Mark 11:1-11
A. A colt for a King, 1-2	Tue.	A King on a Donkey Zechariah 9:9-12
B. Willing supporters, 3-6	Wed.	The Stones Would Shout! Luke 19:28-40
C. The Triumphal Entry, 7-9	Thu.	Cleansing the Temple Mark 11:12-19
II. Cleansing the Temple—15-18	Fri.	'Have Faith in God' Mark 11:20-25
A. The business of faith, 15-16	Sat.	'By What Authority?' Mark 11:27-33
B. House of prayer, vs. plots, 17-18	Sun.	The Wicked Tenants Mark 12:1-12

Verse by Verse

I. Clamor of the Crowds—1-9
A. A Colt for a King, 1-2

1 And when they came nigh to Jerusalem, unto Bethphage and Bethany, at the mount of Olives, he sendeth forth two of his disciples,

2 And saith unto them, Go your way into the village over against you: and as soon as ye be entered into it, ye shall find a colt tied, whereon never man sat; loose him, and bring him.

Although we are little more than halfway through Mark's Gospel, we are already witnessing the beginning of the end. In fact, it is precisely at the book's midpoint (8:31) that Jesus openly tells His disciples of His rendezvous with death, which He knows will be precipitated by His opponents in the Holy City. (The announcement is even earlier in Luke, in 9:51, compared with 24 chapters.) This relatively heavy emphasis on Christ's death or "passion" has prompted some scholars to call Mark a "passion narrative with an introduction."

This scene, commonly called the "Triumphal Entry," is so important that it is recorded in all four Gospels. According to John (12:1, 12), the event occurs at the annual Passover, so Jerusalem would have been teeming with visitors. Many had already heard Him, or heard of Him,

for they acclaim Him as "he that cometh in the name of the Lord" (vs. 9), and as a "prophet" (Matt. 21:11).

Jesus knows Bethany very well, since it was the home of his friend Lazarus and his sisters, Mary and Martha John 11:1). Bethphage was a small village so near Jerusalem (approached on the road from Jericho) that it was virtually a suburb. Just as a modern traveler might "phone ahead" for accommodations as he approaches a large city, so Jesus sends His disciples on into the heart of the city to prepare for His entry.

This is the only time Jesus allows Himself to be positioned as the true King that He was. He will soon enough be treated as a criminal; now it is time to allow His followers to bear witness to His true identity with a gala welcoming parade. Each Gospel describes the mount Jesus sends His disciples to arrange for as a "colt." However, the scene fulfills the prophecy in Zechariah 9:9 so perfectly (see Matt. 21:4-5) that artists' renderings of it invariably picture Jesus riding on a young donkey instead of a young horse.

Three subtle images of the Messiah are communicated here. Although earthly kings prized their horses, donkeys were also coveted by wealthy nomad chieftains. The fact that the colt is young and unspoiled is appropriate, since animals chosen for sacrifice had to be "without spot or blemish," even a yoke-mark (see Num. 19:2).

B. Willing supporters, 3-6

3 And if any man say unto you, Why do ye this? say ye that the Lord hath need of him; and straightway he will send him hither.

4 And they went their way, and found the colt tied by the door without in a place where two ways met; and they loose him.

5 And certain of them that stood there said unto them, What do ye, loosing the colt?

6 And they said unto them even as Jesus had commanded: and they let them go.

Note the miracle of Jesus' foreknowledge of where the colt will be. Having further predicted that its owner would ask why the disciples wanted the animal, Jesus also correctly anticipates the owner's willingness to lend Him the colt. It is possible that saying that "the Lord hath need of him" implies the owner's prior knowledge of Jesus and His claims of Lordship. At the very least, God has prepared the man's heart to cooperate with the "parade."

C. The Triumphal Entry, 7-9

7 And they brought the colt to Jesus, and cast their garments on him; and he sat upon him.

8 And many spread their garments in the way: and others cut down branches off the trees, and strawed them in the way.

9 And they that went before, and they that followed, cried, saying, Hosanna; Blessed is he that cometh in the name of the Lord:

Casting garments on the colt's back provided a cushioned "saddle" for Jesus, and was a sign of deference showing that the people honored Him above their own clothing. The same can be said for those who lay their outer garments on the ground on the roadway, as we might "roll out the red carpet" before an honored visitor today. Paved both with these garments and with branches, the road on which Jesus passes becomes a royal highway . . . although He is also traveling toward His death.

"Hosanna!" means "Save us now," indicating the Messianic expectations of the people. Their cry becomes a chant or even a hymn, since they are quoting Psalm 118:26. Thus, Jesus enters Jerusalem accompanied by expectations that He comes as a king after the manner of David, the psalmist-king, and that as David expanded the kingdom of Israel as a man of war, Jesus would also drive the Roman occupation forces from the Promised Land. Only a few days later Jesus will profoundly disappoint them by dying. The Kingdom He came to establish was a rule over the heart, not a land; and His method of doing so was by giving himself over to His enemies. This gap between expectations and reality will change the cries of Hosanna to weeping, and the crowd's loud support to stealing silently away from the Cross.

II. Cleansing the Temple—15-18
A. The business of faith, 15-16

15 And they come to Jerusalem: and Jesus went into the temple, and

began to cast out them that sold and bought in the temple, and overthrew the tables of the moneychangers, and the seats of them that sold doves;

16 And would not suffer that any man should carry any vessel through the temple.

This next scene must have come as another shock to the people's hopes. Instead of attacking the Roman citadel in the city, Jesus attacks the holy Temple! Actually, He does not oppose the sacrifices, offerings, and prayers authorized by the Law, but the abuses that had built up over the ages. At least two kinds of business thrived in the outer areas of the Temple: buying and selling animals for sacrifice, and changing money brought by Jews from many lands into local currency. The size of this commerce is indicated by one ancient source that holds that a single merchant sold 3,000 sheep in one day of Passover-related business.

Mark is the only Gospel writer who adds that Jesus also prevented people from carrying pots and pans through the Temple, apparently taking a short-cut through the holy grounds instead of going around its huge perimeter.

B. House of prayer, vs. plots, 17-18

17 And he taught, saying unto them, Is it not written, My house shall be called of all nations the house of prayer? but ye have made it a den of thieves.

18 And the scribes and chief priests heard it, and sought how they might destroy him: for they feared him, because all the people was astonished at his doctrine.

As any Jewish rabbi would have done, Jesus follows these dynamic acts with an informal teaching session to explain their significance. Quoting Isaiah 56:7, He reminds His hearers that God conceived the Temple to be a house of prayer for all "nations"— probably referring here not to nationalities but to various classes of people, from the very rich to the very poor. Instead, the competitive business of selling livestock discriminated against the poor; the noise and bustle of the "shoppers" provided little peace and quiet for prayers; and there was some "thievery" involved— perhaps dishonest business practices, short-changing people who were having their money exchanged, or charging exorbitant prices at the shops.

Lurking at the edges of all this activity and teaching were Jesus' ever-present critics, the scribes and chief priests. Some authorities believe that some of the Temple-related shops were actually owned by priests. If so, they were angry not only because the masses were "astonished" and attracted to Jesus and His teachings, but because He threatened their financial well-being. Luke (19:39) and John (12:19) add that Jesus' accusers began planning His death even earlier, moved to alarm and jealousy by the Triumphal Entry. Now they grow deadly serious as they plot His death. That Jesus might actually be their own Messiah does not concern them. He has threatened their control over the people's faith, and now has challenged the way they have been making money from it.

Evangelistic Emphasis

When you get to heaven whom do you want to meet? Do you want to swap recipes with Miriam? She would have some great quail recipes. Would you like to talk about fishing with Jonah or Simon Peter? How about finding Joseph and talking to him about fashion? Maybe you could talk to John the Baptist about being a non-conformist. I want to meet the guy with the donkey in today's lesson, and talk to him about trust and vision. How else could a man who was apparently a stranger to Jesus just let His disciples take away his donkey?

Trust and vision must happen to-gether. One can have a vision of God's plan, but must have trust that God will provide. One who has trust in God usually has a vision beyond what is seen at the moment. The guy with the donkey had both trust and vision. He trusted what the disciples told him about what the donkey was for. He had vision that the Lord could use something of his for a very important task.

The gospel of Jesus is about trust and vision. We must trust that our sins can be forgiven and that God is giving us a second chance. We have a vision of what God wants us to be.

The Church must also have a vision. Our task is to share Christ with our world. There are those in your community who need to hear that God can use their trust and vision in His kingdom.

They need to feel needed.

ഇൗന്ദ്ര

Memory Selection

And they come to Jerusalem: and Jesus went into the temple, and began to cast out them that sold and bought in the temple, and overthrew the tables of the moneychangers, and the seats of them that sold doves.—*(Mark 11:15)*

Sometimes I think I would have loved (in Christian love, of course!) to punch the enemies of the Lord in the nose. Sometimes even today I think that the people who are standing in the way of the work of the Spirit, inside and outside the Church, need a good swift punch! It would not be in anger, but in "righteous indignation." I would want my attitude to be just like Jesus when he drove the money-changers from the Temple.

Of course it's really an absurd idea to take physical action against those who are working contrary to Jesus. We are called to love our enemies . . . to pray for those who do us harm . . . to bless those who persecute us.

Still, kicking over a few tables and swinging the bullwhip around at people might make us feel better. That is why we *all* need a savior, because we all have strong emotions. Because we have those emotions and often take those actions, Jesus had to die for us, and the moneychangers too!

Weekday Problems

The best that could be said for Frank was that he was fickle in his faith. He also faltered in his friendship with the faithful. Frank had fussed and fumed for a fortnight about the failure of the finance committee to forthrightly follow his far-flung fantasies about fixing church finances.

Figuring the finance committee for a flock of fools, Frank fumed that finances were falling because Rev. F. Fred Frazier had failed as the flock's financial fixer. Frank, feeling frisky about his financial acumen, recommended that First Faithful Fellowship Church should invest in the Finest Filter Company of Fairbanks. Frank's financial sheet showed the company had a fantastic financial future and their stock would be a fine find for investment. Foolishly, Frank figured that fooling around in the stock market was more favorable than faithfully following the biblical pattern of financial stewardship.

Frank was flabbergasted when confronted with the folly of his financial fix for the faithful at First Faithful Fellowship Church. Rather than invest their savings they decided to pray and frankly talk about stewardship. When the message about giving was preached, the financial problems were fixed. However, Frank fumed.

*Like the over-use of the letter "f" in this piece, we sometimes do things in the church that drive people away. How have we turned the church into a "den of robbers" rather than a house of prayer?

Smoke Signals

She: Would you like to chew my gum, sir?
He: Of course not! It's been in your mouth!
She: And that, sir, is why, I don't like to breathe the smoke from your cigarette.

❖❖❖❖

The man bought a cigar in a department store, and lit up.
Said the clerk, "We don't allow smoking in the store, sir."
"What?" he asked, "You sell cigars but don't allow smoking?"
"We also sell bath towels," the clerk said sweetly.

❖❖❖❖

Have you heard about the new cigarette that comes with ear plugs in every pack? They're for people who are tired of hearing why they should quit smoking.

❖❖❖❖

Smoking may not send you to hell, but why would anyone want to smell like they've been there?

This Lesson in Your Life

Jesus talked more about money than any other subject. He talked more about money than about prayer, and healing, even about the whole notion of salvation. Even in our lesson, Jesus is addressing the issue of money and He is doing it in a way one might not suspect.

We love the notion of Jesus driving the moneychangers out of the temple. We have fantasies about the moneychangers and whips, when we see the stewardship committee gearing up for the financial drive. If only they would read this section of the New Testament we might not have annual stewardship campaigns. It seems that the finance committee and others have forced many a church into the position of having to sell services in order to raise money. We have, in many places, turned the house of the Lord into a den of robbers. (I won't even start on what I think the television evangelists have done in this realm.)

Jesus was condemning the commerce that was taking place at the Temple. This is the place where this scripture will start rubbing you in the wrong direction: when I explain *He was not criticizing the marketplace so much as the need for that market.*

Every devout Jew was required to tithe. If you will check your Bible you will find that each devout Jew was to pay *three* tithes. Two of those tithes were to be paid annually; the third was to be paid out over a three-year period. By the time Malachi was written, the Jews were cheating on their tithes as frequently as Americans fudge on their income taxes (see Mal. 3:8-10).

A devout Jew was supposed to make sacrifice. The sacrifice for sin was to be a perfect lamb or, for the poor, two turtledoves. It was this sacrificial requirement that was driving the marketplace in the Temple. Many of the Jews were substituting the oldest, sickest lamb for that perfect lamb. A couple of scrawny pigeons would do for the turtledoves. After all these animals were going to be killed anyway, and who would know if they weren't perfect? God hadn't struck anyone dead yet. Because devout Jews were cutting corners when it came to their sacrifices, a whole industry grew up to help them take those short cuts. The very worship of God by devout Jews had created the "den of robbers" hanging out at the Temple. Jesus was attacking the lack of faithful worship that led to the transactions in the Temple.

That was then. Today it is the lack of faithful giving among devout Christians that causes the church to have to "sell services" to raise money.

It is strange what devout people do . . . and don't do.

STRAIGHT

1. Mark 11 begins with Jesus traveling to Jerusalem. Where did the journey begin?
The journey began in Jericho.

2. What places are named in the first verse of Mark 11?
Jerusalem, Bethphage, Bethany, and the Mount of Olives are the place names mentioned in the first verse of this chapter.

3. What were the disciples told to go into the village and find?
The disciples were told to go into a village and find a colt that was tied.

4. What was unique about this colt?
The colt that Jesus directed to be brought was a colt that had never been ridden.

5. If the disciples were interrupted by anyone, what were they to do?
The disciples were to answer all inquiries about their actions by saying, "The Lord has need of it."

6. What happened as the disciples were getting this colt?
Someone saw what the disciples were doing, and they gave the answer the Lord had instructed.

7. What happened when the disciples explained their action in reference to the colt?
They told what the Lord had said and the person (or persons) let them go.

8. Do you think that the owner of the colt knew Jesus, or was this purely a miraculous happening?
This would an excellent discussion question for your class.

9. As Jesus rode into Jerusalem on the colt, how did the crowd react?
Many spread their garments and placed branches on the ground in front of Jesus.

10. What was the significance of Jesus' entry into Jerusalem?
In many ways Jesus entered Jerusalem like a conquering king.

Let's think some more about this man and the donkey.

You know, he was a great hero. His name is never mentioned in the pages of Scripture. Yet I want to talk to him in heaven because I want to know a few things. I want to know if he knew Jesus and had this donkey thing prearranged, thus allowing Jesus to give the disciples a final test. Or maybe this was something he felt led to do and could not ignore the strong feelings he had about what was right. I want to know why the donky had never been ridden. How had this man kept his kids off of the donkey? I know that if he had kids they would want to ride the donkey, and that it just drives children crazy when they are told no.

I want to know if the man ever got his donkey back, and if he did I want to know whether the donkey was more valuable because Jesus had ridden on it.

I really do want to meet this guy, because he is a visionary. He saw in something happening around his village the possibility that God was involved, and that he, a simple person who owned a donkey, could help.

The Bible is filled with stories of people who had simple gifts who were used by God in great ways. Sampson turned a jawbone into a lethal weapon. David made a giant killer out of a sling. Rahab hid some spies in her house.

Some fellow helped Paul down from a wall in a bucket and then out of town. There was the disciple who made room and a pillow so Jesus could sleep in that little fishing boat. There was the man on the road in Jerusalem who helped Jesus carry His cross. The man might not have known Jesus. He simply saw a beaten man who was stumbling under the weight of the cross-piece, a man who needed a hand. This man helped the King of Creation.

God used people who had simple gifts and few worldly possessions and their stories make up the Holy Bible. The hope I glean from this is that if God can use them, then God can use my gifts and me.

Praising God as King is important. Throwing our garments before Him and covering the road with branches and crying Hosanna is our part in worship. But the life changing for others happens when we are back home from the parade finding simple ways and gifts that God can use.

God can use what you have for His glory. But when He uses you, other people are being drawn to Jesus Christ. The interesting thing about how God operates is that one often does not know exactly what impact his life and his faithful actions are having on another individual. The man with the donkey was not looking for a bit part in the New Testament. He never dreamed his story would be told so often. He was simply doing what he knew was right, or what he thought God was leading him to do.

What about you?

A New Meaning for Passover

Mark 14:12-25

And the first day of unleavened bread, when they killed the passover, his disciples said unto him, Where wilt thou that we go and prepare that thou mayest eat the passover?

13 And he sendeth forth two of his disciples, and saith unto them, Go ye into the city, and there shall meet you a man bearing a pitcher of water: follow him.

14 And wheresoever he shall go in, say ye to the goodman of the house, The Master saith, Where is the guestchamber, where I shall eat the passover with my disciples?

15 And he will shew you a large upper room furnished and prepared: there make ready for us.

16 And his disciples went forth, and came into the city, and found as he had said unto them: and they made ready the passover.

17 And in the evening he cometh with the twelve.

18 And as they sat and did eat, Jesus said, Verily I say unto you, One of you which eateth with me shall betray me.

19 And they began to be sorrowful, and to say unto him one by one, Is it I?

and another said, Is it I?

20 And he answered and said unto them, It is one of the twelve, that dippeth with me in the dish.

21 The Son of man indeed goeth, as it is written of him: but woe to that man by whom the Son of man is betrayed! good were it for that man if he had never been born.

22 And as they did eat, Jesus took bread, and blessed, and brake it, and gave to them, and said, Take, eat: this is my body.

23 And he took the cup, and when he had given thanks, he gave it to them: and they all drank of it.

24 And he said unto them, This is my blood of the new testament, which is shed for many.

25 Verily I say unto you, I will drink no more of the fruit of the vine, until that day that I drink it new in the kingdom of God.

Apr. 13

Memory Selection
Mark 14:24
Background Scripture
Mark 14:1-25
Devotional Reading
Matthew 26:17-30

books, *The Kingdom of God Is a Party.*

The Jewish Passover and the Christian Lord's Supper are forecasts of this eventual reality. Today's text focuses on the institution of the Supper. The mood of celebration here is more subdued, including elements of betrayal and death. Yet the teacher should not neglect the brighter note with which the account ends: one day Jesus will eat the bread and drink the wine with the faithful at the great marriage feast of the Lamb of God!

In Scripture, the Kingdom of God is often portrayed as a great banquet or feast (see Matt. 22:1-10; Rev. 19:7-9). This tells us that God's rule is something to celebrate. Having plenty of food at this feast speaks of the end of poverty. Sitting down together at table envisions the end of estrangement from God and former enemies. All this led author Tony Campolo to title one of his

Use a "word-association" exercise to reveal what members of your group think of when they hear the term "party." Does the term evoke scenes of loud music and indulgence? Fond memories of family get-togethers at birthdays or anniversaries? Negative images of not being invited to a party, not having a date to an end-of-school celebration?

Reinforce responses that highlight the celebrative aspect of a party by reading the accounts noted above that portray the Kingdom as a feast or banquet (Matt. 22:1-10; Rev. 19:7-9). Affirm also, however, that the hard realities of life render appropriate the more somber associations some people have with the term. Note that today's lesson on the institution of the Lord's Supper also contains both joyous and painful tones. Challenge group members to identify each kind of responses both in the lesson and the next time they partake of the Supper.

Teaching Outline	Daily Bible Readings	
I. Thrill of Preparation—12-16	Mon.	Anointing Jesus Mark 14:1-9
A. The Passover, 12		
B. Preparation, 13-16	Tue.	Plans for the Passover Mark 14:10-16
1. 'Where is the guest chamber?" 13-14		
2. The upper room, 15-16	Wed.	The Cup and the Bread Mark 14:17-25
II. Tragedy of Betrayal—17-21	Thu.	Washing Feet John 13:1-5
A. 'Someone will betray me,' 17-19		
B. 'Woe to the betrayer,' 20-21	Fri.	Example for Servants John 13:12-20
III. Tasting the Future—22-25	Sat.	Going Ahead John 13:31-35
A. Meaning of the bread, 22		
B. Sharing the cup, 23-24	Sun.	'In Remembrance of Me' 1 Corinthians 11:23-28
C. An end and a beginning, 25		

Verse by Verse

I. Thrill of Preparation—12-16

A. The Passover, 12

12 And the first day of unleavened bread, when they killed the passover, his disciples said unto him, Where wilt thou that we go and prepare that thou mayest eat the passover?

Whether Jesus and His disciples actually partake of the Passover lamb at the feast spoken of here is debated. Those who hold to a strict interpretation of Christ's being in the tomb for three days and nights (Matt. 12:40) say the Crucifixion was on Thursday, not the Good Friday of the traditional Christian calendar. This view would mean that the scene described here, which will include the institution of the Lord's Supper, did not exactly coincide with the Jewish Passover. Mark at least associates it closely with the Passover (vs. 12). The main point is that at the institution of the Supper Jesus portrays himself as the sacrificial "lamb" slain for the sins of the world.

B. Preparation, 13-16

1. 'Where is the guest chamber?" 13-14

13 And he sendeth forth two of his disciples, and saith unto them, Go ye into the city, and there shall meet you a man bearing a pitcher of water: follow him.

14 And wheresoever he shall go in, say ye to the goodman of the house, The Master saith, Where is the guestchamber, where I shall eat

the passover with my disciples?

This scene has several points of similarity with the one in Lesson 6, where Jesus sends disciples ahead to Jerusalem from Bethany to bring a colt on which He will ride into Jerusalem. Perhaps the "goodman" or head of the house where the servant is taking the pitcher of water was a believer. In any case, it is clear that Jesus has supernatural insight into the man's readiness to help set the scene for the Lord's Supper. The "guest-chamber" Jesus sought was one of many provided by private household-ers to the throngs who crowded into Jerusalem for the annual feast.

2. The upper room, 15-16

15 And he will shew you a large upper room furnished and prepared: there make ready for us.

16 And his disciples went forth, and came into the city, and found as he had said unto them: and they made ready the passover.

An ancient tradition holds that this room belonged to the Gospel writer Mark himself. That the mother of Mark had a room later frequented by the disciples is referred to in Acts 12:12. Also, the disciples met for prayers in an upper room while waiting for the promised Holy Spirit, after Jesus' ascension (Acts 1:13).

II. Tragedy of Betrayal—17-21

A. 'Someone will betray me,' 17-19

323

17 And in the evening he cometh with the twelve.

18 And as they sat and did eat, Jesus said, Verily I say unto you, One of you which eateth with me shall betray me.

19 And they began to be sorrowful, and to say unto him one by one, Is it I? and another said, Is it I?

The sad and strange fact that one of Jesus' own disciples would betray Him had alreay been introduced in verses 10-11, where it is revealed that the disciple is Judas. Perhaps his name is withheld here because Jesus wanted the other disciples to examine their own hearts, not others', for any doubts concerning Jesus, and because naming Judas would have incited the other disciples to attack him in anger. (Although Matthew [26:25] and John both show that Judas is identified as the betrayer by eating a "sop" or morsel of bread dipped in the bowl, the other apostles do not associate this with Judas' plan to betray his Lord [see John 13:26-30].)

The self-questioning by the disciples is a good model for believers today. Instead of asking, "Is it Peter? Is it John?" etc., we are challenged to look within, following the biblical injunction to "Examine yourselves, whether ye be in the faith" (2 Cor. 13:5).

B. 'Woe to the betrayer,' 20-21

20 And he answered and said unto them, It is one of the twelve, that dippeth with me in the dish.

21 The Son of man indeed goeth, as it is written of him: but woe to that man by whom the Son of man is betrayed! good were it for that man if he had never been born.

Why does Jesus say "It is one of the twelve" when only they are with Him in the upper room (vs. 17)? Perhaps to say, in effect, "The betrayer isn't an outsider; he is one who has been with us long enough to see my miracles and observe my teachings!"

Those who hold that this meal is the Passover note that Jesus dipping bitter herbs in the "sop" as Jesus seems to do here was a part of the Jewish feast, although it may also have been a part of a regular meal. Saying that "the Son of man goeth" (the opposite of the Messianic title "He who cometh") refers to prophecies such as Isaiah 53:1-2 showing that He would die for our sins. Judas' personal guilt in cooperating with this plan poses the eternal issue of how God's foreknowledge and His scheme of redemption is to be understood in connection with the free will of those who killed His Son.

One way to deal with the question is to perceive the overall plan as foreordained, but its actual implementation involving the choice of those who plotted against Him and killed Him. We have already been told something of Judas' character by a reference to his greed (John 12:6). Apparently he thus allowed Satan to enter his heart (John 12:27) in part to obtain the 30 pieces of silver offered by Jesus' enemies. After all, Judas himself first raised the possibility of betraying Jesus (Matt. 26:14). Of course this question is part of the larger question of God's foreknowledge that all would be so sinful as to require the Son's redemptive act, yet His holding individual sinners responsible for sin.

III. Tasting the Future—22-25
A. Meaning of the bread, 22

22 And as they did eat, Jesus took bread, and blessed, and brake it, and gave to them, and said, Take, eat: this is my body.

Bread has many different connotations in Scripture. It is the "staff of life," a sacred staple on the tabernacle and Temple altars symbolizing dining with (and thus communing with) God, and a symbol of the universal Church. Here the bread of the Passover stands for the body of Jesus Himself, and ceremonially breaking it stands for the way His body will be broken on the Cross. Years later, the apostle Paul will chide Christians for turning the Lord's Supper into a common meal in ways that obscure this symbolism (1 Cor. 11:17ff.).

B. Sharing the cup, 23-24

23 And he took the cup, and when he had given thanks, he gave it to them: and they all drank of it.

24 And he said unto them, This is my blood of the new testament, which is shed for many.

Those who identify what Jesus institutes here with the Passover say that "the cup" is one of the four traditional cups of wine taken at the Jewish feast. Even if this is so, note that Jesus introduces a new element in identifying the wine with His "blood of the new testament" or covenant. Clearly He is distinguishing this cup from Passover wine by showing that it signifies the fulfillment of the prophet Jeremiah's promise of a new covenant (Jer. 31:31).

The important issue in this scene is the fact that Jesus institutes the Supper as a memorial to assist His followers in remembering that His death is the atoning power supplanting the sacrificial system of the Old Covenant. What has been disputed is precisely how the bread and wine are to be considered His body and blood. The four classic ways Christians would later interpret these famous "words of institution" ("This is my body" and "This is my blood") are summarized on page 327.

C. An end and a beginning, 25

25 Verily I say unto you, I will drink no more of the fruit of the vine, until that day that I drink it new in the kingdom of God.

Many Christians take this to mean that Jesus began partaking of the Communion with them when the Kingdom was inaugurated in Acts 2. They hold that Jesus fulfills His promise here by spiritually joining them as they partake of the Supper. Others hold that the promise refers not to the inauguration but the fulfillment of the Kingdom, and that we look forward to "dining with Jesus" at the great wedding feast of the Lamb described in Revelation 19:9. What is held in common is the incomparable blessing of such intimate "table fellowship" with the Lord and each other, which was implied in Jesus' day whenever friends dined together. Like the disciples on the road to Emmaus, it is at such moments that they gain a clearer picture that the Savior once crucified is alive and well and eager to disclose Himself to His followers in this special feast.

Evangelistic Emphasis

Jesus gave new meaning to the Passover. The Seder reminded the Jews that the blood on the doorposts had spared their firstborn when the Lord went across the land of Egypt. The blood of the lamb had saved the Hebrews. The blood protected even Egyptians who were in the households of the Hebrews. This great act of redemption and freedom was recalled at each Passover meal.

When that meal was over, Jesus took the bread still remaining on the table, and with the cup instituted what many Christians call the Lord's Supper. With the memory of one act of salvation being symbolized by the Passover meal, Jesus gave the Church her new symbol to remember His sacrifice. As the Lamb of God, Jesus would point out that the blood of a lamb would again save people.

Like the first time the blood was on the doorpost, the blood dripping from the cross had the power to save anyone who came under its influence. The scandal of the Cross is that Jesus died for everyone, even those persons who would never profess faith in Him. His blood was shed for many for the forgiveness of sins.

We think of salvation in terms of its universal consequences and scope. When we take the Lord's Supper we are reminded that Jesus died for each of us, for you and for me.

ॐ

Memory Selection

And he said unto them, This is my blood of the new testament, which is shed for many.— *Mark 14:24*

I was serving communion in a church once. In that church everyone came to the altar at the same time. It was a small church with a very big altar. I noticed a little tyke named Tyler who was kneeling with his mom and dad. When I said, "This is the body of Christ, take and eat," Tyler was reaching across his parents to take a handful of crackers. He chewed them with a smile on his face. Then he knew what came next.

He took the little communion cup that was on the altar and had it in his hand as well. He was about to put it up to his mouth when I spoke the words, "The blood of Christ, shed for you, drink in remembrance of Him." Tyler looked at that cup, got a funny look on his face and put the cup and the contents back on the altar.

Many people today would like to get rid of the bloody cross. Many good church people are like Tyler: they are repulsed by the blood of Jesus. In whatever way we understand the relationship between the wine of the Supper and the blood of Christ, salvation cannot be separated from the blood He shed on calvary.

326

Weekday Problems

Members of the worship committee at First Church were tackling the age-old mystery of communion, which some call the Lord's Supper. At First Church communion was served on the first Sunday of every month, in both their traditional and contemporary services. Suddenly the members of the worship committee noticed a drop in attendance on first Sundays. It was not a big drop, but the people who kept numbers noted that worship dropped every first Sunday.

The worship committee tried to do what all committees try to do. First they wanted to know "who was to blame for the drop in worship on the first Sunday," and then they asked what could be done about it. Although each member of the committee expressed their emotional responses to the problem, no consensus could be reached. It was therefore decided to form a study committee to investigate the matter further. One member noted that just as communion seemed to have nothing to do with real-life issues, the worship committee could not seem to come to terms with real-life problems.

*What happens to church attendance when communion is served at your church? Why do you think this happens?

Four Views of Communion

Transubstantian. This position, the official view of the Roman Catholic Church, takes Jesus' "words of insititution" literally. At the priest's pronouncement, the inner essence or substance of the bread changes (from Latin trans) into the actual body of Christ, and the wine to His actual blood.

Consubstantiation. Martin Luther taught that although the elements of the Supper do not actually change in substance, Christ's body and blood are truly present "in, with (Latin con), and under" the bread and wine.

The Symbolic View. The Swiss reformer Ulrich Zwingli held that Jesus actually meant "This bread and wine represent my body and blood," and that the elements only symbolize Jesus' body and blood.

The Dynamic View. John Calvin developed a mediating view between those of Luther and Zwingli. He taught that while not physically present in the elements, Christ's body and blood are dynamically or spiritually present, enabling the glorified Christ actually to be present in the Supper.

This Lesson in Your Life

Has this lesson found room in your heart? It is a lesson about the Lord's Supper and the meaning behind this sacred meal of the Church. It is a lesson that is much needed as we seek to understand all the ramifications of what Jesus did for us on the Cross. He gave us such a simple way of remem-bering His sacrifice on our behalf. We remember His death for us by taking the bread and the cup.

The story immediately before the institution of the Lord's Supper is one that needs to find room in your heart. Like the man with the donkey, we are introduced to a nameless individual who gave what ever was needed to the Lord. As the disciples were checking their calendar, they noted that the Passover was upon them. They asked Jesus what they should do in order to make preparation for this meal.

Now there is a great religious tradition behind the Passover meal, and I wish to avoid belittling that tradition. But my suspicion was that the disciples were not so much worried about the theological significance of the meal as they were about the culinary possibilities of the meal. The only American equivalent to the Passover meal would be our Thanksgiving meals. Passover was a time of great, festive celebration. At least three full glasses of wine were served at the meal. The meal itself was an opportunity for the host or hostess to show off his or her cooking skills. It was and is an event to remember.

The disciples wanted to know where they were going to have their Passover party. Jesus had already made a place for that meal. He said, "Go into a city and find a man carrying a jar." What would make this fellow unique was that jar-carrying was a woman's duty. So this man would be someone who stood out in the crowd. This jar-carrying fellow would lead the disciples to the home where the upper room was already prepared.

Two points I wish to make. First of all, we are like the man carrying the jar. Our task as disciples is to point other people to Jesus Christ. We are to take them by the hand and lead them to Christ.

Second, I wonder if in our own lives we have room for the Lord. This householder had made a guest room available for Jesus. This room was furnished and ready for Jesus and His disciples. Have you made a room in your heart for Jesus? With your schedules, your hopes and dreams, your obligations and duties, do you have room in your heart for the Messiah?

Maybe that is why the Lord's Supper bothers so many Christians. It reminds us that Jesus requires only the simplest of things from us, and that often those are the very things we deny Him.

328

GETTING THE FACTS STRAIGHT

1. The chief priests and the scribes were plotting what kind of action against Jesus?

The chief priests and the scribes were plotting how to arrest Jesus and kill Him.

2. What was one of the concerns the plotters had about carrying out their plan?

They were worried that the crowds in Jerusalem for Passover might riot if Jesus were arrested.

3. How did the chief priests and scribes hope to avoid trouble from the Passover crowds?

They plotted to arrest and kill Jesus by stealth and to avoid doing it during the feast.

4. In whose home in Bethany was Jesus when a woman anointed Him with precious ointment?

Jesus was in the home of Simon the leper when the woman anointed Him with the pure nard.

5. What impact did the anointing at Bethany have on Judas?

It might appear that Judas decided after this event to turn Jesus in to the authorities.

6. After Judas went to the religious authorities, what plan was set in motion at that meeting?

The religious authorities would pay Judas to find a way to betray Jesus to them.

7. When was the Passover lamb sacrificed?

The Passover lamb was sacrificed on the first day of Unleavened Bread.

8. How were the disciples to find the place where the Passover meal was to be shared?

The disciples were to go into the city and find a man who was carrying a water jar.

9. What were the disciples to ask of the householder once the jar-carrying man had made the introductions?

The disciples were to ask if the guest room had been prepared for the Teacher.

10. Does it appear as if Judas was at the institution of the Lord's Supper?

There is no indication from the Gospel of Mark that Judas had left the room, so he was there for the institution of the Lord's Supper.

I once pastored two churches, one of them a small country church that had a cemetery. The Sunday of Memorial Day weekend was Decoration Day at the cemetery. Decoration Day, in that setting, involves working around the graves of your relatives. This cemetery was well kept, so they changed the meaning of Decoration Day. No work! Lots of food!

On that Sunday those eight-foot church tables were spread. Ten of them were put end to end, making 80 feet of food. Food almost as far as the eye could see. Chicken in all flavors—fried, barbecued, baked, poached, smothered. Green beans. Baked Beans. Lima beans. White beans. Pinto Beans. Black-eyed peas. Zillions of bowls of potato salad, the kind that looks yellow, and the kind that looks white. The kind with chunks of potatoes and the kind that looks like it had been whipped for hours. Because it was a church function, no bacteria would dare show up in the potato salad left in the sun.

Corn. Sweet corn. On the cob corn. Corn Casserole. And corn out of the Can. Bread. Oh the bread! Rolls. Muffins. Cornbread. The kind with cracklings in it. Now I'm seeing if you are southern. If you need to get a snack, you are getting the point I'm trying to make. Then desserts. Pies. Cakes. Banana puddings. There wasn't a low-calorie dish or a salad within 10 miles of those tables. Health food was not allowed at Decoration Day meals.

The tradition was that these people would bring their food and their families, and wait for the preacher to offer a blessing before eating. On that Sunday, my other church would dismiss services early so I could go back out into the country and pray.

My first Decoration Day service, I made a big mistake. The tables with 80 feet of food were behind me. The people, more than 100 of them, were in front of me. My job was to pray. I discovered my mistake when I uttered the first syllable of the word, "Amen." I didn't get the "Ah" out before I felt the suction from the kids who were blowing past me to the table. The second thing I discovered once I got my eyes opened was that I was about to be mobbed by the adults, who were all heading for Aunt Suzie's fried chicken gizzards. You don't want to get between a Decoration Day crowd and their potluck-fried chicken. I enjoyed the day, though. I had never been invited to a meal that had 80 feet of food. They expected the preacher to eat, and I didn't want to disappoint them.

Jesus has invited you to a heavenly banquet, His supper. The next time your church has the Lord's Supper, remember that Jesus has invited you for some heavenly home cooking. While the Lord's Supper is serious, it is also joyous, for at that table we are remembering Jesus and His love for us. Forgiven sinners should have a smile on their face. So smile at the Lord's Supper. The preacher will wonder what you are up to. It will be good for both of you.

330

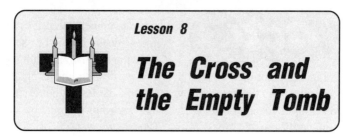

Lesson 8

The Cross and the Empty Tomb

Mark 15:21-24, 34-37; 16:1-8

And they compel one Simon a Cyrenian, who passed by, coming out of the country, the father of Alexander and Rufus, to bear his cross.

22 And they bring him unto the place Golgotha, which is, being interpreted, The place of a skull.

23 And they gave him to drink wine mingled with myrrh: but he received it not.

24 And when they had crucified him, they parted his garments, casting lots upon them, what every man should take.

34 And at the ninth hour Jesus cried with a loud voice, saying, Eloi, Eloi, lama sabachthani? which is, being interpreted, My God, my God, why hast thou forsaken me?

35 And some of them that stood by, when they heard it, said, Behold, he calleth Elias.

36 And one ran and filled a spunge full of vinegar, and put it on a reed, and gave him to drink, saying, Let alone; let us see whether Elias will come to take him down.

37 And Jesus cried with a loud voice, and gave up the ghost.

16:1 And when the Sabbath was past, Mary Magdalene, and Mary the mother of James, and Salome, had bought sweet spices, that they might come and anoint him.

2 And very early in the morning the first day of the week, they came unto the sepulchre at the rising of the sun.

3 And they said among themselves, Who shall roll us away the stone from the door of the sepulchre?

4 And when they looked, they saw that the stone was rolled away: for it was very great.

5 And entering into the sepulchre, they saw a young man sitting on the right side, clothed in a long white garment; and they were affrighted.

6 And he saith unto them, Be not affrighted: Ye seek Jesus of Nazareth, which was crucified: he is risen; he is not here: behold the place where they laid him.

7 But go your way, tell his disciples and Peter that he goeth before you into Galilee: there shall ye see him, as he said unto you.

8 And they went out quickly, and fled from the sepulchre; for they trembled and were amazed: neither said they any thing to any man; for they were afraid.

Apr. 20

Memory Selection
Mark 16:6

Background Scripture
Mark 15:21—16:8

Devotional Reading
John 20:11-18

331

The range of emotions covered in this lesson runs from the deep sorrow of Good Friday to the glad cry of "He is risen indeed!" on that first Easter morning. How realistic! Most significant events in our lives seem to include such extremes. The joy of birth is preceded by the pain of labor. The elation of a wedding can be accompanied by the sadness of "losing" a daughter as she establishes a separate home. The sadness of a loved one's death may be softened by knowing that their suffering has ended.

Yet despite these emotional extremes, the lesson has a single focus: *the redemptive act of Jesus, the Christ, in behalf of sinners.* The separate elements are blended into one story. Good Friday alone would leave us in utter desolation. The account of His rising has an unrealistic ring without the Cross. The plan of salvation meets so well our own needs both for realism and hope!

In what ways do members of your study group celebrate Easter? Or what do they remember most fondly about Easters in their childhood? A discussion of various customs will not only serve as an introduction into this lesson. It may also help group members to shape Easter observances in ways that emphasize the resurrection of Christ more than the fertility and nature-revival celebrations inherited from paganism.

As any holiday, Easter is subject to being commercialized, and to being overwhelmed by cultural traditions. Some complain that the resurrection is often obscured by the Easter egg hunts and candy bunny rabbits. Are such complaints valid, to members of your group? How do they keep the meaning of Easter in perspective?

Teaching Outline	Daily Bible Readings

I. The Crucifixion—15:21-24
  A. Simon the cross-bearer, 21
  B. The cross, 22-23
  C. Gambling for a garment, 24
II. The Death—34-37
  A. Cry of desolation, 34
  B. The Elijah tradition, 35-36
  C. The death of God? 37
III. The Resurrection—16:1-8
  A. Grim expectations, 1-3
  B. Glad evidence, 4-5
  C. Good tidings, 6-8
	Mon. The Place of the Skull
	      Mark 15:21-32
	Tue. Cry of Desolation
	      Mark 15:33-41
	Wed. Asking for Jesus' Body
	      Mark 15:42-47
	Thu. 'He Is Not Here!'
	      Mark 16:1-8
	Fri. The Road to Emmaus
	      Luke 24:13-27
	Sat. He Has Risen Indeed!
	      Luke 24:28-35
	Sun. 'Touch Me and See'
	      Luke 24:36-49

Verse by Verse

I. The Crucifixion—15:21-24
A. Simon the cross-bearer, 21

21 And they compel one Simon a Cyrenian, who passed by, coming out of the country, the father of Alexander and Rufus, to bear his cross.

Exhausted from his all-night ordeal, it is little wonder that Jesus is so weak that His executioners have to find a bystander to carry His cross (perhaps only the cross beam, with the upright portion already in place). We know nothing else of Simon, not even whether he was a believer. No doubt he had little understanding of the honor of carrying the instrument on which God's Son would give his life for our sins.

B. The cross, 22-23

22 And they bring him unto the place Golgotha, which is, being interpreted, The place of a skull.

23 And they gave him to drink wine mingled with myrrh: but he received it not.

"Golgotha" translates a Greek name meaning "bald" or "skull-like." (Its Latin equivalent Calvarium gives us the name "Calvary.") Some tour guides today identify Golgotha with a hill having hollow places resembling the eye-sockets of a skull, but most scholars believe it more likely that Jesus was crucified on a rounded, treeless hilltop, a site now drastically changed, and occupied by the Church of the Holy Sepulchre.

Tradition holds that compassionate Jewish women tried to ease the pain of crucifixion, the cruel Roman method of execution, by offering condemned criminals wine laced with a pain-killing drug. It is generally thought that Jesus declined it because He wanted to identify with the pain of mankind, experiencing fully the "taste" of death. Yet Matthew (26:34) records that He did take a sip of the wine, indicating that it was simply too distasteful to drink deeply.

C. Gambling for a garment, 24

24 And when they had crucified him, they parted his garments, casting lots upon them, what every man should take.

It was the custom to allow Roman executioners to keep any personal effects still clinging to the body of those they crucified. It is John's Gospel (19:23) that indicates that Jesus' garments consisted of, or were torn into, four parts, one of them being the seamless robe made famous in the historical novel *The Robe*, by Lloyd C. Douglas. Although Mark does not say so, the story at this point seems to be told deliberately in the words of Psalm 22, a "Messianic psalm" that figures prominently throughout the crucifixion. (Matthew 23:35 says plainly that dividing

Jesus' garments "fulfills" or is parallel with Psalm 22:18.)

II. The Death—34-37
A. Cry of desolation, 34

34 And at the ninth hour Jesus cried with a loud voice, saying, Eloi, Eloi, lama sabachthani? which is, being interpreted, My God, my God, why hast thou forsaken me?

Jesus Himself, even in His death throes, is so aware of His Messianic mission that He also quotes Psalm 22. This cry of "desolation" or abandonment, from 22:1, first expressed the psalmist David's anguish, perhaps in the days when he was being persecuted by King Saul. Like the words of other prophets who wondered about their ultimate fulfillment, David could not have known that he was also voicing the future cry of the Messiah (see 1 Pet. 1:10-12). It was important for the Gospel writers (especially Matthew) to show how Christ "fit" many prophecies that had previously been obscure, and was thus the fulfillment of the Old Testament hope.

All attempts to explain Jesus' experience of abandonment intrude on what is finally a mystery. The traditional explanation, however, seems the most likely: Jesus was feeling the burden of the sins of all mankind, and while this was God's plan, His justice and holiness called for Him to turn His face from the horrible burden borne by His Son. Yet we have only to recall that in some sense the Son and the Father are one to raise more questions about this cry, and to whom it was addressed, than we can answer.

B. The Elijah tradition, 35-36

35 And some of them that stood by, when they heard it, said, Behold, he calleth Elias.

36 And one ran and filled a spunge full of vinegar, and put it on a reed, and gave him to drink, saying, Let alone; let us see whether Elias will come to take him down.

Recalling that Malachi 4:5 had promised that God would send the prophet Elijah before "the day of the Lord," it is not suprising that Christ's call of "Eloi" was mistaken by some for the name "Elias" or "Elijah." Actually, Jesus had said that Elias had already come, figuratively, in the ministry of John the Baptist (Matt. 17:10-13). The vinegar-soaked sponge was perhaps offered in an attempt to hydrate Jesus and keep Him alive long enough to see if Elijah would in fact appear.

C. The death of God? 37

37 And Jesus cried with a loud voice, and gave up the ghost.

The stark simplicity and bleak barrenness of this verse is appropriate. Little good would be done by embroidering it with speculation about how the eternal Son could die, especially since He was "one" with the Father. In the 1960s it was this description of the sacrifice of the life of the God-Man Jesus that led to discussions that "God is dead." Later Gnostics would claim that Jesus did not really die, or that only His "flesh" was affected by the Cross—prompting Paul and others to insist that Christ's actual death was fundamental to the gospel (1 Cor. 15:3-4). Although it is easy to say that Jesus is dying only in His "humanity," such explanations seem glib and superficial, and were denied by the early Church because they seemed to attribute two natures to Jesus instead of one that was "very God and very man." Scripture simply states that "God was in Christ," who died in the supreme act of reconciling the world unto himself (2 Cor. 5:19).

III. The Resurrection—16:1-8
A. Grim expectations, 1-3

1 And when the Sabbath was past, Mary Magdalene, and Mary the mother of James, and Salome, had bought sweet spices, that they might come and anoint him.

2 And very early in the morning the first day of the week, they came unto the sepulchre at the rising of the sun.

3 And they said among themselves, Who shall roll us away the stone from the door of the sepulchre?

The selected text moves to the third day after Christ's crucifixion. Because His disciples have not understood even that their Messiah must die, much less that He would be raised (Matt. 17:22-23), the women bring the usual embalming spices for Jesus' body. Stones covering the entrance to a sepulchre were heavy enough to discourage grave robbers, and the women expected to need help in temporarily removing this heavy "door."

B. Glad evidence, 4-5

4 And when they looked, they saw that the stone was rolled away: for it was very great.

5 And entering into the sepulchre, they saw a young man sitting on the right side, clothed in a long white garment; and they were affrighted.

Matthew's more elaborate (28:2) account includes the fact that an earthquake was the way God rolled away the stone, and that the "young man" was in fact an angel. The same identification between remarkable "men" and angels occurred in some Old Testament divine-human encounters (e.g., Gen. 18:2; 19:1).

C. Good tidings, 6-8

6 And he saith unto them, Be not affrighted: Ye seek Jesus of Nazareth, which was crucified: he is risen; he is not here: behold the place where they laid him.

7 But go your way, tell his disciples and Peter that he goeth before you into Galilee: there shall ye see him, as he said unto you.

8 And they went out quickly, and fled from the sepulchre; for they trembled and were amazed: neither said they any thing to any man; for they were afraid.

The glad message that shines brightest here agrees with the other Gospels' Easter message that "He is not here." Otherwise, Mark remarkably omits some seemingly important elements recorded in the other Gospels. Christ's post-resurrection appearances are predicted but not described; and the women are not portrayed as overcoming the fear that at first kept them from sharing the good news. No doubt the young man's (or angel's) command that they tell the disciples implies the women's later willingness to do so. Peter seems to be singled out among the disciples because of his special prominence as keeper of the "keys of the kingdom of heaven" (Matt. 16:19).

Evangelistic Emphasis

The story of the cross is a compelling story.

You either believe that Jesus is the Son of God and the Savior of humanity, or you do not. You are either a Christian or you are not. The great divide is caused by the story of the Cross. There are many teachable subjects as you ponder the cross and this lesson.

The text begins when a stranger, a mere passerby, was compelled to carry the cross of Jesus. We know nothing further of Simon of Cyrene, other than he was in Jerusalem and was traveling along the same road that the procession to the crucifixion. Mark makes no mention of Jesus stumbling; he simply tells his audience that someone else was compelled to carry the cross for a distance.

Notice that Jesus told His people that we, like Simon of Crene, are called to *carry* our crosses. He never told us that we would have to be crucified; only that we would have to carry the cross for a while.

The good news of this lesson is compelling news as well. Jesus died for us. He did for us what we could not do. The fact that He calls each of us to take up the cross is disturbing but challenging. It means that we are all participants with Him in the plan of redemption.

In the annual of heaven, one day they will tell the story of how YOU carried YOUR cross for Jesus.

℘℘

Memory Selection

And he saith unto them, Be not affrighted: Ye seek Jesus of Nazareth, which was crucified: He is risen; He is not here: behold the place where they laid Him.—*Mark 16:6*

We have heard this story so many times; we don't understand how radical the message was. The women were looking for a dead body to anoint properly for burial. What better place to look for a dead body than in a cemetery? One does not find many dead bodies in places other than cemeteries.

The fear came when the women did not find Jesus where He naturally should have been found. We know, 2,000 years later, the powerful story of the resurrection. These women were living the story and having all the emotions that came with "not knowing."

Where is Jesus today? Do we keep looking for Jesus in the "natural places"? In what ways do you think we are like those women? In your faith community where are the surprising places that Jesus has turned up? Are there places where you must say, "He is not here, for He has risen." What new and different "resurrection things" do you find Jesus doing in your life?

Weekday Problems

Debbie and Mike had been married for 25 years. They had two children who had grown into adulthood and were starting families of their own. Mike and Debbie had many of the advantages that came since both were college graduates. However, for 20 years of their marriage Mike and Debbie had struggled with Mike's physical problems.

At the age of 26, Mike was diagnosed with Parkinson's disease. The disease had left him unable to drive his own car. He could no longer speak clearly. As the disease progressed into other stages, the doctors became unable to treat his condition. Mike lost control of most of the muscle functions that allowed him to enjoy life. Soon it became evident that Mike would need care beyond Debbie's ability to give.

Debbie, who had a deep faith in the Lord, was changing as Mike's disease progressed. She became angry and bitter about the unfairness of his suffering and the problems his illness had brought to her and her family. She disassociated herself from the people who loved and cared about her. She could scarcely hide her anger at God, and stopped coming to church. She still claimed that she had faith, but she had big questions about why all of this had happened and why God had not heard her prayers for Mike's healing.

*In light of the resurrection of Jesus Christ, how would you help Debbie understand this condition, and where might Mike and Debbie find hope?

If Easter Be Not True

If Easter be not true,
Then all the lilies low must lie;
The Flanders poppies fade and die;
The spring must lose her fairest bloom
For Christ were still within the tomb—
   If Easter be not true.

If Easter be not true,
Then faith must mount on broken wing;
Then hope no more immortal spring;
Then love must lose her mighty urge;
Life prove a phantom, death a dirge—
   If Easter be not true.

If Easter be not true,
'Twere foolishness the cross to bear;
He died in vain who suffered there;
What matter though we laugh or cry,
Be good or evil, live or die,
   If Easter be not true?

If Easter be not true—
But it is true, and Christ is risen!
And mortal spirit from its prison
Of sin and death with him may rise!
Worthwhile the struggle, sure the prize,
   Since Easter, aye, is true!

—Henry H. Barstow, 1866-1944

This Lesson in Your Life

We live in a Good Friday world—a world filled with pain and suffering. We live in a world where science, once seen as a savior, is invading areas reserved for God with an arrogant disregard for consequences. Turn on the news and listen to the stories. Children killing their classmates, no longer over clothes but now just for the "fun" of killing. We hear of parents abusing their children because the children were crying. We read about terrorists bombing their neighbors because of religious or political differences.

It is a Good Friday World. Bad news comes in buckets. A friend has cancer. Another is divorcing. Yet another grieves over a sibling's death.

It is a Good Friday World. Hopelessness is the theme of the day. She works in a dead-end job she hates. He has nothing left to spend after paying the monthly bills. High school kids worry that they won't be able to live the kind of life their parents lived. Some are horrified that they are limited by the same prejudices that have limited their friends.

It is a Good Friday world. We live in the kind of world that is always rolling the rock in front of the tomb. We live in a world that rolls the rock of limitation in our way. A victimized, labeled society. Your ability to succeed or the predictions of your failure are often based on nothing. Your IQ, your socio-economic origin, your genetic code have nothing whatsoever to do with your ability to know joyous living. They are simply labels. If you come from the wrong side of the tracks, if you don't have an education, you can't succeed in a Good Friday world. Any "ism" which can now be blamed on your genetic code gives an excuse to have a Good Friday rock rolled across the path of your life, entombing your choices in hopeless determinism. "I can't . . ."—because of racism, alcoholism, or ageism. Have you heard those excuses, or have you used those excuses as a means of being entombed in a Good Friday world dead end tomb?

Living in a Good Friday world, we had better know the answer to the question, "What is Easter?"

The story of the crucifixion and resurrection of Jesus speaks volumes to the Good Friday world in which we live.

Although we live in a Good Friday world, we have an Easter faith. Because we are an Easter people we don't have to be bound by the dictates of the Good Friday people. The only limitations we know are the ones we give power and place to in our lives. The resurrection of Jesus means that the victory has been won. This victory is one in which we all share, we are no longer VICTIMS we are VICTORS in Jesus Christ.

As you live in a Good Friday world, live with an Easter faith.

1. Simon of Cyrene was compelled to carry the cross. What details were given about Simon?

Simon was coming in from the country. He was the father of Alexander and Rufus.

2. Jesus was crucified on a hill outside of Jerusalem. What two names were given for this place?

Jesus was crucified at a place called Golgotha. The other name for this place was "the skull."

3. Someone offered Jesus something to drink. What was that drink?

Jesus was offered wine mixed with myrrh, but He refused to take the drink.

4. Do you know why Jesus refused to take this drink?

Many scholars speculate the drink was a primitive sedative, thus allowing the one crucified to avoid feeling some pain.

5. After the offer of the drink, Jesus was crucified. What happened next?

After Jesus was crucified, the soldiers cast lots to determine which item of Jesus' clothing they would receive.

6. Why was Jesus killed, according to the inscription over the cross?

The charge against Him read simply, "The King of the Jews."

7. What details are we given about who was near Jesus on the cross?

Two robbers were crucified with Him, one on the right and the other on the left.

8. As the crowds passed by, what were they doing?

Some hurled insults at Jesus, reminding Him of His bold words and tempting Him to come down from the cross and prove His divinity.

9. When some of the bystanders heard Jesus cry, "Eloi, Eloi, lama sabachthani," what did they think?

The crowd heard this and many thought Jesus was caling for Elijah?

10. The crucifixion happened on Friday. What happened on Sunday?

The Good Friday world was defeated when the tomb of Jesus was empty. He is risen indeed!

Not long ago there was a story floating around the Internet about a young man named Jeremy Forrester. He was a student at St. Theresa's Elementary School. Jeremy was 12 years old. He was only in the second grade. Jeremy was a very sick boy. His illness had slowed his progress in school. His parents insisted that Jeremy attend a regular school with the other children.

Jeremy's teacher was Doris Miller. She was not sure it was a good idea to have Jeremy in the regular school, but she was willing to give it a try.

The class was given an assignment to fill a plastic Easter egg with some sign of new life. The children returned the next day with eggs filled with flowers, butterflies, and the like. Jeremy returned with an empty Easter egg. Mrs. Miller thought Jeremy had not understood the assignment. When she opened the empty egg in front of the class. She knew it could only have come from Jeremy. And seeking to spare his feelings, she reached for another egg. But Jeremy called out proudly, "That's my egg!"

"Yes, Jeremy," she said, "but it is empty."

He explained, "Yes, Mrs. Miller it *is* empty. And that's a sign of new life. The egg is empty, just like Jesus' tomb was empty."

Mrs. Miller asked him, "Jeremy, do you know why the tomb was empty?"

"Oh, yes, Mrs. Miller I know why. The tomb was empty because Jesus was killed and put in there. But his Father raised Him up!" The recess bell rang and while the children ran out to play. Mrs. Miller shed a tear. Jeremy understood a lot about new life.

Three months later, Jeremy died. Jeremy's classmates attended the memorial service. After the preacher spoke, the children began to come up and to put something in a basket on his casket. When Jeremy was buried, 19 empty Easter eggs were buried with him.

That story is a good illustration about an Easter faith in a Good Friday world. Our Easter faith does not stop the natural tragedies of life from happening. Our faith gives us the courage to live through those trying times, and not let them become victorious over us. We can live through problems because we know that our Lord has prepared a resurrection for all of us. Our hope and faith is that not even something as powerful as death and the grave has victory over us. Because Jesus was raised from the dead, we believe that we too, will be raised.

Because of resurrection faith we can look at the problems and difficulties of this life as only temporary, because Jesus has planned something much better for His children. Our hope is found in that empty tomb, our faith is in a risen Savior!

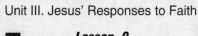

Unit III. Jesus' Responses to Faith

Lesson 9

The Importance of Belief

Mark 5:22-36, 41-42

And, behold, there cometh one of the rulers of the synagogue, Jairus by name; and when he saw him, he fell at his feet,

23 And besought him greatly, saying, My little daughter lieth at the point of death: I pray thee, come and lay thy hands on her, that she may be healed; and she shall live.

24 And Jesus went with him; and much people followed him, and thronged him.

25 And a certain woman, which had an issue of blood twelve years,

26 And had suffered many things of many physicians, and had spent all that she had, and was nothing bettered, but rather grew worse,

27 When she had heard of Jesus, came in the press behind, and touched his garment.

28 For she said, If I may touch but his clothes, I shall be whole.

29 And straightway the fountain of her blood was dried up; and she felt in her body that she was healed of that plague.

30 And Jesus, immediately knowing in himself that virtue had gone out of him, turned him about in the press, and said, Who touched my clothes?

31 And his disciples said unto him, Thou seest the multitude thronging thee, and sayest thou, Who touched me?

32 And he looked round about to see her that had done this thing.

33 But the woman fearing and trembling, knowing what was done in her, came and fell down before him, and told him all the truth.

34 And he said unto her, Daughter, thy faith hath made thee whole; go in peace, and be whole of thy plague.

35 While he yet spake, there came from the ruler of the synagogue's house certain which said, Thy daughter is dead: why troublest thou the Master any further?

36 As soon as Jesus heard the word that was spoken, he saith unto the ruler of the synagogue, Be not afraid, only believe.

41 And he took the damsel by the hand, and said unto her, Talitha cumi; which is, being interpreted, Damsel, I say unto thee, arise.

42 And straightway the damsel arose, and walked; for she was of the age of twelve years. And they were astonished with a great astonishment.

Apr. 27

Memory Selection
Mark 5:36

Background Scripture
Mark 5:21-43

Devotional Reading
Hebrews 11:1-6

341

The power of faith, which is the focus of this lesson, can be deceptively simple to state. It is all too easy for a friend to tell us, as we grieve over the news that our spouse is terminally ill, "Just believe, and everything will turn out all right." At some profound level, this is true; but is this faith in faith, or in God? What will count as "turning out all right"? Will we consider this to be true even if our loved one dies?

Instead of dealing directly with such abstractions, the teacher guiding this lesson may do better by simply unfolding the two incidents of Jesus' healing. Let the accounts themselves both draw out our questions and supply such answers as they might. Emphasize that the "power of faith" lies not in our ability to believe, but in God, through His son Jesus Christ.

ဆာ

How do members of your group respond to the term "faith healing"? Some may react negatively, recalling charlatans who skillfully excite an adrenaline rush in a paralyzed person that enables him to jump from his wheel chair—only to be left still crippled and disillusioned after the "healer" leaves town. Others may have had a genuine experience of healing in response to prayer—an event at which doctors themselves marvel, while still others may hold that people can often heal themselves by faith in the form of a positive attitude. Point out that all healing is in one sense accomplished by God, whether miraculously or through the medications and treatment He enables physicians to discover.

Challenge group members to test their view of healing by the accounts in today's text. Note that neither of these incidents is more "miraculous" than the resurrection of this Healer from the dead, which is the basis of our confidence in His power.

Teaching Outline	Daily Bible Readings	
I. Important Man's Daughter—22-23	Mon.	Touching Jesus' Clothes Mark 5:21-34
II. Interrupted Mission—24-34	Tue.	'Only Believe' Mark 5:35-43
A. An ill but daring woman, 24-26	Wed.	'Believe in God . . . and Me' John 14:1-7
B. Touching His clothes, 27-29	Thu.	'Do You Yet Not Know Me?' John 14:8-14
C. The power of faith, 30-34	Fri.	Belief in the Unseen Hebrews 11:1-6
III. Interfering with Death—35-36, 41-42	Sat.	A Faithless Generation Matthew 17:14-20
A. 'Only believe,' 35-36	Sun.	'Increase Our Faith' Luke 17:1-6
B. 'Damsel, arise!' 41-42		

Verse by Verse

I. Important Man's Daughter—22-23

22 And, behold, there cometh one of the rulers of the synagogue, Jairus by name; and when he saw him, he fell at his feet,

23 And besought him greatly, saying, My little daughter lieth at the point of death: I pray thee, come and lay thy hands on her, that she may be healed; and she shall live.

Jesus has returned from the eastern shore of Galilee (vs. 21), so the synagogue referred to here may have been at Capernaum, where He occasionally preached. Archaeologists believe they have uncovered ruins of this very synagogue. The Old Testament knows nothing of the synagogue, an institution formed during the Captivity.

Jairus was one of several "rulers" who probably occupied the office of synagogue elder. It was the rulers' task to keep order, to invite speakers, and possibly to lead the service. The synagogue ruler in Luke 13:14 felt obligated to object when Jesus performed a healing on the Sabbath. Perhaps Jairus' anguish over his seriously ill daughter, and the trust in Jesus developed during His frequent visits to this synagogue, kept him from such fault-finding. That he falls at Jesus feet may mean that he was a believer, but not necessarily, since this would have been an appropriate way to beg a special favor of any person held in high esteem.

II. Interrupted Mission—24-34
A. An ill but daring woman, 24-26

24 And Jesus went with him; and much people followed him, and thronged him.

25 And a certain woman, which had an issue of blood twelve years,

26 And had suffered many things of many physicians, and had spent all that she had, and was nothing bettered, but rather grew worse,

Jesus' willingness to drop what He was doing and accompany Jairus, a man of importance, will now be matched by equal attentiveness to a "nobody." Although she is not even named, the woman wins Jesus' attention, reminding us of that He regarded all people as created in God's image.

Jesus' trek to Jairus' home, however, is impeded by the throngs of people who crowd around Him. The woman's suffering drives her to make her way through the crowd to seek healing of what was probably a menstrual flow (cp. the NIV, "bleeding for five years"). The "physicians" (lit.

"healers") were usually, at this time, not highly trained medical practitioners but priests, if the woman was a Jew, and shamans or magicians if she was a Gentile. (Luke, a Greek physician, would have been able to take advantage of a more scientific medical training.) At any rate, given the state of the medical arts of the day, it is not surprising that whatever methods had been used in an attempt to cure the woman had failed, and left her in poverty.

B. Touching His clothes, 27-29

27 When she had heard of Jesus, came in the press behind, and touched his garment.

28 For she said, If I may touch but his clothes, I shall be whole.

29 And straightway the fountain of her blood was dried up; and she felt in her body that she was healed of that plague.

Obviously the woman had heard that Jesus was reputed to be a healer. She had some faith, as verse 28 indicates; but it may have been somewhat desperate, based on hope but little first-hand knowledge of Jesus' previous healing miracles.

Several times Scripture refers to the idea that the clothes or other articles belonging to a holy man were involved in healing. Handkerchiefs and other articles of clothing taken from the apostle Paul to the sick and the demonized apparently healed them (Acts 19:11-12). Acts 19:12 calls such instances "special miracles," indicating that whatever healings resulted from the practices were not from some power inherent in the article, but in a disciple in whom God Himself

was the miracle-working power.

By this same power in Jesus, the woman was healed merely by touching His outer garment (vs. 29). We can only imagine how elated she must have been to have a disease that had been plaguing her for 12 years instantly healed. She had found a "physician" with divine power beyond all those she had visited earlier—and He charged nothing!

C. The power of faith, 30-34

30 And Jesus, immediately knowing in himself that virtue had gone out of him, turned him about in the press, and said, Who touched my clothes?

31 And his disciples said unto him, Thou seest the multitude thronging thee, and sayest thou, Who touched me?

32 And he looked round about to see her that had done this thing.

33 But the woman fearing and trembling, knowing what was done in her, came and fell down before him, and told him all the truth.

34 And he said unto her, Daughter, thy faith hath made thee whole; go in peace, and be whole of thy plague.

Verse 30 is remarkable in that it shows that at least at times Jesus was physically aware when miracle working power (NIV) flowed from Him. This mysterious evidence of the union of the divine and the human in Jesus was something more than the mere emotional "drain" a doctor or therapist may experience today. It may have been one reason the Lord sometimes needed to withdraw from the crowds to regenerate both spirit and body.

The woman is so grateful for her experience of healing that she knifes though the disciples' assumption that one person could not be singled out from among the many who were jostling Jesus. His blessing must have removed the fear she would naturally have as a "mere woman" daring to speak publicly with this renowned rabbi. His acknowledgment that her faith had healed her removes all question of there being some healing property in His garment apart from faith.

III. Interfering with Death—35-36, 41-42

A. 'Only believe,' 35-36

35 While he yet spake, there came from the ruler of the synagogue's house certain which said, Thy daughter is dead: why troublest thou the Master any further?

36 As soon as Jesus heard the word that was spoken, he saith unto the ruler of the synagogue, Be not afraid, only believe.

Returning to the account of Jairus and his daughter begun in verse 22, we learn that certain persons came to say that it was too late to bring this rabbi with the gift of healing; his daughter was dead. It may sound shallow when mere humans counsel us to "only believe"; but as we read it in the Gospels, this account comes after Jesus' affirmation that the woman with the issue of blood was healed by faith. Thus His counsel has the unique ring of truth that could only come from God's Son. It is enough to ignite Jairus' faith that Jesus' powers may extend beyond the grave.

B. 'Damsel, arise!' 41-42

41 And he took the damsel by the hand, and said unto her, Talitha cumi; which is, being interpreted, Damsel, I say unto thee, arise.

42 And straightway the damsel arose, and walked; for she was of the age of twelve years. And they were astonished with a great astonishment.

In the intervening text, verse 39 described Jesus' rebuke of those who considered the little girl's situation to be hopeless. "The damsel is not dead," he tells them, "but sleepeth." However, since saying that a dead person is asleep" was a common Jewish way of speaking, and since they could tell when a person stopped breathing, Jesus is probably speaking metaphorically; the girl has actually died. (See the parallel interplay between "sleeping" and death" in the case of Lazarus, John 11:11-14.)

Mark is the only Gospel writer who quotes Jesus' words, "Talitha cumi," and gives their interpretation. They are not a cryptic, magical spell, but a straightforward command in Jesus' native language, Aramaic. If we believe that death will eventually be destroyed at the culmination of the Kingdom of God (Rev. 20:14), we should not stumble at believing that the King Himself could command this little girl to arise from death. Something of the joyous reaction to her "resurrection" is indicated by the fact that the words for "astonish" in verse 42 also give us our word "ecstasy." What better occasion for "ecstasy" than an incident showing that Jesus has power over death!

Evangelistic Emphasis

Jesus touches people at the place of their deepest hurt. That is both very good news and disquieting news. It is good news because Jesus can heal us where we are hurt. He can forgive the sins that have wounded our souls. He can make new the desolate places and bring light into the darkened places in our souls. The disquieting part is that very often we don't want to be that transparent with our Lord.

The woman touched Jesus secretly, but when caught she "told him the whole truth." Now she told Him the truth of her shame and how she didn't want to be singled out as a person who needed healing. She may have told Him more truth. She might have shared her frustrations about all the years of being in the medical care system and not finding healing. She might have even told Jesus the truth about other things in her life.

It is after she has "told Him the whole truth" that Jesus says to her, "Daughter your faith has made you well, go in peace and be healed of your disease." One is left wondering if there was more than just physical healing that happened in this story.

The point is simple, Jesus heals us where we hurt, where we are *really* hurting. Have you opened your heart and soul to His healing, or are you trying to "hide something" from Him?

ഇറ

Memory Selection

Jesus said to the leader of the synagogue, "Do not fear, only believe.—*Mark 5:36*

The opposite of faith is not doubt. The opposite of faith is fear. The essence of fear is not trusting that the Lord is watching over us sufficiently to protect us from the storms of life.

The leader of the synagogue had fear because of a child who was near death. He was worried about the outcome of the child's illness. He was worried about his own faith having an impact on the outcome. His fear was that his daughter would die and that the relationship with her would be lost, as death separates us from the ones we love.

He brought all of this to the feet of Jesus. He may have even had a nagging fear that the request would not be granted by the Lord. None of this was even on a level the man was aware of. He was a quaking mass of emotions.

Jesus' admonition, "Fear not" may be a way of saying "Calm down!" Jesus is watching over His creation and He cares for us.

Do you believe that, or are you still afraid?

Weekday Problems

Evelyn had been to every doctor in town. She had been diagnosed with a terminal illness. After the doctors had tried all of their "cures" and "treatments" they told Evelyn that there was nothing further they could do for her. The doctors told her that she should go home and make preparations for the end of her life.

Evelyn went home, and on the Internet she looked up everything she could find about her disease and most of the known treatments for it. She spent hours researching all of the alternative ways that she might receive beneficial treatments. She tried to get into experimental programs testing new and often exotic treatments for her illness. She became so involved in her research and trying alternative treatments that she added two years to a life that the doctors said wouldn't last six more months.

As the end neared, Evelyn faced death with courage. She talked about all of her "antics" in looking for a treatment or a cure. She faced death not as one who was defeated, but as one who knew she had done everything possible. She faced death knowing that Jesus often brings healing in heaven.

In your class, talk about healing, and those you know who are struggling with chronic or terminal illnesses.

*How can you support them? What message does this lesson have for them?

The Doctor Is In

Epitaph:
> Of all my indignities,
> The shacks, the coops,
> The last was worst—
> The surgeon said "Oops!"

✣✣✣✣✣

Did you hear about the guy who stayed up all night studying for a blood test?

✣✣✣✣✣

Doctor: And how did the accident happen?
Patient: My wife fell asleep in the back seat.

✣✣✣✣✣

Dieting patient: I've been using a "flesh roller" for three months.
Doctor: Any results?
Patient: Oh, yes. The roller's about three inches thinner.

This Lesson in Your Life

The Gospel of Mark was written for a person in a hurry. The action in Mark is fast paced. Even when something important is happening, something else important happens along with it. On His way to heal one person, Jesus heals another. He then continues His journey to the house of Jairus to heal his daughter. The story of the woman with the "issue of blood is a miracle interrupting another miracle.

I relate to this woman in that she had "suffered much under many physicians." One of the things that I think is worse than being sick has to deal with the medical establishment. If you have not been in our medical system for a while, you may not know how complicated things have become. No longer can you walk in and see a physician and have them give a diagnosis. They must run "tests." I have never understood why going to the doctor for a sprained ankle would cause him to run blood tests. I told him how I sprained my ankle and it had nothing to do with my cholesterol level! Such incidents help us understand what this woman had suffered through. She had heard many opinions, many mis-diagnoses, and still she was not made whole.

She didn't know where Jesus was going that day. She simply saw a huge crowd of people and this widely-known rabbi. She knew about His ability to heal others, and perhaps had even witnessed some of that first hand. She knew that she had nothing to lose in reaching out to touch the hem of His garment. She reached out in desperation, frustration, and faith. "If I touch even His garments, I shall be made well." The frustration and desperation led her to act in faith. Immediately, she was healed. The great thing about Mark's Gospel is that no one has to wait long for anything to happen.

The miracle happened on the way to a miracle, and that is important for your life. The great events of life often happen to us in the "in between" times. We discover some spiritual truth while reading the Bible as we are waiting for something else to happen. Some insight might happen as we are cleaning the house and getting ready for the Bible Study group to arrive. Each moment is filled with the power of God. Even those moments we see as mundane can become powerful moments in which God is present with us. If we are looking for God in those moments, we discover His presence in the simple things of life.

I'm afraid some of us think that God only resides in the major holidays on the Church calendar. I wonder: Did you find God to be working in your life on April 23rd, or were you too busy getting ready to teach this lesson? Teaching a lesson is important, but finding Jesus on Wednesday, as you prepared, is what "living for Jesus" is all about.

1. What details are given about the man who comes and falls at the feet of Jesus?

The man's name was Jairus. He was one of the rulers of the synagogue.

2. What request did this man made of Jesus?

Jairus asked if Jesus would come and lay hands on his daughter, who was at the point of death.

3. What hope did Jairus have as he made this request of Jesus?

Jairus hoped that Jesus would lay hands on her and she would "be made well and live."

4. What simple words did Mark use to indicate the response that Jesus gave to Jairus?

Mark wrote, "And He went with him." That is, Jesus followed Jairus home.

5. What happened after Jesus began traveling to Jairus' home?

A great crowd gathered around Jesus and Jairus, and walked along with them.

6. In this crowd was a person. What information was given about this person?

There was a woman in the crowd who had had a flow of blood for 12 years.

7. What other details are given about the woman with the "flow of blood?"

She had been treated by many physicians and had spent all of her money on them, but was no better, and in fact was worse.

8. Why was the woman in the crowd that day?

"She had heard reports about Jesus and came up behind him the crowd."

9. What was the intention of the woman as she came up to Jesus?

She wanted to touch His garments, feeling that even that would bring her healing.

10. What was the response of Jesus to this woman, once she told Him why she touched His robe?

Jesus said, "Your faith has made you well, go in peace and be healed of your disease."

It has been estimated that nearly 20 percent of the gospel narratives are devoted to healing. Indeed a case could be made for arguing that the entire New Testament is one long account of a healing event performed by God, as He heals the rift that has existed between humanity and heaven.

The universe was intended to operate harmoniously, with all creation intimately and intricately coordinated to act, work, love, and live together. But something went terribly wrong. The biblical narrative is an attempt to explain that "something," and to record God's creative response to a now imperfect, unbalanced world.

For humans, an out-of-balance existence is most commonly experienced as a state of illness. Our souls and bodies "ache" when we are separated from God. Health and wholeness remain at the root of creation, but human freedom has enabled us to pound out our own distressingly clashing accompaniment to this universal symphony. Thus we experience disease, injury, anxiety, stress, psychosis, and death.

Thankfully, Romans 8 reminds us that the Spirit of God and the Spirit of Christ are continually making intercession for us, and in words that are too deep to be uttered. Honest physicians realize that the only reason a doctor can produce health is because the human body is biased in favor of health. The universe is prejudiced in our favor, and its powers are working on our side. Albert Einstein used to say,"When a baby drops its rattle out of a crib, not only does the rattle fall to reach the earth, but the earth rises imperceptibly to meet the rattle." We don't have to work at seeking God's favor. God's favor is already built into the structure of the universe.

Theology used to be referred to as "The Queen of the Sciences." But modernism fell so madly in love with science, the scientific method, and quantitative analysis that for a century we have denied the "scientific" validity of anything that we could not weigh, measure, or slide under a microscope. Today some scientiests are reverting to the theological roots of science. In many cases they are talking more about theological issues than are our own preachers and teachers of theology. Prayer is now studied along with anatomy in medical schools. It seems that many have begun writing a new symphony of healing, and are this time allowing God to conduct the song.

Maybe that is why the woman with the issue of blood reached out to Jesus. Maybe she knew that medicine without theology was as useless as all those doctors were. She knew that at the heart of healing was the heart of Jesus.

Healing comes with prayer and a good physician. But we must get the order right.

Lesson 10

Bold Faith

Mark 7:24-37

And from thence he arose, and went into the borders of Tyre and Sidon, and entered into an house, and would have no man know it: but he could not be hid.

25 For a certain woman, whose young daughter had an unclean spirit, heard of him, and came and fell at his feet:

26 The woman was a Greek, a Syrophenician by nation; and she besought him that he would cast forth the devil out of her daughter.

27 But Jesus said unto her, Let the children first be filled: for it is not meet to take the children's bread, and to cast it unto the dogs.

28 And she answered and said unto him, Yes, Lord: yet the dogs under the table eat of the children's crumbs.

29 And he said unto her, For this saying go thy way; the devil is gone out of thy daughter.

30 And when she was come to her house, she found the devil gone out, and her daughter laid upon the bed.

31 And again, departing from the coasts of Tyre and Sidon, he came unto the sea of Galilee, through the midst of the coasts of Decapolis.

32 And they bring unto him one that was deaf, and had an impediment in his speech; and they beseech him to put his hand upon him.

33 And he took him aside from the multitude, and put his fingers into his ears, and he spit, and touched his tongue;

34 And looking up to heaven, he sighed, and saith unto him, Ephphatha, that is, Be opened.

35 And straightway his ears were opened, and the string of his tongue was loosed, and he spake plain.

36 And he charged them that they should tell no man: but the more he charged them, so much the more a great deal they published it;

37 And were beyond measure astonished, saying, He hath done all things well: he maketh both the deaf to hear, and the dumb to speak.

May 4

Memory Selection
Mark 7:37

Background Scripture
Mark 7:24-37

Devotional Reading
Luke 7:1-10

351

This lesson focuses on a rare contact between Jesus and a Gentile woman, and another event showing His power to heal. The first incident provides an interesting commentary on Jesus' promise, "Blessed are the meek." It shows that we misunderstand "meekness" when we interpret it to mean always being passive and not speaking up for the truth.

The Canaanite woman is an example of "holy boldness." She clamors for Jesus to heal her daughter, who was demonized. As a wo-man, it was not customary for her to speak to a man. As a Gentile, it was improper for her to speak to a Jew. Yet, just as in the case of Jesus with the whip, the woman dared to defy "proper" expectations in behalf of the right thing to do. Challenge the members of your group to develop a way to determine when bold faith should take priority over cultural expectations.

Ask your group to recall instances of "holy boldness"—such as: Moses, formerly fearful he could not speak well, confronting Pharaoh with the daring challenge to "Let my people go" (Exod. 7:16) . . . Jesus, driving the moneychangers from the Temple (Mark 11:15-17) . . . Peter and John, told by Roman authorities not to preach, replying, "We ought to obey God, rather than men" (Acts 5:29) . . . Martin Luther, standing accused of heresy before a religious court, but saying, "Here I stand. I can do no other, so help me God" . . . The second-century bishop Polycarp, knowing he would be thrown to the lions for refusing to deny his faith, saying, "Eighty and six years have I served Him, and He has never forsaken me. How can I deny my Lord and my King?"

Teaching Outline	Daily Bible Readings

I. Pushy Woman!—24-30
  A. Interrupted vacation, 24-26
  B. Arguing with Jesus, 27-28
  C. A young girl healed, 29-30
II. Power over Silence—31-35
  A. Speech impediment, 31-32
  B. Healing, hearing, speaking, 33-35
III. Publishing a Secret—36-37
	Mon. Seeking Out Jesus
	Mark 7:24-30
	Tue. Acclaim for a Miracle
	Mark 7:31-37
	Wed. 'Do You Not Understand?'
	Mark 8:11-21
	Thu. A Centurion's Faith
	Luke 7:1-10
	Fri. Boldness of Peter and John
	Acts 4:5-14
	Sat. 'We Can't Be Silent!'
	Acts 4:15-22
	Sun. Prayer for Boldness
	Acts 4:23-31

Verse by Verse

I. Pushy Woman!—24-30
A. Interrupted vacation, 24-26

24 And from thence he arose, and went into the borders of Tyre and Sidon, and entered into an house, and would have no man know it: but he could not be hid.

25 For a certain woman, whose young daughter had an unclean spirit, heard of him, and came and fell at his feet:

26 The woman was a Greek, a Syrophenician by nation; and she besought him that he would cast forth the devil out of her daughter.

Tyre and Sidon were coastal cities to the northwest of Galilee, where Jesus has been ministering. His work has become exhausting, and He finds it necessary to go away into an area where He would not be so well known. While the Godhood in Jesus was all-powerful, in His manhood He needed a vacation!

Jesus' fame has preceded Him even in this mostly Gentile area. The term "Syrophenician" combines "Syria" with "Phoenicia," an empire that extended west as far as Carthage, in northwest Africa. It is important to note her designation as a "Greek" or Gentile, since Jesus' disciples will view this as a cultural barrier. The woman comes in a cause so urgent that she breaks two taboos. As a

woman it was not appropriate for her to speak directly to a man in public, and as a Gentile she shocked bystanders by speaking to a Jew. She even "falls at his feet," and, Matthew adds, worships Jesus (Matt. 15:25).

The demon in the woman's daughter is called an "unclean spirit," reminding us of how closely religious and physical purity were related among the Jews. As noted in previous lessons, being "demonized" was something different to merely being ill, and is still said by many to be witnessed especially in areas where the power of the gospel has not been proclaimed. Obviously the woman had heard of Jesus' previous victories over demons.

B. Arguing with Jesus, 27-28

27 But Jesus said unto her, Let the children first be filled: for it is not meet to take the children's bread, and to cast it unto the dogs.

28 And she answered and said unto him, Yes, Lord: yet the dogs under the table eat of the children's crumbs.

"The children" indicates God's chosen people, the Jews. Jesus' first response to the woman indicates the priority of the Jews in God's plan of salvation. Since the Messiah was to come through the Jews, Jesus was sent first to "the lost sheep of the house of Israel" (Matt. 15:24). Even after Jesus' death and resurrection, the apostle Paul was still commissioned to "go the Jew first," and only then to the Gentiles (Rom. 1:16, etc.).

However, something else is at work in this scene. Referring to Gentiles as "dogs" was certainly not required by the need to preach the gospel first to the Jews, and it is unthinkable that Jesus, who came for the salvation of all mankind, would use the term unkindly. Yet He knew that this was precisely the attitude of His disciples, who overheard this exchange; in fact, His retort may have been a common proverb among the Jews. It is therefore likely that Jesus' harsh language is for His disciples' benefit. He is setting them up with "reverse psychology" to discover the truth that this Gentile woman is as fit a subject of the Kingdom as anyone.

The woman is so bold in faith that she refuses to be put off by Jesus' apparently harsh response. She dares to argue with the Son of God! Yet she accepts the racial epithet Jesus has used, submitting for the sake of argument to her position as a "dog" but using her culturally accepted "place" to argue for "the leftovers" from the Messianic banquet.

C. A young girl healed, 29-30

29 And he said unto her, For this saying go thy way; the devil is gone out of thy daughter.

30 And when she was come to her house, she found the devil gone out, and her daughter laid upon the bed.

Again, it is unlikely that the Son of God simply allowed Himself to be outwitted by this quick-thinking Gen-

tile. He consents to do as she requested not as a reward for her sharp tongue, but because it is time to let His disciples in on the secret: the Messiah's gifts are for all, not just for Jews.

Perhaps because He was weary, or because He did not want to push the acceptance of this Gentile woman too far for the disciples, Jesus accomplishes this exorcism by "long distance." This reminds us of the varieties of circumstance in which He worked His mighty signs and wonders. Present or absent, with victims having faith and not having faith, using "visual aids" as in the healing of the deaf man, below, or not, Jesus can perform both the spiritual and physical wonders that had been predicted of the Messiah.

II. Power over Silence—31-35
A. Speech impediment, 31-32

31 And again, departing from the coasts of Tyre and Sidon, he came unto the sea of Galilee, through the midst of the coasts of Decapolis.

32 And they bring unto him one that was deaf, and had an impediment in his speech; and they beseech him to put his hand upon him.

His time away having come to an end, Jesus and His disciples return to His home country. The "Decapolis," or 10-city area, consisted of cities mostly to the east and north of the Sea of Galilee, and included Gadara, where Jesus cast out the Legions of demons from the man living in a cemetery (Mark 5; see Lesson 3 of this quarter). In the first century B.C. these cities had formed an alliance that won enough respect from the invading Romans that they were allowed to have their own currency and to develop a league for trading purposes. Cities that were members of this alliance and are still thriving are Damascus, in Syria, and Amman, the capital of Jordan.

It is common for deaf people also to have speech difficulties since learning to speak depends so heavily on hearing others speak. We are not told whether this was the extent of the man's "impediment," of whether he had a vocal ailment in addition to his hearing problem. In Matthew 9, a man who could not speak is also said to have been demonized, but in this case only the physical ailment is mentioned.

B. Healing, hearing, speaking, 33-35

33 And he took him aside from the multitude, and put his fingers into his ears, and he spit, and touched his tongue;

34 And looking up to heaven, he sighed, and saith unto him, Ephphatha, that is, Be opened.

35 And straightway his ears were opened, and the string of his tongue was loosed, and he spake plain.

Modern readers search in vain for reasons for the details of this healing account. Why does Jesus take the man aside? What called for the unusual acts of placing His fingers in the man's ears, and touching his tongue with spittle-coated fingers? What is the significance of the sigh, in verse 34, and of Mark's preserving, but translating, the Aramaic command Jesus used, and to whom was it addressed—God or Satan? The incident simply stands on its own, and we should use caution in trying to make profound guesses about the outward signs Jesus uses. After all, He has just exorcised a demon in a young girl even without being present, and He could no doubt have healed this man in this way as well. Physically touching the man's ears and tongue was probably more for his own benefit, to reinforce the focus of Jesus' act, than for any supernatural reasons.

III. Publishing a Secret—36-37

36 And he charged them that they should tell no man: but the more he charged them, so much the more a great deal they published it;

37 And were beyond measure astonished, saying, He hath done all things well: he maketh both the deaf to hear, and the dumb to speak.

Similar charges for those who witnessed Jesus' miracles not to publish them abroad are scattered throughout the Gospels. Often described as the "Messianic Secret," these commands are usually marked by the way they are ignored, and the "secret" scattered far and wide. Why does Jesus so often tell people not to tell about His mighty acts, when later He will charge His disciples to "go into all the world" to tell about them?

The most likely answer is that Jesus is attempting to protect His own time-table for accomplishing his mission. Because His fellow-Jews associated the coming of the Messiah with the arrival of the Kingdom on earth, Jesus knew that His ministry would be seen as a threat to the ruling Roman authorities. He does not want His work cut short by opponents who are threatened by His kingship.

Evangelistic Emphasis

"I have my mind made up." How many times have you expressed that sentiment? Before the evidence was presented you had already decided on the outcome, or the direction you were heading. A "made up mind" is a lonely thing. Think about it. When a bed is made up, no one is in the bed. I have wondered about people who already have their minds made up. I wonder if anyone is "at home" mentally.

We live in a world that is ever changing. The very notion of change is changing. The only way to keep up is to keep an "open mind" about so many of the new issues presented by progress. What are we to believe, and how are we to act in the face of all the change in our world?

The insanity of the Church is to believe that we can keep doing what we have always done and expect different results from those we have experienced. That is why so many are amazed that what worked in the last century does not work today. We must change our mind about what being faithful is all about. Faithfulness must be defined in terms of discipleship and stewardship, not in terms of how much we adopt the "traditions of our fathers."

This lesson talks about change, about Jesus changing His mind about something. Are you ready to change?

ഔരു

Memory Selection

Jesus hath done all things well: he maketh both the deaf to hear, and the dumb to speak.—*Mark 7:37*

Jesus does everything well. We need to remember that. Jesus does *everything* well. There is no indication in this verse that you and I, as disciples, are required to be perfect. Perfection is left to divinity. The fact that Jesus does everything well leaves us free to be human. This is a very positive trait. Perfection is a nice goal to have, but none of us will achieve perfection in this lifetime. We are imperfect beings.

The sooner we are able to admit our imperfections and confess our sins, the sooner we will discover the joys of being human. No longer will we have to strive to put on the perfect tea, have the perfect marriage, or raise perfect children. We can trust that in Jesus, we are whole and complete. We can leave being perfect to Martha Stewart and other people we love to hate, because they seem to be perfect when we know they are not.

Because Jesus does everything well, we can quit trying to be perfect and be human. Let God love you, flaws and all.

Weekday Problems

Oh boy! Don't you get tired of all the trouble we cause in this section? I mean really—some of the things we have these poor people doing, you would think we were all trying to audition to write for the most popular soap operas. "As the Weekday Problem Grows" would be a good title of our soap opera. Of course as a Christian you don't watch anything like that. But even if you don't, surely the people in this section could benefit from an appearance on Oprah, or maybe they need to call Dr. Laura.

Christians have "weekday problems" because only Jesus was perfect. It could be said of Jesus that He did "everything well," but that can't be said of us! I wonder how many of us are so determined to do things perfectly that we won't even try something, because it would not end up being perfect?

Jesus never told us to live a life free of mistakes. When He did say "Be perfect" (Matt. 5:48), the word He used carried with it the idea of *wholeness*, not a life free of mistakes.

The guilt we feel because we are not perfect is a barrier to spiritual growth. We are "sinners saved by grace." Worse than guilt are the expectations of perfection we place on others while not being able to achieve it ourselves.

In other words, all Christians have "weekday problems."

More Terrible Typos

For sale: A full-blooded cow, giving three gallons of milk, two tons of hay, a lot of chickens, and a cook stove.

The general will remain unequaled in history for his accomplishments on the bottlefield.

Help wanted: Adult or mature teenager to baby-sit. One dollar an hour, plus fridge benefits.

The church had a going away part for Pastor Hanson. The congregation was anxious to give him a little momentum.

Marriage announcement: A 25-year friendship ended at the altar.

Headline: Dead policeman on force 17 years.

Testing new explosives, the army recently dropped four-ton blondes on the test site.

For sale: Two plots in lively Fairmount Cemetery.

At asterisks in church bulletin: Ushers will swat latecomers at these points.

Clarkesville, Tenn., held a mule parade yesterday, headed by the governor.

357

This Lesson in Your Life

The story is told of a vacuum cleaner salesman whose technique was to get his foot in the door of a prospective home and throw a bag of manure on the entrance carpet before the resident had a chance to object. One day the salesman approached a home, knocked on the door, and as the elderly owner of the home answered the door, the usual bag of manure was soon on the carpet. Before the woman could object, the salesman explained, "Lady, this vacuum is so powerful, and I have so much confidence in its ability, that I believe this vacuum will pick up every speck of this manure or I will personally get on my hands and knees and pick up every speck by hand."

To which the lady replied, "Well, come right on in, young man. We don't have any electricity."

The only way to sell a vacuum cleaner is turn it on and use it. There is only one way to evangelize (that means making disciples for Jesus Christ), and that is to turn on your faith and use it.

Jesus used a variety of methods—sometimes strange, sometimes plain, and sometimes controversial—to bring wholeness and wellness into people's lives. Jesus tailored His healing techniques to the needs of the person, but there was one unchangeable and unshakable foundation around which everything else revolved. He was who He said He was. He turned over His life to God's Spirit working through Him.

Unless we ourselves are "turned on" to the transforming power of the Spirit, we can't be good instruments for redemption and reconciliation. The essence of evangelism is a life that is "turned on" to the power of the gospel, a life that is so "turned over" to the Word that the Word becomes flesh in us. Anything less than this becomes phony.

The two healing stories in this lesson have one thing in common: They easily rub readers the wrong way. Each of the stories has some aspect about it that we find disturbing to our sense of correctness. Accustomed to reading the gospel and being impressed by the divine power healings reveal, the stories of the Syrophoenician woman and the Decapolis deaf-mute don't quite measure up. One has to beg, the other has to endure behavior from Jesus that was less than proper decorum might tolerate.

Jesus healed both persons, but He did the healing on His terms. Each miracle reveals that God is God and can't be manipulated by our formulas or our theological properness. Jesus does all things well. He even does a good job of being Messiah.

Are you letting Jesus do His job, even as you are doing yours?

1. **Where was Jesus traveling as this lesson begins?**
   Jesus was traveling to the region of Tyre and Sidon.

2. **Mark gave a hint as to why Jesus was traveling in the area of Tyre and Sidon. What might have been the reason?**
   Jesus was trying to get away from the crowds and most likely was seeking some rest and private prayer time.

3. **What happened as Jesus came to the region of Tyre and Sidon?**
   A mother who had a demonized daughter came to ask His help.

4. **What details about this woman's heritage were given in the reading?**
   The lady was a Greek, a Syrophoenician by birth. This meant she was a Gentile.

5. **What request did this mother make of Jesus?**
   She begged Jesus to cast the demon out of her daughter.

6. **What was Jesus' first response to the mother's request?**
   Jesus said, "Let the children first be fed, for it is not right to take the children's bread and give it to the dogs."

7. **What do you think Jesus was telling this woman by His response to her?**
   He was saying that His ministry to the Jews must come first. He may also have been using "reverse psychology" to show His followers that He would accept Gentiles.

8. **Why did Jesus change His mind about healing this woman's daughter?**
   He saw her wit and her faith in response to His remarks, and he wanted His followers to see His acceptance of her.

9. **What did the deaf and dumb man have in common with this woman?**
   He was also a Gentile, because he lived in the Decapolis, a Gentile region.

10. **How did Jesus bring healing to the deaf and dumb man?**
    Jesus put His fingers into his ears, and spat and touched his tongue.

Once I noticed a boy who had some dried-up food on his face. (Not since birth, just since lunch, I imagine.) His mother took out a tissue, spat on it, and rubbed it into the boy's face. I'm not making this up. This goes on, in communities around our country, on a daily basis. It's enough to break your heart. You know that if babies could talk, that would be the first thing they'd bring up. "Hey, don't do that. It's revolting. Would you like it if someone did that to you? Okay, then."

It is disgusting, but it sure does work, doesn't it? There's something in mother's saliva that cleans like nobody's business. Once women give birth, their enzymes seem to change, and saliva becomes Ajax. It'll clean anything: a baby's face, a countertop, a Buick—you get enough mothers, you could do a whole car in 30 or 40 minutes.

If we are honest about the message in this lesson we find interesting emotions. In the first story we are offended. In the second we are repulsed.

But the results are what ultimately matter. The crowds who witnessed this cure were moved to wonder and overcome with zeal. Even when Jesus told them to keep quiet, they were unable to contain their exuberance and eagerly proclaimed the news of this miracle all about. The crowd's ultimate conclusion is one that both recognizes Jesus' power and articulates their faith. Jesus *"has done everything well"* (vs. 37). Jesus not only brings about healing, but knows the best way to accomplish the needed results for each individual who approaches Him.

That's the key. God meets us where we are as we are. His love reaches down to us. In any circumstance in which we need Him to find us. His call is for us to do whatever it takes to "make disciples for Him." The crowd saw His actions, including the results of His touching Gentile people, even though He was a Jewish rabbi. I think we have become overly concerned about the process. God is results-oriented! If winning His world back would take coming to earth as a human, living among humanity, and dying on a cross, God would do it.

Rosanne Bos, who teaches high-school Spanish in Glendive, Montana, was teaching her students to conjugate verbs in the first person—I sing, I read, I speak, I run. After going through several examples, she wanted the students to give it a try.

"Okay, now," she said, "how would you say, 'I need money'" A young man immediately yelled out, "Love ya, Mom!" When everyone laughed, he said, "Well, it works for me."

Whatever works to lead people to Jesus, do it.

Confession of Faith and Affirmation

Mark 8:27-35; 9:2-7

And Jesus went out, and his disciples, into the towns of Caesarea Philippi: and by the way he asked his disciples, saying unto them, Whom do men say that I am?

28 And they answered, John the Baptist: but some say, Elias; and others, One of the prophets.

29 And he saith unto them, But whom say ye that I am? And Peter answereth and saith unto him, Thou art the Christ.

30 And he charged them that they should tell no man of him.

31 And he began to teach them, that the Son of man must suffer many things, and be rejected of the elders, and of the chief priests, and scribes, and be killed, and after three days rise again.

32 And he spake that saying openly. And Peter took him, and began to rebuke him.

33 But when he had turned about and looked on his disciples, he rebuked Peter, saying, Get thee behind me, Satan: for thou savourest not the things that be of God, but the things that be of men.

34 And when he had called the people unto him with his disciples also, he said unto them, Whosoever will come after me, let him deny himself, and take up his cross, and follow me.

35 For whosoever will save his life shall lose it; but whosoever shall lose his life for my sake and the gospel's, the same shall save it.

9:2 And after six days Jesus taketh with him Peter, and James, and John, and leadeth them up into an high mountain apart by themselves: and he was transfigured before them.

3 And his raiment became shining, exceeding white as snow; so as no fuller on earth can white them.

4 And there appeared unto them Elias with Moses: and they were talking with Jesus.

5 And Peter answered and said to Jesus, Master, it is good for us to be here: and let us make three tabernacles; one for thee, and one for Moses, and one for Elias.

6 For he wist not what to say; for they were sore afraid.

7 And there was a cloud that overshadowed them: and a voice came out of the cloud, saying, This is my beloved Son: hear him.

May 11

Memory Selection
Mark 8:29

Background Scripture
Mark 8:27–9:8

Devotional Reading
Philippians 2:5-11

361

When Jesus first began His ministry, He called the 12 in terms that were part command, part invitation: *Follow me*. Gradually, as opposition stiffened, the disciples began to experience some of the cost of responding to those seemingly simple words. In the first part of this lesson, Jesus announces His destiny on a cross in Jerusalem, and the disciples' understanding of what it means to follow Him is taken to a new level.

In the second part of the lesson, the famous event of the Transfiguration exposes yet another level of "followership." There the disciples learn that regardless of the importance of other religious leaders, following Jesus requires that our ultimate allegiance be only to Him. Events change; but for the disciples, and for us, the focus is still *Follow me*.

ഔ൫

This session on the importance of stalwart faith in God can be introduced by discussing the price some have paid for their faith.

Dietrich Bonhoeffer was jailed in Hitler's Germany speaking out against Nazi atrocities, and paid for it with his life. Any of the "heroes of faith" listed in Hebrews 11 can be used of examples of "the cost of discipleship, a phrase associated with Bonhoeffer. The biblical Job said, "Though he slay me, yet will I trust in him" (Job 13:15). Group members may cite cases from their own experience, from modern missionaries to students who are teased for their faith, to show the ongoing power of Jesus to bring out the quiet bravery and stick-to-itiveness in His followers.

Teaching Outline	Daily Bible Readings

I. The Great Confession—8:27-31
  A. Views of Jesus, 27-28
  B. The dangerous truth, 29-30
II. The Enemy Within—31-33
III. The Cost of Discipleship—34-35
IV. The Mount of Transfiguration—9:2-7
  A. The inner circle, 2
  B. Sharing the spotlight, 3-4
C. The exclusive challenge, 5-7
	Mon. 'Who Do You Say I Am?"
	Mark 8:27-33
	Tue. 'Take Up Your Cross'
	Mark 8:34–9:1
	Wed. 'This Is My Son'
	Mark 9:2-8
	Thu. 'You Have the Words of Life'
	John 6:60-69
	Fri. Zacchaeus Sees Jesus
	Luke 19:1-10
	Sat. Every Tongue Shall Confess
	Philippians 2:5-11
	Sun. Confessing His Lordship
	Romans 10:5-13

Verse by Verse

I. The Great Confession—8:27-31
A. Views of Jesus, 27-28

27 And Jesus went out, and his disciples, into the towns of Caesarea Philippi: and by the way he asked his disciples, saying unto them, Whom do men say that I am?

28 And they answered, John the Baptist: but some say, Elias; and others, One of the prophets.

The time has come for Jesus to set the stage for the culmination of His ministry: the Cross that awaited Him in Jerusalem. It is important therefore for Him to help His disciples clarify their view of Him, and to contrast the truth of His identity with mistaken notions. Jesus asks first who the general populace thinks He is. Some, especially if they have been close to the court of King Herod (see 6:14), think He is John the Baptist returned from the dead. Others think He is the prophet Elijah, whose return was associated with the Messianic Age (Mal. 3:1, 4:5-6). Note that both "wrong" answers are partially right, since John was a figurative Elijah preparing the way of the Lord (Matt. 17:12-13).

B. The dangerous truth, 29-30

29 And he saith unto them, But whom say ye that I am? And Peter answereth and saith unto him, Thou art the Christ.

30 And he charged them that they should tell no man of him.

Typically, it is Peter who is first to speak—and first to err, as we shall see. Here, however, he is on-target, and makes what has been called "the great confession" that Jesus is the Messiah (Gr. *christos*). This confession would become basic to becoming a Christian, "for with the mouth confession is made unto salvation" (Rom. 10:10).

In Matthew's account of this scene, Jesus heartily commends Peter for this confession, calls him "Peter the Rock," and promises to give him the keys of the kingdom of heaven (Matt. 16:16-18). Some scholars think this is omitted from Mark's account because his Gospel was based on the preaching of Peter himself, and the apostle was too modest to include this high praise.

The "Messianic secret" examined in Lesson 9 appears again in verse 30. Jesus probably knew that if His true identity is scattered abroad it would be so politically destabilizing that Rome would arrest Him before He can accomplish the full teaching ministry He had planned.

II. The Enemy Within—31-33

31 And he began to teach them, that the Son of man must suffer many things, and be rejected of the elders, and of the chief priests, and

scribes, and be killed, and after three days rise again.

32 And he spake that saying openly. And Peter took him, and began to rebuke him.

33 But when he had turned about and looked on his disciples, he rebuked Peter, saying, Get thee behind me, Satan: for thou savourest not the things that be of God, but the things that be of men.

Some scholars have suggested that any astute observer of the political and religious climate in Judea could have concluded that anyone who taught that "We ought to obey God rather than men" (Acts 5:29) would be hounded and eventually executed. However, the prediction of a resurrection after three days could hardly be assigned to such an observer. Jesus' statement is therefore an indication that the foreknowledge of His future was divinely inspired.

Placing this announcement of Jesus' suffering and death immediately after the confession that He is the Christ is of extreme importance. This kind of future was not at all what Peter had in mind. The Messiah he envisioned when he confessed his faith was a divine Ruler who would rout the hated Romans and set up the Kingdom of God on earth. This required the Christ to be accepted, not rejected, and for Him to be triumphant over His enemies instead of being killed. Obviously these "blinders" prevented Peter from understanding the significance of Christ's promise that He would also rise again.

Peter's mistake may not seem so important to us. After all, many people view Jesus as a great teacher, but deny His resurrection and the saving significance of His death. Why, then, does Jesus object so strongly to Peter's rebuke? Because the view that Messiah could escape dying for our sins is "of men." It cannot be squared with the need for a divine sacrifice for sin, nor even with the abundant prophecies of the Old Testament, especially Isaiah's vision of the Messiah as a Suffering Servant.

Jesus is therefore so adamant on the role His death will play in God's scheme of redemption that He attributes Peter's rejection of this role as satanically inspired.

III. The Cost of Discipleship—34-35

34 And when he had called the people unto him with his disciples also, he said unto them, Whosoever will come after me, let him deny himself, and take up his cross, and follow me.

35 For whosoever will save his life shall lose it; but whosoever shall lose his life for my sake and the gospel's, the same shall save it.

Now Jesus clinches the necessity of His coming death by extending the picture of the Cross even to His followers. If Peter, or anyone else, cannot accept that Christ's redemptive work requires a Cross that takes His life, he certainly will not accept a personal cross as a way to live. It should be noted that this taking up our cross does not mean bearing a burden we are stuck with (as "My bad back is a cross I have to bear"), but the daily crucifixion of subjecting our will to that of the Lord's.

Paradoxically, as verse 35 explains, it is this kind of cross that turns out to be the pathway to life, just as it was for Jesus in His resurrection. Putting up with a bad back or other burden contains no such paradox. It is saying No to our own unregenerate will, putting to death the desires of the flesh, that releases the Spirit to live a "resurrected" life. Someone has written that a coward dies a thousand deaths, dreading anew each dangerous encounter, while a brave man dies only once. Similarly, those who accept the death of self are delivered of that burden and set free to live for Christ.

IV. The Mount of Transfiguration —9:2-7

A. The inner circle, 2

2 And after six days Jesus taketh with him Peter, and James, and John, and leadeth them up into an high mountain apart by themselves: and he was transfigured before them.

The mood of our text changes from the serious business of crucifixion to the shining moment of the Transfiguration—although the theme of "Follow me!" dominates this scene as well. What a privilege it would have been to be among Jesus' inner circle, as were Peter, James, and John! Their inclusion, however, was probably not just a matter of friendship, but had to do with the requirement in the Law that events must be attested by two or three witnesses (Deut. 17:6; 19:15).

B. Sharing the spotlight, 3-4

3 And his raiment became shining, exceeding white as snow; so as no fuller on earth can white them.

4 And there appeared unto them Elias with Moses: and they were talking with Jesus.

The brilliance of Christ's clothing is in contrast to the ordinary appearance of Elijah and Moses (if a vision of these long-dead leaders can be considered ordinary!). Jesus' Messiahship was based on the claim that He fulfilled "the law and the prophets," the two main divisions of the Jewish Bible. The appearance of Moses, the giver of the Law, and Elijah, one of the greatest of the prophets, indicates their importance, while Christ's shining garment and the voice from heaven (below) emphasize their subordinance to Him.

C. The exclusive challenge, 5-7

5 And Peter answered and said to Jesus, Master, it is good for us to be here: and let us make three tabernacles; one for thee, and one for Moses, and one for Elias.

6 For he wist not what to say; for they were sore afraid.

7 And there was a cloud that overshadowed them: and a voice came out of the cloud, saying, This is my beloved Son: hear him.

Although it was common for Peter to speak and act brashly, it is unusual for someone like Mark to add that he said some things simply because he could think of nothing else to say! In this case His suggestion that three "tabernacles" or booths be built as shrines to honor each of the three personages turns out to be not only thoughtless, but wrong. The voice from heaven affirms that as important as Moses and Elijah were, if Jesus is truly the Messiah, He alone is to be venerated as our ultimate authority.

Evangelistic Emphasis

The picture we have of Simon Peter may seem like a caricature. He is so much like "a bull elephant in a china shop" that we don't take him seriously as a person. Simon Peter was as real and as human as a disciple has ever been. His mistakes are legendary.

He wanted to walk on water, but got lead feet only a few steps from the boat. He wanted to build separate monuments for Moses, Jesus, and Elijah on the mountain of Transfiguration. He tried to correct Jesus' theology of the suffering servant at Caesarea Philippi. He fell asleep while Jesus prayed in Gethsemane. He cut off the servant of the High Priest's ear. He denied knowing Jesus three times. He ran away when the shadow of the Cross loomed large over our Lord's last hours. Rather than waiting for instruction from the Lord after the resurrection, Peter said, "I'm going fishing."

Yet, even with this list, Peter was "the rock." He was the one around which the early church was built. For all of his buffoonery, Peter turned out to be a man who was used mightily by the Lord. More like a "bulldog" than a "bull elephant," Peter's faith and witness grew though sheer tenacity. Since Jesus had not quit on him, Peter would not quit on himself.

If Christ has room in His church for Simon Peter, He certainly has room in His kingdom for you.

෨෬

And he saith unto them, But whom say ye that I am? And Peter answereth and saith unto him, Thou art the Christ.—*Mark 8:29*

The same traits that could make Peter look like a buffoon also made him a bold saint. Peter was willing to buck the tide of public opinion and tell Jesus what he (Peter) really thought. Jesus was the long-awaited Messiah, according to Simon Peter.

"Who do people say that I am?" That is a question that Jesus asks throughout the pages of history, and still today. "Who do you say that I am?" That is a question that each of us must answer for himself. On the answer hinges our eternal destiny.

The world is giving some interesting answers about Jesus. Most of those answers are very flattering to Him and His teachings. They, however, ignore His claim to the human soul. Any picture of Jesus that demands less than complete obedience and surrender from us is inadequate. Jesus will not be a mental or scholastic exercise. He desires to become a living reality for all of us.

Jesus Christ must be "the Son of the Living God." It doesn't matter what others say about Him. This is what He claimed for himself.

Weekday Problems

Who do you believe Jesus is? Your eternal salvation rests on your answer. Even your "weekday problems" will be solved or not, depending on who you believe Jesus is. If you believe that He is a religious teacher of the tradition of other great religious teachers, you will look to Him only for advice or wisdom.

If you believe that Jesus was a good man, you will face your problems with that in mind. You might even try to live by the Golden Rule, because Jesus did. I would hope you remember that the Jewish authorities had this good man crucified. Besides, trying to determine how a good person would handle a situation doesn't solve all of your problems.

You might think that Jesus was crazy. Some people believe that He was off of His rocker. I can't imagine how you could face any problem with a concept of Jesus that held He was crazy.

Or, like John Cole in a previous Weekday Problem, you might believe that Jesus is Lord. With Jesus as Lord, you don't have to figure out the solution to all your problems. You simply have to trust that Jesus has a solution for you.

*Who do you believe Jesus is? How has that impacted your "weekday problems"?

Sidelights on Sermons

Preaching what people really need to hear, but may not like, can be like babies: easy to conceive but hard to deliver.

Little Willie grew weary of the long sermon. Finally he turned and whispered to his mom: "If we give him the money now, will he let us go?"

Seminary student: I've heard that a good beginning and a good ending makes a good sermon. Is that true?

Professor: If they're close enough together.

Jill: I thought that sermon was divine. It reminded me of the peace that passes all understanding.

Jack: I thought it was divine, too. I thought it would endure forever.

Many people think that a good sermon is one that goes over their head—and hits a neighbor.

This Lesson in Your Life

Simon Peter is the hero of every preacher! Laypersons seem to identify with Peter as well. He had many positive traits. Peter was bold. One day, as Jesus walked by, He called Peter and Andrew from the fishing boats and asked them to give up their careers and follow Him on the adventure of faith. From Matthew's telling of the story, it appears that Peter went with Jesus without question.

Peter's bold and adventurous spirit was partially responsible for his walking on the water. Sometimes we forget that Peter actually *did* walk on the water, for a moment. For whatever reason he left that boat, we need to be reminded that he did.

Peter was willing to die for Jesus. We see that in his actions in Gethsemane. He was willing to pick a fight even though there were Roman guards all around him.

We know from the book of Acts that Peter was willing to reach out to the Gentiles. We know that he did become great in the eyes of the early Church.

Peter got the answer to Jesus' question in the account of his confession at Caesarea Philippi. Rather than giving back the popular answers to who Jesus was. Peter talked only about what he thought! He thought right, too.

For being a simple fisherman, Peter was a complex and inconsitent man. One minute he would die for the Lord, the next he was running from a fight. One minute he was walking on water, the next he was floundering in the pitching seas. In this, Peter is an example of what God can do with ordinary, inconsistent people like us.

Preachers draw inspiration from Peter because sometimes we are inconsistent, too. We want to minister to all the sheep, but sometimes we miss one or two. We want to preach great sermons, but sometimes we fail to get the thing off the launching pad. On and on we could go about preachers.

Laymen are also inconsistent. Some will reach great spiritual heights. They will have vision and commitment. Then a couple of years later they have been added to an "inactive roll."

Peter is an example of God's patience with our inconsistency. He demands our total obedience, He wants us to mold ourselves perfectly to His will; but He understands that sometimes we fail to do either. We know about Peter's short-comings, and about our own. We also know that Jesus willingly forgave Peter and reissued His call on his life. Can we believe Jeus also forgives us and calls us despite our inconsitencies?

1. How was Peter called into the service of the Lord, according to the Gospels?

Jesus was walking along the Sea of Galilee and called to the brothers Simon Peter and Andrew. They left their fishing duties and followed Him.

2. What other two persons were called at about the same time?

James and John, the sons of Zebedee, were also called from their fishing boats to follow Jesus.

3. In your opinion, who were the younger—the brothers James and John, or Simon and Andrew?

One might guess James and John, since their father Zebedee was still involved with their fishing endeavors.

4. What were the popular opinions concerning who Jesus was?

Some thought Jesus was John the Baptist, Elijah, Jeremiah, or another prophet.

5. What confession did Simon Peter make as an answer to Jesus' inquiry?

Peter confessed that Jesus was the Messiah, the Son of the Living God.

6. What did Jesus do immediately after Peter's confession?

Jesus told the disciples to tell no one about His true identity.

7. What did Jesus begin to teach the disciples after He identified Himself as the Messiah?

He told the disciples that He must suffer many things, be rejected, and killed.

8. What lesson did Jesus then give the disciples about living in the Kingdom of God?

Jesus said that to follow Him involved taking up His cross.

9. What did Jesus say about those persons who might be ashamed of Him?

Jesus said that whoever is ashamed of Him, He would be ashamed of when the Son of Man comes in glory.

10. After Peter's confession, what major event happened next?

Jesus took Peter, James, and John up on a high mountain where He was transfigured before them.

There is a very old pulpit story that tells of a customer who went into a jewelry store to buy a cross necklace. The clerk asked, "Do you want to see a plain one, or do you want to look at the one with a little man on it?"

We want the plain one. We find it difficult to hear the word of the loaded cross, which says that any religious human being sees suffering differently from others. We are hard of hearing when Christ's voice calls us to stay in our suffering, even as we become successful and powerful; and to bear a cross of our own, even when we can do more and go farther with a plain one.

Even in the ministry, "professionalism" has led many to the point where the central motivating symbol of ministry is the ladder, rather than the cross. A prospective student who had decided to enter the ministry after a successful, six-figure-income career in corporate America, illustrates the lethal power resident in the "ladder" paradigm. "Once I reached the top of the ladder and looked around," he reflected, "I realized that all the struggle, all the costs to my family and friendships, all the sacrifices I had made to reach the pinnacle were not worth what I found there. Suddenly it hit me: I had propped my ladder up against the wrong building." Elmer Gantry's pilgrimage from Baptist to Methodist because he wanted to become a bishop immediately comes to mind. Gantry moved up the ladder until the possibility of becoming bishop was in sight. But by that time, he saw higher rungs than those on his own career ladder.

The only ladder the Bible knows anything about is Jacob's ladder. Jacob's ladder was pitched against the spiritual, not the material. Ladders should stand in the Garden of Gethsemane and the temple courtyard, not Madison Square Garden and Wall Street. Actually, Jacob had no ladder. He only had a vision and a mission. And he did not climb the ladder anyway. Angels did. When the theme song of a disciple becomes "We are climbing Jacob's ladder," Jesus' followers become better at climbing ladders than at lifting crosses.

San Francisco Chronicle columnist Herb Caen wrote in 1981, "The trouble with born-again Christians is that they are an even bigger pain the second time around." Could Caen have been right?

Conversion, without *immersion* in the life of Jesus Christ, is *perversion* of the gospel. St. Augustine talked about "the costly grace" of God. Discipleship, servanthood, costs us everything. Everything must go. Genesis 2:25 conveys this powerfully in the image of nakedness: "And the man and his wife were both naked, and were not ashamed."

We stand before God naked, with none of the trappings of success. He doesn't see the ladders we have climbed. He sees only the cross to which we cling.

Lesson 12

Honest Faith

Mark 9:14-29

And when he came to his disciples, he saw a great multitude about them, and the scribes questioning with them.

15 And straightway all the people, when they beheld him, were greatly amazed, and running to him saluted him.

16 And he asked the scribes, What question ye with them?

17 And one of the multitude answered and said, Master, I have brought unto thee my son, which hath a dumb spirit;

18 And wheresoever he taketh him, he teareth him: and he foameth, and gnasheth with his teeth, and pineth away: and I spake to thy disciples that they should cast him out; and they could not.

19 He answereth him, and saith, O faithless generation, how long shall I be with you? how long shall I suffer you? bring him unto me.

20 And they brought him unto him: and when he saw him, straightway the spirit tare him; and he fell on the ground, and wallowed foaming.

21 And he asked his father, How long is it ago since this came unto him? And he said, Of a child.

22 And ofttimes it hath cast him into the fire, and into the waters, to destroy him: but if thou canst do any thing, have compassion on us, and help us.

23 Jesus said unto him, If thou canst believe, all things are possible to him that believeth.

24 And straightway the father of the child cried out, and said with tears, Lord, I believe; help thou mine unbelief.

25 When Jesus saw that the people came running together, he rebuked the foul spirit, saying unto him, Thou dumb and deaf spirit, I charge thee, come out of him, and enter no more into him.

26 And the spirit cried, and rent him sore, and came out of him: and he was as one dead; insomuch that many said, He is dead.

27 But Jesus took him by the hand, and lifted him up; and he arose.

28 And when he was come into the house, his disciples asked him privately, Why could not we cast him out?

29 And he said unto them, This kind can come forth by nothing, but by prayer and fasting.

Memory Selection
Mark 9:24

Background Scripture
Mark 9:14-37

Devotional Reading
John 16:25-33

May 18

371

Focusing on "Honest Faith," as this lesson is titled, implies that faith may also be dishonest. Although few believers can imagine themselves actually lying about their faith, it is the better part of honesty to admit that our faith is weaker at some times than others; or that, at life's "hard edges," our faith may be mixed with doubt.

This lesson shares the book of Job's emphasis: It is better to admit a problem we may have with God than to pretend there is no problem. God had some stern words for Job; but He honored Job's honesty over that of his would-be "comforters." In today's text, a father's faith is tested; but Jesus honors the man's honesty even though part of his faith was only a prayer. Doesn't honesty sometimes compel us to say also, "Lord, I believe; help thou mine unbelief"?

One overall purpose of Scripture study is to encourage and increase faith. Another purpose, however, is to encourage values such as honesty. These two aims come together in this lesson. It can therefore be introduced by asking group members to share any questions they may have had about the faith. Predictable responses may be the question of why the innocent suffer. Some group members may wonder about the validity of some of the miracles in the Bible. Others may think that Genesis is in conflict with science. Some may have had questions about whether God heard their prayers.

Point out that this lesson, like the book of Job, shows the value of honest faith; and that this may lead us to admit doubt. Note that a true believer is not a person who never admits doubt, but one who believes in spite of doubts, and has enough faith to turn his doubts over to God.

Teaching Outline	Daily Bible Readings	

I. Stubborn Demon—14-18
  A. Lively discussion, 14-16
  B. Dumb demoniac, 17-18
	Mon.	Resistant Demon
		Mark 9:14-18

	Tue.	'Help My Unbelief' Mark 9:19-27

II. Honest Father—19-24
  A. Jesus' rebuke, 19
  B. Demonic demonstration, 20-22
  C. Faith and doubt, 23-24
	Wed.	By Prayer and Fasting
		Mark 9:28-32

	Thu.	'Do You Now Believe?' John 16:25-33

III. Powerful Savior—25-27
  A. A cleansing word, 25
  B. Violent exit, 26-27
	Fri.	Prayer for Future Believers
		John 17:20-24

	Sat.	One Thankful Leper Luke 17:11-19
IV. Explanatory Postscript—28-29	Sun.	Eternal Life for Believers John 6:43-48

Verse by Verse

I. Stubborn Demon—14-18
A. Lively discussion, 14-16

14 And when he came to his disciples, he saw a great multitude about them, and the scribes questioning with them.

15 And straightway all the people, when they beheld him, were greatly amazed, and running to him saluted him.

16 And he asked the scribes, What question ye with them?

As the developing story shows, this scene involved Jesus' disciples and their usual opponents in a noisy discussion over a case of demonization or demon possession. Although the scribes may have been harassing the disciples for being unable to exorcise the demon (see below), the phrase "questioning with them," may imply that both groups were discussing a difficult case.

Jesus is famous enough as an exorcist to draw the crowd away from the initial discussion as He approaches. Although we might expect Him to ask His own disciples what was going on, Jesus surprises us by putting the question to the scribes. This may be not just for information but to clarify the issue for the crowd, including His own disciples. It is not a time for sectarian argument: a young boy needs relief from his suffering.

B. Dumb demoniac, 17-18

17 And one of the multitude answered and said, Master, I have brought unto thee my son, which hath a dumb spirit;

18 And wheresoever he taketh him, he teareth him: and he foameth, and gnasheth with his teeth, and pineth away: and I spake to thy disciples that they should cast him out; and they could not.

Now the reason for the discussion between Jesus' disciples and the scribes becomes clear. A man has brought his son to the disciples to be cured of a demon. After all, Christ had given them power over demons (6:7). His poor son's condition sounds like epilepsy; but as in previous lessons we should not assume that all illness was considered to be caused by demons. In several instances Jesus heals people without reference to the demonic.

Although the inability of His disciples to exorcise this demon may have been their lack of faith (see below), "this kind" of demon (vs. 29) was apparently also particularly resistant to being exorcised. We simply lack enough information on the nature of demons to explain this matter-of-fact reference to life in the spirit-world.

II. Honest Father—19-24
A. Jesus' rebuke, 19

19 He answereth him, and saith, O faithless generation, how long shall I be with you? how long shall I suffer you? bring him unto me.

Jesus' impatience is remarkable, reflecting the kind of exasperation that had caused God to cry out to Moses, "How long will this people despise me? And how long will they not believe in me, in spite of all the signs which I have wrought among them?" (Num. 14:11, RSV). Even Jesus has a limit to His patience.

Jesus' rebuke seems to be addressed to the disciples (especially in light of Matt. 17:20). If so, it is similar to His exasperation over their slowness to understand the nature of His Kingdom and His mission (see 8:31-33). However, it is just possible that Jesus could also be rebuking the crowd's lack of faith. After all, the level of faith in those around the victims who needed healing sometimes affected their case. Jesus could not do many miracles in and around His home in Nazareth because of widespread doubt (Matt. 13:58).

B. Demonic demonstration, 20-22

20 And they brought him unto him: and when he saw him, straightway the spirit tare him; and he fell on the ground, and wallowed foaming.

21 And he asked his father, How long is it ago since this came unto him? And he said, Of a child.

22 And ofttimes it hath cast him into the fire, and into the waters, to destroy him: but if thou canst do any thing, have compassion on us, and help us.

"When he saw him" probably refers to the demon's seeing and recognizing Jesus, causing a paroxysm that demonstrated what the boy's father had told Jesus about the case. Jesus' question regarding how long the boy had been affected again indicates how little we know about the malady. Apparently the length of time the boy had suffered may have affected how Jesus would treat the case, or at least why the disciples could not effect a cure.

The self-destructive aspect of some demonization indicated in verse 22 was also illustrated in the account of the Gadarene demoniac (5:5). It is for this reason that Jesus takes demonization seriously, and it is why evil in people today, whether "possessed" or not, is serious. Believers should oppose evil not out of a self-righteous spirit, but because it hurts the people who allow it to dominate their lives.

C. Faith and doubt, 23-24

23 Jesus said unto him, If thou canst believe, all things are possible to him that believeth.

24 And straightway the father of the child cried out, and said with tears, Lord, I believe; help thou mine unbelief.

Jesus seizes on the father's words in verse 22, "If thou canst do anything," but turns them around. The question is not whether Jesus is able to heal the boy, but whether the man is able to believe strongly enough. The Lord has already (probably) rebuked the disciples for their lack of faith; now he places the responsibility of faith squarely on the father. "All things are possible" through faith, with the added provision that what we ask for must be within the will of the One in whom we believe (14:36).

We can discern an element of desperation in the father's outcry in verse 24. The word here for "cried out" is also used to describe the croak of a raven; and Matthew 27:50 uses the same term to describe Jesus' hoarse, thirsty cry from the Cross. Obviously, the boy's father has been driven to desperation not only by his son's suffering but by his struggle with faith. Many who have prayed without apparent success for a loved one to be healed know something of the torturous anxiety of asking God for something that is not forthcoming.

The earnest plea that Jesus would help the man in his unbelief is remarkably candid. Perhaps in another sense it is equally remarkable that anyone would not admit honest doubt, since God sees our hearts. However, it is often the case that we pretend to believe more than we actually do for the benefit of others, fearing their censure or what our doubt may do to their own faith. The book of Job is the Bible's strongest portrayal of a man struggling to believe in the face of doubt. Despite pressure from his friends to confess sin he had not committed, Job clung to his integrity; and this stubborn honesty won God's commendation (see Job 42:8).

III. Powerful Savior—25-27

A. A cleansing word, 25

25 When Jesus saw that the people came running together, he rebuked the foul spirit, saying unto him, Thou dumb and deaf spirit, I charge thee, come out of him, and enter no more into him.

Jesus may have seen that the multitudes of people "running together" might result in someone being trampled. At any rate, He accomplishes another exorcism merely by divine command, which no demon can resist. (The kjv's "foul" spirit translates the same word that usually yields "unclean" spirit.)

B. Violent exit, 26-27

26 And the spirit cried, and rent him sore, and came out of him: and he was as one dead; insomuch that many said, He is dead.

27 But Jesus took him by the hand, and lifted him up; and he arose.

In stark contrast to the demon's last-ditch attempt to harm the boy as it reluctantly left him, the Great Physician tenderly lifts up the lad from apparent death.

IV. Explanatory Postscript—28-29

28 And when he was come into the house, his disciples asked him privately, Why could not we cast him out?

29 And he said unto them, This kind can come forth by nothing, but by prayer and fasting.

In Matthew's account (17:20), Jesus answers the disciples' question with His original charge that they lacked enough faith. Here, He is more consoling. Prayer and fasting are two classical disciplines of the spiritual life which, when more faithfully practiced, can also defeat evil in our own lives.

Evangelistic Emphasis

We are participants in the great journey of faith. We don't walk this path of being a Christian alone. We walk it with Jesus. He is the object of our journey and the power we have to make the journey.

However, we do the walking! The story of Jesus and the boy and his healing points out the truth that we participate in our own salvation. We can't save ourselves, but we participate with Jesus as He saves us. You are responsible for so much in this journey. There are some things that only you can do. You are the only one who can confess your sins to the Father. You must repent of your sins. You have to call upon the name of Jesus to be saved. You are responsible for your continued growth in the knowledge of God through His son Jesus. All this important because ultimately you will be judged for how you responded, or didn't respond, to the saving power of Jesus Christ.

Just as we are not helpless victims, we likewise are not listless victors. We are working with Jesus in bringing about our healing and salvation. Jesus does the saving; we are responsible for putting ourselves in line with His will. Our prayer, like the honest prayer of that father needs to be, "We believe, help our unbelief."

That is good news. We do what we can and trust Jesus to do the rest for us. It is called having faith.

ഈ‍൫

And straightway the father of the child cried out, and said with tears, Lord, I believe; help thou mine unbelief.—Mark 9:24

Fatherhood is under assault in America!

Mother's Day celebrations are a big deal. If you don't believe that is so, talk to a man who has forgotten any woman in his life on Mother's Day. All women get gifts on Mother's Day, even those who are not yet mothers. The female reasoning is that all women have mothers. Hey what about us guys? We weren't just hatched you know!

The father in our text was begging for the life and the health of his son. In a day when the care of the child was left to the mother, this is a dad who is breaking the mold of fatherhood. He is working every angle for his son's benefit.

For some in America, it is not "cool" to be a strong father, showing strong male characteristics. This man is an example of fatherhood. The role that men should take with their children is to beg the Lord for their souls. Fatherhood means praying and working for the benefit of your children.

God, coming to earth and dying for His children, best shows fatherhood.

Weekday Problems

Often we have to have faith *for* others. There are people who will be sitting next to you on Sunday morning, who could only make it because you are believing for them that God will answer their prayer and bring healing to their situation. The desperate father in the lesson for this week voices the way many people feel when confronted with life's tragedies and terrors: "Lord, we believe; help our unbelief!" We want to pull ourselves up by our own bootstraps and deal with our own problems. But some situations require divine intervention.

As you prepare for discussion, think of a time in your life when the problems you were facing were bigger than the faith you had at the time. Can you name the people who believed *for* you that God would do something grand in your life? Can you name the people whose shoulders were broad enough for you when life got tough?

*What examples can you give of someone who encouraged others so much that they could eventually believe for themselves?

The Devil You Say

A dignified old clergyman, a widower, bought a parrot to keep him company. Alas, the bird swore like it was demon-possessed, and the minister decided he would have to put it to sleep. A lady in his church had a last-ditch suggestion: "I have a female parrot who is an absolute saint. It does nothing but pray every day. Why not bring your parrot over and see if my angelic bird can influence him?"

It was worth a try, the minister decided, but when he walked in carrying his naughty parrot, it leered at the female bird and said, "How's about a kiss, toots?"

To the surprise of all, the praying parrot squawked, "My prayers have been answered!"

A man on his way to a Halloween ball in a devil's costume ducked into a church when a sudden rainstorm struck. The congregation fled at the sight, but one lady's coat sleeve was caught on the arm of the seat, and she was trapped. As "Satan" came closer she pleaded, "Satan, I've been a member of this church for 20 years, but all along I've really been on your side!"

This Lesson in Your Life

Nothing will draw a crowd faster than religion gone wrong. It is almost like watching a train wreck in slow motion. We can't bear to look and we can't stand to turn away. One example of religion gone wrong is terrorism. We have all come to understand the high price of terrorism. Whether the terrorists are Irish, Protestant, Catholic, or Islamic fundamentalists, they draw a crowd by their hideous activities. As we ponder what to do about the acts of terrorism in our world, so many times we make religious statements that are also examples of religion gone wrong. A crowd will gather to hear these wrong state-ments because they make the crowd comfortable that they are not part of religion that has turned sour.

The disciples were down in the valley after the great moment of Transfiguration. They had managed to draw quite a crowd when their religious attempt at healing went south. The scene would have challenged the most adept traffic cop trying to keep all the parties in line. The disciples first of all had managed to get into a verbal sparring match with a bunch of scribes. There is nothing worse than two reli-gious people arguing with each other over the finer points of theology, such as whether we are "post-," "pre-," or "a-" something or another.

I told a fellow once that I was a "pan" millennialist. I believe it would all "pan" out the way God wanted it to.

So the disciples have managed to get into a religious war of words. The fray began because they were unable to heal the boy who had been brought to them for healing. They did just enough work on the boy to stir up the demon in him. Now the boy was thrashing about, foaming on the ground, making a spectacle of himself. The father, who was looking for relief, became frantic because his son grew worse. This really looked like a pie fight scene from the Three Stooges.

Then Jesus walked up. I think His rebuke was more about religion gone wrong than a lack of faith. So many times we are so busy de-fending our position on Mount Rightness that we forget that down in the valley people need a word of grace. We even get so busy healing people that we forget to point them to Jesus.

We need to keep Jesus the main focus of our religious activities. Otherwise we will make one noisy mess and gather a gawking crowd when our religion goes wrong. The crowd will not be looking at Jesus but laughing at the mess *we* have made. Let's point all to Christ and not worry about winning an argument, or putting on a show that gathers a crowd.

GETTING THE FACTS STRAIGHT

1. Jesus had been away from the disciples. Where was Jesus before the events of Mark 9: 14-29?

Jesus took Peter, James, and John to a mountain where He was transfigured before them.

2. When they came down off of the mountain, what was their first experience?

They saw a great crowd gathered around with the disciples and scribes arguing with one another.

3. What was the crowd's reaction when they noticed Jesus in their midst?

When the crowd finally saw Jesus they were amazed and ran up to Him and greeted Him.

4. Jesus had seen the crowd and had known something was going on. What was His question to those greeting Him?

Jesus asked , "What are you discussing with them (the scribes)?"

5. One member of this crowd spoke up and explained what the discussion was all about. What was going on?

A man who had a son with a "dumb spirit" had brought the boy to the disciples for healing.

6. What had been the results of the disciples' attempt to heal the boy with the "dumb spirit"?

The disciples had been unable to heal this boy's problem.

7. When they brought the boy to Jesus, what kind of reaction did that produce?

The boy was convulsed and fell to the ground and rolled around. He was also foaming at the mouth.

8. What was Jesus' reaction to this physical display of the boy's malady?

Jesus asked, "How long has he had this?"

9. What other things did the father tell Jesus about his son's condition?

The spirit often cast the boy into fire and water, attempting to destroy him.

10. What was the man's response when Jesus told him that healing would come if he only believed?

"Immediately the father of the boy cried and said, 'I believe, help my unbelief.'"

What "impossible" things have you done so far today? None? Really?

Did you perfectly poach your breakfast egg in 45 seconds in your microwave?

Did you log on to your e-mail site and down-load messages from friends, business associates, and maybe even your grandson?

Did you get out of bed and stroll pain-free around your home using an artificial hip or knee?

Did you swallow a simple aspirin and so reduce your chance of a heart attack?

Did you drive to church in a $30,000-plus computer-assisted car that has a built-in satellite system so that you always know exactly where you are or where you are going?

Did you make a phone call from your car while on your way to church? Did you stop at an ATM and pay a few bills or get some cash?

Did you stop at a 24-hour Taco Bell and grab a burrito with extra hot sauce for breakfast on your way to Sunday school?

All of these things, and a million more, would have been rejected as "impossible" only a decade or two ago. Today, home electronic gadgetry, micro-chip technology, medical, surgical and pharmaceutical wizardry, and a culture with services 24/7/365 have made much of what seemed impossible a decade ago part of common everyday experiences.

Of course some people would rather deny that the impossible is now possible than to learn new ways of doing things or to risk the possibilities of some new experiences in their lives. Some people would rather cook in the same old scarred and seared saucepan they have been using for years rather than try the convenience of a microwave. Some people would rather hobble around on a painfully arthritic knee or hip rather than allow some strange new artificial joint into their body. Some people refuse to believe that anything other than "snail mail" is a legitimate or trustworthy form of communication.

But for most people, the impossible has become possible. If technology can advance, why can't we put our belief in the God of creation? Where in your life do you have "unbelief," and where do you need to claim, "Lord, I believe, help my unbelief?"

The most "impossible" obstacles that stunt our lives are not technological challenges or physical disabilities or the realities of time and space. The most debilitating "impossibilities" we face are those that are rooted in flawed relationships, eroded emotions, hurtful habits, and bad behavior. Every one of us faces in life some looming "impossibilities."

Everyone of us needs to pray, "Lord, help my unbelief." He stands ready to bring powerful healing and the answer to prayer to our lives, but we need His help to remove areas of doubt.

Mark 10:37-52

They said unto him, Grant unto us that we may sit, one on thy right hand, and the other on thy left hand, in thy glory.

38 But Jesus said unto them, Ye know not what ye ask: can ye drink of the cup that I drink of? and be baptized with the baptism that I am baptized with?

39 And they said unto him, We can. And Jesus said unto them, Ye shall indeed drink of the cup that I drink of; and with the baptism that I am baptized withal shall ye be baptized:

40 But to sit on my right hand and on my left hand is not mine to give; but it shall be given to them for whom it is prepared.

41 And when the ten heard it, they began to be much displeased with James and John.

42 But Jesus called them to him, and saith unto them, Ye know that they which are accounted to rule over the Gentiles exercise lordship over them; and their great ones exercise authority upon them.

43 But so shall it not be among you: but whosoever will be great among you, shall be your minister:

44 And whosoever of you will be the chiefest, shall be servant of all.

45 For even the Son of man came not to be ministered unto, but to minister, and to give his life a ransom for many.

46 And they came to Jericho: and as he went out of Jericho with his disciples and a great number of people, blind Bartimaeus, the son of Timaeus, sat by the highway side begging.

47 And when he heard that it was Jesus of Nazareth, he began to cry out, and say, Jesus, thou Son of David, have mercy on me.

48 And many charged him that he should hold his peace: but he cried the more a great deal, Thou Son of David, have mercy on me.

49 And Jesus stood still, and commanded him to be called. And they call the blind man, saying unto him, Be of good comfort, rise; he calleth thee.

50 And he, casting away his garment, rose, and came to Jesus.

51 And Jesus answered and said unto him, What wilt thou that I should do unto thee? The blind man said unto him, Lord, that I might receive my sight.

52 And Jesus said unto him, Go thy way; thy faith hath made thee whole. And immediately he received his sight, and followed Jesus in the way.

Memory Selection
Mark 10:52

Background Scripture
Mark 10:32-52

Devotional Reading
John 20:24-31

May 25

381

Jesus has said that He has a rendezvous with death in Jerusalem. Although His disciples do not understand why this should be, some want to position themselves for leadership roles after their Leader is gone. James and John ask boldly that Jesus would hand to them His mantle of leadership in the Kingdom.

This lesson focuses on Jesus' reply to these disciples. He gently chides them for acting like pagans in their lust for glory. The sign of a good leader in the Kingdom, He insists, is how he *serves*, not in the position he holds. Then He proceeds to illustrate this truth by healing a blind man He finds by the roadside out of Jericho.

The modern Church sometimes suffers from James and John's mistaken notion of what it takes to be a good leader. Christians are not immune to politics and power struggles. Through it all, we must hear the voice of Jesus telling us, "To be great, serve."

ഇൗരു

Have a brainstorming session in which group members select an appropriate symbol of *leadership* in the church—a "logo" for the church's stationery and an emblem on the office door of ministers or bishops.

Would a scepter or a crown like those wielded by a king be suitable? In the same regal vein, how about a lion? Or, closer to a minister's task, how about a sword representing "the sword of the Spirit," or a shield standing for "the shield of faith"? Or what other symbols would more adequately illustrate the role of a leader?

Finally, if no one else suggests it, ask about *a towel*. This symbol of leadership arises from the time Jesus washed the disciples' feet. As humble as it is, doesn't a towel well illustrate Jesus' ideal of a servant leader?

Teaching Outline	Daily Bible Readings	

I. Request for Power—37-40
  A. James and John's plea, 37
  B. Jesus' response, 38-40
    1. 'Qualifying suffering,' 38-39
    2. Submitting to God, 40
II. Redefining Leadership—41-45
  A. Pagan pattern, 41-42
  B. Christian alternative, 43-45
III. Real Leaders Serve—46-52
  A. Blind Bartimaeus, 46-48
  B. Jesus' call, 49-50
  C. Choosing sight, 51-52
	Mon.
	Tue.
	Wed.
	Thu.
	Fri.
	Sat.
	Sun.
		Can You Drink the Cup?
		Mark 10:32-40
		To Be Great, Serve
		Mark 10:41-45
		Jesus Gives Sight
		Mark 10:46-52
		Believing Without Seeing
		John 20:24-31
		Abraham's Faith
		Romans 4:16-22
		Faith from a Distance
		Hebrews 11:8-16
		Looking Ahead
		Hebrews 11:23-28

Verse by Verse

I. Request for Power—37-40
A. James and John's plea, 37

37 They said unto him, Grant unto us that we may sit, one on thy right hand, and the other on thy left hand, in thy glory.

"They" refers to James and John, the sons of Zebedee (vs. 35). Despite their having sat at Jesus' feet for more than two years, they have approached Jesus with a persistent misunderstanding about the nature of the Kingdom of God. For them, the Kingdom was a religious-political regime that the Messiah would create, complete with all the trappings of worldly power. Not until Jesus' death would shatter the disciples' hopes, and His resurrection would revise their concept of power, would they be able to discern the true nature of the Kingdom Jesus inaugurated.

The origin of a ruler's vice-regents sitting at his right and left hands is lost in antiquity. So also is the priority of a "right hand man" over one on the left (an idea, unfortunately for left-handed people, perpetrated by the French *gauche*, "left," also meaning "crude" or "lacking in grace"). In the Bible, this tradition first appears in Genesis 48:13-18, when old Isaac is blessing his grandsons. Joseph tries to guide his father's right hand to Joseph's first-born son so he would get the superior blessing.

B. Jesus' response, 38-40
1. Qualifying suffering,' 38-39

38 But Jesus said unto them, Ye know not what ye ask: can ye drink of the cup that I drink of? and be baptized with the baptism that I am baptized with?

39 And they said unto him, We can. And Jesus said unto them, Ye shall indeed drink of the cup that I drink of; and with the baptism that I am baptized withal shall ye be baptized:

Jesus shows that above all else Kingodm leadership is to be modeled after His own leadership style. He led not by brute strength, but as One so gentle He would not break a bruised reed (Isa. 42:3; Matt. 12:20). More importantly, His authority would be demonstrated by His suffering. He refers to the two time-honored metaphors of a cup (containing bitter medicine) and of a baptism (a figurative "death"; see Rom. 6:3). As the disciples and countless Christian martyrs would eventually learn, being a Christian leader would become a life-threatening position.

We wonder whether James and John really understand the meaning of "the cup" and "baptism," in their eagerness to assure Jesus that they are ready to accept them. In any case, Jesus assures them that they will undergo a level of suffering that was to befall all faithful Christians in the coming periods of persecution.

2. Submitting to God, 40

40 But to sit on my right hand and on my left hand is not mine to give; but it shall be given to them for whom it is prepared.

This remarkable confession reminds us of the limitations imposed upon the Son by nature of His having become flesh, temporarily giving up His heavenly position (Philip. 2:7). This included incomplete knowledge, specifically of when "the End" would come (13:32). Here the Son submits the Father's authority to name those who would occupy positions of honor in the Kingdom. Since Jesus has just stated that these positions would be determined not by rank or the usual princely trappings, He probably is referring to the fact that God alone would name those who would be first in suffering for the sake of the Kingdom.

II. Redefining Leadership—41-45

A. Pagan pattern, 41-42

41 And when the ten heard it, they began to be much displeased with James and John.

42 But Jesus called them to him, and saith unto them, Ye know that they which are accounted to rule over the Gentiles exercise lordship over them; and their great ones exercise authority upon them.

The very resentment of the rest of the apostles toward James and John indicates that they too share the misconception that being "first" in the Kingdom of God was a matter of position, place, and authority. Obviously they are jealous of the two brothers, who were already better connected than the rest since they knew, and were perhaps related to, the high priest (John 18:15).

Jesus chooses to deal gently with James and John by including all the apostles in His teaching about the contrast between Kingdom leadership and the model widely at hand in the culture about them, especially among Gentiles. Although overbearing Jewish leaders could also be found, it was the pagan style of tyrannical leadership that gave us, from the Greek language, our word "despot." A single Greek term is translated here by "exercise lordship." The apostle Peter would later use the same word to counsel church leaders not to "lord it over" the flock in their charge (1 Pet. 5:3). In God's Kingdom, there is only one Lord.

B. Christian alternative, 43-45

43 But so shall it not be among you: but whosoever will be great among you, shall be your minister:

44 And whosoever of you will be the chiefest, shall be servant of all.

45 For even the Son of man came not to be ministered unto, but to minister, and to give his life a ransom for many.

In contrast to the tyranny of leaders of other kingdoms, leaders "among *you*," that is in God's Kingdom, are to be identified by ministering or serving. As Jesus had previously taught, "the first shall be last." The person with the most desirable "leadership skills" is not the one who can best subject a church to a budget, or dictate what members believe, but the one most willing to meet the needs of others in humble service.

Verse 45 is the primer of Christian ministry, grounding it on the pattern of the ministry of Christ, who came not to be exalted as pagans exalt a ruler but to serve—even to the point of giving His life. Obviously this last degree of service is reserved for Christ; it is the principle of serving that is to characterize Christian leaders.

III. Real Leaders Serve—46-52
A. Blind Bartimaeus, 46-48

46 And they came to Jericho: and as he went out of Jericho with his disciples and a great number of people, blind Bartimaeus, the son of Timaeus, sat by the highway side begging.

47 And when he heard that it was Jesus of Nazareth, he began to cry out, and say, Jesus, thou Son of David, have mercy on me.

48 And many charged him that he should hold his peace: but he cried the more a great deal, Thou Son of David, have mercy on me.

Whether by design or not, this incident appropriately follows Jesus' teaching on servant leadership. Jericho was on the road from Galilee to Jerusalem; and since He is approaching the high point of His ministry Jesus could have arranged for His passage through Jericho to take on the appearance of a parade, such as the Triumphal Entry (chap. 11). Instead, He illustrates His teaching on servant leadership by healing a blind man (named only in Mark; cp. several slight differences in Luke 18:35 and Matt. 20:30).

The Messianic title "son of David" might conjure visions of Jesus as the kind of regal ruler His disciples

wanted Him to be. In fact, bystanders rebuke Bartimaeus as though protecting a king's dignity and royal privacy.

B. Jesus' call, 49-50

49 And Jesus stood still, and commanded him to be called. And they call the blind man, saying unto him, Be of good comfort, rise; he calleth thee.

50 And he, casting away his garment, rose, and came to Jesus.

Unlike a Roman emperor or other pagan king, Jesus has time for this blind man. He does not merely send a servant to tend to Bartimaeus, but honors him by inviting him to join His retinue (an act of personal contact with an important lesson to teach the modern church as it seeks to meet human needs). Throwing aside the garment that might impede the halting steps of a blind man, Bartimaeus takes the most important steps of his life.

C. Choosing sight, 51-52

51 And Jesus answered and said unto him, What wilt thou that I should do unto thee? The blind man said unto him, Lord, that I might receive my sight.

52 And Jesus said unto him, Go thy way; thy faith hath made thee whole. And immediately he received his sight, and followed Jesus in the way.

Unlike James and John, Bartimaeus has a more basic request than their quest for glory. He simply wants to see. Once again, the power of faith is emphasized in another healing miracle. Bartimaeus instantly becomes not a prince in the King's court, but one of His humble followers.

Evangelistic Emphasis

It seems to happen about once a year. On an otherwise "slow news day" some media person gets wind of yet another "miracle story" and runs a camera crew out to film the big event. In their most frequent incarnations these momentarily newsworthy miracles usually take the form of a vision of the divine . . . of sorts.

Let's face it, though—these are pretty puny epiphanies! The face of Christ miraculously appears in the cracked bathroom window of some rundown house. The image of a descending angel miraculously floats above the landscape scenery of some cheap painting. And of course who can forget the miraculous transformation of a home-fried tortilla into an icon by the silhouette of Jesus that emerged upon its surface.

Don't all these "miracles" make you mad? It is utterly unfair that God could appear as a pillar of smoke by day and fire by night to the escaping Israelites, that Jesus could walk on the water and bring a dead man back to life in first-century Palestine, while we here near the beginning of the 21st century are supposed to squint our eyes in order to think we can see a miracle on a piece of fried dough!

God is still moving mountains; and best of all He is still saving souls. Those are the kinds of miracles we all need.

♥)(♥

Memory Selection

And Jesus said unto him, Go thy way; thy faith hath made thee whole. And immediately he received his sight, and followed Jesus in the way.—*Mark 10:52*

The story in this text is about "blind Bartimaeus." The irony of this passage is that Bartimaeus is the only person in the tenth chapter of Mark's gospel who can really see. The Pharisees are blind to the love of God. They can't see His love for their understanding of the law.

The people who tried to keep the children away from Jesus were blind to the priorities that He had set for His kingdom.

The Rich Young Ruler was blind to God because he could only see the money and possessions that were so important to him. James and John the disciples were blinded by the pride which would want them to sit one on Jesus' right and one on His left hand.

Strange how the weak lead us, the blind see the children have faith. Maybe those people in the Bible who are blind, can really see things we can't. Those closest to God might be the very ones WE think need Him most. Maybe we need to have our eyes checked by the Lord.

Weekday Problems

You can't get into an elevator today and not be aware that some people are blind. On the panel of the elevator area, floor numbers are indicated by Braille markings. The law requires that we make life easier for people who are blind. There are whole schools dedicated to teaching blind people how to function in our world. Blindness, while personally painful, is no longer considered the tragedy it was 50 years ago.

Yet many people are often blind in another way—to the possibilities that God has placed in their lives. We have people who have 20/20 sight who have no vision of a God who loves them, and who died on the Cross for them.

Do you ever wonder how many people are walking the grocery store aisles with you who are blind to the power of God? Do you wonder how many people are sitting next to you in a pew who are blind to what God can do for them?

The "weekday problem" that we all face is our own spiritual blindness. Some of it is due to the fact that we refuse to see what God is doing in our world. Although He is bringing light to a darkened world, too often we would rather "curse the darkness than light a candle."

Our weekday problem is that we have grown comfortable with spiritual blindness.

*What specific spiritual realities are most urgent for us to "see"?

Temperature Gauges

Some people are like buttons—always popping off.

People who fly into a rage always make a bad landing.

Your life is in the hands of anyone you allow to make you lose your temper.

About the time a man gets his temper under control, he goes out and plays golf again.

Nothing will cook your goose faster than a red-hot temper.

You don't get rid of your temper just by losing it.

Your temper may get you in trouble, but it's your pride that keeps you there.

He who loses his head is usually the last one to notice.

Strike when the iron, not the head, is hot.

He who blows a fuse is usually in the dark.

—From Shredded Wit, by Vern McLellan

387

This Lesson in Your Life

Do miracles still happen, or did God stop working through miracles after the apostolic era? This has been one of the biggest and longest-running controversies in the Church. For at least 500 years believers have been asking, "Does God do miracles today?" The Renaissance, the Reformation, and the Enlightenment each added more and more bricks to the wall between people and the idea that miracles still occur in a rationally-minded world. But it took the Industrial Era to really start erecting a miracle-proof barrier between the ongoing transforming work and presence of God in this world and the "scientific" view of the universe being developed.

As these walls have grown higher and wider, the separation between those who continue to believe in the presence and possibility of miracles and those who utterly deny this kind of experience has become taller and deeper.

Take, for example, the great debate over a long-ago miracle, the virgin birth. Few issues have caused such historic histrionics. Churches have been split and thousands of books have been written on the possibility or impossibility of a miraculous virgin birth.

The debate often has been ugly and nasty on both sides. Reams of papers and teams of scientists have marched before virgin-birth believers, denouncing the belief in that miracle as anti-science, anti-rational, and anti-intellectual. Unfortunately, many of the defenders of the virgin birth miracle considered such designations complimentary. Some evangelicals and fundamentalists adhering to the old "not-since-the-apostolic-era" mandate against miracles are just as restrictive and closed-minded as the clinical white-coated skeptics.

Why is it that science gets all the miracle-making, wonder-working powers, and not God? Why is it we can't say, "God can do anything God wants to do?"

That is a message our world needs. *God can do what God wants to do.* He has never read a textbook on what is physically impossible for Him.

Aren't you glad? Because the greatest miracle was the day He saved your soul!

STRAIGHT

1. **What request did James and John make of Jesus?**
James and John wanted to sit on the right and left hand of Jesus when He entered His kingdom.

2. **What question did Jesus ask them as a response to their power grab?**
Jesus asked if they were able to drink of the cup that He would drink and be baptized with His baptism.

3. **What was James and John's response to Jesus' challenge?**
They said that they would be able to drink His cup and be baptized with His baptism.

4. **When the rest of the disciples heard what James and John had asked, what was their response?**
When the other 10 heard it, they were indignant at James and John.

5. **How did Jesus respond to the rift caused in the disciples by this request of the Zebedee boys?**
Jesus spoke of the last being first and the first being last.

6. **After this encounter, where did the disciples and Jesus travel next?**
They traveled through Jericho on the way to Jerusalem.

7. **As the disciples and Jesus left Jericho, what happened to them?**
A great multitude gathered and followed them through Jericho.

8. **As this throng was leaving Jericho, who did they meet on the roadside?**
They met a blind beggar, Bartimaeus, the son of Timaeus.

9. **What did Bartimaeus do when he heard that Jesus was passing by?**
He started crying out to Jesus, "Jesus, Son of David, have mercy on me."

10. **What did Bartimaeus do when others tried to silence him?**
He cried out even louder, "Jesus, Son of David, have mercy on me."

I came across a sad story this week. This is a story about a honeymoon disaster. The newlyweds arrived at the hotel in the wee hours with high hopes. They'd reserved a large room with romantic amenities. That's not what they found.

The room was pretty skimpy. The tiny room had no view, no flowers, a cramped bathroom and worst of all—no bed. Just a foldout sofa with a lumpy mattress was the only thing to sleep on. It was the kind that has the bar in the middle of your back that makes your back hurt all day the next day. The springs even had the nerve to sag. It was not what the couple had hoped for; consequently, neither was the night.

The next morning the sore-necked groom stormed down to the manager's desk and ventilated his anger. After listening patiently for a few moments, the clerk asked, "Did you open the door in your room?"

The groom admitted he hadn't. He returned to the suite and opened the door he had thought was the closet.

There, complete with fruit baskets and chocolates, was a spacious bedroom.

Can't you just see them standing in the doorway of the room, they'd overlooked? Oh, it would have been so nice . . . .

But they missed it. How sad. Cramped, cranky, and uncomfortable while comfort was a door away. They missed it because they thought the door was a closet.

Why didn't you try? I was asking as I read the piece. Get curious. Check it out. Give it a shot. Take a look. Why did you just assume the door led nowhere?

The great thing about the story of Bartimaeus is that he was willing to give Jesus a try. No one could stop him from being touched by the Lord. Not even the Jericho Chamber of commerce" could keep old blind Bartimeaus quiet when he knew that Jesus, and thus his salvation, was near. Bartimaeus knew what was wrong and knew the One who could fix it.

There is a story circulating about the patient who went to his physician complaining of pain in several places. The doctor asked him to indicate where it hurt. He pointed first to his leg, then to his back, then to his side, finally to his head. "Every time I press on these places, it hurts." After a careful examination, the physician diagnosed his problem: "You have a broken finger."

I wonder how many of us really "see" the truth of our own blindness? To what lengths would we go to make sure that our sight was restored? How many doors would we be willing to open? Will we make a spectacle of ourselves in order that our souls might be saved?

Are we so proper that we are like that bride and groom? Will we fail even try the door that might lead to our richest blessings?

390

Unit I. Beginning the Return

Lesson 1

Return of the Exiles

Ezra 1

Now in the first year of Cyrus king of Persia, that the word of the LORD by the mouth of Jeremiah might be fulfilled, the LORD stirred up the spirit of Cyrus king of Persia, that he made a proclamation throughout all his kingdom, and put it also in writing, saying,

2 Thus saith Cyrus king of Persia, The LORD God of heaven hath given me all the kingdoms of the earth; and he hath charged me to build him an house at Jerusalem, which is in Judah.

3 Who is there among you of all his people? his God be with him, and let him go up to Jerusalem, which is in Judah, and build the house of the LORD God of Israel, (he is the God,) which is in Jerusalem.

4 And whosoever remaineth in any place where he sojourneth, let the men of his place help him with silver, and with gold, and with goods, and with beasts, beside the freewill offering for the house of God that is in Jerusalem.

5 Then rose up the chief of the fathers of Judah and Benjamin, and the priests, and the Levites, with all them whose spirit God had raised, to go up to build the house of the LORD which is in Jerusalem.

6 And all they that were about them strengthened their hands with vessels of silver, with gold, with goods, and with beasts, and with precious things, beside all that was willingly offered.

7 Also Cyrus the king brought forth the vessels of the house of the LORD, which Nebuchadnezzar had brought forth out of Jerusalem, and had put them in the house of his gods;

8 Even those did Cyrus king of Persia bring forth by the hand of Mithredath the treasurer, and numbered them unto Sheshbazzar, the prince of Judah.

9 And this is the number of them: thirty chargers of gold, a thousand chargers of silver, nine and twenty knives,

10 Thirty basons of gold, silver basons of a second sort four hundred and ten, and other vessels a thousand.

11 All the vessels of gold and of silver were five thousand and four hundred. All these did Sheshbazzar bring up with them of the captivity that were brought up from Babylon unto Jerusalem.

Memory Selection
Ezra 1:3

Background Scripture
Ezra 1

Devotional Reading
Isaiah 52:7-12

The first quarter of this year's cycle of lessons focused on God's judgment on His Old Testament people for their disobedience, resulting in the people of the southern kingdom of Judah being carried into Babylonian captivity. This final quarter brings a happier ending to that tragic opening chapter. It all begins with the edict of Cyrus, king of Persia, the focus of this lesson, which allowed the captive Jews to return and rebuild the holy city, Jerusalem.

God had threatened that Israel would be held captive for 70 years (Jer. 25:11-12). Now the time is fulfilled. The return was not accomplished all at once, and the rebuilding that begins in this lesson will continue for more than 50 years. Also, only a remnant of the people return. Still, they rejoice. Deliverance has come!

∞૦રૂ

FOR A LIVELY START...

Going home, went the gospel song several years ago, *Lord, I'm always going home inside.* This lesson on the "homecoming" of a remnant of the Jews from Babylonian captivity who had been in can be introduced by inviting group members to share what "going home" means to them. Why does visiting parents and/or the home where they grew up usually bring joyful memories? Are homecomings associated with special holidays such as Thanksgiving or Christmas? Do the children sometimes object to leaving their present-day friends and activities, or are they always excited to visit their grandparents?

Such feelings and memories are about roots; and anyone who has ever revisited their roots can imagine the emotions that surged in the hearts of God's people as they hear the good news: *We are going home!*

Teaching Outline	Daily Bible Readings	
I. Return Authorized—1-4	Mon.	Cyrus, the Lord's Anointed Isaiah 45:1-5
A. Cyrus' proclamation, 1-2	Tue.	Cyrus to Rebuild Jerusalem Isaiah 45:7-13
B. Invitation to rebuild, 3-4	Wed.	Israel to Be Saved Isaiah 45:14-19
II. Response of the People—5-6	Thu.	'The Lord Will Go Before You' Isaiah 52:7-12
III. Restoring Holy Wares—7-11	Fri.	Preparing to Return Ezra 1:1-5
A. Recovering holy items, 7-8	Sat.	Aid from Neighbors Ezra 1:6–2:2
B. Numbering precious vessels, 9-11	Sun.	Offerings for God's House Ezra 2:65-70

Verse by Verse

I. Return Authorized—1-4
A. Cyrus' proclamation, 1-2

1 Now in the first year of Cyrus king of Persia, that the word of the LORD by the mouth of Jeremiah might be fulfilled, the LORD stirred up the spirit of Cyrus king of Persia, that he made a proclamation throughout all his kingdom, and put it also in writing, saying,

2 Thus saith Cyrus king of Persia, The LORD God of heaven hath given me all the kingdoms of the earth; and he hath charged me to build him an house at Jerusalem, which is in Judah.

God's people in Judah, the southern kingdom, had been taken captive into Babylonia by King Nebuchadnezzer in 587 B.C. Then why does the story of their return begin with *Cyrus,* king of *Persia*? Because in 538 B.C. Persia, under Cyrus' leadership, had conquered Babylon; and in the very first year of his reign he announces plans to allow the Judeans to return and rebuild their holy city. (Although this decree was only 49 years from the final captivity, some Jews had been carried away as early as 605, accomplishing almost 70 years.)

Now it is time to allow another player to take center-stage in history. Just as God had used Nebuchadnezzar as an instrument of punishment, He now uses Cyrus and the Persians as instruments of grace. God's sovereignty even over evil empires, and His ability to "stir up" kings of the earth to accomplish His purposes, is remarkable enough. In this case, however, we are further awed by the fact that God had actually predicted *by name* the king He would use to restore His people to the Promised Land. Writing nearly 200 years earlier, the prophet Isaiah had quoted God as saying that "Cyrus, He is my shepherd, and shall perform all my pleasure, even saying to Jerusalem, Thou shalt be built; and to the temple, Thy foundation shall be laid" (Isa. 44:28).

Centuries later the Jewish historian Josephus would write that faithful Jews had shown Cyrus this text. If so, the king may have been eager to go down in history as having fulfilled this awesome God's prophecy. Also, an archeological discovery called the "Cyrus Cylinder" has revealed that it was the Persian conquerors' practice to let the peoples they subdued continue to worship their own deities, and that Cyrus was eager to please as many "gods" as possible. The cylinder is inscribed with Cyrus' own words: "May all the gods whom I have resettled in their sacred cities ask daily Bel and Nebo [Babylonian gods] for a long life for me." Such language suggests that in calling the Jews' God "the LORD God of heaven" (vs. 2), Cyrus was not professing belief in the one true God but trying to curry favor with what he considered the Jewish god by referring to him in the way they did.

B. Invitation to rebuild, 3-4

3 Who is there among you of all his people? his God be with him, and let him go up to Jerusalem, which is in Judah, and build the house of the LORD God of Israel, (he is the God,) which is in Jerusalem.

4 And whosoever remaineth in any place where he sojourneth, let the men of his place help him with silver, and with gold, and with goods, and with beasts, beside the freewill offering for the house of God that is in Jerusalem.

We might think that Cyrus' open invitation would have attracted all Jews, but this was hardly the case. Many were comfortably settled in their new home; there is even some evidence that some, such as a family of bankers, were becoming wealthy. Also, since they had already been guilty of diluting their faith in the true God by dallying with the gods of the Canaanites, some may have become too disinterested in Yahweh worship to go to the trouble to return and rebuild His Temple in Jerusalem. Whatever the reasons, God would be able to count on only a "remnant" to rise to the challenge of restoring Judaism in the Holy City. This had also been predicted by the prophets: "The remnant shall return, even the remnant of Jacob, unto the mighty God" (Isa. 10:21).

However, this minority of faithful people would return enriched for the worship of God. Verse 4 implies that Persians who lived where Jews "sojourned" were to give them silver and gold and other offerings for the return trip and the restoration of Temple worship. The scene must have ignited exciting memories of the exodus long ago, when their ancestors fled Egypt taking with them jewels and other spoils from their hosts (Exod. 12:35).

II. Response of the People—5-6

5 Then rose up the chief of the fathers of Judah and Benjamin, and the priests, and the Levites, with all them whose spirit God had raised, to go up to build the house of the LORD which is in Jerusalem.

6 And all they that were about them strengthened their hands with vessels of silver, with gold, with goods, and with beasts, and with precious things, beside all that was willingly offered.

Note that the remnant who returned consisted mainly of older Jews, heads of the clans that still comprised the remains of the tribes of Judah and Benjamin, people old enough to be concerned about "the old paths," and priests who longed to point the people back to true worship. Further encouragement came from neighboring Persians who heeded the king's exhortation to donate part of their wealth to the Jews for the work of restoration back in Jerusalem.

III. Restoring Holy Wares—7-11
A. Recovering holy items, 7-8

7 Also Cyrus the king brought forth the vessels of the house of the LORD,

which Nebuchadnezzar had brought forth out of Jerusalem, and had put them in the house of his gods;

8 Even those did Cyrus king of Persia bring forth by the hand of Mithredath the treasurer, and numbered them unto Sheshbazzar, the prince of Judah.

One of the saddest elements in Nebuchadnezzar's sack of Jerusalem in 587 was the looting of the Temple of the sacred and expensive vessels used in the sacrifices and services. It was now Cyrus' right, by conquest, to return these precious items to those from whom they had been stolen. Mentioning the work of the Persian treasurer and of Sheshbazzar, a prince (NEB "chief") of Judah, shows how carefully these valuable articles were catalogued. (Some scholars think Sheshbazzar is another name for Zerubbabel, who figured prominently in the return [3:8]).

B. Numbering precious vessels, 9-11

9 And this is the number of them: thirty chargers of gold, a thousand chargers of silver, nine and twenty knives,

10 Thirty basons of gold, silver basons of a second sort four hundred and ten, and other vessels a thousand.

11 All the vessels of gold and of silver were five thousand and four hundred. All these did Sheshbazzar bring up with them of the captivity that were brought up from Babylon unto Jerusalem.

So important was the return of the gold and silver vessels that had been used in Temple worship that the ancient author now goes to the trouble of offering a partial inventory. (Clearly, since the list does not total 5,400, only some are listed.) The NIV prints the items in list form, portraying the true character of the careful tally that was kept.

Unfortunately, the meaning of the Hebrew words for each item is disputed. "Chargers" (NIV "dishes) may have been bowls that were used to catch the blood from animal sacrifices. Knives would probably have been ceremonial weapons for slaughtering the sacrifices. Some scholars, however, think the word should be translated "pans" (as in the NEB) or even "baskets," in which case they would have been used to carry the grain offerings. "Basons" (the KJV spelling of "basins") were bowls which could have been put to a number of uses.

Recovering the specific meaning of these items is not as important as the fact of their return to Jewish worshipers, an act that is unique in the annals of war. The final words of verse 11 are significant: the vessels of worship crossed a great theological divide in making the trip from Babylon back to Jerusalem, where they belonged. We are led to the conclusion that God is moving in the life of Cyrus in allowing these valuable items to be returned to the Temple so His people will have no excuse for not setting up true worship when they return. After stirring up Cyrus to allow the return, God is equipping the people to worship as they should have before their captivity. The scene reminds us of the modern saying, *Where God guides, God provides.*

Evangelistic Emphasis

The story as told in the book of Ezra is that "everyone whose spirit God had stirred got ready to go up and rebuild the house of the Lord in Jerusalem." If one were an aloof spectator, one could speculate on the interplay between God's initiative in inspiring the families of Judah and Benjamin to return to Palestine. But if one were an exile in Babylon and the word comes, "You can go home again," you know in that moment you must decide. You are not a spectator. You are an actor. Only you can choose.

When the word of God comes to us, inviting us to trust in God alone, we must answer. When the word of God comes calling us to serve, only we can say "Here I am, Lord" or turn away, "no, not now, not there."

Sometimes we love to live in the past, cherishing the stories of ancient heroes. Sometimes we love to dwell in the future, imagining how life will be in God's future kingdom. But we only live in the present, in the now. In the now as God's spirit stirs us we must say "Yes" or "No." Still God's Spirit comes. Still God's word addresses us. In this present moment we respond. In faith we say "Yes" or in fear we say "No." But each of us must answer when the Spirit stirs our spirits.

୨୦୦୪

Memory Selection

Who is there among you of all his people? His God be with him, and let him go up to Jerusalem, which is in Judah, and build the house of the Lord God of Israel, (he is the God,) which is in Jerusalem. – *Ezra 1:3*

What startling news! After a generation living in exile, the king decrees they can go home. Their homeland lived in their hearts only by the stories the old folks told. They had been sustained by the promise of the prophets that one day they would return. Now this pagan king gives them permission to go home.

More than just permission, the king gives them a charge to rebuild the temple in Jerusalem. They were commissioned by the king to create a sacred space in which the Lord God Eternal would dwell.

But the permission was really an invitation. Whoever wishes to may accept this mission. Some had grown so comfortable and secure they blended in with this strange culture. Others heard in the king's decree the call of God to be his people.

Where is God calling you to serve today?

Weekday Problems

Joe was enjoying his ministry. He was a good preacher and teacher. He was especially attentive to the needs of the elder members of his congregation, who composed 90 percent of his flock. The church had no financial problems and provided a good salary with a modest increase every year. It was a good place to be and to raise a family.

But Joe had always longed to go back to the inner city where he grew up. The needs of kids growing up in poverty, in the midst of gang warfare, were always on his mind. Then the phone call came. He was asked to serve as pastor of an inner city church. It was like the neighborhood where he grew up. The church was struggling to stay open. The salary offered was less, and there was no certainty the congregation could pay it. His children would be starting to school soon, and the inner city schools were in bad shape. He had grown use to the stained glass windows, the beautiful organ, the cushioned pews. He enjoyed the affection showered on him. But his roots were in the inner city. He had been helped by a pastor who took a special interest in him. He felt he could make a difference in the lives of children and youth.

*What would you advise Joe?

*Have you ever faced similar choices? How did you discern God's will?

For Those Who Like Lawyer Jokes More than Lawyers

Q: Why do they bury dead lawyers six feet under?
A: Because lawyers are real good down deep.

❖❖❖❖

Q: Is there a criminal lawyer in this town?
A: Well, we think so, but we haven't been able to prove it yet.

❖❖❖❖

Lawyer: Are you positive that the prisoner is the man who stole your car?
Witness: Well, I was until you cross-examined me. Now I'm not sure whether I ever had a car at all.

❖❖❖❖

Crook: I got nearly a million in cash in the bank. Can you get me off?
Lawyer: Believe me, pal, you'll never go to prison with that kind of money.

This Lesson in Your Life

In the story of the return of the Jewish exiles to "the promised land" there is a strange mixture of worldly wisdom and trusting faith, a balance between divine providence and human decision.

The exiles are allowed to return by the permission of King Cyrus of Persia. Many historians and political scientists praise his wise decision to encourage conquered people to continue their traditions. Cyrus' empire was so vast that he could not control the cultural life of every province and city. It was better that his subjects be happy and willingly pay their taxes than to plot endless series of uprisings because of the king's heavy-handed oppression. Allowing refugees to return home was just smart political policy.

But it was not the act of Cyrus alone. His offer had to be met by Jews willing to return to a land which for some was only a distant memory, and for others was a land they had never seen. They were given permission and surprising help, but no guarantees. For all the longing of the elders to return to the holy city, life in Babylon was not too bad. There was plenty to eat. They had grown accustomed to its ways. The empire brought safety and security. They had grown comfortable in Babylon. Who knows what it might be like in that land ravaged by the Babylonians decades before? Yet many of the people decided to return. They would go home. It was a venture of faith.

Many events in our own story are also a mixture of wise and careful thought and a leap of faith. In discerning where and how one's call to discipleship is to be fulfilled, we take into account our gifts and strengths. We calculate the special training required and its cost. We recognize our interests and see how those interests compare with others in that field. We assess the demands of this avenue of serving to see if emotionally and intellectually we can meet its challenge. We seek a broader understanding of the needs of the world and a firmer sense of how we can make a difference. But in the end, we have to choose where and how to invest our lives, with no guarantees. We take a leap of faith.

Like Israel's return to Palestine, our lives are a balance of the divine and the human. Apart from the decree of Cyrus, the exiles would not return. Apart from their courageous decision to return, the exiles would remain forever aliens. Yet it was the Lord who stirred Cyrus' heart. It was God's word that was being fulfilled. It was the Spirit who moved the hearts of the long time refugees to return.

Like so many decisions and turning points in our own lives, we take responsibility for our choices and at the same time discern in retrospect the hand of God.

STRAIGHT

1. **What king of Persia allowed the Jews to return to their homeland?**
   Cyrus was the Persian king who allowed the Jews to return (Ezra 1:1).

2. **When during the king's reign did he allow the Jewish people to return?**
   During the first year of his rule, the king permitted their return (Ezra 1:1).

3. **What did the king charge the Jewish exiles to do when they returned to Jerusalem?**
   They were to rebuild the house of the Lord (Ezra 1:3) .

4. **Why did the king of Persia allow the Jewish exiles to return?**
   The Lord stirred up the heart of King Cyrus of Persia allowing the exiles to return (Ezra 1:1).

5. **Which families are mentioned as returning to Palestine?**
   The heads of the families of Judah and Benjamin, and the priests and the Levites got ready to go (Ezra 1:5).

6. **Who returned to Jerusalem?**
   Everyone whose spirit God had stirred (Ezra 1:5).

7. **How did the neighbors of the returning exiles help?**
   They gave articles of silver and gold, goods, livestock, gifts, and free will offerings (Ezra 1: 6).

8. **What did King Cyrus contribute?**
   The vessels from the Jerusalem Temple that Nebuchadnezzar had carried away (Ezra 1:7).

9. **What prince of Judah was put in charge of the return and rebuilding?**
   The person in charge was Sheshbazzar (Ezra 1:8).

10. **How many articles in all were returned to the Jerusalem Temple?**
    The total number of the gold and silver vessels was 5,400 (Ezra 1:11).

On Easter Sunday morning, the first day of Daylight Saving Time, the telephone in the church office kept ringing. Most of the callers were checking on the time of services or special activities: Sunrise service? Sunday School? Congregational Breakfast? Easter egg Hunt? Morning worship?

With one caller, I could feel the frustration in her voice. She asked simply and directly, "What time is it?" I could almost hear the inner dialogue in her mind (for I debate the same question every year myself.) Do I move the clock *up* an hour or *back* an hour? Do I get up an hour early or sleep in an extra hour? In her uncertainty she called the church. "What time is it?"

After I gave her an accurate and authoritative answer and hung up, I thought of all the bright replies I might have made to this sleepy, frustrated, perplexed early morning caller. "What time is it?" *It's later than you think.* Or *The hour cometh and now is when the true worshipers shall worship the Father in spirit and in truth.* Or had I been really wide awake myself I might have said, *Now is the acceptable time.*

The fact is that *now* is the only time we have. The present moment between the "no longer" and the "not yet" is the only moment we have to live. We can learn from the past, but we can't relive it. We can anticipate the future, but we can't "fast forward" to it. It is in *this* fleeting present moment that ideas are translated into realities, intentions become concrete deeds, and vague feelings become firm decisions.

"What time is it?" the woman had asked. I said prosaically and accurately, "It's 8:10 a.m. I hope to see you at church." But with a more profound and truthful response I might have said, "It's the time of opportunity, the moment of decision, the *now* uniquely given. It's not just a time of "saving day light" but a time ripe with opportunity. "The Kingdom of God is at hand!"

What time is it in your life?

Lesson 2

Beginning to Rebuild

Ezra 3:1-3, 6-7, 10-13

And when the seventh month was come, and the children of Israel were in the cities, the people gathered themselves together as one man to Jerusalem.

2 Then stood up Jeshua the son of Jozadak, and his brethren the priests, and Zerubbabel the son of Shealtiel, and his brethren, and builded the altar of the God of Israel, to offer burnt offerings thereon, as it is written in the law of Moses the man of God.

3 And they set the altar upon his bases; for fear was upon them because of the people of those countries: and they offered burnt offerings thereon unto the LORD, even burnt offerings morning and evening.

6 From the first day of the seventh month began they to offer burnt offerings unto the LORD. But the foundation of the temple of the LORD was not yet laid.

7 They gave money also unto the masons, and to the carpenters; and meat, and drink, and oil, unto them of Zidon, and to them of Tyre, to bring cedar trees from Lebanon to the sea of Joppa, according to the grant that they had of Cyrus king of Persia.

10 And when the builders laid the foundation of the temple of the LORD, they set the priests in their apparel with trumpets, and the Levites the sons of Asaph with cymbals, to praise the LORD, after the ordinance of David king of Israel.

11 And they sang together by course in praising and giving thanks unto the LORD; because he is good, for his mercy endureth for ever toward Israel. And all the people shouted with a great shout, when they praised the LORD, because the foundation of the house of the LORD was laid.

12 But many of the priests and Levites and chief of the fathers, who were ancient men, that had seen the first house, when the foundation of this house was laid before their eyes, wept with a loud voice; and many shouted aloud for joy:

13 So that the people could not discern the noise of the shout of joy from the noise of the weeping of the people: for the people shouted with a loud shout, and the noise was heard afar off.

Memory Selection
Ezra 3:11

Background Scripture
Ezra 3—4

Devotional Reading
Pslam 100:1-5

After nearly 70 years, the Jews have returned to the Land of Promise. Where would they begin in the huge task of rebuilding Jerusalem? Significantly, their first act is *to worship*. At first they use a hastily constructed outdoor altar, since the Temple had been razed. Then, laying the foundations of the new Temple, they look forward to recreating Temple worship as it was when it was instituted under King Solomon. For us, the focus here is not only on the story of a reconstructed Judaism. It is also on how acknowledging God's presence is an important part of marking births and deaths, weddings and funerals, new jobs and retirement—moments that are also "rebuilding" events in our own lives.

ଯ୍ଜର

As suggested in our last lesson, "going home" is a nearly universal source of excitement and joy because it is about rediscovering our roots. *"Nearly"* universal, we now note. Some in your group may have noted that unhappy childhood experiences, conflicts with relatives, or the mere fact that Mom and Dad have aged more than we realized, can sometimes mix happiness with sorrow.

The Jews had a similar experience as they began to rebuild the Temple. Ezra 3:13 notes that amid the rejoicing at laying of the foundation for a new Temple is the sound of weeping. It was a bittersweet experience for those who could remember the glory of the previous Temple. *Yet they worshiped.*

Discuss whether this range of emotions, from joy to sorrow, is appropriate in modern worship. If so, how can it be accommodated, or appropriately expressed?

Teaching Outline	Daily Bible Readings

I. Putting Worship First—1-3
  A. A reunified Israel, 1
  B. Altar of worship, 2-3
 	
II. Plans for the Temple—6-7
 	
III. Praising and Weeping—10-13
  A. Worship in shouts and
     songs, 10-11
  B. Bittersweet note, 12-13
	Mon. Renewed Worship
	       Ezra 3:1-5
	Tue. 'Worship with Gladness'
	       Psalm 100:1-5
	Wed. Laying a New Foundation
	       Ezra 3:6-13
	Thu. Discouragement from Others
	       Ezra 4:1-5
	Fri. Enemies Appeal to the King
	       Ezra 4:6-16
	Sat. Orders to Halt the Work
	       Ezra 4:17-24
	Sun. 'Your Foundation Shall Be Laid'
	       Isaiah 44:24-28

Verse by Verse

I. Putting Worship First—1-3

A. A reunified Israel, 1

1 And when the seventh month was come, and the children of Israel were in the cities, the people gathered themselves together as one man to Jerusalem.

The seventh month in the Jewish calendar (Tishri) was a month of harvest, corresponding roughly to September. While the Jews had been in their own homeland it had been a sacred time, beginning with the Day of Atonement and including the Feast of Tabernacles or Ingathering. A more appropriate or holier time could not have been arranged for the "remnant" of God's people to return from captivity to restore the Temple and the holy city, and to settle "in the cities" surrounding Jerusalem.

According to 2:64, more than 40,000 Jews returned to their homeland. They consist of both those who were born Israelites and converts to the faith, priests and other Levites, servants, the young and the old. Despite this diversity, however, they gather as one for worship—their first corporate act after returning to their homeland. The moment is more than a gesture. 12:7). In bowing before the God who had both loved them and judged them, so near the Day of Atonement, the people are showing their repentance and recommitment.

B. Altar of worship, 2-3

2 Then stood up Jeshua the son of Jozadak, and his brethren the priests, and Zerubbabel the son of Shealtiel, and his brethren, and builded the altar of the God of Israel, to offer burnt offerings thereon, as it is written in the law of Moses the man of God.

3 And they set the altar upon his bases; for fear was upon them because of the people of those countries: and they offered burnt offerings thereon unto the LORD, even burnt offerings morning and evening.

Because animal sacrifice had been prescribed in the Law of Moses, the people's worship requires an altar of sacrifice. Perhaps they searched through the ruins of the Temple for remnants of the previous altar and built a rough-hewn version that would be refined and refinished when the entire structure was completed. In raising the altar, the people are acting out the drama of father Abraham, who had first built an altar to Yahweh near this very spot (Gen. 12:7-8). They work diligently at the task "despite their fear of the peoples around them" (NIV). This fear will be justified when surrounding tribes will jealously oppose the restoration project (Ezra 4:1-6).

The work is supervised by two leaders. The name "Jeshua," being the same as "Joshua," would have stirred the people's memory of the leadership of Joshua in conquering the land in the first place. Jeshua's Zerubbabel is probably the "prince" or tribal chief who had received the precious vessels from the Temple that had first been pilfered by Nebuchadnezzar, then restored by Cyrus (1:7-8).

II. Plans for the Temple—6-7

6 From the first day of the seventh month began they to offer burnt offerings unto the LORD. But the foundation of the temple of the LORD was not yet laid.

7 They gave money also unto the masons, and to the carpenters; and meat, and drink, and oil, unto them of Zidon, and to them of Tyre, to bring cedar trees from Lebanon to the sea of Joppa, according to the grant that they had of Cyrus king of Persia.

Knowing that the altar at which they first worshiped would be temporary, the people set about immediately to provide materials for the permanent altar. The first order of business must be to lay the foundations of the Temple that will house the altar. But how are they to pay for the materials they will need? We recall that the people had been given silver and gold by the Persians (1:4). They have been further financially equipped by a grant from Cyrus.

Apparently the Jews had also gone to work in agriculture immediately upon their return, since they trade for the famous cedars of Lebanon with "meat, and drink, and oil." These giant evergreens would have been either tied together and floated in pods down to Joppa (Jerusalem's nearest port city) or lashed on ships and then unloaded at Joppa. The meat would have been that of sheep, goats, and oxen, while the oil would have consisted mainly of olive oil.

No doubt the people were aware that this commerce echoed the work of Solomon in building the first Temple (see 2 Chron. 2:10, 15ff.). Also, the prophet Isaiah had predicted the scene, citing God's promise that "the wealth of nations" in general and the cedars of Lebanon in particular would flow into the country once the people repented and God restored their fortunes (Isa. 60:11, 13).

III. Praising and Weeping—10-13
A. Worship in shouts and songs, 10-11

10 And when the builders laid the foundation of the temple of the LORD, they set the priests in their apparel with trumpets, and the Levites the sons of Asaph with cymbals, to praise the LORD, after the ordinance of David king of Israel.

11 And they sang together by course in praising and giving thanks unto the LORD; because he is good, for his mercy endureth for ever toward Israel. And all the people shouted with a great shout, when they praised the LORD, because the foundation of the house of the LORD was laid.

The intervening verses 8-9 indicated that some months were required for the materials for the Temple foundation to arrive. Finally they are assembled, and the Levites apparently lead in both work and worship, once again showing the importance of acknowledging God's presence at such momentous occasions. In verse 11, the worship overpowers the work. The blast of ceremonial trumpets and the clash of cymbals herald the setting of the first foundation stones in what will be called "the second Temple."

After being punished so dramatically for disobeying God's Word, the people are now remarkably focused on basing their renewal on new allegiance for the Word. Ezra has cited Moses as the authority for the offering of sacrifices (vs. 2b). Now the work of David, the psalmist-king, is called on as the basis for the great outpouring of music that accompanies these first steps toward a rebuilt Temple. After all, it was David who "set the Levites in the house of the LORD with cymbals, with psalteries, and with harps, according to the commandment of David, and of Gad the king's seer, and Nathan the prophet: for so was the commandment of the LORD by his prophets" (2 Chron. 29:25). The people accompany the instruments by chanting a refrain from David's Psalm 136: "for His mercy endureth for ever."

B. Bittersweet note, 12-13

12 But many of the priests and Levites and chief of the fathers, who were ancient men, that had seen the first house, when the foundation of this house was laid before their eyes, wept with a loud voice; and many shouted aloud for joy:

13 So that the people could not discern the noise of the shout of joy from the noise of the weeping of the people: for the people shouted with a loud shout, and the noise was heard afar off.

Many thoughtful people can identify with the sadness of these "ancient men" as they watched the foundations of a restored Temple being laid. Those, especially from among the priests, who had seen the majesty of the first Temple were reminded of the horror of its destruction. Some features in the first Temple simply could not be duplicated, such as its "almug" wood (perhaps sandalwood, 1 Kings 10:12). Faithful priests no doubt also mourned not just the loss of the Temple's previous material splendor, but the disobedience of Israel that had brought about its destruction. Their joy at the laying of new foundations could not be separated from the sense of tragedy that lay behind needing a new Temple in the first place.

Neither could the noise of the joyful shouts be separated from the mournful cries among the crowd of people attending the foundation-laying ceremony. The observation that this noise "was heard afar off" sounds a deliberately ominous note. The enemies of the Jews were listening. Their opposition will help cause the work of rebuilding the city and the Temple to be delayed for almost 100 years.

This development will discourage many of the people. Distracted from the work of rebuilding the Temple, they will turn to their own needs and interests. Not until the work of Nehemiah will the work so gloriously celebrated here—and wept over—be completed.

Evangelistic Emphasis

It had been a long time since the Jewish exiles had gathered at the site of the ancient temple in Jerusalem to offer sacrifice and praise. Only a few of the most elderly could remember the splendor of Solomon's temple. But now God's promise has been fulfilled, and they are on that holy ground. They offer praise and thanks, "for God is good and God's steadfast love endures forever."

Their act of praise and worship points us to the essence of the gospel. The good news is not that we shall always be successful. The good news is not that we shall be protected from the world and its problems. The good news is not that we have a protective charm that wards off illness, accident, tragedy and grief. The good news is that God's love endures. God's faithfulness and loyalty endures forever. We are not saved *from* the world and its troubles. We are saved *for* the world, raised up to tell of the love of God that is with us in the midst of sorrow, defeat, suffering and tragedy.

After six decades of being exiles in a strange land, the Jews return to their homeland. They come not complaining of the hard times. They come praising God and giving thanks: "For he is good, for his steadfast love endures forever toward Israel."

ℬℭ

Memory Selection

And they sang together by course in praising and giving thanks unto the Lord; because he is good, for his mercy endureth for ever toward Israel. And all the people shouted with a great shout, when they praised the Lord, because the foundation of the House of the Lord was laid.—*Ezra 3:11*

When the foundation for the altar of the temple was complete, the people of God held a prayer and praise service. It could have been a gripe session. Why did God let that beautiful temple of Solomon be destroyed by pagans? Why did they have to stay in Babylon for decades? When they got back to the "promised land" it wasn't all milk and honey. The land was poor. Those who had stayed in Jerusalem were sullen and suspicious. There was a lot to complain about.

But when the foundation of the altar was completed they gathered to praise God. Trumpets and cymbals and songs of praise were in order. They had a long way to go. But they had made a good start. Once again there would be a holy temple, a dwelling place for God in Jerusalem. They remembered God's gracious acts in creation, in liberation from slavery in Egypt, in bringing them back from captivity. So they sang, prayed, and shouted: "Give thanks to the Lord for he is good, for his steadfast love endures forever!"

Do you do more complaining or thanking?

Weekday Problems

Jane had been gone from her hometown for 40 years. She had fond memories of her childhood there. When she moved back, there was a new school, a new library, and a new church building. The congregation was somewhat smaller, but loyal members had worked together to replace the old building, which had major structural damage. Everyone was so pleased with the new building—everyone but Jane. She kept reminding everyone of the good old days. To hear her tell it, the church was crowded every Sunday, the choir was larger, the children's Sunday School bursting at the seams. The massive, high ceilinged (expensive to heat and impossible to cool), oak paneled, carpeted, stained glass sanctuary looked the way a church ought to look. The truth is, nothing about the town was quite like Jane remembered it. The children of the neighborhood, who came for tutoring after school, were not "our kind." She turned off people with her continual reminder, "It's just not like it used to be."

In today's lesson, some of the elders wept at the dedication of the altar of the new Temple—perhaps because they realized that at their age they would not live to see the new Temple restored, or because they remembered (with some idealizing) the way things were.

*What do people miss when they can only recall an idealized past?

Commenting on the Contribution

An usher was passing the collection plate. "What is this?" a surprised parishioner asked him. "This is a wedding, for goodness' sake."

"I know," the usher whispered back. "The father of the bride requested it."

Mother to son: Now remember to put some of your allowance in the offering plate. It's better to give than to receive.

Son: Then why don't I just buy some ice cream and let the cashier give the money?

As reimbursement, the visiting preacher passed his hat at the close of a service at which he had preached. When the hat had made the rounds, he looked into it intently, then said: "Let us offer thanks for the offering. I thank thee, dear Lord, that I got my hat back from these people!"

This Lesson in Your Life

The rebuilding of the temple in Jerusalem is an indication of the essential role of worship in the life of the people of Israel. They knew that God could be worshiped anywhere, anytime. But for the Jew there was a special sacredness about the Temple. There the young prophet Isaiah had sensed the holiness of God, with his vision of seraphim singing "Holy, Holy, Holy." There the ritual sacrifices of burnt offerings were made. Once a year the high priest would enter the holy of holies, the very dwelling place of God.

Martin Buber, the Jewish scholar from whom Christians have learned so much, goes so far as to say: "God cannot be expressed, he can only be addressed." No attempt to describe worship can be successful. There is only one way to find out what worship is, and that is to worship. Evelyn Underhill writes, "Worship is the little human spirit's humble, adoring acknowledgment of the measureless glory of God, the only Reality, the Perfect, the Unchanging, the entirely Free."

It was because Israel yearned for this experience of the Holy One that soon after their return to Jerusalem they began to restore the Temple. In our experience the sense of awe and wonder before the Holy God is no less important. In worship we begin not by telling God of our needs. We simply acknowledge His awesome and mysterious presence.

Grady Hardin says that *awe* is the definitive spirit of worship. "All emotions or feelings in worship are valid as worship feelings to the extent that they accord with awe, for awe is the direct personal relatedness to God, who is the object of worship. Awe is the awareness by thought and feeling that God is God and we are creatures. It is the seeing at once God's holiness in power and goodness and our creatureliness in weakness and wrongness. It is the vital, overwhelming awareness that nothing in life has real meaning except our being accepted by God and that we ourselves cannot cause this acceptance to happen."

It is not enough to know about God. It is not even enough to know God. The important thing is to be known by God (Gal.4:9). Robert McAffee Brown observed, "When people are known by God they do not first of all write books or work out a philosophy of history, or start analyzing their religious experiences. They sing, or they pray, or they sing and pray at the same time."

Worshipers say or pray, "Thank you, Lord! Bless the Lord! Alleluia! Praise the Lord for his steadfast love endures forever!" These acts we call worship—singing, praying, listening, adoring, shouting, being silent and aware. The returning Jews built a temple because worship was of first importance. Worship is no less important to the believer today.

GETTING THE FACTS STRAIGHT

1. Who was in charge of the Temple building project (Ezra 3:2)?
Jeshua and Zerubbabel were in charge.

2. What festival was observed when the altar was set on the foundation (Ezra 3:4)?
They kept the festival of booths (tabernacles) as prescribed.

3. Who were appointed to have oversight of the work on the house of the Lord (Ezra 3:8)?
Levites from 20 years old and upward were to have oversight of the work.

4. Who wept when the foundation of the Temple was laid (Ezra 3:12)?
Many of the priests and Levites and heads of family, old people who had seen the first house on its foundations.

5. Why did they weep?
The beginnings of the new Temple seemed poor in comparison with their memory of the old Temple.

6. What did the Jews' adversaries request (Ezra 4:2)?
The adversaries asked that they might be allowed to help build the Temple.

7. How did the leaders of Israel respond to this offer to help (Ezra 4:3)?
They said, "You shall have no part with us in building a house to our God; but we alone will build to the Lord."

8. What did the people of the land (the adversaries) do (Ezra 4: 4-6)?
They discouraged the people of Judah, made them afraid to build, and wrote an accusation against them and sent it to the Persian King, Artaxerxes.

9. What accusation did they send to the king (Ezra 4:13)?
They said that if the city were rebuilt and its walls finished, the Jews would not pay tribute, custom, or toll, and the royal revenue would be reduced.

10.What was the reply of King Artaxerxes (Ezra 4:22)?
He commanded that the construction stop and the work of rebuilding halted.

All worship in the Judeo-Christian tradition is a response. It is always a response to God's initiative. Evelyn Underhill puts it: "It is the self giving of that Infinite God to us, His showing of himself to us which is the true cause of the impulse to worship that springs up in men's hearts."

Grady Davis sees here the distinguishing mark between Christian and pagan worship. "The worship of a pagan is searching upward to the divine. The worship of a Christian is a glad response to the God who reaches down to him. The worship of the pagan is search; the worship of a Christian is recognition."

J. B. Phillips has a gift for putting things in an unusual way. During World War II he was working at a Youth Center in London. He writes, " I had had a very exciting evening. There had been a concert and dancing and speeches and cheers and singing ' For he's a jolly good fellow' and all the rest of it. When it came to closing time I suggested to the leaders that they might close with worship. One of them said, 'You know we haven't a clue to what you really mean by worship.' 'Haven't you? Well, its three cheers for God!'"

"Three cheers for God!"

Worship is a glad and joyful response to what God has done and is doing. It is God's initiative that draws us back to worship, week after week, year after year, generation after generation. We return to worship at a special time, in a sacred place not because of a dreary sense of duty. We come not to gain a future reward. We come again and again not primarily to hear one person's ideas about God. We come not even to listen to good music. Rather we are drawn to worship in order to acknowledge God's greatness, to give thanks for God's goodness, and to join all creation in adoring God.

The gathering to dedicate the foundation, the beginning of restoration of the temple in the time of Ezra, is an anticipation of another gathering described in the vision of the prophet on the Isle of Patmos in the book of Revelation "After this I looked, and there was a great multitude which no one could count, from every nation, from all tribes and peoples and tongues, standing before the throne and before the lamb robed in white with palm branches in their hands. They cried with a loud voice, saying, 'Salvation belongs to our God who sits upon the throne and to the Lamb!' And all the angels stood round the throne ... and they fell on their faces before the throne and worshiped God singing, 'Amen! Blessing and glory and wisdom and thanksgiving and honor and power and might be to our God forever and ever! Amen!'" (Rev.7:9-12)

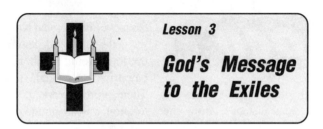

Lesson 3

God's Message to the Exiles

Haggai 1:2-14

Thus speaketh the LORD of hosts, saying, This people say, The time is not come, the time that the LORD's house should be built.

3 Then came the word of the LORD by Haggai the prophet, saying,

4 Is it time for you, O ye, to dwell in your cieled houses, and this house lie waste?

5 Now therefore thus saith the LORD of hosts; Consider your ways.

6 Ye have sown much, and bring in little; ye eat, but ye have not enough; ye drink, but ye are not filled with drink; ye clothe you, but there is none warm; and he that earneth wages earneth wages to put it into a bag with holes.

7 Thus saith the LORD of hosts; Consider your ways.

8 Go up to the mountain, and bring wood, and build the house; and I will take pleasure in it, and I will be glorified, saith the LORD.

9 Ye looked for much, and, lo, it came to little; and when ye brought it home, I did blow upon it. Why? saith the LORD of hosts. Because of mine house that is waste, and ye run every man unto his own house.

10 Therefore the heaven over you is stayed from dew, and the earth is stayed from her fruit.

11 And I called for a drought upon the land, and upon the mountains, and upon the corn, and upon the new wine, and upon the oil, and upon that which the ground bringeth forth, and upon men, and upon cattle, and upon all the labour of the hands.

12 Then Zerubbabel the son of Shealtiel, and Joshua the son of Josedech, the high priest, with all the remnant of the people, obeyed the voice of the LORD their God, and the words of Haggai the prophet, as the LORD their God had sent him, and the people did fear before the LORD.

13 Then spake Haggai the LORD's messenger in the LORD's message unto the people, saying, I am with you, saith the LORD.

14 And the LORD stirred up the spirit of Zerubbabel the son of Shealtiel, governor of Judah, and the spirit of Joshua the son of Josedech, the high priest, and the spirit of all the remnant of the people; and they came and did work in the house of the LORD of hosts, their God.

Memory Selection
Haggai 1:4

Background Scripture
Haggai; Ezra 5:1-2

Devotional Reading
1 Corinthians 3:10-17

411

Although this lesson seems to "jump" a great distance, from the book of Ezra to Haggai, it portrays historically adjacent events. The prophet Haggai prophesied after those who were rebuilding Jerusalem and its Temple were beginning to see some results from their labor. Unfortunately, enemies from the Samaritan cities near Judea wrote to the successors of the Persian King Cyrus and warned that if Jerusalem were rebuilt, the Jews would revolt, and no longer pay tribute to Persia (see Ezra 4). Their protest worked, and the restoration was abandoned.

God's people then went about constructing elaborate houses for themselves instead of pressing for permission to continue work on the Temple. The focus in this lesson is therefore on Haggai's message: *Don't dishonor God by placing our own interests above His.*

ഇരുള

Bring to class a novel or some other object connected with a hobby such as sewing or a golf club. Pretend to be absorbed in reading, sewing, or practicing your golf swing.

Before class, instruct a helper to dress in a prophet's garment (a terry-cloth bathrobe will do!), and carry a cross as he comes up behind you. His or her task is to mime an appeal for you to leave your hobby and come tend to the work of the cross (which can be lifted up and pointed to repeatedly). After ignoring the "prophet" for awhile, relent and follow him out of the room.

Resuming leadership of the class, ask what is wrong with having a hobby, or our own work to do. Nothing, of course, unless we become so focused on them that we forsake the work of God. That is what the prophet Haggai warns against.

Teaching Outline	Daily Bible Readings

I. Neglecting God's Work—2-4
  A. Not working for God, 2
  B. Working for self instead, 3-4
	Mon. Time to Rebuild
	        Haggai 1:1-6
	Tue. God Stirs Up the People
	        Haggai 1:7-15

II. Suffering the Consequences—5-11
  A. 'Where does it all go?,' 5-6
  B. A wiser investment, 7-8
  C. Judgment on the land, 9-11
	Wed. 'Take Courage, I Am With You'
	        Haggai 2:1-9
	Thu. Working Despite Criticism
	        Ezra 5:1-5
	Fri. 'We Are God's Servants'
	        Ezra 5:6-12

III. Responding to God's Call—12-14
  A. Enjoying God's presence, 12-13
  B. Doing God's work, 14
	Sat. From that Time Until Now
	        Ezra 5:13-17
	Sun. Blessings from This Day
	        Haggai 2:13-23

Verse by Verse

I. Neglecting God's Work—2-4
A. Not working for God, 2

2 Thus speaketh the LORD of hosts, saying, This people say, The time is not come, the time that the LORD's house should be built.

Verse 1 has identified the speaker here as the prophet Haggai. As noted in the "Focus" section, the enemies of the Jews had written to their Persian overlords, warning that if the Temple in Jerusalem were rebuilt the Jews would find in it the motivation to throw off Persia's yoke (Ezra 4:1-13). Eventually their complaints would have the desired effect, at least temporarily, for King Artaxerxes (the third king after Cyrus, who had authorized the return) halted the restoration project (4:23-24).

Even earlier, however, Jewish morale sagged, and the strength of will necessary to complete the huge task of rebuilding the Temple wilted under the pressure of their enemies' complaints to King Darius (Ezra 4:5). This is where the prophet Haggai comes into the picture. Looking about him, he saw that the land that was supposed to be flowing with milk and honey was actually drab and desolate. He connected the withholding of rain from heaven with the people's having insulted God by not having the moral backbone to continue work on the Temple despite the pressure from surrounding political enemies. (Ezra 4:10 notes that some of these critics were Samaritans, an insight into part of the reason relations between the Samaritans and Jews were still tense even in Jesus' day; see John 4:9.)

Claiming that "the time is not come" to rebuild the Temple may be a hint that some Jews were taking the prediction that the captivity would last 70 years (Jer. 25:11-12) very literally, and had stopped work on the building because their sentence had not quite expired. They had quite a different interpretation of why drought ruled the land—for them it was because the time of "desolation" had not run its course.

B. Working for self instead, 3-4

3 Then came the word of the LORD by Haggai the prophet, saying,

4 Is it time for you, O ye, to dwell in your cieled houses, and this house lie waste?

Haggai's perceptive prophetic voice pierced through the deceitfulness of this argument. If the desolation was a fixed part of a 70-year punishment willed by God in judgment for the former disobedience of the Jews' forefathers, then why were they able to expend so much money and effort on their own houses? The word for "ceiled" may refer either to a house with a ceiling or with the more lavish feature of paneling (as in the NIV). Certainly the prophet would have nothing against the people building a basic house with a roof to keep out the weather. The implication is that the work of rebuilding their houses and the Temple could have progressed alongside each other.

While it is certainly true that even today believers can become so focused on the luxury of their own homes that they neglect to provide an adequate place of worship, this is not a precise parallel to the situation Haggai faced. Under the New Covenant, the house of God is the Church—His people, rather than the edifice where they meet (1 Tim. 3:15). A more direct parallel is to point out how easy it is for us to focus our energies and wealth on personal concerns, including our homes, than on the work of building up God's family.

II. Suffering the Consequences—5-11

A. 'Where does it all go?,' 5-6

5 Now therefore thus saith the LORD of hosts; Consider your ways.

6 Ye have sown much, and bring in little; ye eat, but ye have not enough; ye drink, but ye are not filled with drink; ye clothe you, but there is none warm; and he that earneth wages earneth wages to put it into a bag with holes.

Haggai usually asserts that his words are not his own, but God's, which calls for the people to grant that they bear the authority of God, not man. Also, the line "Consider your ways" is a true prophetic call designed to draw hearers up short from a tendency not to think seriously about their manner of life and to revise their

plans with God's will in mind instead of our own.

Many people even in our own day can verify the experience described in verse 6. How often do we feel that we "come to the end of the money before the end of the month, seem to have more income than ever but less to show for it, and can never fill our purse with money because holes drain it faster than we can put more in? The prophet points out to the Jews why they are having this experience.

B. A wiser investment, 7-8

7 Thus saith the LORD of hosts; Consider your ways.

8 Go up to the mountain, and bring wood, and build the house; and I will take pleasure in it, and I will be glorified, saith the LORD.

Based on the repetition of his appeal, we may conclude that Haggai is calling the people to *re*consider their ways. The best investment takes into consideration the needs of the Kingdom of God, not just our own comfort. So the people are urged to bring timber from the surrounding hills (which, unlike today, were well-wooded) for use in the Temple. Rock was plentiful without going to the mountains; and both wood and rock were used in the Temple walls (Ezra 5:8), the connecting timbers perhaps minimizing damage from earthquakes.

C. Judgment on the land, 9-11

9 Ye looked for much, and, lo, it came to little; and when ye brought it home, I did blow upon it. Why? saith the LORD of hosts. Because of mine house that is waste, and ye run every man unto his own house.

10 Therefore the heaven over you is stayed from dew, and the earth is stayed from her fruit.

11 And I called for a drought upon the land, and upon the mountains, and upon the corn, and upon the new wine, and upon the oil, and upon that which the ground bringeth forth, and upon men, and upon cattle, and upon all the labour of the hands.

The prophet now returns to the theme of not being able to experience God's blessings because our hearts are on a different track. This reminds us that God can marshal the forces of nature to send a message to people. Even today, He may use such natural events as the drought described here to get our attention and cause us to examine our priorities.

Of course Jesus will later remind us that mere humans cannot always determine when outward events such as drought or disease are the result of disobedience: God sends rain on the just and the unjust (Matt. 5:45). However, He is still Lord of the natural world; and even at a more obvious level, we know that the sinful abuse of the environment can cause nature to rise up in protest.

III. Responding to God's Call—12-14
A. Enjoying God's presence, 12-13

12 Then Zerubbabel the son of Shealtiel, and Joshua the son of Josedech, the high priest, with all the remnant of the people, obeyed the voice of the LORD their God, and the words of Haggai the prophet, as the LORD their God had sent him, and the people did fear before the LORD.

13 Then spake Haggai the LORD's messenger in the LORD's message unto the people, saying, I am with you, saith the LORD.

Unlike their forefathers before the Captivity, the people actually heed the prophet's warning. Haggai's strong words from God are joined with the influence of the priest Zerubbabel. Both Zerubbabel and Shealtiel seem to be descendants of others with the same name. To say that Zerubbabel is "the son" of Shealtiel must mean "descendant," since the Zerubbabel who was Shealtiel's son lived when the people first returned under Cyrus, rather than in the says of Darius when Haggai prophesied (see Ezra 3:2).

B. Doing God's work, 14

14 And the LORD stirred up the spirit of Zerubbabel the son of Shealtiel, governor of Judah, and the spirit of Joshua the son of Josedech, the high priest, and the spirit of all the remnant of the people; and they came and did work in the house of the LORD of hosts, their God,

Twice now, in verses 12 and 14, the word "remnant" has been used to describe the people, reminding us that only a minority of the Jews accepted Cyrus' challenge to return to the Promised Land. Note also that the combination of both the prophetic and priestly leadership roles succeeds in moving this remnant to reconsider their misplaced values. Even today, in church leadership, the need for the sharp challenge of the prophet-like voice is balanced with the need for those who, like the Jewish priest, can effectively lead the people in meaningful worship.

Evangelistic Emphasis

We know little of the prophet Haggai. We do know that he was commissioned as God's spokesperson. He had a message to deliver. "The word of the Lord came by the prophet Haggai" (Hag. 1:3). He had a message for the high priest and for the governor. His task was to deliver God's message to rebuild the Temple.

As surprising as it may be to us, we are also called to deliver God's word. That is the mission of the Church. It is as though the message of the gospel is a special delivery letter with some person's name upon it. Benjamin R. Garrison reminds, "Christians are God's postmen, not his letter. We dare not deliver ourselves. When the patrons on our route express surprise that we have been chosen to deliver the Gospel's letter the most seemly reply is, 'Yes, it seems strange to us also. But it is a registered letter we bear with your name upon it. We beg your pardon for messing it up with our gummy thumb prints. But we have been commissioned to deliver it.'"

We spend a lot of time and effort getting people to come to church. Inviting others to church is one way of delivering the message; but it is not the good news itself. Our aim is to bring others to a trust in and obedience to Christ as Lord. We may stumble and fall in our task, but we have no choice but to share the Word.

ഇൗരു

Memory Selection

Is it time for you, O ye, to dwell in your ceiled houses, and this house lie waste? —*Haggai 1:4*

The prophet Haggai has a single focus. The word he is to bring to the governor, to the high priest, to the people is that it is time to get their priorities straight. God has stirred the ruler of Persia to allow them to return to the promised land. It was not all they had expected. The times were hard. The harvest was just enough to get by on. What little extra they had to spend they spent on their own houses, while the Temple still lay in ruins.

The Holy Temple in Jerusalem was the symbol of God's presence in their midst. Yet the people were giving first loyalty to their own comfort and security. Until they put God first, then nothing else would bring wholeness and healing to the land. The ancient words ,"Thou shalt have no other gods before me" were ignored as they embellished their houses while neglecting God's Temple.

What do we put ahead of God's claim on our life? What is our first love? How long will we put off giving God first place?

Weekday Problems

Improvements were being made throughout the small rural community. The old ramshackle, frame school house had been replaced by an attractive, modern school with the latest equipment. The small section of the corner grocery where mail could be picked up or left off was replaced by a state of the art brick post office. New ranch-style houses equipped with all the modern conveniences were replacing small frame houses that great-grandparents of the modern, prosperous population had built.

However, the community's church building had been neglected. The paint was peeling, the floor was uneven and creaky, the pews were rough. The piano was out of tune and beyond repair. There was no running water. Broken windows invited dirt daubers to make their home inside. It was clear to children growing up in that community what was most important to their parents. A drive through town made plain what was of least importance.

Finally the leaders decided it was not right that God's house should be so shabby when their own homes were much improved. The congregation worked, gave, and sacrificed that it would be restored to a place of beauty, and a witness to the value which the family of faith put on the worship of God.

*Have you seen signs that people in your own community value their building? What are they?

*Why was the temple so important to the Jews returning to Jerusalem?

Interesting Introductions

Ladies and gentlemen, the speaker and I have a strange and wonderful relationship. He's strange and I'm wonderful.

You have been giving your attention to a turkey stuffed with sage. You are now about to hear from a sage stuffed with turkey.

✦✦✦✦✦

Our speaker needs no introduction. What he needs is a conclusion.

✦✦✦✦✦

You will appreciate our speaker tonight. He is the type of person who approaches everything with an open mouth.

✦✦✦✦✦

Our speaker has accomplished some great deeds. Don't let him weary you with the patter of little feats.

✦✦✦✦✦

Few can equal the creative mind of our speaker. He can wrap up a one-minute idea in a one-hour speech.

This Lesson in Your Life

God did not need a material dwelling place. When the Temple was destroyed and they were carried off in captivity, God went with them. God was not limited to one place, however sacred. Yet, for the prophet Haggai the rebuilding of the temple was of the highest priority.

In their long tradition, going back to the time of Moses, the tabernacle (tent) was where God would meet Moses. The magnificent temple built by Solomon was God's chosen place where human beings should expect to encounter God, to be challenged and renewed by God's divine presence. The new Temple would be a constant reminder of the presence of God and a declaration of God's authority.

The rebuilding of the Temple was an appropriate way of honoring God. It was not a magical way of gaining God's approval. Through their sacrifice and work, the people were giving themselves to God.

Always and everywhere God's people were taught to bring the first-fruits of the harvest as an offering. They were to bring the best, not the left overs, not the culls. In a similary way, the Temple was an expression of that devotion, "Our utmost for His highest."

Once while visiting in a gift shop owned by a church member, I noted a beautiful crystal pitcher that was drastically marked down in price. It was very slightly damaged. I inquired if the owner would consider giving the damaged pitcher to the church for use in Holy Communion services. She quickly replied there was no way she would give that pitcher to her church—but that she would gladly give a perfect, unblemished one for use in holy worship. Only her best was suitable for God.

In the Scriptures, the Temple as the dwelling place of God goes through several transformations. The Temple in Jerusalem in Jesus' time was not the one rebuilt during Haggai's time. It was a more elaborate structure built by King Herod. But the Church came to understand that the dwelling place of God was not limited to houses of brick and stone, wood or steel. The Word made flesh came and dwelt among us. The body of Jesus was the temple referred to by Jesus when He was asked for a sign: "Destroy this temple, and in three days I will raise it up" (John 2:19, 21). Peter refers to the Church, God's people, as the temple of God. "Come to him, a living stone, and like living stones let yourselves be built into a spiritual house" (1 Pet. 2:4). And Paul asks, "Do you not know that you are God's temple and that God's Spirit dwells in you?" (1 Cor. 3:16). We sometimes sing a prayer-song: "Lord, prepare me / to be a sanctuary, / pure and holy, tried and true, / With thanksgiving, / I'll be a living / Sanctuary for you."

GETTING THE FACTS STRAIGHT

1. When were Haggai's speeches given (Hag. 1:1)?
The speeches of Haggai were given during the second year of the rule of Darius, king of Persia, between the sixth and ninth months, 520 B.C.

2. To whom did Haggai deliver the Word of the Lord (Hag. 1:1)?
To Zerubbabel, governor, and to Joshua, high priest.

3. What was the popular opinion about rebuilding the Temple (Hag.1: 2)?
The people say the time is not right.

4. How are the people of Judah faring (Hag. 6)?
They sow much but harvest little; they eat but never enough; they drink but are not satisfied; they have clothes but no one is warm; their wages seem to disappear.

5. According to Haggai, why were the people fairing so poorly (Hag. 1: 9)?
"Says the Lord of hosts. Because my house lies in ruins, while all of you hurry off to your own houses."

6. What further calamities does Haggai see coming because of the people's neglect of the Temple?
The Lord will call for a drought affecting land, grain, wine, oil, human beings, and animals.

7. How does the new Temple appear to those who remember Solomon's temple in its glory (Hag. 23)?
"Is it not in your sight as nothing?"

8. What does the prophet say to those to whom the new Temple seems as nothing (Hag. 2:4-6)?
"Take courage, for I am with you. My spirit abides among you; do not fear."

9. What was Haggai's vision of the future?
The treasures of all nations shall come, the house will be filled with God's splendor, and the later splendor of the temple shall be greater than the former.

10. What is the Lord's promise to Zerubbabel the governor through Haggai (Hag. 2:20-23)?
The Lord will overthrow the kingdoms of the nations and will make Zerubbabel like a signet ring, God's chosen one.

I went on a deer hunt. It was a chilly, misty morning. The day before, my wife and I had come upon a family of four deer. They were so quick, so agile, so timid, so graceful! They were a joy to behold.

So today I would track them down for a second look. I got an early start. Perhaps they would be out for an early breakfast. Armed with two eyes and my usual bifocals, I started out. Two ducks caught my eye. As they heard my footsteps they scurried away, fussing about this invasion of their space. A great gray heron spread his majestic wings as he gracefully rose from the lake, giving a command performance before my very eyes. A mocking bird, lost in song, took no note of my intrusion. Robins were out in force, both the early birds and late. Crows were everywhere to police the park grounds. But the deer I never found. The day before, without a passing thought of seeing a deer, we saw them. They suddenly appeared, in plain sight, as though returning from a mid-morning romp in the playground of the park. But when I went hunting for them, there was neither hide or hair. The hike was well rewarded though, with delights of eye and ear. It was the fleeting sight of yesterday's deer that lured me back to drink in more of nature's grace.

How often does God come, not when we look for God, but when we least expect to find God! How often do we experience God, not in a form and manner we expect but in a surprising way. When we go looking for God, just at the place and in the way some one said they found the Lord, we wander on and on. Just when we need God most, it seems God is absent, nowhere to be found. Then it dawns on us that the God we search for high and low has been with us all the time, hidden in plain sight.

Through the ancient prophet Haggai, the Lord declares, "I am with you" (Hag. 1:13). Again the Lord promises: "Take courage, all you people; work, for I am with you" (Hag 2:4). Then, just in case we missed it, he promises again: "My spirit abides among you; do not fear" (Hag. 2:5).

Sometimes we cry with Job: "O that I knew where I might find him" (Job 23:3). Other times we know the psalmist's truth: "Whither shall I go from thy Spirit? Or whither shall I flee from thy presence?" (Ps. 139:7). The words of the ancient prophet find a new fulfillment in the birth of Mary's child, whom they called "Emmanuel," which means, "God with us!" (Matt. 1:23).

Happy hunting! Happy being found!

Lesson 4

Hope for a New Era

Zechariah 8:1-13

Again the word of the LORD of hosts came to me, saying,

2 Thus saith the LORD of hosts; I was jealous for Zion with great jealousy, and I was jealous for her with great fury.

3 Thus saith the LORD; I am returned unto Zion, and will dwell in the midst of Jerusalem: and Jerusalem shall be called a city of truth; and the mountain of the LORD of hosts the holy mountain.

4 Thus saith the LORD of hosts; There shall yet old men and old women dwell in the streets of Jerusalem, and every man with his staff in his hand for very age.

5 And the streets of the city shall be full of boys and girls playing in the streets thereof.

6 Thus saith the LORD of hosts; If it be marvellous in the eyes of the remnant of this people in these days, should it also be marvellous in mine eyes? saith the LORD of hosts.

7 Thus saith the LORD of hosts; Behold, I will save my people from the east country, and from the west country;

8 And I will bring them, and they shall dwell in the midst of Jerusalem: and they shall be my people, and I will be their God, in truth and in righteousness.

9 Thus saith the LORD of hosts; Let your hands be strong, ye that hear in these days these words by the mouth of the prophets, which were in the day that the foundation of the house of the LORD of hosts was laid, that the temple might be built.

10 For before these days there was no hire for man, nor any hire for beast; neither was there any peace to him that went out or came in because of the affliction: for I set all men every one against his neighbour.

11 But now I will not be unto the residue of this people as in the former days, saith the LORD of hosts.

12 For the seed shall be prosperous; the vine shall give her fruit, and the ground shall give her increase, and the heavens shall give their dew; and I will cause the remnant of this people to possess all these things.

13 And it shall come to pass, that as ye were a curse among the heathen, O house of Judah, and house of Israel; so will I save you, and ye shall be a blessing: fear not, but let your hands be strong.

Memory Selection
Zechariah 8:3

Background Scripture
Zechariah 8

Devotional Reading
Psalm 48:1-14

In the previous lesson we noted that enemies of the Jews had persuaded Persian authorities to shut down the work of rebuilding Jerusalem and the Temple. Later, that prohibition was relaxed, and the prophet Haggai was able to revive interest in the work of restoration.

Still, there is widespread discouragement; and the present lesson focuses on how God raised up another prophet, Zechariah, to balance Haggai's stern warnings with new hope. If the people will only continue what they have started, all of God's previous promises to bless them will be fulfilled. Beyond personal success, God's people will also become a blessing to the nations.

What examples of "encouraging words" have members of your group experienced, at crucial times in their lives? Recall the earlier lesson on Barnabas, whose name means "son of encouragement." Older persons may remember the encouragement President Roosevelt offered during the Great Depression, when he rallied a nation by the counsel, "All we have to fear is fear itself." Others may cite a

minister, an older Christian, a mentor at work, or a community leader. Emphasize the way God often sends such encouragers when our spirits are low, our zeal flagging.

This is the role God carved out for the prophet Zechariah. As the previous lesson showed, they had assembled many of the materials needed for rebuilding the Temple in Jerusalem. Yet they lacked was enthusiasm, goals, and a vision of victory. Zechariah supplied these missing elements.

I. God's Return to Zion—1-3
  A. Pattern of prophecy, 1-2
  B. God's Presence, 3
	Mon. God Will Return to Zion
	Zechariah 8:1-6

	Tue. 'Let Your Hands Be Strong' Zechariah 8:7-12

II. Gracious Future—4-8
  A. The good life for all, 4-5
  B. Everyday miracles, 6-8
	Wed. 'You Shall Be a Blessing'
	Zechariah 8:13-17

	Thu. Many Will Seek the Lord Zechariah 8:18-23
III. 'Get to work!'—9-11	Fri. Great Is the Lord Psalm 48:1-8

IV. Good to Come—12-13
  A. Abundant harvests, 12
  B. Blessing to others, 13
	Sat. Let Zion Be Glad
	Psalm 48:9-14

	Sun. Praise Among the Nations Psalm 57:7-11

Verse by Verse

I. God's Return to Zion—1-3

A. Pattern of prophecy, 1-2

1 Again the word of the LORD of hosts came to me, saying,

2 Thus saith the LORD of hosts; I was jealous for Zion with great jealousy, and I was jealous for her with great fury.

As early as the giving of the Law, shortly after the Jews had been freed from Egyptian bondage, they learned that the God who delivered them was a *jealous* God (Exod. 20:5). The repetition of the term in verse 2 forms a play on words. God is often portrayed as a jealous lover who burns in anger at His beloved, Israel, when she "plays the harlot." Here, however, the context suggests that God's jealousy is now burning *in favor* of the people. As Haggai (a contemporary of Zechariah) has indicated, God longs for the people whom He loves jealously to be reestablished in the land. The word for "fury," therefore, may better be translated "zeal," or "burning" as in the NIV. God is not expressing anger at His people so much as intense desire to bless them in their renewed efforts to rebuild the Temple in Zion (another name for Jerusalem).

B. God's Presence, 3

3 Thus saith the LORD; I am re-turned unto Zion, and will dwell in the midst of Jerusalem: and Jerusalem shall be called a city of truth; and the mountain of the LORD of hosts the holy mountain.

Although Yahweh is a universal God, whom even the heavens cannot contain, He had withdrawn His presence from Jerusalem, allowing the Babylonians to overrun the city when the people abandoned the Covenant. Now, as noted in preceding lessons, the term of their sentence has been served. With the return of both God's presence and His people, a new age is dawning. The hope is that instead of a city that stands for the "lie" of boasting of God's presence while worshiping idols, it will stand for truth; instead of just any mountain, Zion will stand for God's *holy* citadel.

Historically, the rebuilt city did not reach such status. This fact, and the several Messianic references in Zechariah, prompt many Christian interpreters to see a "bulge" in such statements—a meaning that swells beyond its original application and points to the Christian era. The prophet has therefore become known as a "Messianic" prophet second only to Isaiah. The Gospel writers point to Zechariah as background for Jesus' riding into Jerusalem on a donkey (cp.

9:9 with Matt. 21:5); a servant who will be a "Branch" or root (3:8; Rom. 15:12); the price of 30 pieces of silver that was "cast unto the potter" (11:12-13; Matt. 27:9); people looking on the divine One whom they have pierced (12:10; John 19:37); and the fact that people will "smite the shepherd and the sheep shall be scattered" (13:7; Mark 14:27). (Also, several of Zechariah's, symbols reappear in the book of Revelation.)

II. Gracious Future—4-8
A. The good life for all, 4-5

4 Thus saith the LORD of hosts; There shall yet old men and old women dwell in the streets of Jerusalem, and every man with his staff in his hand for very age.

5 And the streets of the city shall be full of boys and girls playing in the streets thereof.

But what if Israel's enemies (see Ezra 4) succeed in their campaign to have the work stopped, or, worse still, attack the workers and destroy all the work required to rebuild the city? The prophet reassures the workers that the city will be safe from such enemies, a place where people can grow old (cp. "very age" with the NIV's "ripe old age), and young children can play.

B. Everyday miracles, 6-8

6 Thus saith the LORD of hosts; If it be marvellous in the eyes of the remnant of this people in these days, should it also be marvellous in mine eyes? saith the LORD of hosts.

7 Thus saith the LORD of hosts; Behold, I will save my people from the east country, and from the west country;

8 And I will bring them, and they shall dwell in the midst of Jerusalem: and they shall be my people, and I will be their God, in truth and in righteousness.

As a nation, Israel was small compared to its neighbors; and only a remnant of that small nation had returned to rebuild Jerusalem. To them, it would require a miracle; but not to God, for whom "all things are possible." Not only will the task of rebuilding be possible with God's aid; the city will regain at least something of the importance it had under David, and under his son Solomon, when the queen of Sheba saw its wonders and exclaimed that "the half was not told me" (1 Kings 10:1-7).

Again, because Jerusalem has hardly become the center of world attention described here, some authorities believe that Zechariah is describing the End Time, when Jerusalem is transformed into the spiritual center of the reign of God over the earth. Note that the last phrase of verse 8 is in fact applied to the Messiah's reign in Revelation 21:3.

III. 'Get to work!'—9-11

9 Thus saith the LORD of hosts; Let your hands be strong, ye that hear in these days these words by the mouth of the prophets, which were in the day that the foundation of the house of the LORD of hosts was laid, that the temple might be built.

10 For before these days there was no hire for man, nor any hire for beast; neither was there any peace to him that went out or came in because of the affliction: for I set all men every one against his neighbour.

11 But now I will not be unto the residue of this people as in the former days, saith the LORD of hosts.

Here Zechariah supports the call of his fellow-prophet Haggai for the people to take heart and return to the task of rebuilding the Temple (Hag. 1; see Lesson 3). It is time to build on the foundations that had been laid. If anything is to come of Cyrus' edict allowing the Jews to return, the people must be strong in their resolve.

When Israel's enemies had caused the work to be halted, there was no work ("hire") in the public sector for man or beast; and people had turned to building their own accommodations instead of the Temple. The situation was worsened by God's sending a spirit of division and dissension among the people because of their lack of zeal for His work. Now Zechariah promises that this negative economic and spiritual climate will be reversed.

IV. Good to Come—12-13
A. Abundant harvests, 12

12 For the seed shall be prosperous; the vine shall give her fruit, and the ground shall give her increase, and the heavens shall give their dew; and I will cause the remnant of this people to possess all these things.

When God had first given the Covenant, He asserted His sovereign blessings in both spiritual and physical ways. If the people remained in covenant relationship, he would bless both the soil of their souls and of the land, the fruit of the ground and the fruit of flocks and herds (see Deut. 28:1-6, 11-12). Both the Captivity

and the poor production in agricultural were the direct result of their having abandoned the Covenant. Now, along with the restoration of the Temple, God promises also to restore the earth to productivity. Obviously not every drought can now be traced to disobedience (Matt. 5:45). Long-term, however, God retains the ability to send and withhold the rain; and the drastic failure of any agricultural or economic system should get our attention and ask ourselves whether such conditions might coincide with widespread disobedience. The devastation of the land by war, for example, can sometimes be traced to rebellion against godly principles.

B. Blessing to others, 13

13 And it shall come to pass, that as ye were a curse among the heathen, O house of Judah, and house of Israel; so will I save you, and ye shall be a blessing: fear not, but let your hands be strong.

When God's people repent and realign their behavior with the Covenant, blessings spill over onto surrounding peoples. The unfolding history since the Restoration has shown partial fulfillment of this promise. Jewish statesmen, philosophers, businessmen, and tradesmen have made astonishing contributions to society as a whole, compared with their numbers. Yet, again, there seems to be an end-time and Messianic overtone to this prophecy. Perhaps it envisions the coming of all nations to "the new Jerusalem" of Revelation, when every knee shall bow and every tongue proclaim that the Jewish Messiah is Lord of all.

Evangelistic Emphasis

No amount of church advertising, newspaper, bill boards, radio, or television is as effective as word of mouth. When the word is out on the streets, when neighbors tell new residents, when it's the talk over coffee about what is happening at church, then people begin to take notice.

It happened in Jerusalem. People in other cities, people from other nations, people who spoke other languages had heard the news, "God is with you." They would take hold of the hem of the robe of a Jew and say, "Let us go with you for we have heard that God is with you." (Zech. 8:23)

What would be the signs of God's presence in your congregation? What would convince others that God is with you? Perhaps the way you care for one another? Perhaps the way you make the outcast welcome? Perhaps the joy that pervades your gatherings? Perhaps the involvement in helping children and old people in your community? What would lead others to say to you, "Let us go with you for we have heard that God is with you"?

80C3

Memory Selection

Thus saith the Lord; I am returned unto Zion, and will dwell in the midst of Jerusalem: and Jerusalem shall be called the city of truth; and the mountain of the Lord of hosts, The holy mountain. —*Zech. 8:3*

One of the most familiar passages from John's gospel is the promise of Jesus, "In my father's house are many mansions or many dwelling places. (John 14:2).

This promise is a source of hope and comfort to know that we shall be with Jesus after death. But in this passage, Zechariah 8:3, there is the promise that the Lord comes to dwell with us now. "I will dwell in the midst of Jerusalem."

God's dwelling place may also be in our church: "Where two or three are gathered in my name, there am I in the midst of them."

God may dwell in our home. Some have left a chair at the family table as a reminder of the unseen but ever-present guest.

God may dwell in our hearts, even as we pray, "Come into my heart, Lord Jesus."

God may dwell in our city. It is God's presence that makes a person, a group, or a place a holy place. Wherever we live or work or play is "holy ground," for God is there!

Weekday Problems

John had a problem. It was bigger than he could manage. He was addicted to his wealth. It was what brought him self worth and value. No matter how much he had, he always worked for more. His security was bound up with his stocks. The meaning of his life was found in things he could acquire. He was most miserable. But he had been addicted so long, he could not change. Others agreed that John would never, could never, change. But in Zechariah 8:6 we read, "Thus says the Lord of hosts, 'Even though it seems impossible to the remnant of this people in these days, should it also seem impossible to me?'" The Lord could set him free. The Lord could make him whole. The Lord can save!

Another man, James, had a dream—that every child would have a chance at decent education, good health care, a safe and healthy place to play, parents or caring adults to help them learn to know God. He wanted every child to have a head start, a safe start, a healthy start, a moral start. He knew that all this was impossible by his own effort. But he remembered what the Lord said: "For mortals it is impossible, but not for God for with God all things are possible" (Mark 10:27).

*How could God's "possibilities" impact the lives of both John and James?

Wrong Numbers

Irate man on the phone: "Operator, why can't you get me the zoo?"
Operator: "Because the lion is busy."

Jim: "What became of the hired man you got from the city?"
Slim: "He crawled under a mule to see why it wouldn't go."

Bossy scoutmaster: "We've had enough bad food at this camp. Let me taste the soup in that kettle you're carrying."
Scout: "But sir—" one boy began.
Scoutmaster: "No buts!" He swallowed a big spoonful, then exclaimed. "Yuck! You don't call this soup, do you?
Scout: "No sir, like I tried to tell you, we call it dishwater."

Bill: "I wish you guys wouldn't call me Big Bill.
Phil: "Why not?"
Bill: "Those college names stick—and I plan to be a doctor."

This Lesson in Your Life

In the eighth chapter of Zechariah there are 10 messages, each beginning, "Thus says the Lord of hosts." Each message gives us a partial glimpse of the nature of God revealed by what God says to and through the prophet. Each one suggests, directly or implicitly, an appropriate human response.

"I am jealous for Zion" (vs. 2). God wants our first love and undivided loyalty. When we serve other gods it brings disaster.

"I will return to Zion" (vs. 3). God chastises Israel but does not abandon her. When we respond in faith and trust, broken relations can be restored.

"Old men and women shall sit in the streets and children safely play. (vss. 4-5)." God's plan is for a peaceable kingdom, and God invites us to be peacemakers.

"Should it be impossible to me?" (vs.6). Though it seems impossible to people, God's we cannot measure or control power. We are called to dare great things for God and leave the outcome in God's hands.

"They shall be my people and I will be their God" (v.8). The ancient Covenant made with Abraham and his descendants, renewed with Moses, still stands. God is faithful. We are called to be faithful people of the Covenant.

"There shall be a sowing of peace, the vine shall yield its fruit and the ground give its produce and I will cause the remnant to possess all these things" (vs. 12). God is portrayed as in charge of crops and harvest. Knowing that all is from God we are called to be faithful stewards, nurturing the earth, protecting the environment, and sharing the abundance we did not create.

"I have purposed in these days to do good to Jerusalem" (v. 15). For a time God had disciplined Israel for her unfaithfulness. But now that affliction is over.

"The fasts shall be seasons of joy (v. 19). God is one who calls for fasts and festivals as appropriate worship. Ritual and rites have their place as a people offers praise and thanks to God. It is one way we respond to God. But God would have our worship be full of joy and gladness.

People will come from many cities and nations (v. 20). God is a God for all people, all nations. Israel, God's chosen, is chosen not for privilege but as a light to the Gentiles.

People will come because they heave heard "God is with you"(v.23). God is one who makes His presence known. Even those outside Israel can recognize God's presence. No skill or gifts of eloquence are required of the people whom God has blessed. We have only to let the light shine.

1. **What is the consequence of the Lord's returning to Zion and dwelling in Jerusalem?**

Jerusalem will be called a faithful city and the mountain of the Lord called the holy mountain (Zech. 8:3).

2. **What does the future hold for the elderly and for the children (Zech. 8:4-5)?**

Old men and women, as well as children, will be safe in the streets.

3. **What is the difference in perspective between the people of the "remnant" and the Lord?**

What is seen as impossible to the remnant is not seen as impossible to the Lord (Zech 8:6).

4. **What is the ancient covenant to be renewed (Zech 8:8)?**

They shall be my people and I will be their God.

5. **What changes will come since the Temple foundation has been laid (Zech 8:10-13)?**

Before, there were no wages, no safety from foes, antagonism, a cursing among nations. Now there is to be peace, fruit, produce, dew, and a blessing among nations.

6. **What has changed in God's purpose toward Judah(Zech. 8:14)?**

Before the Lord purposed to bring disaster; now He purposes to do good.

7.**What things does the prophet command the people to do(Zech. 8:16)?**

They are to speak the truth, render judgements that make for peace; they are not to devise evil in their hearts or to love false oaths.

8. **How many fasts does the prophet call for, and what is to be their mood (Zech. 8:18)?**

Four fasts are called for, to be observed with joy and gladness.

9. **What qualities or virtues are the people to love(Zech 8:19)?**

They are called to love truth and peace.

10. **Why do people of many cities want to go with the Jews to Jerusalem (Zech. 8:23)?**

"Let us go with you, for we have heard that God is with you."

Part of Zechariah's vision of the peace of Jerusalem was that old men and women shall sit again in the streets, and that they shall be full of boys and girls playing (Zech 8:4).

The measure of any society is not its gross national product, its buildings, bridges, and highways, but the way it treats its elders and its children. Sister Mary Gemma Brunke reflects this respect and honor for "Beautiful Old People." She writes: "It is the old apple trees that are decked with the loveliest blossoms. It is the ancient redwoods that rise to majestic heights. It is the old violins that produce the richest tones. It is the aged wine that tastes the sweetest. It is ancient coins, stamps, and furniture that people seek. It is old friends that are loved the best. Thank God for the blessings of age and the wisdom, patience, and maturity that go with it."

Marion Wright Edelman, a modern prophetic voice in behalf of children, has the watchword, "Leave no child behind." Her prayer for children, in her book *Guide My Feet,* calls us to pray and work for the day when all children can safely play in the streets and neighborhoods of every community. She writes:

We pray for children who sneak Popsicles before supper, who erase holes in math workbooks, who can never find their shoes. And we pray for those who stare at photographers from behind barbed wire, who can't bound down the street in a new pair of sneakers, who were born in places we wouldn't be caught dead, who never go to the circus, who live in an X-rated world. We pray for children who bring us sticky kisses and fistfuls of dandelions, who hug us in a hurry and forget their lunch money. And we pray for those who never get dessert, who have no safe blanket to drag behind them, who watch their parents watch them die, who can't find any bread to steal, who don't have any rooms to clean up, whose pictures aren't on anybody's dresser, and whose monsters are real. We pray for children who spend all their allowance before Tuesday, who throw tantrums in the grocery store and pick at their food, who like ghost stories, who shove dirty clothes under the bed and never rinse out the tub, who get visits from the tooth fairy, who don't like to be kissed in front of the car pool, who squirm in church and scream in the phone, whose tears we sometimes laugh at and whose smiles make us cry. And we pray for those whose nightmares come in daytime, who will eat anything, who never have seen a dentist, who aren't spoiled by anybody, who go to bed hungry and cry themselves to sleep, who live and move, but have no being. We pray for children who want to be carried and for those who must, for those we never give up on and for those who never get a second chance, for those we smother with love and for those who will grab the hand of anyone kind enough to offer it.

Lesson 5

Dedication of the Temple

Then Tatnai, governor on this side the river, Shethar-boznai, and their companions, according to that which Darius the king had sent, so they did speedily.

14 And the elders of the Jews builded, and they prospered through the prophesying of Haggai the prophet and Zechariah the son of Iddo. And they builded, and finished it, according to the commandment of the God of Israel, and according to the commandment of Cyrus, and Darius, and Artaxerxes king of Persia.

15 And this house was finished on the third day of the month Adar, which was in the sixth year of the reign of Darius the king.

16 And the children of Israel, the priests, and the Levites, and the rest of the children of the captivity, kept the dedication of this house of God with joy,

17 And offered at the dedication of this house of God an hundred bullocks, two hundred rams, four hundred lambs; and for a sin offering for all Israel, twelve he goats, according to the number of the tribes of Israel.

18 And they set the priests in their divisions, and the Levites in their courses, for the service of God, which is at Jerusalem; as it is written in the book of Moses.

19 And the children of the captivity kept the passover upon the fourteenth day of the first month.

20 For the priests and the Levites were purified together, all of them were pure, and killed the passover for all the children of the captivity, and for their brethren the priests, and for themselves.

21 And the children of Israel, which were come again out of captivity, and all such as had separated themselves unto them from the filthiness of the heathen of the land, to seek the LORD God of Israel, did eat,

22 And kept the feast of unleavened bread seven days with joy: for the LORD had made them joyful, and turned the heart of the king of Assyria unto them, to strengthen their hands in the work of the house of God, the God of Israel.

Memory Selection
Ezra 6:16

Background Scripture
Ezra 5–6

Devotional Reading
Psalm 96:1-13

As we have seen, the restoration of Jerusalem and the Temple after Judah was allowed to return to the Promised Land has not been easy. Cyrus, king of Persia, decreed that the Jews could return and begin the work. However, their enemies persuaded his successor to halt the program. Disheartened workers then turned to building houses for themselves. The prophets Haggai and Zechariah called them to give higher priority to God's work.

Now, however, King Darius rebukes Israel's enemies, and the construction of the Temple proceeds. Finally, it is finished; and it is time to celebrate! The focus of this text is on (1) the *perseverance* usually required to complete any worthwhile task; and (2) the importance of *celebrating* major events in the life of God's people.

ജ്ഞൽ

You can capture the attention of your class by bringing a tape recorder or CD and playing a recording of the pop song "Celebrate!" The lyrics, *"Celebrate! Celebrate! C'mon and celebrate!"* carry the theme of people abandoning themselves to joy. Unfortunately, among religious folk, doctrinal disputes, hard times, everyday worry and stress, and a dour, sour spirit too often squelch the mood of celebration.

Point out that the Jews who returned to rebuild Jerusalem had their share of troubles, too. Finally, however, they finish rebuilding the Temple. Nothing can restrain their joy. With appropriate decorum, of course, *it's party time!*

Teaching Outline	Daily Bible Readings

I. The Temple Completed—13-15
  A. Darius' orders followed, 13
  B. The building finished, 14-15
 	
II. The Task Celebrated—16-18
  A. Worship leaders, 16, 18
  B. Sacrifices, 17
 	
III. The Passover Resumed—19-22
  A. Purified priests, 19-20
  B. Separated people, 21-22
	Mon. Decree to Rebuild
	    Ezra 6:1-5
	Tue. 'Leave Them Alone'
	    Ezra 6:6-12
	Wed. Joyous Dedication
	    Ezra 6:13-18
	Thu. 'Sing to the Lord!'
	    Psalm 96:1-6
	Fri. 'Ascribe to the Lord Glory'
	    Psalm 96:7-13
	Sat. God's Marvelous Deeds
	    Psalm 98:1-6
	Sun. 'Extol the Lord Our God'
	    Psalm 99:1-5

Verse by Verse

I. The Temple Completed—13-15

A. Darius' orders followed, 13

3 Then Tatnai, governor on this side the river, Shethar-boznai, and their companions, according to that which Darius the king had sent, so they did speedily.

Israel's opponents warned the Persians, who had by now overrun Babylonia, warning that the Jews should not be allowed to rebuild Jerusalem and the Temple. The Persian king Darius had in fairness researched court records and found that Cyrus had indeed authorized the return (6:1ff). Accordingly, Darius now sends word that the work is to proceed; and Israel's enemy Tatnai and his deputies hastily arrange for the restoration to proceed.

B. The building finished, 14-15

14 And the elders of the Jews builded, and they prospered through the prophesying of Haggai the prophet and Zechariah the son of Iddo. And they builded, and finished it, according to the commandment of the God of Israel, and according to the commandment of Cyrus, and Darius, and Artaxerxes king of Persia.

15 And this house was finished on the third day of the month Adar, which was in the sixth year of the reign of Darius the king.

Verse 14 does not list everyone involved in the work of restoration. It also included masons and carpenters, seamen who brought cedar from Lebanon (Ezra 3:7), elders, prophets, priests and a governor (Zech. 2:3).

An inclusive note is inserted by the mention of the non-Israelite kings whose edicts contributed to the work of restoration. Since the project has been criticized by Israel's enemies, the author is careful to show that it is on the sound legal ground of the commandments of kings under whom Israel was now a vassal state. Although Artaxerxes is not enthroned until after Darius, he is mentioned here because he too was involved in reasserting Cyrus' original decree (Ezra 5:23). The mention of these foreign rulers reminds us that in His sovereignty God can use even leaders who do not honor Him to accomplish His will.

II. The Task Celebrated—16-18

A. Worship leaders, 16, 18

16 And the children of Israel, the priests, and the Levites, and the rest of the children of the captivity, kept the dedication of this house of God with joy,

18 And they set the priests in their divisions, and the Levites in their courses, for the service of God, which is at Jerusalem; as it is written in the book of Moses.

Now follows a religious festival and building dedication that is a highlight in Israel's history. Although the original Temple had been dedicated with an even greater celebration (1 Kings 8:62-66), this time the fervor and joy are heightened by the fact that the people have lived through their captivity to see a renewed emphasis on the worship of the one true God. Several times, the phrase "the children of the captivity" is used in this section, marking the sharp turnaround in their fortunes. Their celebration includes their "graduation" from servile childhood in Babylon to their new freedom to worship in their homeland.

Verses 16 and 18 mark the important role of priests and Levites in leading Israel in worship. Originally the two groups were apparently the same (Deut. 17:18). By this time, however, not all members of the tribe of Levi were priests appointed to formal service in offering sacrifice. The terms "divisions" and "courses" (NIV "groups") indicate this distinction.

B. Sacrifices, 17

17 And offered at the dedication of this house of God an hundred bullocks, two hundred rams, four hundred lambs; and for a sin offering for all Israel, twelve he goats, according to the number of the tribes of Israel.

While in Babylon, God's people had lamented, "How shall we sing the LORD's song in a strange land? (Ps. 137:4). They are not the first or last people to feel more comfortable worshiping in a familiar setting; and these people now have the added joy of worshiping in the land that God had given their ancestors. They not only sing, they sacrifice animals. Although the numbers of the animals slaughtered were tiny compared to those killed at the dedication of the First Temple (1 Kings 8:63), they no doubt represented a greater degree of sacrifice on the part of the people after their captivity.

It may be hard for Christians to identify with the emphasis here on animal sacrifice. However, under Moses' system, this presence of death in the midst of a lively celebration was important for at least two reasons. First, bringing animals for sacrifice represented the people's willingness to give up a part of their wealth to show that they honored God. He was more worthy than their material possessions, and His unique holiness was recognized in the selection of animals without blemish. Second, animal sacrifice symbolized the forgiveness of sins, and after their captivity in punishment for sin, forgiveness would have been especially on the minds of these worshipers.

Even today, in Christian worship, the "death" symbolized by baptism (Rom. 6:3-5) and by the Lord's Supper retain this element of sacrifice, focusing on the redemptive death of Jesus on the Cross.

III. The Passover Resumed—19-22
A. Purified priests, 19-20

19 And the children of the captivity kept the passover upon the fourteenth day of the first month.

20 For the priests and the Levites were purified together, all

of them were pure, and killed the passover for all the children of the captivity, and for their brethren the priests, and for themselves.

Without doubt the priests had been in the forefront of seeing that even in captivity the people remembered the central importance of the feast of the Passover. Although they apparently did not observe it in Babylon, it remained a symbol of God's power to deliver them, just as the first Passover was a memorial of their flight from Egypt. Now what was a mere memory becomes a reality again. To heighten the significance of the feast, it is celebrated on the anniversary of their preparation for the exodus from Egypt (Exod. 12:6). Just as the first Passover was the "beginning" of a new nation (Exod. 12:2), so now the rebuilding of the Temple offers a new beginning also.

B. Separated people, 21-22

21 And the children of Israel, which were come again out of captivity, and all such as had separated themselves unto them from the filthiness of the heathen of the land, to seek the LORD God of Israel, did eat,

22 And kept the feast of unleavened bread seven days with joy: for the LORD had made them joyful, and turned the heart of the king of Assyria unto them, to strengthen their hands in the work of the house of God, the God of Israel.

Who participated in this grand and festive occasion? The answer is uncertain, depending on the meaning of "the land" in verse 21. If this refers to Palestine, we may conclude that the Passover included people who had remained in Palestine and had kept themselves separate from pagan worship while their brethren were taken to Babylon. However, "the land" may instead refer to Babylon, referring to the people who returned from captivity who had similarly remained untainted by heathen worship.

The reference to Assyria in verse 22 is strange, since that regime had long since been conquered by the Babylonians, who had in turn fallen to the Persians. Some scholars think this is merely an error by a manuscript copyist. Others believe that since Assyria had begun the captivities by devastating northern kingdom of Israel in 621/22, the term had become a generic way to refer to all nations whom God had used to punish His disobedient people. Specifically, it would therefore refer here to Cyrus, whose heart the Lord had turned toward the Jews in allowing them to return to the Promised Land.

Part of the joy with which the people celebrated this Passover stemmed from the Jewish concept of "corporate personality. They not only reveled in the fact that they had been allowed to return home, and to experience renewed worship and a new Passover themselves. They were connected both by spiritual and genetic ties to other children of Abraham, Isaac, and Jacob. They are caught up in the sense that these ancestors were participating with them both in the celebration and in symbolizing the continuance of the long line of people whom God had elected for His special blessing—as well as for special responsibility.

Evangelistic Emphasis

When the exiles returned to Jerusalem and rebuilt the temple, they celebrated the Passover Festival. As they shared the unleavened bread and bitter herbs, they retold the story of how they were led to freedom. The Passover Meal celebrated in Jewish homes today allows parents, aunts, and uncles to tell the story of the deliverance of their people from slavery in Egypt. They recall how the angel of death "passed over" the houses of the Hebrew slaves. They recount how they left in such a rush the bread had no chance to rise.

It is essential for us to share the story of how God has worked in our lives. Our witness may be the connection for God's Spirit to reach another person. For some the decisive change may be liberation from drugs. Others may be encouraged to turn from making work and possessions the chief aim of life, or to find a sense of purpose and meaning in life. Or a celebration of faith may simply produce a moment of grace when one comes to know deep down in their hearts that he is accepted by God. The ways that God comes to us are varied. The circumstances through which we find new life in God may differ with each person. But each of us has a story to tell. Our story may be the way God touches another's heart. Evangelism is simply sharing our story.

ಐಂಡಿ

Memory Selection

And the children of Israel, the priests and Levites, and the rest of the children of the captivity, kept the dedication of this house of God with joy. –*Ezra 6:16*

What a joy it was to be back in the house of God! During all their years of captivity in Babylon, the Jews remembered the great Temple in Jerusalem. Its destruction was a tragedy hard to accept. Even though they gathered together to sing the psalms of the Temple in a strange land, it was not the same as praising God in the Holy Temple.

They remembered in captivity the stories of Abraham, Isaac and Jacob. But reciting them in the Temple had special meaning. The elders told what they had learned about God's deliverance of the slaves from Egypt, about God's sustaining them in the wilderness. But fewer and fewer elders were around to tell about the Temple, to recall its awesome majesty, the odors of the burning sacrifices, the smoke billowing from the great altar.

Now at last they were back in the holy city. Finally the holy Temple had been rebuilt. The narrator leaves us to imagine the shouts and songs, the tears and hugs, the warm glow, the mysterious awe. The narrator simply says, "The people of Israel celebrated the dedication of this house of God with joy."

Weekday Problems

In a counseling session before their wedding, John and Joan were guided by their pastor to think about the traditions of the families from which they came. How did they celebrate Christmas? How did they spend vacations? What was Sunday like, and even meal times?

John and Joan discovered their family traditions were different. The pastor reminded them that starting a new family meant establishing their own traditions.

Weeks became months, and months became years. They were blessed with two healthy children. Their lives became busier each year. They saved Sundays for catching up on all the chores. Meals were grabbed on the run. Christmas was filled with too many parties and exhaustive shopping. Joan realized how much she missed time for the family around the table. She missed making worship a part of Sunday.

Finally they determined to reestablish their own traditions. The whole family would spend one evening at home together. They would share at least one unhurried meal together every day. They would take turns saying grace. Sunday they would be at church. Each week during Advent they would light a candle on the Advent Wreath, read a Bible story, and sing a carol. They felt rewarded when they heard their Johnny, their youngest, explain to a sleepover guest about about spending Tuesday night at home with all the family, about going to church each Sunday. "That's just the way we do it," Johnny said.

*What special traditions does your family observe?

The Joy of Remembering

Recollection is the only paradise from which we cannot be turned out.—*John Paul Richter*

❖❖❖❖❖

What we learn with pleasure we never forget.—*Alfred Mercier*

❖❖❖❖❖

The joys I have possessed are ever mine; out of thy reach, behind eternity, hid in the sacred treasure of the past, but blest remembrance brings them hourly back.—*John Dryden*

❖❖❖❖❖

As dew to the blossom/and bud to the bee,/as the scent to the rose,/are those memories to me.—*Amelia B. Welby*

❖❖❖❖❖

We will be glad and rejoice in thee, we will remember thy love more than wine.—*Song of Solomon 1:4*

This Lesson in Your Life

When the Jewish exiles returned to Jerusalem, they rebuilt the Temple. They restored old traditions. They kept the Passover (Ezra 6:19). In reenacting that ancient liturgy they found a spontaneous joy, " for the Lord had made them joyful" (Ezra 6:22).

Their worship then and ours today is an interaction of the ordered and spontaneous, the structured and the free, the planned and the unexpected.

Even the most informal service has a structure. We gather on the first day of the week, and at a scheduled hour, in a designated place. The traditional elements in most worship include music: congregational hymns, anthems by the choir, vocal solos, and musical instruments. Services usually include prayers, Scripture lesson, and sermon. Regular elements in many worship services include praying the Lord's prayer, singing the Doxology, reading from the Holy Bible. Woe be to the visiting preacher who fails to take up the offering.

Because the Holy Spirit moves among us no one can tell what may happen here. Even where a printed order of worship or bulletin is used, the unexpected and unscheduled can happen. The same words are read for the umpteenth time. Then one time they speak to you with new meaning, as though the Spirit interprets them afresh. You sing a hymn a thousand times, but this time it unlocks the tears and inexplicably you cry. Someone is moved to join the church, to confess his faith, to request or even offer prayer.

Richard Foster observes, "Singing, praying, praising all may lead to worship, but worship is more than any of these. Our spirit must be ignited by the divine fire." William Willimon likens worship to a couple in love. People who are in love tend toward extravagant behavior. They will sing, write poetry, acquire new hairstyles, cry, shout, dance. That's the way love is. The starry-eyed teenager, the dozen red roses, kissing, they are all part of loving excess. The question, "What good does that do anybody?" will appear laughable to lovers. Here is the scandal of Sunday morning behavior. We love because we have been loved (1 John 4:19). The church's worship on Sunday is a way of being in love."

Willimon goes on to point out that there is a needed balance between the spontaneous and the regular in healthy marriages. "Romantic love involves momentary, sporadic encounters. But if this love is to last and deepen through time, it must eventually become habitual, ritualized. Most good marriages know that we must do certain things together out of habit —like kissing, saying 'I love you', spending time together."

So Christian worship is both spontaneous and ordered. Even when we don't feel like it, we come to worship. It is a time for singing, hearing Scriptures, renewing our love for God and neighbor. The Lord makes us joyful.

GETTING THE FACTS STRAIGHT

1. Who were the prophets in Judah and Jerusalem in the time of Ezra?
Haggai and Zechariah prophesied to the Jews in Ezra's day (Ezra 5:1).

2. Who set out to rebuild the house of God in Jerusalem?
Zerubbabel set out to rebuild the house of God in Jerusalem.

3. Who was the governor of the "Province Beyond the River"?
Tattenai was the governor of the "Province Beyond the River" (Ezra 5:3).

4. Who was the king of Persia during this period of rebuilding the Temple?
Darius was the Persian king (Ezra 5:5).

5. What document persuaded King Darius to allow the rebuilding of the Temple in Jerusalem to continue?
A decree issued by King Cyrus was found authorizing the rebuilding of the temple in Jerusalem (Ezra 6:3).

6. Beyond giving permission for the temple to be rebuilt, what did King Darius do to help the project?
He decreed that the taxes and revenues from the province would be used to pay for the construction work.

7. What punishment was decreed for any one who altered the decree of the king?
Anyone altering the decree would be impaled on a beam pulled from his own house. The house was to be made a dunghill.

8. When was the Temple completed?
The house was finished on the third day of the month of Adar, in the sixth year of the reign of King Darius (516 B.C.).

9. What animal sacrifices were offered at the dedication of the Temple?
At the dedication, 100 bulls, 200 rams, 400 lambs, and 12 male goats were offered (Ezra 6:17).

10. What festival was celebrated in the new Temple?
The returned exiles kept the Passover (Ezra 6:19).

When I was growing up, we went to church on Sunday. I can't remember ever deciding to go to church. It was a part of Sunday. It's what we did on Sunday. It was a family affair.

We went through several preachers, from blue surge suits to Prince Albert coats and striped trousers. In the summer they switched to white linen suits. Pulpit robes and stoles were not in style long ago in my home church. We went through several choir directors. Some were good and some were very good. But I couldn't tell the difference. All I knew was that the anthem was considerably shorter than the sermon, and that was very good.

I grew up with a variety of music in church on Sunday mornings and Sunday evenings. I was exposed to the gospel beat of "I was sinking deep in sin, far from the peaceful shore" and to the majestic stirrings of "Holy, Holy, Holy, Lord God Almighty." My heart and voice would quiver with the lofty challenge of "Are ye able, said the master, to be crucified with me? Yea the sturdy dreamers answer, to the death we followed thee." More than once I made the trip to the altar to kneel and dedicate my life to Christ, moved by the invitation hymn "Only trust Him, only trust Him, only trust Him now."

When I go back to that old First Church downtown where I went every Sunday, I still delight to pick out the pew where I spent so many hours sitting, squirming, drawing, dreaming, sometimes listening, often singing (always off-key) sometimes even praying.

I like to kneel at the table from which I received gifts of God's grace. And I remember other times when I knelt about that table on Sunday mornings with my family. I am sure I didn't understand all that it meant. I don't pretend to understand the mystery now. But there was a sense of awe and specialness in that holy place. When I visit there from time to time I remember the feeling of awe as we would gather there as a family.

Now, I know that God is just as fully present in other houses of worship. And I know that God can be experienced in nature, at home, at work, and at play. God's holy presence may be found when we are alone, at anytime and anywhere. But for me that particular holy space, that century-old building, has special meaning. It was there I made the first dedication of my life to Christ. In that old, traditional church, full of imperfect, struggling, incomplete, loving persons, the gospel was declared in song and sermon, through loving Sunday School teachers, and by a community of caring. I knew what it was to be a part of a larger family.

I know what the psalmist meant when he said, "I was glad when they said unto me, 'Let us go unto the house of the Lord'" (Ps. 122:1). I have some sense of the joy of those returning exiles in Ezra's day, who once more could worship in the house of the Lord.

Lesson 6

Nehemiah's Work Begins

Nehemiah 1:1-4, 2:4-5, 13, 16-18

The words of Nehemiah the son of Hachaliah. And it came to pass in the month Chisleu, in the twentieth year, as I was in Shushan the palace,

2 That Hanani, one of my brethren, came, he and certain men of Judah; and I asked them concerning the Jews that had escaped, which were left of the captivity, and concerning Jerusalem.

3 And they said unto me, The remnant that are left of the captivity there in the province are in great affliction and reproach: the wall of Jerusalem also is broken down, and the gates thereof are burned with fire.

4 And it came to pass, when I heard these words, that I sat down and wept, and mourned certain days, and fasted, and prayed before the God of heaven,

2:4 Then the king said unto me, For what dost thou make request? So I prayed to the God of heaven.

5 And I said unto the king, If it please the king, and if thy servant have found favour in thy sight, that thou wouldest send me unto Judah, unto the city of my fathers' sepulchres, that I may build it.

13 And I went out by night by the gate of the valley, even before the dragon well, and to the dung port, and viewed the walls of Jerusalem, which were broken down, and the gates thereof were consumed with fire.

16 And the rulers knew not whither I went, or what I did; neither had I as yet told it to the Jews, nor to the priests, nor to the nobles, nor to the rulers, nor to the rest that did the work.

17 Then said I unto them, Ye see the distress that we are in, how Jerusalem lieth waste, and the gates thereof are burned with fire: come, and let us build up the wall of Jerusalem, that we be no more a reproach.

18 Then I told them of the hand of my God which was good upon me; as also the king's words that he had spoken unto me. And they said, Let us rise up and build. So they strengthened their hands for this good work.

July 6

Memory Selection
Nehemiah 2:18

Background Scripture
Nehemiah 1–2

Devotional Reading
Isaiah 26:1-9

This lesson is about the ability to *follow through*. Some 13 years after Ezra the priest led a remnant of the Jews back to Palestine to rebuild Jerusalem and its Temple, the scene shifts to a political leader. A governor, Nehemiah, has been appointed over Judea by a later Persian king, Artaxerxes.

To his dismay, Governor Nehemiah learns that despite Cyrus' earlier commission, the city of Jerusalem and its walls still lie in shambles. We have been informed earlier that King Artaxerxes himself had been persuaded by the Jews' enemies to halt work on the Temple (Ezra 4:23). With every indication of being a good planner, organizer, and motivator, Nehemiah marshals the people into an organized labor force to rebuild the walls. God has worked through pagan kings to give Israel a new start. Nehemiah intends to follow through.

ဆာငာ

To introduce this lesson you may want to walk where angels fear to tread by raising a question about local politics.

Ask your group what they would like to see your community's leaders do to make your town or city a better place to live. Do streets need paving, or water and sewer service improved?

After a brief discussion of such issues, ask why your community's *religious* leaders haven't already accomplished such improvements. An obvious answer is that those aren't their primary areas of responsibility. At any rate, the high ideals of believers aren't enough. Sometimes our communities need civic and political leaders who can move beyond good ideas, and simply get things done.

Point out that Nehemiah was this kind of person. He got things done.

Teaching Outline	Daily Bible Readings

I. Sad Assessment—1:1-4
  A. Briefing on Palestine, 1-2
  B. Dismal diagnosis, 3-4
II. Sent by the King—2:4-5
III. Stimulating Leadership—13, 16-18
  A. Private survey, 13, 16
  B. Motivating the leaders, 17-18
	Mon. Mourning Ruined Walls
	     Nehemiah 1:1-4
	Tue. Prayer of Confession
	     Nehemiah 1:5-11
	Wed. Request to the King
	     Nehemiah 2:1-5
	Thu. Making Plans
	     Nehemiah 2:6-10
	Fri. Inspecting the Walls
	     Nehemiah 2:11-15
	Sat. 'Let Us Begin!'
	     Nehemiah 2:16-20
	Sun. 'We Have a Strong City!'
	     Isaiah 26:1-6

Verse by Verse

I. Sad Assessment—1:1-4

A. Briefing on Palestine, 1-2

1 The words of Nehemiah the son of Hachaliah. And it came to pass in the month Chisleu, in the twentieth year, as I was in Shushan the palace,

2 That Hanani, one of my brethren, came, he and certain men of Judah; and I asked them concerning the Jews that had escaped, which were left of the captivity, and concerning Jerusalem.

Nehemiah was one of the Jews who had stayed in Persia when many returned to Palestine to rebuild the Temple. By now, the king of Persia is Artaxerxes, and Nehemiah is his cup-bearer (Neh. 1:11; 2:1).

The city of Shusan (or Susa) was the summer capital of the Persian kings, and was the place where the Jewess Esther would become famous (Esth. 1:2). Its ruins have been identified, and have yielded many important archeological finds, including the famous obelisk on which were written the laws of Hammurabi, (possibly a contemporary of Abraham).

Nehemiah may be a servant in the king's court, but he has a leader's heart and a true believer's concern for the progress of restoration that has been going on in the land God had given His people. When he learns that Hanani his "brother" (whether by blood or by race and religion we do not know) has just come from Palestine, Nehemiah is eager to know how the work is going there. "The Jews that had escaped" refers not to some band who had fled in secret, but, as the NIV reads, those who "survived the exile"—in other words, those who had taken advantage of Cyrus' decree allowing them to return.

B. Dismal diagnosis, 3-4

3 And they said unto me, The remnant that are left of the captivity there in the province are in great affliction and reproach: the wall of Jerusalem also is broken down, and the gates thereof are burned with fire.

4 And it came to pass, when I heard these words, that I sat down and wept, and mourned certain days, and fasted, and prayed before the God of heaven,

The news from Jerusalem was not good. Non-Jews in the land surrounding the city had warned the Persian authorities that allowing the Jews to rebuild their capital city and its Temple would mean insurrection (Ezra 4). They had persuaded Artaxerxes himself to halt the work (4:23-24). As a result, the city's walls and gates are still in the state in which the Babylonians left them during their invasion in 587.

Nehemiah is not merely a potential politician, but a dedicated Jew whose heart is broken by this sad state of affairs. His first act is to turn to God;

443

and to pray the moving prayer recorded in verses 5-11. Nehemiah begs God's attention as he confesses the sins that caused Judah's captivity in the first place, and prays that the Lord will hear the prayer of His now-chastened people. Such a beginning makes a good model for church leaders today.

II. Sent by the King—2:4-5

4 Then the king said unto me, For what dost thou make request? So I prayed to the God of heaven.

5 And I said unto the king, If it please the king, and if thy servant have found favour in thy sight, that thou wouldest send me unto Judah, unto the city of my fathers' sepulchres, that I may build it.

The calendar references in 1:1 and 2:1 indicate that Nehemiah has brooded for four months over the Jerusalem's plight. King Artaxerxes has noticed that his cupbearer is disturbed, and Nehemiah has explained his distress over the news from Jerusalem (vss. 2-3). The king's kind inquiry here, and his subsequent actions, indicate that not all Jews were badly treated or ignored by their Persian masters. Yet, before he dares to respond to the king's question, notice that Nehemiah breathes another quick prayer that God would guide him in his request. Obviously Nehemiah believes in a God who can guide both his own words and the response of a king. This "formula" of praying to God and petitioning a human authority has stood many a believer in good stead at crucial moments in history.

Nehemiah's petition is brief and to

the point; and as the verses following indicate, the king gives a favorable response. What is left unexplained is how Artaxerxes arranged to cancel his earlier orders to discontinue the work that he now allows Nehemiah to take up again. After all, once something was issued as an official "law of the Medes and the Persians" it could not be rescinded (Dan. 6:8; Esth. 1:19). A possible explanation is that Artaxerxes' edict halting the work was only a verbal edict instead of written and sealed with the king's ring, as in the case of laws that were considered unchangeable.

III. Stimulating Leadership–13, 16-18

A. Private survey, 13, 16

13 And I went out by night by the gate of the valley, even before the dragon well, and to the dung port, and viewed the walls of Jerusalem, which were broken down, and the gates thereof were consumed with fire.

16 And the rulers knew not whither I went, or what I did; neither had I as yet told it to the Jews, nor to the priests, nor to the nobles, nor to the rulers, nor to the rest that did the work.

Although archeologists have found the rubble from Nebuchadnezzar's destruction of Jerusalem, the devastation was so thorough and the time-lapse so great that the route Nehemiah takes in verses 13-15 can only be a matter of conjecture now. A consensus is that the "valley gate" was on the west side of the city, and that from there Nehemiah picked his way through the debris around to the east side.

Aside from the details mentioned, why was this scene recorded? Probably to indicate Nehemiah's conscientiousness and thoroughness in pre-planning, before trying to organize a work force. It is also noteworthy that he made this survey of what needed to be done before consulting with local "rulers" or city leaders. Although the effectiveness of "consensus leadership" can be impressive, a strong leader will at times take it on himself or herself to gather facts before deputies, who may have vested interests, can put their own "spin" on them.

Later texts will indicate that Jerusalem's leaders were given particular portions of the wall, and particular gates, to rebuild (see chap. 3). It may be that even before the work started such portions had been assigned, and that Nehemiah wanted to make his original survey without being influenced by anyone wanting to put their portion of the work ahead of others for the sake of their own reputation and authority.

B. Motivating the leaders, 17-18

17 Then said I unto them, Ye see the distress that we are in, how Jerusalem lieth waste, and the gates thereof are burned with fire: come, and let us build up the wall of Jerusalem, that we be no more a reproach.

18 Then I told them of the hand of my God which was good upon me; as also the king's words that he had spoken unto me. And they said, Let us rise up and build. So they strengthened their hands for this good work.

After making his own private assessment of what needed to be done, Nehemiah now calls together the city's leaders. His agenda for the meeting is clear, and interesting as a model for many situations modern church leaders may face. First, he *outlines the problem.* Obviously, with walls and gates destroyed, the city is open and vulnerable to attack from the enemies who had first objected to the work of restoration.

Second, Nehemiah *motivates the leaders,* who will need to be so personally committed to the project that they can pass along some of this enthusiasm to their workers. Their courage must endure the taunts and opposition of their enemies (see chap. 4). At times, the workers will need to have a tool in one hand and a weapon in another (4:17).

The third item on Nehemiah's agenda is to *inspire the leaders* with the obvious fact that God is with them (vs. 18a). How else could Nehemiah's own elevation from cupbearer to governor be explained? Unless the city's leadership is convinced that the renewed work is authorized by God, and is not just Nehemiah's idea, their zeal will flag at the first sign of difficulty.

Finally, Nehemiah's agenda includes *explaining his authority,* so recently given to him by the king himself. This was obviously necessary since it had been Artaxerxes who had previously caused the work to be discontinued.

With such obvious leadership skills and spiritual preparation, it is little wonder that the city's leaders response indicates a spirit akin to what every modern church leader longs to hear and witness: *Let us rise up and build.*

Evangelistic Emphasis

The story of Nehemiah suggests various ways God's call comes to us. Nehemiah heard reports of the broken walls and destroyed gates in the holy city of Jerusalem. Others had heard these reports and simply muttered, "What a shame!" But for Nehemiah the report became a personal burden. Sometimes a troubling awareness of a need becomes the beginning of a call of God to service.

Nehemiah turns to God in prayer. In his prayer he is reminded both of the warning of God's judgement upon those who do not keep His commandment, and of God's promise to gather His people again in Jerusalem.

Others might remember the ancient stories, but for Nehemiah those stories carried a personal message.

Nehemiah recognizes he has a special gift in his position as the royal cup bearer. He had an easy access to the king that most of the exiles did not have. The king's support of the project meant that Nehemiah could use the timber from the king's forest to repair the walls. The king's approval was an outward confirmation of his inner call.

So God calls servants today, sometimes through an awareness of need, sometimes through a special inner call to mission, sometimes through a recognition of our gifts and strengths, sometimes through the confirmation of those who know us best. Through all of these ways we may be called to serve God and share the story of God's love.

⊗ℭ⅋

Memory Selection

Then I told them of the hand of my God which was good upon me; as also the king's words that he had spoken unto me. And they said, Let us rise up and build. So they strengthened their hands for this good work.—*Nehemiah 2:18*

Nehemiah is not ashamed to speak of his calling of God. His choice to go back to Jerusalem and rebuild the city was not a career choice. It was a mandate from God, a burden on his heart. All this he is willing to share with the people. "The hand of God has been gracious upon me." Nehemiah was also wise. He knew that the people would be more likely to follow him if they knew his project had the approval of the king. "He told them also the words that the king had spoken to him." Nehemiah also knew the deep, patriotic loyalty the people had to the kingdom of Israel and their memories of the distant past of the great King David. The broken down walls around the holy city are a national disgrace. Divine blessing, political approval, national pride are all a part of his challenge. When he gives the call, "Come, let us rebuild the wall of Jerusalem," they are ready. "Let's start building!"

Weekday Problems

Joe served as chairperson of a committee to nominate a lay leader for their congregation. He was clearer about what he did *not* want in a leader than what he did want. He did not want a leader who expected to be served and obeyed. The church didn't need someone who felt it was his or her job to run the church. On the other hand, he had  seen leaders who were more concerned to be well liked than to accomplish the mission of the church. There was a place for friendship and fellowship, but the church was more than a cozy club. They needed a leader who would lift their sight beyond the four cozy walls of the church.

Neither did the people need a leader who tried to do all the work himself, or make all the decisions. He had seen some faithful saints who felt they were the only ones who could do a job, so they did it year after year, asking for no help, and wanting no suggestions, and living for the praise and recognition they received. His ideal leader would enable them to do ministry.

The church needed a leader who would keep before them their larger mission. They needed a leader who was eager to discern the will of God and would help them learn God's will. They wanted a leader who had the courage to stand for his or her convictions, even when others didn't agree. Joe realized that he needed to pray that God might raise up such leaders for the church.

*What qualities do you look for in a church leader?

Following the Leader

People, like sheep, tend to follow a leader—occasionally in the right direction.—*Alexander Chase*

The most important quality of a leader is to be acknowledged as such. All leaders whose fitness is questioned are clearly lacking in force.—*André Maurois*

I never came to this through driving personal ambition. A combined opportunity and duty presented itself and I took it.— *Margaret Thatcher*

Teacher—Johnny, if there were 11 sheep in a field and six jumped the fence, how many would be left?
Johnny—None, ma'am.
Teacher—Why yes there would, Johnny. Five would be left.
Johnny—Ma'am, you may know 'rithmetic, but I know sheep.

This Lesson in Your Life

From Nehemiah we learn some lessons about leadership. He had a vision of a rebuilt Jerusalem. For one thing, its walls need rebuilding, not so much for military defense as a means of consolidation of Jewish traditions and a purification of Jewish culture.

Nehemiah had a charisma about him. It seemed as if God's hand was on him. Those Jews living in Jerusalem were discouraged. The broken walls made them a joke among surrounding nations. But when Nehemiah spoke, he inspired them to do what had seemed impossible. He brought hope where there had been only despair. When he finished speaking, they were ready to start on a task neglected for generations.

Nehemiah showed a compassion for the poor. As governor he did not levy the tax for the upkeep of his administration which was his legal right. He insisted that Jews who had been sold into slavery to other Jews, in payment of their debts, be set free. He persuaded the nobles to return land and property claimed when crops were bad and loans could not be repaid. He persuaded others to follow his example of refusing to charge interest to fellow Jews.

Nehemiah was a person with courage. He had a comfortable, secure position with the King of Persia. He was set for life. He had it made. To ask to go to a distant province was to put at risk all he had achieved in prestigious position in the king's court. His very request could change the king's attitude toward him from one of trust to ill will. Nehemiah risks all this to answer the call of God to go back to his native land and bring about needed reforms—economic, social, and religious.

Above all Nehemiah was a man of faith. God called him to this task. He trusted God to see him through the task to which he was called. He did not seek glory for himself, but continually gave the praise to God.

We need leaders with vision, charisma, compassion, courage, and faith in God. Jesus has given an example of servant leadership. Leaders with natural gifts are always tempted to use their power to exploit others. Jesus reminds us that we are not called to be like "the kings of the gentiles who lord it over them . . . "; instead, "The greatest among you must become like the youngest, and the leader like one who serves." (Luke 22:25-27)

Is God is calling you to a role of leadership in your church or community? Have you a vision of what God calls your church to be? Have you the gift to move others to join you in an important task? Do you genuinely care about people? Have you the courage to do what is right, no matter the cost? Do you believe God can work through you to accomplish God's purposes? Can you pray, "Here I am, Lord, send me"?

STRAIGHT

1. What was the message to Nehemiah from Hanani and others from Judah?
The survivors are in trouble and shame. The wall of Jerusalem is broken down and the gates have been destroyed by fire (Neh. 1:3).

2. Who was the king of Persia at the time of Nehemiah?
Artaxerxes was king of Persia.

3. What was Nehemiah's role in court?
Nehemiah was cupbearer to the king (Neh. 1:11).

4. What was Nehemiah's request of the king?
He asked that he be sent to Judah so that he might rebuild Jerusalem and the Temple (Neh. 2:5).

5. What help did Nehemiah ask of the king?
He asked for letters to the governors for safe passage and to the keeper of the forest to provide timber for the temple and wall (Neh. 2:7-8).

6. What was Nehemiah's challenge to the people of Jerusalem?
"Come let us build the wall of Jerusalem so we may no longer suffer disgrace" (Neh. 2:17).

7. What authority did Nehemiah claim for this project of rebuilding?
"The hand of God has been gracious to me and the words of the king had been spoken to me" (Neh. 2:18).

8. What was the response of the people?
"Let us start building" (Neh. 2:18).

9. What was the mocking insinuation of his opponents?
"Are you rebelling against the king?" (Neb. 2:19).

10. How did Nehemiah answer the critics?
"The God of heaven is the one who will give us success and we his servants are going to start building" (Neh. 2:20).

One morning I was startled to see a turtle on our patio. He was a large, dull, sleepy snapper. He wasn't doing anything. He was just there. He had intruded himself into the very private space of our patio. I'm sure he was as surprised to find himself in the midst of lawn chairs, tables, hummingbird feeders, wind chimes, and barbecue grills, as I was to see him there. He was displaced, an alien, out of his element, wandering and lost.

I thought I'd help him go back home. I gave a glowing description of the lake not far away, with water to swim in, stumps to sun on, and other turtles of his kind. He was unmoved. I gave explicit and clear directions to the lake, "Down Whitehaven to Brame, turn left on Hyacinth at the second traffic light, a quick left and then right and you are at the lake." But he remained as stationary as the house.

With faultless logic and gentle persuasion, I urged him to travel on, but it was plain we were not communicating. I seized a shovel to nudge him in the right direction, But this tool, which was meant only to guide him home, he perceived as a threat to his life. He snapped viciously. He perceived my make-shift shepherd's staff as a weapon of war. With strong jaws he snapped at the blade. It was a stand-off. I could not speak a language he could understand. Only if I became a turtle, with all its risks and limitations, could I tell him that I wished for him only good, that the shovel was meant for life, not death.

Nehemiah also needed a personal language to use with his own people. He wrote letters of encouragement to the exiles who had returned to Jerusalem. He even secured permission for them to harvest timber from the King's forest. But they needed more than letters and lumber. Nehemiah must give up his position of privilege and become one with them, to share the disgrace of that ravaged city, to share the bewilderment that things have gotten so bad. When they saw that he was one of them, they would listen. Not as a remote government official, but as one of them, he could issue the challenge to rebuild.

Moses had a clear call to lead his people to freedom. He might have sent letters of encouragement. He might have described the burning bush. He might have told them that God had seen their misery. But living in the peaceful security of the sheep's pasture, he could exert no leadership. He had to go back to Egypt where Hebrews were slaves. He had to become one with them to lead them out of bondage.

For those of us who often wander far from home, live in alien places where we do not belong, and don't know how to find our rightful place in God's world, the good news is that "The word became flesh and dwelt among us." God became incarnate, coming as man with men to dwell.

Joy to the world, even in July!

The Wall Completed

Nehemiah 6:1-9, 15-16

Now it came to pass, when Sanballat, and Tobiah, and Geshem the Arabian, and the rest of our enemies, heard that I had builded the wall, and that there was no breach left therein; (though at that time I had not set up the doors upon the gates;)

2 That Sanballat and Geshem sent unto me, saying, Come, let us meet together in some one of the villages in the plain of Ono. But they thought to do me mischief.

3 And I sent messengers unto them, saying, I am doing a great work, so that I cannot come down: why should the work cease, whilst I leave it, and come down to you?

4 Yet they sent unto me four times after this sort; and I answered them after the same manner.

5 Then sent Sanballat his servant unto me in like manner the fifth time with an open letter in his hand;

6 Wherein was written, It is reported among the heathen, and Gashmu saith it, that thou and the Jews think to rebel: for which cause thou buildest the wall, that thou mayest be their king, according to these words.

7 And thou hast also appointed prophets to preach of thee at Jerusalem, saying, There is a king in Judah: and now shall it be reported to the king according to these words. Come now therefore, and let us take counsel together.

8 Then I sent unto him, saying, There are no such things done as thou sayest, but thou feignest them out of thine own heart.

9 For they all made us afraid, saying, Their hands shall be weakened from the work, that it be not done. Now therefore, O God, strengthen my hands.

15 So the wall was finished in the twenty and fifth day of the month Elul, in fifty and two days.

16 And it came to pass, that when all our enemies heard thereof, and all the heathen that were about us saw these things, they were much cast down in their own eyes: for they perceived that this work was wrought of our God.

July 13

Memory Selection
Nehemiah 6:16

Background Scripture
Nehemiah 6

Devotional Reading
Isaiah 49:13-18

This realistic lesson focuses on how to face criticism and negativism. Nehemiah is again the leading actor in the drama. His critics are, like Judea, under the rule of Persia. They have spoken against the work of restoration before. Now they become more vocal as they see that Nehemiah and his crew are about to finish work on the walls about Jerusalem. With taunts and jibes and lies, they try to distract Nehemiah; but to no avail. With single-heartedness, he focuses on the task at hand.

We may protest that there is a fine line between "focus" and ignoring the testimony of others, between tending to our own business and arrogantly refusing to listen to the viewpoint of others. These *are* fine lines; but what makes this lesson intriguing is that Nehemiah sees the difference, and has the character to live by them.

℘℩

Introduce the plight of Nehemiah described in this lesson by a brief discussion of the effects of criticism and negativism. Ask what effect such tactics commonly have in our own lives. Responses might include:

1. Discouragement, low morale, and a wilting of the spirit.

2. Self-doubt. ("Maybe my critics have a point.")

3. Defensiveness and counter-charges. ("You have no right to criticize because you're worse than I am!")

4. Quitting under fire (and thus lending credibility to false criticism).

Note that as governor of Judea, Nehemiah had a high-profile job and carried out duties that might easily earn criticism. Imagine a newspaper headline: "GOVERNOR CHOOSES CRONY FOR WALL CONTRACTOR." How would Nehemiah respond?

Teaching Outline	Daily Bible Readings	

I. Negative Comments—1-2
  A. The critics, 1
  B. The invitation, 2
II. Nehemiah's Response—3-4
III. False Report—5-7
  A. Royal revolt? 5-6
  B. Prophetic support? 7
IV. Nehemiah's Denial—8-9
V. The Wall Is Finished—15-16
	Mon.	People with a Mind to Work
		Nehemiah 4:1-6

	Tue.	Plot Against the Workers Nehemiah 4:7-14
	Wed.	Setting a Guard Nehemiah 4:15-23
	Thu.	'Strengthen My Hands!' Nehemiah 6:1-9
	\Fri.	The Wall Is Finished Nehemiah 6:10-19
	Sat.	Rites of Purification Nehemiah 12:27-31b
	Sun.	Joy Heard from Afar Nehemiah 12:43-47

Verse by Verse

I. Negative Comments—1-2
A. The critics, 1

1 Now it came to pass, when Sanballat, and Tobiah, and Geshem the Arabian, and the rest of our enemies, heard that I had builded the wall, and that there was no breach left therein; (though at that time I had not set up the doors upon the gates;)

Ezra the priest had faced just this kind of criticism when he first led a return to the Promised Land in response to a decree by Cyrus, king of Persia (Ezra 4). The situation invited jealousy, with neighboring vassal states under Persian rule vying with each other for the king's favor. At first, some Palestinians, probably Samaritans, professed to want to help with the rebuilding of the Temple (Ezra 4:1-2), perhaps because they had heard of the funds and treasures Cyrus was making available to the Jews. When their offer was declined, they predictably opposed the project.

Sanballat, mentioned first, is named as the "governor of Samaria" in papyrus documents discovered in an area where the Persian capital was located. In 2:10 he is called a "Horonite" or Moabite, a people with a long history of enmity against the Jews. To have Nehemiah named governor of Judah, just to the south, may have provoked Sanballat's jealousy. Furthermore, his daughter married a member of the priestly tribe in Judah, and Nehemiah would later insist that they part in order to start anew in service to God with a pure line of Jews (Neh. 13:28). Little wonder that Sanballat opposes Nehemiah's vision of restoring not only the Temple but the city itself.

Tobiah, an Ammonite, is called "the servant" in 2:10, apparently a title he cherished as designating him a faithful servant of the king of Persia. In 4:3 he joined Sanballat in ridiculing the Jews working on the city walls, saying that they would be so flimsy that a fox could break them down. Later, Tobiah was engaged in even more secretive subterfuge, hiring spies from Nehemiah's own people to report Tobiah's "good deeds" and supply information about the work (6:17-19).

"Geshem" (apparently also spelled "Gashmu, vs. 6) ruled Arabia, another Persian-dominated province to the southeast. In addition to sharing Sanballat's jealousy, he had less interest even than a Samaritan in supporting a Jewish presence in the area, for the Samaritans could at least claim to have originally stemmed from the Jews.

All these enemies, and others (see 4:7) no doubt saw the remaining gaps in the wall about Jerusalem, places where gates were yet to be installed, as an open invitation to raid the city—hence the workmen also became armed guards (4:17-18).

B. The invitation, 2

2 That Sanballat and Geshem sent unto me, saying, Come, let us meet together in some one of the villages in the plain of Ono. But they thought to do me mischief.

The word for "villages" may also be taken as the actual name of a village (see the New English Bible). Many authorities think that Ono has been located about 30 miles northwest of Jerusalem. It has become a byword in some circles as a place for a meaningless or even harmful distraction. This is exactly how Nehemiah treats the invitation, since he sees through his critics' words to their real intent. Ono was very near Judea's border with Samaria, and the "mischief" he perceived could have even included an attack on his life on the pretended charge of trespassing.

II. Nehemiah's Response—3-4

3 And I sent messengers unto them, saying, I am doing a great work, so that I cannot come down: why should the work cease, whilst I leave it, and come down to you?

4 Yet they sent unto me four times after this sort; and I answered them after the same manner.

Although the King James reading makes it sound as though Nehemiah is boasting about how great his task is, he is actually only affirming that it is a "project" (NIV) so important that he cannot leave it for a pointless chat in the desert. We may assume that he could have found time for the meeting

had he not already known that the invitation is from three enemies who actively oppose his work. Their ridicule (4:1-3) has already removed any possibility that a conference might result in a truce or anything else productive. Convinced that his work is God's will, and that he has accurately assessed his enemies' intent, Nehemiah's grip on himself enables him to reject their offer four times.

III. False Report—5-7
A. Royal revolt? 5-6

5 Then sent Sanballat his servant unto me in like manner the fifth time with an open letter in his hand;

6 Wherein was written, It is reported among the heathen, and Gashmu saith it, that thou and the Jews think to rebel: for which cause thou buildest the wall, that thou mayest be their king, according to these words.

Now Sanballat's invitation becomes a threat. He and Gashmu (probably the "Geshem" of verse 1) concoct the rumor that Nehemiah is actually building a capital city for a rebel Jewish empire where he could reign as king. If he does not consent to meet, this story will be taken to Artaxerxes. Anyone who dares to provide strong leadership, as Nehemiah did, is open to the charge of pride. At this point Nehemiah had to depend on the king's having come to know and trust him while serving as Artaxerxes' cupbearer.

B. Prophetic support? 7

7 And thou hast also appointed prophets to preach of thee at Jerusalem, saying, There is a king in Judah: and now shall it be

reported to the king according to these words. Come now therefore, and let us take counsel together.

A second trumped-up charge in Sanballat's letter is that Nehemiah had surrounded his "royal court" with prophets to ensure the people's acceptance of their "king" as the will of God. Of course this was the actual practice of unscrupulous kings of the day, even in Israel. For example, King Ahab gathered a huge band of such false prophets to endorse his own decisions (1 Kings 22:6). Nehemiah had only his character to refute this charge. His honesty of heart is indicated several times when, in such situations, he turns from narrating the story to direct a prayer to God (see 4:4; 6:14).

IV. Nehemiah's Denial—8-9

8 Then I sent unto him, saying, There are no such things done as thou sayest, but thou feignest them out of thine own heart.

9 For they all made us afraid, saying, Their hands shall be weakened from the work, that it be not done. Now therefore, O God, strengthen my hands.

Nehemiah's answer in verse 8 projects a quiet confidence and self-assuredness indicating he is still not disturbed by the enemies' threats. The origin of the notion that he is building his own kingdom, and gathering prophets who approve, is in the mind of Sanballat, not in fact. However, in verse 9, he seems to include himself among those who became fearful and whose resolve was weakened by the constant barrage of criticism, negativism, and threats. Yet another interjection finds Nehemiah not only bravely maintaining his own courage but turning to God in prayer. It is a threat too great to bear without divine aid.

V. The Wall Is Finished—15-16

15 So the wall was finished in the twenty and fifth day of the month Elul, in fifty and two days.

16 And it came to pass, that when all our enemies heard thereof, and all the heathen that were about us saw these things, they were much cast down in their own eyes: for they perceived that this work was wrought of our God.

In the midst of fear, God answered Nehemiah's prayer for boldness and strength. In the intervening verses (10-14), and in the verses to follow (17-19), the record shows that this great leader of God's people even had to face temptation from false brothers and sisters. His classic response to them is of the sort that has characterized persecuted prophets and martyrs through the ages who have relied on God's strength: *"Should such a man as I flee?"* (vs. 11). Again, there is plenty of room here for accusing such a leader of pride; but "by their fruits ye shall know them."

In this case, the fruit of Nehemiah's stalwart stand against criticism and false charges is the completion of Jerusalem's walls, with no signs of rebellion against the Persian king who authorized the restoration of the city. That the project was completed in the astounding span of 52 days is rightly taken by Judah's enemies as a sign that God was with them after all.

Evangelistic Emphasis

Walls can be a boon or a barrier to evangelism. There is a time in the Church's life when we must pull in, withdraw, consolidate, claim our own distinct identity. It is all too easy to accommodate to a secular culture, reflecting the values of its materialism, its nationalism, and its racism. When the Church seems to have accommodated to the culture, to have sold out for cheap success, it is time to pull in.

There are times in the history of the Church, as in Israel's history, when if we are to survive as a people of God, we have to be willing to be set apart, to be a "peculiar people" (1 Pet. 2:9).

When we perceive ourselves to be a minority in society, an island of morality in a sea of paganism, then we have to pull back and teach our children a new way.

The building of the wall around Jerusalem was to give God's people that chance to claim their identity. Sometimes the Church's strongest witness is simply to be the Church, to demonstrate a different way of life. Its witness is to live out a commitment to care and nurture each other that stands in contrast to "the every man for himself" philosophy that pervades society. The pagans said of the early Church, "Behold how these Christians love one another."

However, too often the invisible walls of the Church are used to keep out, exclude those outcasts and misfit whom Jesus welcomed.

∞)(રુ

Memory Selection

And it came to pass, that when all our enemies heard thereof, and all the heathen that were about us saw these things, they were much cast down in their own eyes; for they perceived that this work was wrought of our God. —*Nehemiah 6:16*

The restoration of the walls around Jerusalem was perceived by the heathen as the work of God. It was not simply good engineering. It was not a human achievement of architectural beauty. It was not simply a tribute to the courage of the workers who had a sword in one hand and a trowel in the other. It was not seen as a victory for the persistence of the leader, Nehemiah.

The completion of the project against all odds was seen by the Gentile nations around Israel as a sign of God's help and presence. Their own pride and arrogance was diminished in light of these returning refugees' bringing off such a great work. It made the pagans wonder about the power of the gods they served. It left them troubled and depressed. Though strangers to the stories of Israel, and devotees to various pagan deities, they recognized the hand of a powerful God in this work. The only explanation was that the God of Abraham, Isaac and Jacob had done this.

Weekday Problems

Estelle was chair of the finance committee of her church. They had big dreams of a new family life center and additional parking space. But the million dollar price tag seemed far beyond their means.

Several proposals could help them realize the dream. A private, white academy was looking for space to lease. The church's children's building was empty six days a week. With a reasonable charge for use of the building beyond utilities and maintenance, they could buy extra land, pave it, and pay for it in five years. The church consultant had warned that without additional off-street parking the church would never grow. But would the private school encourage white flight from public schools? What was their obligation to all the children of the community?

A major chemical company had suffered bad press because of toxic chemicals leaking into the water supply of a small community near the plant. As a public relations gesture, the Chemical company offered to build the family life center with a gymnasium, to be used by the whole community, and provide funds for a youth worker to set up year-round activities. Estelle wondered how they could hold the chemical plant accountable to be good stewards of the environment if the church were dependent on them for financial support.

*How would you advise Estelle?

This and That

I now have a library of some 500 or 600 books, but no bookcase. No one will lend me a bookcase.

❖❖❖❖❖

Texans DO NOT LIE. They just remember big.

❖❖❖❖❖

He: I haven't slept for days.
She: Why?
He: I only sleep at night.

❖❖❖❖❖

One out of four Americans is mentally ill. Next time you're in a group with three other people, observe their words and actions carefully. If they're not crazy, guess who is.

❖❖❖❖❖

Clem: Whur ah come from, them's fightin' words.
Lem: Then why don'tcha put up yer dukes an' fight?
Clem: 'Cause we ain't whur ah come from."

This Lesson in Your Life

Nehemiah was a person sent on a mission. He had a single goal in view: to repair the wall. He would not be dissuaded. When summoned to a conference to talk about it, he replied: "I am doing a great work and I cannot come down." When his enemies threatened to send a letter accusing him of plotting a rebellion, he refused to be frightened into negotiating with them. When the prophet sought to have him discredit himself, urging him to flee to the Temple, he refused to be diverted. No threats or diversions could turn him from his goal.

Jesus said, "Seek ye first the kingdom" (Matt 6:33). It's easy to get side-tracked, to spend one's life on side issues. It's easy to wake up too late to discover how much of life has been wasted. In our pursuit of the latest, the fads, we miss the everlasting. Too often we just survive without making any difference in the world.

The writer John Gunther has written many biographies. In trying to get to know a person from the inside, he asks, "What is the one thing you love more than anything else in the world?" How would you answer that question about yourself?

Pastor Kenneth Shamblin tells of visiting a banker friend who was dying with a heart disease. The banker asked his pastor, "I want to ask you about my boy. How is he getting along?"

His pastor replied, "Well, he is doing fine. He is highly respected in his new work, and everybody believes he has a great future. Everything I hear about him is good."

With tears in his eyes the banker said: "That's not what I am talking about. I want to know how he is doing in the church. What is he doing for Christ? What is he doing with his stewardship? The one thing I am more concerned about than anything else is that my son put God first in his life." It is so easy to miss the main thing as we pursue the trivial.

Joe Harding tells the story of a little boy who grew up far out in the country. On one of the family's infrequent trips to town for supplies, he saw a poster announcing that a circus was coming to town. He had never seen a circus, but the pictures of the animals made it seem wonderful to him. He saved his money and counted the days. By the crack of dawn on the day of the circus, he was on his pony riding to town. He stood in the crowd and watched the circus parade. Amazed at the tigers, lions, and bears, his eyes grew even wider as he saw the elephants, the jugglers, the clowns, and the band. When the end of the parade came into sight, he stepped out of the crowd, handed the money he had saved to the last marcher, got on his pony and rode home. It was a few years later that he realized he had missed the main event in the big top.

How about you?

STRAIGHT

1. Who were Nehemiah's enemies?
His enemies were Sanballat, Tobiah, and Geshem (Neh. 6:1).

2. What was the real intention of the conference with Nehemiah which they proposed?
They intended to do Nehemiah harm (Neh. 6:2).

3. What was Nehemiah's response to their proposed meeting?
"I am doing a great work and I cannot come down" (Neh. 6:3).

4. What was reported about Nehemiah's wall rebuilding project in the letter to the king?
It was reported that Nehemiah and the Jews intended to rebel and to make Nehemiah king (Neh. 6:6).

5. What was Nehemiah's response to the charge?
"No such things as you say have been done; you are inventing them out of your own mind" (Neh. 6: 8).

6. How long did it take to rebuild the wall?
The wall was finished in 52 days (Neh. 6:15).

7. What perception of the wall project was held by surrounding nations?
That this work had been accomplished with the help of God (Neh. 6:16).

8. Who was the prophet hired by Nehemiah's enemies?
Shemaiah. He was hired to make Nehemiah sin and get a bad name (Neh. 6:13).

9. Why did Nehemiah reject the word of the prophet to flee to the Temple?
He did not want to be a coward; as a lay person he had no right to enter the Temple; he perceived God had not sent Shemaiah (Neh. 6:10-13).

10. Why would the advice to flee to the Temple and close the doors be considered sinful?
As a layman Nehemiah had no right to go inside the Temple because that space was reserved for the priest. Violation of the law was a capital crime.

It was no easy task to rebuild the wall around Jerusalem. Armed guards had to be posted to ward off invading enemies. The workers would carry a tool in one hand and a sword in other, ready to build or ready to defend the city. Their leader Nehemiah was besieged with entreaties to come to a conference and talk about the project. He was threatened that a letter would to be sent to the King of Persia accusing him of setting himself up as king. A respected prophet, paid by Nehemiah's enemies, warned him of personal danger. The prophet urged him to take refuge in the Holy Sanctuary. That safety would have been bought at the price of appearing to be a frightened refugee. It would make Nehemiah appear to have no regard for the solemn precincts of the Sanctuary, reserved only for the priests.

The obstacles, the threats, the harassment made the completion of the project all the more remarkable. In fact, had it been a project easily accomplished, others might not have even taken notice. But in overcoming such great odds, it was apparent even to unbelievers that the hand of God was in the completion of the wall. God used the meanness, jealousy, and petty strife to God's greater glory.

Recently I received a lovely and thoughtful gift, a beautiful silver pen. After a few day's use I discovered a scratch on the side of it. These ugly marks marred the sleek beauty of the pen. At first I thought I had rubbed it against some keys. Then I realize that there had been nothing in my shirt pocket that could possibly have scratched the pen. It must have been sold with the scratch on it. How cheap to pass off that a shoddy pen as a beautiful writing instrument to an unsuspecting buyer! How embarrassed the gracious donors would be had they realized that the gift they had chosen with such care was in fact defective!

A day or two later, I glanced at the pen, still irritated at the scratch marks. I realized to my chagrin that the marks were not random scratches at all. Seen as a whole, they were my initials beautifully engraved with a master artist's touch. Each letter was in perfect proportion, gracefully curved and meticulously spaced. It was just like my young friends not only to give an attractive and functional gift, but also to give it that special personal touch.

Sometimes when we view an experience piecemeal, seeing it only in bits and pieces, our perceptions are misleading. Paul wrote: "Now we see through a glass darkly, but then face to face" (1 Cor. 13: 12). What seems at first ugly and mean is made by the grace of God a part of a larger design of God's redemptive purpose.

Nehemiah's task was viewed by the enemies of the Jews as a seditious plot. Viewed rightly, as the fulfillment of a divine commission, rebuilding the walls was a beautiful and obedient response to a loving God.

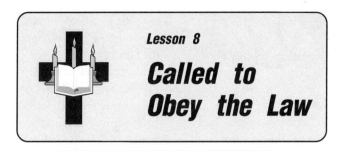

Called to Obey the Law

Nehemiah 8:1-3, 5-6, 8-12

And all the people gathered themselves together as one man into the street that was before the water gate; and they spake unto Ezra the scribe to bring the book of the law of Moses, which the LORD had commanded to Israel.

2 And Ezra the priest brought the law before the congregation both of men and women, and all that could hear with understanding, upon the first day of the seventh month.

3 And he read therein before the street that was before the water gate from the morning until midday, before the men and the women, and those that could understand; and the ears of all the people were attentive unto the book of the law.

5 And Ezra opened the book in the sight of all the people; (for he was above all the people;) and when he opened it, all the people stood up:

6 And Ezra blessed the LORD, the great God. And all the people answered, Amen, Amen, with lifting up their hands: and they bowed their heads, and worshiped the LORD with their faces to the ground.

8 So they read in the book in the law of God distinctly, and gave the sense, and caused them to understand the reading.

9 And Nehemiah, which is the Tirshatha, and Ezra the priest the scribe, and the Levites that taught the people, said unto all the people, This day is holy unto the LORD your God; mourn not, nor weep. For all the people wept, when they heard the words of the law.

10 Then he said unto them, Go your way, eat the fat, and drink the sweet, and send portions unto them for whom nothing is prepared: for this day is holy unto our Lord: neither be ye sorry; for the joy of the LORD is your strength.

11 So the Levites stilled all the people, saying, Hold your peace, for the day is holy; neither be ye grieved.

12 And all the people went their way to eat, and to drink, and to send portions, and to make great mirth, because they had understood the words that were declared unto them.

July 20

Memory Selection
Nehemiah 8:8

Background Scripture
Nehemiah 8

Devotional Reading
Psalm 119:33-40

God's people have celebrated the completion of the rebuilt Temple in worship. The observance of the Passover, the blood flowing from animal sacrifices, the smoke of the incense— all this was an outpouring of what might be called today "right-brained" expressions of the heart. In today's lesson the people celebrate the completion of the walls about the city. This time the ceremony is more cerebral or "left-brained." It features a reading of the Law of the Lord, along with careful explanations of its meaning.

These two celebrations illustrate the essential need for worship that involves both the heart and the head, emotions and rationality, feelings and reason. A centerpiece of this lesson is the renewed commitment of the people to align their lives with God's will as expressed in the Law. From this day onward, God's people have been known as a "people of the Book."

𝄢𝄢

What is the role of Scripture in the lives of group members? Ask such questions as: *Did you memorize Bible verses as a child? Do you still do so (as in the "Memory Verses" of these les-sons)? Do you have a systematic plan for Bible study? Can we be guilty of "biblioatry"—worshiping the Book instead of the God of the Book?*

What's the difference between honoring Scripture and "legalism"?

It is important to avoid judgmental comments. Some people have virtually been "beaten over the head" with dogmatic approaches to the Bible. The discussion should be *descriptive,* to raise awareness of various attitudes toward Scripture, not *prescriptive,* to make rules where the Bible does not. It should also serve to introduce the importance Scripture had in this scene when God's people celebrated the rebuilding of the walls at Jerusalem.

Teaching Outline	Daily Bible Readings	
I. Calling for Scripture—1-3	Mon.	The People Gather Nehemiah 7:66–8:1
A. A people-movement, 1	Tue.	Reading from the Law Nehemiah 8:2-6
B. Ezra's role, 2-3	Wed.	'This Day Is Holy' Nehemiah 8:7-12
II. Convening for Instruction—5-12	Thu.	Continuing to Learn Nehemiah 8:13-18
A. Honoring the Word, 5-6	Fri.	'Teach Me Your Statutes' Psalm 119:33-40
B. Understanding the Word, 8-9	Sat.	Wisdom from the Law Psalm 119:97-104
C. Holiness with Joy, 10-12	Sun.	Longing for the Law Psalm 119:129-136

Verse by Verse

I. Calling for Scripture—1-3
A. A people-movement, 1

1 And all the people gathered themselves together as one man into the street that was before the water gate; and they spake unto Ezra the scribe to bring the book of the law of Moses, which the LORD had commanded to Israel.

"The watergate" was on the east side of Jerusalem. It gave access to the principal spring that provided water for the city. Convening at this relatively "secular" setting, rather than in the Temple, the people are laying the groundwork for treating Scripture as fundamental to the life of the believer, not just a holy book whose use is restricted to the priests in the context of formal worship. This is also indicated in the oldest Greek translation of the Old Testament, which uses the word *laos* for "people" —the word that eventually gave Christendom the term "laity."

B. Ezra's role, 2-3

2 And Ezra the priest brought the law before the congregation both of men and women, and all that could hear with understanding, upon the first day of the seventh month.

3 And he read therein before the street that was before the water gate from the morning until midday, **before the men and the women, and those that could understand; and the ears of all the people were attentive unto the book of the law.**

Note that while Ezra is referred to as "scribe" in verse 1, his more common designation as "priest" appears here. Both functions were ascribed to this remarkable man when he was introduced in Ezra 7:1-6. Many Christians are so accustomed to scribes being associated with the enemies of Jesus (as in "the scribes and Pharisees") that we sometimes forget that many were dedicated believers.

Originally, priests served as worship leaders, superintendents of the Temple sacrifices and services, and teachers of the Law. With Ezra, however, scribes began to be trained for and looked to for more of the studying and interpretation of the Law. Some reached outside Jewish circles and became literate in the learning of other cultures. Many also served as civil and legal secretaries, as well as general teachers who provided tutoring services for those who could afford them.

We cannot estimate now how much of the books of Moses Ezra was able to read "from the morning until midday." What is emphasized in the text is the care taken not only to *read* the Law but to *explain* it so the people "could understand." The assembly is not just to give the Law a "hearing," but to open up insights and understanding into its intended application in the life of the people. (Note this emphasis in verses 2, 3, 7, 8, and 12.)

The evolution of the concept of Law and Scripture in the Bible is interesting. It begins with God's writing the Ten Commandments (literally "ten words") on tables of stone. It progresses to summaries of this code written on thin leather or papyrus and bound on the foreheads of believers and attached to their doorposts (Deut. 6:8-9). Throughout this history, however, God's intent was not just that His *words* be preserved but that the principles they embody be "written on the heart" and practiced in daily life.

Slowly the Old Testament is pointing the way to a time when the real significance of Scripture (which originally simply meant "writing") is that it is written as God's Word on the heart (see Jer. 31:31-33; 2 Cor. 3:3).

In the New Testament, the idea of Jesus as the Word made flesh (John 1:1, 14) overwhelms all previous views of even divine "writings." Still, the writings of the Old Testament are considered the divinely inspired Word of God (2 Tim. 3:16). Finally, before the close of the New Testament period, the writings of Paul were also given the status of "scripture" (2 Pet. 3:16), along with other apostolic or apostolically-authorized writings.

II. Convening for Instruction—5-12

A. Honoring the Word, 5-6

5 And Ezra opened the book in the sight of all the people; (for he was above all the people;) and when he opened it, all the people stood up:

6 And Ezra blessed the LORD, the great God. And all the people answered, Amen, Amen, with lifting up their hands: and they bowed their heads, and worshipped the LORD with their faces to the ground.

Ezra and his helpers were "above all the people" because a wooden platform (an early pulpit?) had been erected for them so they could be easily seen and heard (vs. 4). Familiarity with opening the Bible in Christian assemblies should not blind us to the drama here. Imagine a people, many of whom were illiterate, and most of whom were only vaguely aware of the role of God's Word in their history, watching Ezra as he unrolls a scroll that contained both their "constitution and by-laws" and the very words of God that they have been neglecting for so long.

In passing, we may note the typical Semitic body postures of the day, which here includes standing, lifting the hands, and falling prostrate, face down. All positions communicate honor, respect, and reverence. Some modern critics of the more sedate body positions in most Christian worship have pointed out that these ancient forms actually illustrate the modern recognition that animated and "kinetic" worship can reestablish the connection between body and soul that is neglected in "frozen" worship styles.

B. Understanding the Word, 8-9

8 So they read in the book in the

law of God distinctly, and gave the sense, and caused them to understand the reading.

9 And Nehemiah, which is the Tirshatha, and Ezra the priest the scribe, and the Levites that taught the people, said unto all the people, This day is holy unto the LORD your God; mourn not, nor weep. For all the people wept, when they heard the words of the law.

Again we are shown the emphasis not just on listening to the Law, but understanding it. Never again could those present have an excuse for treating Scripture as a magic talisman. Its "holiness" lies not in the parchment or papyrus roll on which it is written, but its inspired capability of impacting lives.

Now Nehemiah the governor (which is what "Tirshatha" means) is shown to be working side-by-side with Ezra, the priestly scribe. As they explain the true meaning of the Law the people have so long and widely ignored, they see its power to pierce and convict the heart. Here is an explicit illustration of the fact that "the word of God is living and active. Sharper than any double-edged sword, it penetrates even to dividing soul and spirit, joints and marrow; it judges the thoughts and attitudes of the heart" (Heb. 4:12, NIV). The Word, properly understood, has not only shown the people the error of their ways, but that God has nonetheless graciously enabled them to rebuild the Temple and the city walls. It is this combination of "law and gospel," conviction of sin and awareness of grace, that still has the power to convict those

who hear the Word even to the point of weeping.

C. Holiness with Joy, 10-12

10 Then he said unto them, Go your way, eat the fat, and drink the sweet, and send portions unto them for whom nothing is prepared: for this day is holy unto our Lord: neither be ye sorry; for the joy of the LORD is your strength.

11 So the Levites stilled all the people, saying, Hold your peace, for the day is holy; neither be ye grieved.

12 And all the people went their way to eat, and to drink, and to send portions, and to make great mirth, because they had understood the words that were declared unto them.

As Nehemiah has already said in verse 9, it is inappropriate only to weep on this day of dedication and accomplishment. It is also a time of rejoicing. This two-fold emotional response is an important aspect of truly understanding the Word. Those who resist the power of the Word to break down the strongholds of evil in their lives resist also weeping, and cannot know the cleansing power of tears. Those whose sorrow over sin destroys their hope cannot bring themselves to rejoice in the power of forgiveness. For those who allow both responses, eating and drinking, sharing food with others, and even "great mirth" are entirely appropriate reactions to having been convicted, then forgiven, by the living Word.

As one commentator concludes, this entire scene shows that "holiness and gloom go ill together" (Derek Kidner, *Ezra and Nehemiah*, p. 107).

Evangelistic Emphasis

The story in Nehemiah 8 reminds us of the power of the Word. As Ezra read from the ancient stories of Israel, they were deeply moved.

There is power in the Word no less today. An important part of public worship is the reading of the Scripture. An important part of personal devotions is meditating on the written Word. An important part of growing as a disciple is a life long study of the Bible. An important part of sharing our faith with others is sharing the stories of the Bible.

Time and again, when persons are in danger, through the Bible they find new faith. Persons in prison have found God in a diligent study of the word. People who are moving toward death will find the Scriptures speak in a new and deeper way.

The more we are immersed in Scripture the better we are able to share the appropriate word at the right time to fit the circumstance of danger, temptation, or discouragement. Again and again these ancient words, read by Ezra to his people, have been a source of renewal and redemption.

Martin Luther spoke of the Scriptures as "the cradle of Christ." We do not worship the Bible, but it is through the Bible that we come to know the love of God in Christ, the love which brings eternal life.

&)CR

Memory Selection

So they read in the book in the law of God distinctly, and gave the sense, and caused them to understand the reading. —*Nehemiah 8:8*

The memory selection emphasizes the importance both of the written Word and its interpretation. We are blessed to have a book, the Bible, that keeps us anchored to the sacred traditions of Israel and of the Church. Generation after generation returns to the written Word. God made known the way His people should live in the Law given through Moses. In the stories of Israel and the stories of Jesus the nature of God is shown to be holy and loving, just and merciful.

But we also need faithful interpreters of the Word. We need the scholars who know the language, the customs, and the history that shed light on the meaning of the texts. We need teachers who can help us apply the meaning of the Scriptures to our everyday lives. With help in understanding the meaning of the texts when first written, with guidance in discovering the meaning of the texts for our lives today, the ancient written Word becomes the lively, life-giving Word of God for us today.

Weekday Problems

Jim was having trouble reading his Bible. Many times he had resolved to read the Bible through. But along about Leviticus with all the Temple rules he got discouraged and gave up. His pastor suggested several different approaches to Bible reading and study.

Jim enlisted in a year long survey of the Bible taught at his church. It helped him learn who wrote the books of the Bible, when and why they were written. The questions from the group helped him realize that others had the same questions he had.

The pastor also encouraged him to read the Bible with a small group. They would focus each week on a single passage. Often it was the passage on which the preacher would base his sermon that week. They would ask what the passage meant to its first readers. Then they would probe to learn what God might be saying to them through the passage. They shared their experiences.

Then the pastor encouraged Jim to read the Bible devotionally. He suggested, "Take an event from the Gospels and read it with imagination, as though you are present with Jesus. Or take a single verse from a psalm, read and reread it aloud, memorize it, repeat it all day. Let the psalm shape your prayers."

Jim found the Bible coming alive through academic study, through group sharing, and through personal meditation.

*What ways of Bible reading have you found helpful? What problems?

Words About the Word

So great is my veneration for the Bible that the earlier my children begin to read it, the more confident will be my hope that they will prove useful citizens to their country, and respectable members of society.—*John Quincy Adams*

There are 10 men who will fight for the Bible to one who will read it.—*L. R. Akers*

The reason people are down on the Bible is that they're not up on the Bible.—*William Ward Ayer*

The word of God tends to make large-minded, noble-hearted men.—*Henry Ward Beecher*

Almost any fool can prove the Bible ain't so—it takes a wise man to believe it.—*Josh Billings*

467

This Lesson in Your Life

In the story in today's lesson from Nehemiah 8, we are told that Ezra read from the book of the law of Moses to all the people. When the people heard the words of the Law, they wept because their lives fell far short of what was expected by the Law. Surprisingly, Ezra exhorts them not to grieve, but to rejoice and celebrate. The theme of joy moves through the story. Why should they rejoice on the hearing of the book of Moses?

They rejoiced because now they knew the way they were to live. It was as if they had been wandering around for most of their lives, not sure what God expected. The Gentiles around them lived one way. The Jews who had stayed and married the Gentiles lived another way. They had been exposed to different shrines and ceremonies in Babylon. They were confused as to what the God of Abraham, Isaac, and Jacob required of them. The reading of the Law was like finding a path out of a dense forest. They knew they had a long way to go, but finally they knew the direction of their journey. They could go rejoicing on their way.

They rejoiced because now they were right with God. The stories in the book of Moses helped them understand who they were, a people created in God's own image, a people called to share in God's redemptive mission. In their time of captivity, some had lost sight of what it meant to be a child of God, living in obedience, trust, and love. E. Stanley Jones suggests that living at cross-purposes with God is like trying to ride a bicycle with the handle bars on backwards. When you get your life straightened out, with God at the center, it's like riding a bike the way it was designed to be used. Now that the Jews knew "how the handle bars went on," they shared the joy of the Lord.

When they were instructed in the proper celebration of the festival of booths, they were glad to obey. This was not the reluctant, surly obedience of a slave. Rather it was the delight of pleasing One whom they loved and adored. Persons whose daily work is a fulfillment of God's calling find contentment and joy in their work, though it may be exhausting, stressful, or frustrating. They could find other work with better hours, better pay, less stress. But their joy in the Lord is doing what they know they are called to do.

When the prodigal son in Jesus' parable returns home to the waiting father, there is a great party with much rejoicing. The reading of the Law marked the beginning of that long road home for the prodigal Jews. It was not a day to mourn in sackcloth and ashes for their sins, but a day of new beginning. "Joy in the Lord is your strength."

GETTING THE FACTS STRAIGHT

1. Who read from the book of the Law of Moses to the people gathered together?
Ezra, the priest and scribe, read from the scroll (Neh. 8:1-3).

2. How long did the reading of the Law last?
The reading lasted about six hours, from early morning to midday (Neh. 8:3).

3. What gestures were made by the people, and what do they signify?
They raised their hands in expectancy and repentance. They bowed their heads and fell prostrate in obedience and submission (Neh. 8: 6).

4. Who helped the people understand the Law?
The Levites helped the people understand the Law, moving among them while the people remained in their places (Neh. 8:7).

5. What was the response of the people to the reading of the Law?
The people wept because they had not followed the Law perfectly.

6. What did Ezra command the people do as a more appropriate response to the law?
They were to celebrate in joy and feast, eating the fat (best) meat, drinking sweet wine, and sharing portions with those not prepared for the feast.

7. What festival is described in the Law read on the second day?
The festival of booths (Neh. 8:13-14).

8. What trees were to be used in building the booths?
Branches of olive, wild olive, myrtle, palm and other leafy trees were used to make booths (Neh. 8:15).

9. How long had it been since the the festival of booths had been celebrated?
Not since the time of Jeshua (Joshua) son of Nun, during the time of the conquest of the Holy Land, had this festival been observed (Neh. 8:17).

10. Of what was the feast of booths intended to remind the people?
It was to remind Israel of their 40 years of wandering in the wilderness, when they lived in such shelters or "booths."

Nearly 30 years ago, *Guideposts* carried the story of the courageous and compassionate Corrie Ten Boom. Corrie told of her experience in prison. Her family was arrested for concealing Jews in their home in Holland during the reign of Nazi terror. After eight months in prison, Corrie and her sister Betsie were sent to the dreaded Ravensbruck Concentration Camp in Germany.

It was notorious as a death camp. As Carrie and others were shipped in boxcars from Holland to Germany, her only possession was a Bible. She carried it in a small cloth bag tied on a string around her neck. It was midnight when they reached the processing barracks at Ravensbruck. Under the harsh ceiling lights, they saw a dismaying sight. As they reached the head of the line, each woman had to strip off every scrap of clothing, throw it all on a pile guarded by soldiers, and walk naked past the scrutiny of a dozen guards to the shower room. Coming out of the shower the women wore only the regulation prison dress and a pair of shoes.

The Bible . . . how could they take it past all those watchful eyes? Corrie begged a passing guard to show her the toilets. He jerked his head in the direction of the shower room. Timidly she stepped out of line and walked toward the huge room with its row on row of overhead spigots. It was empty waiting for the next batch of 50 naked, shivering women. In a few minutes they would return there, stripped of everything they possessed. Then Corrie and Betsie saw a pile of old wooden benches stacked in a corner, crawling with cockroaches. To Corrie and Betsie it seemed the furniture of heaven itself. In an instant, Corrie stuffed the little bag holding her Bible behind the benches.

The women were herded into that room 10 minutes later, and Corrie reclaimed her precious sack from its hiding place. When she came to her barracks, her only possession was a flimsy prison dress and a copy of the Bible. But, as she put it, at Ravensbruck the women "were not poor but rich, rich in the care of God." Soon they were holding secret Bible study groups. The number of believers was growing. Barracks 28 became known throughout the camp as 'the crazy place where they hope."

How blessed we are to have copies of the Bible available for us to read and study. It can be for us as well a source of strength and guidance. It is the channel of God's Word to us.

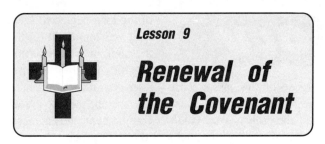

Lesson 9

Renewal of the Covenant

Nehemiah 10:28-37

And the rest of the people, the priests, the Levites, the por ters, the singers, the Nethinims, and all they that had separated themselves from the people of the lands unto the law of God, their wives, their sons, and their daughters, every one having knowledge, and having understanding;

29 They clave to their brethren, their nobles, and entered into a curse, and into an oath, to walk in God's law, which was given by Moses the servant of God, and to observe and do all the commandments of the LORD our Lord, and his judgments and his statutes;

30 And that we would not give our daughters unto the people of the land, nor take their daughters for our sons:

31 And if the people of the land bring ware or any victuals on the sabbath day to sell, that we would not buy it of them on the sabbath, or on the holy day: and that we would leave the seventh year, and the exaction of every debt.

32 Also we made ordinances for us, to charge ourselves yearly with the third part of a shekel for the service of the house of our God;

33 For the shewbread, and for the continual meat offering, and for the continual burnt offering, of the sabbaths, of the new moons, for the set feasts, and for the holy things, and for the sin offerings to make an atonement for Israel, and for all the work of the house of our God.

34 And we cast the lots among the priests, the Levites, and the people, for the wood offering, to bring it into the house of our God, after the houses of our fathers, at times appointed year by year, to burn upon the altar of the LORD our God, as it is written in the law:

35 And to bring the firstfruits of our ground, and the firstfruits of all fruit of all trees, year by year, unto the house of the LORD:

36 Also the firstborn of our sons, and of our cattle, as it is written in the law, and the firstlings of our herds and of our flocks, to bring to the house of our God, unto the priests that minister in the house of our God:

37 And that we should bring the firstfruits of our dough, and our offerings, and the fruit of all manner of trees, of wine and of oil, unto the priests, to the chambers of the house of our God; and the tithes of our ground unto the Levites, that the same Levites might have the tithes in all the cities of our tillage.

July 27

Memory Selection
Nehemiah 9:38

Background Scripture
Nehemiah 10:28-39

Devotional Reading
Psalm 66:8-20

The purpose of this lesson is to describe the way the people of Judah rededicated themselves to God's Covenant after rebuilding the walls about Jerusalem. The commitment they express here is an extension of the gathering described in Lesson 8, when a "lay" movement called for Ezra the priest to organize a reading of the long-neglected Law.

It was important for the author of the book of Nehemiah to record the specific promises the people made after their recommitment to the Law. For it is one thing to profess faith and commitment, and another to get down to specifics such as how to finance the institutions required for the *practice* of the faith. At this point in their history, God's people show their willingness to get down to the "brass tacks" of the Covenant.

ഏറ്റ

Recount Jesus' parable of the two sons, in Matthew 21:28-32. Jesus told this parable to confront His critics with the question of whether they were actually religious, or merely protective of their "religious turf." He said that a father asked his two sons to go work in his vineyard. The first son said he would not go, but then changed his mind and went to work.

The second son said he would oblige his father, then did not.

Jesus compared the first son with sinners who professed no faith, but repented and believed when they heard the preaching of John the Baptist. He compared the second with his opponents, who professed faith, but rejected John's preaching.

In today's lesson, the people of Judah choose to follow the path of the first son. Having confessed their waywardness, they proceeded to *act* on their renewed faith rather than merely to talk about it.

Teaching Outline	Daily Bible Readings

I. Determination to Obey—28-29
  A. Mass movement, 28
  B. Commitment to obey, 29
 	
II. Details of Obedience—30-37
  A. No intermarriage, 30
  B. Sabbath observance, 31
  C. Temple taxes, 32-33
  D. Rotating wood-cutting, 34
  E. Firstfruits committed, 35-37
	Mon. Confession and Worship
	      Nehemiah 9:1-5
	Tue. Ezra Prays
	      Nehemiah 9:6-12
	Wed. Disobedient Ancestors
	      Nehemiah 9:16-21
	Thu. God's Long Patience
	      Nehemiah 9:26-31
	Fri. A Firm Agreement
	      Nehemiah 9:32-38
	Sat. Commitment to Obey
	      Nehemiah 10:28-34
	Sun. Tithing for God's House
	      Nehemiah 10:35-39

Verse by Verse

I. Determination to Obey—28-29

A. Mass movement, 28

28 And the rest of the people, the priests, the Levites, the porters, the singers, the Nethinims, and all they that had separated themselves from the people of the lands unto the law of God, their wives, their sons, and their daughters, every one having knowledge, and having understanding;

We have noticed that the completion of the restoration of Jerusalem's walls was marked by a mass public reading of the Scriptures (Neh. 8). This remarkable event was followed by the consecration of the Levites for their renewed task of offering sacrifice and leading the people in worship. Their first act was to recite the sad history of their forefathers, who, ignoring the mighty acts of God in leading them out of Egypt and giving them the Promised Land, turned to idols (chap. 9).

Now it is time for the people of Judah other than the Levites to respond. God's work will not be adequately fulfilled if only the leaders are dedicated; "the rest of the people" (vs. 28) must also be committed.

Many among the people assisted in the complex details of Jewish worship. The "porters" (NIV "gate-keepers") were attendants posted at the entrances to the Temple to enforce the Law's prohibitions on Gentiles and women entering certain areas. Special singers, as well as players of musical instruments, had been installed in the Temple worship at the commandment of David (1 Chron. 15:16ff.). "Nethinims" literally means "the given ones," and refers to servants who were "given" to the Levites to perform special tasks (Ezra 8:20).

Finally, the list of those who rededicated their lives to God is broadened to include those who had been left behind when Judah and Benjamin had been carried into Babylonian captivity, and who had intermarried with surrounding pagans. The return of many of the captives and the work of restoration had encouraged these "former" Jews to renew their commitment to their faith.

B. Commitment to Obey, 29

29 They clave to their brethren, their nobles, and entered into a curse, and into an oath, to walk in God's law, which was given by Moses the servant of God, and to observe and do all the commandments of the LORD our Lord, and his judgments and his statutes;

The broader "people movement" attaches itself to their leaders, binding themselves by an oath or covenant to forsake their wanton ways and to cling not only to the nobles but to the Law. A "curse" accompanying an oath called down punishment on those making the oath if they failed to live up to their covenant. A common example is the phrase "God do so to me, and more also, [if I fail to fulfill the oath]" (see 2 Sam. 19:13). The combination of oath and "curse" shows the seriousness with which the people take their renewed vows of faithfulness.

II. Details of Obedience—30-37

A. No intermarriage, 30

30 And that we would not give our daughters unto the people of the land, nor take their daughters for our sons:

Now comes a "bill of particulars" affirming the people's intent to keep specific parts of the Law, along with other duties deemed necessary for a renewed Judaism to be effective in the lives of the people. The first seems aimed at those referred to above who had intermarried with pagans in the land. This was a long-standing commandment dating from the time of Moses himself (Deut. 7:1-3); but it was frequently ignored. This separation of Jews from the non-Jews they had married caused great heart-ache (see Ezra 10), but the people see that, as when Solomon married many "foreign women," intermarriage tended to dilute the keeping of the Law.

While this may seem harsh to us, far more than religious legalism is involved here. Pagan influence had previously led to immoral worship, including even human sacrifices, and polluted the high ethical standards of monotheism. Ironically, the demand

for separatism would later benefit pagans, as God preserves a pure line of Jews through whom the Messiah to the Gentiles would come.

B. Sabbath observance, 31

31 And if the people of the land bring ware or any victuals on the sabbath day to sell, that we would not buy it of them on the sabbath, or on the holy day: and that we would leave the seventh year, and the exaction of every debt.

Observing the Sabbath was one of the most visible marks of being a faithful Jew. From the beginning, they were to "remember the Sabbath, and keep it holy." Yet under the pressure of trading with pagans, many Jews had neglected laws concerning Sabbath observance. No reform would have been complete without a rededication to this fundamental platform of Judaism. The people also vow to restore the practice of forgiving debts and leaving land fallow every seventh year (see Exod. 23:11; Deut. 15:1ff.).

C. Temple taxes, 32-33

32 Also we made ordinances for us, to charge ourselves yearly with the third part of a shekel for the service of the house of our God;

33 For the shewbread, and for the continual meat offering, and for the continual burnt offering, of the sabbaths, of the new moons, for the set feasts, and for the holy things, and for the sin offerings to make an atonement for Israel, and for all the work of the house of our God.

The many sacrificial offerings required by the Law, including grain and large and small animals, did not come without cost. Even commodities made available for worshipers to purchase had been bought from some source. Here the people voluntarily tax themselves a nominal amount for this purpose (see also Exod. 30:13ff.).

D. Rotating wood-cutting, 34

34 And we cast the lots among the priests, the Levites, and the people, for the wood offering, to bring it into the house of our God, after the houses of our fathers, at times appointed year by year, to burn upon the altar of the LORD our God, as it is written in the law:

The wood for burning the vast number of sacrifices had to be cut and gathered; and here the people develop a common-sense rotation according to clans. As the hills immediately surrounding the city yielded their timber, taking turns at making longer trips would have become increasingly important. This was a gift or sacrifice of time as well as money, since it involved time away from the people's regular work.

E. Firstfruits committed, 35-37

35 And to bring the firstfruits of our ground, and the firstfruits of all fruit of all trees, year by year, unto the house of the LORD:

36 Also the firstborn of our sons, and of our cattle, as it is written in the law, and the firstlings of our herds and of our flocks, to bring to the house of our God, unto the priests that minister in the house of our God:

37 And that we should bring the firstfruits of our dough, and our offerings, and the fruit of all manner of trees, of wine and of oil, unto the priests, to the chambers of

the house of our God; and the tithes of our ground unto the Levites, that the same Levites might have the tithes in all the cities of our tillage.

Now the people commit themselves to returning to the law of giving the firstfruits and the tithe (tenth) to God. This practice is older than the Bible; the first mention of it is when Abraham gave tithes to King Melchizedek, "priest of the most high God" (Gen. 14:18-20). It was also a firmly established principle of the Law of Moses, with Jews required to give the first offspring of animals and a tenth of ground and orchard crops to the Levites, as their suppor. Although giving God the "firstborn of our sons" is spoken of here in the same terms as crops and animals, Jewish law carefully provided for a child to be ransomed with money (Num. 18:16), in marked distinction from human sacrificed practiced by some Gentiles.

In summary, both people and priests have been moved by the completion first of the Temple and then the walls of Jerusalem to recommit themselves to keeping the Covenant with their Covenant-giving God. Critics might point out that some of these promises were made in the emotional "high" of the moment, and were as short-lived as some conversions to emotional appeals at a Christian revival. Yet the recommitment that marked the return from Babylonian captivity was strong enough to give a rebirth of Judaism that lasted until history repeated itself and the Temple was again destroyed, and Jerusalem razed, by the Romans in A.D. 70, more than 500 years later.

Evangelistic Emphasis

The beauty of the Temple and the richness of its worship showed the value the Jews placed on worship. It was a way they gave glory to God.

Today the ways we share the good news of God's love are varied. The worship center says a lot about the importance we place on the worship of God. The whole church facility can be welcoming to strangers or a turn-off. When visitors come a little late and cannot find a parking place, they feel that church has no place for them. Church consultants remind us that for couples with small children, the nursery may be the most important room in the church. If it is clean, bright, well equipped, they will leave their infant there with a good feeling. If it seems to them dirty, dull, supplied with cast-off toys, they will look for another church that welcomes children. When the church is inaccessible to persons in wheel chairs, it says they are not welcome.

Ezra gave detailed instructions so the people would not neglect the worship of God. Our church buildings may be a part of our welcome and outreach when they make everyone welcome. All through the week the church building can be a silent witness to God and a persistent call to worship.

ഇൽ

Memory Selection

And because of all this we make a sure covenant, and write it; and our princes, Levites and priests, seal unto it. —*Nehemiah 9:38*

"Because of all this we make a sure covenant." The preceding part of the ninth chapter of Nehemiah relates God's mighty acts: in creation, in freeing the Hebrews from slavery, in leading them across the Red Sea, in guiding them with a pillar of cloud in the day time and a pillar of fire at night, in giving them bread to stay hunger and water from a rock to quench their thirst, in sustaining them for forty years in the wilderness. It is "because of all this" that the people respond by entering a sacred covenant with God.

Always the covenant between Israel and God is initiated by God. The obligations which Israel takes on are in response to what God has already done. Abraham responds to God's promise to make of him a great nation. Jeremiah speaks of a new covenant, written on the heart, initiated by God. Jesus speaks of the new covenant, sealed with his blood, God's supreme expression of love. As written in John's letter, "We love because He first loved us." (1 John 4:19)

Weekday Problems

Robert Goodrich tells of a couple who celebrated their Golden wedding anniversary. They recalled for their pastor the first Sunday of their marriage. The bride asked of her husband, "How much are we going to give to the church?" The truth is he had not even planned on going to church on that first Sunday after their wedding, much less given thought to how much they would give. He recovered quickly, saying, "I don't know. We surely want to give something." He was really worrying whether they would have enough gas money to get home from the honeymoon.

"Well," his bride said, "I've always given a tithe and I like it." So that first Sunday they began giving a tenth to the church. Thereafter, each Saturday night they prepared their little tithe box and kept it separate and sacred. It didn't amount to much those first Saturdays—$1.50 or $2. Yet they eventually opened a special ledger account, and kept it faithfully. On that 50th anniversary celebration the husband said: "One of the greatest satisfactions we have had in our married life is to realize that of everything we ever had, 10 percent has gone in to the work of God's kingdom."

* How do you decide what to give to the church?

*What proportion do you give? Do you give the leftovers or the first fruits?

Offerings on Tithing

Deacon: Weren't you nervous when Brother Brown contributed $5,000 to our building fund?
Minister: Nope. I just kept calm . . . and collected.

Minister: Brother Hank, I notice that you're behind on your tithes.
Brother Hank: Well, you know—money flies.
Minister: Yes, but all we've seen from you lately are its tail feathers.

Minister at church business meeting: Why are contributions are down?
Member: It takes twice as much these days to live beyond our means.

Minister: Brother Gibbs, have you forgotten your $500 pledge?
Gibbs: Of course not! Didn't you see me try to duck into the alley to avoid you?

477

This Lesson in Your Life

The book of Moses read by Ezra is very specific about support of the Temple and worship. In a previous age, the Temple was supported by the king. But now there was no Jewish king in Israel. The support of corporate worship was the responsibility of all the people. Moses urged them to bring a tithe to the priest. The tithe is a percentage—in biblical tradition, 10 percent—set aside, and given first. In Leviticus 27:30,32 the Mosaic law is spelled out: "All the tithe of the land, whether of the seed of the land or the fruit of the trees is the Lord's . . . And all the tithe of the herds and flocks, every tenth animal of all that pass under the herdsman's staff shall be holy to the Lord." Many Christians have continued the tithe, not primarily as a means of supporting the church, but as an essential discipline in spiritual growth. It is a systematic and regular way of reminding ourselves that all that we have belongs to God.

It may be surprising to discover that money is the subject Jesus talked most about. He wasn't trying to raise funds for a new Temple. His teachings on possessions had to do with his concern for the spiritual well-being of the giver.

When we face the radical demands of Christ, when we face the challenge of giving primary love to Him, we discover areas not yet surrendered. Sometimes we discover that rather than our possessing possessions, they assume such an importance in our lives that our possessions possess us. They become the source of our security, our identity, our worth. In truth, possessions and money can become our God. Jesus said "No man can serve two masters" (Luke 16:13). One significant spiritual discipline is the practice of regularly setting aside a portion of our income, and setting it aside first, for the work of God's Kingdom. It is a means of removing a blockage to our spiritual growth.

One of the delights of giving in a systematic, proportionate way is that it brings new joy to your giving. It is not a painful parting from funds you really wanted to use in another way. It is as though you are entrusted to make a wise use of funds entrusted to you, funds of which you are the administrator, not the owner. Tithing reminds us that we are trust officers of the Lord. The amount set aside first and regularly is yours only to invest in the Kingdom of God. Such a spiritual discipline reminds us that all that we have is from God. We are the stewards not only of the 10 percent set aside first, but of the other 90 percent as well. Each time we offer our gifts to God we are reminded that our time, our talents, our influence, as well as our money are only entrusted to us for a season. The discipline of setting aside first a proportion of what we have received for the Lord's work helps us to better live the whole of life.

1. **What was the policy on marriage of Jews with Gentiles?**
   They were not to give their daughters in marriage to the people of the land nor to take Gentile daughters for their Jewish sons (Neh. 10:30).

2. **What were the rules concerning trade on the Sabbath?**
   If the "people of the land" bring in merchandise or any grain on the Sabbath, the Jews were not to buy from them (Neh. 10:31).

3. **What is special about the seventh year?**
   Every seventh year the land was to lie fallow, and all debts were to be forgiven (Neh. 10:31).

4. **What tax would the people take on to support the house of God?**
   An annual contribution of one-third of a shekel.

5. **What is a shekel?**
   A shekel is a measure of weight, equal to 1/8-ounce or 4 grams. A one-third shekel coin was introduced into Palestine during the Persian period.

6. **What did the Temple tax cover?**
   Bread for the table, grain and animals for various offerings, festifals and feasts, and support of the priests as they performed their duties (Neh. 10: 32-33).

7. **How was the wood for the altar to be provided?**
   Priests, Levites, and the people cast lots to determine when each of the families was to bring wood to burn on the altar of the Lord (Neh. 10:34).

8. **What firstfruits were to be brought to the Temple?**
   Firstfruits of crops, fruit trees, first born of sons and of cattle, ground meal, new wine and oil (Neh. 10: 35-36).

9. **What is a tithe?**
   A tithe is a tenth.

10. **What was the overall purpose of these obligations to the Temple?**
    In order not to "neglect the house of our God" (Neh. 10:39).

The Scripture passage for this lesson reminds us that one of the important, distinctive, identifying traditions of the Jewish community of faith is observation the Sabbath. They were not to buy, or sell, or trade on that holy day. It was a day of rest. It marks a rhythm of work and rest essential to our well being.

In our seven-day-a-week world of commerce, it is difficult to observe a Sabbath day. Hospitals, industries, stores, restaurants, service stations are open seven days a week. Sunday is the busiest day of the week for pastors. But the need for a pattern of rest and work is not less important for our day. Some persons who must work on Sunday, as pastors do, choose a day other than Sunday as a Sabbath day, a day of rest, reflection, play.

In some traditions the list of prohibited activities is so long and so restricted, that children dread the Sabbath instead of looking forward to it. Some families seek to observe the Sabbath in creative ways. Going to church together, having a leisurely meal together, taking an outing, a short hike, sharing books or music together may mark that day as special. Stepping out of the daily routine and constant stress gives one a fresh perspective. It can open the channels of renewal.

What are the identifying marks of Christians today? If people were to draw conclusions about the teachings of your congregation from the way you live, what would they see as distinctive about your faith group?

I was startled one Sunday morning when the phone rang in my office at church shortly before the services were to begin. The caller was a bride wanting to reserve the church for her wedding, on a Sunday morning. She seemed surprised and annoyed that the sanctuary would not be available on any Sunday morning. I wondered how anyone could be so far removed from church life not to realize that Sunday morning was the major gathering day for Christian congregations. Could it be that this bride knew some members of our congregation in her neighborhood, and that as she drove by their houses she saw cars in car ports, heard the sounds of TV emanating from the house, smelled the delicious aroma of barbecue steaks on the grill, and noticed the Sunday morning paper still in the front yard of the late sleepers? Going by such habits of some church members, I can understand why she may have concluded that the church had closed down for the summer.

If people were to base their conclusions about the faith practices that are important for your congregation, would observance of the Sabbath be an identifying trait? How do you observe the Lord's day in your household? "Remember the Sabbath and keep it holy" (Exod. 20:8).

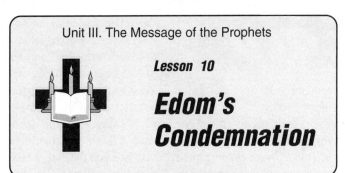

Lesson 10

Edom's Condemnation

Obadiah 1-4, 10-11, 15-16, 21

The vision of Obadiah. Thus saith the Lord GOD concerning Edom; We have heard a rumour from the LORD, and an ambassador is sent among the heathen, Arise ye, and let us rise up against her in battle.

2 Behold, I have made thee small among the heathen: thou art greatly despised.

3 The pride of thine heart hath deceived thee, thou that dwellest in the clefts of the rock, whose habitation is high; that saith in his heart, Who shall bring me down to the ground?

4 Though thou exalt thyself as the eagle, and though thou set thy nest among the stars, thence will I bring thee down, saith the LORD.

10 For thy violence against thy brother Jacob shame shall cover thee, and thou shalt be cut off for ever.

11 In the day that thou stoodest on the other side, in the day that the strangers carried away captive his forces, and foreigners entered into his gates, and cast lots upon Jerusalem, even thou wast as one of them.

15 For the day of the LORD is near upon all the heathen: as thou hast done, it shall be done unto thee: thy reward shall return upon thine own head.

16 For as ye have drunk upon my holy mountain, so shall all the heathen drink continually, yea, they shall drink, and they shall swallow down, and they shall be as though they had not been.

21 And saviours shall come up on mount Zion to judge the mount of Esau; and the kingdom shall be the LORD's.

Aug. 3

Memory Selection
Obadiah 15

Background Scripture
Obadiah

Devotional Reading
Isaiah 43:1-7

The next three lessons are drawn from "minor prophets"—those rugged preachers and "seers" God chose both to warn and to encourage Israel. They are "minor" only because their writings are not "major" in length. Their powerful words reinforced the message that God will bless the nation if it will remain faithful.

This first lesson from Obadiah, also illustrates the "universality" of the prophets. That is, they often speak to nations other than the Jews, asserting that God is sovereign over all. For Obadiah, although Edom has been a thorn in Israel's flesh, they have reached the end of God's tether. Now they will be judged by the same righteous standard by which He judged Israel.

ℰℐℭℛ

Bring a newspaper with international datelines on some of its stories to introduce this class. Read to the group such headlines as "Iraq fires missiles at U.S. planes" . . . "Jewish soldiers fire on Palestinian crowd". . . "African AIDS crisis worsens" . . . "Greenpeace attacks U.S. position on global warming."

Ask the group whether they think that God is concerned with such events. Or is He mainly interested in "religious" issues, especially those faced by our own church? Point out that in this lesson God, through the prophet Obadiah, holds the nation of Edom accountable for its treatment of His people, the Jews. While the Bible usually focuses on what happens to God's people, such glimpses as this show that He is Lord over all nations. The lesson also serves as an invitation to each believer today to become a "world Christian," actively concerned about issues of justice and righteousness throughout God's world.

Teaching Outline	Daily Bible Readings	
I. Complaint Against Edom—1-4	Mon.	Report from the Lord Obadiah 1-9
A. Ambassador to the Heathen, 1	Tue.	Rejoicing at Calamity Obadiah 10-16
B. Fall from the Heights, 2-4	Wed.	Taking Possession Obadiah 17-21
II. Sins Against Brethren—10-11	Thu.	'Give Them Up' Isaiah 43:1-7
A. Sin of commission, 10	Fri.	God Is Israel's Savior Isaiah 43:8-13
B. Sin of omission, 11	Sat	Israel Will Be the Lord's Isaiah 44:1-8
III. Reaping What Was Sown—15-16	Sun.	God Will Comfort Israel Isaiah 66:10-14
IV. Salvation vs. Judgment—21		

Verse by Verse

I. Complaint Against Edom—1-4
A. Ambassador to the Heathen, 1

1 The vision of Obadiah. Thus saith the Lord GOD concerning Edom; We have heard a rumour from the LORD, and an ambassador is sent among the heathen, Arise ye, and let us rise up against her in battle.

Although several men named Obadiah are mentioned elsewhere in the Bible, all we know of Obadiah the prophet is what is contained in this one-chapter book, the shortest in the Old Testament. His name means "Servant (or Worshiper) of Yah; and, filled with righteous indignation, he was sent as Yahweh's "ambassador" to announce His judgment against the nation of Edom. This is the culmination of many years of tension between the two nations, whose founders, ironically, were brothers.

Edom means "red," and was the fitting nickname given to Jacob's brother Esau, for two reasons. From infancy he was covered with red hair (Gen. 25:25); and as a man he sold his birthright to Jacob for a bowl of red pottage (Gen. 25:29-34). In the division of land between the two brothers, Esau settled in the rugged area of Mt. Seir, to the south of the Dead Sea. Much of the land is red-hued wasteland and sandstone, again making "Edom" or "red" a very suitable name. A dramatic example of the area's coloration is the city of Petra, which was carved out of red sandstone (and which can still be visited today).

In addition to Jacob and Esau's (Edom's) conflict over the birthright, much of the long-standing enmity between their descendants stemmed from the later Edomites' refusal to allow the Jews who were fleeing from Egyptian captivity to cross Edomite territory on their way to Canaan (Num. 20:14-21). Such opposition is perhaps behind Obadiah's inclusion of the Edomites among the "heathen." Intermittent war with Edom occurred throughout the reigns of the kings of Israel despite God having forbidden it because of the family relationship (Deut. 23:7).

B. Fall from the Heights, 2-4

2 Behold, I have made thee small among the heathen: thou art greatly despised.

3 The pride of thine heart hath deceived thee, thou that dwellest in the clefts of the rock, whose habitation is high; that saith in his heart, Who shall bring me down to the ground?

4 Though thou exalt thyself as the eagle, and though thou set thy nest among the stars, thence will I bring thee down, saith the LORD.

Edom was much higher in altitude

than the surrounding countryside. Its inhabitants took pride in their ability to spy out people approaching them from lower elevations, and would often swoop down to attack them. One of their central strongholds was Mt. Seir, which rises to about 3,500 feet (compared to the nearby Dead Sea to the north, which is below seal level). The red sandstone "cleft" that would later accommodate the city of Petra was a favorite hiding place.

It is this arrogance of position that God rebukes through Obadiah, and for which He had allowed other nations to subdue them. The forces of Egypt, Syria, and Babylonia repeatedly brought the Edomites "down to the ground" from their airy home where eagles soared. From a nation of aggressors they descended to the level of a despised people.

II. Sins Against Brethren—10-11
A. Sin of commission, 10

10 For thy violence against thy brother Jacob shame shall cover thee, and thou shalt be cut off for ever.

Israel's trouble with the Edomites had begun years earlier. The "violence" or injustice the Edomites committed against their brethren, the Jews (descendants of Esau's brother, Jacob), probably includes their refusing to allow them to cross Edom on their way to the Promised Land, as well as the later wars between the two nations. Their first war was when Israel was ruled by King Saul (1 Sam. 14:47). David slew 18,000 in one fight, and shortly afterward his deputy Joab "cut off every male in Edom" (1 Kings 11:15). Although Edom was subservient to Israel

through much of this time, they constantly showed themselves to be rebellious servants. Now Obadiah is promising final judgment for these years of opposition to God and His people.

B. Sin of omission, 11

11 In the day that thou stoodest on the other side, in the day that the strangers carried away captive his forces, and foreigners entered into his gates, and cast lots upon Jerusalem, even thou wast as one of them.

Although some scholars date the book of Obadiah in the eighth or ninth century B.C., the Babylonian invasion of Judah in the sixth century is probably referred to here. The prophet seems to have in mind the Edomites standing by and watching while an enemy sacked Jerusalem and carried its inhabitants into captivity; and the Babylonian captivity is the most likely reference.

It is also possible that the latter part of the verse accuses the Edomites of casting lots with other nations and winning the right to loot Jerusalem after Babylon destroyed it. It is therefore likely that Obadiah was a prophet God raised up after the Jews returned and rebuilt their capital and their Temple, and charged him to reassure the people that enemies such as Edom would be punished.

III. Reaping What Was Sown—15-16

15 For the day of the LORD is near upon all the heathen: as thou hast done, it shall be done unto thee: thy reward shall return upon thine own head.

16 For as ye have drunk upon my holy mountain, so shall all the

heathen drink continually, yea, they shall drink, and they shall swallow down, and they shall be as though they had not been.

It is significant that the judgment promised against Edom here is "the day of the LORD," the same come-uppance that the disobedient among God's own people will face. This great event, variously described as a moment in time and a final time-beyond-time, is to be a joyful day for the faithful, but a day of doom for the unfaithful, whether Jew or Gentile. Those who live by God's Covenant can expect that great Day to be one of deliverance from their enemies. However, prophets such as Amos described the other side of this coin: "Woe unto you that desire the day of the LORD! to what end is it for you? the day of the LORD is darkness, and not light" (Amos 5:18).

God's sovereign ability to balance "free will" with His will is implied here. On the one hand, He has allowed "heathen" such as the Edomites to pursue their wayward course against the Jews as punishment against His people's disobedience. On the other hand, God holds these enemies of His people account-able for their opposition. They will reap what they have sown.

In the case of Edom, God uses the figure of drinking at a banquet to describe this two-fold nature of the Day of the Lord. Apparently Edomites had stood by and virtually "toasted" the destruction of Jerusalem, on the hill of Zion, when the Babylonians had overrun the city. In turn, the tables will be turned on them; they

and other heathen foes of God's people will be poisoned by the same cup they lifted in delight over the destruction of Jerusalem.

IV. Salvation vs. Judgment—21

21 And saviours shall come up on mount Zion to judge the mount of Esau; and the kingdom shall be the LORD's.

A persistent feature of many pro-phetic passages is that they can be read as referring both to immediate and future events. The introduction of the word "savior" and "kingdom" in verse 21 prompts many commenta-tors to see here a double meaning. The word for "savior" means "deliverer" or "messiah"; and may easily refer to leaders such as Ezra, Zerubbabel, and Nehemiah, whose work help deliver the Jews from captivity. In this im-mediate sense, "saviors" may be taken literally.

However, none of the temporary "saviors" such as those who led in the rebuilding of the Temple and the walls of Zion were as gloriously successful as many "kingdom" pas-sages predict. We know that prophets did not always understand the full implication of their predictions (1 Pet. 1:11). Perhaps Obadiah knowingly or unknowingly envisions a "deliverer" who would in fact be the Messiah; and uses "the mount of Esau," or Edom, to stand for all of God's enemies. On this reading, the prophet speaks of an even greater defeat for the "Edoms" of the world, and the establishment of God's future King-dom that would be far more glorious than the mere seed that had been planted by the return from captivity.

Evangelistic Emphasis

For all the fearful judgments Obadiah pronounces upon the nation of Edom, he ends his brief work on a note of hope and confidence. "The kingdom shall be the Lord's" (Obad. 21). The ultimate outcome is not in doubt. In the end, God will be victorious.

An ancient rabbi once asked his pupils how they could tell when the night had ended and the day was on its way back. "Could it be," asked one student, "when you can see an animal in the distance and tell whether it is a sheep or a dog?"

"No," said the Rabbi.

"Could it be," asked another, "when you look at a tree in the distance and tell whether it is a fig tree or a peach tree?"

"No," said the Rabbi. "

Well what is it then?" his disciples demanded.

"It is when you look on the face of any person and can see your brother or sister. Because if you cannot do this, then no matter what time it is, it is still night."

The Kingdom of God on earth will be real when we see our brother or sister in the face of every person. Until that happens, we live in darkness, no matter what the time. But the good news is "the light shines in the darkness and the darkness did not overcome it" (John 1:5). The Kingdom shall be the Lord's!

ᔓᐤᙦ

Memory Selection

For the day of the Lord is near upon all the heathen: as thou hast done, it shall be done unto thee: thy reward shall return upon thine own head.—*Obadiah 15*

The great day of the Lord was long heralded as a time when all wrongs would be righted and evil punished. It was a judgment to be faced by all nations, with no exceptions. The fearful part of the coming judgment on the day of the Lord is that precisely what you have done to others will be done to you. If you have been merciful, you can expect mercy. If you have taken advantage of the oppressed, you will in turn be exploited. If you have been indifferent to those in need, your needs will be ignored. If you have excluded others, you will yourself be left out.

There is an echo of this warning/ promise in Jesus' words: "For with the judgment you make you will be judged, and the measure you give will be the measure you get" (Matt. 7:2). The prophet's words seem almost a negative way of stating the Golden Rule. Jesus said: "Do unto others as you would have them do to you (Matt. 7:12). Obadiah makes his word a warning: "As you have done, it shall be done to you."

Weekday Problems

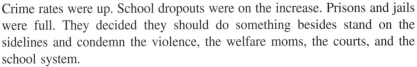

The Edomites were condemned by the prophet Obadiah because they stood and watched—and even gloated—as Jerusalem was being ravaged.

A women's group in a church in West Virginia was concerned that their community was also being ravaged. Crime rates were up. School dropouts were on the increase. Prisons and jails were full. They decided they should do something besides stand on the sidelines and condemn the violence, the welfare moms, the courts, and the school system.

They started a tutoring program. Carol was asked to help one youth, Wayne. It was a commitment of at least one hour a week. But as Carol got involved with helping Wayne, her commitment of energy, care, and love went far beyond. Wayne testifies, "Without tutoring I would have failed some classes and not graduated from high school . . . I really thank my tutor because she helped me out. She pushed me toward things I wanted to do and goals I set. It's great to have someone like that who cares and helps kids."

Wayne recently graduated from high school and is making plans to build and market low-income housing on the land his grandmother left him in her will.

*How can you get involved in helping kids in your community?

Judgment Now

During the days of the Cold War, a Russian about to be sentenced to Siberia said to the court: "If the United States is such a terrible place, why not send me there instead of to Siberia?"

❖❖❖❖❖

A boy who had gone fishing after school instead of going straight home met one of his school chums. Seeing that the first boy was carrying a stick fashioned into a fishing pole, his friend asked, "Catch anything?"

"Nope," was the reply. "But I ain't been home yet."

❖❖❖❖❖

Thief, to the lawyer about to defend him: How long do you think this business is gong to last?"

Lawyer: For me, about two hours. For you, two years."

❖❖❖❖❖

Judge: I hereby sentence the prisoner to a fine of $100 and seven days' imprisonment.

Prisoner: Aw, judge, I wish you would just reverse your sentence.

Judge: Oh well, okay: $7 and 100 days' imprisonment.

This Lesson in Your Life

Abraham Lincoln, in his second inaugural address, interpreted the War Between the States as God's righteous judgment on the institution of slavery. "Fondly do we hope—fervently do we pray—that this mighty scourge of war may speedily pass away," he said. "Yet, if God wills that it continue, until all the wealth piled by the bondman's two hundred and fifty years of unrequited toil shall be sunk, and every drop of blood drawn with the lash, shall be paid by another drawn with the sword, as was said three thousand years ago, so it must be said, 'the judgments of the Lord are true and righteous altogether'" (Ps. 19:9). Or in Obadiah's words: "As you have done it, it shall be done to you"—truly some of the most frightening words in Scripture.

Two-thirds of our human family suffer the ravages of hunger and malnutrition. More than 30,000 of our brothers and sisters around the world die every day from hunger and preventable diseases. George McGovern insists, "The earth has enough knowledge and resources to eradicate this ancient scourge. Hunger has plagued the world for thousands of years. But ending it is a greater moral imperative now than ever before, because for the first time humanity has the instruments in hand to defeat this cruel enemy at a very reasonable cost."

Middle-class and affluent Americans waste more food in one day than many families have to eat in a week. Arthur Simon has put the contrast of our plenty in the midst of great hunger in a picture difficult to forget: "Imagine ten children at a table dividing up the food. The three healthiest load their plate with the largest portions, including most of the meat, fish, milk and eggs. They eat what they want and discard the leftovers. Two other children get just enough to meet their basic requirements. Three of them, sickly, nervous, apathetic children, manage to stave off the feeling of hunger by filling up on bread and rice. The other two cannot even do that. One dies from dysentery and the second from pneumonia, which they are too weak to ward off. These children represent the human family. If the present food production were evenly divided among all the world's people with minimal waste, every one would have enough." The prophet warns, "As you have done it, it shall be done to you."

Obadiah's words are underscored by those of Jesus: "When the Son of Man comes in all his glory . . . then he will sit on his throne of glory. All nations will be gathered before him . . . Then he will say to those at his left, "You are accused, depart from me unto the eternal fire . . . ; for I was hungry and you gave me no food." "Lord, when was it we saw you hungry?" "Truly I tell you just as you did not do it to one of the least of these, you did not do it to me" (Matt 25).

STRAIGHT

1. **To what nation are the prophet's words addressed in Obadiah 1-14?**
   These verse are addressed to the nation of Edom.

2. **What punishment will come upon Edom?**
   It shall be least among nations, utterly despised, brought down by the Lord, pillaged, and its treasures searched out (Obad. 2-6).

3. **What had been the actions of Edom's allies?**
   Their allies have deceived them, driven them to the border, prevailed against them, and set a trap for them (Obad. 7).

4. **What happens to the wise, the warriors, everyone?**
   The wise are destroyed, the warriors are shattered, and everyone is cut off (Obad. 8).

5. **What were the crimes for which Edom is punished?**
   At the time when Israel (Jacob) was being violently slaughtered, Edom stood aside, gloated, looted, and handed over the fugitives (Obad 10-14).

6. **What will the day of the Lord bring to all nations?**
   "As you have done so shall it be done to you. Your deeds shall come back and be on your own head" (Obad. 15).

7. **What hope is there for the house of Jacob?**
   The house of Jacob shall once again possess Mt. Zion, with all its holiness.

8. **What is the connection between Esau and Edom?**
   The Edomites were descendents of Esau, son of Isaac and Rebekah, twin brother of Jacob (Gen. 25:19-25).

9. **When did the enmity between Jacob and Esau start?**
   When Jacob tricked their father, Isaac, into giving him the blessing intended for Esau (Gen. 27).

10. **Ultimately, to whom does the kingdom belong?**
    "The kingdom shall be the Lord's" (Obad. 21).

Obadiah ends on a triumphant, hopeful note: "The kingdom shall be the Lord's." Jesus teaches us to pray for the Kingdom to come. Then in the same prayer, he helps us understand the kingdom: "Thy will be done."

To pray "Thy kingdom come, Thy will be done" is a prayer of commitment, an enlisting in the Kingdom. It represents both trust in God's final victory and involvement in God's present struggle. To pray "Thy will be done" does not mean "I surely hope that the Church may be equal to her task to feed the hungry, to find shelter for the homeless, to help the unemployed find work, to free those who are victims of prejudice. But at the present time there is not much I can do. Rather it is to say "Here I am. Send me."

It is all too easy glibly to pray for peace in the world and yet not to pay the painful cost of reconciliation with a cantankerous neighbor or a competitive fellow worker. It is all too easy to advise the President or the Congress on how to solve the famine in Africa and ignore the embarrassed silence and bruised ego of the unemployed in our circle of friends. It is all too easy to decry the cruel aggression of oppressive dictatorship and to fail to welcome the refugee at our door. To pray "Thy kingdom come, Thy will be done" is to say, "in me, this day, thy will be done."

As I read Obadiah's condemnations of the descendants of Esau for standing aloof in the time when Jacob's descendants were being ravaged, I was reminded of Jesus' parable of the Good Samaritan. In seeking to define for the questioning lawyer, "Who is my neighbor?" Jesus speaks of the priest and Levite who pass by the wounded man, on the other side of the road.

One of the favorite songs of the children at Vacation Bible School one summer was about this Good Samaritan. I missed the closing program, but I was blessed to have a command performance by my three-year-old granddaughter, Bernadette. The song she sang to us summarized the story pretty well: "They hit'm on the nose and took his clothes and stole his money, it was not funny!"

I was a little shocked at what they had taught my little granddaughter to sing, "The preacher didn't help. The teacher didn't help. They closed their eyes and didn't even try." But the song had a good ending, an action ending: "If I were there that day, this is what I'd say: 'I want to be your helper . . . .'" As she sang, she went around the family circle shaking every hand and saying, "I want to be your helper and show God's love to you."

Jesus said "Go and do likewise."

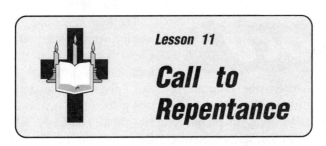

Call to Repentance

Joel 2:1-2, 12-17, 28-32

low ye the trumpet in Zion, and sound an alarm in my holy mountain: let all the inhabitants of the land tremble: for the day of the LORD cometh, for it is nigh at hand;

2 A day of darkness and of gloominess, a day of clouds and of thick darkness, as the morning spread upon the mountains: a great people and a strong; there hath not been ever the like, neither shall be any more after it, even to the years of many generations.

12 Therefore also now, saith the LORD, turn ye even to me with all your heart, and with fasting, and with weeping, and with mourning:

13 And rend your heart, and not your garments, and turn unto the LORD your God: for he is gracious and merciful, slow to anger, and of great kindness, and repenteth him of the evil.

14 Who knoweth if he will return and repent, and leave a blessing behind him; even a meat offering and a drink offering unto the LORD your God?

15 Blow the trumpet in Zion, sanctify a fast, call a solemn assembly:

16 Gather the people, sanctify the congregation, assemble the elders, gather the children, and those that suck the breasts: let the bridegroom go forth of his chamber, and the bride out of her closet.

17 Let the priests, the ministers of the LORD, weep between the porch and the altar, and let them say, Spare thy people, O LORD, and give not thine heritage to reproach, that the heathen should rule over them: wherefore should they say among the people, Where is their God?

28 And it shall come to pass afterward, that I will pour out my spirit upon all flesh; and your sons and your daughters shall prophesy, your old men shall dream dreams, your young men shall see visions:

29 And also upon the servants and upon the handmaids in those days will I pour out my spirit.

30 And I will shew wonders in the heavens and in the earth, blood, and fire, and pillars of smoke.

31 The sun shall be turned into darkness, and the moon into blood, before the great and the terrible day of the LORD come.

32 And it shall come to pass, that whosoever shall call on the name of the LORD shall be delivered: for in mount Zion and in Jerusalem shall be deliverance, as the LORD hath said, and in the remnant whom the LORD shall call.

Aug. 10

Memory Selection
Joel 2:13

Background Scripture
Joel 1–2

Devotional Reading
Acts 2:14-23, 32-33

We have noted the principle of "double fulfillment" which sometimes seems to apply to prophecy. Although we are not sure of the date of Joel, its first fulfillment seems to have been a disastrous drought and a plague of locusts that God sent in judgment, symbolizing the "day of the Lord." The plague will be lifted when the people repent.

The Roman legions that swarmed like locusts in Palestine in the time of Christ is probably a second fulfillment of this prophecy. Relief from that "plague" is the forgiveness of sins poured out in Acts 2, when the Holy Spirit poured out salvation after the resurrection of Christ. The apostle Peter said, "This is that which was spoken by the prophet Joel," then cited the text for today. This twofold working of God in the life of Israel and in the opening of the Kingdom of God is the focus of today's lesson.

You can illustrate not only today's lesson but a principle for interpreting Bible prophecy by bringing to class two balls, one large (such as a basketball), and one small (perhaps a tennis ball). Hold the large ball in one hand and explain that "this is the earth." Holding the smaller ball in the other hand, tell the group that "This is the moon," and move it around the large ball in an "orbit" or circle, like the moon orbits the earth.

Now ask the group the difference between what you have said and done, and *reality itself*. Obviously you have not used the earth and moon themselves, but *symbols* or *illustrations* of them, and their relationship. Point out that this was the task of the prophet Joel in today's lesson: to use current events as symbols to describe another reality that is coming in the future.

Teaching Outline	Daily Bible Readings	
I. 'Sound the Alarm!'—1-2 A. The Day of the Lord, 1 B. A terrible 'people,' 2	Mon.	Sound the Alarm! Joel 2:1-11
	Tue.	Return to the Lord Joel 2:12-17
II. 'Let the People Repent!'—12-14 A. The people's part, 12-13a B. God's response, 13b-14	Wed.	God Had Pity Joel 2:18-22
III. 'Assemble for Prayer!'—15-17	Thu.	'I Will Pour Out My Spirit' Joel 2:23-29
IV. The Ultimate Meaning—28-32 A. Outpouring of the spirit, 28-29 B. Miraculous wonders, 30-31 C. Saving grace, 32	Fri.	God Is a Stronghold Joel 3:16-21
	Sat.	The Day of Pentecost Acts 2:14-23
	Sun.	God Has Made Jesus Lord Acts 2:29-36

Verse by Verse

I. 'Sound the Alarm!'—1-2
A. The Day of the Lord, 1

1 Blow ye the trumpet in Zion, and sound an alarm in my holy mountain: let all the inhabitants of the land tremble: for the day of the LORD cometh, for it is nigh at hand;

The prophet Joel sounds an alarm, warning that God will judge unfaithful Israel in a terrible "day of the Lord." We do not know when this judgment struck, but 1:4 says that it came in the form of a plague of locusts; and 1:19; 2:23 show that it was accompanied by a drought.

Joel perceived this "natural disaster" to be punishment for the people's faithlessness. Yet he also prophesies the land's future return to productivity as God's gracious forgiveness when they returned to Him.

The Bible speaks of the day of the Lord as both judgment and salvation. Israel largely ignored the aspect of judgment, and looked forward to the Day as a kind of "party" God would throw for them at the end of the age simply by virtue of their being part of God's elect. The prophets, however, warned that it would be a time of calamity and judgment if the people neglected the responsibility of their election and became faithless (Amos 5:18-20). Joel describes both of these aspects.

B. A terrible 'people,' 2

2 A day of darkness and of gloominess, a day of clouds and of thick darkness, as the morning spread upon the mountains: a great people and a strong; there hath not been ever the like, neither shall be any more after it, even to the years of many generations.

The language here reminds us of the "double fulfillment" of many prophecies. Here, most scholars think "a great people and a strong" actually describes the locusts themselves. The militant hordes of insects could easily be compared with an invading army. Other authorities search for human armies in the future that the locusts might describe—such as the Roman invaders of Palestine at the time of the Messiah.

II. 'Let the People Repent!'—12-14
A. The people's part, 12-13a

12 Therefore also now, saith the LORD, turn ye even to me with all your heart, and with fasting, and with weeping, and with mourning:

13 And rend your heart, and not your garments, and turn unto the LORD your God:

Joel's primary aim, calling the people to repentance, is clear regardless of what or who the "great people" represent. God frequently used both

493

natural disasters and pagan armies to punish His people for disobedience. They were a "wake-up call," designed to pierce the people's indifference and their tendency to worship idols and mistreat the weak. God would tolerate no "jail-house conversions" or "trips down the aisle" to profess repentance if it was not grounded in sincerity.

B. God's response, 13b-14

13b for he is gracious and merciful, slow to anger, and of great kindness, and repenteth him of the evil.

14 Who knoweth if he will return and repent, and leave a blessing behind him; even a meat offering and a drink offering unto the LORD your God?

Joel is not just a "gloom and doom" prophet. He is as affirming of God's gracious mercy as he is of the necessity that the people genuinely repent. To say that God "repenteth him of the evil" is to remind us that "repentance" means a change of mind that results in a change of course, not primarily an admission of sin (see Gen. 6:6, the first time repentance is attributed to God). Verse 14 expresses the hope that if the people will repent, God will reverse the usual meaning of sacrifice, making an offering to the people as a sign that their own offering of changed lives has been accepted.

III. 'Assemble for Prayer!'—15-17

15 Blow the trumpet in Zion, sanctify a fast, call a solemn assembly:

16 Gather the people, sanctify the congregation, assemble the elders, gather the children, and those that suck the breasts: let the bridegroom go forth of his cham-

ber, and the bride out of her closet.

17 Let the priests, the ministers of the LORD, weep between the porch and the altar, and let them say, Spare thy people, O LORD, and give not thine heritage to reproach, that the heathen should rule over them: wherefore should they say among the people, Where is their God?

The disaster, whether from the invasion of locusts or enemy armies, is so serious that Joel calls for all Israel to halt their normal activities and gather in solemn assembly for fasting and prayer that God would spare them. Even important events such as marriages are worth being interrupted because the nation's very life is at stake.

Although the fear that "heathen" might rule Israel seems at first to refer to human armies, it is still possible that Joel is giving a "military face" to the hordes of locusts that were plundering the land. Both natural disasters and conquering invaders can cause a people to ask in desperation, "Where is God in all this?" Here the question is posed in derision by the enemy itself; and Joel's hope for release is in part to prove to the enemy, whether insect or man, that God is alive and will yet rescue His people. Israel often lived in fear that negative events among them would cause outsiders to scorn their God (see Micah 7:8-10).

IV. The Ultimate Meaning—28-32

A. Outpouring of the spirit, 28-29

28 And it shall come to pass afterward, that I will pour out my spirit upon all flesh; and your sons and your daughters shall prophesy, your old men shall dream dreams,

your young men shall see visions:

29 And also upon the servants and upon the handmaids in those days will I pour out my spirit.

Beginning in 2:18, God's tone of voice begins to change from doom to hope. If the people will return to Him, the day of the Lord will be one of joy instead of sadness. The "enemy," whether insects or men, will be driven away, and the land will blossom again. No doubt the primary application of these promises was for those who first heard the prophet, assuring them that they would live to see deliverance if they return to God.

However, the fact that this passage is also the foundation of the preaching of the first gospel sermon after the resurrection of Christ, in Acts 2, invites us to consider again the principle of "double fulfillment." The apostle Peter uses this very passage to explain the miracle of "tongues" that resulted from the outpouring of the Holy Spirit on the first Pentecost after Christ was raised from the dead—the event that enabled the Good News to be understood by people from many nations (Acts 2:17ff.)

B. Miraculous wonders, 30-31

30 And I will shew wonders in the heavens and in the earth, blood, and fire, and pillars of smoke.

31 The sun shall be turned into darkness, and the moon into blood, before the great and the terrible day of the LORD come.

Understanding the rest of this quotation as it is used in Acts 2 requires another basic principle of interpreting prophecy: we cannot always track down the precise

fulfillment of each detail. Some interpreters find Joel's reference to blood and fire and cosmic disturbances to be fulfilled in the destruction of Jerusalem and the Jewish order, some 40 years after Peter's sermon in Acts 2. While this is certainly possible, it may also be true that Peter merely quotes the entire context in which the passage he wants to use appears, not intending for us to search for specific fulfillment of the rest of the text. What is important is that we recognize that Acts 2 records God's deliverance from the Old Regime into the "Church Age" of the Kingdom of God, and that Peter finds Joel's prophecy to apply to this momentous event.

C. Saving grace, 32

32 And it shall come to pass, that whosoever shall call on the name of the LORD shall be delivered: for in mount Zion and in Jerusalem shall be deliverance, as the LORD hath said, and in the remnant whom the LORD shall call.

As noted in the previous lesson, the prophets were not always fully aware of the long-term import of the words the Spirit gave them (1 Pet. 1:10-11). Although relief from locusts and drought might be envisioned in this language, it once again seems to point toward a grander and more worldwide fulfillment such as the salvation Peter promises in Acts 2. For it was from Zion (Jerusalem), and out of the mouths of apostles who were "remnants" of God's original chosen people, that the promise of salvation for all time, not just Joel's day, was first issued.

Evangelistic Emphasis

The prophet Joel describes a great day when God's Spirit will be poured out on all people. On the day of Pentecost, when the disciples were gathered together, they were filled with the Holy Spirit and began to speak in other languages. Some thought the disciples were drunk. Peter explains that the strange phenomenon they were witnessing was in fact the fulfillment of Joel's prophecy, "In the last days, God declares I will pour out my spirit upon all flesh" (Acts 2:1-4, 15-17).

"All flesh" indicates among other things that the task of telling of God's love is not limited to ordained clergy.

All can be endowed with God's spirit, young and old, men and women, slave and free. Each person has a story to tell. Your story may be just the one to reach another's heart. With God's spirit in our hearts, guiding, leading, nudging, we will find the words to speak to another person.

For some, that place of witness may be the pulpit of a church. For another the place may be a support group for the grief stricken or the drug addicted. Some physicians find effective and helpful ways to share their faith with patients before surgery, testifying to the healing power of God. In the work place some find the opportunity to tell what faith in God means to them. Around the family table parents have a chance to share their faith. God's Sprit is being poured out today, and all are called to bear witness to God's love.

ଛଠେ

Memory Selection

Therefore also now, saith the Lord, turn ye even to me with all your heart, and with fasting, and with weeping, and with mourning: And rend your heart, and not your garments, and turn unto the Lord your God: for he is gracious and merciful, slow to anger and of great kindness, and repenteth him of the evil.—Joel 2: 12-13

Joel calls the people to return to God. It is a change that involves the whole heart. The change can be so dramatic and life-changing that it may bring weeping. The prophet goes beyond the ritualistic mourning of tearing garments in an outward show of sorrow. The change God looks for is a change of heart, a change that wells up from the soul.

The basis of that returning to God is not that the sinner can do anything to gain God's favor, or manipulate a pardon. The hope of coming back to God is based simply on who God is, "for he is gracious and merciful, slow to anger and abounding in steadfast love."

Weekday Problems

George is a family man, a churchgoer, active in civic affairs. He began gambling as a happy diversion. He would calculate how much he could afford for an evening out. When he lost that amount, he would quit and figure that was a reasonable price for an enjoyable and exciting evening. But he got hooked. He couldn't quit. He ran up debts he couldn't handle.

George worked for a government agency, receiving bids on major purchases, and deciding which bid to accept. The bids often ran in the hundreds of thousands of dollars. It was so easy to ask for a kick-back from the bidder. As his gambling debts grew, so grew the bribes he demanded and received. But he was caught, then indicted, found guilty, and sentenced to five years in prison.

George hated that he had brought shame upon himself and embarrassed his family. In prison he asked for God's forgiveness. His repentance was more than being sorry he was caught. He looked honestly at himself. For the first time, he put his life in God's hands. He asked his pastor if God could forgive him.

*How would you answer George?

*What might Joel's words mean to George?—"'Yet even now,' says the Lord, 'return to me with all your heart'" (Joel 2:12).

Let Us Pray

Little Billy was kneeling beside his bed and prayed, "Dear God, I'd sure appreciate if You could find some way to put the vitamins in candy and ice cream instead of in spinach and broccoli."

Little Mary's dad was practicing at home to become a radio announcer. When Mary was invited to say table grace while visiting a friend, she cleared her throat, looked at her watch, and intoned, "This food, friends, is coming to you through the courtesy of Almighty God."

Sunday School teacher: We shouldn't just pray for ourselves. Who can give us an example of an unselfish prayer?

Jake: Every night I pray that God will come through with a new bike—not for myself, but one for my brother that we can both ride.

Jimmy had been in trouble, and was punished by his father. That night he prayed, "And please don't give my folks any more children. They don't know how to treat those they've got now."

This Lesson in Your Life

Joel speaks of God as "gracious and merciful, slow to anger, and abounding in steadfast love." His call to sinners to return to Him is based on the affirmation that forgiveness is possible. We can be forgiven, cleansed, made new, set right with God. The Bible proclaims again and again the possibility of new beginnings.

Always this forgiveness is offered as a gift of God's grace. It is not a new relationship we can earn. In Jesus' parable, the prodigal son knew he had no claim on the father. He had squandered his share. It was not his carefully crafted, well rehearsed speech that changed his Father's mind. His welcome from the father was so lavish , so extravagant, that it was beyond any neatly calculated system of exchange. It was sheer grace.

In Luke's story of Jesus' crucifixion, we hear of the two criminals crucified on either side of Jesus. The one thief taunts Jesus, echoing the jeers of the crowd around the cross. The other, with amazing trust, regards Jesus as a king about to receive his coronation, saying, "Remember me when you come into your kingdom." Jesus did not ask for his credentials, his record of attendance at synagogue, his gifts to the temple, or even a letter of reference from his rabbi. The thief had already confessed that his sentence was just. Like all persons, he was a sinner who fell short of the glory of God. Jesus said to him, "Truly I tell you, this day you shall be with me in paradise" (Luke 23:42-43). Forgiveness is not the remission of a penalty; it is the restoration of a relationship.

Donald J. Selby tells of an Army man who had been a heavy drinker for 35 years. He told a group of doctors of his transformation of personality. Now he was considerate as he had once been severe, concerned for others as he had once been self-serving. A psychiatrist, who believed that personality was so set early in life that no one can change, protested to the colonel that no one could have such a radical transformation. "Well," replied the soldier, "at least I'm under new management. I now answer to another authority, the highest and truest that there is."

But the gift of grace is not cheap. The cross of Christ reminds us that God does not make light of sin. Paul teaches, "For all have sinned and fall short of the glory of God: they are now justified by his grace as a gift, through the redemption that is in Christ Jesus, whom God put forward as a sacrifice of atonement by his blood, effective through faith" (Rom. 3:23-25). Paul's use of "sacrifice of atonement" or in some translations "expiation by his blood" points to the suffering of God, who loves us so much He sent His only Son into the world not to condemn the world but that the world might be saved through him (John 3:16-17).

GETTING THE FACTS STRAIGHT

1. According to Joel, what are the signs that go with returning to God with all one's heart?

The Lord requires a sincere return with all your heart, with fasting, with weeping, with mourning (Joel 2:12).

2. In the act of repentance, what is preferable to the ritualized tearing of garments?

What God wants is a rending of the heart. not clothing (Joel 2:13).

3. What are the qualities of God mentioned by Joel as an encouragement to repentance?

God is gracious, merciful, slow to anger and abounding in steadfast love, and relents from punishing (Joel 2:13).

4. Will God return and repent (relent) and leave a blessing?

It depends on whether the people truly repent (see Joel 2:14).

5. On whom did God promise to pour out His Spirit?

On all flesh (all Israel), sons and daughters, old men and young men, male and female slaves God (Joel 2:28).

6. What are the signs and portents of the coming of day of the Lord?

Blood and fire and columns of smoke, the sun turning to darkness and the moon to blood (Joel 2:30-31).

7. Who will be saved?

Everyone who calls on the name of the Lord shall be saved (Joel 2:32).

8. What apostle quoted from Joel 2:28-32?

The apostle Peter quoted from the prophet Joel on the day of Pentecost (Acts 2: 17-21).

9. What event was Peter interpreting when he quoted Joel?

On the day of Pentecost the disciples began to speak in other languages. Some thought they were drunk. Peter says they were filled with the Spirit.

10. What promise did God make to Israel after the plague of locusts and drought?

"You shall know that I am in the midst of Israel, and that I, the Lord am your God . . . My people shall never again be put to shame" (Joel 2:27).

"THERE IS NO GRACE!" In bold black letters this bad news was posted at the entry to the university library. I've learned to ignore profane graffiti scribbled on walls, to tune out four-letter words in movies, and even to "bleep" out the blasphemies of the peddlers of hate. But this blatant heresy I could not shake off.

I soon discovered as I paid my 35-cent fine that the bold and blasphemous billboard was not intended as a theological statement but a proclamation of a new library policy. I was happy enough to do my part to help meet the university's financial crisis.

But what if the grace of God were in short supply? What if we received exactly what we deserved? What if in the final accounting there were only justice and no mercy? What if the final word of God were "There is no grace!"

The dying thief on the Cross beside Jesus would have had his earnest plea, "Remember me," met with cold silence. Zacchaeus would still be in the sycamore tree. The publican in Jesus story would have gone home condemned even as the Pharisee. Jacob and David, Peter and Paul, would be missing from the company of the redeemed.

Whenever I go past that library sign with its dark, foreboding proclamation, I whistle a happy tune, "Amazing grace! How sweet the sound that saved a wretch like me." I thank God for the gospel expressed by Paul, "For by grace you have been saved through faith; and this is not your own doing, it is the gift of God —not the result of works, so that no one may boast" (Eph. 2:8).

A lady had her picture taken by a professional portrait photographer. She was displeased with the result and complained that the portrait did not do her justice. The photographer replied that what she needed was not justice but mercy. So do we all.

David Roberts paraphrased a passage from Kierkegaard thus: "No man who is aware of God's presence can regard himself in a strong position for making demands. He will realize that once strictness gets started God can always, so to speak, overbid him."

If we should say, "I demand justice!" a voice from heaven will reply, like an echo, "I demand justice!" Who is bold enough to think we can pass this test. But if we fall on our knees and cry out: "Grace!" the answer comes back from heaven, "Grace!"

Thank God for His word to us through the prophet Joel, "Return to the Lord, your God, for he is gracious and merciful, slow to anger, and abounding in steadfast love" (Joel 2:13).

500

A Promise to the Faithful

Malachi 3:1-4, 16-18; 4:1-3,5-6

Behold, I will send my messenger, and he shall prepare the way before me: and the Lord, whom ye seek, shall suddenly come to this temple, even the messenger of the covenant, whom ye delight in: behold, he shall come, saith the LORD of hosts.

2 But who may abide the day of his coming? and who shall stand when he appeareth? for he is like a refiner's fire, and like fullers' soap:

3 And he shall sit as a refiner and purifier of silver: and he shall purify the sons of Levi, and purge them as gold and silver, that they may offer unto the LORD an offering in righteousness.

4 Then shall the offering of Judah and Jerusalem be pleasant unto the LORD, as in the days of old, and as in former years.

16 Then they that feared the LORD spake often one to another: and the LORD hearkened, and heard it, and a book of remembrance was written before him for them that feared the LORD, and that thought upon his name.

17 And they shall be mine, saith the LORD of hosts, in that day when I make up my jewels; and I will spare them, as a man spareth his own son that serveth him.

18 Then shall ye return, and discern between the righteous and the wicked,

between him that serveth God and him that serveth him not.

4:1 For, behold, the day cometh, that shall burn as an oven; and all the proud, yea, and all that do wickedly, shall be stubble: and the day that cometh shall burn them up, saith the LORD of hosts, that it shall leave them neither root nor branch.

2 But unto you that fear my name shall the Sun of righteousness arise with healing in his wings; and ye shall go forth, and grow up as calves of the stall.

3 And ye shall tread down the wicked; for they shall be ashes under the soles of your feet in the day that I shall do this, saith the LORD of hosts.

5 Behold, I will send you Elijah the prophet before the coming of the great and dreadful day of the LORD:

6 And he shall turn the heart of the fathers to the children, and the heart of the children to their fathers, lest I come and smite the earth with a curse.

Memory Selection
Malachi 3:18

Background Scripture
Malachi 3–4

Devotional Reading
Psalm 90:1-17

Aug. 17

This lesson offers guidelines for what to do when church gets dull! The prophet Malachi was charged with enlivening the fervor of the Jews whose forefathers had returned to Jerusalem from captivity and rebuilt the Temple. Although some hoped that all this activity might usher in the Messianic Age, the people grew discouraged when nothing seemed to happen. They began to dishonor God (Mal. 1:6), return to pagan worship (2:11), and withhold tithes (3:8).

Malachi promises that even though we cannot always see God at work, He is busy preparing a rewarding future for the faithful. Meanwhile, we are to be "people of the long haul," finding fulfillment in faithful worship, ordinary acts of kindness, living in community with others who hope . . . and wait.

❧

Offer your group a lively review of what the Jews who returned from Babylonian captivity have done, as recounted in previous lessons. Make it exciting as you recall the bustle of activity as they rebuilt the Temple. The people dedicated their time and money. Cedar was imported from Lebanon. True worship was restored.

Then the walls around Jerusalem were built, despite threats from surrounding enemies. Men laid the stones of the wall with one hand while holding weapons in the other. What an exciting time to be alive!

Now the work is done. What's next? *Everyday life . . . business as usual . . . going to Temple regularly.* Does this sound like church sometimes? The prophet Malachi calls God's people to find fulfillment in being faithful, not in constant motion and frantic activity.

Teaching Outline	Daily Bible Readings	
I. Preparing the Way—3:1-4	Mon.	Charge to the Priests Malachi 2:1-9
A. Messenger of the Covenant, 1	Tue.	Purifying Trials Malachi 3:1-5
B. Purifying worshipers, 2-4	Wed.	'Return to Me!' Malachi 3:6-12
II. Preparing a Book—16-18	Thu.	God's Own Possession Malachi 3:13-18
A. Book of remembrance, 16	Fri.	Sun of Righteousness Malachi 4:1-6
B. God's own treasure, 17-18	Sat.	God's Steadfast Love Psalm 89:19-29
III. Preparing a People—4:1-3	Sun.	God Keeps His Covenant Psalm 89:30-37
IV. Preparing for Messiah—5-6		

Verse by Verse

I. Preparing the Way—3:1-4
A. Messenger of the Covenant, 1

1 Behold, I will send my messenger, and he shall prepare the way before me: and the Lord, whom ye seek, shall suddenly come to this temple, even the messenger of the covenant, whom ye delight in: behold, he shall come, saith the LORD of hosts.

About 100 years have passed since the Persians had allowed a remnant of the Jews to return and rebuild the city and the Temple of God. Many Israelites had become discouraged because, after the exciting years of restoration, they could see nothing much happening. God says through He will send His messenger to the recently rebuilt Temple—but where is He?

The message here is that God is at work even though the people could not see His presence among them. He was simply working on a different schedule. Whereas the people expected Him to send "the messenger of the covenant," the Messiah, shortly after the Temple was rebuilt, by God's time-table it was to be another 400 years before He came. Greece would rise and fall, and Rome would replace it, teaching people that salvation would not come through politics but setting the stage for the coming of the Messiah. The difficulty is that the people of Malachi's day

wanted to see some immediate fruits of their labor. They did not fully trust God's timing.

B. Purifying worshipers, 2-4

2 But who may abide the day of his coming? and who shall stand when he appeareth? for he is like a refiner's fire, and like fullers' soap:

3 And he shall sit as a refiner and purifier of silver: and he shall purify the sons of Levi, and purge them as gold and silver, that they may offer unto the LORD an offering in righteousness.

4 Then shall the offering of Judah and Jerusalem be pleasant unto the LORD, as in the days of old, and as in former years.

Malachi joins Amos and other prophets who warned that the coming Day of the Lord would not be a joyful time for those whose faith and obedience had lapsed. In some ways, Malachi says, the day of the Lord will not be so much like a banquet as a jeweler's workshop. As a jeweler heats silver and gold to refine it, the time of the Messiah will be a time of testing, not just a time of vindictiveness over the Gentiles. We cannot help but note that when God finally did send His Messiah, most of the Jews failed to pass this test because of unbelief.

Note also that this refining process would begin with the priests, the sons of Levi. In 1:6-7, God had charged that it was the priests who had "despised my name" by making pagan sacrifices on the altar in the newly rebuilt Temple! Obviously God would like to see a great deal of reforming before the exciting "day of the Lord" comes and the Messiah appears.

II. Preparing a Book—16-18
A. Book of remembrance, 16

16 Then they that feared the LORD spake often one to another: and the LORD hearkened, and heard it, and a book of remembrance was written before him for them that feared the LORD, and that thought upon his name.

Unlike many of God's prophets, Malachi is privileged to see some of the fruits of his labors. Genuine God-fearers among the Jews listened to his message. Just as believers today often discover, the faithful found strength in sharing their concerns with each other, and in going to God in prayer together. As a result, God promises that their names will be written in a "book of remembrance." Despite the widespread faithlessness among the people, God will be faithful to His Covenant, remembering those who keep it.

The role of books and writings in some ways makes the Jewish and Christian faiths distinct from many other religions. While some other faiths seek salvation by looking within, or having a special experience, the Jewish and Christian way of salvation is recorded in books. Lesson 8 noted the emphasis the people who first returned from Babylon placed on having the book of the Law read in a public ceremony

(Neh. 8). Here we see that God's response to the faithful also involves a book—one in which He assures us that He records our very names (see also Rev. 3:5). When the faithful think "nothing is happening," let them remember that God is busy writing!

B. God's own treasure, 17-18

17 And they shall be mine, saith the LORD of hosts, in that day when I make up my jewels; and I will spare them, as a man spareth his own son that serveth him.

18 Then shall ye return, and discern between the righteous and the wicked, between him that serveth God and him that serveth him not.

God's tone of voice softens here as He issues another explicit word of assurance that those who remain dedicated to Him during exciting times or dull are as precious to Him as jewels, or as a man's own son. It is important to notice that this promise is grounded in God's promise when He gave the Law through Moses. A part of the Covenant was that the obedient will be "a peculiar treasure unto me above all people" (Exod. 19:5).

From this we can assume that the "return" mentioned in verse 18 refers to returning to the Law. Although "law-keeping" could become a badge of arrogance, as it was to many in Jesus' day, Malachi preached in a time of laxness toward the Law. He calls for more than a sentimental attachment to God, pleading for a faithful keeping of the Law that would result in a visible difference between believers and unbelievers, the righteous and the wicked.

III. Preparing a People—4:1-3

4:1 For, behold, the day cometh, that shall burn as an oven; and all the proud, yea, and all that do wickedly, shall be stubble: and the day that cometh shall burn them up, saith the LORD of hosts, that it shall leave them neither root nor branch.

2 But unto you that fear my name shall the Sun of righteousness arise with healing in his wings; and ye shall go forth, and grow up as calves of the stall.

3 And ye shall tread down the wicked; for they shall be ashes under the soles of your feet in the day that I shall do this, saith the LORD of hosts.

Now the hard realities of the coming Day of the Lord that await the wicked are laid side-by-side with the blessings reserved for the righteous. Although the faithful have nothing to fear, the arrogant and the wicked will be destroyed. It was this kind of black-and-white choice that the coming of the Messiah brought. His arrival was viewed by the earliest Christian preachers as the beginning of the Day of the Lord (Acts 2:20), although there would yet be a Judgment Day, a last Day of the last days (1 Thess. 5:2).

The justification of the faithful by the "Sun of righteousness" with "healing in his wings" will be taken as a "treading down" of the wicked. This imagery, found only here in the Bible, is drawn from Egypt, Assyria, and Assyria. Ancient tablets portray a winged sun presiding over important events; and Malachi borrows the symbol as a sign of God's benevolent protection of the faithful during the Day of the Lord.

IV. Preparing for Messiah—5-6

5 Behold, I will send you Elijah the prophet before the coming of the great and dreadful day of the LORD:

6 And he shall turn the heart of the fathers to the children, and the heart of the children to their fathers, lest I come and smite the earth with a curse.

Finally the dread associated with the Day of the Lord overwhelms the joy awaiting the righteous. Yet God will send the fieriest of His prophets, Elijah, as one final act of grace—a gracious warning for unbelievers to repent. This prophecy is another pointer to the fact that the coming of Christ was taken as the first day of the great Day of the Lord, for Jesus expressly identifies John the Baptist as Elijah (see Matt. 11:14). Curiously, John himself denied that he was Elijah (John 1:21). Probably John meant that he was not actually the literal reincarnation of Elijah, while Jesus meant that John's stern preaching and fierce warnings made him a figurative Elijah, and a definite fulfillment of Malachi's prophecy. Also, John the Baptist's preaching picks up Malachi's theme of fiery judgment as a characteristic of Messiah's coming (Matt. 3:11-12).

Yet John, as "the second Elijah," had an effect on those who heard him. People streamed out from the cities into the wilderness where John preached to express their penitence—and in that way to avoid the smiting of those who refused to do so (Matt. 3:5-6).

Evangelistic Emphasis

"I am sending my messenger to prepare the way before me." Some scholars suggest the messenger was Malachi himself, since his name means "My Messenger." Later Malachi speaks of Elijah as the one who would be sent before the day of the Lord. The Gospel writers identify John the Baptist as the messenger sent to prepare the way.

Perhaps it is more important for us to identify the messengers of God today. Perhaps it is a leader in prayer like Frank Laubach, a teacher of holiness like Dietrich Bonhoeffer, an advocate for social justice like Martin Luther King, Jr., a great evangelist reaching millions like Billy Graham. Perhaps the messengers are not only the great and famous, but persons who have born God's message to us, parents, teachers or friends. In a time of despair, they brought hope. In a time of temptation, they brought guidance. In a time of weakness, they lent strength. In a time of depression, they were there for us. Their words, their love, their presence brought us strength from God. For us, these persons, known only to their friends and family, were in truth the messengers of God to us.

Could it be that God is calling us to be His messengers, too? Could it be that messengers are needed today to help prepare for Messiah's return? What message would we carry? To whom might God be sending us?

ഇരു

Memory Selection

Then ye shall return, and discern between the righteous and the wicked, between him that serveth God and him that serveth him not.— *Malachi 3:18*

Much of the preaching of the prophet Malachi addresses the question of the people, "Where is the God of justice?" (Mal. 2:17). To them it seemed that those "who do evil are good in the sight of the Lord."

In this memory selection, the prophet affirms that on the Day of the Lord the prosperity of the wicked will be reversed, and the innocent will be rewarded. On that day they will once again see the difference between the righteous and the wicked, between those who serve God and those who do not serve God.

In the short run it sometimes seems that the evil prosper, and those who look out only for themselves get ahead. But on the Day of the Lord there will be an ultimate reckoning. Then it will be clear who truly serves the Lord. Despite appearances now, the day is coming when it will be clear who have faithfully served God and who have only given lip service.

Stay faithful. God is not finished yet.

This Lesson in Your Life

Judy had worked hard as a case manager with the children in foster care. She often spent her Saturdays shopping with the children. She took workshops to improve her skills. Her reports were always complete, turned in on time. She was popular with her fellow workers. They had urged her to apply for the position of supervision when it came open. After six years with the office, it would be a nice promotion.

But Jane was chosen instead: Jane, who was always late for work, never got her reports in on time; Jane, who was always asking other workers to cover for her at court when she was ill-prepared. The word was that her father, a prominent state official, pulled some strings. Judy felt hurt, even bitter. If she had felt that Jane was better qualified, she could have accepted it. But formal process was just a pretense. It wasn't what you knew but who you knew that counted. "Life is not fair," Judy concluded.

Malachi reminds us that there is a new day coming, the Day of the Lord. In that day, hard work will be rewarded and dishonesty exposed. Meanwhile, in this imperfect world, we keep on doing our best, leaving the outcome in the hands of God. For those who honor God's name in all they do, there will come a day of joy, exuberant joy, like that of a calf released from the stall (Mal. 4:2).

*What wrongs do you especially look forward to being righted at the Day of the Lord?

Dining Out ('Way Out)

Customer: Waiter! There's no chicken in my chicken soup!
Waiter: Well, there's no horse in horse radish, either.

❖❖❖❖❖

Waiter: May I help you with the soup, sir?
Customer: What do you mean, help me? I don't need help.
Waiter: Sorry, sir. From the sound of it, I though you might need to be dragged ashore.

❖❖❖❖❖

Customer: Waiter, this food is terrible! I won't eat it. You'd better get the manager.
Waiter: Won't do any good, sir. He won't eat it either.

❖❖❖❖❖

Customer: Waiter! There's a twig in my soup!
Waiter: Sorry, sir, I'll get the branch manager.

This Lesson in Your Life

Good news/bad news/good news. That's what this story is about. The good news is that God is sending a messenger before God Himself comes. Isn't that good news that God Himself will be coming to His Temple? His messenger will come before him to get the Temple ready, to help get the people ready. Isn't that good news? Well, yes and no. It's great that God will visit His people. But who can face the Holy One when God comes in full glory and power. "Who can endure the day of his coming, and who can stand when he appears?" (Mal. 3:2)

The young prophet Isaiah felt this way when he realized he was in the presence of the Holy God. "Holy, Holy, holy is the Lord of hosts. The whole earth is full of his glory." But then he said, "Woe is me! I am lost, for I am a man of unclean lips, and I live among a people of unclean lips, yet my eyes have seen the King, the Lord of hosts!" (Isa. 6: 3,5).

Luke tells the story of Simon Peter, who had fished all night. At Jesus' instructions Simon lowered his nets one more time. They caught so many fish the nets began to break. When Peter saw it, and realized they were in the presence of the holiness of God, he cried, "Depart from me, Lord, for I am a sinful man!" (Luke 5:8). Good news/bad news.

When we grow aware of God's holy presence, in purity, in holiness, in power, in love, we know we are unworthy. We know we are known as we are without pretense or disguise. We come into God's presence, "to whom all hearts are open, all desires are known, and from whom no secrets are hid." We can but pray that God will cleanse us, and help us grow to love as God loves us. "Who can stand when He appears?" (Mal. 3:2). Who can boast of his good works? Who can claim a special place of favor? Paul painfully reminds us, "There is no distinction, since all have sinned and fall short of the glory of God" (Rom. 3:23). The messenger's experience is like a refiner's fire. The white hot heat does not destroy but purges away the dross. The live coal brought by one of the seraphs to Isaiah's mouth blots out his sin (Isa. 6:7).

In the familiar words of the hymn, "How Firm a Foundation," we begin to get a hint of the good news that follows the bad. "When through fiery trials thy pathways shall lie, / my grace all sufficient, shall be thy supply. / The flame shall not hurt thee, I only design, / thy dross to consume and thy gold to refine."

The psalmist knew of this experience: "Purge me with hyssop, and I shall be clean; wash me, and I shall be whiter than snow." (Ps. 51:7) The good news after the bad news is that the refiners fire burns away the dross, and the fuller's soap makes us whiter than snow. The God who comes to us, comes to dwell in us. We are the temple of the Holy Spirit. God dwells with us. That's good news!

1. What is the messenger's task as described in Malachi 3:1-4?

The messenger is to prepare the way for the Lord by purifying the temple and its priests.

2. To what is the messenger's work compared in Malachi 3:2?

He is like a refiner's fire and like fullers' soap.

3. In Malachi 3:5, who are those against whom the Lord will bear witness when He comes?

Adulterers, those who lie, who oppressed hired workers, widows, orphans, aliens, who do not fear the Lord

4. According to Malachi 3:16, whose names will be written in the book of remembrance?

Those who revered the Lord and who thought on His name will be written in the book of remembrance.

5. How had the Israelites spoken against the Lord, according to Malachi 3:13-15?

When they said, "It is vain to serve God. What do we profit by keeping his command? The arrogant are happy and the evil doers prosper."

6. What is promised to come in the future in Malachi 3:18?

Once more you shall see the difference between the righteous and the wicked, between the one who serves God and one who does not serve him.

7. What is the promise to the faithful at the day of the Lord? (Mal. 3:2).

For those who revere God's name, the sun of righteousness shall rise, with healing in His wings. You shall leap like calves released from the stall.

8. Where did the image of "the sun of righteousness" come from?

It is a symbol from Egyptian religion where the winged disk of the sun is often represented as a source of protection and blessing.

9. What will be the prophet Elijah's role before the Day of the Lord? (Mal. 4:5-6).

He will turn the hearts of parents to their children, and the hearts of children to their parents.

10. Malachi 3:1 is cited in Matthew, Mark, and Luke. To whom does it refer?

In each of the Gospels the Malachi text, "I am sending my messenger ahead of you who will prepare the way for you" refers to John the Baptist.

For more years than I can remember I've loved the Christmas carol of Charles Wesley, "Hark the Herald Angels sing." I've sung and heard the words a thousand times: "Hail the heaven born Prince of Peace! Hail the Sun of Righteousness! Light and life to all he brings, risen with healing in his wings." Until this study of Malachi I never realized where the image of the "sun of righteousness" came from. Malachi borrowed it from ancient Egyptian religious art, which often pictured the sun as a disk with wings, flying through the sky. To those in his time who wondered where the God of justice was, the prophet says, your day is coming, the day of the Lord, when "for you who revere my name the sun of righteousness will rise, with healing in its wings" (Mal. 4:2). Wesley borrowed this image from the obscure prophet Malachi to describe the newborn king, the Christ of Bethlehem.

Those who have waited through the dark hours of the night have experienced what an apt image for Christ the rising sun can be. In the darkness our fears loom large. We experience blindness. We cannot see the way ahead. We cannot make sense of what is around us. Every tree or movement become a threat. When you cannot sleep it seems like dawn will never come. Fears and doubts fill the void of the night. When finally the sun comes up, its first rays begin to color the eastern sky. In the light of day, the dark, foreboding shapes are lovely trees providing welcome shade. The scaring, unknown sound that terrorized us is only the tent flap blowing in the wind. The ominous, moving monsters are the cows in a nearby pasture. In the bright light of the rising sun, we see the world in a new dimension. Our mood is changed from "Out of the depths I cried unto thee" to " this is the day which the Lord hath made, let us rejoice and be glad in it."

"Hail the Sun of righteousness! Light and life to all he brings. Risen with healing in his wings." The Christ of whose birth Charles Wesley sings is one who brings healing in his wings. Those who are gathered under his wings, like chicks gathered by a mother hen for protection, find healing. It is a healing within as fears are displaced. They learn to love because they are loved. A healing comes with others with whom they find reconciliation. A oneness with God is given, in whom alone is life. The root meaning of the word for healing is the same word for wholeness, and for salvation.

It may seem to be rushing the Christmas season to reflect upon a carol in the heat of August, but its message is for all seasons. Christ brings light, dispelling the darkness of our hearts, helping us to find meaning and purpose in life. In His gracious wings we find a security not dependent upon outward circumstance. In him we find life, life abundant and life eternal. So every day we may join in singing with the herald angels: "Glory to the new born king."

Lesson 13

An Eternal Reign

Daniel 2:26, 36-45

The king answered and said to Daniel, whose name was Belteshazzar, Art thou able to make known unto me the dream which I have seen, and the interpretation thereof?

36 This is the dream; and we will tell the interpretation thereof before the king.

37 Thou, O king, art a king of kings: for the God of heaven hath given thee a kingdom, power, and strength, and glory.

38 And wheresoever the children of men dwell, the beasts of the field and the fowls of the heaven hath he given into thine hand, and hath made thee ruler over them all. Thou art this head of gold.

39 And after thee shall arise another kingdom inferior to thee, and another third kingdom of brass, which shall bear rule over all the earth.

40 And the fourth kingdom shall be strong as iron: forasmuch as iron breaketh in pieces and subdueth all things: and as iron that breaketh all these, shall it break in pieces and bruise.

41 And whereas thou sawest the feet and toes, part of potters' clay, and part of iron, the kingdom shall be divided; but there shall be in it of the strength of the iron, forasmuch as thou sawest the iron mixed with miry clay.

42 And as the toes of the feet were part of iron, and part of clay, so the kingdom shall be partly strong, and partly broken.

43 And whereas thou sawest iron mixed with miry clay, they shall mingle themselves with the seed of men: but they shall not cleave one to another, even as iron is not mixed with clay.

44 And in the days of these kings shall the God of heaven set up a kingdom, which shall never be destroyed: and the kingdom shall not be left to other people, but it shall break in pieces and consume all these kingdoms, and it shall stand for ever.

45 Forasmuch as thou sawest that the stone was cut out of the mountain without hands, and that it brake in pieces the iron, the brass, the clay, the silver, and the gold; the great God hath made known to the king what shall come to pass hereafter: and the dream is certain, and the interpretation thereof sure.

Memory Selection
Daniel 2:44

Background Scripture
Daniel 2

Devotional Reading
Revelation 21:1-7

Aug. 24

This lesson shows that while God allows earthly kings limited freedom, He remains in ultimate control of history. This truth is shown when Nebuchanezzar, king of Babylon, has a dream which is interpreted by the Israelite captive Daniel.

In the dream, a series of world powers are represented in an image. Although the kind cannot even remember the dreams details, God enables Daniel both to recall and interpret the dream. It represents the sweep of history up to the time of the Messiah. At the expense of any long-lasting power of Nebuchadnezzar or successive world powers, God is assuring His people that He will reign supreme.

೫೦೦೩

Show your class a picture of the image seen by King Nebuchadnezzar in the dream which Daniel interprets. Many Christian bookstores have cardboard representations of this image, or you can make your own using various colors of foil and construction paper. Here is a guide, from Daniel 2 :31-35:

(1) Make the head of gold foil, and (2) the breast and arms of aluminum foil (silver). (3) Use dark gold or bronze construction paper for the brass on the belly and thighs. (4) Make the legs of a gray paper that resembles iron, and (5) the feet a patchwork of gray and red-orange paper (for the clay).

Point out that while scholars debate what each kingdom represents, the overall lesson is that God's "stone" (vs. 34) is probably Christ, "the stone that was made the head of the corner"(Acts 4:11). The overall point is not a history lesson, but the affirmation that God's Kingdom supersedes all others.

Teaching Outline	Daily Bible Readings	
I. Interpreter of Dreams—26, 36	Mon.	The King's Dream Daniel 1:18–2:6
II. Image of Kingdoms—37-43	Tue.	Daniel the Interpreter Daniel 2:7-16
A. The gold: Babylon, 37-38	Wed.	Praying for Wisdom Daniel 2:17-23
B. Silver: Medo-Persia?, 39a	Thu.	God Reveals Mysteries Daniel 2:24-28
C. Brass: Greece?, 39b	Fri.	Daniel Tells the Dream Daniel 2:29-35
D. Iron: Rome?, 40		
E. Iron and Clay: Rome in decay?, 41-43	Sat.	The Eternal Kingdom Daniel 2:36-45
III. Immortal Kingdom—44-45	Sun.	The Alpha and Omega Revelation 21:1-7

Verse by Verse

I. Interpreter of Dreams—26, 36

26 The king answered and said to Daniel, whose name was Belteshazzar, Art thou able to make known unto me the dream which I have seen, and the interpretation thereof?

36 This is the dream; and we will tell the interpretation thereof before the king.

Daniel, only a teenager when he was carried into Babylonian captivity, has been brought before King Nebuchadnezzar of Babylon because the king's court magicians and wizards had been sentenced to death because they could not recall a dream the king could not recall the king's disturbing dream. Seeking to spare their lives, Daniel had asked God for aid; and because he relied on God, not just on what he had learned from his pagan teachers, God revealed to him both the king's dream and its interpretation (2:19).

The name "Daniel" means "God (Heb. *el*) is my judge." The Babylonians, however, had renamed Daniel after their own god, Bel— "Belteshazzar" means "May Bel protect his life." Daniel's three friends, famous for enduring trials with Daniel, are also best known by their Babylonian names—see 1:7.

II. Image of Kingdoms—37-43

A. The gold: Babylon, 37-38

37 Thou, O king, art a king of kings: for the God of heaven hath given thee a kingdom, power, and strength, and glory.

38 And wheresoever the children of men dwell, the beasts of the field and the fowls of the heaven hath he given into thine hand, and hath made thee ruler over them all. Thou art this head of gold.

Although the identity of the rest of the kingdoms represented in the image in the king's dream is widely debated, this first one is clearly identified in 38b as Nebuchadnezzar himself: "Thou art this head of gold." To have been rated at the "gold standard" must have been flattering to an egotistical king—so much so that he probably missed the point of the dream, which is that God's Kingdom will crush to dust all opposing kingdoms of the world.

In verse 38, Daniel probably deliberately overstates the extent of Nebuchadnezzar's rule, leading him into a trap of pride that will be his downfall in 4:24-28, when he will be reduced to the level of an animal. The fact is that it had been God who made the king great, giving him the power to punish the disobedient Jews through the Captivity.

B. Silver: Medo-Persia?, 39a

39 And after thee shall arise another kingdom inferior to thee,

513

Some interpreters think that the other kingdoms in Nebuchanezzar's image are to be identified with various nations along the path of history toward the end of time, ending with the *consummation* of God's Kingdom. The interpretation to follow differs from that approach, finding the image to represent world powers immediately following Babylon, ending with Rome and the *inauguration* of God's rule. This approach attempts to take seriously the fact that Jesus said that the Kingdom of God was "at hand," and that those who responded to Him were "translated into the kingdom of His dear son" (Col. 1:13).

In this approach, the nation "after thee," or following Nebuchadnezzar, would be the Medo-Persian Empire. A hint of this identification is given in 5:28, where a succeeding Babylonian king, Belshazzar, is told that the Medes and Persians will be heirs of his kingdom. The Medes had been allies of Nebuchadnezzar, but revolted and combined forces with Cyrus, king of Persia. The new empire thus formed did not become as powerful or as influential as had Babylon, making it "inferior" and suiting the comparison of silver to gold.

C. Brass: Greece?, 39b

. . . and another third kingdom of brass, which shall bear rule over all the earth.

The Greeks, under the young genius Alexander the Great, were the next nation to strut across the stage of history, just as Daniel predicts in 10:20. Alexander's conquests were legendary, and so far-flung that he is said to have wept, while still in his 20s, that there were no more nations to conquer. Yet Greek rule would be aptly described only by brass, a still less precious metal, because of its very breadth "over all the earth." Eventually Greek troops came to be spread over such great distances that they were cut off from their supply lines. Administration became difficult as well. The advances Alexander had made became conquerable with the rise of the administrative geniuses of the next world power.

D. Iron: Rome?, 40

40 And the fourth kingdom shall be strong as iron: forasmuch as iron breaketh in pieces and subdueth all things: and as iron that breaketh all these, shall it break in pieces and bruise.

The iron part of the image seems to stand for the Roman empire, which followed the Greeks. The lesser value of iron perhaps implies a judgment against Rome's lack of cultural and intellectual contributions, compared to the "silver" rule of Alexander. Although Rome gave the world an impressive administrative system, Daniel accuses it of "breaking in pieces and bruising" those who stood in its way. The cruelty of Rome became legendary, as it subdued nation after nation. The Roman senate made some strides toward an international system of laws, but its emperors gradually took on the role of dictator in the latter days of the Empire. This leads us to the last part of Nebuchadnezzar's image, the feet.

E. Iron and Clay: Rome in decay?, 41-43

41 And whereas thou sawest the feet and toes, part of potters' clay, and part of iron, the kingdom shall be divided; but there shall be in it of the strength of the iron, forasmuch as thou sawest the iron mixed with miry clay.

42 And as the toes of the feet were part of iron, and part of clay, so the kingdom shall be partly strong, and partly broken.

43 And whereas thou sawest iron mixed with miry clay, they shall mingle themselves with the seed of men: but they shall not cleave one to another, even as iron is not mixed with clay.

As oil and water do not mix, so iron and clay do not bond. By the time of Christ, the Roman empire's decline could be fittingly described in these terms. Gone were the days when great generals prided themselves on being able to endure long marches and conquer kingdoms for the sake of empire building. As the historian Gibbon is famous for noting, Rome became rotten at the core, in its capital city, with its politicians seeking not a just society but personal gain and competition for position and power weakened the Empire from within. Financial difficulties left the far-flung Roman outposts without supplies or leadership. The glory days were over; and "clay" was a fitting description.

III. Immortal Kingdom—44-45

44 And in the days of these kings shall the God of heaven set up a kingdom, which shall never be destroyed: and the kingdom shall not be left to other people, but it shall break in pieces and consume all these kingdoms, and it shall stand for ever.

45 Forasmuch as thou sawest that the stone was cut out of the mountain without hands, and that it brake in pieces the iron, the brass, the clay, the silver, and the gold; the great God hath made known to the king what shall come to pass hereafter: and the dream is certain, and the interpretation thereof sure.

A final reason for adopting this approach to Daniel's interpretation of the king's dream is the fact that the "kingdom which shall never be destroyed" is obviously Christ's reign, which was inaugurated in the times of the "kings" or caesars of the late Roman Era. Only the spiritual Kingdom of the Messiah could be destined to consume all others. It was Christ who was the "stone" that became at once the cornerstone on which the Kingdom was erected (Acts 4:11), and the "stone of stumbling" for those who resist His rule (1 Pet. 2:8). Only the Kingdom of God will be eternal.

The valuation of God's reign over these great political powers is sobering. It means that to label such nations as Greece and Rome "great" on the basis of their vast territories and military might is to use the wrong standard. God's rule, characterized by love and justice, is greater. Daniel's "rating system" is also a source of reassurance for believers. Amid the political uncertainties that plague their lives, God promises that the rule of Christ in the heart supplies long-term and dependable hope.

Evangelistic Emphasis

When Daniel is able not only to interpret the meaning of the king's dream but also to narrate the strange vision, the king was amazed. Daniel is quick to make it plain that the revealing of this mystery was not a great achievement of his. His ability to decipher both the dream and its meaning was not because of his great study or brilliant mind. Daniel attributes this gift to the working of God. He is only the messenger.

In leading others to know Christ, to trust in God's love, it is always tempting to take pride, as if conver-sions were something we accom-plished. Rather when we see the transformation that God's Spirit can bring in a person's life, we give God thanks for what God has accom-plished. If God used us to bear the message, to embody God's love, we are simply amazed and grateful.

One of the hundreds of persons who had come forward at a evangelis-tic rally was seen staggering on the streets the next day, drunk again. A cynic, pointing him out to the famous evangelist, said, "Is that the man you converted yesterday?"

The preacher replied, "It must have been me, because if *God* had converted him he would be truly transformed." Paul reminds us we have this treasure in earthen vessels that the glory may be given to God.

ଓଙ

Memory Selection

And in the days of these kings shall the God of heaven set up a kingdom, which shall never be destroyed: and the kingdom shall not be left to other people, but it shall break in pieces and consume all these kingdoms, and it shall stand forever. — *Daniel 2:44*

The prophet was writing for a people facing persecution and oppression. It seemed that the king was all powerful. He held the power of life and death. He could reduce them to poverty with taxes or confiscate their property. He could carry them off to a foreign land. He could take away their freedom and make them slaves. There seemed no limit to his power, no accounting for his cruelty.

But as Daniel interprets the king's vision of the great statue reduced to dust, it is clear there is a greater power. Ultimately tyrants will fall and even the greatest kingdoms will collapse. But there is a greater kingdom to come. It is the kingdom of God. It will last forever. So we pray, "Thy kingdom come." So we live faithfully as those who know that in the end, God is in control. God's reign is forever.

516

Weekday Problems

Pete was a popular and effective pastor. He had been serving his present congregation for six years. Under his leadership there had been a healing, a coming together of factions. They had exciting plans for a major renovation project. Following his leadership, the congregation had gained a new vision of outreach into the community. It seemed a promising beginning to a long and fruitful ministry.

Then came an offer from another congregation. It was an unsolicited offer. The congregation's leaders had sought him out. Their needs were great. They felt their church was at a crossroads. They needed strong, dynamic leadership. With a television ministry in place, the pastor could reach many persons outside the church.

Like Daniel, the young pastor called together a small group of his most trusted friends. Before he attempted to interpret the king's dream, Daniel went home and prayed with his companions (Dan. 2:17-18). Pete and his friends also prayed about the decision he must make, earnestly seeking to discern God's will.

*How can prayer groups, covenant groups, or family groups help us make important decisions about how our calling from God is to be answered?

The Politics of the Kingdom

Whatever makes men good Christians makes them good citizens.—*Daniel Webster*

With God in charge of our defenses, there will be peace within.—*T. T. Faichney*

❖❖❖❖❖

God will keep no nation in supreme peace that will not do supreme duty.—*William McKinley*

❖❖❖❖❖

The world will be safe and secure in its peace only when nations adopt the principles of Christ and play fair with them.—*William Pierson Merrill*

❖❖❖❖❖

Great peace have they which love thy law: and nothing shall offend them.—*Psalm 119:165*

❖❖❖❖❖

Righteousness exalteth a nation.—*Proverbs 14:34*

This Lesson in Your Life

As in many stories in the Bible, there is a mixture of divine initiative and human responsibility in the story for this week. In the vision of King Nebuchadnezzar, the statue is destroyed by a stone cut from the mountain. Yet it is a stone not cut by hands. The final destruction of the kingdoms is accomplished by God, in God's good time.

Daniel's message is one of encouragement to believers. All the outward evidence suggested that the king was invincible. Their sufferings would go on and on. There was no relief in sight. But in that dark hour, Daniel speaks of a new Kingdom that will last forever. The old order will be destroyed. A new order will begin. This is God's doing!

For many in our day, that reminder that God is in control is a needed word of encouragement. Afro-Americans have suffered discrimination, low wages, poor health care, inadequate education, and outright lynchings. Those who based their power on fear and hate and prejudice are an embarrassment to their children, and a disgrace to the nation. In a land of plenty, there is still hunger. Children are those who suffer most from poverty. But Daniel's message to the politically and economically oppressed in our day is the same. Another Kingdom is coming.

Sometimes it seems as if we have more than we can bear. Illness or accident brings collapse to our brightest dreams and dearest hopes. Job cut backs, stock market fluctuations, hurricanes, invasive cancer—and our secure little world comes crashing down. An indifferent, if not evil, fate seems to rule the world. But Daniel's message is that despite all the signs to the contrary, God is in control. His kingdom comes.

In one sense, Daniel seems to assert it is all up to God. The stone that pulverizes the imperial statue was not made with human hands. It is all the work of God. Yet Daniel writes to encourage the people to be faithful. There are pressures to conform, to blend in. Some advise: *Go along to get along. Let old values go. Don't risk yourself. Play it safe. Be tolerant of pagan ways. Become like one of them.* Daniel's message is not one of safe conformity but rather of radical transformation. They are to be faithful to the God of Moses and Abraham. God will use their faithful witness. So the message to us is a call to faithfulness. In our fear to live faithfully we miss out on really living.

The picture is a mixture of divine initiative and human responsibility. We pray as if it is all up to God. We work and serve as if it were up to us. So faith and work are held in a healthy tension.

The archway at Scarritt College in Nashville, Tenn., bears a double inscription. On one side it reads, "Attempt great things for God." The other side reads, "Expect great things from God."

1. What was the request of King Nebuchadnezzar?
He asked his wise men both to tell his dream and to interpret it (Dan. 2: 2, 5).

2. What punishment would be given if the wise men could not do what the king commanded?
If they did not tell both the dream and its interpretation, they would be torn limb from limb and their houses destroyed.

3. Who were Daniel's friends?
Hananiah, Mishael, and Azariah (Dan. 2:17).

4. What Babylonian names were given to these companions of Daniel?
Shadrack, Meshach, and Abednego (Dan. 1:7, 2:49).

5. Who revealed to Daniel the king's dream and its meaning?
Daniel said that it is God in heaven who reveals mysteries, and that He had disclosed what will happen at the end of the king's days (Dan. 2:28).

6. What was the king's dream?
He saw a statue made of gold, silver, copper, iron, and clay. A stone struck the statue and destroyed it (Dan. 2: 31-35).

7. What was Daniel's interpretation of the king's dream?
There would be four successive kingdoms, all destroyed, followed by another kingdom which would not be destroyed (Dan.2:36-45).

8. What was the King's response to Daniel?
He worshiped Daniel, commanding that grain and incense be offered to him (Dan. 2: 46).

9. What did the king say about Daniel's God?
"Your God is God of gods, and Lord of kings and a revealer of mysteries.

10. What happened to Daniel after he told the king his dream and its meaning?
The king promoted Daniel and made him ruler over the whole province (Dan. 2:48).

Stones are among the most common objects mentioned in Scripture. The role they play can be good or bad, destructive or redeeming.

When Jesus was placed in the cave-like tomb, a great stone was rolled against the cave to lock Him in, to be done with him. The women hurrying to the tomb in the early morning were worried about how they might roll away the stone that kept them from the body of Jesus. The stone symbolized the world that would be done with Jesus.

In Nebuchadnezzar's dream, Daniel described a stone that was cut from a mountain, and that destroyed the succession of kingdoms with all their pomp and power. That stone becomes a mountain, filling the whole earth, the symbol of God's sovereignty.

The Scriptures speak Jesus as the stone which was rejected by the builders. It becomes the chief cornerstone of the true Temple. The story of the crucifixion is a stumbling block to the Jews, but to believers it is the power and salvation of God.

John's Gospel reminds us that stoning was the preferred method of execution for some crimes. A woman taken in adultery was brought before Jesus. Her self-righteous neighbors were eager to get started on their bloody job, ready with stones in hand. Yet Peter talks of becoming living stones, brought together as the Temple, where Christ is the foundation stone, in whose midst God dwells.

Treacherous rocks in a harbor are the bane of all seafarers. The ship on which Paul traveled as a prisoner crashed against a reef on the island of Malta. Jesus tells that the person who hears His words and acts on them is like a man who builds his house upon the rock. Neither wind nor rain nor flood can destroy the house built upon the rock.

In the barren desert wilderness, the refugees from Egypt complained to Moses of their thirst. All they saw was sand, sun, and rocks. But Moses sees one particular rock with different eyes. He strikes the rock, and out flows living water. So still we sing, "Rock of ages, cleft for me, let me hide myself in thee."

It is better, says Jesus, to have a millstone tied around your neck and be cast into the sea, than to lead a little one astray. Yet the psalmist teaches us to pray, "Let the words of my mouth, and the meditations of my heart be acceptable in thy sight, O Lord, my *rock* and my redeemer."

How strange and beautiful that Jesus should call impetuous and fickle Simon, "Rock," "Petros," "Peter." At times he was as "flaky" as slate, yet he could also be as steady as a foundation rock for the church.

How is it with you? Are you a stumbling block or a stepping stone?

The End of the Days

Daniel 12:1-9

And at that time shall Michael stand up, the great prince which standeth for the children of thy people: and there shall be a time of trouble, such as never was since there was a nation even to that same time: and at that time thy people shall be delivered, every one that shall be found written in the book.

2 And many of them that sleep in the dust of the earth shall awake, some to everlasting life, and some to shame and everlasting contempt.

3 And they that be wise shall shine as the brightness of the firmament; and they that turn many to righteousness as the stars for ever and ever.

4 But thou, O Daniel, shut up the words, and seal the book, even to the time of the end: many shall run to and fro, and knowledge shall be increased.

5 Then I Daniel looked, and, behold, there stood other two, the one on this side of the bank of the river, and the other on that side of the bank of the river.

6 And one said to the man clothed in linen, which was upon the waters of the river, How long shall it be to the end of these wonders?

7 And I heard the man clothed in linen, which was upon the waters of the river, when he held up his right hand and his left hand unto heaven, and sware by him that liveth for ever that it shall be for a time, times, and an half; and when he shall have accomplished to scatter the power of the holy people, all these things shall be finished.

8 And I heard, but I understood not: then said I, O my Lord, what shall be the end of these things?

9 And he said, Go thy way, Daniel: for the words are closed up and sealed till the time of the end.

Memory Selection
Daniel 12:2

Background Scripture
Daniel 12

Devotional Reading
Revelation 7:9-17

Aug. 31

521

Although Christians differ on the interpretation of Bible prophecy, this lesson has a single focus: *to reassure and strengthen the faithful in the face of an uncertain future.*

Some find here a reference to end of the world. Others think that Daniel is completing a description that began in 10:21 of Jewish history during the rule of the Syrian king, Antiochus Epiphanes in the third century B.C. Still others read the passage as a prophecy about the destruction of Jerusalem, which occurred in A.D. 70; and some say the predictions have double application and speak of events both past and future.

Rather than arguing for one or another of these "angles of vision," you can focus on an underlying aim of all biblical prophecy: To show that despite opposition from Satan's forces, in whatever political form, the faithful "shall rest" in the end (12:13).

ॐ

Ask your group to describe the most wickedly powerful world figures they can think of. Does King Herod come to mind? Or Josef Stalin, Adolph Hitler, or Saddam Hussein? If we were Jews living in the second century B.C. we would certainly mention Antiochus Epiphanes, a Syrian ruler who set up an altar to Zeus in the Jewish Temple in Jerusalem, and killed not only those who refused to worship Zeus, but who even kept a copy of the Law.

Whoever the world's most evil figure is, *God* knows their evil deeds. He is concerned both about their blasphemies against Him and about the people they abuse. An underlying message of this lesson is that God knows those who are for Him and against Him; and there will come a Day when His judgment in both cases will be revealed.

Teaching Outline	*Daily Bible Readings*	
	Mon.	The Sealed Book Daniel 12:1-7
I. What About the End?—1-4	Tue.	Happy Are Those Who Wait Daniel 12:8-13
A. Deliverance of God's People, 1		
B. General resurrection, 2	Wed.	'I Will Make You a Pillar' Revelation 3:7-13
C. Work of the wise, 3-4		
	Thu.	Inherit the Imperishable 1 Corinthians 15:50-56
II. When will this Be?—5-12		
A. Questions at the river, 5-6	Fri.	Multitude Before the Throne Revelation 7:9-17
B. Fall of the holy ones, 7		
C. Unanswered question, 8-9	Sat.	The Lord, Their Light Revelation 22:1-7
	Sun.	'Come Inherit the Kingdom!' Matthew 25:31-40

Verse by Verse

I. What About the End?—1-4

A. Deliverance of God's People, 1

1 And at that time shall Michael stand up, the great prince which standeth for the children of thy people: and there shall be a time of trouble, such as never was since there was a nation even to that same time: and at that time thy people shall be delivered, every one that shall be found written in the book.

In the previous lesson we read in awe of how God gifted Daniel with the ability to interpret a dream of the rise and fall of kingdoms leading up to the time of Christ and the Kingdom that "shall never be destroyed" (2:44). Since that scene, the prophet has had many other revelations; but now we come to the grand climax of them all—a prophecy dealing with "the time of the end" (vs. 3).

The words "at that time" connect this section with a revelation that began in chapter 10. Most scholars believe that this section deals with the time "between the Testaments" when Assyria and Egypt were at war with each other, with the land of the Jews lying between them and suffering the consequences. These were the days of the Maccabean kings in Israel, and of Antiochus Epiphanes, the hated Syrian ruler who cruelly persecuted the Jews and forced them to commit sacrilege, as recounted in parts of the Apocrypha—books written by Greek-speaking Jews that are included in Roman Catholic editions of the Bible, but not in most Protestant editions.

Those days end with such trouble that Michael the archangel stands up to deliver God's people, perhaps referring to the destruction of Jerusalem in A.D. 70. This wondrously powerful "prince" of angels" first appeared in 10:21. In the few references to Michael, he is the supernatural defender of the faithful, appearing to destroy the attacks of Satan just when all seems lost (see Rev. 12:7-9). Although prophecies such as this leave many unanswered questions, Michael's appearance here provides solid and consistent reassurance to the believer that the future is in God's hands, and that the gates of hell will not prevail over His kingdom. The solemn promise to Daniel is extended to all believers: *"Thy people shall be delivered."*

The statement that the trouble was "such as never was since there was a nation" (along with vs. 2, below) seems so strong that many interpreters sense that this section refers not only to a great conflict toward the end of the Maccabean period but also to the end of the world. Once more we are facing the possibility that prophecy may point to more than one event. Perhaps this text, as Matthew 25 seems to do, describes the destruction of Jerusalem in the same terms as the end of the world, since both events contain the same kind of terror and deliverance.

B. General resurrection, 2

2 And many of them that sleep in the dust of the earth shall awake, some to everlasting life, and some to shame and everlasting contempt.

Here is even stronger evidence that Daniel's vision extends to the end of time, since we could hardly imagine a more explicit reference to the general resurrection predicted in other passages (see 1 Cor. 15: 20-24, 51-55; 1 Thess. 4:13-18). The word "many" does not refer to a third class, in addition to those rising to inherit eternal life on the one hand and everlasting "contempt" on the other. As in the NIV, the word simply means a "multitude," and actually includes all who have died.

C. Work of the wise, 3-4

3 And they that be wise shall shine as the brightness of the firmament; and they that turn many to righteousness as the stars for ever and ever.

4 But thou, O Daniel, shut up the words, and seal the book, even to the time of the end: many shall run to and fro, and knowledge shall be increased.

What are the spiritually "wise" to do in the light of this firm prediction of conflict, the end of time, and the future fate of heaven or hell? They are to let their "light shine before men" (Matt. 5:16), shining the light of the Gospel into every dark corner of unbelief and ignorance. It should be no surprise that the light will "rub off" on those who faithfully engage in this work, making them shine like stars.

Verse 4 also indicates another, less glorious, piece of work for Daniel and other teachers of the truth to do while prophecy is in the process of fulfillment: shutting up the words and sealing the book. Perhaps part of what this means is that we should not speculate about the meaning of prophetic events when that meaning was "shut up" from Daniel himself (see also vs. 9).

II. When will this Be?—5-12

A. Questions at the river, 5-6

5 Then I Daniel looked, and, behold, there stood other two, the one on this side of the bank of the river, and the other on that side of the bank of the river.

6 And one said to the man clothed in linen, which was upon the waters of the river, How long shall it be to the end of these wonders?

In addition to Michael the archangel, two other heavenly messengers now appear at both sides of a river. Presumably this is the river Hiddekel, where Daniel was when the preceding vision was revealed (10:4). Hiddekel is another name for the Tigris River, which, joining the Euphrates, flows into the Persian Gulf through ancient Babylon and Persia.

Apparently one of these unnamed figures, probably angels, hovers "above" (as in the NIV) the river, and is asked the question always asked when end-time prophecy is brought up: *When will this occur?* Specifically, the questions are: When will the errors and deliverances just mentioned be concluded? When can the righteous expect to be vindicated for their faithfulness? When will the wicked receive their due? When will God draw the curtain on the final act of the drama of history?

B. Fall of the holy ones, 7

7 And I heard the man clothed in linen, which was upon the waters of the river, when he held up his right hand and his left hand unto heaven, and sware by him that liveth for ever that it shall be for a time, times, and an half; and when he shall have accomplished to scatter the power of the holy people, all these things shall be finished.

Holding up one's hand when making a solemn statement made the statement into an oath, as when a judge swears in a witness who has one hand on the Bible and the other raised. The mysterious, angel-like figure doubles the dependability of his words by raising both hands, and swearing by none other than God Himself. Only much later will this practice be taken so lightly and abused so often that Jesus is prompted to forbid it (Matt. 5:34).

Unfortunately, this solemnly-sworn answer is shrouded in mystery. A "time" may be taken as one; "times" as two; and with the half added the total is three and a half. This strange number first appears in 7:25, and is often taken to mean three and a half *years*. However, it is impossible to pinpoint such a period during the evil reign of Antiochus and the troubles of the Jews under him. Other scholars

believe the number is symbolic, and means an indefinite period such as "once, and again, and again, and half that." This too can only be speculation, whether we apply it to the reign of Antiochus, or the period when Rome destroyed the Temple in A.D. 70, or the end of the world. The meaning of the number is simply a part of the book that is "sealed."

Whatever its meaning, "the end" will not come until after "the power of the holy people" is scattered. Apparently whatever "end" is referred to here, it will come after God's people have exhausted all their own resources. Their salvation, although certain, will be accomplished "Not by might, nor by power, but by my spirit, saith the LORD of hosts" (Zech. 4:6).

C. Unanswered question, 8-9

8 And I heard, but I understood not: then said I, O my Lord, what shall be the end of these things?

9 And he said, Go thy way, Daniel: for the words are closed up and sealed till the time of the end.

Joining many others who have to honestly admit that they do not understand the answer to his question, Daniel asks another slightly different question, which the NIV words, "What will the outcome of all this be?" Again, however, the prophet is told that the answer of this question is also "sealed." In this light, it is amazing how many prophecy specialists since Daniel have "unsealed" answers about the end of the world, asserting that they *do* understand what Daniel could not. We do know that those who endure will be protected by God's power.

Evangelistic Emphasis

In the book of Daniel we read, that "those who lead many to righteousness (shall shine) like the stars forever and ever" (Dan 12:3). I started remembering the many persons who have led me: parents who took me to church, a Sunday School teacher who encouraged me to read the Sermon on the Mount every day for a month, a campus minister who raised hard questions and had time to listen to me, a church pastor who encouraged me, mentors in ministry. For me they shine like stars forever.

In your life, who do you remember who helped you on the way, persons who were there when you needed them, persons you couldn't have made it without, those who shine like stars forever?

Ponder another question. Who may be looking to you to lead them to righteousness, teach them right from wrong, to model integrity in business or profession, to manifest commitment to family, to live out the faith? Is it possible some may look to you as an example even though you are not even aware of it?

The prophet Isaiah said, "The people that walked in darkness have seen a great light." Jesus said, "I am the light of the world." But He also said to His disciples, "You are the light of the world. Let your light shine."

ഇᏍᏝᏋ

Memory Selection

And many of them that sleep in the dust of the earth shall awake, some to everlasting life, and some to shame and everlasting contempt.— *Daniel 12:2*

Some scholars identify this verse as the first unambiguous teaching about resurrection in the Old Testament. It is amplified in the New Testament in the words of Jesus and in the teachings of Paul.

Our hope in life after death is not based on clinical evidence of the reports of those who have been declared dead and have been revived. Our hope grows out of our trust in God. There is much we don't know about the life to come; but when we fully trust God we don't need to know the details. It is not essential to know the furniture of heaven or the temperature of hell. It is enough to know that the God who made us also loves us into life. We are His children.

At death we commit ourselves into God's hands. Having come to trust in God, and God alone for our salvation, we are content to leave the outcome in His hands, knowing that His plan for us is greater than any we could conceive.

Weekday Problems

Don MacLeod tells of a man who was told by his physician that he had an incurable disease. His death would be in a few months. When he received the news, he went to his home and looked at the river and the mountain which he loved. As twilight deepened he looked at the stars glimmering in the sky. He said to them, "I may not see you many times more. But River, I shall be alive when you cease running to the sea. Mountain, I shall be alive when you have sunk down into the plain. Stars, I shall be alive when you have fallen in the ultimate disintegration of the universe."

Christ changes the face of death. It is not a dead-end street but a highway. It is not the end, but a passage to a new, more glorious and eternal life. Jesus said to Martha, as she was grieving for her brother Lazarus, "I am the resurrection and the life; he who believes in me shall never die."

A little girl whose path from school led across a graveyard was asked if she was afraid. "No," she said, "I just cross it to reach home."

*How does Jesus' promise change the way you face your own mortality?

On Glimpsing the Future

The grand difficulty is to feel the reality of both worlds, so as to give each its due place in our thoughts and feelings: to keep our mind's eye and our heart's eye ever fixed on the land of promise, without looking away from the road along which we are to travel toward it.—*August W. Hare*

I feel my immortality o'ersweep all pains, all tears, all time, all fears, and like the eternal thunders of the deep, peal to my ears this truth—"Thou livest forever."—*George Byron*

Belief in a future life is the appetite of reason.—*Walter S. Landor*

Everything that looks to the future elevates human nature; for life is never so low or so little as when occupied with the present. —*L. E. Landon*

Trust no future, howe'er pleasant;/let the dead past bury its dead./Act—act in the living present,/heart within, and God o'erhead.—*Wm. Longfellow*

This Lesson in Your Life

Bruce Larson writes: "In a profound sense we all become what we aim at. You are your dreams."

The Christian hope of the "resurrection of the body" and "life everlasting" impacts us in at least three ways. First it puts our day-to-day concerns in a true perspective. This awareness of eternity helps us sort out the more important from the less important. Emil Brunner reminds us, "The less men have hope beyond this life, the more they will ruin themselves with pleasures and goods." The hedonist with no hope says "You only go around once, so get yours while you can"; and "Eat, drink, and be merry, for tomorrow you die." But with the hope of life after death we come to value love, truth, and beauty. Jesus helps us find a new perspective: "Lay up for yourselves treasures in heaven."

Second, the Christian hope in resurrection impels us to participate in what God is doing here and now. Some charge that belief in a life after death distracts us from the tasks at hand, that it provides an easy escape from reality. But the opposite is true. Those who are certain of life everlasting set out to alleviate human suffering. They do not idly wait for the second coming of Christ or for their own death. Undergirded with prayer, these believers seek to make their years count in bringing peace and justice on earth. A Mother Teresa feeding the hungry in India, a Dietrich Bonhoeffer resisting oppression in Nazi Germany, an Albert Schweitzer healing the sick in Africa, a Martin Luther King, Jr., mobilizing non-violent resistance to the unjust laws of our land—all were impelled by a hope of a Kingdom still to come. Knowing that their lives were secure with God, they were freed from fears of what others might do to them. Their certain hope of resurrection was not an invitation to withdrawal. Rather it was that hope which impelled them to participate in God's work of redemption and liberation.

Finally, this Christian hope in resurrection imparts power in the living of this life. The early Christians were empowered by a faith that only God had the final word. Courts or armies might kill their bodies, but death could not separate them from God. Principalities and powers held no power over them, for they knew Christ in all His risen power.

The same power by which God raised Christ from the dead is available to us. Chester Pennington observes, "God's victory over death is the promise of our increasing victory over the powers which cause little deaths of our daily anxieties and fears."

The gift of life eternal not only gives us hope for the future. It is also an inseparable relation with the living Christ here and now.

GETTING THE FACTS STRAIGHT

1. Who was the angel sent to Daniel?
The angel Michael, patron angel of the Jews was sent to stand with Daniel and his people (Dan. 12:1).

2. According to Daniel 12:2, who shall be delivered in times of trouble?
Everyone whose name is found written in the book.

3. What is the first clear reference to the resurrection found in the Old Testament?
Daniel 12:2: "And many of them that sleep in the dust of the earth shall awake, some to everlasting life."

4. At the resurrection, what happens to the righteous?
They shall awake to everlasting life (Dan. 12:2).

5. At the resurrection, what happens to evil persons?
They shall awaken to shame and everlasting contempt (Dan. 12:2).

6. What shall happen to the wise?
They will shine like the brightness of the sky (Dan. 12:3).

7. What is the reward for those who turn many to righteousness?
They will shine like the stars forever and ever (Dan. 12: 3).

8. What answer was given to Daniel's question, "How long will it be until the end?"
A time, two times and a half, or three and a half years (Dan. 12: 7).

9. When Jesus was asked when the kingdom would be restored, what did He say?
It is not for us to know the times and seasons God has fixed by His own authority (Acts 1:6).

10. What is promised to Daniel in Daniel 12:13?
Daniel shall rest and shall stand in his allotted place at the end of his days.

The promise is made to Daniel: "You shall stand at your allotted place at the end of the days" (Dan. 12:13). Jesus assures us that we have a reserved place as well:

> In my father's house are many rooms. I go to prepare a place for you. And if I go and prepare a place for you, I will come again and take you to myself, that where I am, you may be also (John 14:2-3).

That may be all we can ever know. But it is all we need to know. The "resurrection of the body" points to the uniqueness, the essence, the special self that is made to live again. The mortal puts on immortality. The "spiritual body is raised." We know and we are known. Most importantly, we are with God, the God made known in Jesus Christ.

J. R. MacPhail passes on an old story about a physician. The good doctor was visiting a patient who knew he was dying. He asked the doctor what the doctor believed about the next life. The doctor wasn't accustomed to talking much about his faith, or interpreting the Bible or Christian doctrine. He was wondering what to say, where to begin.

At that moment the doctor heard his dog scratching at the door. The dog had somehow escaped from the car. Following the familiar scent of the doctor, he found out where his master was. He could hear his master's voice. The doctor let the little dog into the room. He pointed out to his dying patient friend that the dog had never been in the room before. He had no idea of what the room might be like. The dog only knew that his master was there; and that was enough for him. He just wanted to be with him.

Our journey through life will lead us into unknown passages. It will lead us to a door we cannot open. Yet if we know that on the other side is Jesus and that He will let us in, that's enough.

"In my father's house are many rooms. I go to prepare a place for you that where I am you may be also." There are mysteries we cannot begin to comprehend. But we shall be with Him.